Using Symphony,
Special Edition

David Paul Ewing

Geoffrey T. LeBlond

Revised for Release 2.2
by Rebecca Bridges Altman

Rosemary Colonna

Ricardo Dobson

David Maguiness

Timothy Stanley

Brian Underdahl

QUE ®
CORPORATION
LEADING COMPUTER KNOWLEDGE

EDITING AND PRODUCTION STAFF

Product Director

David P. Ewing

Acquisitions Editor

Terrie Lynn Solomon

Production Editor

Mike La Bonne

Contributing Editor

Alice Martina Smith

Technical Editors

Jay Jacobson
Don Roche Jr.
Timothy S. Stanley

Book Design

William Hartman

Book Production

William Hartman
Dan Armstrong
Stacey Beheler
Travia Davis
Charles A. Hutchinson
Jennifer Matthews
Dennis Sheehan
Mae Louise Shinault
Bruce D. Steed

Indexer

Sharon Hilgenberg

Composed in Garamond and OCRB by

Hartman Publishing

DEDICATION

To Sheila

D.P.E.

To my grandfather

G.T.L.

ABOUT THE AUTHORS

Rebecca Bridges Altman has a degree in economics from Stanford. She owns her own microcomputer training and consulting business. Her specialty is developing computer training materials. She is technical editor for *Absolute Reference: The Journal for 1-2-3 and Symphony Users* and the revision author for Que's *1-2-3 Release 2.2 Quick Reference; 1-2-3 QueCards,* 2nd Edition; and *Using Symphony,* 2nd Edition.

Rosemary Colonna is a software engineer who has developed course materials and trained instructors on networking, and operating systems such as DOS, UNIX, and ULTRIX. She also has worked as a software quality assurance engineer for several computer companies, and is the author of user and system administrator manuals for a variety of computer products.

Dr. Ricardo Dobson directs Commonwealth Computer Assistance for Business, Inc., a personal computer consulting firm specializing in *Symphony, 1-2-3, Freelance, LaserJet printer,* and *Paradox* applications. Since earning his Ph.D. in 1969 at Arizona State University, Dobson has gained practical business experience by working for such firms as General Motors, Chase Manhattan Bank, and the General Electric Company.

David Paul Ewing is publishing director for Que Corporation. He is the author of Que's *1-2-3 Macro Library, Using 1-2-3 Workbook and Instructor's Guide;* co-author of Que's *Using Symphony, Using Q&A, Using Javelin,* and *1-2-3 Macro Workbook;* and contributing author to *Using 1-2-3 Release 3, Using 1-2-3,* Special Edition, *1-2-3 Quickstart,* and *Upgrading to 1-2-3 Release 3.*

Geoffrey T. LeBlond, president of LeBlond Software, received his B.A. degree from Brown University and his M.B.A. in finance from Indiana University's Graduate School of Business. He is co-author of *Using 1-2-3* and contributing author to *1-2-3 for Business,* both published by Que Corporation. He also was a technical editor at Que Corporation for the *IBM PC Update* magazine, and Editor-in-Chief of *Absolute Reference: The Journal for 1-2-3 and Symphony Users.*

David Maguiness, a financial analyst with Que Corporation, was editor-in-chief of *Absolute Reference: The Journal for 1-2-3 and Symphony Users,* Que's monthly technical journal. He also was a product development specialist with expertise in spreadsheet, database, and integrated software. He is the revision author for *1-2-3 for Business,* 2nd Edition, and co-author of *Using 1-2-3* Special Edition, *1-2-3 Quick Reference,* and *Upgrading to 1-2-3 Release 3.*

Timothy S. Stanley has worked for Que since 1985 as a technical editor. In addition to technical editing a number of Que's books, he has contributed to *Using 1-2-3 Release 3; Upgrading to 1-2-3 Release 3; 1-2-3 Macro Library; Introduction to Business Software Instructor's Guide; Using Symphony,* Special Edition; and *Absolute Reference: The Journal for 1-2-3 and Symphony Users.*

Brian Underdahl, an independent consultant based in Reno, Nev., studied electrical engineering at the University of Minnesota. He later worked at Graybar Electric for 18 years where, most recently, he was responsible for all PC-related projects. He specializes in *Symphony* applications development and support.

CONTENTS AT A GLANCE

TABLE OF CONTENTS

Part VI: Symphony Communications Module

Part VII: Symphony Macros and the Command Language

Part VIII: Quick Reference Guide to Using Symphony

TRADEMARK ACKNOWLEDGMENTS

Que Corporation has made every effort to supply trademark information about company names, products, and services mentioned in this book. Trademarks indicated below were derived from various sources. Que Corporation cannot attest to the accuracy of this information.

Apple II is a registered trademark of Apple Computer, Inc.

Ashton-Tate, dBASE II, dBASE III, and dBASE III Plus are registered trademarks of Ashton-Tate Company.

AST Premium, AST Rampage, and EEMS are registered trademarks of AST Research Inc.

AT&T is a registered trademark of American Telephone & Telegraph Company.

Avery is a registered trademark of Avery International.

Commodore PET is a registered trademark of Commodore Electronics Ltd.

COMPAQ and COMPAQ PLUS are registered trademarks of COMPAQ Computer Corporation.

CompuServe Information Service is a registered trademark of CompuServe Incorporated and H&R Block, Inc.

Context MBA is a trademark of Contest Management Systems, Inc., and LeMain, Inc.

EPSON is a registered trademark of Epson Corporation. Epson FX-80, Epson FX-100, Epson LQ-800, Epson RX-80, and Epson printer are trademarks of Epson America, Inc.

Extrak is a trademark of Lerman Associates.

Hayes Smartmodem 1200 is a trademark of Hayes Microcomputer Products, Inc.

HP LaserJet, and LaserJet are trademarks of Hewlett-Packard Co.

IBM, PC XT, OS/2, Personal System/2, and IBM Graphics Printer are trademarks of International Business Machines Corporation.

intel is a registered trademark of Intel Corporation.

Microsoft and MS-DOS are registered trademarks of Microsoft Corporation.

MOS Technologies and 6502 are trademarks of MOS Technologies.

Norton Utilities is a trademark of Peter Norton Computing.

Popcom X100 is a trademark of Prentice Corporation.

SuperCalc is a registered trademark of Computer Associates International, Inc.

1-2-3, Allways, DIF, Freelance Plus, Graphwriter II, Jazz, LIM, Lotus, Magellan, Symphony, and VisiCalc, are registered trademarks of Lotus Development Corporation.

TRS-80 and Radio Shack are registered trademarks of Radio Shack, Division of Tandy Corporation.

WordStar is a registered trademark of MicroPro International Corporation.

Z80 is a registered trademark of Zilog, Inc.

CONVENTIONS USED IN THIS BOOK

Using Symphony, Special Edition, uses several conventions to help you learn the program.

Boldface letters indicate that the word is a Symphony command and that you can select the command by typing the boldface letter after you have retrieved the appropriate menu. For example, SERVICES **W**indow **C**reate indicates that you retrieve the SERVICES menu, type w, and then type c to select this command.

Words printed in all capital letters signify the following:

> Function keys for retrieving Symphony menus: ACCESS SYSTEM, SERVICES, TYPE, and MENU. (When the book refers to the specific menus for spreadsheet, word processing, graphics, data-form, or communications environments, then SHEET, DOC, GRAPH, FORM, and COMM are used.) For example, SHEET **E**rase indicates that you retrieve the spreadsheet menu and select the **E**rase command.
>
> Mode indicators that appear on the screen in all capital letters are printed in all capital letters.
>
> Range names, including those used for macros, appear in all capital letters.
>
> In general, words appearing in all capital letters within the Symphony control panel are printed in all capital letters.

Function key names are used in the text with function key numbers appearing often in parentheses after the name. GoTo (F5), for example, indicates to press the GoTo key, which is F5 on the keyboard. Whenever the Symphony function requires that you press the Alt key and a function key simultaneously, the function key name is given, followed by the Alt and function key in parentheses — for example, Learn (Alt-F5).

Worksheet cell addresses are shown as they are in the Symphony control panel; for example, A1..G5, or a range name (SALES).

Features new to Release 2.2 are indicated by an icon in the margin.

Introduction

Symphony® is the integrated software package from Lotus® Development Corporation, creator of 1-2-3®, the nation's best-selling software program. First released in 1984, Symphony is used worldwide by more than one million people in business, finance, government, and the nonprofit sector.

Symphony provides users with not only the best of 1-2-3 technology—spreadsheet, graphics, and database—but also word processing and communications. Symphony's capability to integrate its five environments makes it one of the most powerful and useful software programs available. With the latest release (2.2), Symphony also includes the major new features of Release 2.2 of 1-2-3, such as file linking, enhanced macro debugging, spreadsheet publishing, and much more.

Although 1-2-3 users may find Symphony similar to 1-2-3 in many respects, Symphony is more versatile and integrated than its predecessor in several ways. First, Symphony's word processor provides users the features of many stand-alone word processing programs. Second, Symphony's database and database-entry form features go well beyond 1-2-3's data management capabilities. Third, Symphony's communications program enables users to connect to time-sharing services such as CompuServe and send or receive data to and from other personal computers. Finally, the program's window capabilities enable users to integrate Symphony's multiple programs to create sophisticated applications.

Using Symphony, Special Edition

With the added features of Symphony comes complexity. Although learning how to use some of Symphony's applications may be easy, learning how to use windows, to integrate applications, and to take advantage of the @functions and Command Language, can take months to master.

Using Symphony, Special Edition, helps both experienced and new users of Lotus spreadsheet programs to learn all of Symphony's powerful features. This book explains Symphony's command menu system and special features in a clear, easy-to-understand style. Users may appreciate the detailed discussions of Symphony's five environments, supported by figures showing spreadsheets, word processing documents, databases, and graphs that illustrate program operations. Learning is further enhanced by tips in the text and, in most sections of the book, cues, cautions, and reminders in the margins to help users remember important Symphony features. Another margin feature is a special icon that flags a new command or feature in Symphony 2.2. In addition, many examples of commands and functions, along with hands-on practice sections, help users apply the program to help solve their business problems.

Who Should Use This Book?

If you own Symphony, you should own this book. *Using Symphony,* Special Edition, picks up where the Symphony manual leaves off. This book explains both the basics and the fine points of the program. Every chapter includes clear explanations and examples, and special care has been taken to cover in detail those topics that are not thoroughly explained in the Symphony manual. For instance, many chapters give specific examples of how to integrate one Symphony environment with another. Chapter 17 shows you how to use the full range of Symphony's database capabilities with the program's database entry form. Chapters 21 and 22 explain Symphony's keyboard macro and Command Language capabilities by providing sample macros and a powerful set of commands that you can use during your Symphony sessions.

If you do not own Symphony, but are considering purchasing the program, this book is also for you. This book will help you understand Symphony's unique features and how to apply them to your advantage.

About This Book

Using Symphony, Special Edition, is divided into eight parts. The book also includes a tear-out command menu, a command reference section, a troubleshooting section, an appendix on installing Symphony, and an appendix on new 2.2 features.

Part I: Understanding and Getting Started with Symphony

Chapter 1, "Building with Symphony: An Overview," explains Symphony's basic concepts. This chapter describes in detail Symphony's SHEET, DOC, FORM, GRAPH, and COMM environments and their capabilities, and illustrates with a practical example how you can integrate the different applications.

Chapter 2, "Getting Started," covers the Symphony menu system, the display screen and keyboard features, and the program's window capabilities. Chapter 2 also discusses Symphony's help system.

Part II: Learning Symphony Worksheet Basics

Chapter 3, "Using the Symphony SHEET Environment," introduces the foundation of the program—the spreadsheet—and covers its size and memory capacity. If you are new to spreadsheets, and to Lotus spreadsheets in particular, this chapter teaches you the fundamentals of entering data into the Symphony worksheet. You also learn how to use one of Symphony 2.2's most important new features, worksheet linking, and are introduced to the new VIEWER add-in, a version of Lotus Magellan®. Magellan is the popular disk utility program from Lotus that helps you quickly find, view, and use information stored on your hard disk. VIEWER enables you to see the contents of your files without having to first retrieve them. VIEWER also helps you create links to worksheets on disk.

Chapter 4, "Learning Fundamental SHEET Window Commands," discusses the basic Symphony spreadsheet commands, including **R**ange, **C**opy, **M**ove, and **E**rase.

Chapter 5, "Formatting the Worksheet," teaches you how to customize the appearance of your data on-screen and in printouts by using the **F**ormat and other commands.

Chapter 6, "Using @Functions," explains Symphony's mathematical, trigonometric, statistical, financial, data-management, logical, and string functions. Also discussed are date and time arithmetic functions, Symphony functions used with ASCII/LICS, and special functions that give you information about the contents and locations of cells (or ranges) in the worksheet.

Chapter 7, "Managing Files," covers the commands for saving and retrieving files. The chapter also explains commands you use for file management, including erasing, consolidating, and translating files into formats other than Symphony's.

Chapter 8, "Learning SHEET Window: Hands-On Practice," is the first of a series of hands-on practice chapters that provide you with practical experience in working with Symphony's environments. The chapter shows you step by step how to create, save, retrieve, and expand a simple spreadsheet.

Part III: Using the Symphony Word Processor

Chapter 9, "Working in a Symphony DOC Environment: Word Processing," introduces you to Symphony's word processing capabilities. You learn the word processing commands and how to use them to create and edit text, and how to apply formats to your documents. The chapter also covers Symphony's word processing display, and the function and cursor-movement keys.

Chapter 10, "Learning DOC Window: Hands-On Practice," enables you to enter, edit, and format a document in Symphony's word processing environment.

Chapter 11, "Using Word Processing Add-Ins: Spelling Checker and Text Outliner," introduces you to Symphony's two word processing add-ins. This chapter shows you how to use these applications to enhance and extend Symphony's word processing capabilities.

Part IV: Creating Symphony Reports and Graphs

Chapter 12, "Printing Spreadsheets and Word Processing Documents," teaches you how to print spreadsheet reports and word processing documents. Through an explanation of the print commands and examples of printouts, the chapter explains how to take advantage of Symphony's print capabilities.

Chapter 13, "Using Allways: The Spreadsheet Publisher," explains how to use the Allways add-in to create professional-quality reports and graphs.

Chapters 14 and 15, "Creating and Displaying Graphs: Hands-On Practice" and "Printing Graphs," cover in detail Symphony's graphics capabilities. Chapter 14 provides examples of the types of graphs you can create, and explains how you can integrate Symphony's GRAPH environment with the other features of the program. Chapter 15 describes how to use and take advantage of the PrintGraph program.

Chapter 16, "Creating and Printing Graphs: Hands-On Practice," enables you to practice the commands and procedures you learned in Chapters 14 and 15.

Part V: Data Management with Symphony

Chapter 17, "Managing Data," tells you how to use Symphony's data-management capability by integrating the data-entry form features with the data-management commands and database statistical functions. You also learn about Symphony 2.2's new @BASE add-in, which enables you to read and write dBASE records to and from disk and work simultaneously with multiple databases.

Chapter 18, "Managing Data: Hands-On Practice," shows you step-by-step how to generate a database; enter, sort, and locate data; and produce reports.

Part VI: Symphony Communications Module

Chapter 19, "Using the Symphony Communications Module," shows you how to link your computer with many types of computers. The chapter also explains how to access a bulletin board system and how to communicate with another user's personal computer.

Chapter 20, "Learning Communications: Hands-On Practice," teaches you how to use Symphony's communications capabilities. In this chapter, you connect with a popular time-sharing service called CompuServe Information Service.

Part VII: Symphony Macros and the Command Language

Chapters 21 and 22, "Creating and Using Macros" and "An Introduction to the Command Language," provide you with the essential information you need to create and use keystroke macros and Command Language programs, and explain how to take advantage of Symphony's Macro Library Manager add-in. Chapter 21 shows you how to create, use, and debug macros, and shows sample macros that you can use with each Symphony environment. Chapter 22 covers in detail the features of Symphony's programming language—the Symphony Command Language.

Part VIII: Quick Reference Guide to Symphony

The **Troubleshooting Section** can be a valuable resource for you. This section addresses many of the problems other Symphony users have encountered while using the program, and offers a variety of solutions.

Using the Symphony Command Reference is a quick, easy-to-use, and comprehensive guide to using almost every command on the command menus. This section also gives reminders, important cues, and cautions that greatly simplify and expedite your day-to-day use of Symphony.

The book also includes two appendixes: Appendix A helps you install Symphony; Appendix B gives you a thumbnail sketch of new commands and features in Symphony 2.2.

Summary

USING SYMPHONY, Special Edition is designed to help you quickly master Symphony's powerful features. As a tutorial or reference, this book is the leading and most comprehensive source of information available on Symphony software.

Part I

Understanding and Getting Started with Symphony

An Overview of Symphony

Getting Started

1

An Overview of Symphony

Expanding 1-2-3

Symphony is an expansion of 1-2-3, the popular integrated spreadsheet program from Lotus Development Corporation. To 1-2-3's three business applications programs—electronic spreadsheet, business graphics, and data management—Symphony adds word processing, data-form management, and communications capabilities. Symphony makes all these expanded applications available in one sophisticated program.

The Symphony program is an impressive integration of five microcomputer software applications: spreadsheet, word processing, business graphics, database management, and communications. These environments are available as soon as you access the program, and are identified on-screen as window types.

Symphony's exciting window feature enables you to create bordered areas on-screen and to perform different applications within these areas with a great deal of flexibility (see fig. 1.1). You can create a spreadsheet in one window, word processing text in another window, a database in a third window, and a graph in a fourth window. At the same time, in a fifth window, you can receive data from another computer or send data to that computer. You can make these different windows appear on-screen simultaneously. (Whether graphs will appear on-screen with other applications depends on your equipment.) Or you can use the full-screen area to work on one application and then, by pressing one key, retrieve any other window you have created in the worksheet.

Reminder:

Graphs may or may not appear on-screen simultaneously with other applications, depending on your equipment.

9

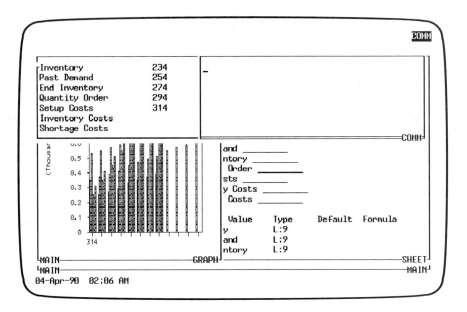

Fig. 1.1.

An example of Symphony's window feature.

The five Symphony environments include the following features:

❏ In the SHEET window, you can create many kinds of spreadsheets by using Symphony's large worksheet area (256 by 8,192 cells), sophisticated SHEET command menu, and multiple functions.

❏ In the DOC window, you can draft, revise, and edit documents through Symphony's word processing capability.

❏ In the GRAPH window, you can create and save graphs, display them in color (with the proper equipment), and also display them on-screen with other Symphony environments, such as spreadsheets, databases, and word processing text.

❏ In the FORM window, you can create a data form, generate a database, and perform sort and query operations.

❏ In the COMM window, you can send and receive data through telecommunications lines.

The following special features increase your productivity by using the power of Symphony:

❏ The *macro facility* creates macros that repeats frequently used keystrokes. You associate this macro with a particular key and when you need these keystrokes you press the key.

❏ With the *command language*, you get an extension of the macro facility that enables you to create sophisticated programs to customize Symphony. You can even design menus and commands by using this special feature.

❏ *Data integration* enables you to combine data created with the different Symphony capabilities. You can insert word processing data into a spreadsheet. You also can merge information from a database into a document to create form letters.

❏ The *add-in applications* are programs, such as Allways (a desktop-like publishing add-in), that are fully integrated with Symphony.

Each of the five Symphony environments, used singly, is an extremely potent tool. Symphony's real power, however, is best illustrated by the program's capability to integrate applications. If you use Symphony to create a spreadsheet and then retrieve the spreadsheet, create a new window, and build a graph on the screen while your spreadsheet is still displayed, you are using Symphony's integrative power. Whenever you create a database and then use it on-screen to help you compose an important report, you are also using Symphony's integrative power. And if you use Symphony's communications environment to receive on-line data, transfer it into a spreadsheet, graph the information to help you analyze it, then use both the spreadsheet and the graph to prepare a report, you are taking further advantage of Symphony's capability to integrate.

The best way to introduce you to Symphony is to present a simple example showing how you can use and then coordinate four of the environments (data management, spreadsheet, graphics, and word processing). Suppose that you want to use Symphony at home to maintain a record of payments you have made on household bills. You can begin by creating a data form like the one in figure 1.2, which was made in Symphony's FORM environment. In this environment, you can create a data form and then enter records into it. From the information you put in the form and from the records themselves, Symphony creates a database similar to that in figure 1.3.

Now suppose that you want to find out how much your gas bills increased during the fall and winter months of 1989-90 over the previous year's bills. By using Symphony's spreadsheet feature (referred to as **SHEET** in the top right corner of the screen), you can view a database that includes only gas utility costs (see fig. 1.4). Such a database, although originating from records entered in a FORM environment, can be changed within a SHEET environment by using Symphony's Query commands. The database in figure 1.4 was created from the larger database in figure 1.3, which contains not only gas but also electric, water, and telephone utility costs.

When you shift from Symphony's FORM environment to the SHEET environment, you can perform data query and sort operations on the database that was created in the FORM environment. You can also apply to the database the same functions used to create spreadsheets. For example, by using Symphony's spreadsheet environment, you can format columns in your database and adjust column width. Sorting the database, extracting certain categories (or fields), changing the format of values, and changing column width are operations provided by Symphony's spreadsheet function.

Fig. 1.2.
A data form.

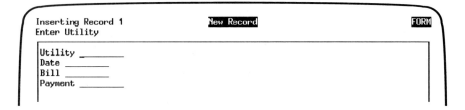

Fig. 1.3.
A database created from a form.

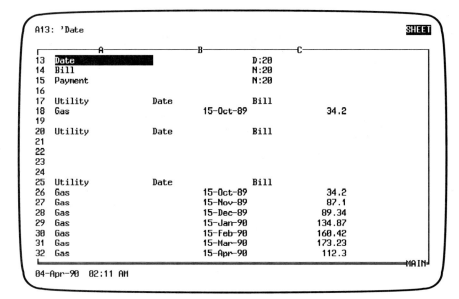

Fig. 1.4.
Viewing a database in the SHEET environment.

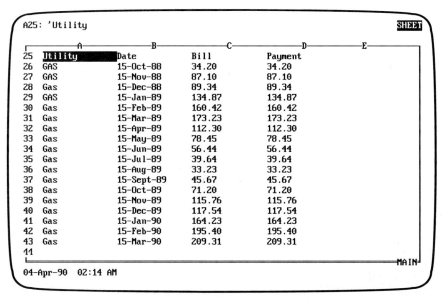

The database of gas costs in figure 1.4 provides a much better idea of how your gas bills have increased than does the database in figure 1.3. But Symphony's GRAPH environment enables you to quickly view the relationship between gas costs for the fall and winter of 1988-89 and costs for the fall and winter of 1989-90. By using the values in the "Gas Costs" database, Symphony created the graph shown in figure 1.5. As the graph indicates, your gas costs are steadily and significantly increasing.

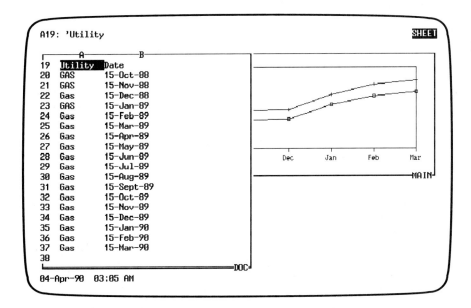

Fig. 1.5.
Creating a graph from a database.

Now assume that your discovery of this steady increase prompts you to write a letter to your state's public service commission to voice your concern about rising utility rates. While leaving both your database and graph on the screen, you can write your letter and even include with it a copy of the database that dramatically emphasizes how much gas costs have increased (see figs. 1.6 and 1.7). To make your point even more emphatic, you can attach to the letter a print of the graph shown in figure 1.8.

If this simple example has not convinced you of Symphony's power and capabilities, read on. The following sections, containing background to the program and an introduction to Symphony's features, provide further evidence.

Building the Symphony System

Symphony takes 512K of memory, or 640K of conventional or main memory when you use add-ins. To take full advantage of Symphony's capabilities, you need equipment to display graphs, to display text and graphs on-screen at the same time, and to use Symphony's communications feature. Table 1.1 provides a summary of the system requirements.

Fig. 1.6.

Three windows displayed on-screen simultaneously.

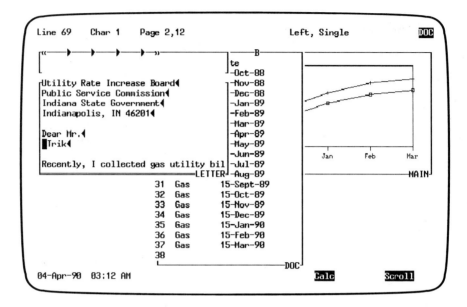

Fig. 1.7.

Incorporating database material in a word processing document.

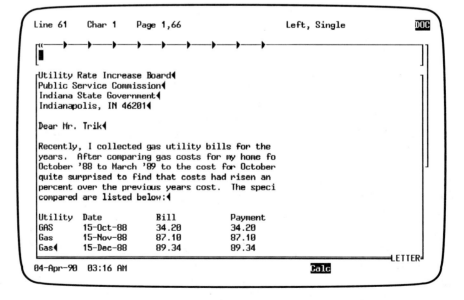

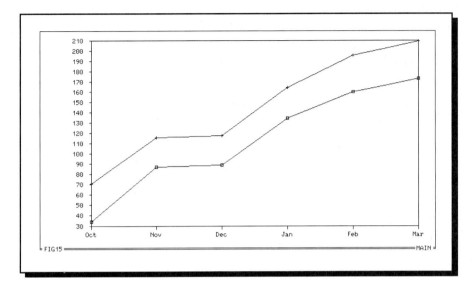

Fig. 1.8.
A printed graph.

Table 1.1
Symphony at a Glance

Published by:	Lotus Development Corporation 55 Cambridge Parkway Cambridge, Massachusetts 02142
System Requirements:	*Computer:* IBM® PC, IBM PC XT™. IBM AT, IBM Portable, IBM PS/2, COMPAQ® Portable, COMPAQ Plus. Toshiba, and other IBM-compatibles
	Display: color or monochrome.
	Minimum disk capacity: one double-density, double-sided disk drive
	Memory size: 512K; 640K when used with add-ins
	Operating system: PC DOS V2.0, V2.1, V3.0, V3.1, V3.2, V3.3; OS/2 V1.0
	Optional hardware: color/graphics adapter, printer, plotter, modem or acoustic coupler, additional monitor, add-on memory board, expanded memory board and math coprocessor

Appendix A includes the procedure for installing your Symphony disks so that they can operate with your equipment. Before you begin this installation procedure, though, keep these points in mind: You can use Symphony only with DOS Versions 2.0, 2.1, and later. If you want to display graphs on-screen simultaneously with other environments—such as spreadsheets, databases, and word processing text—you need to check the equipment requirements listed within the Symphony Install program.

Gauging The Worksheet and its Effect on RAM

Symphony's worksheet contains 8,192 rows and 256 columns (2,097,152 cells). Each column is assigned a one- or two-letter name ranging from A for the first column to IV for the last. A good way to visualize the worksheet is to imagine a giant sheet of grid paper about 21 feet wide and 176 feet high!

Compared to the tremendous overall size of the Symphony worksheet, the video display is capable of showing on-screen only 20 rows and 72 characters at a time. As illustrated in figure 1.9, the screen represents one small window on the Symphony worksheet. Because of the worksheet's size, you have plenty of room to create many windows within the same worksheet; windows containing different kinds of spreadsheets; databases; and notes, memos, or short reports.

Fig. 1.9.

Area of spreadsheet appearing on-screen.

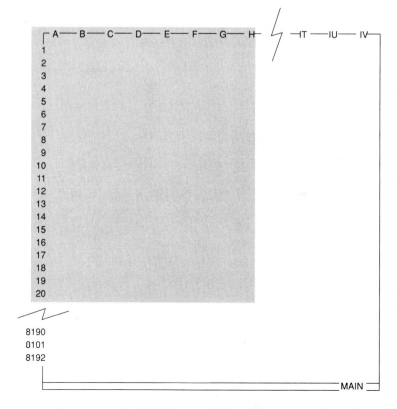

Symphony has some limitations, however, to using the entire sheet. In practical terms, you must consider memory limitations when you are determining the size and complexity of a spreadsheet or database.

The Symphony program with DOS requires approximately 350K of RAM. Symphony's large size stems primarily from the programming required for all the extra features that Symphony provides. Such features as windows, settings sheets, and extensive use of range names require memory on top of the memory required for your data.

In addition to the size of the Symphony program, you must consider the size of the worksheet in RAM. The number of active cells in a worksheet cannot simply be equated to its RAM requirements, because the contents of cells can vary greatly. Perhaps the best way to get a realistic notion of the potential size of a worksheet is to conduct two simple tests. In the first test, you can relate the size of the worksheet to the number of standard 8 1/2-by-11-inch pages that can fit into the worksheet. In the second test, you can experiment with filling cells in the worksheet, using the **C**opy command, and then see when you run out of main memory. From these two tests, you can draw realistic conclusions about the worksheet size.

To begin the first test, use a configuration of 640K of RAM. After you subtract 350K for the Symphony program and DOS, a worksheet size of 290K remains. If you divide the remaining RAM by the number of characters that fit on a standard 8 1/2-by-11-inch page with pica type (approximately 3,000 characters), you get approximately 96 pages. This figure points out the theoretical capacity of the Symphony sheet. In the second test, again use the configuration of 640K. Begin by entering the label **ABCDEF** in cell A1. Then duplicate this cell until you run out of main memory.

These tests indicate that you can fill columns A, B, and most of C, or approximately 24,000 cells. Assuming that 448 cells are on a printed page (8 columns by 56 rows), you can build a 53-page spreadsheet. The results from these two tests demonstrate the difference between theory and reality. Because of the way Symphony allocates memory, in reality your worksheets may be approximately half the size that you may expect.

As you can see, an important consideration when using Symphony is the size of the worksheets you create. Symphony requires a computer with at least 384K of memory; if you are operating Symphony with 384K, you are limited in the amount of space you can use on your worksheet. You may particularly find memory restricted when you create multiple windows in various sections of your worksheet.

A few guidelines, however, may help you get the most from the amount of memory you have available. First, try to monitor your memory use by periodically checking how much memory is available for your worksheet. you can easily check memory by selecting **S**ettings from the SERVICES menu.

Second, you need to understand how Symphony allocates and consumes memory. Symphony takes a columnar view of things. In other words, space is consumed from the first cell that contains data in a column down to the last cell that contains data in that column. Although blank cells between the first and last cells that contain data in a column still take up space, each column is viewed independently. Although Symphony's memory allocation scheme uses an efficient columnar orientation, you should strive to keep the active areas within any column packed as close as possible. If you spread out your entries too much, you may find yourself running out of memory because RAM is required to store the contents of cells between entries, even though only blanks may be in the cells. For example, the spreadsheets in figures 1.10 and 1.11 contain the same information, but the first spreadsheet requires about 8 percent more RAM than the second.

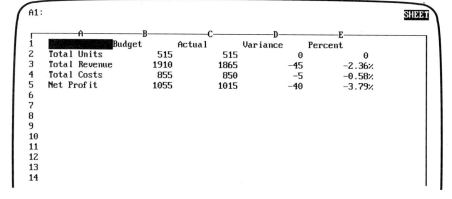

Fig. 1.10.

A spreadsheet that doesn't economize on space.

Fig. 1.11.

A spreadsheet that economizes on space.

Finally, remember that when you delete part of a worksheet, the main memory requirements for that worksheet do not diminish completely until you save the worksheet to your disk, then load the worksheet back into RAM. Symphony's optimization routines are not totally activated until you store a worksheet. Also, using the SERVICES **F**ile **X**tract command to shrink the memory requirements further may help. (The commands for storing and retrieving worksheets are covered in Chapter 7, "Managing Files.")

Examining Symphony's Capabilities

As mentioned previously, Symphony is an integrated collection of five microcomputer software applications: spreadsheet, word processing, data management, graphics, and communications. These applications are combined with the additional features of windows and a programming language called the Symphony Command Language.

Creating The Spreadsheet

Symphony's spreadsheet component is the most powerful of its features. The spreadsheet environment is an electronic replacement for the traditional financial modeling tools: the accountant's columnar pad, pencil, and calculator. In some ways spreadsheet programs are to these tools what word processors are to typewriters. Spreadsheets offer dramatic improvements in creating, editing, and using financial models.

Tip
To save you time, effort, and frustration when building your first electronic spreadsheet report, do the initial report by using pencil and paper, and then transfer the data over to your Symphony spreadsheet.

The typical electronic spreadsheet configures the memory of a computer to resemble an accountant's columnar pad. Because this "pad" exists in the dynamic world of the computer's memory, the pad is different from paper pads in some important ways. For one thing, electronic spreadsheets are much larger than their paper counterparts. Symphony has 8,192 rows and 256 columns.

Each row in Symphony's spreadsheet environment is assigned a number, and each column is assigned a letter or a combination of letters. The intersections of the rows and columns are called "cells," which are identified by their row-column coordinates. For example, the cell located at the intersection of column A and row 15 is called A15. The cell at the intersection of column X and row 55 is called X55. You can fill these cells with three kinds of information: numbers; mathematical formulas, as well as special spreadsheet functions; and text (or labels).

A cell pointer enables you to write information into the cells in much the same way that a pencil enables you to write on a piece of paper. In the Symphony spreadsheet environment, the cell pointer looks like a bright rectangle on the computer's screen. Typically, the cell pointer is one row high and one column wide.

Reminder:

In Symphony, you can create different windows in the worksheet area, all containing different applications.

Because the Symphony grid is so large, you cannot view the entire spreadsheet on the screen at one time. The screen thus serves as a "window" on the worksheet. As mentioned at the beginning of this chapter, this window can contain within it other windows. To view other parts of the sheet, you can scroll across the worksheet with the cursor-movement keys; or if you have created multiple windows on the worksheet, you can retrieve another window to take you to that part of the worksheet. In Symphony, you can create different windows in the worksheet area, all containing different applications, such as word processing and data management.

The spreadsheet feature is the foundation of the program. For example, when you are working in a word processing (DOC) window or data-form (FORM) window, all data is entered and stored within the worksheet boundaries. Because of this setup, entries and changes in a DOC or FORM window can affect a spreadsheet entered on the same worksheet.

To understand this concept, you may imagine a large grid containing 256 columns across the top and 8,192 rows along the side—which is the size of the Symphony worksheet. Then imagine various work areas that you have created on this worksheet (see fig. 1.12). In the upper left corner of the worksheet is a balance sheet. Directly to the right of the balance sheet is a database (created either by you or by Symphony through its FORM capability). Then below the balance sheet are a few of your notes—important points relating to the information in the balance sheet or database.

Cue:

To keep one data range from affecting another, restrict each work area or window so that the cell pointer does not move outside the restricted area.

Furthermore, to prevent one range of data from affecting another, you can restrict each work area or window so that the cell pointer doesn't move outside the window and so that some command operations affect data only within the restricted area.

Symphony's window feature enables you to create a spreadsheet, a database, and word processing text on the same worksheet within the worksheet's 256 by 8,192 boundaries. How much of this worksheet area you can use and how far apart you can keep one application from another depend on your machine's memory (as discussed in "Worksheet Size and its Effect on RAM," earlier in this chapter.)

Symphony 2.2 introduces you to the new Advanced Expanded Memory feature, which is discussed at the end of this chapter. This is memory in addition to the 640K conventional memory limit that meets the Lotus/Intel/Microsoft® Expanded Memory Specification (LIM specification, versions 3.2 and 4.0). Although AEM enables you to build much larger worksheets, keep in mind that AEM takes more time to process your data than does conventional memory.

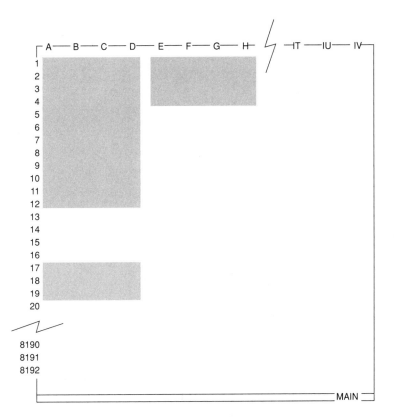

Fig. 1.12.
*Symphony's
worksheet area.*

Adding Expanded Memory Specification

Symphony Version 1.1 and higher can take advantage of the Lotus/Intel/
Microsoft® Expanded Memory Specification, and combination hardware/
software trick to fool the operating system into recognizing more memory than
it usually can. Until this method was developed, any program (including
Symphony) that operated under normal DOS could not access more than 640K
of RAM; Symphony worksheet creation was thus limited to about 290K of
memory.

Plug-in memory boards that support expanded memory are now available. By
adding one of these boards to your computer, you can break through the DOS
memory barrier of 640K RAM. In fact, Symphony Version 1.1 and higher can
address up to about four megabytes of memory under EMS. That is quite a jump.

EMS is not, however, the perfect solution to the need for more memory. Even
with plenty of expanded memory available, you can fill conventional memory
(up to 640K) to the point that Symphony does not allow you to proceed.
Expanded memory stores only certain kinds of information, and conventional

memory is needed to do much of the "bookkeeping" associated with keeping track of such information. Furthermore, depending on the exact nature of your worksheets, you may notice that speed decreases as your worksheet expands to fill the available space.

Symphony incorporates many functions and commands. For example, Symphony contains statistical and date functions and offers a wide variety of formats for numeric entries. These formats also enable you to display or print numbers with embedded commas, dollar signs, parentheses, and percent signs. You also can specify the exact number of digits to display to the right of the decimal. For example, Symphony can format the number 12345 to look like $12,345.00, 12,345, 1.23E3, or 12345. You can have the number -12345 appear as ($12,345.00) or -12,345. And the number .45 can look like 45% or $.45.

Symphony provides the full range of commands for entering and changing individual cells and ranges, adjusting columns and rows, creating and using range names, and recalculating a worksheet (see Chapters 3 and 4).

Playing "What If... ?"

The act of building a model on a spreadsheet establishes all the mathematical relationships in the model. Until you decide to make changes, every sum, product, division, subtraction, average, and net present value remains the same. Each time you enter data into the model, computations are calculated at your command with no effort on your part. All these computations are calculated correctly; spreadsheets do not make math errors. And next month, when you decide to use the same model again, the formulas will still be set, ready to calculate at your command.

Reminder:

Once you have built a set of mathematical relationships into your spreadsheet, Symphony can recalculate it with amazing speed.

Even more important, spreadsheet software enables you to play "What if ... ?" with your model, particularly when you use Symphony's command, function, and graphics capabilities. Once you have built a set of mathematical relationships into the sheet, Symphony can recalculate it with amazing speed, by using different sets of assumptions. If you use only paper, a pencil, and a calculator to build a model, every change to the model requires recalculating every relationship in it. If the model has 100 formulas and you change the first one, you must make 100 calculations by hand to flow the change through the entire model. If, on the other hand, you use a spreadsheet, the same change requires the press of only a few keys—the program does the rest. This capability permits extensive "what if" analysis.

Two specific parts of the Symphony program that enable you to easily perform "what if" analysis are the "what if" graphing capability and the SHEET **R**ange **W**hat-If command. Symphony's graphics can be an integral part of "what if" analysis by enabling you to fine-tune projections, budgets, or projects. Symphony's GRAPH window helps you understand the effect on your model of changes in your data. For example, you can create one window to display spreadsheet data and another window to display a related graph. You can then display both windows simultaneously on the screen. When you make a change in the data, the GRAPH window immediately reflects the change.

Reminder:

You can create one window to display spreadsheet data and another window to display a related graph. You then can display both windows simultaneously on-screen.

Symphony's SHEET **R**ange **W**hat-If command, on the other hand, enables you to conduct extensive sensitivity analysis and to display the results in a tabular form. The SHEET **R**ange **W**hat-If command enables you do the kind of thorough analysis that you may not do otherwise, given the time required to perform the analysis.

These are only two examples of how Symphony can help you with "what if" analysis. As you use the program, you may find numerous ways for conducting sophisticated "what if" analysis through the power of Symphony's functions and Command Language.

Performing Data Management

Symphony's integration capability, which was mentioned earlier, enables you to perform database operations within the program's spreadsheet environment. Some of the tasks you may want to perform on a Symphony database can be accomplished with the Symphony SHEET commands. For example, you can add records to a database with the SHEET **I**nsert **R**ows command. Editing the contents of a database is like editing the contents of any other cell in the worksheet.

Release 2.2 provides the add-in @BASE (discussed later in this chapter), a powerful database manager that enables you to work with database files from within Symphony, thereby enhancing Symphony's database operations.

In Symphony, you also can sort data. You have three options for sorts: primary key, secondary key, or third-order key. You can conduct a sort in ascending or descending order by using alphabetical or numeric keys. In addition, Symphony enables you to perform various kinds of mathematical analyses on a field of data over a specified range of records. For example, you can count the number of items in a database that match a set of criteria; compute a mean, variance, or standard deviation; and find the maximum or minimum value in the range.

Reminder:

Symphony enables you to perform various kinds of mathematical analyses on a field of data over a specified range of records.

The full power of Symphony's data-management capabilities is especially evident when you make use of the data-form environment (FORM window), the data-management commands included in Symphony's spreadsheet menu, and the database statistical functions.

With its data-management capabilities, Symphony can handle many chores for you, such as setting up database ranges, criterion ranges, and output ranges. When you work in a FORM window, much of the work is done for you by the program itself.

While you are in a FORM window, you rarely see the entire database at one time. You view the records through a special data form that you build with Symphony's help. To create a data form, such as the one shown earlier in this chapter, begin in a SHEET or DOC window and enter the field names you want in your form. After you enter the field names, shift to a FORM window to have Symphony generate an actual data form and then to begin entering records in the form. (The specific procedures for creating and using a data form are covered in Chapter 17.)

After you enter records into your data form, you can use the data commands in the FORM menu to perform data-sort operations. You also can sort records by using the SHEET environment. In fact, when you switch from a FORM window to a SHEET window, Symphony provides a number of data-management operations that you can use on the database you have created. In a spreadsheet environment, for example, you can have Symphony (1) find records that match the given criteria, (2) copy to a specified area of the worksheet all or some of the records in certain fields that match given criteria, and (3) delete records in a database. In a SHEET environment, you also can change the width of columns in the database, change the format of values, and insert or delete columns or rows.

After you begin using Symphony's data-management operations, you will find how high-powered they are.

Creating Graphs

You can create graphs in two parts of the program: the spreadsheet menu, and the GRAPH environment.

Symphony can create bar, stacked-bar, line, scatter, and pie (including exploded pie) graphs and high-low-close-open charts. The exploded pie graph is like a standard pie graph, except that one or more of the slices is separated from the pie for emphasis. High-low-close-open charts are useful for graphing the prices of stocks over time and for evaluating trends.

Other graphics features in Symphony include crosshatchings, nonzero origins, logarithmic graph scales, and the ability to control scaling factors manually.

With the right equipment and the correct driver set, you can display both the graph and the spreadsheet on-screen at the same time. This feature is further enhanced by use of the Allways add-in. If your system cannot display the graph and spreadsheet simultaneously, you can shift back and forth between the spreadsheet and the graph by pressing one key repeatedly.

Using Word Processing

When you use Symphony's DOC environment, you have the full range of commands and operations that are included in sophisticated stand-alone word processing programs. And when you use Symphony's Command Language to create macros for simplifying word processing operations, you may find that the word processor is easy to use and very powerful.

Symphony's word processor provides a number of capabilities. You can move the cursor forward or backward character by character, word by word, or from the beginning to the end (and vice versa) of a line, paragraph, or page. In addition, Symphony enables you to move the cursor to any character by pressing End and then pressing that character. Furthermore, a command for naming lines in your text enables you to use Symphony's GoTo key for moving quickly from any location in your text to the named line.

Besides being able to move the cursor in various ways, you also can regulate and change the format of your text. You can set and store configuration settings for margins, spacing, tabs, and paragraph justification. When you store these settings in Symphony's configuration file (see the section on **C**onfiguration in Chapter 2), the margins, spacing, tabs, and paragraph justification are automatically set for your text every time you begin a new word processing session.

If you want to change these configuration settings temporarily for a particular document, you can use Symphony's DOC **F**ormat **S**ettings command. And if you need to change format in the middle of a document, Symphony's **F**ormat **L**ines enables you to change margins, spacing, paragraph justification, and tabs for only one section, then return to the original settings for your document.

Symphony's word processor also includes complete editing and revising capabilities. With Symphony's **E**rase command or **E**rase key (a special function key for initiating erase operations), you can erase any number of characters, from single characters to large blocks of text. Symphony makes possible the marking and erasing of large blocks of text with a couple of keystrokes. And when you create macros for erase operations, the number of keystrokes is reduced to one. (See Chapter 21 for more information on creating word processing macros.)

In addition, Symphony's **S**earch and **R**eplace commands can help you edit text. When you use **S**earch, you can search either forward or backward and easily exit from the search at any time. Although the **R**eplace command performs only forward search-and-replace operations, you can incorporate this command with a macro that automatically moves the cursor to the top of your file to begin a search.

For composing and revising, you can use Symphony's **C**opy, **M**ove, File **X**tract, and **F**ile **C**ombine commands to create form letters, combine parts of one document with another, and reorganize sections of text.

Reminder:

Symphony's DOC environment gives you as much processing power as many sophisticated stand-alone word processing programs.

Reminder:

By using the Configuration file, you can set and store for future use margin, spacing, tab, and paragraph justification settings.

Cue:

To speed up Symphony's Replace capability, create a macro that automatically moves the cursor to the top of the file to begin a search.

Symphony's DOC environment is an integral part of the program for many reasons. First, using Symphony's word processing environment is similar to using the other program applications—spreadsheet, graphics, data management, and communications. Second, you can easily integrate a DOC window with other types of windows. Being able to display a SHEET or GRAPH window along with a DOC window can help you to draft certain kinds of reports. In addition, you can readily incorporate parts of spreadsheets and databases into your text and have your text printed with tables or figures inserted right where you want them.

Beginning with Release 2.0, Symphony includes two word processing add-in applications: Spelling Checker and Text Outliner. When the Spelling Checker is attached, you can check your documents for spelling errors and typing mistakes. An additional option appears on the DOC menu: **V**erify. When the Text Outliner is attached, you can use the OUTLN window type to create and edit text outlines.

Communicating with Symphony

Symphony's communications capability (COMM environment/window) is quite sophisticated, rivaling that of many stand-alone packages. With Symphony, you can use your personal computer to receive database information from a corporate mainframe computer or minicomputer. You also can connect to a time-sharing service to get current news, stocks, weather, and other information. Finally, Symphony's communications capability enables you to exchange information with another microcomputer. You can even connect with many different kinds of computers.

Symphony supports asynchronous communications transmission and several types of protocol for file transfer. With asynchronous transmission, a clock in the computer is used to time the sampling of incoming data and the recording of the number of bits in each sample. You specify the transmission speed (the baud rate or bits per second) for the clock. Protocol, a special system of rules established for exchanging information between computers, is specified during installation. You can select from three different types: XMODEM, BLAST, or B Protocol. XMODEM, developed by Ward Christensen, has become a standard in the microcomputer industry for communications protocols. BLAST (Blocked Asynchronous Transmission) is used on some large systems, while B Protocol can be used to communicate with CompuServe Executive Information Service.

Like other Symphony environments, the communications environment enables you to enter settings for a specific COMM window in the **S**ettings selection from the COMM menu. In the COMM **S**ettings sheet, for example, you enter such settings as the protocol parameters: baud rate, byte length, stop bits, and parity. Also included in the COMM **S**ettings sheet are selections for automatic dialing (if your modem has an auto-dial feature) and settings for matching the characteristics of the COMM window you are using with the service or computer you are calling.

Available through CompuServe, the time-sharing service, is a source of information called "The World of Lotus." When you access CompuServe's Executive Information Service (EIS), you can receive messages from Lotus Development. These messages may contain, for example, information on Symphony product services, tips and techniques for Symphony users, a Symphony user newsletter, and a library of Command Language programs, worksheet models, and add-in applications. In addition, you can send and receive messages to and from other Symphony users.

Reminder:

Symphony users can link with time-sharing services to obtain messages on program and product services, tips and techniques for Symphony users, and a Symphony-user newsletter.

When you mail in your Symphony registration card, you will receive a list of CompuServe's services and one hour of free connect time. This on-line time gives you an introduction to The World of Lotus. One other benefit is that the free on-line time gives you a chance to try out Symphony's COMM environment.

Creating Window Features

As indicated at the beginning of this chapter, with Symphony's window capability you can move among any of the five applications and view different parts of the same worksheet. In other words, you can create and work within multiple windows on a single screen.

Symphony keeps track of the windows you create by requiring a name for each window. When you use the **W**indow **C**reate command, the program displays a list of existing windows. You then must name the new window, using a name that does not appear in the list. The name can contain up to 15 characters, and can include any alphanumeric characters, spaces and punctuation marks. Whenever you are working in a particular window, it is bordered at the bottom with a double line. The double line tells you that the window is currently the "active" window. That is, the active window is the one in which you can perform command operations, enter data, and make changes.

Reminder:

The double line at the bottom of the window tells you that the window is the active window in which you can perform command operations, enter data, and make changes.

The **W**indow command menu and special window function keys enable you to change the type of window, create new windows, change the size and shape of windows, and split a window horizontally and vertically. You also can restrict a window to a specific range in the worksheet so that data you enter and changes you make won't interfere with data entered in other windows on the worksheet. As mentioned earlier, you can organize a single worksheet into different parts, or applications, by creating multiple windows of different types. And if you store the worksheet with the SERVICES **F**ile **S**ave command, these different windows are stored in one file.

Once you begin using Symphony's window features, you discover unlimited possibilities for integrating various types of windows on one screen. Creating windows enables you, for example, to compare and analyze spreadsheet data from different areas of the worksheet. You also can write memos and short reports as you view spreadsheets and databases. And you can see data displayed in graphs and modify those graphs as you change the data.

Using the Command Menu System

When you access Symphony through the ACCESS SYSTEM, the first menu to appear is the ACCESS SYSTEM menu, which provides options for starting Symphony, PrintGraph, Install, and File Translate.

Seven command menus also are available. These menus include (1) a SERVICES menu for global operations such as **F**ile **S**ave, **R**etrieve, and **E**rase, (2) a TYPE menu for changing the type of window you are working in (SHEET, DOC, GRAPH, FORM, and COMM), (3) a SHEET menu for spreadsheet work, (4) a DOC menu for word processing, (5) a GRAPH menu for graphics, (6) a FORM menu for data-form operations, and (7) a COMM menu for communications. If the Text Outliner application is attached, an OUTLN menu is also available.

Many of Symphony's command menus are multilevel (menus within menus). After you select a choice from a menu, Symphony, if it needs more information, provides you with another menu from which to choose.

Using Settings Sheets

In the seven Symphony menus listed, you will find settings sheets. Except for the DOC menu, all command menus contain settings sheets at the first level. These settings sheets enable you to enter settings for such operations as creating graphs, printing reports and documents, or using Symphony's communications capability.

Reminder:

Symphony displays multiple settings on a single screen, which is helpful when you need to remember special print or graph settings.

Symphony displays multiple settings on a single screen. This feature is helpful when you need to remember special print or graph settings. Another advantage of settings sheets is that you can create a catalog of some types of sheets and retrieve these types when needed. To store and reuse a settings sheet, you must assign a name that Symphony can attach to the sheet.

Working with Functions

Symphony includes a wide assortment of built-in mathematical, statistical, financial, logical, date, time, and string functions. In addition, a set of special functions is available that gives you detailed information about the contents of cells (or ranges) and their locations in a spreadsheet. In Chapter 6 you will find a detailed explanation of all the Symphony functions. Here, however, is a brief introduction.

Symphony has a variety of string functions that give you significantly more power to manipulate strings than do earlier integrated packages. The @FIND function, for example, enables you to locate the starting position of one string within another string. The @MID, @LEFT, and @RIGHT functions enable you to extract one string from another. You can use these string functions, only a few of the many functions available in Symphony, to increase the power of Symphony's database and Command Language capabilities.

The date and time functions in Symphony include @DATEVALUE, @NOW, @TIME, and @TIMEVALUE. @DATEVALUE, a variant of the @DATE function, accepts a date-string rather than a numeric argument. With @DATEVALUE, you can enter @DATEVALUE*("6/21/88")*, and the function produces a serial number, just as @DATE does when you enter @DATE*(88,6,21)*. The @TIME function arrives at a serial number for a specified time of day that you enter in numeric arguments: @TIME*(3,12,30)*. @TIMEVALUE, on the other hand, uses string arguments to produce a serial number from the information you provide for the hour, minute, and second:

> @TIMEVALUE*("12:30:59")*.

The special functions in Symphony include @CELL, @CELLPOINTER, @ROWS, @COLS, @TRUE, and @FALSE. All of these provide information about the contents of cells or ranges and their locations in a spreadsheet. For example, if you enter @CELL*("width",B12..B12)*, Symphony returns the width of column B as viewed in the current window. In addition to indicating width, the @CELL function can indicate the address of a cell, the type of value, the label prefix, the format, and the row or column number location. (See Chapter 6 for a listing of the special functions' capabilities.)

Cue:
Use @CELL to indicate the address of a cell, the type of value, the label prefix, the format, and the row or column number location.

Symphony offers a comprehensive set of built-in functions. And when you use these functions with Symphony's Command Language, you have the ingredients of a sophisticated programming language.

Using International Formats and Character Set

One other special feature of Symphony is the availability of international formats and an international character set. First, through the configuration settings, you have the options of changing **C**urrency, **D**ate, and **T**ime formats to international formats. The **C**urrency option, for example, enables you to change the default dollar sign ($) to a foreign currency sign, such as the British pound (£), if you are going to use that format regularly throughout your worksheet. Second, the international character set, referred to as the Lotus International Character Set (LICS), provides characters from many languages. You can enter these characters at any keyboard. In Symphony's *Reference Manual*, you will find a complete list of international and special characters available in LICS.

Using Symphony's Security System

Symphony enables you to protect cells in a worksheet so that changes cannot be made in cells containing, for example, important formulas. Symphony's range-protection capability, however, also extends to protecting a section of word processing text in a DOC window. In addition, you can use a special password security system to lock an entire worksheet or range of cells.

Whenever you protect an area of your worksheet, whether the area is part of a spreadsheet or part of word processing text, you use two commands: Symphony's SERVICES **S**ettings **G**lobal-Protection command and the SHEET **R**ange **P**rotect command. These two commands, which enable you to protect a range of cells, prevent users from erasing, moving, or changing the cells, although the cell contents are displayed on-screen. If you want not only to protect cell contents from being changed but also to keep them from being displayed on-screen, you can use the two commands mentioned previously along with the SHEET **F**ormat **O**ther **H**idden command. (See Chapter 4 for details on protecting a range in the worksheet.)

In addition to the range-protection capability, Symphony enables you to "lock" an entire worksheet or range of cells. With Symphony's security system, you create a password for locking and unlocking the worksheet. Only by using the password can a user make changes or even see cell contents.

The last form of security that Symphony provides is the ability to password-protect a file when you save it. This system prohibits anyone even from retrieving the worksheet without the password.

To use the security system, you must select a number of commands in a specific order. The commands and steps for locking a worksheet are provided in table 1.2.

The first four steps listed in table 1.2, after you have completed them, will have certain effects on your worksheet. A user cannot change the cell protection setting that you entered in SHEET **R**ange **P**rotect. The SERVICES **S**ettings **G**lobal-Protection setting also cannot be changed. Finally, a user cannot redisplay "hidden" cells. With the security system, cell contents do not appear either in the worksheet or in the control panel. If you choose to **F**ile **S**ave the file with a password, a user who doesn't know the password cannot retrieve the file. When you do a **F**ile **R**etrieve of a file that has been saved with a password, Symphony prompts you to enter the password.

Whenever you want to unlock a worksheet that you have locked, retrieve the worksheet and select SERVICES **S**ettings **S**ecurity **U**nlock. At the **Password** prompt, enter your password. As long as you enter the password in the exact form in which you created it, you can control any of the settings that were previously frozen.

Table 1.2
Steps for Using the Security System

1. Turn on global protection (SERVICES **S**ettings **G**lobal-Protection **Y**es) and set SHEET **R**ange **P**rotect.

2. Hide cells from being displayed on the screen by selecting **F**ormat **O**ther **H**idden from the SHEET menu. This command applies to cell entries that you made in a SHEET environment, so don't use **F**ormat **O**ther **H**idden with entries made in a DOC or FORM environment.

3. Once you go through the steps for locking a worksheet, you can unlock it only with the password you have created. You may therefore want to create a backup file of your worksheet at this point, in case you forget the password. To create a backup, save your worksheet under a file name different from the one containing the security system.

4. Lock the worksheet by selecting the SERVICES **S**ettings **S**ecurity **L**ock command. Enter a password when the password prompt appears. Before pressing enter, write down the password and check the spelling closely. To unlock a worksheet, you must enter the password exactly as you originally created it, including upper and lower case letters. Symphony is case sensitive when it comes to security and accepts a password only as specified. For example, if you create the password MYBUDGET, Symphony will not retrieve the file if you enter the password as mybudget or MYbudget.

5. You can further protect the worksheet by saving it with a password. Select SERVICES **F**ile **S**ave, type a **P** (at least one space after the specified file name), and press Enter. Symphony prompts you for a password and after you press Enter, prompts you to verify the password by typing it again.

Symphony's security system goes beyond simply protecting ranges. With the security system, you not only can protect ranges from change, but also prevent users from viewing important data or even from retrieving a worksheet.

Programming with the Command Language and Macros

Symphony provides not only a keyboard macro capability, but also a sophisticated programming language. The Symphony Command Language is the programming language available to you for automating repetitive keyboard tasks.

The Symphony Command Language contains a nearly full-featured programming language, including the capability to call subroutines, iterative looping, improved conditional logic, and error trapping. Through these tools, you can develop special applications programs to run by using Symphony.

Another feature of Symphony's Command Language is the program's capability to store commands automatically. With Symphony's Learn mode, you can easily create keyboard macros that are usable with little or no editing. When you use the Learn mode, Symphony converts into Command Language statements the commands and keystrokes you enter and then stores the statements in a special worksheet range that you set. Through a name that you assign to this range of statements, you can invoke the macro to simplify an operation.

If you want to go beyond the Learn mode capability and build your own macros to perform many types of complex operations, Symphony's Command Language enables you to do so. These commands do not simply duplicate keystrokes, as does creating a macro with the Learn mode. The Command Language enables you to program, which is much like using a programming language such as BASIC.

With Release 2.2, Symphony has enhanced Step mode (a macro integrity-checking feature) to make it easier for you to locate problems in the execution of a macro.

Symphony's Command Language has its own special grammar and set of keywords. For example, if you want to enter a command in your macro to cause it to stop processing temporarily so that you can enter a label, you use the following:

{GETLABEL *"Enter label: ",FIRST FIELD*}

GETLABEL is one of the Command Language's keywords. The items that come after the keyword are examples of arguments that you include in Command Language statements. (For a detailed look at Symphony's Command Language, see Chapter 22.)

Cue:

For more efficient use of memory, store your macros in separate macro libraries.

Symphony can place macros into separate macro libraries that you can call from any worksheet. These libraries load into a separate area of memory (nicknamed "hyperspace" by Lotus) where they remain resident until explicitly removed. In addition to removing the "clutter" of many macros from your worksheets, this capability enables you to achieve more efficient use of memory; commonly used macros need not appear in every worksheet.

Naming in Symphony

Besides Symphony's window and integration features, another important feature for you to know before you jump into the program is "naming." You will do a lot of naming when you use Symphony. Naming, in fact, is fundamental to the program. Naming files, of course, is one kind of naming, but file naming is only the beginning.

By using range names, you can get around the worksheet quickly and enter ranges in commands. When you are working in the word processing environment, you can name lines in your document. These lines may include lines of text or special lines you insert in a document whenever you want to vary the format of the text. You also can name settings sheets for printing, creating graphs and databases, and communications.

In some cases, Symphony gives you the option of providing names for all the windows you create on the screen for different applications. And when you don't name the windows, Symphony takes the initiative and names them for you, by using numbers.

Reminder:
If you forget to name your window, Symphony automatically names it for you by using numbers.

Whenever you assign names, Symphony keeps track of them for you. By keeping track of named print settings, lines of text, format lines, and so on, Symphony helps you get more out of the program. If you want to use a name again and again, Symphony saves the name (and what's attached to it) for you. Then when you want to print, for example, a letter with most if not all of the same print settings you used in another letter in the worksheet, you can call up those original settings—but only if you gave them a name.

Reminder:
Before you can print a document by using settings from previous documents, you must first have given the previous settings a name.

As you begin using Symphony, watch out for the special commands that refer to names. When you become accustomed to Symphony's naming feature, you may find that it is quite an advantage.

New Features in Symphony Release 2.2

Symphony Release 2.2, although retaining the familiar menu structure and ease of use, provides a number of new features to further enhance its wide range of capabilities. Those of you who have upgraded to this version may appreciate the many different improvements to the program. Symphony now offers:

❏ Lotus Magellan VIEWER add-in to simplify file management

❏ Full integration of the Allways add-in

❏ The @BASE add-in that supplies disk-based database functionality

❏ File linking support

❏ An improved use of expanded memory

❏ Enhanced Step mode for macro debugging

Using the Lotus Magellan VIEWER Add-in

This add-in is provided to improve file management tasks by allowing the user to view a list of files and their contents on a two-window display (as shown in fig. 1.13), before loading them into memory or linking them (see Linking Files later in this chapter for a more complete explanation).

Fig. 1.13.

The Lotus Magellan VIEWER Add-in

```
 FIG01.WR1       A1: 'Inventory                                    SHEET
 FIG02.WR1
 FIG04.WR1
 FIG15.WR1        Inventory            234   334   434   534
 FIG16.WR1        Past Demand          254   354   454   554
 FIG22.WR1        End Inventory        274   374   474   574
 IMPORT.WR1       Quantity Order       294   394   494   594
 MINDLESS.WR1     Setup Costs          314   414   514   614
 TAB1KC.WR1       Inventory Costs
 TEST.WR1         Shortage Costs
 WINDOWSH.WR1
                  Inventory _____
                  Past Demand _____
                  End Inventory _____
                  Quantity Order _____
                  Setup Costs _____
                  Inventory Costs _____
                  Shortage Costs _____
                                                                   COMM
 File 1 of 12     FIG01.WR1        4/03/90   8:21p      6,314 Bytes
```

You also gain the capability to browse through all the files in a directory and view their contents. It is important to note that although you may view files in a variety of directories, you must first select the desired directory as the default directory using the SERVICES **F**ile **D**ir menu option before you can view the file with the viewer. An example of this is when you want to view a file in another directory that you want to link to. You would have to change directories by using the previously prescribed method.

Four viewers are available. They provide a method for you to identify a file by its contents, rather than by its file name. You will see the first screen of a Symphony worksheet file, a 1-2-3 worksheet file, a dBASE file, or a text file.

The default viewer is the text file viewer and it is used if the file does not match one of the other three viewer file formats. This viewer strips out any graphics in the file and displays only alphanumeric characters.

If you need to view other kinds of files, other than those described previously, you will need to use Lotus Magellan, an additional software product available from Lotus Development Corporation.

Once you have invoked the VIEWER and located the file you desire, you may **B**rowse, **L**ink or **R**etrieve the file.

Using the Allways Add-in

The Allways add-in is now fully integrated into the Symphony program directory. The installation of Allways occurs during the routine installation of Symphony. To use the Allways add-in you must have at least 640K of conventional memory.

Reminder:
To use the Allways add-in, you need at least 640K of conventional memory.

Allways gives you a complete formatting and printing system for your Symphony worksheets. You can use up to eight fonts in any printout, make text and numbers bold or underlined, adjust row height and column width, add light, dark and solid black shades to worksheet areas, draw horizontal and vertical lines, enclose cells in boxes or outline ranges, double underline, include Symphony graphs in the same printout as your worksheet, print in color (if you have a color printer) and print to PostScript printers.

Allways provides a WYSIWYG (What-You-See-Is-What-You-Get) display, if you have the proper type of display adapter.

Using the @BASE Add-in

This add-in is a powerful database manager that brings you the capability to work with data in dBASE file structure. (It will also read Foxbase files, for example). @BASE does not restrict the size of your database to the worksheet capacity. It enables you to work with multiple databases at the same time.

To use @BASE you need the three add-in files included with Symphony. They are: BASE.APP, BASEUTIL.APP and BASEFUNC.APP. Each of these files may be invoked through the SERVICES **A**pplication menu option.

With the use of the @BASE add-in you can bring data files into the worksheet for processing, work directly with the database files on disk, and transfer Symphony database records to database files on disk. You also can work with @BASE databases by using Symphony macros.

Linking Files

This new feature enables you to bring data from worksheet files on disk into the current file for use in calculations. This move is accomplished by entering a linking formula in the current file that refers to a cell in a file on disk. To keep things clear, the current file is called the "target file," because it receives data. The file referred to by the linking formula is called the "source file" because it supplies the data.

Reminder:
With Linking Files, you can bring data from worksheet files on disk into the current file for use in calculations.

File linking provides you with an effortless means of updating worksheets affected by a change of data in another worksheet. You can use this to consolidate data from a number of worksheets into a summary worksheet. Advantages of consolidating data include reduced recalculation time and reduced memory consumed by your worksheets. You also eliminate large quantities of unnecessary data in the target worksheet because the data already exists in the linked source files.

To use the Linking File feature, you must create a linking formula by using the following special format:

> +<<*file reference*>>*cell reference*

Symphony 2.2 cannot link to 1-2-3 Release 3.0 worksheet files (WK3 files). To link to these files you must first save them as a WK1 file.

New File Commands

By adding the File Linking feature, Symphony 2.2 includes the following new file commands:

Command	Function
❏ Updating Linked Cells	Ensures that Symphony is using the most recent data by recalculating all linking formulas in the current worksheet. You access this command by using SERVICES (F9) **F**ile **A**dmin **L**ink-Refresh
❏ Listing Linked Files	Displays a list of all files on disk that are referenced by linking formulas in the current worksheet. Access this command by invoking SERVICES (F9) **F**ile **L**ist **L**inked
❏ Creating File Tables	Creates a table of all files that are linked by formula references to the current worksheet. This table takes up three columns and lists the file names in alphabetical order, the date and time each file was last modified and the file size. Access this command by using SERVICES (F9) **F**ile **T**able

Debugging Macros

Release 2.2 includes an enhanced STEP mode to simplify locating problems in a macro. If a macro does not perform as you expect and produces an error, you need to debug the macro (find out which instruction is causing the problem). Although at times you may be able to find the cause of this error by observation, there may be times when you need to go through the macro and evaluate the problem. This chore is better handled through use of the Step mode.

Reminder:
If a macro does not perform as you expect and produces an error, you need to debug the macro.

The Step mode is accessed by using Alt-F7 to turn it on. This produces an indicator at the bottom of the screen telling you that the Step mode is on (as shown in fig. 1.14).

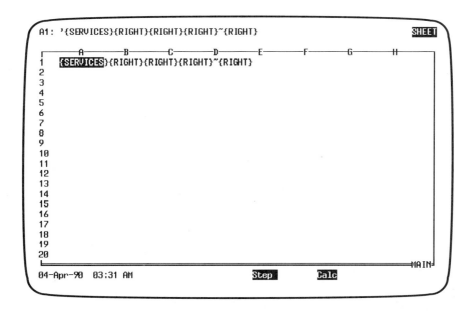

Fig. 1.14.
Indicator showing that the Step mode is on.

Once the Step mode is activated, proceed to run the macro. Each time you press a key to execute another instruction in the macro, Symphony replaces the Step indicator to display information about the macro instructions that are being executed. You may be able to locate and edit errors to correct the problem.

Using Advanced Expanded Memory (AEM)

Symphony's Advanced Expanded Memory (AEM) feature is designed to manage memory for Symphony users. Because of the large size of the Symphony program, there may be times when handling large worksheets presents a memory limitation. AEM takes full advantage of expanded memory for users who have expanded memory available.

To use AEM you must enable the feature. Enabling is handled through the **C**onfiguration **O**ther menu option. You access this option by using SERVICES (F9) **C**onfiguration **O**ther **M**emory. Please note that AEM is set to **Y**es by default and it will stay active until you specifically disable it. You may change the default to **N**o and use the **C**onfiguration **U**pdate option to save the setting.

If you are using add-ins with AEM, you must first attach the add-in, then enable AEM.

Disabling AEM

At times, you may need to disable AEM. For example, when you are using a non-Lotus add-in. When this occasion occurs, first save the current worksheet and then clear the worksheet on the screen with SERVICES (F9) **N**ew menu option and follow the procedure described previously by selecting **N**o to disable the AEM.

Chapter Summary

This chapter summarizes what Symphony is all about. The chapter gives you a comprehensive view of Symphony by introducing you to the program's main features and capabilities. As a first step in learning Symphony, you now have an overview of the features and concepts that make Symphony what it is—an outstanding integrated software package.

For a more specific look at Symphony's powerful spreadsheet, word processing, graphics, data management, and communications applications capabilities, turn to the following chapters. In the next chapter, you learn how to get started by understanding the program's command system, special screen display features, and uses of the keyboard. You also learn in later chapters how to use each of Symphony's five environments (SHEET, DOC, GRAPH, FORM, and COMM), how to print reports and graphs, how to use Symphony's Command Language, and how to integrate Symphony's five applications.

Getting Started

You have read Chapter 1 and been introduced to Symphony's main features and capabilities, and are ready to start using the program. However, before you start, Symphony requires some preparation. You must install and set up the Symphony software on your computer. These operations are detailed in Appendix A. Also, you must know how to load the Symphony program. This chapter gives you the kind of background you need for getting started with Symphony.

This chapter discusses the following Symphony features:

❏ The menu structure
❏ Special uses of the keyboard
❏ General features of the Symphony display screen
❏ The functions and operations of Symphony's windows

Beginning and Ending Symphony

You may enter Symphony directly from the DOS prompt or from the Symphony Access menu. By using the DOS prompt method, you enter directly into the Symphony program. You are then ready to begin working in Symphony. If you choose the Access method to enter Symphony, you bring up a menu displaying the additional functions (**P**rintGraph, **I**nstall, **F**ile-Translate) of Symphony, along with the option to enter Symphony.

Entering Symphony Directly

The DOS prompt handles entering Symphony whether you have the program installed on a hard disk or you are using dual drives and loading from floppies.

39

If you are using a system with two disk drives, you should place the System disk into drive A and a formatted disk into drive B. Then at the **A>** prompt, type **symphony**. This command takes you directly into the Symphony program. If you have Symphony on your hard disk, first change to your Symphony directory (for example, type **cd \symphony**); then type **symphony**.

Entering Symphony by Using the Access Menu

At the DOS menu (following the steps outlined previously for dual drives or hard disk), type **access**. The Symphony Access System command menu, as shown in figure 2.1, displays the following five available functions:

Symphony **P**rintGraph **I**nstall **F**ile-Translate **E**xit

With the Access System, you can move back and forth between the **S**ymphony, **P**rintGraph, **I**nstall, and **T**ranslate programs.

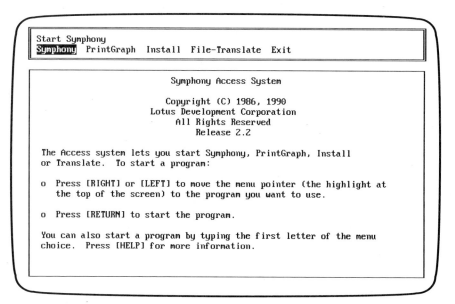

```
Start Symphony
Symphony  PrintGraph  Install  File-Translate  Exit

              Symphony Access System

              Copyright (C) 1986, 1990
              Lotus Development Corporation
                 All Rights Reserved
                   Release 2.2

  The Access system lets you start Symphony, PrintGraph, Install
  or Translate.  To start a program:

  o  Press [RIGHT] or [LEFT] to move the menu pointer (the highlight at
     the top of the screen) to the program you want to use.

  o  Press [RETURN] to start the program.

  You can also start a program by typing the first letter of the menu
  choice.  Press [HELP] for more information.
```

The first option in the Symphony Access System menu is to enter Symphony. To do so, either point to Symphony in the menu by using the cursor-movement keys (→ ←) and then press Enter, or simply type **S**. (All Symphony menus enable you to select commands either by moving the cursor and pressing Enter, or by typing the first letter of the command.)

Several seconds may pass before the next screen appears. For a hard disk system, you will see only the SYMPHONY box and then the first spreadsheet window.

To exit the Symphony program, select **E**xit from the SERVICES menu. Afterward, Symphony reminds you to save your work if you haven't done so beforehand. If you entered Symphony from the Access System, **E**xit returns you to the Access System. To exit from the Access System, again select **E**xit.

Using The Symphony Menus

Four main menus make up the Symphony menu system: the Access System menu, the SERVICES menu, the command MENU system, and the window TYPE menu. You retrieve each of the four main menus in the following manner:

❑ To retrieve the Access System, you must type access (plus the name of the driver set if you are not using the default "Lotus") at the DOS prompt.

❑ To retrieve the SERVICES menu, press SERVICES (F9).

❑ To retrieve the command MENU for each application (SHEET, DOC, FORM, GRAPH, and COMM), press Menu (F10).

❑ To retrieve the window TYPE menu, press Type (Alt-F10).

The menus are hierarchical (menus within menus) and enable you to generate a command with several steps. To select a command from any menu, you can either move the cursor to the selection and press Enter, or you can type the first letter of the command. If you want to move out of a command menu completely, press Ctrl-Break. To move back to a prior command-menu level, press Esc.

Using PrintGraph

The **P**rintGraph option in the Access System menu initiates the PrintGraph program for printing graph files. When you choose this option for a two floppy drive system, you must load the PrintGraph disk before you can run the program. (See Chapter 13 for a detailed discussion of the PrintGraph program.) As with other programs, you can proceed directly to the PrintGraph program without going through the Symphony Access System. Type **pgraph** at the operating system prompt. If the driver name is not "Lotus," you must enter the driver name after typing **pgraph**.

Working with Install

You can start up the **I**nstall program from the Access System menu by selecting **I**nstall from the menu options or directly from the system prompt by simply typing **install** and pressing Enter.

Using File-Translate

The **F**ile-Translate option accesses the Translate utility. This utility provides a link between Symphony, 1-2-3, Jazz, and outside programs, including VisiCalc and dBASE III. As with the other programs, you can access the Translate utility directly from the operating system prompt. To access the program from the system prompt, type **trans** and press Enter. If the name of your driver is not "Lotus," you must type **trans** and the driver name. (The Translate utility is discussed in detail in Chapter 7.)

Using the SERVICES Menu

No matter which method you select to access the main Symphony program, once Symphony is loaded, three types of command menus are available for retrieving commands and performing operations: SERVICES, TYPE, and command menus specific to each Symphony application. Within the SERVICES and application command menus you find a number of settings sheets. (Fig. 2.2 shows an example of a database settings sheet in the FORM environment. Also refer to this chapter's section on "Settings Sheets.") These settings sheets contain various characteristics that either relate to a particular environment, or are global to the Symphony program. Most of the characteristics in the settings sheets can be modified.

Fig. 2.2.

A sample database settings sheet.

```
Database, Criterion, Output ranges                                    MENU
Basic  Form  Underscores  Sort-Keys  Report  One-Record  Name  Cancel  Quit

Basic Ranges                              Report Ranges
   Database:                                 Main:
   Criterion:                                Above:
   Output:                                   Below:
Form Ranges                                  Type         Single
   Entry:                                       Entry list:
   Definition:                                  Input cell:
Underscores:      Yes                      One-Record:      No
Sort-Keys
   1st-Key:                   2nd-Key:                   3rd-Key:
   Order:                       Order:                     Order:
                                                =Database Settings: MAIN
```

The SERVICES menu provides utilities that are common to all Symphony window types, along with configuration, special settings, and add-in program options. The window types are also referred to as the Symphony environments (SHEET, DOC, GRAPH, FORM and COMM). You can retrieve the SERVICES menu (see fig. 2.3) as you are working in any window.

```
Modify current window or use another window                          MENU
Window  File  Print  Configuration  Application  Settings  New  Exit
      A        B        C        D        E        F        G        H
1   ████████
2
```

Fig. 2.3.
The SERVICES menu.

The first selection in the SERVICES menu is **W**indow. **W**indows are work environments where you can use Symphony's many capabilities to view data in different ways depending on the type of window. You can retrieve a window already created; create and name new windows; delete windows; change window size or location; hide, isolate, or expose windows; or split one window into two or four.

The **F**ile selection contains commands for saving, retrieving, and erasing files, as well as commands for special file operations, such as copying files (or parts of files) into worksheets (see Chapter 7).

The **P**rint selection provides the commands for printing all Symphony documents except graphs. **C**onfiguration enables you to change default settings.

Another selection, **A**pplication, enables you to access add-in programs and use them when needed. For example, adding DOS through **A**pplication enables you to perform such operations as copying or formatting disks without having to exit from the Symphony program.

The **S**ettings selection displays and enables you to change operations for (1) creating and using macros, (2) locking a worksheet, (3) protecting cells in a worksheet, and (4) automatically loading a communications file. The final two commands in the SERVICES menu, **N**ew and **E**xit, enable you to create a new worksheet (after you have saved the current one) and exit Symphony.

Using Windows

The best way to describe a Symphony **W**indow, is to compare it to a work environment that Symphony provides to display data in the worksheet in a variety of ways. Creating multiple windows is useful when you are attempting to view a Symphony worksheet that is too large to fit on the screen. Normally, you would be limited to the portion that fits within your display screen. Using the **W**indow menu option enables you to view different portions of the worksheet simultaneously. You also may need to do more than one type of work in the same worksheet. With the Symphony **W**indow menu option you can view two or more different spreadsheets in the same worksheet or a spreadsheet and a word processing document through a separate window on the screen.

Reminder:
You can create multiple windows to view a Symphony worksheet that is too large to fit on the screen.

You can place the windows anywhere on the screen you desire. They may even overlap and vary in size (up to the size of the display screen). By using the **R**estrict **R**ange option, you can restrict the area the cell pointer can move in and confine different activities to different parts of the same worksheet.

Symphony consists of five work environments that may be viewed through a selection of a window type. A portion of the worksheet is displayed through the SHEET and DOC windows. Database information displays one record at a time through the FORM window. Graphs are displayed in a GRAPH window, and the COMM window acts as a computer terminal screen.

Reminder:

To shift from working in a spreadsheet window to working in a word processing window, press Type and select DOC.

Once you have selected the **W**indow type, by using Type (Alt-F10), the window's type appears in the upper right corner of the screen. At any time you may shift from one type of window to another by pressing Type (Alt-F10), then selecting the type of window you want. For example, if you want to shift from working in a spreadsheet window to working in a word processing window, press Type and select DOC; if you want to work in the data forms window, select FORM; and so on. (See the section in this chapter titled "Function Keys Working in All Windows," for a detailed explanation of specific **W**indow commands.)

While you may have more than one window on the screen, Symphony limits your working activity to one window at a time. The window that you are working in is called the current window.

Symphony's window capability enables you to move among any of the five components—spreadsheet, word processing, data-management, graphics, and communications—and view different parts of the same worksheet. Figure 2.4, shows three different views of a window on-screen at the same time.

Fig. 2.4.

Multiple windows on the screen.

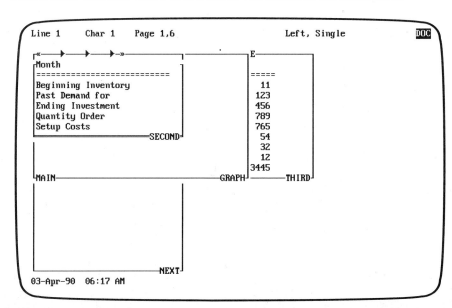

Through the SERVICES **W**indow command menu, you can change the type of window, create new windows, change the size of windows, split windows horizontally and vertically, and easily change the number of windows that appear on the screen at any one time. Menu options also include capabilities for restricting a SHEET or DOC window to a specific range in the worksheet, changing the type of border around a window, and automatically redisplaying a worksheet after changes. Use of the function keys and the SERVICES **W**indow menu make it possible to access the many window operations Symphony provides.

Symphony provides a default window, called MAIN. This window is as large as your display screen will allow. Unless you choose to create additional windows, you will be working in the MAIN window. The default window may be used for all the work you do and you never have to create another window. If you would like to create additional windows, take a closer look at the options Symphony provides.

Creating Windows and Files

Once you begin using Symphony's window feature, you find that the feature enables you to organize a single file into many different parts, displaying information in different forms. With the Symphony window feature, you can create multiple windows of different types, or shift easily from one type of window to another.

For example, if your file contains a spreadsheet beginning at cell A1 and ending at cell M90, and a database beginning at cell AA1 and ending at cell AT300, you can easily display sections of both the spreadsheet and the database in two separate windows. If you want to view a graph that analyzes the spreadsheet data, you can add a third window to your screen. Finally, if you want to use the information from your spreadsheet, database, and graph to prepare a word-processed report, you can create a fourth window.

All these windows are created and can be stored within the same file. Although you may be writing the report in a separate window, the text is entered into the same worksheet file in which you created your spreadsheet and database. Changes that you make in one window can affect all other windows, unless you have set restrict ranges (see the section on restricting ranges). When you are working within a window, make sure that different spreadsheets, databases, and texts are far enough away from each other so that one doesn't erase part of or interfere with another. Remember also that when you initiate the **F**ile **S**ave command, windows are saved within a file as they appear on-screen. You can store windows, like data, within individual files, unless you delete the window by using the **W**indow **D**elete command.

Cue:
To keep changes made in one window from affecting other windows, set your restrict ranges

You also can create two or more separate screens and view data from different files. If you want to view data from different files, use the **F**ile **C**ombine command to pull data from one file into another (see Chapter 7).

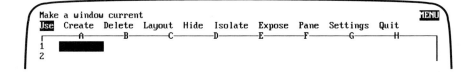
Reminder:

By using Windows you can write memos and short reports at the same time you view spreadsheets and databases.

After you begin using Symphony's window feature, you may find the possibilities limitless for integrating various types of windows onto one screen. Creating windows enables you to compare and analyze spreadsheet data from different areas of the worksheet. Windows enable you to write memos and short reports at the same time you view spreadsheets and databases. And with windows, you can not only see data displayed in graphs, but also watch graphs change as you modify the data.

Using Function Keys for Window Operations

Five function keys control special window operations, such as changing the type (TYPE—Alt-F10), switching between two types of windows (SWITCH—Alt-F9), moving the cursor from one window to another (WINDOW—F6), zooming from a small-screen window to a full-screen window (ZOOM—Alt-F6), and redrawing a window (DRAW—Alt-F8).

Creating the Window Menu

The **W**indow menu, like other primary menus from the SERVICES menu, contains numerous levels that require different types of responses (see fig. 2.5). And like other menus, the **W**indow menu contains a settings sheet, which indicates the current settings for the current window: the name, the type, the range for which pointer movement and data entry are restricted, the display of borders, and the redisplay of a window after spreadsheet changes are made. In addition to the **S**ettings command, other commands control creating, retrieving, and deleting windows; removing and redisplaying windows; changing the size and position of windows; and dividing a window into two or four parts.

Fig. 2.5.
The SERVICES Window menu.

```
Make a window current                                                    MENU
Use   Create  Delete  Layout  Hide  Isolate  Expose  Pane  Settings  Quit
      A        B       C       D      E        F       G      H
1
2
```

Creating, Using, and Deleting Windows

Within the **C**onfiguration selection of the SERVICES menu, both window type and name are preset. When you first enter Symphony, you may find that the initial window type is SHEET, and the window name is MAIN. You can change these settings if you want, but an initial window type and name must be set at all times. For example, if you find yourself using the FORM window more frequently than the SHEET window, you can change the **C**onfiguration setting to FORM. Then every time you enter Symphony, a FORM window appears as the first one.

For creating new windows, Symphony provides two procedures. In the first procedure, you (1) select **C**reate from the **W**indow menu, (2) provide a name for the new window, (3) select the window type (SHEET, DOC, GRAPH, FORM, or COMM), (4) identify the size and shape of the new window, and (5) make changes in the **W**indow settings sheet.

The second procedure is to select **P**ane from the **W**indow menu and indicate the type of split—vertical, horizontal, or both. Symphony automatically names each window and creates each one in the same size and shape. If you want to change the type or name of a window, select **W**indow **S**ettings; if you want to change the size and shape of the window, select **W**indow **L**ayout.

Reminder:
Symphony automatically assigns a number to each window created with the **P**ane *menu command.*

To use windows you have previously created, select the **U**se command from the **W**indow menu, then indicate which window you want displayed on-screen. When you retrieve another window, the cursor moves from the current window to the window just retrieved. To return the cursor to the other window, press Window (F6). This function key also retrieves previously created windows and displays multiple windows on-screen at the same time. Switch (Alt-F9), on the other hand, switches the current window type, such as DOC, to a previous window type, such as SHEET.

To delete windows, select **W**indow **D**elete. If you want to remove a window from the screen only temporarily, use the **W**indow **H**ide command.

Removing and Redisplaying Windows

Sometimes you may want to create three or four windows and be able to use any one of them when needed, but also have access at times to a full screen. Three commands—**H**ide, **I**solate, and **E**xpose—and a function key enable you to remove any or all windows from the screen and to expand a single window to full-screen size. **H**ide and **I**solate do not delete a window; you can at any time redisplay the window on-screen. If you use the **H**ide and **I**solate commands then save your file, all previously created windows still exist when you retrieve the file later. As illustrated in figures 2.6A and 2.6B, you can easily change from a screen containing three or four windows to a screen with one window expanded to full-screen size, then redisplay all windows again. If you remove all but your main window, use Zoom (Alt-F6) to expand the remaining window to full-screen size.

Changing Window Shape and Size

In addition to using Zoom (Alt-F6) to expand a window, you can use the **W**indow **L**ayout command to expand or decrease the size of any window as well as regulate its shape and position on the screen. When you select **W**indow **L**ayout, you can position the window anywhere on the screen by anchoring the cursor at a spot that may become one of the four corners of the new window.

Fig. 2.6A.

A screen with three windows.

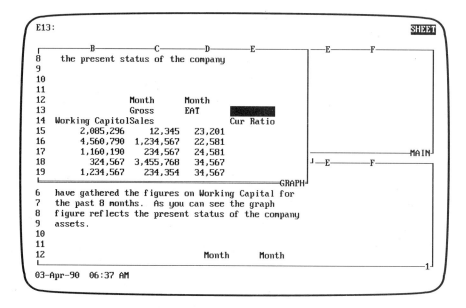

Fig. 2.6B.

Zooming to a full-screen window.

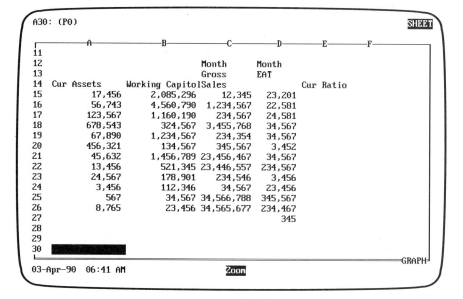

Position the cursor in any corner of the window by pressing either the period (.) or Tab key. (Pressing **H**ome moves the cursor to the top left corner of the current window.) Next, highlight the size and shape of the screen you want, by using the cursor-movement and PgUp and PgDn keys (see fig. 2.7). Then press

Enter. If you decide to change the position of a window but want to retain the current size and shape, select **W**indow **L**ayout, press Scroll Lock, and move the cursor.

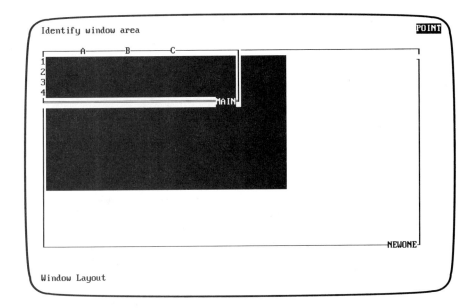

Identify window area   POINT

          A   B   C
        1
        2
        3
        4
                                MAIN

                                                    NEWONE

Window Layout

Fig. 2.7.
Regulating the size and shape of a window.

As mentioned earlier, one quick way to create multiple windows is by using the **W**indow **P**ane command. This command enables you to divide an existing window into two parts, horizontally or vertically, or into four windows (see fig. 2.8). After you have created two or four windows with the **W**indow **P**ane command, you can then change the position, shape, and size of any of the windows. If window size or location causes one window to overlap another, the window in which you are currently working remains on top until you move to work in another window. That window then cycles to the top of the stack.

Restricting Ranges in Windows

Restricting your work area within a SHEET, DOC, FORM, or COMM window is an important step in creating windows for two reasons. First, restricting the area in which you can enter text in a DOC window, or data in a SHEET window, prevents you from accidentally erasing or changing work in another part of the worksheet. Second, restricting the work area can speed up the operation of certain commands. Restricting your work area is particularly important when you are working within a DOC window on a worksheet containing spreadsheet data, because changes in the DOC window can affect the spreadsheet.

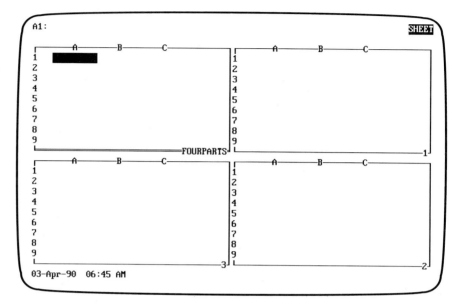

Fig. 2.8.

*After selecting
SERVICES **W**indow
Pane.*

To restrict a window area, (1) press Services (F9); (2) select **W**indow, then **S**ettings; (3) select **R**estrict; (4) select **S**creen if you are going to use only the space in the current window, but select **R**ange if your work area will be larger than the current window; (5) select **Q**uit to enter the restrict range; and (6) then select **Q**uit once more to return to DOC mode. Note that when you select **R**ange, you also must indicate the area either by typing the beginning and end points or by moving the cursor.

Using File

The **F**ile menu in Symphony contains **S**ave, **R**etrieve, **C**ombine, **X**tract, **E**rase, **B**ytes, **L**ist, **T**able, **I**mport, and **D**irectory selections. You most often will use **R**etrieve and **S**ave, respectively, to load from and save your worksheets to disk. Combine and **X**tract allow you to load or save selected portions of worksheets. With **I**mport, you can bring into a worksheet ASCII print files created by Symphony or another program. The other commands, as you will see, provide additional file management capabilities. For example, **B**ytes indicates the available disk space on the current drive. The **T**able selection creates in a specified range of the worksheet a table with information on files in the specified directory. This information includes file names and extensions, the date and time that each file was last changed, and the number of bytes for each file. (For more information on the Symphony **F**ile menu, see Chapter 7, "Managing Files.")

Using Print

You can use the SERVICES **P**rint menu to print all documents—spreadsheets, databases, and word processing documents—but not graphs. The Symphony **P**rint menu contains a settings sheet (see fig. 2.9) that displays print options and either default or changed settings. Because the settings sheet is displayed as soon as you retrieve the **P**rint menu, you can tell immediately what settings you need to change before saving a print file or printing your report.

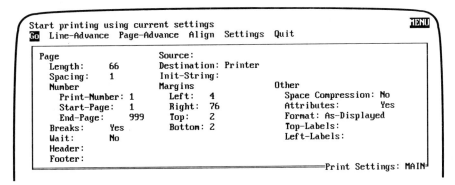

Fig. 2.9.
The SERVICES
P*rint Settings*
sheet.

Symphony enables you to name and save **P**rint settings sheets so that you won't have to reset a sheet every time you need to change margins, headings, etc. (See Chapter 12, "Printing Spreadsheets and Word Processing Documents," for specific explanations of commands.)

Cue:
*To avoid resetting a sheet every time you need to change margins and headings, name and save your work through **P**rint settings sheets.*

Using Configuration

Configuration, the fourth selection from the SERVICES menu, provides an easy way for viewing and changing default settings (see fig. 2.10). **C**onfiguration settings affect numerous operations, from changing the type of window that initially appears after you access Symphony to changing the size of margins for printing reports. When you display the configuration settings for the first time (press F9 and select **C**onfiguration), you see the default settings provided by Lotus. You can easily change any setting by selecting the appropriate category in the menu, entering the change(s), and then choosing **U**pdate to store the new setting.

Symphony stores configuration settings in a configuration file named SYMPHONY.CNF. Whenever you make a change in these settings, you have the option of updating the configuration file. To update the file, select **U**pdate from the **C**onfiguration menu after entering all the changes you want to make. Whenever you select **U**pdate, Symphony stores all current settings in the file. If you do not select **U**pdate, all newly entered settings are in effect only until the end of your current work session or until you exit from the Symphony program.

Reminder:
*If you do not select **U**pdate, all newly entered settings remain in effect until the end of your current work, or until you exit from Symphony.*

Fig. 2.10.

The SERVICES Configuration settings sheet.

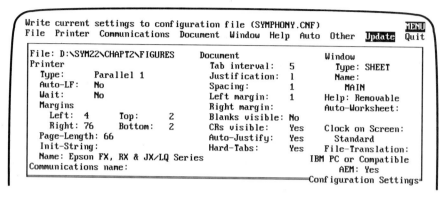

Throughout the remaining chapters of the book, various configuration settings are mentioned. Here are the types of settings you can enter in **C**onfiguration:

Setting	Function
File	Stores the disk drive and current directory for the start of a Symphony session (see Chapter 7)
Printer	Contains the configuration settings for the type of printer, line advance, pause between printing pages, margins, page length, initialization string, and printer selection (see Chapter 12)
Communications	Indicates which communications configuration file should be loaded at the beginning of a session; also used to cancel an existing file (see Chapter 19)
Document	Stores default format settings for Symphony's DOC (word processing) environment; these default settings are for tabs, paragraph justification, spacing, margins, automatic justification of paragraphs, and display of hard spaces, carriage returns, and hard tabs (see Chapter 9)
Window	Controls what window type and name are first displayed when you begin a Symphony session or create a new worksheet file by selecting SERVICES New (see the section earlier in this chapter on "Creating, Using, and Deleting Windows")
Help	Controls whether the Symphony Help file remains open throughout a session (**I**nstant), or opens only when you press Help and closes once you return to Symphony (**R**emovable)

Setting	Function
Auto	Enables you to automatically load a worksheet file as soon as you begin a Symphony session
Other	Contains the default settings for (1) **C**lock, which regulates the date and time format appearing in the bottom left corner of your screen; (2) **F**ile-Translation, which regulates character-code translation tables; (3) **I**nternational, which regulates **P**unctuation and **N**egative display in values, and arguments in functions and in **C**urrency, **D**ate, and **T**ime formats (see Chapter 4); and (4) **A**pplication, which regulates automatically loaded add-in programs
Update	Updates the Symphony configuration file (CNF) to include any changes in settings

Although the SERVICES **C**onfiguration settings provide global default settings, you can override many of these settings within the specific type of window in which you are working. Settings sheets in the SHEET, DOC, GRAPH, FORM, and COMM environments enable you to override the default settings (see the section in this chapter called "Settings Sheets").

Using Application

The **A**pplication selection in the SERVICES menu enables you to add outside programs and retrieve and use those programs without leaving Symphony. The **A**pplication selection enhances Symphony in two ways. First, the selection enables you to use operating system commands without having to leave Symphony. Second, **A**pplication provides the flexibility for adding other programs, such as Allways, the Macro Library Manager, Spelling Checker, the Lotus Magellan VIEWER, @BASE and Text Outliner.

Four **A**pplication commands control the loading and unloading of add-in programs: **A**ttach, **D**etach, **I**nvoke, and **C**lear. The **A**pplication **A**ttach command loads an add-in program into main memory, except when you have entered add-in programs into the **C**onfiguration **O**ther **A**pplication setting of the SERVICES menu. In that case, the add-in program(s) automatically load when you select **A**pplication. Whenever you add a program, Symphony adds the file extension APP when the program is attached.

After you load a program into main memory (either automatically or with **A**ttach), you select **I**nvoke. This command activates the program so that you can begin to use it. **D**etach and **C**lear are necessary when you need to free up the memory space being used by add-in programs. **D**etach unloads a single add-in program, and **C**lear unloads all add-in programs, completely freeing the memory space for add-ins.

Reminder:
*When you need to free up the memory space being used by add-in programs, invoke the **Detach** and **Clear** commands.*

The function of the **A**pplication selection is illustrated in Chapter 7. The "Making Backup Copies of Files" section of that chapter describes the procedure for using the DOS add-in application to access the operating system without leaving Symphony.

Using Settings

The **S**ettings selection permits you to enter special global settings and indicates the amount of both conventional and expanded memory available as you work within Symphony. It also indicates whether a math coprocessor chip is installed in your system to speed up certain calculations. The following chapters present specific applications of the **S**ettings options. Provided here, however, is a brief description of each selection.

With the **S**ettings menu, you can change and save special settings for creating and executing macros (see Chapter 21 on keyboard macros). To create keyboard macros automatically, select **L**earn. To execute a macro automatically at the beginning of a worksheet, select **A**uto-Execute.

Reminder:

Symphony enables you to protect a worksheet so that the only way to view and change it is by entering a password.

Settings also enables you to secure a worksheet so that the only way to view and change the worksheet is by entering a password that you have created (see Chapter 4 on SHEET window commands). If you want to prevent someone else from viewing and modifying a worksheet, use the **S**ecurity selection in combination with **G**lobal-Protection, and the **R**ange Protect and **F**ormat **O**ther **H**idden commands of the SHEET menu (see Chapter 4). Finally, through the SERVICES **S**ettings **C**ommunications selection, you can automatically load a communications configuration file. (Communications is discussed in Chapter 19.)

Using New

If you finish working in a worksheet and want to begin a new one, as well as a new file, you select **N**ew from the SERVICES menu. Be certain that you save your current worksheet first. Once you have selected **N**ew, Symphony asks whether you want to erase everything. If you select **Y**es, the current worksheet data is lost, unless you first use the **F**ile **S**ave command.

Reminder:

If you want to save your file, you must select File Save before exiting the program. Symphony does not automatically save your file.

Using Exit

The **E**xit selection returns you to the main Symphony Access System (or the operating system prompt, if you started up the program by typing symphony). Here again, you need to make sure that you have saved your work before exiting. Symphony does not automatically save your file, so you must select **F**ile **S**ave before exiting the program.

Learning the Command Menu

The SERVICES menu contains the primary operations relating to all applications; each application also has its own command menu, invoked by Menu (F10). Although the command menus of the different applications are somewhat similar, each is tailored to a particular environment. The SERVICES menu is used for all windows and remains the same no matter which one you are working in; but, the second kind of menu, the command menu, changes with each type of window (see fig. 2.11). You can retrieve the primary command menu for each window by pressing F10. (When working within a SHEET window, you can retrieve the command menu either by pressing F10 or by pressing the slash (/) key in the lower right corner of the alphanumeric keyboard.)

```
 Use a database and its associated entry-form           MENU
  Attach  Criteria  Initialize  Record-Sort  Generate  Field  Settings
```

Fig. 2.11.
Command menu for the FORM window.

Using Settings Sheets

In both the SERVICES menu and the command menus, you find settings sheets. Figure 2.12 shows an example of a SHEET settings sheet. These sheets enable you to store settings for everything from **G**lobal-Protection in a worksheet to **S**pacing settings in a word processing work area.

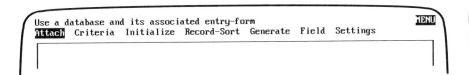

Fig. 2.12.
A sample settings sheet in the SHEET environment.

Except for the DOC command menu, all command menus contain settings sheets on the first command line. Settings is the final selection in the SHEET, FORM, and COMM menus; **1**st-Settings and **2**nd-Settings are the second and third selections in the GRAPH menu. Special settings sheets, however, are located within first-level commands. For example, the SHEET **G**raph command contains two settings sheets, the SHEET **Q**uery command contains one, and the DOC **F**ormat command contains one.

For example, if you want to set horizontal or vertical titles in a worksheet, you find **T**itles within the SHEET **S**ettings window. In addition, you enter numerous kinds of DOC format changes, including changes in tabs, margins, and spacing, through the **F**ormat **S**ettings sheet.

Tip

By creating a catalog of named settings sheets, you can retrieve them quickly for use in printing various kinds of document formats.

Settings sheets make it possible for Symphony to display multiple settings on-screen at once. Symphony updates the settings sheet as you select menu commands to change the current settings. These settings are saved when you save the worksheet so that you do not have to re-enter the same information the next time you perform the same operation. You also can create a catalog of named settings sheets and retrieve them when needed. Such a catalog is useful when you have various kinds of document formats to print, such as memos or letters, each with its own special margin, heading, and spacing formats.

A catalog of print settings sheets can make the job of printing these documents quite simple. As you read other chapters in this book, you will find examples of specific settings sheets and suggestions on how you can use them to make your tasks easier in spreadsheets, word processing, graphics, data management, and communications.

Reminder:

The SERVICES Configuration Settings menu options contain the default settings for every environment screen.

You may find in many cases that settings sheets located in the specific menus of the SHEET, DOC, GRAPH, FORM, and COMM environments contain the same settings as those in the **C**onfiguration settings of the SERVICES menu. The effect of SERVICES **C**onfiguration settings on settings sheets in the SHEET, DOC, GRAPH, FORM, and COMM windows may be a bit confusing at first. The important fact to remember is that the SERVICES **C**onfiguration **S**ettings menu options contain the default settings for every environment screen. To override these settings for a particular environment screen, you may use the settings sheet contained in that environment's settings menu option. These varied settings will apply to that one document only. The next time you use the **N**ew menu option, you will be using the settings contained in the SERVICES **C**onfiguration **S**ettings menu option. To help you understand this, take a look at the following example.

Suppose that the SERVICES **C**onfiguration setting for the left margin of a DOC window is 5 spaces, and the right margin setting is 65 (see fig. 2.13). Suppose also that you are just beginning a new worksheet and have created a DOC window for writing a memo. When you create the DOC window, the setting for the left margin is 5 spaces, and for the right margin the setting is 65. If you begin entering text into this DOC window, all lines are indented 5 spaces on the left, as in figure 2.14.

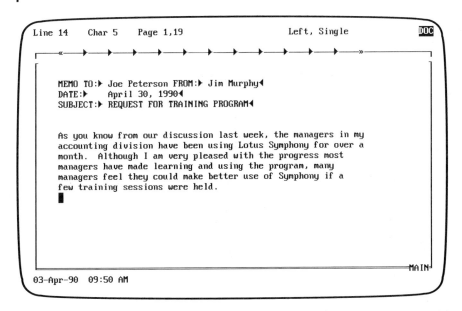

Fig. 2.13.
The left margin at 5, right margin at 65.

Fig. 2.14.
Margin appearing in the document.

If, however, you decide to change the default left margin setting to 10 spaces, you do so by changing the settings sheet in the DOC menu. To change the DOC settings sheet, retrieve the DOC menu by pressing Menu (F10), select **F**ormat from the menu, and then choose **S**ettings. After you select **S**ettings, Symphony displays a settings sheet containing format settings. If you compare the settings in the settings sheet in SERVICES **C**onfiguration **D**ocument with the settings in **F**ormat **S**ettings, you see that the settings are the same. After you change the left margin setting in the DOC settings sheet, however, the new setting overrides the setting in SERVICES **C**onfiguration **D**ocument. When you finish the memo, suppose that you decide to write a letter. You then create another DOC window on the same worksheet. When you create the new window, it inherits the settings sheet of the previous (memo) window. The DOC settings sheet still overrides the SERVICES Configuration settings, even though you have shifted to a new window.

You can change the Format Settings for the second window. When you do, the first DOC window retains its format settings, and the second DOC window retains its settings. If you create a third DOC window, that window inherits the format settings of the second window. But once you save the worksheet file and begin a new worksheet in a later session, the SERVICES Configuration Document settings will be in effect for the first DOC window in that later session.

Learning The TYPE Menu

In addition to the SERVICES and command menus, one other menu, called TYPE, is part of the Symphony menu tree. The TYPE menu is shown in figure 2.15.

Fig. 2.15.
The TYPE menu.

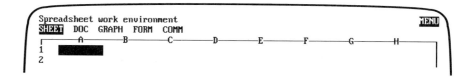

The TYPE menu enables you to change the window environment in which you are working. To retrieve this menu, press Type (Alt-F10) and either move the cursor to the new window type and press Enter or type the first letter of the window. Besides using the Type key to change window type, you can use two other methods. One is to use the SERVICES Window Settings Type command. The other method is to press Switch (Alt-F9), but only when you already have been using different types of windows in one worksheet. The Switch key returns you to the window type you used previously.

Using Automatic Exit versus "Sticky Menu"

Symphony offers two ways to exit from a menu. Many menus return you to the current window mode—SHEET, DOC, GRAPH, FORM, or COMM—once you have finished selecting commands or entered a response. Other menus, however, require that you select Quit to exit and return to the current window mode. Selecting Quit, like pressing Enter, tells Symphony that you have entered a command or changed a setting. To assure yourself that a command has been entered, you need to complete the following:

❑ Move the cursor to the appropriate selection and press Enter, or type the first letter of the selection

❏ To change a setting, such as for margins in **P**rint **S**ettings, press Enter or select **Q**uit after making the changes

Remember that you can move out of a command menu by pressing Esc or Ctrl-Break. If you select either Esc or Ctrl-Break before you enter a change in a setting by pressing Enter or selecting **Q**uit, however, the change is not entered. Suppose, for example, that you are working in Symphony's word processing environment (a DOC window) and want to change margin settings. You first retrieve the DOC command menu.

Second, you select **F**ormat by moving the cursor to **F**ormat on the menu and pressing Enter or by typing **F**. The following options appear:

    Create   **E**dit   **U**se-Named   **S**ettings

Then you select **S**ettings, again either by moving the cursor and pressing Enter or by typing **S**. When the next screen appears, you select **L**eft and then enter the new margin when Symphony indicates `Default Left Margin:1`. You enter the new margin simply by typing in the number, such as **4**, and pressing Enter. If you were to press Esc or Ctrl-Break at this point rather than Enter, your new setting would not be entered. Once you have pressed Enter and Symphony returns to the prior menu (see fig. 2.16), you can exit by selecting **Q**uit, pressing Esc three times (to exit to each previous menu level one at a time), or pressing Ctrl-Break.

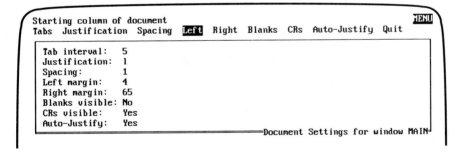

Fig. 2.16.

After typing a new margin and pressing enter.

Using The Symphony Keyboard

Symphony makes considerable use of the various parts of the IBM keyboard, particularly function keys and the Alt and Ctrl keys used in combination with others. The keyboard is divided into three sections: (1) the alphanumeric keyboard in the center, (2) the numeric keypad on the right, and (3) the special-function key section on the left. With this arrangement in mind, you can more easily understand the functions of the Symphony keyboard.

The IBM Personal Computer keyboard is shown in figure 2.17. Although the keyboard layout is almost the same for the IBM Personal Computer AT, shown in figure 2.18, some minor differences exist. The IBM Enhanced Keyboard, shown in figure 2.19, differs considerably from the others, but the actions of the keys are the same. (Function keys F11 and F12, unique to the Enhanced Keyboard, have no effect in Symphony.)

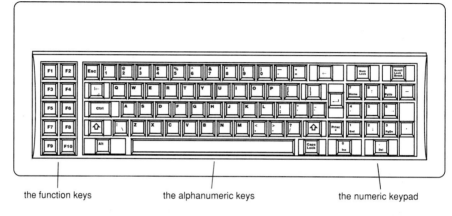

Fig. 2.17.
The IBM Personal Computer Keyboard.

the function keys   the alphanumeric keys   the numeric keypad

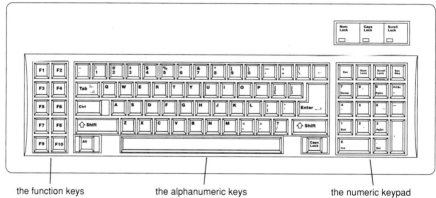

Fig. 2.18.
The IBM Personal Computer AT Keyboard.

the function keys   the alphanumeric keys   the numeric keypad

the function keys

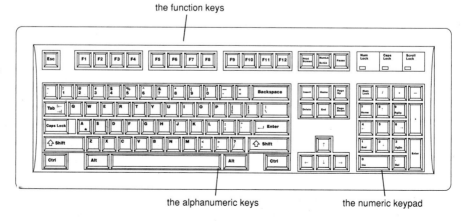

Fig. 2.19.
The IBM Enhanced Keyboard.

the alphanumeric keys   the numeric keypad

Although the functions of certain keys change as you change windows, the Symphony keyboard sections have certain general characteristics.

Most of the keys in the alphanumeric section at the center of the keyboard are found on any common typewriter. These keys maintain their normal functions in Symphony. Keys that take on unique functions, however, are Esc, Tab, Shift, Ctrl, and Alt.

The numeric keypad on the right side of the keyboard is normally used for entering numbers in most programs on the IBM PC. You can use this keypad for numbers whenever Num Lock is set. In Symphony, however, the main purpose of the numeric keypad is cursor movement.

The special-function keys on the left side of the keyboard (on the IBM PC and compatibles) are designed for special uses ranging from getting help (F1) to retrieving the command menus (F10).

Using The Alphanumeric Keyboard

Although most of the alphanumeric keys (see figs. 2.17-2.19) have the same functions as those on a typewriter, several keys have special functions in Symphony. If some of the functions do not make much sense the first time through, don't worry. Their meanings become clearer as you read more of this chapter and those that follow.

Key	Function(s)
Esc	Erases current entry when you specify a command line or range, erases a command menu, or returns from a help screen; removes a graph from the screen and returns you to the graph menu in SHEET mode
Tab	Moves the cursor to each tab setting in DOC mode; moves the cursor to the left when you use Tab with the Shift key; anchors cells or the cursor when you are indicating a range
Alt	When used in combination with the function keys, changes function key operations; used simultaneously with other alpha keys to invoke keyboard macros (Alt is covered in detail in Chapter 21)
Shift	Changes the central section of the keyboard to uppercase letters and characters; enables you to key in numbers by using the numeric keypad on the right when you are working in a SHEET window, (Shift is equivalent to a temporary Num Lock)
Ctrl	When used with Break, takes you out of a command operation and back to the SHEET, DOC, GRAPH, or COMM mode; used simultaneously with other alpha keys to invoke accelerator keys in DOC mode (see Chapter 9)

Using The Numeric Keypad

The keys in the numeric keypad on the right side of the keyboard (see figs. 2.17-2.19) are used primarily for cursor movement. You also can use them for scrolling the screen up or down, deleting characters, and inserting records into a database. In some cases a key's function is specific to the type of window in which you are working. These specific functions are indicated subsequently.

(See the section in this chapter on "Cursor-Movement Keys and the Cell Pointer" for detailed explanations of the Home, End, PgUp, and PgDn keys used alone or in combination with other keys.)

Key	Function(s)	Windows
Backspace	When you are defining the contents of a cell, it erases the character to the left of the cursor; erases characters in DOC and FORM windows	SHEET DOC FORM
/ (Slash)	Retrieves the SHEET command menu; used in its normal function as a division sign	SHEET
(Period)	Separates cell addresses when you designate ranges of cells; anchors cell addresses or the cursor when you are are pointing; also used as a decimal point (See the section called "Ranges" in Chapter 3)	SHEET DOC FORM GRAPH COMM
Home	Returns to cell A1 or the beginning of a restrict range from any location in the worksheet in the SHEET window; used after the End key to position the cursor at the active end of the worksheet or restrict range; used in EDIT mode to jump to the beginning of the edit line; returns to the beginning of the file or restrict range from any location in the DOC window; moves to the first record in the FORM window (See the section in this chapter on "Cursor Movement Keys and the Cell Pointer")	SHEET DOC FORM
PgUp	Moves the cursor 20 rows up in the column where it currently resides in a SHEET window; moves the cursor one window up in a DOC window; moves to a previous record in a FORM window	SHEET DOC FORM

Key	Function(s)	Windows
PgDn	Moves the cursor 20 rows downin a SHEET window and one window down in a DOC window; moves to the next record in a FORM window	SHEET DOC FORM
Ins	Inserts a record into the database; clears form for next entry; used to switch from Insert to Overstrike mode in a DOC window	FORM DOC

Using the Lock Key Indicators

Three "lock" keys are on IBM and compatible computers: Num Lock, Caps Lock, and Scroll Lock. Whenever you use any of these keys, Symphony indicates that the keys are operating. Each key has its own reverse-video indicator that appears in the lower right corner of the screen when the key is on (see fig. 2.20).

03-Apr-90 07:28 AM   MAIN
                                                CapsNumScroll

Fig. 2.20.
The lock key indicators in lower right corner.

Using the Function Keys

The special-function keys in Symphony generally do the same thing regardless of the window type. A few special-function keys change their functions, however, when you change the window environment. You use F2, for example, to edit cell entries when you are working in a SHEET window, but this same key justifies paragraphs when you are in a DOC window.

Lotus Development provides for Symphony users a function key template that fits over the function keys of your computer. Fig 2.21 is a diagram of this template. The figure distinguishes those keys that operate by pressing a function and a function key. On the template, operations in light tan are initiated by simultaneously pressing the Alt key and the function key. Like the lock keys, the function keys remain "turned on" until you press the key(s) a second time. Such toggle keys include Alt-F6 (Zoom), Alt-F7 (Step), and F7 (User).

Using Function Keys that Work in All Windows

Some keys operate in all types of windows, whereas other keys function only with specific window types. The three keys that you may use most frequently for all window types are Services (F9), Type (Alt-F10) and Menu (F10). Function keys operating in all windows include the following:

Key	Function(s)
F1 (Help)	Retrieves the help screens
Alt-F1 (Compose)	Creates special characters by combining standard characters
Alt-F5 (Learn)	Records keystrokes for creating macros
F7 (User)	Initiates a macro
Alt-F7 (Step)	Operates a macro in single-step mode for debugging
F6 (Window)	Rotates windows; brings a bottom window to the top; moves the cursor from one window to another; rotates; the settings sheets for windows of the same type
Alt-F6 (Zoom)	Creates a full screen after isolating a window
Alt-F8 (Draw)	Redraws all windows after making changes
F9 (Services)	Retrieves the SERVICES menu
Alt-F9 (Switch)	Changes window to previous type

Fig. 2.21.
The function key template.

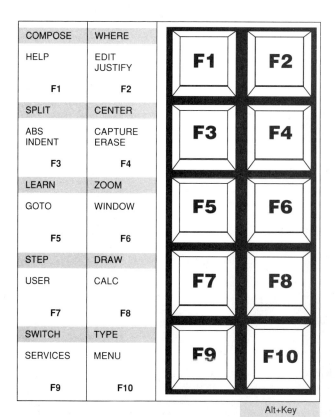

Key	Function(s)
F10 (Menu)	Retrieves the command menus for each Symphony environment
Alt-F10 (Type)	Retrieves the TYPE menu

Using Function Keys for Specific Windows

The function keys listed in the previous section are available for any Symphony window (SHEET, DOC, GRAPH, FORM, and COMM). As mentioned earlier, many function keys have particular uses for specific window types. Here are these keys and their functions:

Key	Window	Function(s)
Alt-F1 (Compose)	DOC FORM	Inserts special print commands (such as those for boldfacing and underlining) in the text; creates special characters
F2 (Justify)	DOC	Justifies paragraphs
F2 (Edit)	SHEET FORM	Edits a cell entry in a spreadsheet; edits entries in a form
Alt-F2 (Where)	DOC	Indicates page and line location on printed copy of current on-screen line
F3 (Indent)	DOC	Indents lines
F3 (Abs)	SHEET	Changes a formula to absolute reference
Alt-F3 (Split)	DOC	Splits a line without leaving carriage return
F4 (Capture)	COMM	Captures data to a worksheet range or printer
F4 (Erase)	DOC	Erases a block
Alt-F4 (Center)	DOC	Centers a line
F5 (GoTo)	SHEET DOC FORM	Goes to a range
F8 (CALC)	SHEET	Calculates formulas in a worksheet

Using Other Special Key Combinations

Besides the special uses of the Alt key with function keys, many other key combinations have special functions, particularly in the DOC and SHEET windows. In many cases, these combinations involve moving the cell pointer in a SHEET window or moving the cursor in a DOC or FORM window.

In addition, many special key combinations, called "accelerator keys," are available in DOC mode. For example, rather than selecting the **M**ove command from the DOC menu, you can press Ctrl-M. A complete list of these accelerator keys appears in Chapter 9.

Cursor-Movement Keys and the Cell Pointer

Cursor movement occurs in all Symphony environments. In some cases, cursor movement within a window is primarily for identifying ranges; in other windows, cursor movement is important for entering, editing, and deleting data and for making selections from menus. Cursor movement occurs when you use keys alone and in combination with others, as listed in the following tables. (In a SHEET environment, note that the cursor is referred to as the cell pointer.)

Moving the Cell Pointer in a SHEET Window

Symphony provides several ways for moving around a worksheet, whether you are identifying a range, or entering or changing data. Eleven keys in all, used alone and in combination, control cell-pointer movement throughout the worksheet. These keys include the following:

The cursor keys: ($\leftarrow$, $\rightarrow$, $\uparrow$, $\downarrow$)

The PgDn and PgUp keys

The Home key

The End key

The F5 function key

The Ctrl key (used only in combination with others)

The Scroll Lock key (used only in a combination with others)

Here's how to use these keys to move the cell pointer around the worksheet (fig 2.22 illustrates how the keys operate):

To move the cell pointer:	Use the following:
One cell up	$\uparrow$
One cell down	$\downarrow$
One cell left	$\leftarrow$
One cell right	$\rightarrow$

To move the cell pointer:	*Use the following:*
To the upper left corner	Home
To the lower right corner	End + Home
One window up	PgUp
One window down	PgDn
One window left	Ctrl-←
One window right	Ctrl-→
Window up one row	Scroll Lock on, then ↑
Window down one row	Scroll Lock on, then ↓
Window left one column	Scroll Lock on, then ←
Window right one column	Scroll Lock on, then →

To jump the cell pointer to:	*Use the following:*
Specific cell position or named range	F5 function key
Next filled cell above	End then ↑
Next filled cell below	End then ↓
Next filled cell to left	End then ←
Next filled cell to right	End then →
First row of window restrict range	End then PgUp
Last row of restrict range	End then PgDn
First column of restrict range	End then Ctrl-←
Last column of restrict range	End then Ctrl-→
Upper right corner of restrict	Scroll Lock on, then Home

Moving the Cursor in a DOC Window

Moving the cursor in a DOC window is similar to moving the cell pointer in a SHEET window. You can use many more keys, however, to move the cursor in a DOC window. These keys include the following:

The cursor keys: (←, →, ↓, ↑)
The PgUp and PgDn keys
The Home key
The End key
The Ctrl key (used only in combination with others)
The Scroll Lock key (used only in combination with others)
The F2 function key (used with the End key)
The Alt-F2 key combination (used with the End Key)
Enter (used with the End key)
Any typed character (used with the End key)

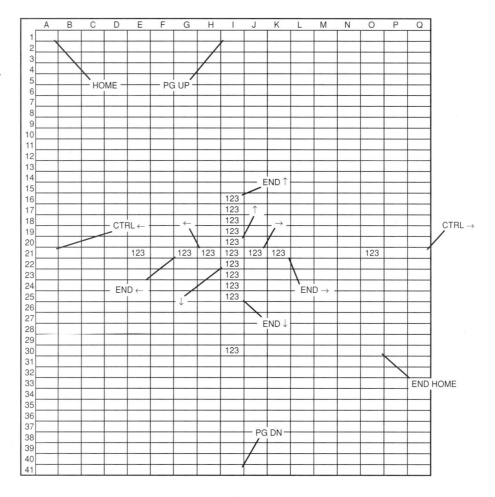

Fig. 2.22.

Moving the cell pointer in a SHEET window.

These keys enable you to move the cursor around a DOC worksheet in the following ways:

To move the cursor:	Use the following:
One line up	↑
One line down	↓
One format line up	End then Alt-F2
One format line down	End then F2
To preceding character	←
To next character	→
To any specific character	End then specific character

To move the cursor:	Use the following:
To next word	Ctrl-→
To preceding word	Ctrl-←
To beginning of paragraph	End then ↑
To end of paragraph	End then ↓
One window up	PgUp
One window down	PgDn
Window up one line	Scroll Lock on, then ↑
Window down one line	Scroll Lock on, then ↓
Window 25% to left	Scroll Lock on, then ←
Window 25% to right	Scroll Lock on, then →
To upper left corner of a document or restrict range	Home
To end of a document or restrict range	End then Home
To next carriage return	End then Enter

Moving the Cursor in a FORM Window

Cursor movement is important not only for operating within a SHEET or DOC window, but also for the work you do in a FORM window. When you enter information into data forms and criterion records, use the following keys for cursor movement:

The cursor keys: ←, →, ↓, ↑

The Tab key

The Home key

The End key

The Ctrl key (used only in combination with others)

These keys enable you to move the cursor in a FORM window in the following ways:

To move the cursor:	Use the following:
To the previous field	↑ or ←
To the next field	↓, →, or Tab
To the first field of a record	Ctrl-←
To the last field of a record	Ctrl-→
To the first record	Home
To the last record	End

Learning The Symphony Display

Descriptions of the Symphony display, like those of many other features of the program, vary according to the type of window being used. Some general remarks, however, can be made about the Symphony display. For all types of windows, the work or display area is bordered on all four sides. You can change this border or remove it completely by using the SERVICES **W**indow **S**ettings **B**orders command. The border for a SHEET window contains letters and numbers that mark columns and rows (see fig. 2.23).

Reminder:

The double line at the bottom of the window means that the window is the current window.

A particularly important part of the border of any window is the bottom line. The double line indicates the current window. Important areas outside the window border include the control panel, the mode indicator, the date-and-time indicator, the error message area, and the lock key indicator.

Fig. 2.23.

The border for a SHEET window.

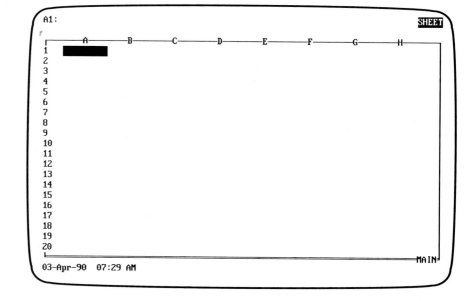

Using The Control Panel

The area directly above the top line of the border is the menu area for all windows. In Symphony, the command menu line appears in this position, but the explanation of the command appears on the first line above the command menu line (see fig. 2.24).

Whenever a SHEET, DOC, or FORM window is in the mode ready to receive data, the area above the top border contains information about the data or the operations that you must complete before you can enter data.

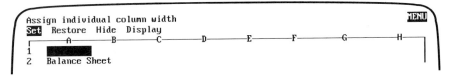

Fig. 2.24.
The command menu line with explanations above it.

In the SHEET window mode, the first line contains all the information about the current cell, which is the cell where the pointer is currently located (see fig. 2.25). The first item is the address of the cell, such as A9. And the second item is the display format, such as (D1), which is always displayed in parentheses. (Display formats are covered in detail in Chapter 4.) The last item is the actual contents of the current cell, such as @DATA*(90,4,23)*.

The line underneath the current cell information is the edit line. As you enter or edit data, characters display on this line. It is blank in figure 2.25 because the formula has already been entered.

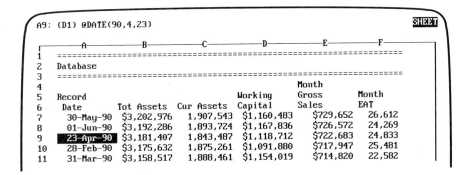

Fig. 2.25.
Current cell information displayed in the first line of a SHEET window.

In the DOC window mode, the first line indicates the line, character, and page position of the cursor, as well as the type of justification and spacing that are set (see fig. 2.26). Whenever an asterisk (*) appears in the middle of the control panel, it indicates that the cursor is positioned on data that was entered in another type of window, or positioned on a special DOC format symbol (see Chapter 9).

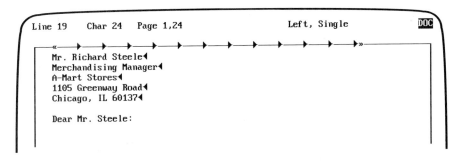

Fig. 2.26.
Information displayed in the first line of a DOC window.

In the FORM window mode, the control panel is reserved as a special message area (see fig. 2.27). For example, this area tells you that you need to set a range for creating a form. But more important, the control panel tells you which record is being entered or edited and indicates the entry slot where the cursor is currently positioned.

Fig. 2.27.

A special message area in the first line of a FORM window.

```
Inserting Record 1          New Record              FORM
Enter Name
Name _____
Address _____
City _____
State _____
Zip Code _____
Phone _____
```

Using the Mode Indicators

Symphony provides several modes, one of which is always in effect, depending on what you are doing. The mode indicator is located in the upper right corner of the screen and always shows the current mode. The mode indicators and related modes include these:

Modes Indicating Current Window

Mode Indicator	Description
SHEET	You can enter a command or make a cell entry in the spreadsheet.
DOC	You can enter a command or text or perform editing operations in a word processing window.
GRAPH	You can enter a command to create graphs and charts and attach them to a GRAPH window.
FORM	You can enter a command or data and change data in the forms you have created in a FORM window.
COMM	You can enter a command or data in the COMM window.
OUTLN	When the Outliner application is attached, you can enter headings and subheadings, or commands, in the OUTLN window.

Modes Working in All Windows

Mode Indicator	Description
MENU	You must select from the SERVICES menu or from a SHEET, DOC, GRAPH, FORM, COMM, or OUTLN menu. (Or you can press Esc to return to a window mode.)
POINT	A range is being pointed to.
HELP	You are using a help screen.
ERROR	An error has occurred, and Symphony is waiting for you to press Esc or enter to acknowledge the error.
WAIT	Symphony is in the middle of an operation and cannot respond to commands.
EDIT	A settings sheet or cell entry is being edited.

SHEET Window Modes

Mode Indicator	Description
VALUE	A number or formula is being entered.
LABEL	A label is being entered.
FIND	Symphony is in the middle of a Query Find operation and cannot respond to commands.
NAMES	A range name (or line marker in a DOC window) is being pointed to).

FORM Window Mode

Mode Indicator	Description
CRIT	A criterion record is being edited.

Using Other Indicators

In addition to the mode indicators in the top right corner, other indicators are displayed in the area at the bottom of the screen (see fig. 2.28). On the left, Symphony displays date and time whenever you are in a window mode. When you have selected a command, the command name is displayed in the bottom left corner. Also displayed here are error messages and the `Memory full` message. In the bottom right corner, a number of other indicators appear. These inform you of certain conditions, such as lock keys being on, and also of operations for creating, edition, and using macros.

Fig. 2.28.

Indicators at the bottom of the screen.

Following is a list of other indicators.

Indicator	Description
Calc	You need to recalculate the worksheet.
CAPS	The Caps Lock key is on.
Capture	Data from a COMM environment is being logged in a worksheet range to the printer.
Circ	Symphony has found a circular reference in the worksheet.
Draw	You need to update windows because of changes in one of them.
End	The end key is on.
Learn	You can store keystrokes automatically for creating macros.
Macro	A macro is in operation.
Mem	Only a small amount of memory remains.
New Record	A new record is being entered (FORM window).
Num	The Num Lock key is on.
OnLine	In the COMM window, a connection with another computer is signified.
Ovr	You are in the Overstrike mode in a DOC window.
Pause	You need to input something so that a macro can continue.
Scroll	The Scroll Lock key is on.
Step	Step mode is set for running macros.
User	You can execute a macro by entering the macro name.

Using The Help Feature

Symphony makes available a series of help screens that you can easily refer to as you're working in the program. Press the F1 function key to access these screens.

Each screen contains information on a topic listed in the Help Index (see fig. 2.29). To retrieve the Help Index, simply move the cell pointer to the bottom of the screen, position it over Help Index, and press Enter. When the Help Index appears, you may notice that it is arranged alphabetically according to general topics. To select a help screen topic, position the cursor over a heading and press Enter.

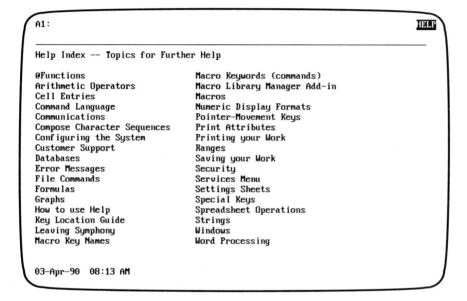

Fig. 2.29.
The Help Index.

Each heading within the Help Index consists of a series of screens, which are organized in two ways. First, screens are organized according to the topics in the Help Index; the @Function help screen, for example, lists all the types of functions. Second, many help screens contain cross-references listed in the bottom left corner of the help screen. For example, if you select the **D**atabase **S**tatistical **F**unctions help screen, it contains cross-references to **D**atabase **R**anges and **C**riterion **R**anges, among other things (see fig. 2.30). By positioning the cursor on either of these cross-references, you can retrieve the help screen for either Database Ranges or Criterion Ranges.

You also can invoke help immediately after you encounter an error. If you press F1 as the ERROR indicator is still flashing in the upper right corner, a Help screen pops up with detailed information concerning the error.

Fig. 2.30.

Cross-references in the Help Index.

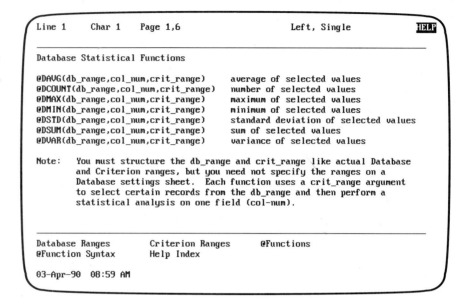

```
 Line 1     Char 1     Page 1,6                Left, Single        HELP

 Database Statistical Functions

 @DAVG(db_range,col_num,crit_range)      average of selected values
 @DCOUNT(db_range,col_num,crit_range)    number of selected values
 @DMAX(db_range,col_num,crit_range)      maximum of selected values
 @DMIN(db_range,col_num,crit_range)      minimum of selected values
 @DSTD(db_range,col_num,crit_range)      standard deviation of selected values
 @DSUM(db_range,col_num,crit_range)      sum of selected values
 @DVAR(db_range,col_num,crit_range)      variance of selected values

 Note:   You must structure the db_range and crit_range like actual Database
         and Criterion ranges, but you need not specify the ranges on a
         Database settings sheet.  Each function uses a crit_range argument
         to select certain records from the db_range and then perform a
         statistical analysis on one field (col-num).


 Database Ranges        Criterion Ranges     @Functions
 @Function Syntax       Help Index

 03-Apr-90  08:59 AM
```

Chapter Summary

This chapter has provided information for helping you begin to use Symphony. The chapter has presented an overview of Symphony: the Symphony Access System, the menu structure, the window feature, the keyboard, and the display. Now that you have had a chance to discover Symphony, read the following chapters for a closer view of Symphony's capabilities. These include creating spreadsheets; using file commands; using word processing; printing reports; creating and displaying graphs; and using data-management, communications, and macro features.

Part II

Learning Symphony Worksheet Basics

The Symphony SHEET Environment

Learning Fundamental SHEET
Window Commands

Formatting the Worksheet

Using @Functions

Managing Files

Learning the SHEET Window:
Hands-On Practice

3

The Symphony SHEET Environment

If you have used 1-2-3 or another worksheet, then you are familiar with Symphony's SHEET environment. Examining this environment is a good way to learn about Symphony, because you may spend most of your Symphony sessions in the SHEET environment. Symphony and 1-2-3 use almost identical commands when entering and editing data, moving the cell pointer, and identifying and using ranges.

As in 1-2-3, the worksheet is Symphony's foundation. You make entries in the SHEET, DOC, and FORM environments and store those entries in worksheet cells. You create graphs based on entries in a worksheet. And you load data, up or down, through the COMM environment and store it in a worksheet. Finally, similar to 1-2-3 macros and Command Language programs, you create, edit, and invoke macros in a worksheet.

In this chapter, you will learn how to do the following:

❏ Enter and edit labels, numbers and formulas
❏ Use Symphony's @functions
❏ Create string formulas
❏ Create formulas that link files
❏ Use, shape and designate ranges

Entering Data

If you have worked with other worksheets, you know that you can make three types of cell entries: labels, numbers, and formulas (including functions). You enter data in a cell by positioning the cell pointer on the cell, typing the entry, and pressing Enter or one of the cursor keys. Symphony interprets the type of cell entry from the first character that you enter. If you enter one of the following characters:

0 1 2 3 4 5 6 7 8 9 + − . (@ # $

Symphony treats the entry as either a number or a formula. If you enter a character other than one of those listed, Symphony treats the entry as a label.

Entering Labels

The first character of any label you enter causes Symphony to shift from SHEET to LABEL mode. Labels commonly are used for row and column headings. A label can be up to 240 characters long and can contain any combination of characters and numbers. If a label is too long for the width of a cell, the label displays across the cells to the right, as long as these cells are empty. If the cell to the immediate right of the label contains an entry, only the default width of nine characters (or whatever width you use) is displayed in the cell, as shown at the cursor in cell A3 (see fig. 3.1).

Fig. 3.1.

How a label continues across cells.

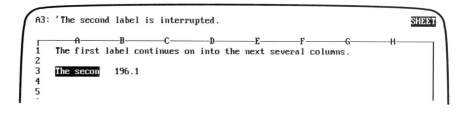

Reminder:

The program does not automatically add the label prefix to repeat, center- and right-justified labels.

You also can left-, center-, or right-justify labels when you display them (see fig. 3.2), as long as you precede the label with one of the following label-prefix characters:

Character	Action
'	Left-justifies
"	Right-justifies
^	Centers
\	Repeats

Symphony's default label display is left-justification, and Symphony automatically adds the prefix when you enter the label. For example, when you type **Net Income**, the label appears on-screen as `'Net Income.`

If you want to enter a header that begins with a numeral, such as 1990 Sales, you must type the prefix before 1990 (**'1990 Sales**). Symphony then interprets 1990 as a label and automatically left-justifies it, as the program does for other labels. If you want to center this header, you type ^**1990 Sales**. To learn how you can control label alignment automatically, see Chapter 5.

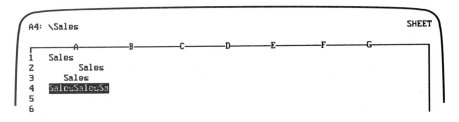

Fig. 3.2.
Left-aligned, right-aligned, centered, and repeating labels.

Tip

Symphony does not right-justify labels that are less than a column's width. For example, if you type **"profit** (using the right-justify label prefix) in a column with Symphony's default width of nine spaces, the "t" does not fit flush with the right side of the cell.

To right-justify labels less than a column's width, press the keyboard space bar the number of spaces that matches the difference between the column width and the label, type the label, and then press Enter. For instance, in the preceding example, the column width is nine spaces, the word length is six spaces, for a difference of three spaces. Press the space bar three times, then type **profit** (without the right-justify label prefix), and then press the space bar again. Symphony automatically enters the left-justify character ('), and the spaces you entered force the label to the right-hand side of the cell.

A convenient label prefix is the backslash (\), which is used for repetition. You can use any character, label, or value with the backspace for repetition. One of the most frequent uses of this prefix is to create a separator line. The first step is to enter \= in the cell where you want the line to begin (cell A3 in fig. 3.3). The \= makes the equal sign appear across the entire cell. Once you have made this entry, you then use the **C**opy command to duplicate the cell across the row or to other parts of the worksheet (see fig. 3.4). For more information about the **C**opy command and duplication, see Chapter 4.

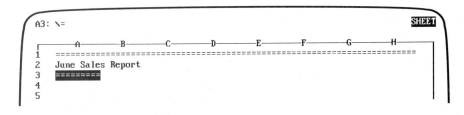

Fig. 3.3.
A repeating label prefix.

Fig. 3.4.
Creating a separator line.

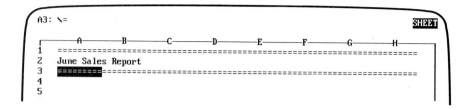

Entering Numbers

As you learned earlier in this chapter, if you begin an entry with one of the following characters:

    0 1 2 3 4 5 6 7 8 9 + − . (@ # $

Symphony interprets the entry as a number or formula. Here are some simple rules to follow for entering numbers:

1. You can end a number with a percent sign (%), which tells Symphony to divide by 100 the number that precedes the sign.

2. You cannot have more than one decimal point in a number.

3. Although you may not use commas or dollar signs when you enter a number, you can display numbers with commas, and dollar signs by using the **F**ormat command. You also can suppress the display of a number, or you can display the formula rather than the number itself. (See Chapter 5.)

4. You can enter a number in scientific notation.

Reminder:

When you make a mistake while entering a number, Symphony alerts you with a beep.

If you fail to follow these rules when entering a number, Symphony beeps when you press Enter. Symphony also automatically shifts to EDIT mode just as if you had pressed F2. (See the "Editing" section in this chapter for an explanation of how to correct this situation.)

Entering Formulas

Symphony can calculate formulas relating numbers, and formulas connecting text strings. For example, if cell C1 contains the formula: +A1+B1, then C1 displays the sum of the contents of cells A1 and B1. The cell references serve as variables in the equation. No matter what numbers you enter in A1 and B1, cell C1 always returns their sum. For example, if cell A1 contains the number 5, and cell B1 contains the number 10, then the formula in C1 (+A1+B1) returns the number 15. If you change the number in cell A1 to 4, C1 also changes—to 14. Of course, formulas can be more complex than this example. A cell can be added to, subtracted from, multiplied by, or divided by any other cell. You also can enter @functions into the cells.

To enter a formula into a cell, you need to follow some basic rules. Suppose, for example, that you want to create a formula that adds the row of numbers in fig. 3.5—the amounts in cells B1, C1, D1, and E1—and place the result in cell F1.

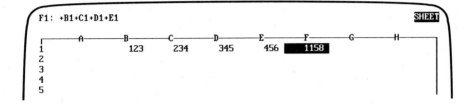

F1: +B1+C1+D1+E1   SHEET

	A	B	C	D	E	F	G	H
1		123	234	345	456	1158		
2								
3								
4								
5								

Fig. 3.5.
A formula that adds a row of numbers

One formula that calculates the total is +B1+C1+D1+E1. The plus sign (+) at the beginning of the formula tells Symphony to interpret the entry as a formula, not a label. Remember, for Symphony to recognize an entry as a formula, the entry must begin with one of the following characters:

0 1 2 3 4 5 6 7 8 9 + − . (@ # $

Entering Cell Addresses in Formulas

You can use two methods to enter cell addresses in formulas: typing and pointing. Both accomplish the same result, and you can mix and match the two techniques within the same formula. Typing cell addresses is self-explanatory, but pointing to cell addresses requires some explanation. The method used is the same as that used in pointing to cell ranges (see the section titled "Pointing to Cells: The Expanding Cell Pointer" in Chapter 4), but in this case the range is only a single cell.

To enter the formula +B1+C1+D1+E1 by pointing, place the cell pointer in cell F1, press the plus sign, and move the cell pointer to B1. Notice that the address for the cell (B1) appears after the plus in the second line of the control panel, and that the mode indicator in the upper right corner of the screen shifts from **VALUE** to **POINT**.

To continue to the next address in the formula, type another plus sign. Your cell pointer moves immediately from cell B1 back to the cell where the cell pointer was located when you began entering the formula—in this case, cell F1. Also, the mode indicator shifts back to **VALUE**. You continue this sequence of pointing and entering plus signs until you have the formula you want, and then press Enter. Remember that nothing prohibits you from using a combination of the two methods of pointing and typing. Use whatever method works best for you.

As you gain experience with Symphony, you find it easier to point to cells that are close to the cell you are defining, but simpler to type references to distant cells. Symphony makes pointing to distant cells simple, however, because of the End, PgUp, PgDn, and Ctrl keys that help you move quickly around the worksheet.

Tip

You can create formulas easier and increase their accuracy by using range names. Naming cells enables you to use terms that are meaningful to you, and frees you from remembering cell addresses that may be in remote areas of the worksheet.

Understanding Operators

Operators indicate arithmetic operations in formulas. Operators come in three types: mathematical, logical, and string. Logical operators are discussed in Chapter 6. The mathematical and string operators are:

Operator	Meaning
^	Exponentiation
+,−	Positive, Negative
*,/	Multiplication, Division
+,−	Addition, Subtraction
&	String Concatenation

To understand operators, you must know their order of precedence in calculation. The previous list is arranged in order of precedence. Operators with the highest order of precedence are at the top; operators with equal precedence are listed on the same line and evaluated from left to right. You also can use parentheses, to specify the order of precedence Symphony uses to calculate formulas. Similar to the rules of arithmetic, Symphony calculates functions and formulas enclosed in parentheses first.

To test your understanding of precedence, determine the order of precedence in the following formulas, where B3 = 2, C3 = 3, and D3 = 4. Are your answers the same as those given? In the first two formulas, notice particularly how parentheses affect the order of precedence as well as the answer.

Formula	Answer
+C3–D3/B3	1
(C3–D3)/B3	–.5
+D3*C3–B3^C34	+D3*C3*B3/B3^C3–25/5–2

Symphony can process complex formulas that contain many levels of parentheses. However, the number of levels is limited. If Symphony is unable to process a formula because the formula contains too many levels of parentheses, ERR is displayed in the cell.

Tip

If you receive an ERR message in response to entering a formula, do not press the Esc key. Rather, press the Home key, the apostrophe key ('), and then Enter. In this manner, instead of losing the formula (which happens if you first press the Esc key), you preserve it as a label. This technique enables you to test and debug the formula without having to re-enter it.

Using Functions

Symphony includes a large assortment of built-in functions (called @functions) that you can use to perform calculations. You can use them also in formulas you create. All functions are considered formulas by Symphony. In fact, the functions are abbreviations for long or complex formulas. Each function consists of three parts: the @ sign, a function name, and an argument or range. Some @functions require both an argument and a range, for example, @CELL*("width," range)*. The @ sign signals to Symphony that a function is being entered; the name (CELL) indicates which function is being used; and the argument *("width,")* or range *(range)*, is the data required by Symphony to perform the function. (Ranges are discussed later in this chapter and also in Chapter 4.) Although Chapter 6 provides a detailed discussion of Symphony functions, a brief illustration is provided here to help you begin to understand them.

Reminder:
Use Symphony's functions to perform calculations.

In figure 3.5, four cell references were used to create the desired formula *(+B1+C1+D1+E1)*. But you can use the @SUM function to total, or "sum" the numbers in the example. (The concept of ranges is important to the @SUM function. For now, think of a range as simply a continuous group of cells.) When you use the @SUM function, the equivalent to the *+B1+C1+D1+E1* formula is *@SUM(B1..E1)*. The only difference between the two formulas is one of convenience. Had several more entries extended across the row, the @SUM function would change only slightly in order to use the address of the last cell to be summed. For example, @SUM*(B1..Z1)* would sum the contents of the first row all the way from cells B1 to Z1.

> **TIP**
>
> Use the @SUM function whenever possible when you need to total a row or column of cells. For example, the @SUM function calculates totals faster and requires less memory than alternately typing the plus (+) sign and the cell addresses shown in figure 3.5. The @SUM function is discussed fully in Chapter 6, @Functions.

Using String Formulas

Symphony's string arithmetic enables you to create formulas for joining words, phrases, or even sentences. Special functions enable you to perform various operations on strings, including joining them together, converting them to numbers, and indicating the total number of characters in a string. (These special functions are discussed in Chapter 6.)

String formulas can join words, phrases, and sentences originally entered in SHEET, DOC, or FORM environments; the string formula, however, must be entered in the SHEET environment. String formulas also are discussed in Chapter 6, but some general principles you should know are as follows:

1. As in formulas for numbers, formulas containing strings must begin with the plus sign (+).

2. The ampersand (&), which is the special operator for strings, tells Symphony to join items together.

3. As in formulas involving numbers, string formulas also use cell addresses. For example, if you enter John in cell B1 and Smith in cell B2, the formula +B1&B2 results in JohnSmith.

Reminder:

Whenever you want to include an element in a formula that is not the cell address itself or a range name, enclose that element in double quotations.

To put a space between the first and last name in (3), you add a space and two double quotation marks between the two names. Thus, the original formula becomes: +B1&" "&B2, which results in John Smith. Whenever you want to include an element in a formula that is not the cell address itself or a range name, you must enclose that element in double quotation marks.

String formulas involving functions follow the same rules as mathematical formulas. That is, string functions begin with an @ sign, followed by the function name and an argument and/or range in parentheses. You also can indicate cell addresses or ranges by either typing or pointing to them, similar to numerical formulas.

Symphony's string arithmetic enables you to apply many types of functions to strings stored in databases, in worksheets themselves, and in documents created in Symphony's word-processing environment.

Creating Formulas that Link Files

Symphony 2.2 enables you to reference a cell in a worksheet in memory with a cell in a worksheet on disk. This capability is known as linking files—you add data from a worksheet on disk to a worksheet in memory. In file linking, the worksheet on disk is the source file, since it supplies data to the worksheet in memory, the target file. Using linked files is particularly useful for combining totals from a number of worksheets into a summary worksheet.

For example, figures 3.6, 3.7, and 3.8 display three separate worksheet files. The WORLD worksheet in fig. 3.8 refers to cells in the AM_01 (North and South America) and EA_01 (Europe and Asia) files in Figures 3.6 and 3.7 as follows:

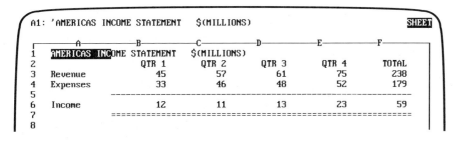

A1: 'AMERICAS INCOME STATEMENT $(MILLIONS)   SHEET

	A	B	C	D	E	F
1	AMERICAS INCOME STATEMENT	$(MILLIONS)				
2		QTR 1	QTR 2	QTR 3	QTR 4	TOTAL
3	Revenue	45	57	61	75	238
4	Expenses	33	46	48	52	179
5		----	----	----	----	----
6	Income	12	11	13	23	59
7		====	====	====	====	====
8						

Fig. 3.6.

The AM_01 worksheet that contains data to be used in figure 3.8.

A1: 'EUR_ASIA INCOME STATEMENT $(MILLIONS)   SHEET

	A	B	C	D	E	F
1	EUR_ASIA INCOME STATEMENT	$(MILLIONS)				
2		QTR 1	QTR 2	QTR 3	QTR 4	TOTAL
3	Revenue	76	98	104	148	426
4	Expenses	49	68	73	73	263
5		----	----	----	----	----
6	Income	27	30	31	75	163
7		====	====	====	====	====
8						

Fig. 3.7.

The EA_01 worksheet that contains data to be used in figure 3.8.

B4: +<<C:\S_22\AM_01.WR1>>B3   SHEET

	A	B	C	D	E	F
1	WORLDWIDE INCOME STATEMENT	$(MILLIONS)				
2		QTR 1	QTR 2	QTR 3	QTR 4	TOTAL
3	Revenue					
4	Americas	45	57	61	75	238
5	Eur_Asia	76	98	104	148	426
6						
7	Tot Revenue	121	155	165	223	664
8						
9	Expenses					
10	Americas	33	46	48	52	179
11	Eur_Asia	49	68	73	73	263
12						
13	Tot Expenses	82	114	121	125	442
14						
15	Total Income	39	41	44	98	222
16		====	====	====	====	====
17						

Fig. 3.8.

The WORLD worksheet that contains formulas that link it to the worksheets in figures 3.6 and 3.7.

Linking files enables you to summarize data from separate files automatically. In this manner, you are able to create a Symphony application that relies on smaller, logically organized worksheets that use less memory than large, complex, single worksheet applications.

Creating Links To Files On Disk

To create a link from the worksheet in memory to one on disk, you use a formula. You type a plus (+) sign, the name of the source file in double angle brackets (<< >>), and the cell address. For example, to create the link in cell B4 of WORLD in figure 3.8, you type the following:

> **+<<AM_01>>B3**

Note the similarity between referencing a cell on disk to referencing a cell in another area of the worksheet in memory—both begin with the plus (+) sign.

When the file you want to link to is not in the default directory, you must include the entire path, such as:

> **+<<C:\SYMPHONY\DATA\AM_01>>B3**

Reminder:

When the file you want to link to is not in the default directory, you must include the entire path.

Using Range Names in Linking Formulas

You also can use range names in your linking formulas. In the preceding example, you can use the MENU **R**ange **N**ame **C**reate command to name cell B3 AM_QTR1. The link in cell B4 of WORLD can then be entered as follows:

> **+<<AMERICAS>>AM_QTR1**

Using the range names in file-linking formulas has two advantages: The names help you remember the cell you want to link to; and, if the data location in the source worksheet changes, you may reference incorrect or no data. (Changes could occur by inserting or deleting rows or columns, or by using the MENU **M**ove command.) To resolve this situation, press EDIT (F2) and correct the formula. On the other hand, Symphony automatically adjusts range names to their new locations.

Other Linking Formula Techniques

You can link only single cells and not ranges in worksheets on disk. In addition, a linking formula can contain only the plus (+) sign and not one of Symphony's

@functions. For example, cell F4 in figure 3.8 totals the cells in row 4 with the formula @SUM*(B4..E4)*. The formula

@SUM(<<*AM_01*>>*B3..*<<*AM_01*>>*E3*)

results in Symphony beeping and changing to EDIT mode. Symphony does not accept linking formulas as components of another formula and you should edit or enter the formula properly.

Fortunately, once you enter a linking formula, you can use the MENU **C**opy command to copy the formula to other cells in the worksheet. If the cell reference is a relative reference, Symphony adjusts the formula accordingly. For example, if you copy the formula <<AM_01>>*B3* in cell B4 to cell C4, the formula adjusts to <<AM_01>>*C3*. If the cell reference in the linking formula is absolute *($B$3)* or mixed *($B3* or *B$3)*, and you copy the formula to another area in the worksheet, Symphony copies the formula as usual.

Recalculating Linked Worksheets

When you retrieve a file from disk into memory, or enter or edit linking formulas, Symphony automatically recalculates and updates the links for you.

However, if you have an application that contains many linking formulas, the application may take a long time to update. You may want to use the MENU **S**ettings **A**uto-Link **N**o command, to control when you want the links updated. If you have links that need updating, the **LINK** indicator will appear at the bottom of the screen. When you set **A**uto-Link to **N**o, use the SERVICES **F**ile **A**dmin **L**ink-Refresh command to update the links. Be aware that links are not updated when you press the F8 (Calc) key.

Reminder:
*Update links with the SERVICES **F**ile **A**dmin **L**ink-Refresh command.*

Creating Multilevel Linked Applications

Whenever you retrieve a file from disk to memory that contains linking formulas, Symphony automatically reads the referenced cells from each linked file and recalculates each linked formula. This feature enables you to create large applications that update automatically and use less memory.

In figure 3.9, revenue and expenses of the AMERICAS file are dependent on the revenue and expenses of North and South America. Similarly, the revenue and expenses of the EUR_ASIA file are dependent on the revenue and expenses of Europe and Asia. If you examine the worksheets, the WORLD worksheet—the top-level worksheet—contains formulas that link to AMERICAS and EUR_ASIA, the second-level worksheets. These worksheets, in turn, contain formulas that link to the continent, or third-level, worksheets.

Fig. 3.9.

*A multilevel
summary
application.*

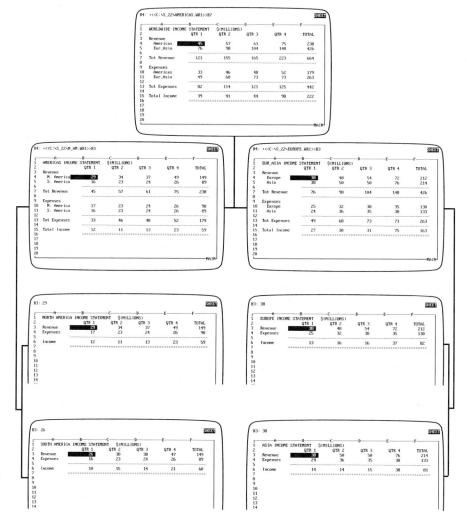

To create a multilevel linked application, you enter the revenue and expense values at the lowest level in worksheets N_AM, S_AM, EUROPE, and ASIA (see figure 3.9). The AMERICAS and EUR_ASIA worksheet contains linking formulas to access this information. Finally, the summary worksheet, WORLD, contains linking formulas to pull this data up another level.

When you use linking formulas in this manner, be careful how you update the worksheets. For example, if you change the data at the continental level, the summary worksheet does not reflect the change until you update the AMERICAS or EUR_ASIA worksheet. To update a worksheet, use the SERVICES File Retrieve command to retrieve the worksheet and then save it under the same name with the SERVICES File Save command.

> ### Tip
> You can use Symphony's Macro Library Manager add-in and a macro to help you update a multilevel linked application. The macro should retrieve then save each file with its same name, beginning with the lowest to the highest worksheet in your hierarchy. Symphony will then automatically update all the links in your application. By using the Macro Library Manager, you can update the links from any worksheet. Chapter 21, "Creating and Using Macros," contains File Retrieve and Save macros, and an explanation of the Macro Library Manager.

> ### Tip
> If you perform consolidations of similarly structured worksheets, such as annual budgets, you should use the SERVICES **F**ile **C**ombine **A**dd **E**ntire-File command and a macro. Using linked worksheets for this type of consolidation will require a lengthy recalculation period.

Linking Files with VIEWER.APP

Symphony 2.2 includes an add-in application to help you create linked files. VIEWER.APP is a version of Lotus Magellan, the file management program from Lotus. VIEWER.APP enables you to see the contents of the worksheet files on disk, retrieve them, and create links.

Using VIEWER.APP

After you attach VIEWER.APP with the SERVICES **A**pplication **A**ttach command, you invoke the add-in with the SERVICES **F**ile **V**iew command. You have the choice of retrieving, linking, or browsing through the files, as shown by the menu in figure 3.10.

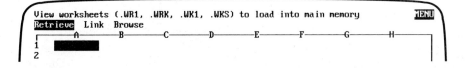

Fig. 3.10.
The VIEWER add-in menu.

VIEWER enables you to view, retrieve, or link the files in the current directory, shown in the Directory Path Line. The **L**ist **W**indow, the far left of the screen, displays a list of the worksheet files in the current subdirectory. You use the up-and-down arrow keys to select a file, which is displayed to the right of the file list, in the **V**iew **W**indow. Along the bottom of the screen is the Information

Line, which displays information about the file: Its name, the date and time you last updated it, and its size in bytes, similar to the information the SERVICES **F**ile **T**able command provides you.

To create a link to another file, retrieve the file you want to be the target file. Next, attach the VIEWER add-in with the SERVICES **A**pplication **A**ttach command. Once you have VIEWER attached, use the SERVICES **F**ile **V**iew command to use VIEWER.

Now, select **L**ink, and select the source file from the list of files using the up-and-down arrow keys. After you have selected the proper file, press the right-arrow key and move the cell pointer to the cell you want to link to, as shown in figure 3.11. You can move to the cell with any of Symphony's pointer movement keys, including PgUp, PgDn, Home, and End+Home. Finally, press Enter. The link is created and you are returned to the target worksheet and Symphony's SHEET mode.

Fig. 3.11.

Creating a link by using Symphony's VIEWER add-in.

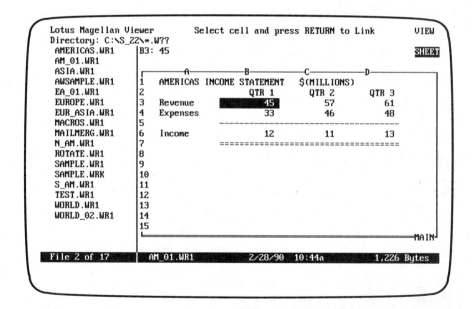

Note, however, that you can only view the worksheet files, and not edit or make changes to them. In addition, to change to another directory or drive, you exit VIEWER by pressing Ctrl-Break or Esc, and using the SERVICES **F**ile **D**irectory command.

Other Uses for VIEWER

Once you have attached VIEWER, you can use the add-in to help you find the worksheet file you need. For example, if you are having difficulty remembering the name of one of the files, issue the SERVICES **F**ile **V**iew **B**rowse command to see the contents of the files. After finding the file, use the SERVICES **F**ile **V**iew **R**etrieve command to retrieve the file. After the file is retrieved, Symphony returns to SHEET mode. Similar to the SERVICES **F**ile **R**etrieve command, any file currently in memory is replaced with the new file.

Tip

Unlike 1-2-3, Symphony does not display the width of a column in the control panel. VIEWER, however, displays in the View Window the widths of worksheet columns other than the default of nine.

Editing in Symphony

Symphony offers different ways to edit material. You can edit data that you are entering in response to a command. For example, you can edit range names, cell addresses, or special entries that you are making in settings sheets. You can edit this data if you have not entered it by pressing Enter.

The other three kinds of editing involve data that you are entering or have already entered in SHEET, DOC, and FORM windows. This section covers the keys and procedures for editing only in the SHEET environment, which includes editing labels, numbers, and formulas. (For procedures on editing ranges by erasing ranges and deleting rows and columns, see Chapter 4.)

Reminder:
Use the F2 key to edit a cell entry.

Editing an entry in the SHEET environment is easy to do. You begin by moving the cell pointer to the appropriate cell and pressing the F2 key (the Edit key). If you are in the process of typing the entry, press F2.

When you press F2, Symphony switches from SHEET to EDIT mode. (The mode indicator in the upper right corner of the screen changes from **SHEET** to **EDIT**.) The cell contents are duplicated in the second line of the control panel and are then ready for editing.

In EDIT mode, the following keys function differently than they do in SHEET mode:

Key	Action in EDIT Mode
[←]	Moves the cursor one position to the left
[→]	Moves the cursor one position to the right
Home	Moves the cursor to the first character position of the edit line
End	Moves the cursor one position to the right of the last character

Ctrl-[→]	Moves the cursor five characters to the right
Ctrl-[←]	Moves the cursor five characters to the left
Backspace	Deletes the character just to the left of the cursor
Del	Deletes the character above the cursor
Esc	Clears the edit line (also cancels data that you have not finished typing)

To show how these keys are used, consider two examples. First, suppose that you want to edit an entry in cell E4 that reads **Sales Comparisson**. After you position the cell pointer in cell E4, press the following keys:

Key	Edit Line	Explanation
F2	'Sales Comparisson_	The cursor always appears at the end of the edit line when you press F2
Del	'Sales Comparison	The Del key deletes the character above the cursor
Enter		You must press Enter to update the entry in the worksheet and return to SHEET mode

Reminder:

When you enter a cell for the first time and make a mistake, use EDIT mode to reduce retyping.

Keep in mind that you can use EDIT mode when you are entering a cell for the first time and you make a mistake. With EDIT mode, you can reduce retyping.

Now suppose that you want to change a formula in cell G6 from +D4/H3*(Y5+4000) to +C4/H3*(Y5+4000). After you move the cell pointer to cell G6, press the following keys:

Key	Edit Line	Explanation
F2	+D4/H3*(Y5+4000)_	Again, the cursor always appears at the end of the edit line when you first press F2
Home	+D4/H3*(Y5+4000)	The Home key takes you to the first position in the edit line
→	+D4/H3*(Y5+4000)	The right-arrow key moves the cursor one position to the right

C	+CD4/H3*(Y5+4000)	Whenever you enter a character in EDIT mode, the character is inserted to the left of the cursor. Entering a character never causes you to write over another one. You can eliminate unwanted characters with the Del and Backspace keys	**Reminder:** *The "C" in this formula appears in lowercase unless C A P S is visible on-screen.*
Del	+C4/H3*(Y5+4000)	The Del key deletes the character above the cursor	
Enter		Again, you must press Enter to update the entry in the worksheet and return to SHEET mode	

You can use the F2 (Edit) and F8 (Calc) function keys together to convert a formula stored in a cell to a number. Normally, you use F8 to recalculate the worksheet when you have recalculation set to Manual. (Symphony's default is automatic; the **R**ecalculation command is covered in Chapter 4.) When you are in EDIT mode, however, pressing F8 causes a formula to be converted to a number.

Reminder:
Convert a formula to a number by pressing F8 while in the EDIT mode.

For example, suppose that you want to use F8 to convert the formula in the previous example to a number (assumed to be 64,000) and store the result. You should perform the following steps:

Key	*Edit Line*	*Explanation*
F2	+C4/H3*(Y5+4000)_	F2 puts Symphony in EDIT mode
F8	64000_	F8 converts the formula to its current number (64,000)
Enter		Enter stores the entry in the current cell and shifts Symphony to SHEET mode

Using Ranges

Symphony often requires you to designate a group of cells in response to a command or to complete a function. This group is called a range. A range is one or more cells shaped like a rectangle. The smallest range is one cell and the largest is Symphony's entire worksheet.

Reminder:

Naming ranges and indicating them in settings sheets saves you from having to search the worksheet for cell addresses.

Using ranges makes the work in Symphony easier and faster. Because of the worksheet size and the possibility that you may have worksheet analyses, databases, and word-processing documents in various parts of the worksheet, naming the ranges and indicating ranges in settings sheets saves you from having to search the worksheet for cell addresses. Ranges also enable you to process blocks of cells in commands and formulas at the same time.

Although you can choose when to use ranges, you soon learn that if you use them frequently you can simplify, increase the accuracy of, and accelerate many operations. (Ranges are covered in more detail in Chapter 4.) Once you begin using Symphony extensively, you find that the range feature is more than a convenience; ranges often are necessary for processing commands and moving to various parts of the worksheet. Most of the commands that use ranges in the SHEET environment are included in the next chapter.

Shaping Ranges

As you can see from fig. 3.12, ranges are rectangles. Symphony's expanding cell pointer feature enables you to view the shape of ranges. When you designate a range, Symphony displays it in reverse video. As the cell pointer moves, the reverse-video rectangle expands. Defining a range is easy because you can always tell where its borders are.

Fig. 3.12.

A reverse-video expanding rectangle.

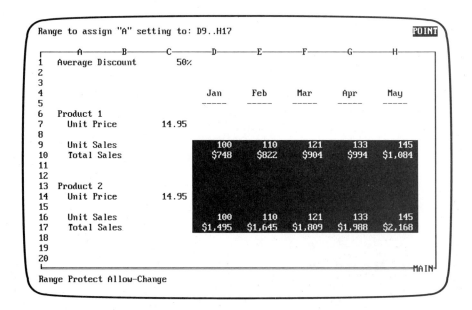

Designating Ranges

You can designate ranges by entering cell addresses, pointing to cells, and specifying range names. These methods enable you to indicate the corners of the rectangular group of cells that the range represents.

Ranges are specified by diagonally opposite corners—the upper left and lower right cells (see fig. 3.13). Indicating the other set of corners, however, is also permissible. For example, the range shown in figure 3.10 can be identified as A1..D5 or D1..A5.

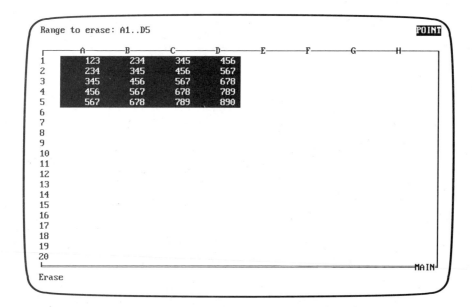

Fig. 3.13.

Range specified by diagonally opposite corners.

Getting the Most From Symphony

Thus far, most of this chapter has focused on the SHEET environment as a separate window in Symphony. But even though you can use the SHEET environment apart from the DOC, FORM, GRAPH, and COMM environments, you get the most from Symphony by including the other four environments with the applications you create.

Many possibilities exist for combining the SHEET environment with one or more of the other four environments. The following suggestions show you a few ways to create powerful and useful applications:

❑ Similar to 1-2-3 Rel. 3.0, you can display a graph and a worksheet on the screen simultaneously. If you change a number that the graph is based on, Symphony updates the graph instantly. Having a SHEET and a GRAPH window together is an important tool in "What If" analysis, as shown in fig. 3.14.

❑ You can use the DOC environment to create a document that contains worksheet data, as shown in fig. 3.15.

❑ You also can use Symphony's word processing capability to document the worksheet applications, as shown in fig. 3.16.

❑ Symphony's FORM environment enables you to create a data entry form to quickly enter data into a database that resides on a worksheet, as shown in fig. 3.17.

❑ Finally, Symphony's COMM environment is also dependent on the SHEET environment. For example, you download data from the COMM environment and store the data in a worksheet.

Fig. 3.14.

Viewing a SHEET and GRAPH window.

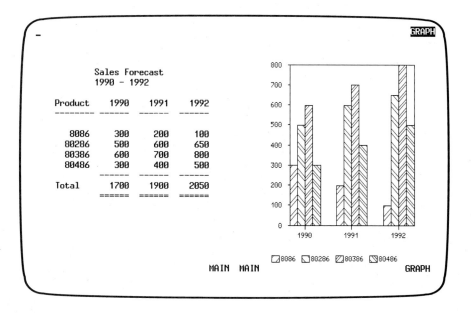

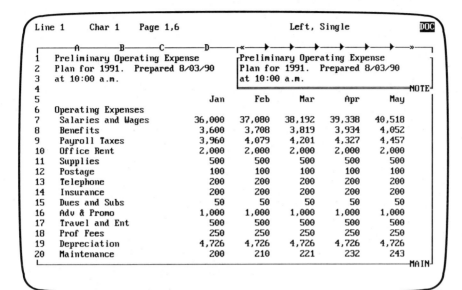

Fig. 3.15.

Adding notes to a worksheet with a DOC window.

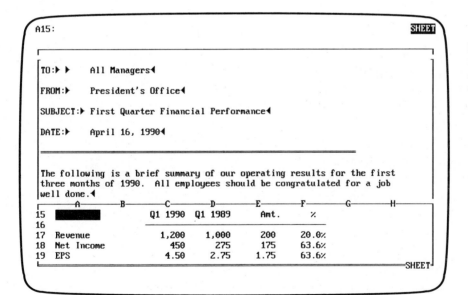

Fig. 3.16.

Using the DOC and SHEET environments in a report.

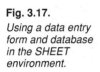

Fig. 3.17.

Using a data entry form and database in the SHEET environment.

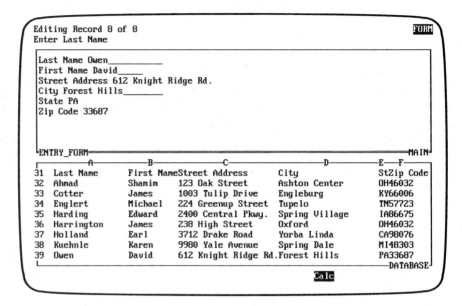

```
Editing Record 8 of 8                                    FORM
Enter Last Name
  Last Name Owen_____
  First Name David_____
  Street Address 612 Knight Ridge Rd.
  City Forest Hills_____
  State PA
  Zip Code 33687



 ENTRY_FORM                                            MAIN
     A           B          C            D          E  F
 31  Last Name   First NameStreet Address  City      StZip Code
 32  Ahmad       Shamim     123 Oak Street  Ashton Center OH46032
 33  Cotter      James      1003 Tulip Drive Engleburg  KY66006
 34  Englert     Michael    224 Greenup Street Tupelo   TN57723
 35  Harding     Edward     2400 Central Pkwy. Spring Village IA86675
 36  Harrington  James      238 High Street  Oxford    OH46032
 37  Holland     Earl       3712 Drake Road  Yorba Linda CA98076
 38  Kuehnle     Karen      9980 Yale Avenue Spring Dale MI48303
 39  Owen        David      612 Knight Ridge Rd.Forest Hills PA33687
                                                      DATABASE
                                       Calc
```

Chapter Summary

This chapter introduced you to the basics of using Symphony's SHEET environment, which is similar to using 1-2-3 or other worksheets. You learned about the value of ranges, how to enter and edit cell entries, and how to create formulas. In addition, you learned how to take advantage of Symphony as an integrated program.

In the next chapter, you learn how to take charge of the SHEET environment by mastering Symphony's SHEET commands.

4

Learning Fundamental SHEET Window Commands

Symphony's command system is the gateway to harnessing the power of the program. You use Symphony's SHEET-environment commands to perform a task or sequence of tasks. You also use SHEET commands in macros and Lotus Command Language programs to automate repetitive tasks and create custom applications.

In the SHEET environment, some of the more common tasks are copying, moving, and erasing cell entries; creating and deleting range names; and inserting and deleting rows and columns. This chapter explains how you can use the SHEET commands to do these tasks.

In this chapter, you learn how to do the following:

❑ Access Symphony's SHEET commands

❑ Use ranges and range names

❑ Copy, move, and erase data

❑ Insert and delete rows and columns

❑ Protect data

❑ Use absolute, mixed, and relative cell addresses

❑ Set column widths

❑ Freeze titles on-screen

❑ Control recalculation

101

Several SHEET commands are explained in Chapter 5, "Formatting the Worksheet," because these commands affect how cell entries are displayed on-screen and in printouts. The **F**ormat, **R**ange **L**abel-Alignment, **S**ettings **Z**ero, and **S**ettings **L**abel-Prefix commands are covered fully in Chapter 5, where you learn to customize the display of your applications. In addition, the **G**raph and **Q**uery commands are treated separately in Chapters 14 and 17, respectively.

Accessing the SHEET Commands

Reminder:

Access the SHEET menu by pressing Menu (F10); you also can press slash (/).

Like Lotus 1-2-3, Symphony uses a horizontal rolling-bar command menu that is displayed in the control panel. In Symphony, you access the SHEET commands (or any other environment's commands) by pressing Menu (F10). If you are upgrading to Symphony from 1-2-3, know that you also can access the commands by pressing slash (/).

Figure 4.1 shows the SHEET command menu on the second line of Symphony's control panel. A brief description of the highlighted command appears on the first line of the control panel. When you select a command, Symphony displays the name of the command in the lower left corner of the screen until you complete the command sequence. This feature helps you keep your place in Symphony's command menus.

Fig. 4.1.

The SHEET menu.

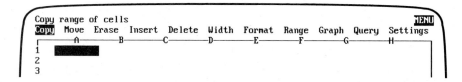

You can select a command in two ways. The first is to point to the command by using the cursor keys or the space bar. When the cell pointer is positioned on the desired command, press Enter. You can move the cell pointer rapidly to the far left and far right commands by pressing the Home and End keys, respectively. If you move the cell pointer to the last command in the menu bar and then press →, the cell pointer appears on the first command in the menu bar. Similarly, if the cell pointer is on the first command in the menu, pressing ← moves the cell pointer to the last command in the menu.

Reminder:

Select a command quickly by typing its first letter.

The second and faster way to select commands is to type the first letter of the command. As is true with 1-2-3, all Symphony commands begin with a different letter so that you can select a command rapidly. For example, to select the **R**ange **T**ranspose command, press Menu (F10) or slash (/), then press R to select **R**ange. A second command menu appears (see fig. 4.2). To select **T**ranspose from the second menu, press T. Symphony then displays prompts to which you respond to complete the command.

```
Maintain list of range names                                    MENU
Name  Transpose  Values  Label-Alignment  Protect  Fill  Distribution  What-If
    ───A───    ───B───  ───C───  ───D───  ───E───  ───F───  ───G───  ───H───
  1  █████████
  2
  3
```

Fig. 4.2.
*The SHEET **R**ange menu.*

If you make an incorrect selection, press Esc at any time to return to the previous command menu. For instance, if you wanted to select **D**istribution instead of **T**ranspose, press Esc to return to the **R**ange menu. To move to previous command menus or to leave MENU mode altogether, continue pressing Esc. You also can press Ctrl-Break to return to SHEET mode quickly.

The **R**ange commands are discussed first because creating and using range names are fundamental spreadsheet tasks. The **M**ove, **E**rase, **I**nsert, **D**elete, **C**opy, and **W**idth commands, and two of the **S**ettings commands (**T**itles and **R**ecalculation), are discussed later in the chapter.

Using the Range Commands

The **R**ange commands enable you to name ranges, transpose values, convert formulas to values, protect ranges, and perform other similar operations. When you press Menu (F10) or slash (/) and select **R**ange, the **R**ange commands appear in Symphony's control panel, as shown in figure 4.2.

The specific range commands are explained in the following sections. The **R**ange **L**abel-Alignment command is discussed in Chapter 5.

Designating a Range

Before you learn any of the specific **R**ange commands, you should learn what a range is and how to *specify*, or *highlight*, one. A *range* is a group of cells as small as a single cell or as large as an entire worksheet. Cells in a range usually have some relationship to each other: they all may be values you want to sum, or they may be a group of people's names.

Ranges are designated by the cell addresses at their opposite corners. For example, a range that contains the cells A1, A2, B1, and B2 forms a square of four cells that can be referred to as A1..B2, A2..B1, B1..A2, or B2..A1. Notice that it doesn't matter in which order the range addresses are given, as long as the addresses are for the diagonal corners of the range. If these four cells contained information you wanted to copy, for example, you could issue the **C**opy command and type **A1..B2** in response to the `Range to copy FROM:` prompt.

You typically specify ranges in response to command prompts or when specifying a formula. For example, if you select **C**opy, the prompt `Range to copy FROM:` appears. You can respond to this prompt in one of two ways: you can type the addresses of the range (for example, **A1..A10**), or you can point to the range. *Pointing to a range* simply means that you use the arrow keys to highlight the desired range. Pointing to a range can be easier and safer than typing the address of the range. Because you actually see the range highlighted on-screen, you know you are selecting the correct range. If you type the range address, you run the risk of mistyping one of the cell addresses.

In most cases, the command prompt shows a default range of one cell. This range is the *current cell* (where the cell pointer is located when you select the command). If the cell pointer is in cell A1 when you select **C**opy, for example, the prompt reads `Range to copy FROM: A1..A1`.

If the range that Symphony shows in the command prompt is not correct, you can change it easily. Just type a new range or point to the desired range.

To point to a range in response to a command prompt, follow these steps:

1. Notice that the indicator in the upper right corner of the screen is POINT. When you can use the arrow keys to point to a range, Symphony displays the POINT indicator to let you know you are in POINT mode. (If you start typing an address at this point, the indicator changes to EDIT and you must press Esc to return to POINT mode.)

2. Use the arrow keys to expand the highlight to encompass the entire range you want to specify. The current cell is the "anchor"; the highlight expands and contracts around this cell. Notice that the range address in the control panel changes as you press the arrow keys.

3. Press Enter to indicate that you are done defining the range.

Reminder:

When you want to point to a range, anchor the highlight by pressing the period or Tab key.

If the range you want to indicate does not begin with the current cell (the anchor cell displayed in the control panel), press Esc to "unanchor" the cell pointer. Then move the cell pointer to one of the corners of the range you want to specify and press the period (.) or Tab key. The period or Tab key anchors the highlight at that cell. Now use the arrow keys to expand the highlight. When you have highlighted the desired range, press Enter.

You also can use the End key to help point to ranges. When you press the End key and one of the arrow keys, the cell pointer moves in the direction of the arrow to the last cell that has data. For example, if an otherwise empty worksheet contains data in cells A1..A10 and the cell pointer is in cell A1, pressing End ↓ moves the cell pointer to cell A10. If you anchor the cell pointer in cell A1 before you press End ↓, the entire range A1..A10 is highlighted. As you can see, End can help you specify a range quickly.

Tip

Quickly move to the last active cell in the worksheet by pressing End Home (first press End and then press Home).

When you want to specify a range in a formula, you can type the range name or the address or point to the range. For example, to enter the formula @SUM*(A1..D1)* in cell E1, you can move the cell pointer to cell E1 and type **@SUM(A1..D1)**. Alternatively, you can type **@SUM(** and press one of the arrow keys to access POINT mode. Move the cell pointer to cell A1, press period to anchor the cell, move the cell pointer to D1 to expand the highlight, and press Enter. Finish the formula by typing **)**, the closing parenthesis; press Enter to enter the formula into cell E1.

If you start to point to a range and realize that you are specifying an incorrect range, press Esc. The range you entered is erased from the control panel and the highlight contracts to the anchor cell. However, that cell is no longer anchored; you can move the cell pointer to a new location and specify the correct range.

The Backspace key is similar to the Esc key when you want to cancel range specifications. Where Esc contracts the highlighted range to the anchor cell, however, Backspace contracts the highlight and returns the cell pointer to the cell that was current when you issued the command. Backspace doesn't care whether you specified an anchor cell different from the one that was current when you started; it always returns the cell pointer to the location it occupied before you issued the command or began typing the formula.

Reminder:
Use the Backspace key to cancel a range specification and return the cell pointer to its previous location.

Now that you know how to specify ranges by pointing and typing, you are ready to learn about the commands that affect ranges.

Naming Ranges

You can assign a name of up to 15 characters to a range of cells. Make the range names descriptive to help you recall what ranges the names represent. The advantage to naming ranges is that range names are easier to understand and remember than cell addresses; range names also enable you to work more intuitively. For example, describing gross margin with the phrase SALES–COGS is more understandable than using +A17–B10.

Reminder:
A range name can be up to 15 characters long.

Creating Range Names

You create range names with the **R**ange **N**ame **C**reate and **R**ange **N**ame **L**abels commands. Once you establish names, you can use them in commands and formulas. Use the **R**ange **N**ame **C**reate command to specify a name for any range, even one cell. You specify ranges by one of two methods: entering the cell address or pointing. You also can use **R**ange **N**ame **C**reate to respecify a range if its location has changed. (If a range is affected by minor changes, however, such as the deletion of a column or row, Symphony modifies the range for you).

The **R**ange **N**ame **L**abels command is similar to **R**ange **N**ame **C**reate, except that **R**ange **N**ame **L**abels uses label entries in adjacent cells to name the ranges. Consider figure 4.3. If you use the **R**ange **N**ame **L**abels command and specify that cell A1 contains the range name for cell B1, you can assign the name CASH to the range B1. If you assign the label ACCOUNTS RECEIVABLE as a range name, Symphony assigns the name ACCOUNTS RECEIV. Remember that Symphony accepts a maximum of 15 characters (including spaces) for a range name.

Fig. 4.3.

*Using the **Range** Name Labels command.*

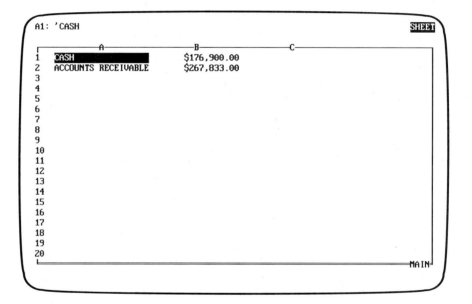

You also use range names to create a macro. You use the **R**ange **N**ame **C**reate command to name a macro. (Keyboard macros are discussed in detail in Chapter 21.)

Refer to figure 4.3 and follow these steps to create range names by using both of the methods just discussed:

1. Select **R**ange **N**ame **C**reate.

2. Type the name **CASH** and press Enter.

3. Type B1 to specify the address of the range you want to name and press Enter.

    The range B1 has been named CASH.

4. Select **R**ange **N**ame **L**abels.

5. Select **R**ight.

6. Press Esc to unanchor the cell pointer; use the arrow keys to move the cell pointer to cell A2. (Alternatively, type **A2** in response to the prompt.)

7. Press Enter.

    The label in cell A2 has been assigned to the cell to its right (cell B2).

Deleting Range Names

You can delete range names individually or all at once. The **R**ange **N**ame **D**elete command enables you to delete a single range name. You may want to delete unused range names to save memory; you also delete range names if you want to assign the range name to a different range of cells. The **R**ange **N**ame **R**eset command deletes all range names simultaneously. Use **R**ange **N**ame **R**eset with caution.

Caution:

Range Name Reset deletes all range names simultaneously.

Follow these steps to delete the range name CASH created in the last section:

1. Select **R**ange **N**ame **D**elete.

2. Use the arrow keys to move the highlight through the list of range names that appears on the second line of the control panel. When the range name that you want to delete is highlighted, press Enter.

Creating a Table of Range Names

You can create a table of range names and their cell addresses with the **R**ange **N**ame **T**able command. This command creates a two-column list of range names. The first column lists in alphabetical order the range names in the worksheet; the second column lists the corresponding cell addresses. **R**ange **N**ame **T**able enables you to view and print the range names used in the worksheet (see fig. 4.4).

To create a range-name table, select the **R**ange **N**ame **T**able command. Next, indicate the location in the worksheet where you want the table to appear by pointing to or typing a cell address; press Enter. Be careful where you place the range-name table, however. Because the table will overwrite any existing data, place the table in an area that won't interfere with other cell entries.

Reminder:

When you use Range Name Table, select an area of the worksheet that won't overwrite existing cell entries.

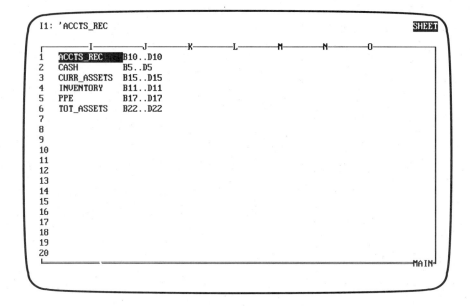

Fig. 4.4.

A table of existing range names.

Using Range Names

Range names are useful tools in processing commands and generating formulas. In both cases, whenever you want to designate a range, you can enter its range name instead. Using names eliminates the repetitive task of entering cell addresses or pointing to cell locations whenever a range is called for. Suppose that you designate SALES as a range name for the range A5..J5 in one of your worksheets. The simplest way to compute the sum of this range is to use the formula @SUM*(SALES)*. Similarly, to determine the maximum value in the range, use the formula @MAX*(SALES)*. You can always use range names in place of cell addresses in functions and formulas.

Another advantage of range names is that once you establish a range name, you can use that name throughout the worksheet in place of the corresponding cell address. If you delete a range name, Symphony no longer uses that name but reverts to the corresponding cell address in functions, formulas, and macros.

Consider a few examples of using range names. Figure 4.5 shows a simple case of totaling two rows of numbers.

If you assigned the range name SALES to the range D3..G3, and the name CGS to range D4..G4, you can define cell H3 with the function @SUM*(SALES)*. Similarly, you can define cell H4 with @SUM*(CGS)*. Cell H6 can contain the function @SUM*(SALES)*–@SUM*(CGS)*.

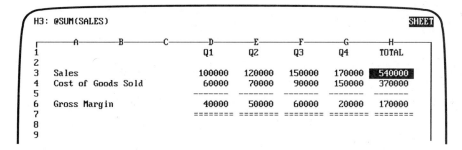

```
H3: @SUM(SALES)                                                    SHEET
 ┌──────A───────B───────C───────D──────E──────F──────G──────H──────
 1                              Q1     Q2     Q3     Q4    TOTAL
 2
 3    Sales                  100000 120000 150000 170000  540000
 4    Cost of Goods Sold      60000  70000  90000 150000  370000
 5                           ------- ------ ------ ------  ------
 6    Gross Margin            40000  50000  60000  20000  170000
 7                           ======= ====== ====== ====== ======
 8
 9
```

Fig. 4.5.
Range name used in a formula.

Another example uses names to designate the ranges of cells to be printed or saved. Suppose that you create range names corresponding to different pages of a worksheet and want to print or save them to another worksheet. When Symphony prompts you for a range, you can enter a range name rather than the actual cell addresses. For example, if you select SERVICES **P**rint **S**ettings **S**ource **R**ange, you can enter the range name **PAGE 1** in response to the prompt.

A third range-name example involves the GoTo (F5) key. Recall that the GoTo key enables you to move the cell pointer directly to a cell when you specify the cell's address. You also can provide a range name rather than a cell address. For example, suppose that you gave the name INSTRUCT to the range of cells A1..C10. Press GoTo (F5) and enter **INSTRUCT** in response to the `Address to go to:` prompt. The cell pointer moves to the upper left corner of the named range.

You can display a list of range names when you are prompted for a range by pressing the Menu (F10) key. For example, press GoTo (F5) followed by Menu (F10) and select from the list of range names the range to which you want to move the cell pointer.

Cue:
Display a list of range names when prompted for a range by pressing Menu (F10).

Suppose that you assign the name CGS to the range D4..G4 in the example in figure 4.5. You can erase this portion of the worksheet by pressing Menu (F10), selecting **E**rase, and entering the range name **CGS** rather than the cell address **D4..G4**.

However, suppose that you cannot remember the name of the range you want to erase after selecting the **E**rase command. Press Menu (F10) again to display a list of the range names in the worksheet. If you have more than five range names, press Menu again. Symphony displays a complete list of the range names in the control panel. Figure 4.6 shows a screen with two range names displayed in the control panel. After this list appears, use the cell pointer to point to the range you want to delete and select it by pressing Enter.

Cue:
Display a full-screen list of range names when prompted for a range by pressing Menu (F10) twice.

Fig. 4.6.
Range names listed in the control panel.

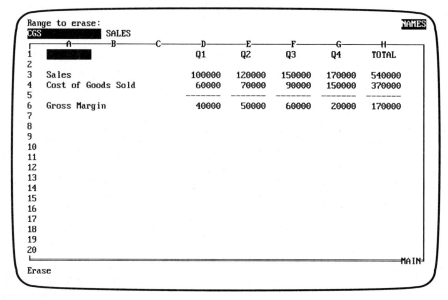

Transposing Rows and Columns

You can copy the contents of rows to columns or columns to rows with the **R**ange **T**ranspose command. This feature is useful, for example, if you want to use column headings as row labels. In figure 4.7, for example, the range to copy FROM is B3..H3; the range to copy TO is A5.

Fig. 4.7.
Transposing columns to rows.

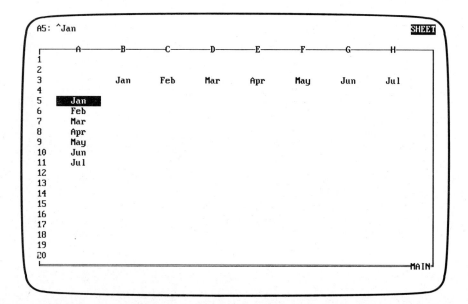

The **R**ange **T**ranspose command enables you to copy labels, values, and formulas from rows to columns or from columns to rows. To transpose ranges, select **R**ange **T**ranspose, indicate the range of the original column or row, and then specify the range for the new row or column.

When you use **R**ange **T**ranspose, be aware of the following possibilities. First, if you transpose values or formulas, Symphony either recalculates or indicates that you should press the Calc (F8) key once you complete the transpose operation. If the range you are transposing contains relative cell addresses (refer to "Understanding Relative and Absolute Addressing" later in this chapter), Symphony cannot convert the cell addresses. In this case, formulas do not recalculate correctly; use the **M**ove command instead. Second, make sure that the range to which you are moving the cell contents (the TO range) won't interfere with other cell entries. Transposed columns and rows overwrite any previously entered data.

Copying Values

You can copy a range of values from one part of a worksheet to another with the **R**ange **V**alues command. This feature is useful when you want to preserve values that would change when you recalculate or enter new values. The **R**ange **V**alues command converts formulas to values. You don't have to worry, therefore, about formulas that depend on cell references. (Copying formulas that contain cell addresses is discussed in more detail in "Copying Cell Contents," later in this chapter.)

Reminder:

Range Values changes to values any formulas in the specified range to be copied.

Now consider the following example of the **R**ange **V**alues command. Suppose that you calculate monthly totals from values entered into an income statement (see fig. 4.8). Because you change the sheet every month, the Year-to-Date (Y-T-D) totals change as well. If you want to save the Y-T-D totals to compare them with previous years or quarters, you can use the **R**ange **V**alues command to do so (see fig. 4.9).

To copy a range of formulas to values, select **R**ange **V**alues. When Symphony prompts you for `Range to copy FROM:`, indicate the range of values you want copied (H56..H69, in the example shown in fig. 4.8). Then indicate where you want the values copied TO (M56, as shown in fig. 4.9); be careful that you don't overwrite existing data with the newly copied values. Notice that you can give a single cell as the TO address; Symphony makes an exact copy of the FROM range at the specified TO address, regardless of the size of the TO address.

Fig. 4.8.

A monthly income statement.

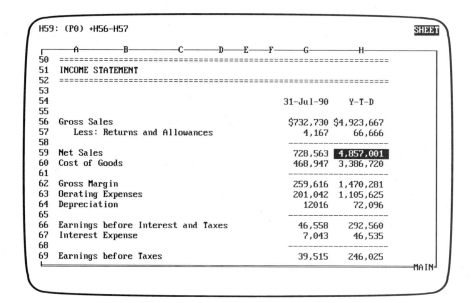

Fig. 4.9.

Copying a range of values.

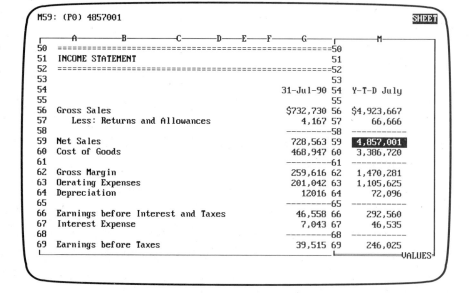

Protecting Ranges

You use the **R**ange **P**rotect command to prevent intentional or unintentional changes to cell entries. (For more information about range protection, see the section titled "Using Symphony's Security System" in Chapter 1). The **R**ange

Protect command is particularly beneficial when you are creating applications for other people that shouldn't be changed or modified.

In a new worksheet, every cell has the potential of being protected, but no cell is protected unless you invoke the SERVICES **S**ettings **G**lobal-Protection command. Lotus uses the analogy of a series of electric fences erected around all the cells in the worksheet. The "electricity" to these fences is turned off when a new worksheet is brought into memory. In other words, all the cells in the worksheet can be modified. This arrangement is appropriate because you want to have access to all the cells in the worksheet as you are creating it. Once you finish creating the worksheet application, however, you may have areas that you don't want changed, or you may want to disallow cell-pointer movement elsewhere.

To protect a range of cells in a worksheet, you must follow several steps. First, select the SERVICES **S**ettings **G**lobal-Protection command. At the `Allow changes only to cells with the "A" setting:` prompt, select **Y**es and press Enter. Once you issue this command, *all* cells are protected.

To continue the "electric fence" analogy, the SERVICES **S**ettings **G**lobal-Protection command is the switch that activates all the electric fences in the worksheet. After you turn on this switch, the next step is to tell Symphony which fences should be "turned off" so that you can enter data in those cells.

Turn off protection for selected cells by issuing the **R**ange **P**rotect command and choosing **A**llow-Changes. Then indicate the range of cells where you want to allow changes. You can reprotect these cells at any time by issuing the **R**ange **P**rotect **P**revent-Changes command. If you want to make changes possible in any cell in the worksheet, select SERVICES **S**ettings **G**lobal-Protection **N**o to "turn off all the electricity." Figure 4.10 can help you understand the relationship between SERVICES **S**ettings **G**lobal-Protection and SHEET **R**ange **P**rotect.

	SERVICES Global-Protection No: allow changes to all cells	SERVICES Global-Protection Yes: allow changes to cells with only "A" setting
SHEET **R**ange **P**rotect **A**llow-Changes "A" setting: Allow changes to cells even if **G**lobal-Protection = Yes	No Restriction Changes can be made in all cells	Restricted Changes can be made in only "A" cells
SHEET **R**ange **P**rotect **P**revent-Changes Remove "A" setting: Prevent changes to cells when **G**lobal-Protection = Yes	No Restriction Changes can be made in all cells	Restricted The "A" marker is removed; no changes can be made

Fig. 4.10.
The relationship between Global-Protection and Range Protect.

If you create an application that contains many complex formulas, you may want to protect these areas against accidental modification by using Symphony's protection capability. But what if you have to change several of these formulas? Allow the formulas to be changed by issuing the **G**lobal-Protection **N**o command to "lower the fences" around all cells. After you make the necessary changes, use **G**lobal-Protection **Y**es to restore protection to all the cells. Notice that the **R**ange **P**rotect **A**llow-Changes command is in effect until you specifically remove it with **R**ange **P**rotect **P**revent-Changes, regardless of what global protection is applied.

Reminder:

Use SERVICES Window Settings Restrict Range to restrict the movement of the cell pointer to a specified range.

For even more protection, you can limit the movement of the cell pointer by using the SERVICES **W**indow **S**ettings **R**estrict command. Setting a restrict range means that the cell pointer can move only to those cells within the range you specify. For example, suppose that you want to restrict cell-pointer movement to the area occupied by the data in figure 4.11. To restrict the cell pointer to this area, select SERVICES **W**indow **S**ettings **R**estrict **R**ange. When Symphony prompts you with `Restrict range for this window:`, type **A57..H76** or move the cell pointer to highlight that range. To restrict the cell pointer to what is on the screen, select **R**estrict **S**creen. The restrict range remains in effect until you reset it with SERVICES **W**indow **S**ettings **R**estrict **N**one.

The SERVICES **W**indow **S**ettings **R**estrict and SHEET **R**ange **P**rotect commands are useful tools for decreasing the possibility of lost data.

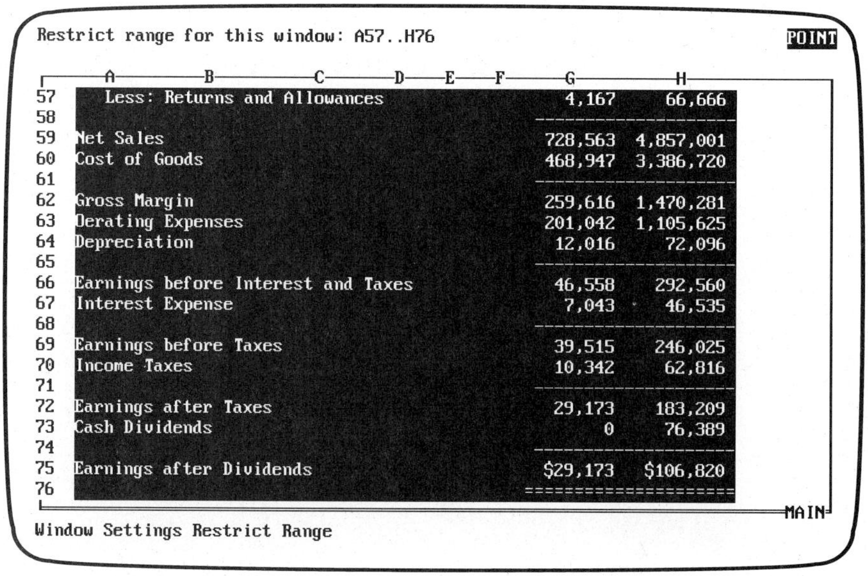

Fig. 4.11.

Setting a restrict range.

	A	B	C	D	E	F	G	H
Restrict range for this window: A57..H76								POINT
57	Less: Returns and Allowances						4,167	66,666
58								
59	Net Sales						728,563	4,857,001
60	Cost of Goods						468,947	3,386,720
61								
62	Gross Margin						259,616	1,470,281
63	Oerating Expenses						201,042	1,105,625
64	Depreciation						12,016	72,096
65								
66	Earnings before Interest and Taxes						46,558	292,560
67	Interest Expense						7,043	46,535
68								
69	Earnings before Taxes						39,515	246,025
70	Income Taxes						10,342	62,816
71								
72	Earnings after Taxes						29,173	183,209
73	Cash Dividends						0	76,389
74								
75	Earnings after Dividends						$29,173	$106,820
76								MAIN

Window Settings Restrict Range

Filling Ranges with Numbers

The **R**ange **F**ill command enables you to enter a series of values or dates that automatically increase or decrease by an increment you specify. The range of values can include a range of numbers listed in increments of 1, or a list of years (as shown in cells B5..F5 in fig. 4.12).

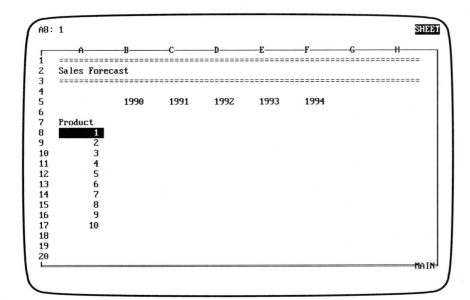

Fig. 4.12.
*Two examples of using **Range Fill**.*

Following are the specific steps for entering a sequence of numbers with **R**ange **F**ill:

1. Select **R**ange **F**ill.

2. Symphony displays the prompt `Fill range:`. Indicate the range in the worksheet where you want the numbers to be entered. In figure 4.12, this is **A8..A17**. Press Enter.

3. Symphony displays the prompt `Start value:`; enter **1** as the value at which you want the range of numbers to start.

4. Symphony displays the prompt `Step value:`; this is the increment of the numbers. Type **1** for this prompt also.

5. Symphony displays the prompt `Stop value:`; specify **10**. The default stop value is 8191; you can fill an entire column with numbers if you indicate that in the fill range.

Cue:

*Use **R**ange **F**ill to assign consecutive numbers to the records of a database before you sort it. Re-sort on the numbers to restore the original order.*

One use for the **R**ange **F**ill command is with databases to be sorted. If you assign consecutive numbers to each record in a database (placing the numbers in a separate column), no matter how much you change the order of the database, you can re-create the original order. You simply sort the database according to the numbers you assigned with **R**ange **F**ill. Using **R**ange **F**ill in this way is particularly helpful if the database has an order other than numeric.

Tip

You can enter dates by using the @DATE function as the start value. For example, enter @DATE(90,1,1) as the start value and 1 as the step value to produce a list of dates one day apart. The stop value should be a particular date, entered with the @DATE function, or any number greater than 73050 (the maximum serial-number date that Symphony understands).

Creating Frequency Distributions

You use the **R**ange **D**istribution command to create frequency distributions, which are often used with databases. A *frequency distribution* is a representation of the relationship between a set of measurement classes and the frequency of occurrence of each class. An example of a frequency distribution and the use of **R**ange **D**istribution is a list of consumers and their product preferences (see fig. 4.13).

Fig. 4.13.

A frequency distribution.

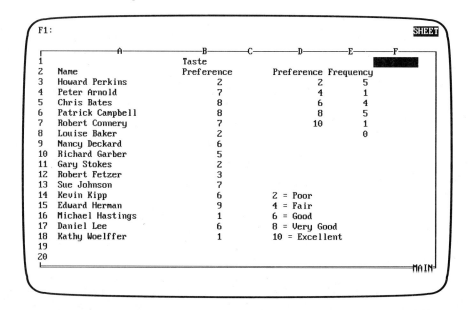

```
F1:                                                          SHEET
      ┌────A────────────B────────C─────────D──────────E──────────F────
    1                 Taste
    2   Name          Preference           Preference Frequency
    3   Howard Perkins    2                     2          5
    4   Peter Arnold      7                     4          1
    5   Chris Bates       8                     6          4
    6   Patrick Campbell  8                     8          5
    7   Robert Connery    7                    10          1
    8   Louise Baker      2                                0
    9   Nancy Deckard     6
   10   Richard Garber    5
   11   Gary Stokes       2
   12   Robert Fetzer     3
   13   Sue Johnson       7
   14   Kevin Kipp        6         2 = Poor
   15   Edward Herman     9         4 = Fair
   16   Michael Hastings  1         6 = Good
   17   Daniel Lee        6         8 = Very Good
   18   Kathy Woelffer    1        10 = Excellent
   19
   20   └                                                         ──MAIN─
```

Before you use **R**ange **D**istribution, you must create a *value range*, that is, you must list the values you want to include in the frequency distribution. In figure 4.13, this range is B3..B18. You also must create a range of *intervals*, also known as a *bin range* in Symphony. The bin range is a list of the numerical intervals for the frequency distribution of values in the value range. In figure 4.13, this range is D3..D7. If you want evenly spaced intervals, use the **R**ange **F**ill command to specify the values to be used in the bin range.

Once the value range and the bin range are created, select **R**ange **D**istribution. Symphony prompts you for the value range. Type or point to the appropriate range and press Enter. Symphony then prompts you for the bin range; specify this range and press Enter. Symphony calculates a results column (E3..E8 in figure 4.13) to the right of the bin range; this is the frequency distribution. (Make sure that the column to the right of the bin range is empty; Symphony uses this column for the distribution results by default.)

Reminder:

Symphony places the frequency distribution results in the column immediately to the right of the bin range.

The values in the results column represent the frequency of occurrence of numbers in the values range that fall within the intervals. The first interval in the bin range is for values greater than 0 and less than or equal to 2; the second interval is for values greater than 2 and less than or equal to 4; and so on. The final result of 0 in cell E8 is the frequency of values that don't fit into a specified interval classification.

Performing "What-If" Analysis

The **R**ange **W**hat-**I**f commands enable you to consider multiple business scenarios with a minimal amount of effort. The commands take a set of values and substitute them one at a time into a model. You need to specify only the values and the location for the results; Symphony calculates and displays the results for you. This procedure may sound complicated at first, but is actually very simple. All you have to know is how to create the appropriate ranges. Symphony takes care of the rest.

You may find the **R**ange **W**hat-**I**f commands difficult to understand at first. Once you understand how to use them, however, you'll find them one of Symphony's most powerful features. In fact, these commands rival similar capabilities in some of the most sophisticated management-information systems. When you consider that this power is available to you now with Symphony, the **R**ange **W**hat-**I**f commands can be some of your most important business-decision tools.

Using the Range What-If 1-Way Command

An example of how the **R**ange **W**hat-**I**f **1**-Way command operates is shown in figure 4.14. The figure shows a table of interest rates and their effects on the monthly payments of a 30-year mortgage.

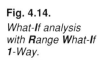

Fig. 4.14.

*What-If analysis
with Range What-If
1-Way.*

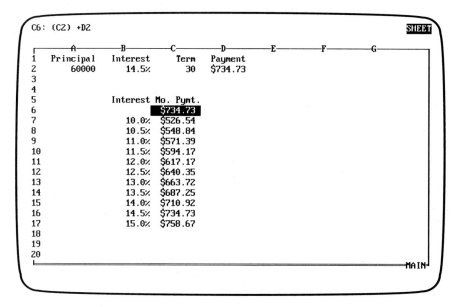

```
C6: (C2) +D2                                              SHEET
    ┌───A────────B────────C────────D──────E───────F───────G──────
  1 │ Principal  Interest   Term  Payment
  2 │   60000      14.5%      30  $734.73
  3 │
  4 │
  5 │            Interest Mo. Pymt.
  6 │                     $734.73
  7 │             10.0%   $526.54
  8 │             10.5%   $548.84
  9 │             11.0%   $571.39
 10 │             11.5%   $594.17
 11 │             12.0%   $617.17
 12 │             12.5%   $640.35
 13 │             13.0%   $663.72
 14 │             13.5%   $687.25
 15 │             14.0%   $710.92
 16 │             14.5%   $734.73
 17 │             15.0%   $758.67
 18 │
 19 │
 20 │
    └──────────────────────────────────────────────────MAIN─
```

Reminder:

*What-If 1-Way uses
one formula that
references one
variable to create a
matrix table of
results.*

The **R**ange **W**hat-If **1**-Way command substitutes the interest rates entered in column B into the appropriate input cell (B2). The *input cell* is the cell referenced in the formula in cell D2; each of the interest rates in column B is substituted into cell B2 and used in a separate calculation. Symphony lists the results of the individual calculations—in this case, the monthly payments—in the column next to the interest rates.

In figure 4.14, you enter the principal, interest, and term values in cells A2, B2, and C2, respectively. In cell D2, you enter the following formula for calculating the payment:

@PMT*(A2,B2/12,C2*12)*

Note: Functions are explained in detail in Chapter 6.

In B7..B17, you enter the various interest rates that you want to "plug into" the formula. (You can use the **R**ange **F**ill command to enter a list of incrementing interest rates).

Reminder:

*Put the formula
used to calculate
the 1-way what-if
table in the cell one
column to the right
and one row above
the list of variables.*

The next step is to enter the formula for calculating the results—or the cell address of the formula—in the cell one column to the right and one row above the first interest rate (cell C6). In figure 4.14, you can either copy the formula in cell D2 to cell C6 or enter in cell C6 the cell address of the formula: +D2.

Invoke the **R**ange **W**hat-If **1**-Way command. Symphony prompts you for a table range. The *table range* must include the list of variables (the interest rates in column B) and the column in which you want to place the results (column C). In figure 4.14, the table range is B6..C17. Notice that the formula's cell (cell C6) must be included in the table range. Symphony next prompts you for the input cell. In this example, the input cell is B2: the cell into which the various interest rates are to be substituted. Symphony flashes the **WAIT** indicator while calculating the results and returns to SHEET mode when finished.

Tip

If you work with what-if tables frequently, consider upgrading your computer's microprocessor. What-if tables recalculate more quickly if you have a more advanced microprocessor. For example, if you use an IBM PC or XT, consider adding an 80286 accelerator board to your computer.

Another alternative is to add a math coprocessor chip to your computer, which also results in faster calculation of what-if tables. See your computer retailer about the appropriate enhancement for your computer and the type of work you do.

As your expertise with macros increases, you can create macros that emulate the function of what-if tables but require less recalculation time. Macros are introduced in Chapter 21.

Using the Range What-If 2-Way Command

You can use the **R**ange **W**hat-**I**f **2**-Way command for more complex analysis than you can achieve with **R**ange **W**hat-**I**f **1**-Way. The **2**-Way command requires two input variables rather than one.

Figure 4.15 displays the effect of changes in order quantity and order point on total cost. In this example, you want to know which combination of order point and order quantity minimizes "Cumulative Costs to Date" at the end of a 12-month period.

The lower left portion of figure 4.15 shows how the **W**hat-**I**f **1**-Way command is used to determine the effect of different order quantities on cost. The lower right portion of figure 4.15 shows how **W**hat-**I**f **2**-Way is used to determine the effect of different order quantities *and* additional order points, for a more complete analysis.

To use **W**hat-**I**f **2**-Way, you use two sets of variables. In figure 4.15, you use the order-quantity and order-point values as the first and second variables, respectively. Enter the values for variable 1 (order quantity) in the range B22..B57. Enter the values for variable 2 (order point) in the range F21..J21 (the row above the first entry of variable 1). Cell M12 contains the formula +M10+M11; enter the formula **+M12**—the cell address of the "Cumulative Cost to Date" formula—in the row directly above the first entry of variable 1.

Reminder:
What-If 2-Way uses one formula that references two variables to create a matrix table of results.

Fig. 4.15.

*What-If analysis with **Range What-If** 1-Way and 2-Way.*

```
              A        B      C      D      E      F      G      H      I      J       K       L       M
 1 Month               Jan    Feb    Mar    Apr    May    Jun    Jul    Aug    Sep     Oct     Nov     Dec
 2 ------------------------------------------------------------------------------------------------------------
 3 Beginning Inventory 43     51     35     60     42     30     46     33     45      35      59      40
 4 Past Demand for Month 28   16     11     18     12     20     13     24     10      12      19      22
 5 Ending Inventory    15     35     24     42     30     10     33      9     35      23      40      18
 6 Quantity Ordered    36      0     36      0      0     36      0     36      0      36       0      36
 7 Setup Costs ($10 per order) $10.00 $0.00 $10.00 $0.00 $0.00 $10.00 $0.00 $10.00 $0.00 $10.00 $0.00 $10.00
 8 Inventory Costs ($.2/unit) $3.00 $7.00 $4.80 $8.40 $6.00 $2.00 $6.60 $1.80 $7.00 $4.60 $8.00 $3.60
 9 Shortage Costs ($1/unit) $0.00 $0.00 $0.00 $0.00 $0.00 $0.00 $0.00 $0.00 $0.00 $0.00 $0.00 $0.00
10 Total Costs for Month $13.00 $7.00 $14.80 $8.40 $6.00 $12.00 $6.60 $11.80 $7.00 $14.60 $8.00 $13.60
11 Cum Cost From Last Month $0.00 $13.00 $20.00 $34.80 $43.20 $49.20 $61.20 $67.80 $79.60 $86.60 $101.20 $109.20
12 Cumulative Costs to Date $13.00 $20.00 $34.80 $43.20 $49.20 $61.20 $67.80 $79.60 $86.60 $101.20 $109.20 $122.80
13
14
15 Order Quantity Input Cell  36
16 Order Point Input Cell     28
17
18                      Order Cumulative
19     What-If 1-Way--> Quant  Cost       What-If 2-Way -->     Order Quantity
20                      -----  -----      ------------------------------------------------------------
21                      +M12              +M12   25      26      27      28      29    Average
22                      25 $137.40          15 $150.40 $150.40 $150.40 $150.40 $150.40 $150.40
23                      26 $136.00          16 $163.60 $163.60 $163.60 $163.60 $163.60 $163.60
24                      27 $144.60          17 $143.00 $149.80 $160.00 $160.00 $160.00 $154.56
25                      28 $137.60          18 $154.80 $154.80 $154.80 $154.80 $154.80 $154.80
26                      29 $140.20          19 $141.40 $145.20 $149.00 $149.00 $149.00 $146.72
27                      30 $130.40          20 $148.40 $148.40 $148.40 $152.40 $152.40 $150.00
28                      31 $131.80          21 $132.40 $136.60 $136.60 $150.80 $150.80 $141.44
29                      32 $122.80          22 $138.00 $142.40 $142.40 $142.40 $142.40 $141.52
30                      33 $130.00    O     23 $138.60 $138.60 $143.20 $143.20 $147.80 $142.28
31                      34 $130.40    r     24 $133.20 $133.20 $133.20 $138.00 $138.00 $135.12
32                      35 $123.40    d     25 $132.40 $137.40 $137.40 $137.40 $142.40 $137.40
33                      36 $122.80    e     26 $136.00 $136.00 $136.00 $136.00 $141.20 $137.04
34                      37 $129.20    r     27 $123.80 $134.60 $144.60 $144.60 $144.60 $138.44
35                      38 $128.00          28 $120.80 $126.40 $132.00 $137.60 $137.60 $130.88
36                      39 $124.20    P     29 $128.60 $128.60 $128.60 $140.20 $140.20 $133.24
37                      40 $130.40    o     30 $124.40 $124.40 $124.40 $130.40 $142.40 $129.20
38                      41 $128.40    i     31 $131.80 $131.80 $131.80 $131.80 $131.80 $131.80
39                      42 $134.40    n     32 $122.80 $122.80 $122.80 $122.80 $129.20 $124.08
40                      43 $123.20    t     33 $130.00 $130.00 $130.00 $130.00 $130.00 $130.00
41                      44 $128.80          34 $110.00 $116.80 $130.40 $130.40 $130.40 $123.60
42                      45 $134.40          35 $116.40 $116.40 $116.40 $123.40 $123.40 $119.20
43                      46 $121.60          36 $122.80 $122.80 $122.80 $122.80 $122.80 $122.80
44                      47 $126.80          37 $121.80 $121.80 $129.20 $129.20 $129.20 $126.24
45                      48 $122.00          38 $110.40 $118.00 $118.00 $128.00 $128.00 $120.48
46                      49 $127.20          39 $116.40 $116.40 $124.20 $124.20 $124.20 $121.08
47                      50 $122.40          40 $122.40 $122.40 $122.40 $130.40 $130.40 $125.60
```

After you invoke **Range What-If 2**-Way, Symphony prompts you for a table range and the input cells for variables 1 and 2. Enter the following responses:

Prompt	Response
Table range	E21..J47
Input cell 1	B15
Input cell 2	B16

Similar to the **What-If 1**-Way command, the **What-If 2**-Way command requires one table range; however, **2**-Way requires input cells for *two* variables. After you enter this information, Symphony begins calculating a table of results.

The power of the **R**ange **W**hat-**I**f commands enables you to perform analyses that you might not do otherwise, given the time required to perform a similar analysis manually. You can combine the results of these two commands with macros and database statistical functions to create important management information.

Resetting What-If Tables

You can change the settings of what-if tables by specifying new ranges at the appropriate prompt. You also can cancel all what-if table settings with the **R**ange **W**hat-**I**f **R**eset command.

Cutting and Pasting Cell Entries

Five SHEET commands enable you to perform the same process of "cutting and pasting" used in the days of paper worksheets: copying, erasing, and moving data; and inserting and deleting rows and columns. In Symphony, the commands are **C**opy, **M**ove, **E**rase, **I**nsert, and **D**elete.

These commands enable you to rearrange your cell entries so that you can control the appearance of your applications easily. The **C**opy and **M**ove commands, as their names indicate, copy and move cell contents. The **E**rase command removes the contents of a single cell, a row, a column, or range of cells. The **I**nsert command adds blank rows or columns; the **D**elete command removes rows or columns. Each of these commands is explained in the following sections.

Moving Cell Contents

You can move cell entries easily from one area of a worksheet to another with the **M**ove command. For example, to move the contents of range C1..D3 to range E1..F3 in figure 4.16, select **M**ove from the SHEET command menu. Symphony displays the prompt `Range to move FROM:`. Specify the range C1..D3 and press Enter.

Reminder:
*Use **M**ove to move the contents of one range to another range.*

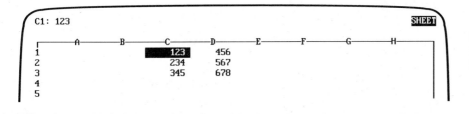

Fig. 4.16.
*The worksheet before using **M**ove.*

Note: If you use range names, you can enter the name of the range in response to the range prompts.

Symphony next displays the prompt `Range to move TO:`. Specify a TO range by typing or pointing to the cell address. You can enter the single-cell address **E1** for the TO range; Symphony understands that E1 is the upper left corner of the range. As soon as you press Enter, Symphony moves the contents of C1..D3 to E1..F3 and returns the cell pointer to the position it occupied before you invoked the **M**ove command (see fig. 4.17).

Fig. 4.17.
The result of using Move.

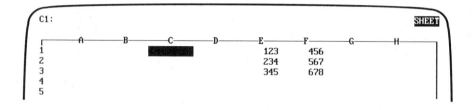

Reminder:
You can specify any TO or FROM range, regardless of the position of the cell pointer.

Keep in mind that when you designate ranges in response to a command, Symphony doesn't require you to position the cell pointer at the beginning of a TO or FROM range. You can specify any range, regardless of the location of the cell pointer.

Tip

When you copy and move cell entries, you frequently want to work on the cell entries that were just moved. Instead of moving the cell pointer back to the TO range after you complete the **C**opy or **M**ove command, consider the following technique.

Move the cell pointer to the upper left corner of the TO range. Issue the **C**opy or **M**ove command and press the Esc key to "unanchor" the FROM range. Move the cell pointer to the cell or range you want to copy or move, highlight the range, and press Enter. The cell pointer automatically returns to the original location: the TO range. Press Enter to complete the operation. Now you can work with the data without having first to move the cell pointer to it.

Moving Formulas—A Warning

When you move a range that contains formulas, all formulas are recalculated automatically. For example, suppose that you enter the following into a worksheet:

Cell	Entry
A1	+D1*100
C1	15
D1	+C1
E1	—blank—

Now suppose that you move the contents of cell D1 to cell E1. The formulas in your worksheet become as follows:

Cell	Entry
A1	+E1*100
C1	15
D1	—blank—
E1	+C1

Notice that the reference to cell D1 in the formula in A1 changed to accommodate the cell's new location. The formula in D1 did not change at all. Symphony automatically adjusts cell references in formulas for you.

Be careful how you use the **M**ove command. When you move a range of cell entries to another location, any existing contents of the TO range are completely overwritten by the contents of the FROM range. In addition, if you have a formula that depends on a cell entry that has been overwritten, the formula returns ERR. For example, as a continuation of the preceding example, if cell E2 contains the formula +E1 and you repeat the move operation (move the contents of cell D1 to cell E1), cell E2 displays **ERR**. Cell E2, which originally referenced the contents of cell E1, now returns ERR as a result of the move operation. Any formula that refers to a range you have moved returns ERR.

Caution:
Don't copy ranges over cells referred to by formulas; the formulas will return ERR.

Erasing Cell Contents

You use the **E**rase command to remove the contents of unprotected cells. **E**rase doesn't alter any global settings, such as column widths or label prefixes. You can erase the contents of a single cell, a range, or an entire worksheet. When you erase, the cell contents disappear, but the cells themselves remain.

To use **E**rase, simply select SHEET **E**rase, indicate the range you want to erase, and press Enter. When you erase a range, any formulas in the worksheet are recalculated.

The SERVICES **N**ew command clears the entire worksheet from your computer's memory. When you select SERVICES **N**ew, Symphony replaces the current

Reminder:
Use SHEET Erase to erase a cell, range, or entire worksheet; use SERVICES New to replace the current worksheet with a new one.

application with a new worksheet, just as if you reinvoked Symphony. You can use SERVICES **N**ew from any environment to begin a new application.

Tip

Before you issue SERVICES **N**ew, make sure that you have a recent copy of the current file saved to disk. Issue SERVICES **F**ile **S**ave to back up important work. You should routinely save your work to disk whenever you make changes to an application.

Remember the difference between the two commands. Fortunately, Symphony reduces the chance of selecting the wrong command by placing the **N**ew and **E**rase commands in the SERVICES and SHEET menus, respectively.

Inserting Blank Columns and Rows

The SHEET **I**nsert command enables you to add one or more blank rows and columns to a worksheet. The **I**nsert command is helpful, for example, if you want to add an expense category to an annual budget you've completed. Or you may want to "dress up" a finished application by adding descriptive labels to it.

When you select **I**nsert, Symphony asks whether you want to insert columns or rows. You also have the option of inserting columns or rows within the restrict range or beyond it. If you want to insert a column or row within the restrict range, select either **C**olumns or **R**ows and then enter the range where you want to insert the column or row. If you want to insert a column or row through the entire worksheet, regardless of the window's restrict range, select **G**lobal, indicate whether you want a column or row inserted, and enter the range where you want to insert the column or row.

Symphony's capability of inserting columns and rows within restrict ranges is a useful feature. In this way, you're prevented from unknowingly changing cell entries in other windows. If you have multiple windows in an application, and you want to insert a row or column in only one window, using **I**nsert **C**olumns or **R**ows limits the inserted column or row to the current window. If you select **G**lobal, on the other hand, columns or rows are inserted in all the windows. **I**nsert **G**lobal also affects "hidden" windows. (See the description of the **W**indow **H**ide command in Chapter 2 for more information.)

Reminder:

Inserted columns appear to the left of the specified range; inserted rows appear above the specified range.

When you insert a column, it appears to the left of the specified range; inserted rows appear above the specified range. For example, if you start with the worksheet shown in figure 4.18, issue the **I**nsert **C**olumns command, and enter an insert range of **A10..A10**, a single blank column is inserted to the left of the labels in column A (see fig. 4.19). Symphony moves all cell entries over one column and modifies all formulas to reflect the change. If you select **I**nsert **R**ows and specify a range of **A10..A10**, Symphony inserts a blank row above row 10 (see fig. 4.20).

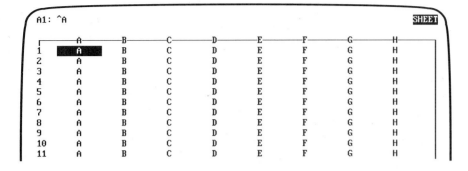

Fig. 4.18.
A sample worksheet.

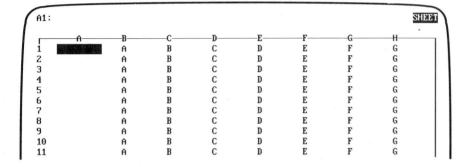

Fig. 4.19.
Inserting a column.

```
A10:                                              SHEET
        A       B       C       D       E       F       G       H
1       1       1       1       1       1       1       1       1
2       2       2       2       2       2       2       2       2
3       3       3       3       3       3       3       3       3
4       4       4       4       4       4       4       4       4
5       5       5       5       5       5       5       5       5
6       6       6       6       6       6       6       6       6
7       7       7       7       7       7       7       7       7
8       8       8       8       8       8       8       8       8
9       9       9       9       9       9       9       9       9
10
11      10      10      10      10      10      10      10      10
```

Fig. 4.20.
Inserting a row.

Symphony also adjusts range names if you insert a column or row. For example, suppose that you have created two range names in the worksheet shown in figure 4.21. These range names are CA (Current Assets) at cell G16, and TNCA (Total NonCurrent Assets) at cell G23.

If you insert a column to the left of column D, Symphony changes the names CA and TNCA to represent cells H16 and H23, respectively. This adjustment of range names occurs whether you use the global **I**nsert or the restricted **I**nsert, with one exception: only the **I**nsert **G**lobal command expands the restrict range of a window; **I**nsert **C**olumns or **R**ows does not affect the size of the restrict range.

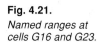

Fig. 4.21.

Named ranges at cells G16 and G23.

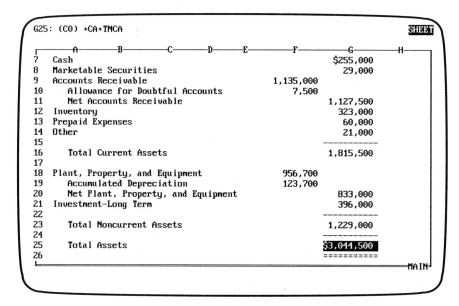

```
G25: (C0) +CA+TNCA                                          SHEET
 ┌─────A────────B────────C────────D────E────────F────────G───────H─
 7   Cash                                             $255,000
 8   Marketable Securities                              29,000
 9   Accounts Receivable                    1,135,000
 10     Allowance for Doubtful Accounts         7,500
 11     Net Accounts Receivable                        1,127,500
 12   Inventory                                          323,000
 13   Prepaid Expenses                                    60,000
 14   Other                                               21,000
 15                                                  ────────────
 16      Total Current Assets                          1,815,500
 17
 18   Plant, Property, and Equipment           956,700
 19      Accumulated Depreciation              123,700
 20      Net Plant, Property, and Equipment              833,000
 21   Investment-Long Term                               396,000
 22                                                  ────────────
 23      Total Noncurrent Assets                       1,229,000
 24                                                  ────────────
 25      Total Assets                                 $3,044,500
 26                                                  ════════════
 └                                                              ─MAIN─
```

Deleting Columns and Rows

The opposite of the **I**nsert command is the **D**elete command. You can delete columns and rows in either a restricted range or throughout the entire worksheet. When you select **D**elete, you then choose **C**olumns, **R**ows, or **G**lobal. As **I**nsert does, **D**elete allows you to confine the column or row deletion to the current window or to delete columns or rows globally. If you have multiple windows, **D**elete **G**lobal affects all windows, whether or not they appear on-screen when you initiate the command.

Reminder:

Include at least one cell from the column or row you want to delete in the specified range.

If you choose **D**elete **R**ows, Symphony prompts you for the range to be deleted within the window restrict range. The range you specify should include at least one cell from the row you want to delete. For example, to delete rows 2 and 3 from the worksheet in figure 4.22, you could enter **A2..A3**. Examples of other ranges you could enter are **B2..B3**, or **A2..B3**, or **C2..G3**. The results of the deletion are shown in figure 4.23. Notice that Symphony automatically moves up all the cell entries below row 3. In addition, Symphony adjusts all formulas and range names. Be aware that formulas containing references to any deleted cells return ERR.

The easiest way to designate the range to be deleted is by pointing to the appropriate cells. Although you can enter the cell addresses from the keyboard, pointing to cells helps avoid errors in selecting the range. Remember that when you use **D**elete, the rows or columns you delete are removed. The data is gone permanently unless you have saved the application to disk. If you haven't saved a copy, the data in the deleted rows and columns is lost.

```
A1: ^1                                                              SHEET
┌─────────────────────────────────────────────────────────────────────┐
│        A       B       C       D       E       F       G       H      │
│ 1      1       1       1       1       1       1       1       1       │
│ 2      2       2       2       2       2       2       2       2       │
│ 3      3       3       3       3       3       3       3       3       │
│ 4      4       4       4       4       4.      4       4       4       │
│ 5      5       5       5       5       5       5       5       5       │
│ 6      6       6       6       6       6       6       6       6       │
│ 7      7       7       7       7       7       7       7       7       │
│ 8      8       8       8       8       8       8       8       8       │
│ 9      9       9       9       9       9       9       9       9       │
│10     10      10      10      10      10      10      10      10       │
│11     11      11      11      11      11      11      11      11       │
│12     12      12      12      12      12      12      12      12       │
│13     13      13      13      13      13      13      13      13       │
│14     14      14      14      14      14      14      14      14       │
│15     15      15      15      15      15      15      15      15       │
│16     16      16      16      16      16      16      16      16       │
│17     17      17      17      17      17      17      17      17       │
│18     18      18      18      18      18      18      18      18       │
│19     19      19      19      19      19      19      19      19       │
│20     20      20      20      20      20      20      20      20       │
└───────────────────────────────────────────────────────────────MAIN───┘
```

Fig. 4.22.

The worksheet before deleting rows 2 and 3.

```
A2: ^4                                                              SHEET
┌─────────────────────────────────────────────────────────────────────┐
│        A       B       C       D       E       F       G       H      │
│ 1      1       1       1       1       1       1       1       1       │
│ 2      4       4       4       4       4       4       4       4       │
│ 3      5       5       5       5       5       5       5       5       │
│ 4      6       6       6       6       6       6       6       6       │
│ 5      7       7       7       7       7       7       7       7       │
│ 6      8       8       8       8       8       8       8       8       │
│ 7      9       9       9       9       9       9       9       9       │
│ 8     10      10      10      10      10      10      10      10       │
│ 9     11      11      11      11      11      11      11      11       │
│10     12      12      12      12      12      12      12      12       │
│11     13      13      13      13      13      13      13      13       │
│12     14      14      14      14      14      14      14      14       │
│13     15      15      15      15      15      15      15      15       │
│14     16      16      16      16      16      16      16      16       │
│15     17      17      17      17      17      17      17      17       │
│16     18      18      18      18      18      18      18      18       │
│17     19      19      19      19      19      19      19      19       │
│18     20      20      20      20      20      20      20      20       │
│19                                                                     │
│20                                                                     │
└───────────────────────────────────────────────────────────────MAIN───┘
```

Fig. 4.23.

The worksheet after deleting rows 2 and 3.

The procedure for deleting one or more columns is similar to that for deleting rows. Select **D**elete **C**olumns and specify a range of columns within the window's restrict range. Specify a range that includes one or more cells from each column to be deleted.

> **Tip**
>
> Unlike 1-2-3 Releases 2.2 and 3.0, Symphony does not have an UNDO feature. If you use **E**rase or any of the **D**elete or **I**nsert commands, the file is permanently changed. Before you issue these commands, save the file to disk with the SERVICES **F**ile **S**ave command. If you erroneously change the worksheet, you can retrieve the backup file with SERVICES **F**ile **R**etrieve.

Reminder:

Delete removes the specified columns or rows from the worksheet; Erase just removes the cell contents.

Keep in mind the differences between the **D**elete and **E**rase commands. The **D**elete command removes entire columns and rows from the worksheet; **E**rase clears the contents from a range of cells. When you use **D**elete, Symphony automatically adjusts all addresses, range names, and formulas. Symphony also automatically moves data to the left to fill in the deleted column or up to fill in the deleted row as a result of a **D**elete **R**ows or **D**elete **C**olumns command. With **E**rase, the cell entries are merely blanked; no cell movement takes place.

The difference between **D**elete and **E**rase can be best explained by using the analogy of a paper spreadsheet. The manual equivalent of **D**elete is to use scissors to cut out unneeded columns and rows and then glue the spreadsheet back together. The equivalent of **E**rase is to use an eraser that removes ranges of data from the spreadsheet but doesn't change the relationship of rows and columns to each other.

Copying Cell Contents

The SHEET **C**opy command enables you to copy the contents of cells from one location to another in a worksheet. You can use the **C**opy command to copy labels, values, and formulas from one cell or range to another in four different types of copy operations.

All the copy operations use the following basic steps:

1. Select **C**opy.
2. Specify the FROM range.
3. Specify the TO range.

The only elements that change in the different operations are the size, shape, and locations of the FROM and TO ranges.

The first type of copy operation is copying from one cell to another. Consider figure 4.24. To copy the contents of cell A1 to A2, issue the **C**opy command. Symphony prompts you for a FROM range, as it does for the **M**ove command. Because you want to copy cell A1, enter **A1**. (If the cell pointer was on A1 before you issued the command, you can simply press Enter.) Symphony then prompts for a TO range. Enter **A2**. Figure 4.25 displays the results of this copy operation.

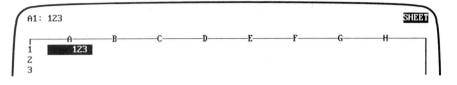

Fig. 4.24.
*A sample worksheet before using the **Copy** command.*

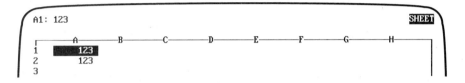

Fig. 4.25.
Copying from one cell to another cell.

A second type of copy operation is copying from one cell to a range of cells. Suppose that you want to copy the contents of cell A1 to the range B1..H1, as shown in figure 4.26. To do this, issue the **C**opy command, specify **A1** as the FROM range, and indicate **B1..H1** as the TO range. You can type the cell address of the range or point to the range with the arrow keys.

Reminder:
You can copy a single cell to a range of cells.

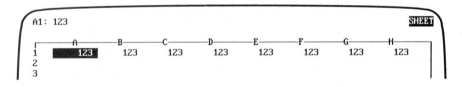

Fig. 4.26.
Copying from one cell to a range of cells.

The third type of copy operation is a bit more complicated. You may want to copy a row of cells to another row in a worksheet. Suppose that you want to copy the range A1..H1 in figure 4.26 to A2..H2. To do this, issue the **C**opy command and specify **A1..H1** as the FROM range. Then specify a TO range of **A2**. The result of this operation is shown in figure 4.27.

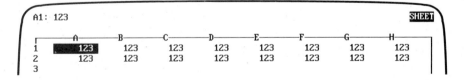

Fig. 4.27.
Copying a row of cells.

Although the TO range you specified is not the same size as the FROM range, Symphony copies all the cells in the FROM range to the cell designated as the TO range. Symphony automatically furnishes the rest of the TO range, as it does with the **M**ove command. In this case, Symphony assumes that you want to create an exact duplicate of range A1..H1 beginning in cell A2.

The same principle applies when you copy cells in columns. Look back at figure 4.25, which shows the results of the first copy operation. Suppose that you want to copy the range A1..A2 to the range B1..B2. To do this, issue the **C**opy command and specify a FROM range of **A1..A2**. Specify a TO range of B1. The results are shown in figure 4.28.

Fig. 4.28.

Copying a column of cells.

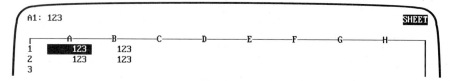

A fourth kind of copy operation is copying a range of cells to a larger range of cells elsewhere in the worksheet. Suppose that you want to copy the range A1..H1 in figure 4.26 to the range A2..H20. To do this, issue the **C**opy command and specify **A1..H1** as the FROM range. Specify a TO range of **A2..A20**. The results are shown in figure 4.29.

Fig. 4.29.

Copying a range of cells to an even larger range.

```
A1: 123                                                          SHEET
        A         B         C         D         E         F         G         H
1      123       123       123       123       123       123       123       123
2      123       123       123       123       123       123       123       123
3      123       123       123       123       123       123       123       123
4      123       123       123       123       123       123       123       123
5      123       123       123       123       123       123       123       123
6      123       123       123       123       123       123       123       123
7      123       123       123       123       123       123       123       123
8      123       123       123       123       123       123       123       123
9      123       123       123       123       123       123       123       123
10     123       123       123       123       123       123       123       123
11     123       123       123       123       123       123       123       123
12     123       123       123       123       123       123       123       123
13     123       123       123       123       123       123       123       123
14     123       123       123       123       123       123       123       123
15     123       123       123       123       123       123       123       123
16     123       123       123       123       123       123       123       123
17     123       123       123       123       123       123       123       123
18     123       123       123       123       123       123       123       123
19     123       123       123       123       123       123       123       123
20     123       123       123       123       123       123       123       123
                                                                     MAIN
```

Cue:

Specify a large TO range rather than copying the FROM range multiple times.

Think of this last example as an extension of the third type of copy operation. You can achieve the results shown in figure 4.29 by repeating the **C**opy command 19 times and specifying 19 different single-row TO ranges. The first TO range would be A2; the second, A3; the third, A4; and so on. You can use either method, but you save time by specifying **A2..A20** as the TO range, thus completing the copy operation in one step.

Now you know the copy operations you'll use most frequently while working in the SHEET environment. The best way to become familiar with the effects of copying with different TO and FROM ranges is to experiment on your own. With practice, copying will become second nature to you.

Understanding Relative and Absolute Addressing

One of the most powerful features of the **C**opy command is its capacity to copy formulas and adjust them appropriately. However, Symphony needs to know how to adjust a formula it copies to create the correct results. The original formula must contain the right kind of cell address. You can use three different methods of addressing cells when you copy: relative, absolute, and mixed. These three methods are also important when you build formulas. Following are general definitions.

In *relative addressing*, when you copy a formula, the cells in the formula change relative to the new formula's location. For example, suppose that cell A5 in the worksheet contains the formula +A2+A3, which means you want Symphony to add the contents of these cells. If you copy +A2+A3 to cell B5, the formula in cell B5 is +B2+B3 (see fig. 4.30).

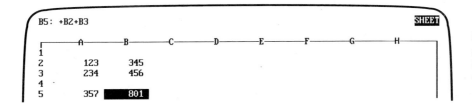

Fig. 4.30.
Copying a formula with relative addresses.

In *absolute addressing*, when you copy a formula, the original cell addresses as well as the relationships of the cells are copied. For example, if you want to copy the formula +A2+A3 in cell A5 to cell B5 as you originally entered it, you must enter the formula in cell A5 as follows:

+$A$2+$A$3

The dollar signs ($) in the cell addresses create absolute cell addresses. When you copy this formula to cell B5, the formula remains +$A$2+$A$3 (see fig. 4.31).

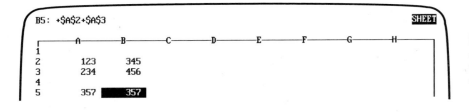

Fig. 4.31.
Copying a formula with absolute addresses.

In mixed addressing, when you copy a formula, part of the address is absolute and so does not change; the other part of the address is relative and can change. For example, if you copy the formula +$A2+$A3 from cell A5 to cell B6, the formula reads +$A3+$A4: the rows changed but the columns didn't.

Using Relative Addressing

Suppose that you want to total the contents of several columns of numbers, but only want to enter the @SUM function once. The worksheet in figure 4.32 displays five columns of numbers. Only column C has been totaled by using @SUM*(C3..C7)* in cell C8.

Fig. 4.32.

A sample worksheet with an @SUM formula in column C.

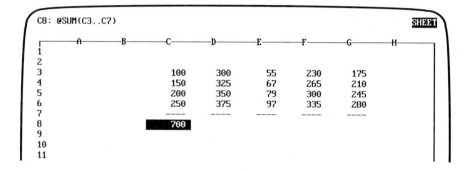

You want to total columns D, E, F, and G in the same way as column C. To perform this operation, issue the **C**opy command, indicate C8 as the range to copy FROM, and press Enter. Then specify D8..G8 as the range to copy TO. After you press Enter, Symphony copies the @SUM function in cell C8 to the range D8..G8, as shown in figure 4.33.

Fig. 4.33.

Copying the @SUM formula.

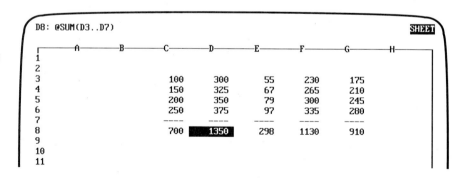

Notice the formula in the first line of Symphony's control panel. The formula contains the proper cell addresses for totaling cells in column D. Symphony knows that you wanted the *relative* addresses of cells in column C, not their *absolute* addresses.

Using Absolute and Mixed Addressing

Sometimes you want to copy a formula with an address that shouldn't change. As you know, you can create formulas with cell addresses that don't change as the formula is copied (you use a $ in front of both the column letter and the row number of the cell addresses). Such an address is called an absolute address. You also can create a *mixed address*: an address where parts of the address change, and other parts don't. The following examples help you understand the concepts of absolute and mixed addresses.

Mixed cell addressing is a combination of relative and absolute addressing. You can make either the row portion or the column portion of a cell address absolute. Suppose that you want to perform a projection of monthly sales for Product 1 in dollars. In the initial analysis, you want to use a specific retail price, an average discount rate, and a unit volume for the projection. Later, you'll vary these parameters to determine the effects of the changes. Figure 4.34 shows an example projection.

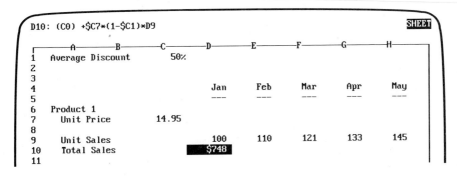

Fig. 4.34.

An example of mixed cell addressing.

Notice the dollar signs in the formula in the control panel. The dollar signs indicate an absolute address in the column portion (the column letters) of the cell addresses of column C. Because dollar signs don't appear in front of the row numbers of these addresses, Symphony uses relative cell addresses there.

To understand the advantage of this type of referencing, copy cell D10 to the range E10..H10, using the **C**opy command (see fig. 4.35).

Fig. 4.35.

Copying a formula with mixed addresses.

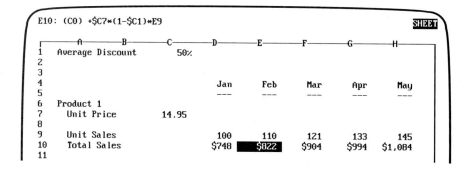

```
E10: (C0) +$C7*(1-$C1)*E9                                    SHEET
   ┌──────A───────B────C─────D─────E─────F─────G─────H──
  1 │ Average Discount     50%
  2 │
  3 │
  4 │                      Jan    Feb    Mar    Apr    May
  5 │                      ---    ---    ---    ---    ---
  6 │ Product 1
  7 │   Unit Price   14.95
  8 │
  9 │   Unit Sales         100    110    121    133    145
 10 │   Total Sales        $748   $822   $904   $994   $1,084
 11 │
```

Now compare the formula in cell E10 with the original formula in cell D10:

$$E10 = \$C7*(1-\$C1)*E9$$
$$D10 = \$C7*(1-\$C1)*D9$$

The formulas are identical except for the last cell addresses. Symphony holds the column portions of the addresses for C7 and C1 constant. (Because you are copying across a row, you don't have to make the row portion of the address absolute.) In summary, the copied formulas translate to "using a constant price (C7) and a constant discount (C1), compute the dollar sales for Product 1 at each month's sales volume (specified in the range D9..H9)."

Now, suppose that you need a projection for a Product 2. To accomplish this, copy the labels in the range A6..A10 to A13 and change the product name to Product 2. Then copy the range C7..H10 to C14..H17 (see fig. 4.36).

Fig. 4.36.

An incorrect reference in the formula to cell C8.

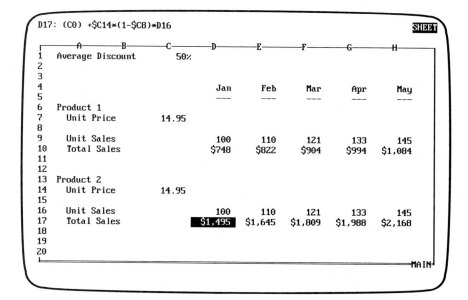

```
D17: (C0) +$C14*(1-$C8)*D16                                 SHEET
   ┌──────A───────B────C─────D─────E─────F─────G─────H──
  1 │ Average Discount     50%
  2 │
  3 │
  4 │                      Jan    Feb    Mar    Apr    May
  5 │                      ---    ---    ---    ---    ---
  6 │ Product 1
  7 │   Unit Price   14.95
  8 │
  9 │   Unit Sales         100    110    121    133    145
 10 │   Total Sales        $748   $822   $904   $994   $1,084
 11 │
 12 │
 13 │ Product 2
 14 │   Unit Price   14.95
 15 │
 16 │   Unit Sales         100    110    121    133    145
 17 │   Total Sales        $1,495 $1,645 $1,809 $1,988 $2,168
 18 │
 19 │
 20 │                                                    MAIN
```

Notice that the numbers in row 17 aren't correct. Even though you assigned the same price and unit sales volumes to Product 2, that product shows monthly dollar sales that are double those for Product 1. To understand why, look at the formula in cell D17:

`+$C14*(1-$C8)*D16`

The references to cell C14 and cell D16 are correct—these cells contain the unit price and unit sales for Product 2. But notice that the reference to the average discount in cell C1 has changed to refer to cell C8. This change occurred because the row designation in the address $C1 was relative and not absolute, and because you copied down the column. When you copied the formulas containing the address $C1, Symphony assumed that you wanted to adjust the row component of the address.

You can correct the problem by changing the reference to cell C1 from a mixed to an absolute reference. Move the cell pointer to cell D10, press Edit (F2), and change the formula to the following:

`+$C7*(1-$C$1)*D9`

The only difference between this formula and the formula in cell D10 of figure 4.34 is the addition of a dollar sign in front of the 1 in the address $C$1. The additional dollar sign changes the address from mixed to absolute.

Copy the new formula in cell D10 to the range E10..H10 so that all the formulas in row 10 are the same. Then use **C**opy to copy the range D9..H10 to D16..H17 (see fig. 4.37).

Reminder:
With mixed addressing, the relative portion of the address may change, giving you inaccurate results.

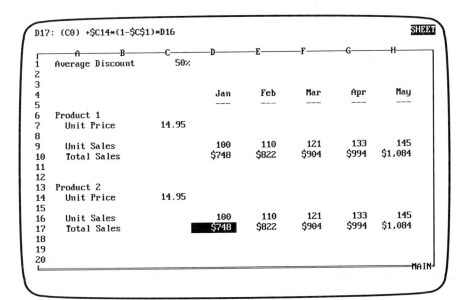

Fig. 4.37.
Adjusting the reference to an absolute address.

The numbers in cells D17..H17 are now correct. Compare the original formula in cell D10 to the formula in cell D17 to verify that the reference to cell C1 remained fixed:

D10 = +$C7*(1–$C$1)*D9

D17 = +$C14*(1–$C$1)*D16

Another example of mixed cell addressing appears in figure 4.38. This example displays a table for exploring the effect of different interest rates and years to maturity on the present value of an annuity that pays $1,000 a year. (See the discussion of the @PV function in Chapter 6 for an explanation of present value.) The syntax of the @PV function is as follows:

@PV*(payment,interest,term)*

where

payment = amount per period

interest = interest rate

term = period number

Fig. 4.38.

Another example of mixed addressing.

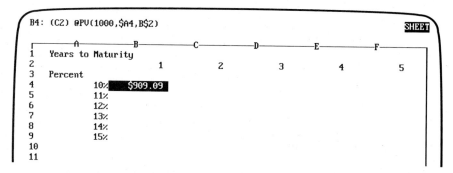

You can see the cells with mixed cell references in the control panel. The idea behind this example is to use a single formula for the model, with an absolute address for the column portion (column A) of the interest-rate address, and a relative address for the row portion (row 4). Conversely, you use a relative address on the column portion of the years-to-maturity address (column B), and an absolute address on the row portion (row 2).

Compare the formula in cell B4 in figure 4.38 with the formula in cell D8 of figure 4.39. Notice that column A (the interest rate) and row 2 (the years-to-maturity) have not changed, but the other parts of the cell addresses have.

Another way you can use mixed cell addressing is to accumulate a running total across a row of numbers. Enter in cell B2 the formula **@SUM($A$1..B1)** and copy the formula to C2..H2, as shown in figure 4.40. Compare the cell addresses when you complete the copy operation.

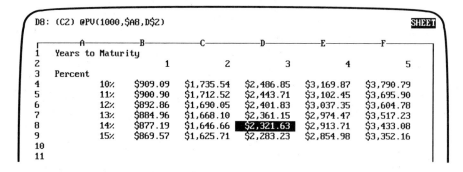

Fig. 4.39.
The worksheet after copying the formula.

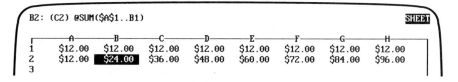

Fig. 4.40.
Accumulating a running total.

The best way to become comfortable using mixed cell addresses is to experiment. Try different uses and examine the results.

Copying—Some Guidelines

When you use the **C**opy command in the SHEET environment, be sure to keep the following points in mind:

1. When you copy a cell, Symphony also copies the format of the TO range to the FROM range. (See Chapter 5, "Formatting the Worksheet" for more information). This capability eliminates the need for you to format ranges before copying to them.

2. In a few rare instances, the TO and FROM ranges may overlap when you copy. If you don't overlap the end points for the FROM and TO ranges, the results will be fine. If you do overlap them, portions of the FROM range are overwritten by the TO range. The one time you can safely overlap the ranges is when the FROM and TO ranges have the same upper left corner.

3. Remember the finality of the **C**opy command. If you copy over the contents of a cell—even a cell in another environment—you cannot recover the original contents unless you saved a copy of the file to disk. Make sure that you designate the FROM and TO ranges properly before you press Enter.

4. You can copy between two windows; for example, from one SHEET window to another SHEET window, from a SHEET window to a DOC window, and vice versa. To copy from one SHEET window to another SHEET window, select **C**opy and specify the FROM range. When Symphony asks for the TO range, press the Window (F6) key and point to the range. If you want to copy from a DOC window to a SHEET window, change from the SHEET environment to the DOC environment, invoke the **C**opy command, indicate the FROM range in the DOC environment, and then indicate the TO range in the SHEET environment. If you want to copy from a SHEET window to a DOC window, start in the SHEET environment before invoking the **C**opy command.

Setting Cell References

To use absolute and mixed addresses in formulas, you first identify which cell addresses should be relative, mixed, and absolute. Then you enter the appropriate dollar signs to create the type of address you need. This section discusses how to create absolute and mixed cell addresses from relative addresses.

You can create a mixed or absolute address in two ways. You can type dollar signs as you enter the cell address, or you can use the Abs (F3) key to have Symphony enter the dollar signs for you. Symphony must be in POINT mode before you can use the Abs key. In Chapter 3, you learned that you must use the cell pointer in POINT mode to enter addresses in formulas.

To use the Abs key to enter dollar signs in the formula +$C14*(1–$C$1)*D16, begin by typing **+**. To create a formula with absolute addresses, change to POINT mode by moving the cell pointer to cell C14; press Abs (F3). The formula in the control panel is $C$14. Press Abs again to change the address to C$14. If you press Abs a third time, the address changes to $C14, the address you need. Complete the formula by pointing and using the Abs (F3) key to enter the dollar signs for absolute references.

Following is a summary of what happens to a cell address when you press the Abs key in POINT mode:

Original address	C14
First press	$C$14
Second press	C$14
Third press	$C14
Fourth press	C14

Cue:

Use the Abs (F3) key in POINT mode to change relative addresses into mixed or absolute addresses and back again.

> ### Tip
> If you have already entered a formula that needs mixed or absolute cell addresses, position the cell pointer on the cell that contains the formula and press the Edit (F2) key. Move the cursor to the column letter or row number of the cell address you want to change and press Abs (F3). Symphony cycles through the four reference types. When you finish modifying the formula, press Enter to complete the operation.

Setting Column Widths

With Symphony, you can specify that all columns in an application have the same width, or you can set the width of individual columns. Symphony's default column width is nine characters; Symphony displays values wider than the column width as asterisks (*********). Labels too wide for the column are truncated in the display (although all the data is still in memory) if the adjacent cells contain entries. If the adjacent cells do not contain entries, the entire long label is displayed across the adjacent columns. To adjust the width of columns, you use Symphony's SHEET **W**idth **S**et command.

Reminder:
Values wider than the column width display as asterisks; labels are truncated.

You change the width of a column by either entering a number or using the ← and → keys, and pressing Enter. The advantage of using the left and right arrows is that you can see the column width expand and contract each time you press these keys. At a minimum, you should widen a column until the asterisks disappear and labels no longer display in a truncated fashion.

Keep in mind two things about the **W**idth **S**et command. First, move the cell pointer to the column you want to adjust before you initiate the command (any row in the column will do). If you don't, you'll have to initiate the command again. Second, to reset the column width to the default of nine, use the **W**idth **R**estore command.

You also can set the widths of *all* columns with the SHEET **S**ettings **W**idth command. This global command creates an entry in the settings sheet for that window and is particularly useful when you begin creating a new application. The **W**idth **R**estore command resets the width of a column to the value designated with the **S**ettings **W**idth command.

The width of any column you set with the **W**idth command is not affected by a change in the global setting. For example, if you use the **W**idth command to set the width of column A to 12, and then use the **S**ettings **W**idth command to change all the columns in the worksheet to a width of five, every column except A has a width of five. Column A remains at 12. To change column A to five, you must set the width of that specific column to five with the **W**idth **S**et or **W**idth **R**estore command.

Both the **W**idth and **S**ettings **W**idth commands affect only the current window. For example, the three windows in figure 4.41 contain different column widths. The columns in window 1 are set at Symphony's default of nine; the columns in window 2 are set at a width of six; the columns in window 3 are set at various widths. Each window also has a different value for its width in its settings sheet. If you scrolled through each window, you would see that the column width of one window doesn't affect the column width of another. Each window maintains its own widths until you either delete the window with the SERVICES **W**indow **D**elete command or change the width of an individual window with the **S**ettings **W**idth command.

Fig. 4.41.

Three windows with different column widths.

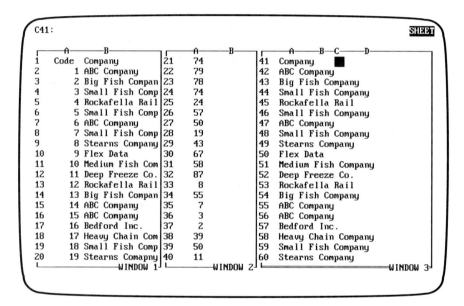

You can hide a column with the **W**idth **H**ide command. You can designate the columns to be hidden either by pointing with the cell pointer across the columns or by typing cell addresses. If you type the cell address, enter a horizontal range. For example, to hide columns D through F, issue the **W**idth **H**ide command, type **D1..F1**, and press Enter. Alternatively, you can move the cell pointer to highlight column D through column F and then press Enter. Figure 4.42 displays a worksheet with hidden columns.

Cue:

Hide columns to keep them from printing.

Hidden columns aren't displayed on-screen; they do retain their contents and format, however. Any formulas that depend on cells in hidden columns retain that dependence. Hiding columns is a convenient method to keep sensitive information confidential while you're printing your application.

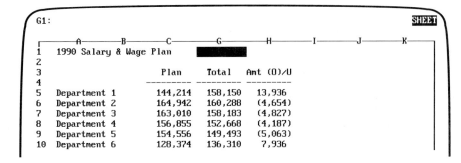

Fig. 4.42.
A worksheet with columns D through F hidden.

Tip

Any time you are in POINT mode, Symphony's hidden column feature is disabled entirely, and all hidden columns are displayed. When you return to SHEET mode, the columns are automatically "rehidden." Keep this in mind if you're using **W**idth **H**ide as a data-security technique.

To redisplay hidden columns, use the **W**idth **D**isplay command. Symphony prompts you for a range of cells whose columns you want displayed. The currently hidden columns are displayed temporarily (with an asterisk next to the column letters), so that you can decide which columns you want to display (see fig. 4.43). As when you hide columns, you select the columns to redisplay by using the cursor keys or typing the cell addresses.

```
Columns to Display: G1..G1                                          POINT
    ┌──A────────B────────C─────────D*──────E*──────F*────────G────────H──┐
  1 │ 1990 Salary & Wage Plan                              ▮▮▮▮▮▮▮▮
  2 │
  3 │                     Plan     Jan     Feb     Mar     Total   Amt (O)/U
  4 │                   ────────  ──────  ──────  ──────  ────────  ────────
  5 │ Department 1      144,214   38,444  34,943  84,763  158,150   13,936
  6 │ Department 2      164,942   37,815  33,277  89,196  160,288   (4,654)
  7 │ Department 3      163,010   40,256  30,344  87,583  158,183   (4,827)
  8 │ Department 4      156,855   38,656  31,098  82,914  152,668   (4,187)
  9 │ Department 5      154,556   38,890  29,088  81,515  149,493   (5,063)
 10 │ Department 6      128,374   35,591  26,225  74,494  136,310    7,936
```

Fig 4.43
The hidden columns displayed during the Width Display command.

Using Other Settings Commands

In the preceding section, you learned about the SHEET **S**ettings **W**idth command. The **S**ettings **T**itles and **R**ecalculation commands are discussed next. The **S**ettings **L**abel-Prefix, **F**ormat, and **Z**ero commands are discussed in Chapter 5, "Formatting the Worksheet," because these commands affect how your applications are displayed on-screen and on printouts.

Freezing Titles On-Screen

Cue:

Freeze columns and rows to form an on-screen border that doesn't move when the rest of the worksheet scrolls.

The **S**ettings **T**itles command enables you to freeze column labels, row labels, or both, on-screen. The command freezes all the cells to the left of or above the cell pointer's current position so that the cells don't move when you scroll the screen with PgUp, PgDn, and other cell-pointer keys.

An example of the advantage of this command is shown in figure 4.44. If you scroll the screen down, the column labels (months) disappear, and you no longer know which month an amount represents. Similarly, if you scroll the screen to the right, to review the later months of the year, you no longer know which expense category an amount represents.

Fig. 4.44.

A sample balance sheet and income statement that needs titles.

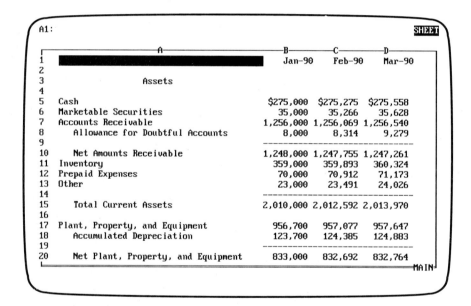

To keep the column and row titles in figure 4.44 on-screen at all times, move the cell pointer to cell B2 and issue the **S**ettings **T**itles command. The following options appear:

> **B**oth **H**orizontal **V**ertical **C**lear

If you select **B**oth, Symphony freezes the rows above the cell pointer and the columns to the left of the cell pointer. The frozen rows and columns do not move off the screen if you scroll up and down or left and right. If you select **H**orizontal, only the rows above the cell pointer are frozen. If you select **V**ertical, only the columns to the left of the cell pointer are frozen. To unfreeze all titles, choose **C**lear.

Figure 4.45 shows the worksheet after selecting **S**ettings **T**itles **B**oth. All titles remain on-screen regardless of which direction you scroll.

```
G26: (P0) +G24+G15                                            SHEET
┌──────────────A──────────────────────E────────F────────G────┐
 1                                    May-90   Jun-90   Jul-90
 8       Allowance for Doubtful Accounts  9,725   10,501   10,941
 9                                    ─────────────────────────
10       Net Amounts Receivable      1,248,592 1,247,974 1,248,420
11   Inventory                         360,917   360,962   361,241
12   Prepaid Expenses                   72,677    72,905    73,566
13   Other                              25,215    25,964    26,959
14                                    ─────────────────────────
15       Total Current Assets        2,020,872 2,022,295 2,025,131
16
17   Plant, Property, and Equipment    959,505   960,452   960,868
18       Accumulated Depreciation      125,846   126,171   126,438
19                                    ─────────────────────────
20       Net Plant, Property, and Equipment  833,659  834,281  834,430
21
22   Investment Long-Term              409,222   409,222   409,222
23                                    ─────────────────────────
24       Total Noncurrent Assets     1,242,881 1,243,503 1,243,652
25                                    ─────────────────────────
26   Total Assets                    3,263,753 3,265,798 3,268,783
└────────────────────────────────────────────────────────MAIN┘
```

Fig. 4.45.
*An example of using **Settings** Titles **Both**.*

When you use **S**ettings **T**itles to freeze rows or columns, you cannot move the cell pointer into the titles area. For example, Symphony beeps if you try to move the cell pointer to column A or row 1 in figure 4.45 and prevents you from doing so. In addition, if you press the Home key, the cell pointer moves to cell B2, not cell A1. Home moves you to the upper left cell in the unfrozen area.

The one exception to Symphony's restriction on cell-pointer movement with titles is the GoTo (F5) key. You can jump to a cell within the titles area by using this key. However, Symphony displays another copy of the titles area. This second set of titles provides you with the opportunity to edit the titles in the usual way. Figure 4.46 shows the effect of pressing GoTo (F5) and moving to cell A1.

To remove a second set of titles from the screen, scroll the screen until the second set of titles disappears. The screen now displays only one set of titles.

Understanding Recalculation

One of Symphony's primary purposes is to quickly recalculate applications when values or formulas change. Symphony's default recalculation settings are automatic and optimal, which means that Symphony automatically recalculates only formulas that depend on values that have changed since the last recalculation. In most cases, Symphony's default recalculation settings are the ones you should use.

However, Symphony also provides other recalculation methods for different situations. If you select the **S**ettings **R**ecalculation command, the menu shown in figure 4.47 appears.

Reminder:

Symphony recalculates automatically only those formulas that depend on values that have changed since the last recalculation.

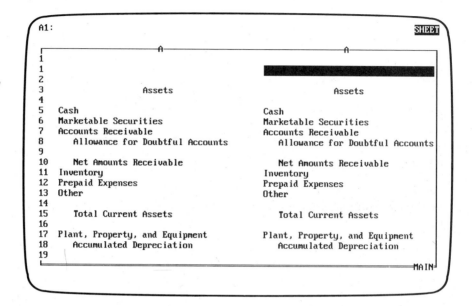

Fig. 4.46.

Results of pressing GoTo to move to a titles area.

```
A1:                                                                    SHEET
 1
 1
 2
 3                    Assets                             Assets
 4
 5   Cash                                   Cash
 6   Marketable Securities                  Marketable Securities
 7   Accounts Receivable                    Accounts Receivable
 8      Allowance for Doubtful Accounts        Allowance for Doubtful Accounts
 9
10      Net Amounts Receivable                 Net Amounts Receivable
11   Inventory                              Inventory
12   Prepaid Expenses                       Prepaid Expenses
13   Other                                  Other
14
15      Total Current Assets                   Total Current Assets
16
17   Plant, Property, and Equipment         Plant, Property, and Equipment
18      Accumulated Depreciation               Accumulated Depreciation
19
                                                                       MAIN
```

Fig. 4.47.

Default recalculation settings under SHEET Settings Recalculation.

```
Automatic or Manual                                                    MENU
Method  Order  Iterations

  Circular           (none)
  Label-Prefix:      '
                                             Titles
  Recalculation                                Columns:  0
    Method:          Automatic                 Rows:     0
    Order:           Optimal                   Format:   (G)
    Iterations:      1                         Width:    9
                                             For window: MAIN
  Zero Suppression:  No
  Auto-Link:  Yes
                                                           Sheet Settings
```

As you can see from figure 4.47, Symphony provides you with three recalculation categories so that you can select a recalculation setting appropriate for your application:

Method **O**rder **I**terations

Each of these options is explained in the following sections.

Selecting a Method

The **S**ettings **R**ecalculation **M**ethod command enables you to specify whether you want Symphony to recalculate values automatically as you change them, or to recalculate them only when you press the Calc (F8) key.

Large applications that contain many interdependent formulas and functions or what-if tables may take a long time to recalculate. To reduce recalculation time, you should change from Symphony's default setting of **A**utomatic recalculation to **M**anual. You can then enter new values or edit existing ones; after you complete data entry, press Calc (F8) to recalculate the application. By turning on Manual recalculation, you don't have to wait for the application to recalculate before you can enter another value.

Cue:
*Use Settings
Recalculation
Method Manual
with large
worksheets that
have many
formulas to speed
up data-entry time.*

Selecting an Order

You can change the order of recalculation from **O**ptimal (Symphony's default) to **N**atural, **C**olumn-by-Column, or **R**ow-by-Row with the **S**ettings **R**ecalculation **O**rder command. In **O**ptimal order, Symphony recalculates only the formulas affected by changes in the application. In **N**atural order, Symphony doesn't recalculate a cell until the cells on which it depends have been recalculated. Because formula relationships are rarely linear, this method of recalculation is not linear. Instead, recalculation occurs in a "topographical" manner, beginning with the lowest level and working up. The **O**ptimal order also uses this hierarchical method.

With **N**atural and **O**ptimal recalculation, the problem of forward references (a cell refers to another cell located physically lower in the worksheet) and the order of recalculation is eliminated. For example, consider a worksheet with the following cell entries:

Cell	Entry
A1	+C3
C1	100
C2	200
C3	+C1+C2

Notice that A1 and C3 both calculate to 300. Now, suppose that you change the value in cell C2 to 100.

If the cells are recalculated by using forward references, recalculation begins in the upper left corner of the worksheet, and cell A1 is evaluated first. Because the previous value of C3 (300) has not changed, A1 retains the value 300. Recalculation continues, either column by column or row by row (depending on the **S**ettings **R**ecalculation **O**rder you select), across the worksheet, until Symphony comes to cell C3. Because the value of cell C2 has changed, the value in C3 changes to 200.

The forward-reference order of recalculation results in a value of A1, different from that of C3, although the cells are defined to be equal. Although recalculating the worksheet again eliminates the inequality, it does not remove the basic problem. Be careful if you create large and complex models; unintentional forward references are possible.

Column-by-Column and **R**ow-by-Row calculations tell Symphony to calculate by columns and rows, respectively. In **C**olumn-by-Column calculation, Symphony calculates cells beginning in cell A1 and down column A, then down column B, and so forth. In **R**ow-by-Row calculation, Symphony calculates cells beginning in cell A1 and across row 1, then row 2, and so forth.

These two calculation methods are important if you import a file from an older spreadsheet program, such as VisiCalc, that calculates using one of these methods.

Selecting the Number of Iterations

Normally, you need only one pass to recalculate an application. However, if the application contains a circular reference, one pass isn't sufficient. A common example of a circular reference occurs when you try to determine the amount of borrowing required by a firm. Following is the logic behind this process:

1. Borrowings = Assets − (Total Liabilities + Equity). Borrowings equal the difference between projected asset requirements and the sum of total projected liabilities and equity.
2. The level of equity is a function of net income and dividends.
3. Net income is a function of gross margin and interest expense.
4. Interest expense and gross margin are functions of borrowings.

You can see the circular pattern in this scenario. In this situation, Symphony displays **C i r c** in the lower right corner of the screen. When you recalculate the application, using **N**atural or **O**ptimal calculation, Symphony does not accurately recalculate all the values. Because each value in the relationship depends directly or indirectly on all other values, Symphony cannot get a "toehold." In other words, Symphony cannot find the most fundamental, or lowest level, cell for **N**atural order recalculation because no such cell exists.

Iterative, or repetitive, recalculation helps Symphony solve the problem. When you specify a value with the **S**ettings **R**ecalculation **I**terations command, Symphony recalculates the application the specified number of times each time you press Calc (F8). Normally, Symphony recalculates once each time you press Calc. If you have circular references in an application, specify a higher number of iterations.

Iterative recalculation overcomes a circular reference because the formulas' results more closely approach correct values with each successive recalculation. Suppose that the worksheet contains the following:

Cell	Entry
A3	0.05*A5
A4	100
A5	+A3+A4

When you first enter these formulas, A3 has a value of 0, A4 equals 100, and A5 equals 100. Assume that the number of iterations has been set to 5 with the **S**ettings **R**ecalculation **I**terations command. The values of each cell after each recalculation are as follows:

Recalc Number	A3	Cell A4	A5
1	5	100	105
2	5.25	100	105.25
3	5.2625	100	105.2625
4	5.263125	100	105.2631
5	5.263156	100	105.2631

With each recalculation, notice that the difference between the previous and current values of cells A3 and A5 becomes smaller. After only 5 passes, the difference is small enough to be insignificant. After 20 passes, the difference is probably too small even for Symphony to recognize. At that point, the problem with the circular reference is eliminated.

You should note two points about iterative recalculation. First, you may possibly create a set of circular references too complicated for Symphony to sort out, even in 20 recalculations. Second, the maximum number of iterations you can set is 50. Keep in mind, however, that 20 (and certainly 50) calculations of a large application can take some time, depending on your computer system.

Reminder:
The maximum number of iterations you can set is 50.

Chapter Summary

In this chapter, you learned about the fundamental SHEET environment commands. You learned how to access the SHEET command menu and select commands. Specifically, you learned how to create and use range names; copy, move, and erase cell entries; insert and delete rows and columns; transpose values and convert formulas to values; fill a range with values; protect cell entries; and perform data distribution and what-if analysis.

In Chapter 5, you are introduced to the formatting commands that enable you to customize the appearance of Symphony applications on-screen and for your reports.

5

Formatting the Worksheet

Symphony provides 11 different ways to display numeric data. Changing how the data is displayed on-screen and in reports makes the results clearer and easier to understand. When you change the appearance of cell entries, you are *formatting* the worksheet.

When you format data, you change only the way Symphony displays the data, and not the contents of the cells. You can format a single cell, multiple cells, or your entire spreadsheet. You also can use as many formats in a Symphony spreadsheet as you like.

In this chapter, you will learn the following:

❏ The commands you use to format cells

❏ The types of formats available for values

❏ How to automatically align labels

❏ How to suppress the display of zeros

Using Format Commands

Symphony provides two commands for applying formats to cells: MENU (F10) **F**ormat and MENU (F10) **S**ettings **F**ormat. The **F**ormat command formats specific ranges in the spreadsheet; the **S**ettings **F**ormat command controls the format of all spreadsheet cells. A third command, SERVICES (F9) **C**onfiguration **O**ther **I**nternational, enables you to specify the type of international format you apply to date and time values. Figure 5.1 and table 5.1, respectively, provide examples and a list of the formats available.

Fig. 5.1.

Examples of Symphony Formats.

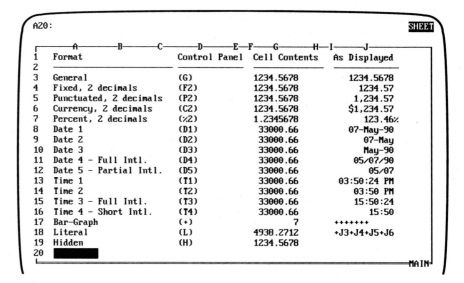

Table 5.1
Available Symphony Formats

Format	Example	Application
General	1234.5	Numeric data
Fixed	1234.50	Numeric data
Punctuated	1,234.50	Numeric data
Currency	$1,234.50	Numeric data
Percent	35.4%	Numeric data
Scientific	1.2345E+03	Numeric data
Date	10/10/90	Special date serial numbers
Time	06:23 AM	Special time fractions
Bar–Graph	+++++	Numeric data
Literal	+C6	All formulas
Hidden	No display	All data

In general, you should use **S**ettings **F**ormat before you begin creating a new application. You want to select a format for the majority of the cells in your application. Symphony's default format is **G**eneral, which means cell contents are displayed and printed in the same way you entered them. Use the **S**ettings **F**ormat command if you need a format other than **G**eneral for your applications.

The SERVICES **C**onfiguration **O**ther **I**nternational command enables you to control the display of currency signs, punctuation (separating thousands), negative values, and date and time values. If you work with values not denominated in U.S. dollars, or in a country other than the United States, this command helps you customize your Symphony display to those non-U.S. formatting standards. Symphony's international formats are discussed later in this chapter.

Formats applied with the MENU **F**ormat command take precedence over formats applied with the MENU **S**ettings **F**ormat command. For example, you may have a financial application that has **G**eneral as its **S**ettings **F**ormat, but also has values formatted with dollar signs (**C**urrency) and with commas (**P**unctuated).

Reminder:
Formats applied with the MENU Format command take precedence over formats applied with the MENU Settings Format command.

When you select **F**ormat from the SHEET command menu, the menu in figure 5.2 appears.

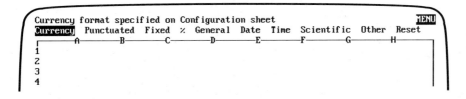

Fig. 5.2.
The Symphony Format menu.

Symphony displays 10 format options, eight of which format the cells in the spreadsheet. The **O**ther option contains three additional formats for special uses; and the **R**eset option restores the worksheet to its default format. These formats will be discussed next, beginning with the **G**eneral format.

General Format

General is the fifth choice in Symphony's **F**ormat menu, but is discussed first because it is Symphony's default format setting for new worksheets. In other words, when you begin a new application, all cells are formatted as **G**eneral, which is represented by the (G) on the SHEET **S**ettings sheet in figure 5.3.

Reminder:
When you begin a new application, all cells are formatted as General.

When you display values in **G**eneral format, Symphony suppresses insignificant zeros to the right of the decimal point. If values are too large or too small to be displayed normally in **G**eneral format, Symphony uses **S**cientific notation. The following are values formatted as **G**eneral:

Fig. 5.3.

The Symphony SHEET environment Settings sheet.

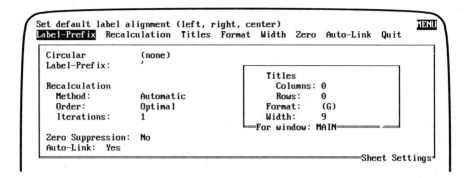

```
Set default label alignment (left, right, center)         MENU
Label-Prefix  Recalculation  Titles  Format  Width  Zero  Auto-Link  Quit

  Circular          (none)
  Label-Prefix:     '
                                         Titles
  Recalculation                            Columns: 0
    Method:         Automatic              Rows:    0
    Order:          Optimal                Format:    (G)
    Iterations:     1                      Width:     9
                                         For window: MAIN
  Zero Suppression: No
  Auto-Link:  Yes
                                                   Sheet Settings
```

Typed Entry	Displayed Result
123.45	123.45
−123.45	−123.45
1.2345678912	1.234567
150000000	1.5E+08
−.00000002638	−0.00000

General format affects values only and not how the labels are displayed. Labels are displayed as left-justified, centered, or right-justified, depending on the settings you make with the **R**ange Label-Alignment and **S**ettings Label-Prefix commands. Symphony's default label alignment is left-justified. Later in this chapter, you learn how to use the **S**ettings Label-Prefix and **R**ange Label-Alignment commands to change label justification from the default of left alignment. (**G**) appears in Symphony's control panel of cells formatted with the **F**ormat **G**eneral command.

Fixed Format

Reminder:

Use Fixed format when you want a column of numbers to line up on the decimal point.

Symphony's **F**ixed format is similar to the **G**eneral format, except that **F**ixed enables you to align a column of values on the decimal point. **F**ixed format also enables you to display from 0 to 15 decimal places. If the value has more decimal digits than the number you specify in the format, Symphony rounds the display of the value. The underlying value, however, is used in calculations. Depending on the value and the number of decimal places you specify in the format, rounding is either up or down.

The following are some examples of cells formatted as **F**ixed in the default column width of nine characters:

Typed Entry	Cell Format	Display Result
123.46	(F0)	123
123.46	(F1)	123.5
−123.46	(F2)	−123.46
123.46	(F4)	123.4600
−123.46	(F4)	*********
12345678	(F2)	*********

(**F n**) appears in Symphony's control panel of cells formatted with the **F**ormat **F**ixed command, where *n* is the number of decimal places you specify.

Punctuated Format

Symphony's **P**unctuated format (P) enables you to use commas in large values to separate hundreds from thousands, thousands from millions, and so forth. You can choose to display from 0 to 15 decimal places, similar to **F**ixed format. The **P**unctuated format is most frequently used in financial applications.

Cue:
Use Punctuated format to make large numbers easier to read.

If the value has more decimal digits than the number you specify in the format, Symphony automatically rounds the display of the value, but uses its full value in calculations. Several examples of cells formatted with the **P**unctuated format in a column width of nine are as follows:

Typed Entry	Cell Format	Display Result
123.46	(P0)	123
1234.6	(P2)	1,234.60
−1234.6	(P0)	(1,235)
−1234	(P2)	*********

(**P n**) appears in Symphony's control panel of cells formatted with the **F**ormat **P**unctuated command, where *n* is the number of decimal places you specify.

Currency Format

Reminder:

Use the Currency format to display values with a dollar ($) sign.

Symphony **C**urrency format (C) is similar to the **P**unctuated format in that commas are used as separators, but includes a leading dollar sign. Keep in mind that the dollar sign will take up one space in the cell to be formatted as **C**urrency. You can choose to display from 0 to 15 decimal places, similar to the **F**ixed and **P**unctuated formats. The **C**urrency format is most frequently used with the **P**unctuated format in financial applications.

The section on **I**nternational formats discusses how you can change the currency symbol from Symphony's default of U.S. dollars ($).

Several examples of cells formatted with the **C**urrency format in a column width of nine are as follows:

Typed Entry	Cell Format	Display Result
123	(C2)	$123.00
−123.124	(C2)	($123.12)
1234.12	(C0)	$1,234
1234.12	(C2)	*********

(C n) appears in Symphony's control panel of cells formatted with the **F**ormat **C**urrency command, where *n* is the number of decimal places you specify.

% Format

Reminder:

Use the % format to display values as percentages.

You use the **%** (**P**ercent) format to display percentages. You can display from 0 to 15 decimal places, similar to the **F**ixed, **P**unctuated, and **C**urrency formats discussed previously. If the value has more decimal digits than the number you specify in the format, Symphony automatically rounds the display of the value. The percent sign (**%**) is displayed in the farthest right space of the cell.

When you enter a value formatted as **%**, Symphony displays it as multiplied by 100, although the underlying value remains unchanged. Therefore, you should enter values formatted as **%** as decimal fractions, not whole numbers. For example, enter .5 and use the **F**ormat **%** 0 command to display the value as 50%.

Reminder:

Enter percentages as decimal fractions, not whole numbers.

Several examples of cells formatted with the **%** format in a column with a width of nine are as follows:

Typed Entry	Cell Format	Display Result
.2	(%2)	20.00%
−1.3528	(%2)	−135.28%
30	(%0)	3000%
30	(%4)	*********

(**%n**) appears in Symphony's control panel of cells formatted with the **F**ormat **%** command, where *n* is the number of decimal places you specify.

Scientific Format

Symphony's **S**cientific format (S) enables you to display very large or very small values. Very large and very small numbers usually have a few significant digits and many zeros. Symphony automatically displays in **S**cientific format those values that are too large to display in **G**eneral format.

Cue:
Use Scientific format to display very large or very small numbers.

Similar to the formats discussed previously, you can specify 0 to 15 decimal places. If the value has more significant digits than the value you specify in the **F**ormat **S**cientific command, the number is rounded in the display. As always, the underlying value remains unchanged.

A number displayed in **S**cientific notation contains two parts: a *mantissa* and an *exponent.* The mantissa is a number from 1 to 10 that contains the significant digits. The exponent tells you how many places to move the decimal point to get the actual value of the number.

Examples of cells formatted with the **S**cientific format in a column with a width of nine are as follows:

Typed Entry	Cell Format	Display Result
1632116750000	(S2)	1.63E+12
1632116750000	(S0)	2E+12
−1632116750000	(S1)	−1.6E+12
−1632116750000	(S2)	*********
.00000000012	(S2)	1.20E−10
−.00000000012	(S0)	−1E−10

(**Sn**) appears in Symphony's control panel of cells formatted with the **F**ormat **S**cientific command, where *n* is the number of decimal places you specify.

Using Date and Time Formats

Thus far, you have learned how to format numbers as numeric values. In this section, you learn how to format values as dates and times. You use the **F**ormat **D**ate and **F**ormat **T**ime commands to format cells as dates and times, respectively. You also use these formats when you use the @DATE and @TIME functions to enter dates and times, respectively, in your Symphony applications. These and Symphony's other date and time functions are covered fully in Chapter 6, "Using @Functions."

Date Formats

Caution:

Symphony is one day off in serial–number calculations beginning with March 1, 1990.

Symphony represents any given date as an integer equal to the number of days from Dec. 31, 1899, to the specified date. For example, Jan. 1, 1900, is represented by 1; Dec. 31, 2099, which is the last date in Symphony's calendar, is represented by 73050. If a number is less than 0 or greater than 73050, and formatted as **D**ate, Symphony displays asterisks in the cell.

When you select the **F**ormat **D**ate command, the menu in figure 5.4 appears.

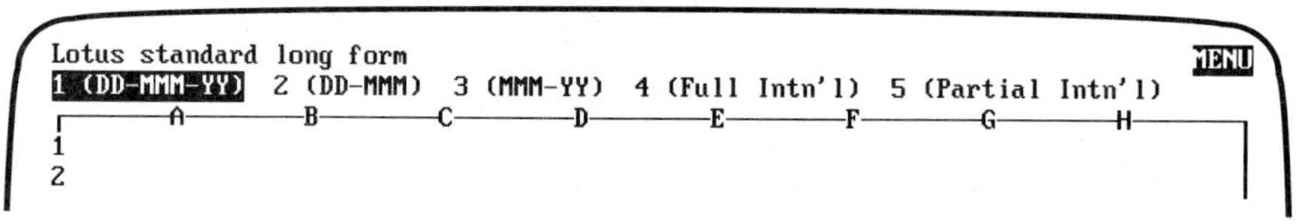

Fig. 5.4.

The Format Date menu.

You have a choice of three commonly used date formats in the United States. In addition, you have access to eight **I**nternational formats, as shown in table 5.2.

Selecting an international date format is covered later in this chapter.

Examples of cells formatted with **D**ate **4** (Full International) format, using the default of MM/DD/YY, in a column with a width of nine characters are as follows:

Typed Entry	Cell Format	Display Result	Cell Contents
15	(D4)	01/15/00	15
32888	(D4)	01/15/90	32888
32888.4538	(D4)	01/15/90	32888.4538
–32888	any date	********	–32888

Table 5.2
Symphony's International Date Formats

Menu Choice	Format	Description	Example
1	(D1)	Day–Month–Year	15–Jan–90
		DD–MMM–YY	
2	(D2)	Day–Month	15–Jan
		DD–MMM	
3	(D3)	Month–Year	Jan–90
		MMM–YY	
4	(D4)	Full International	
A		MM/DD/YY	01/15/90
B		DD/MM/YY	15/01/90
C		DD.MM.YY	15.01.90
D		YY–MM–DD	90–01–15
5	(D5)	Partial International	
A		MM/DD	01/15
B		DD/MM	15/01
C		DD.MM	15.01
D		MM–DD	01–15

(Dn) appears in Symphony's control panel of cells formatted with the **F**ormat **D**ate command, where *n* represents the **D**ate format selection from Symphony's **F**ormat **D**ate menu.

Time Formats

Symphony's **T**ime format is similar to the **D**ate format. Times, like Dates, are represented as integers. However, when you enter a time function into Symphony, Symphony stores the time as a decimal fraction (from 0 to 1) that represents the fraction of the 24-hour clock. Thus, the time fraction for 3 a.m. is 0.125; the time fraction for noon is 0.5; the time fraction for 6 p.m. is 0.75, and so forth. Fortunately, you need not deal with the fractions; Symphony takes care of that for you by displaying them as times.

Reminder:

Symphony stores the time as a decimal fraction that represents the fraction of the 24-hour clock.

When you select **F**ormat **T**ime, the menu in figure 5.5 appears.

You have a choice of two common **T**ime formats and eight International formats, as shown in table 5.3.

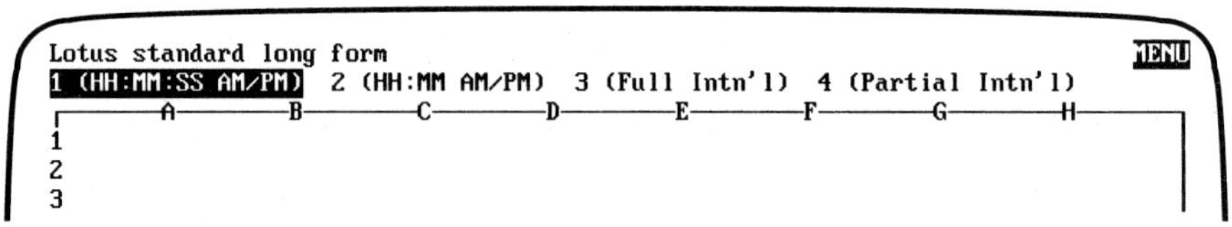

Fig. 5.5.

The Format Time menu.

```
Lotus standard long form                                          MENU
1 (HH:MM:SS AM/PM)  2 (HH:MM AM/PM)  3 (Full Intn'l)  4 (Partial Intn'l)
   A          B          C         D          E          F          G          H
1
2
3
```

Table 5.3
Symphony's International Time Formats

Menu Choice	Format	Description	Example
1	(T1)	Hour:Minute:Second HH:MM:SS AM/PM	06:23:57 PM
2	(T2)	Hour:Minute HH:MM AM/PM	06:23 PM
3	(T3)	Full International	
A		HH:MM:SS	18:23:57
B		HH.MM.SS	18.23.57
C		HH,MM,SS	18,23,57
D		HHhMMmSSs	18h23m57s
4	(T4)	Partial International	
A		HH:MM	18:23
B		HH.MM	18.23
C		HH,MM	18,23
D		HHhMMm	18h23m

Selecting an international time format is covered later in this chapter.

Examples of cells formatted with the **T**ime **2** format in a column with a width of nine are as follows:

Typed Entry	Cell Format	Display Result	Cell Contents
2	(T2)	12:00 AM	2
.25	(T2)	06:00 AM	0.25
−.25	(T2)	*********	−0.25

(**Tn**) appears in Symphony's control panel of cells formatted with the **F**ormat **T**ime command, where *n* represents the **T**ime format selection from Symphony's **F**ormat **T**ime menu.

Using Other Formats

Symphony's **F**ormat **O**ther command provides you with access to three additional formats: **B**ar-Graph, **L**iteral, and **H**idden.

Bar-Graph Format

Symphony's **B**ar-Graph format creates a horizontal bar graph of plus (+) or minus (–) signs, depending on the value of the number you enter in the cell. A positive number displays as a row of plus signs; a negative number displays as a row of minus signs; and a zero displays as a period (.). Decimals and numbers between 0–1 also display as a period. The number of pluses or minuses can be no wider than the cell.

The **B**ar-Graph format was originally created when spreadsheet programs lacked graphing capability. However, you can use the **B**ar-Graph format in project management applications, such as Gantt charts.

Examples of cells formatted with the **B**ar-Graph format in a column with a width of nine are as follows:

Typed Entry	Cell Format	Display Result
6	(+)	++++++
4.9	(+)	++++
–3	(+)	- - -
0	(+)	.
17.2	(+)	********

(+) appears in Symphony's control panel of cells formatted with the **B**ar–Graph format.

Literal Format

Symphony's **L**iteral format displays formulas instead of values in a cell. Numbers formatted as **L**iteral display similar to **G**eneral format. However, if the formula is longer than the width of the cell, its display is truncated, unlike long labels that display across blank cells. Labels are unaffected by **L**iteral format.

Literal format is useful when you need to debug your formulas. In this manner, you can display your formula to locate and correct errors. **L**iteral format also is convenient when you are working with the MENU **Q**uery and **W**hat **I**f commands. All cells in figure 5.6 are formatted with the **L**iteral format.

Reminder:
When you need to debug your formulas, use the Literal format.

Fig. 5.6.

An example of Symphony's Literal format.

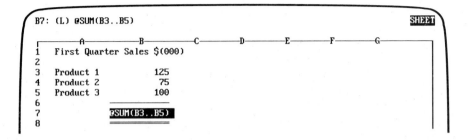

```
B7: (L) @SUM(B3..B5)                                          SHEET
        A          B          C       D       E       F       G
1   First Quarter Sales $(000)
2
3   Product 1              125
4   Product 2               75
5   Product 3              100
6                      _____
7                      @SUM(B3..B5)
8                      ==========
```

Notice that Symphony displays range names rather than cell addresses when the formula uses named ranges and is formatted as **L**iteral.

(**L**) appears in Symphony's control panel of cells formatted with the **L**iteral format.

Hidden Format

Caution:

Do not rely on Hidden format to hide sensitive information.

Cells formatted with **H**idden format display blank, regardless of their contents. However, if you move the cell pointer to a cell formatted as **H**idden, its contents will be displayed in Symphony's control panel. The SERVICES **S**ettings **G**lobal-Protection used in combination with **H**idden format helps you to hide cell contents. See Chapter 1, "Security System," for more information about worksheet protection.

Even though a cell's contents are not displayed on-screen when you use **H**idden format, Symphony continues to calculate and readjust all formulas and values when values are changed.

(**H**) appears in Symphony's control panel of cells formatted with the **H**idden format.

Using International Formats

You can change the way Symphony displays some **D**ate and **T**ime formats, and characters Symphony uses to display currency, the decimal point, the thousands' separator, and negative values. If you work outside the United States, or in a currency other than U.S. dollars, or just prefer one of the international formats, you can customize your display by using Symphony.

You use Symphony's SERVICES **C**onfiguration **O**ther **I**nternational command to select the formats you want as your international defaults. When you invoke this command, the menu in figure 5.7 appears.

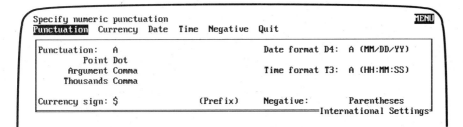

Fig. 5.7.
*The SERVICES
Configuration Other
International menu.*

This command enables you to change the way Symphony displays international dates, times, punctuation, currency, and negative values. Keep in mind that when you use a **C**onfiguration command, you make a global change, one that affects all your applications. To make your changes permanent, use the SERVICES **C**onfiguration **U**pdate command. Otherwise, the changes remain in effect only for the current Symphony session.

To use a new **I**nternational format, you simply use the same commands you used for Symphony's default formats. Use the **S**ettings **F**ormat command to set formats for your entire application and the **F**ormat command to set formats for individual cells and ranges. As always, any formats you set with the **F**ormat command have precedence over those set with the **S**ettings **F**ormat command.

Reminder:
*Formats you set
with the **Format**
command have
precedence over
those set with the
Settings Format
command.*

Displaying International Currency Formats

Symphony's default currency symbol is the U.S. dollar sign. If you are using a different currency, use the SERVICES **C**onfiguration **O**ther **I**nternational **C**urrency command to specify another currency. You can select a character from the Lotus International Character Set (LICS) as your new currency symbol.

Reminder:
*Change the default
currency symbol
with the SERVICES
Configuration
International
Currency
command.*

As an example, to change your currency sign to the British pound after selecting the SERVICES **C**onfiguration **O**ther **I**nternational command, press your backspace key to remove the $. Next, press the Compose key (Alt-F1), then type L=, the LICS character for the British pound sign. Finally, select Prefix or Suffix if you want the sign placed before or after the value, respectively. When you retrieve another file, any cells you have formatted as **C**urrency will display the British pound sign.

Remember to use the SERVICES **C**onfiguration **U**pdate command to make your new currency sign a permanent setting.

Displaying International Date and Time Formats

Select **D**ate and **T**ime from the SERVICES **C**onfiguration **O**ther **I**nternational command to change the **I**nternational **D**ate and **T**ime formats. The format options are displayed in figure 5.1. Notice as you change a Full International format, its Partial International format changes also, and vice-versa. For example, if you select Full International A, Partial International A is also selected.

Because the settings are similar to the **C**urrency format, remember to use the SERVICES **C**onfiguration **U**pdate command to make the new date or time formats permanent.

Displaying International Punctuation Formats

Symphony provides you with a combination of eight different punctuation settings, as shown in table 5.4.

Table 5.4
Symphony's International Punctuation Formats

	A	B	C	D	E	F	G	H
Decimal point	.	,	.	,	.	,	.	,
Argument separator	,	.	;	;	,	.	;	;
Thousands separator	,	.	,	.				

Symphony's default punctuation setting is A. A period (.) is used to separate the integer part of a number from its fractional part; a comma (,) separates arguments in @functions and macro statements; and a comma (,) separates thousands. The thousands separator for settings E through H is a space.

Similar to the **C**urrency, **D**ate, and **T**ime formats, remember to use the SERVICES **C**onfiguration **U**pdate command to make the new punctuation settings permanent.

Displaying Negative Numbers

Symphony provides the following two formats for displaying negative numbers:

Typed Entry	Cell Format	Display
–123.45	Parentheses	(123.45)
–123.45	Minus	–123.45

Reminder:
Change the default negative format with the SERVICES Configuration Other International Negative command.

Symphony's default is Parentheses, but you can change it to a minus sign (–) if you prefer. Similar to the other International formats, use the SERVICES Configuration Update command to make the settings permanent.

Aligning Labels Automatically

In Chapter 3, you learned how to enter and align labels with the left-('), center-(^), and right-(") justification characters. However, suppose that you have entered a series of labels, but decide instead to have a different alignment. You can change each label prefix manually, or you can change them all at once with the **R**ange **L**abel-Alignment command. When you select this command, the following options appear in Symphony's control panel:

    Left Center Right

After you choose **L**eft, **C**enter, or **R**ight, Symphony asks you to designate a range of cells to change. When you specify a range and press Enter, the cells in that range are displayed according to the option you choose.

Another option for changing label prefixes automatically is to change Symphony's default label alignment setting. To accomplish this, you use the **S**ettings **L**abel-Prefix command. This command gives you the same options as **R**ange **L**abel-Alignment — **L**eft, **C**enter, and **R**ight. Similar to formatting values with the **S**ettings **F**ormat and **F**ormat commands, **R**ange **L**abel-Alignment has precedence over the **S**ettings **L**abel-Prefix command.

Reminder:
*The **R**ange **L**abel-Alignment command has precedence over the **S**ettings **L**abel-Prefix command.*

Keep in mind that the **R**ange **L**abel-Alignment command affects only the cells containing labels you specify in the range. However, labels entered *after* you issue the **S**ettings **L**abel-Prefix command will change alignment.

Controlling Display of Zeros

You can control the display of zeros in your applications with the **S**ettings **Z**ero command. If you select **S**ettings **Z**ero **Y**es, cells containing a value of zero will not be displayed on the screen or printout; these cells will appear blank. To redisplay zeros, select the **S**ettings **Z**ero **N**o command. Note that the **S**ettings **Z**ero **Y**es is a temporary setting. If you always want zeros suppressed, you must use the **S**ettings **Z**ero **Y**es command each time you retrieve a file.

TIP

The (MENU)szy macro suppresses the display of zeros. If you designate the macro as your autoexecuting macro in your applications, Symphony will automatically display zeros as blank as soon as you retrieve the file. See Chapter 21, "Creating and Using Macros," for information about macros and autoexecuting macros.

Chapter Summary

In this chapter, you were introduced to the many options available in Symphony to control and customize the display of applications. You learned how to format the values in the spreadsheet with Symphony's 11 format options. You also learned about the international formatting options available in Symphony. Finally, you learned how to automatically align labels and suppress the display of zeros.

In the next chapter, you learn how to use @functions to tap the analytical power of Symphony.

6

Using @Functions

You can think of *functions* (also called *built-in functions*) as abbreviations of formulas. Symphony's functions are quick ways to perform tasks that would take much longer (or in many cases could not be done at all) with standard mathematical and string concatenation symbols such as +, /, and &.

Symphony includes a comprehensive set of built-in functions. If you use Symphony's functions with some of its more high-powered features, such as the database or Command Language, you will find that Symphony has many of the ingredients of a sophisticated programming language.

This chapter begins with an examination of function basics. The functions then are covered by application: mathematical, trigonometric, statistical, financial, data management, logical, special, string processing, ASCII/LICS, date, and time.

Understanding Function Basics

You announce Symphony's functions to the computer by typing @ in front of the function name. The @ distinguishes the formula from a normal label entry.

To evaluate functions, most functions use one or more arguments. An *argument* is one of three different types: a single numeric value, a single string value, or a range. (Remember that all ranges in Symphony are rectangular in shape.) In Symphony, arguments are always written in parentheses after the function. For example, the following function (which you can assume is in cell B21) computes the total of a range of eight cells:

@SUM(*B12..B19*)

Reminder:

Type @ to indicate to the computer that you are typing a function and not a normal label.

The @ signals that the entry is a function, *SUM* is the name of the function, and the range *B12..B19* is the argument. This function tells Symphony to compute the sum of the numbers located in cells B12, B13, B14, B15, B16, B17, B18, and B19, and to display the result in cell B21.

A few functions, such as @ERR and @NA, do not use arguments. These functions are discussed in detail later in the chapter.

Following are examples of different functions with the three argument types:

@SUM(*A2..H14*)	Computes the sum of the numbers in the rectangular range A2..H14.
@COUNT(*TOTALS*)	Returns the number of nonblank cells in the range called TOTALS.
@MAX(*C15..H32*)	Returns the maximum value in the rectangular range C15..H32.
@SUM(*A2..H14,A15*)	Computes the sum of the numbers in the range A2..H14 and in cell A15.
@DATEVALUE(*AA1*)	Converts the string value in cell AA1 (such as "12/23/88") to a serial number representing the number of days since December 31, 1899.
@NPV(*.15/12,A1..A17*)	Computes the net present value of the 17-month range A1..A17 at the monthly rate of 1.25 percent.
@LOWER(*"TIMES"*)	Converts the word TIMES to lowercase.

Like mathematical and string-concatenation formulas, functions can be much more complex than those listed. For example, you can combine several functions in a single cell by using functions as the arguments for the original function. This technique is called *nesting*. In practice you will find that you nest functions quite frequently.

Note: The term *string* refers to a group of characters that Symphony treats as a label. The term *concatenation* refers to the joining of strings. If you have the string `Using Symphony` in cell A1 and the string `Secial Edition` in cell A2, you can use the concatenation formula +A1&", "&A2 in cell A3 to produce the result `Using Symphony, Special Edition` in cell A3.

Using Mathematical Functions

Symphony contains several functions that you can use to perform mathematical operations. These functions include the following:

@ABS(*number***)**

Computes the absolute value of *number*. You also can use a cell reference in place of *number*. For example, the function @ABS(–4) returns the value 4; the function @ABS(–556) returns the value 556; the function @ABS(3) returns 3.

@EXP(*number***)**

Computes the value of the constant *e* (approximately 2.718) to the power specified by *number*, often used to reverse the @LN function. For example, the function @EXP(5) returns 148.4131. If cell A1 contains the value 2.75, the function @EXP(A1) returns 15.64263. Also, if @LN(2) is placed in cell AA1, the number that appears in that cell is 0.693147. If @EXP(AA1) is then placed in cell AB1, the number that appears in that cell is 2. If you use a number greater than 230 with @EXP, Symphony returns asterisks in the cell.

Reminder:
If you use a number greater than 230 with @EXP, Symphony returns asterisks in the cell.

@INT(*number***)**

Computes the integer portion of *number*. For example, the function @INT(4.356) returns the value 4. If cell A1 contains the value 55.666, the function @INT(A1) returns the value 55. Notice that unlike the @ROUND function (explained in the next section), @INT simply truncates all the digits to the right of the decimal.

Tip

To ensure that a date field in a database contains a pure date serial number, use the @INT function to convert the date and time serial number returned by @NOW. Do this by using @INT(*@NOW*) instead of @NOW alone. If you enter dates in this fashion, you can compare a field value to an exact date.

@LN(*number***)**

Computes the natural logarithm (base *e*) of *number* or cell reference. For example, the function @LN(17.634) returns the value 2.869828. *number* must be positive; otherwise, the function returns ERR. (Refer to the description of @EXP to see how the two functions work.)

@LOG(*number***)**

Computes the logarithm (base 10) of *number* or cell reference. For example, the function @LOG(4.56) returns the value 0.658964. If cell A1 contains the value 3.555, the function @LOG(A1) returns the value 0.550839.

@SQRT(*number*)

> Computes the square root of *number* or cell reference. For example, the function @SQRT(5) returns the value 2.236067. If cell A1 contains the value 16, the function @SQRT(A1) returns the value 4.

Using Special Mathematical Functions

The following mathematical functions require special explanation:

@RAND   Generates random numbers

@ROUND   Rounds numbers to a given precision

@MOD   Returns the remainder (the modulus) from division

Generating Random Numbers: @RAND

Reminder:

Use @RAND to generate random numbers.

The @RAND function requires no argument and is used to generate random numbers. The function generates random numbers between 0 and 1, with up to 10 decimal places. If you enter the function @RAND in a cell, that cell displays a different value between 0 and 1 each time the worksheet is recalculated. Figure 6.1 shows two versions of the same worksheet filled with @RAND functions. Notice that in the second sheet, which has been recalculated, each cell has a different value from that in the first.

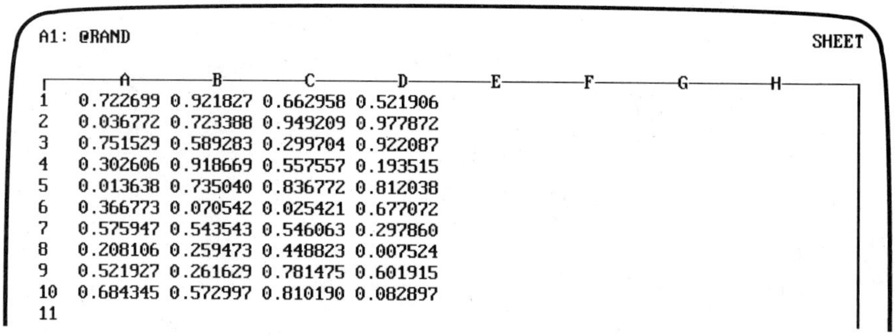

Fig. 6.1.

A worksheet using @RAND, before and after being recalculated.

```
A1: @RAND                                               SHEET
      A          B          C          D      E      F      G      H
 1   0.722699  0.921827  0.662958  0.521906
 2   0.036772  0.723388  0.949209  0.977872
 3   0.751529  0.589283  0.299704  0.922087
 4   0.302606  0.918669  0.557557  0.193515
 5   0.013638  0.735040  0.836772  0.812038
 6   0.366773  0.070542  0.025421  0.677072
 7   0.575947  0.543543  0.546063  0.297860
 8   0.208106  0.259473  0.448823  0.007524
 9   0.521927  0.261629  0.781475  0.601915
10   0.684345  0.572997  0.810190  0.082897
11
```

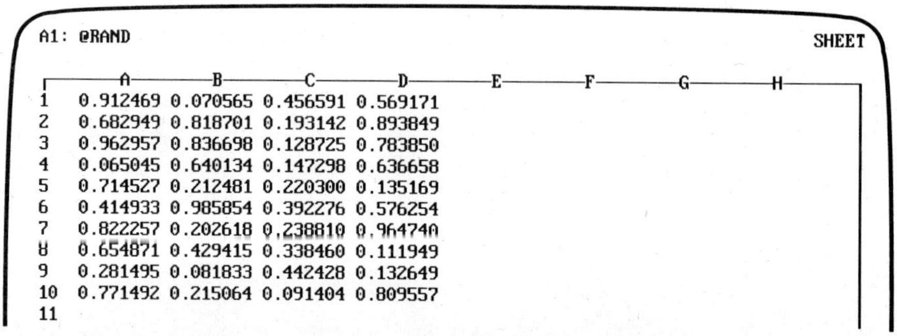

```
A1: @RAND                                               SHEET
      A          B          C          D      E      F      G      H
 1   0.912469  0.070565  0.456591  0.569171
 2   0.682949  0.818701  0.193142  0.893849
 3   0.962957  0.836698  0.128725  0.783850
 4   0.065045  0.640134  0.147298  0.636658
 5   0.714527  0.212481  0.220300  0.135169
 6   0.414933  0.985854  0.392276  0.576254
 7   0.822257  0.202618  0.238810  0.964740
 8   0.654871  0.429415  0.338460  0.111949
 9   0.281495  0.081833  0.442428  0.132649
10   0.771492  0.215064  0.091404  0.809557
11
```

Rounding Numbers: @ROUND

The @ROUND function rounds numbers to a specified precision. The general form of the function is as follows:

@ROUND($x, numb\_digs$)

In this format, x is the number to be rounded, and *numb_digs* is a number between 15 and –15 representing the number of digits to the right of the decimal. Here are some examples of this function:

@ROUND(*123.456,3*) = 123.456   @ROUND(*123.456,2*) = 123.46

@ROUND(*123.456,1*) = 123.5   @ROUND(*123.456,0*) = 123

@ROUND(*123.456,–1*) = 120   @ROUND(*123.456,–2*) = 100

The advantage of the @ROUND function over the SHEET **F**ormat **F**ixed command is that with @ROUND you avoid the errors that may appear when you add rounded currency amounts. If you add the following two sets of numbers with the formula +A1+A2 in cell A4, the numbers in the right column appear to have the wrong total:

Cue:
Use @ROUND to avoid apparent errors in math caused by the format of the worksheet.

Cell	Value Stored	Value Displayed in Currency Format to Nearest Cent
A1	123.025	$123.03
A2	123.025	$123.03
A4	246.05	$246.05

The @ROUND function gets around this problem by making the columns total properly. The total displayed in cell A4 ($246.06) is derived from using the formula @ROUND(*A1,2*)+@ROUND(*A2,2*) instead of just +A1+A2 in cell A4.

Cell	Value Stored	Value Displayed in Currency Format to Nearest Cent
A1	123.025	$123.03
A2	123.025	$123.03
A4	246.05	$246.06

Tip

Don't confuse the formula @ROUND(*A1,2*)+@ROUND(*A2,2*) with @ROUND(+*A1+A2,2*). Although you may think that this is a good shortcut, the two formulas produce different results. The first formula rounds the numbers before adding them; the second formula adds the numbers and rounds the result.

Returning a Remainder: @MOD

The @MOD function returns the remainder (the modulus) from a division operation. @MOD's general form is as follows:

@MOD(*number,divisor*)

The following examples show how @MOD works:

@MOD(*7,3*) = 1
@MOD(*71.3,21*) = 8
@MOD(*31,0*) = ERR

If you specify 0 as the divisor, Symphony displays **ERR**.

Here's an example of how the @MOD function can be helpful. Suppose that you have 500 items and you want to determine the number of parts that will be left over if you run equal-sized batches of 33 items. The result is 5 items, determined by @MOD(*500,33*) = 5.

Tip

You can use @MOD to determine the day of the week. @MOD(*@INT(@NOW),7*) returns the number corresponding to today's position in the week (Sunday is 1, Monday is 2, and so on). If you combine @MOD with one of the date functions that returns a date serial number, you can determine the day of the week for any date.

Using Trigonometric Functions

Symphony has a complete set of trigonometric functions. Many people never use these functions because they have little application in the world of accounting or finance. But people who use Symphony to solve engineering problems will find these functions invaluable. Symphony's trigonometric functions include the following:

@PI

> This function, which requires no argument, returns the value of the constant pi (π), accurate to 10 decimal places, or 3.1415926536.

@SIN(*number*) @COS(*number*) @TAN(*number*)

> These functions compute the common trigonometric functions. The values returned are expressed in radians. For example, the value of the function @SIN(*2*) is 0.909297 (radians). The value of @TAN(*136*) is 1.290401 (radians).

@ASIN(*number*) @ACOS(*number*) @ATAN(*number*) @ATAN2(*number*)

These functions compute the arcsine, arccosine, arctangent, and four-quadrant arctangent of a number or cell reference. The @ASIN, @ACOS, and @ATAN functions reverse the @SIN, @COS, and @TAN functions, respectively. For example, for the @ACOS function, you specify a number between 1 and –1, representing the cosine of an angle; the value of the function is the size of the angle in radians. The value of @ACOS(.33) is 1.234492 in radians.

Note: All the trigonometric functions use radians. If your calculations use degrees, convert the input to radians and the results back to degrees. To convert degrees to radians, multiply the value by @PI/180. To convert radians to degrees, multiply the value by 180/@PI. Therefore, the value of @COS(.33)*180/@PI is approximately 71 degrees.

Reminder:
All the trigonometric functions use radians instead of degrees.

Using Statistical Functions

Symphony has several functions that perform simple statistical analyses. These statistical functions are typically used with an argument consisting of a range of cells. As you may recall, a *range* is a single cell or a series of contiguous, or adjoining, cells. Symphony's statistical functions include @SUM, @MAX, @MIN, @COUNT, @AVG, @VAR, and @STD.

Computing a Sum: @SUM

Perhaps the most important statistical function is @SUM, which computes the sum of a range of entries. The range is usually a partial row or column but can also be an entire block of cells consisting of several rows and columns. For example, in the simple worksheet shown in figure 6.2, the function @SUM(*A1..A2*) returns the value 11110 or 345+765. The function @SUM(*A1..C2*) returns the value 3330, which is the total of all the numbers in the six-cell range. Notice that the range in this case consists of two partial rows.

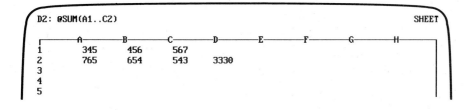

Fig. 6.2.
An example of @SUM.

You can even define the argument of the @SUM function as a discontinuous set of cells. For example, the function @SUM(*A1,B2,C1*) returns the value 1566.

This function is equivalent to the formula +A1+B2+C1. A more useful hybrid is the function @SUM(*A1..B2,C1*), which computes the total of the range *A1* to *B2* plus the value in *C1* for a total of 2787.

Cue:

Use @SUM instead of a longhand arithmetic formula when you have a lengthy range to add.

In the preceding example, using @SUM takes about the same amount of time as using the longhand arithmetic +A1+A2+B1+B2+C1. But when you have a lengthy range, @SUM can save time.

Another advantage of the @SUM function (and other functions where you use a range such as A1..C1 instead of individual cell-address arguments like A1, B1, C1) is that @SUM is more adaptable than a formula to changes made in the sheet with cut-and-paste commands. For example, in the sheet in figure 6.2, the function @SUM(*A1..C1*) is equivalent to the formula +A1+B1+C1. If you use the SHEET **D**elete **C**olumn command to delete column B, the sheet looks like figure 6.3. The formula has changed to +A1+ERR+B1, which returns the message ERR. The function, on the other hand, has changed to @SUM(*A1..B1*) and returns the correct answer: 912.

Fig. 6.3.

The +A1+B1+C1 formula after deleting column B.

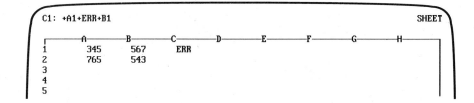

What happens if you use this example and insert a column using SHEET **I**nsert **C**olumn? The sheet resembles figure 6.4. The formula is +A1+C1+D1 and still has the value 1368. The function is now @SUM(*A1..D1*). If you insert a number in the new cell B1, the function includes that number in the new total, but the formula does not.

Fig. 6.4.

The +A1+B1+C1 formula after inserting a column.

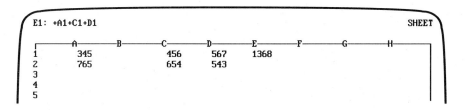

> ### Tip
>
> Here is a practical application for @SUM. Whenever possible, define a sum range to include an extra cell at the end of the range. For example, in the worksheet shown in figure 6.5, you can enter the formula @SUM(A1..A4) in cell A5. Because the label in cell A4 has a mathematical value of 0, the label does not affect the sum. But because you include the label in the formula, you can add an extra item to the list simply by inserting a row at row 4. The sheet then looks like figure 6.6. The formula in cell A6 is now @SUM(*A1..A5*). If you insert the number 114 in cell A4, the formula displays the value 2100 in cell A6.
>
> Be careful when you include an extra label cell in the argument of a function, however. As you will see, some functions such as @COUNT, @AVG, @MAX, and @MIN do not ignore the extra cell and give unexpected results.

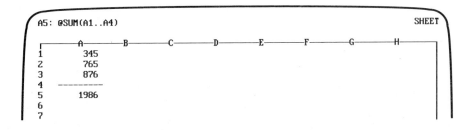

Fig. 6.5.

Including an extra cell in the @SUM formula.

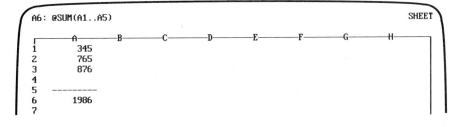

Fig. 6.6.

Adding another item to the list.

Finding the Maximum and Minimum Values: @MAX and @MIN

The @MAX and @MIN functions return the maximum and minimum values in a range. As with the @SUM function, the range can be a partial row or column, a block of several partial rows and columns, a named range, or a discontinuous group of cells joined by commas. Both @MAX and @MIN assign a value of 0 to labels but completely ignore empty cells. For example, in the worksheet shown in figure 6.7, the function @MAX(*A1..A5*) returns the value 777. The function @MIN(*A1..A5*) returns the value 134, and the function @MIN(*A1..A6*) also

Reminder:

If you include cells with labels in the @MAX or @MIN range, Symphony evaluates the labels as 0; blank cells are ignored.

returns 134, because cell A6 is blank. If you enter the label ABCD in cell A6, the function @MIN(*A1..A6*) returns the value 0, because Symphony evaluates labels as zero.

Fig. 6.7.
An example of @MAX and @MIN.

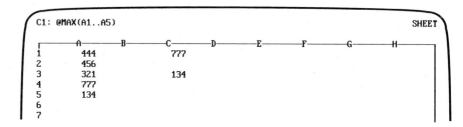

```
C1: @MAX(A1..A5)                                              SHEET
    ┌───A────────B────────C────────D────────E────────F────────G────────H──┐
  1           444              777
  2           456
  3           321              134
  4           777
  5           134
  6
  7
```

Counting Nonblank Entries: @COUNT

The @COUNT function is similar to the @MIN, @MAX, and @SUM functions. @COUNT returns the count of the number of nonblank entries in a range. In the worksheet in figure 6.7, the function @COUNT(*A1..A6*) returns the value 5. If you enter a label or number in cell A6, the value of the function is 6. Cells containing spaces also increment the @COUNT.

Caution:
If you specify a single blank cell, @COUNT returns 1. Make the single cell into a range (A1..A1) to avoid this problem.

One interesting feature of the @COUNT function is the way it reacts to a single blank cell. If cell A1 is blank, the function @COUNT(*A1*) returns the value 1. The function @COUNT(*A1..A1*), however, returns the value 0. In fact, every @COUNT function that refers to a single cell without specifying a range (such as A1..A1) has a value of 1. The most reliable technique for avoiding the single-cell problem is always to specify a range with the @COUNT function.

Calculating the Mean: @AVG

Another simple statistical function is @AVG. This function computes the mean, or average, of all the cells in a range. Essentially, the @AVG function is similar to the @SUM function divided by the @COUNT function. Because @AVG ignores blank cells, an @AVG function that refers to a range with all blank cells returns ERR.

Tip

You easily can forget that a cell containing a label affects the results produced by the statistical functions. Make sure that your results aren't skewed incorrectly because you included a label cell in the calculation range. If your results seem wrong, check to make sure that a "blank" cell doesn't include an empty label.

Reviewing Statistics

A quick review of statistical concepts may be worthwhile at this time. If you are already quite familiar with the concepts of mean, variance, and standard deviation, as well as population and sample statistics, you may want to skip to the next section.

The *mean*, often called the *arithmetic average*, is commonly used to mark the midpoint of a group of data items. The mean is calculated by adding the items in a group and dividing the total by the number of items. Don't confuse the mean with the median or mode, which also are measures of central tendency. The *median* is the value midway between the highest and lowest value in the group in terms of probability. Half the items in the group have values above the median, and half have values below. The *mode* is the most commonly occurring value in a group of items (that is, the value you see most often).

Variance and *standard deviation* are related dispersion statistics. To calculate the variance, you subtract the mean of a group of numbers from each number in the group and square each result. You then add the squares and divide the total by the number of items in the group. To compute the standard deviation, you take the square root of the variance. Symphony's @VAR and @STD functions automatically make these calculations for you.

What does the standard deviation tell you? As a general rule, about 68 percent of the items in a normally distributed population fall within a range that is plus or minus one standard deviation of the mean. About 95 percent of the items fall within plus or minus two standard deviations of the mean.

Reminder:
When you determine the standard deviation, you can assume that about 68 percent of the population falls in a range plus or minus one standard deviation of the mean.

To understand Symphony's @VAR and @STD statistical functions, you should know the difference between population and sample statistics. *Population statistics* are used when you know the values of all the items in a population. When the number of items is quite large and you don't know them all (which is usually the case), you cannot compute the population statistics. You must instead rely on *sample statistics* as estimates of the population statistics. For more information on statistics, refer to *Statistical Methods* by Donald Harnett (Addison-Wesley Publishing Company, Philippines, 1982).

Finding Variance and Standard Deviation: @VAR and @STD

These slightly more complex statistical functions have the following formats:

@VAR(*list*) Computes the population variance

@STD(*list*) Computes the standard deviation of a population

A simple example that uses both functions is shown in figure 6.8. The worksheet shows a list of the number of items each salesperson sold during a given period. The list of the number of items sold is the population in this example. The population is used as the range for all the statistical functions.

Fig. 6.8.

A practical application of @VAR and @STD.

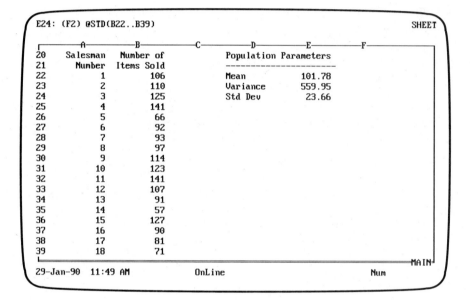

```
E24: (F2) @STD(B22..B39)                                        SHEET
     ──A──   ──B──      ──C──    ──D──        ──E──      ──F──
20   Salesman  Number of        Population Parameters
21    Number  Items Sold        ─────────────────────
22       1       106            Mean           101.78
23       2       110            Variance       559.95
24       3       125            Std Dev         23.66
25       4       141
26       5        66
27       6        92
28       7        93
29       8        97
30       9       114
31      10       123
32      11       141
33      12       107
34      13        91
35      14        57
36      15       127
37      16        90
38      17        81
39      18        71
                                                          ─MAIN─
29-Jan-90  11:49 AM            OnLine                    Num
```

The mean of the population (101.78, shown in cell E22) is computed by using the @AVG function. The standard deviation, shown in cell E24, is about 24, which means that roughly 68 percent of the salespeople sold between 77 and 125 items.

If you do not have the entire population of sales figures but only a small portion of it, you can compute the sample statistics. This approach is more realistic because you are more likely to be told that the actual population is all the monthly sales for the year and to be given only one month's worth of sales. You can see that moving into the realm of sample statistics involves more sophisticated concepts.

To calculate the sample variance for the sales data used in the previous example, multiply the population variance by n/n–1 (degrees of freedom), where *n* equals the number of items in the sample. Multiplying by n/n–1 adjusts the variance for the size of the sample used in the calculation. Because n/n–1 is always less than one, multiplying this figure by the population variance has a conservative influence on the sample variance. The results of this calculation are shown in figure 6.9.

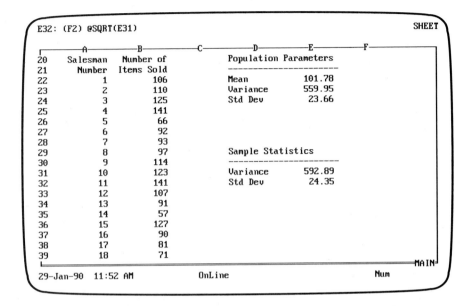

```
E32: (F2) @SQRT(E31)                                          SHEET
   ┌────A────────B────────C───────D───────E───────F──────┐
  20    Salesman   Number of        Population Parameters
  21     Number   Items Sold        ─────────────────────
  22       1        106             Mean          101.78
  23       2        110             Variance      559.95
  24       3        125             Std Dev        23.66
  25       4        141
  26       5         66
  27       6         92
  28       7         93
  29       8         97             Sample Statistics
  30       9        114             ─────────────────────
  31      10        123             Variance      592.89
  32      11        141             Std Dev        24.35
  33      12        107
  34      13         91
  35      14         57
  36      15        127
  37      16         90
  38      17         81
  39      18         71
                                                        ─MAIN─
   29-Jan-90  11:52 AM          OnLine                     Num
```

Fig. 6.9.
Calculating the sample statistics.

To compute the sample variance in figure 6.9, you can use @COUNT to determine the degrees of freedom:

Sample Variance = @COUNT(*list*)/(@COUNT(*list*)–1)*@VAR(*list*)

To compute the standard deviation of the sample, you can take the square root of the sample variance. A convenient way to do this is to use the @SQRT function:

Sample Standard Deviation = @SQRT(*Sample Variance*) =
@SQRT(*@COUNT(list)/(@COUNT(list)–1)*@VAR(list)*)

Using Financial Functions

Symphony also has several financial functions. These functions include @NPV, @PV, @FV, @TERM, @IRR, @PMT, @RATE, @CTERM, and the depreciation functions @SLN, @SYD, and @DDB.

Determining the Net Present Value: @NPV

The @NPV function computes the net present value of a stream of cash flows. The form of this function is as follows:

@NPV(*discount_rate,range*)

Reminder:

The interest rate must be given in the same intervals as the intervals between the cash flows.

The *discount_rate* is the interest rate that Symphony uses to compute the net present value; *range* is the stream of flows to be discounted. The interval between the flows must be constant and is determined by the specified rate. For example, if the flows occur one year apart, you should use an annual discount rate. If the rates occur every month, you should use a monthly rate.

You can use the @NPV function to evaluate a variety of investment opportunities. Suppose that you have a chance to buy a piece of property that will create the following stream of income in the next five years:

Year 1	100,000
Year 2	120,000
Year 3	130,000
Year 4	140,000
Year 5	50,000

To evaluate this investment, you can create a simple worksheet as shown in figure 6.10. The function @NPV(*A3,A1..E1*) returns the value 368075.1631, which is the net present value of that stream at the discount rate of 15 percent. If this rate accurately represents the rate you earn on the investment, and the price of the property is equal to or less than $368,075, the property is a good investment.

Fig. 6.10.

The net present value.

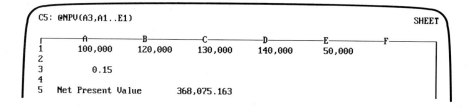

Notice that a cell reference, A3, is used to enter the discount rate into the function. Because the formula @NPV(*0.15,A1..E1*) is just as easy to enter, why wasn't it used instead? In fact, neither method has an advantage until you want to make a change in the rate.

For example, assume that you want to evaluate this same investment with a rate of 14 percent. With the method in figure 6.10, all you do is enter the number 0.14 in cell A3. If you embed the rate in the formula, you must edit the formula, replacing 0.15 with 0.14. As you can see, if several changes are required, this operation consumes much time unnecessarily. You can apply the simple technique of using a cell reference to enter a rate in a variety of situations to facilitate changing a worksheet.

Determining the Present Value of an Annuity: @PV

The @PV function calculates the present value of an ordinary annuity, given *payment* per period, *interest_rate*, and the number of periods (or *term*). An ordinary annuity is a series of payments made at equally spaced intervals. Present value is the value today of the payments to be made or received later, with the value discounted at a given interest or discount rate. Calculating the present value of an ordinary annuity gives you a way to compare different investment opportunities or potential obligations while taking into account the time value of money. The general form of the @PV formula is as follows:

@PV(*payment,interest_rate,term*)

The actual equation for calculating the present value of an ordinary annuity is shown here:

$$PV = payment * \frac{1 - (1 + interest)^{-term}}{interest}$$

Figure 6.11 shows an example of how you can use the @PV function.

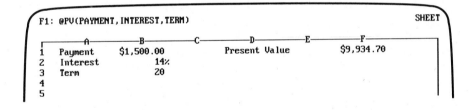

Fig. 6.11.
The present value.

The difference between @NPV (the function for net present value) and @PV stems from the difference in cash flows and the way they are laid out in the worksheet. @NPV calculates the net present value of a series of flows that may or may not be equal but which are all contained in a range of cells in the worksheet. The cash flows in the @PV function must all be equal, and the amount of the flows must be contained in a single cell or entered as a value in the @PV function.

Reminder:
With the @PV function, all cash flows are equal; with @NPV, the cash flows do not have to be equal.

Determining the Future Value of an Annuity: @FV

The @FV function is similar in form to the @PV function, but @FV calculates the future value of an ordinary annuity. Future value is the value at a given day in the future of a series of payments or receipts, discounted at a given interest or discount rate. Calculating the future value of an annuity enables you to compare different investment alternatives or potential obligations. The form of the @FV function is as follows:

@FV(*payment,interest,term*)

The @FV function uses this equation for calculating the future value of an ordinary annuity:

$$FV = payment * \frac{(1+interest)^{term-1}}{interest}$$

An example using the @FV built-in function is shown in figure 6.12.

Fig. 6.12.
The future value.

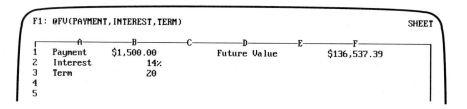

Determining the Number of Time Periods of an Annuity: @TERM

You can use the @TERM function to calculate the term (number of time periods) of an ordinary annuity, given the *payment*, periodic *interest*, and *future_value*. The form of the @TERM function is as follows:

@TERM(*payment,interest,future_value*)

For example, you can use the @TERM function to compute the length of time necessary for a periodic investment to grow at a given interest rate to some predetermined amount.

The equation for calculating the number of time periods is given here:

$$TERM = \ln(1+(future\_value*interest)/payment)/\ln(1+interest)$$

In this formula, *ln* is the natural logarithm.

Reminder:

Use @TERM when payments are made at the end of each time period; adjust the formula for payments made at the beginning of each time period.

Use @TERM for an annuity in which payments are made at the end of each time period. For payments made at the beginning of each time period, adjust the @TERM function by dividing it by the factor (1+*interest*):

@TERM(*payment,interest,future_value*)/(1+*interest*)

Determining the Internal Rate of Return: @IRR

Internal rate of return (IRR) is the discount rate that equates the present value of the expected cash outflows with the present value of the expected inflows. In simple terms, IRR is the rate of return, or profit, that an investment is expected to earn. Like the other financial calculations, IRR determines the attractiveness of an investment opportunity.

The @IRR function is built around an iterative process in which you provide an initial "ballpark" guess for a discount rate (somewhere between 0 and 1), and Symphony calculates the actual discount rate that equates the present value of a series of cash outflows with the present value of a series of inflows. Although Symphony's method may seem awkward, it is actually very logical. The same iterative method is used when you calculate IRR manually.

Given the format of the equation, all the inflows and outflows must be in the same range. The general form of the @IRR function is as follows:

@IRR(*guess,range*)

After 20 iterations, Symphony should reach convergence on a discount rate within 0.0000001, or the program returns ERR. Figure 6.13 shows an example of how the @IRR function is used. The internal rate of return, or profit, for the project in figure 6.13 is about 16 percent.

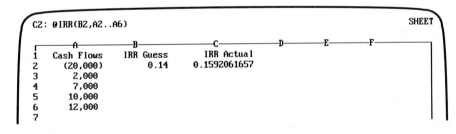

```
C2: @IRR(B2,A2..A6)                                          SHEET
     A          B             C          D      E      F
1   Cash Flows   IRR Guess    IRR Actual
2    (20,000)       0.14      0.1592061657
3     2,000
4     7,000
5    10,000
6    12,000
7
```

Fig. 6.13.
Finding the internal rate of return.

You may encounter two possible problems with the @IRR function. First, Symphony may not converge on a value for one of two reasons. One reason is that you have more than a single sign change between negative and positive cash flows. For example, you may have the sporadic cash flows that appear in figure 6.14. Because Symphony cannot reach convergence on a single IRR value, the program returns ERR.

Fig. 6.14.

The result of using a sporadic cash flow with @IRR.

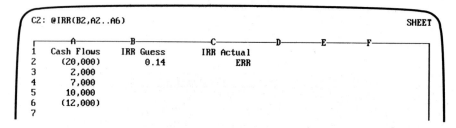

```
C2: @IRR(B2,A2..A6)                                          SHEET
       A            B                 C          D      E      F
  1  Cash Flows    IRR Guess      IRR Actual
  2   (20,000)       0.14            ERR
  3     2,000
  4     7,000
  5    10,000
  6   (12,000)
  7
```

Another possible problem with the @IRR function is that, depending on the guess value you enter, the value returned may be unreasonable. For example, figure 6.15 shows a series of 11 cash flows, an IRR guess of 0.20, and an IRR of approximately –289 percent. Even though Symphony has not reached the proper convergence, the ERR message is not displayed. The proper IRR for this series of cash flows is approximately 138 percent. To get Symphony to display 138 percent, your guess must be between 0.74 and 11.99. Remember that a guess that is too high returns ERR; a guess that is too low can return an incorrect and misleading result.

Fig. 6.15.

The result of using a low IRR guess.

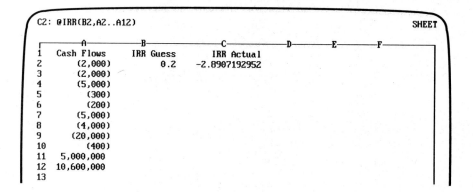

```
C2: @IRR(B2,A2..A12)                                        SHEET
       A            B                 C          D      E      F
  1  Cash Flows    IRR Guess      IRR Actual
  2    (2,000)       0.2        -2.8907192952
  3    (2,000)
  4    (5,000)
  5     (300)
  6     (200)
  7    (5,000)
  8    (4,000)
  9   (20,000)
 10     (400)
 11   5,000,000
 12  10,600,000
 13
```

Cue:

With @IRR, use a guess value on the high side and double-check any answers by trying two more guesses.

A good way to avoid this problem with the @IRR function is to guess on the high side. You should also double-check any answer you get by trying two or more guess values.

Determining the Payment per Period: @PMT

Another Symphony financial function calculates the mortgage payment required for a given *principal*, *interest_rate*, and number of periods (*term*). The format of this function is as follows:

@PMT(*principal,interest_rate,term*)

The formula behind the @PMT function calculates the present value of an ordinary annuity, but the formula is rearranged to yield the period payment as the result:

$$PMT = principal * (interest - \frac{interest}{1 - (1+interest)^{term}})$$

You can use @PMT to build a table of mortgage-rate payments. Such a table is easy to construct (see fig. 6.16).

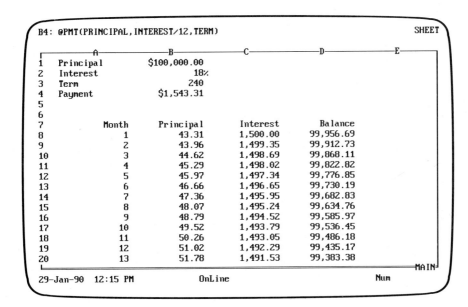

B4: @PMT(PRINCIPAL,INTEREST/12,TERM)   SHEET

	A	B	C	D	E
1	Principal	$100,000.00			
2	Interest	18%			
3	Term	240			
4	Payment	$1,543.31			
5					
6					
7	Month	Principal	Interest	Balance	
8	1	43.31	1,500.00	99,956.69	
9	2	43.96	1,499.35	99,912.73	
10	3	44.62	1,498.69	99,868.11	
11	4	45.29	1,498.02	99,822.82	
12	5	45.97	1,497.34	99,776.85	
13	6	46.66	1,496.65	99,730.19	
14	7	47.36	1,495.95	99,682.83	
15	8	48.07	1,495.24	99,634.76	
16	9	48.79	1,494.52	99,585.97	
17	10	49.52	1,493.79	99,536.45	
18	11	50.26	1,493.05	99,486.18	
19	12	51.02	1,492.29	99,435.17	
20	13	51.78	1,491.53	99,383.38	

29-Jan-90   12:15 PM   OnLine   Num

MAIN

Fig. 6.16.
A table of mortgage rate payments created with @PMT.

Determining the Periodic Interest Rate for an Investment: @RATE

The @RATE function computes the interest rate per period for an investment. The form of this function is as follows:

@RATE(*future_value,present_value,term*)

As with all investment or annuity functions, the periodic interest rate (not necessarily the annual rate) is the rate calculated. For example, to calculate a monthly interest rate for an investment of $1,000 to grow to $10,000 in eight years, you use this formula to achieve a a monthly interest rate of 2.4275:

@RATE(*10000,1000,8*12*)

The annual interest rate equivalent is 12*2.4275 percent, or 29.13 percent.

The @RATE function uses the followings formula to compute the periodic interest rate:

RATE = ((future_value/present_value)^(1/term))–1

Determining the Number of Time Periods for an Investment: @CTERM

The @CTERM function is basically a mirror image of the @RATE function. You can use @CTERM to calculate the number of periods based on the present value, future value, and periodic interest rate of an investment. The form of the function is as follows:

@CTERM(*interest,future_value,present_value*)

If you know the interest rate and want to compute the number of years needed for an investment to grow from $1,000 to $10,000, you can use @CTERM.

Reminder:
@CTERM uses a onetime investment; @TERM uses a series of constant periodic payments.

@CTERM is a variation of the @TERM function. @TERM deals with a series of constant periodic payments; @CTERM works from a one-time investment (the present value).

The formula underlying the @CTERM calculation is as follows:

CTERM = ln(future_value/present_value)/ln(1+interest)

In this equation, *ln* is the natural logarithm.

Using Depreciation Functions

Symphony includes three depreciation functions for dealing with different methods of depreciation: straight-line, sum-of-the-years'-digits, and double-declining-balance. An asset's depreciation expense is calculated based upon the asset's cost, useful life, and salvage value.

Calculating Straight-Line Depreciation: @SLN

As the name implies, straight-line depreciation simply takes the depreciable cost (initial cost less salvage value) and divides it evenly over the asset's useful life. The form of this function is as follows:

@SLN(*cost,salvage_value,life*)

Thus, a $100,000 asset with a salvage value of $20,000 and a useful life of 10 years is calculated by using @SLN(*100000,20000,10*). The asset depreciated at $8,000 per year.

The formula used by @SLN is given here:

SLN = (cost–salvage_value)/life

Calculating Sum-of-the-Years'-Digits Depreciation: @SYD

The @SYD function computes depreciation based on the so-called sum-of-the-years'-digits formula. This method accelerates depreciation; greater depreciation occurs in the early periods. The form for this function is as follows:

@SYD(*cost,salvage_value,life,period*)

Unlike straight-line depreciation, the sum-of-the-years'-digits depreciation amount varies by period, so the time period must be one of the arguments specified. For a $100,000 asset with a salvage value of $20,000 and a useful life of 10 years, the depreciation amount for the fifth year is calculated by using @SYD(*100000,20000,10,5*). The depreciation amount is approximately $8,727.

The underlying formula for @SYD is given here:

SYD = (cost–salvage_value)*(life–period+1)/(life*(life+1)/2)

Calculating Double-Declining-Balance Depreciation: @DDB

Like the sum-of-the-years'-digits method, the double-declining-balance method of depreciation generates amounts that are higher in earlier years than in later years. You also must specify the period for which you want the deprecation calculated. The function syntax is like that of @SYD:

@DDB(*cost,salvage_value,life,period*)

The formula for calculating double-declining-balance depreciation is given here:

DDB = (Cost–total depreciation taken in earlier periods)*2/life

Reminder:
The sum-of-the-years'-digits and double-declining-balance methods of depreciation return higher depreciation values in earlier years.

Using the @DDB function as is, however, can lead to a situation in later time periods in which the asset's *book value* (cost less cumulative depreciation) exceeds its salvage value. The @DDB function in Symphony has been modified to ensure that such a situation does not occur. Thus, when the cumulative depreciation equals the asset's cost less its salvage value, the function results in a zero value.

Using Data-Management Functions

Symphony has four data-management functions: @CHOOSE, @VLOOKUP, @HLOOKUP, and @INDEX. These functions are called "special" functions by Lotus, but in this book they are called *data-management functions* because they retrieve data from lists and tables. Do not confuse these functions with Symphony's database statistical functions, which operate only on databases. (Database statistical functions are discussed in Chapter 17.)

Selecting from a List: @CHOOSE

The @CHOOSE function uses a key value, which you provide, to select a number from a list. The form of this function is as follows:

@CHOOSE(*key,argument0,argument1,...,argumentN*)

In this function, *argument0* is the first argument, *argument1* is the second argument, and so on.

Reminder:

When specifying a key, remember that Symphony counts the first item in the list as item 0, the second as item 1, and so on.

@CHOOSE returns the argument whose position in the list matches *key*. For example, the function @CHOOSE(*2,3,4,5*) returns the number 5 because 5 is in the second-argument position in the list. If you change the key to 1, as in @CHOOSE(*1,3,4,5*), the function returns 4.

As with other functions, the arguments in the @CHOOSE function can be numbers, formulas, or functions. You also can use @CHOOSE to select formulas that vary in different situations. For example, the percentage rate used to compute depreciation under the Accelerated Cost Recovery System (ACRS) depreciation system varies with the useful life of the asset. Thus, an asset with a three-year life is depreciated in the first year of the asset's life at a rate different from that of an asset with a five-year life. A function like the following one dramatically simplifies the computation:

@CHOOSE(*year of life,rate for 3-year asset,rate for 5-year asset...*)

Tip

@CHOOSE selects the first argument in the list if *key* evaluates to zero. Be certain that you account for this either by adding an extra argument to your list or adjusting the key value. Consider the following formula:

@CHOOSE(@MOD(@DATE(*90,1,25*),*7*),*"Sun","Mon","Tue","Wed","Thu","Fri","Sat"*)

This formula returns the incorrect value of F r i instead of T h u. To correct the formula, move the "Sat" argument into position zero in the list.

Looking up Values: @VLOOKUP and @HLOOKUP

@VLOOKUP and @HLOOKUP are two variations of a basic LOOKUP function. As their names suggest, these functions, based on the value of a test variable, "look up" a value from a table. The forms of these functions are as follows:

@VLOOKUP(*test_variable,range,column_offset_number*)

@HLOOKUP(*test_variable,range,row_offset_number*)

A *test_variable* can be either a number or a string. The *range* should contain at least one partial row or column. The range can include the entire lookup table from the top left corner of the comparison column to the bottom right corner of the last data column. Alternatively, you can specify just the range of the lookup column or row. (You can use a range name for this argument instead of actual cell references.)

The third argument, called the *offset_number*, determines which data column supplies the data to the function. In every case, the comparison column, which is the first column in a vertical lookup table, has an offset-number of 0 (zero); the first data column has an offset-number of 1; and so on. An offset-number can be negative in Symphony, and the number can also exceed the number of columns or rows in the lookup table. (Some examples of negative and excessive offset-numbers are shown later.)

To use the lookup functions, you need a lookup table, which must consist of two or more adjacent partial rows or columns. An example of a numeric vertical lookup table is shown in figure 6.17.

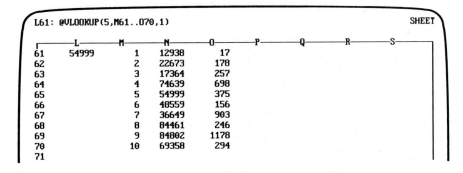

Fig. 6.17.
A numeric vertical lookup table.

Reminder:
The first column in a numeric vertical lookup table contains numbers arranged in ascending order.

What differentiates this table from a string vertical lookup table is the contents of the first column, M. In a numeric vertical lookup table, the comparison column contains numbers arranged in ascending order. In a string vertical lookup table, the comparison column can contain labels in any order.

In figure 6.17, the comparison column (M) contains the values that Symphony uses to look up the data shown in the second and third columns (N and O). To access this columnar table, you use the @VLOOKUP or *vertical lookup*, function.

In figure 6.17, the function @VLOOKUP(*5,M61..O70,1*) returns the value 54999. To return this result, Symphony searches the comparison column for the largest value that is not greater than the key (in this case, 5) and returns the corresponding value from the data column that has an offset number of 1 (in this case, column N). Remember that the comparison column has an offset number of 0. Column N, therefore, has an offset number of 1; column O has an offset number of 2.

Because the LOOKUP function does not search for a specific match, but for the largest value in the comparison column that is not greater than the key, the formula @VLOOKUP(*5.5,M61..O70,1*) also returns 54999. Similarly, a key of 100 returns 69358: the number corresponding to the largest value in the comparison column. If you use 0 as the key in this example, an ERR message appears because no key in the table is less than or equal to 0.

To return results form column O in figure 6.17, use an offset number of 2. For example, the function @VLOOKUP(*10,M61..O70,2*) returns the value 294.

Lookup tables must follow specific rules. As mentioned earlier, the comparison-column values for numeric lookups must be arranged in ascending order, and a comparison value cannot be repeated. For example, the lookup table in figure 6.18 does not work because the comparison values in column M are not in ascending order. The table in figure 6.19 is also not allowed because the value 5 is repeated.

Fig. 6.18.

Using comparison values that are not in ascending order.

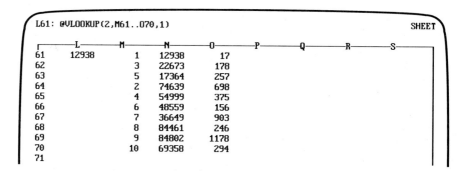

L61: @VLOOKUP(2,M61..O70,1)								SHEET
	L	M	N	O	P	Q	R	S
61	12938	1	12938	17				
62		3	22673	178				
63		5	17364	257				
64		2	74639	698				
65		4	54999	375				
66		6	48559	156				
67		7	36649	903				
68		8	84461	246				
69		9	84802	1178				
70		10	69358	294				
71								

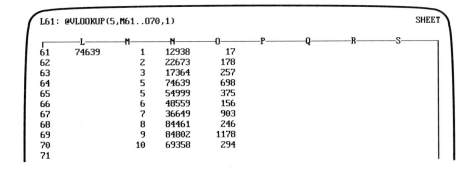

Fig. 6.19.
Using comparison values that repeat.

A modification of the table in figure 6.19 shows the effects of using a negative offset number. Using the formula @VLOOKUP(*5,N81..P90,–1*) for the vertical lookup table in figure 6.20, you can see that Symphony selects the appropriate value from the column just to the left of the lookup table. Here the value returned from the table lookup is **Shelf 8** (see cell L81).

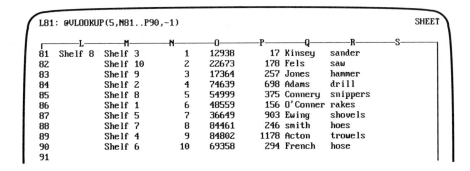

Fig. 6.20.
Using a negative offset number.

Similarly, an offset number that exceeds the last column in the lookup range is also acceptable. Figure 6.21 shows the result of setting the offset number to 4. In this case, the value returned is **snippers**, a value taken from the column that is two columns to the right of the rightmost column in the lookup table.

In addition to numeric-table lookups, Symphony also can perform string-table lookups. In performing string-table lookups, Symphony looks for a perfect match between a value in the comparison column and the key. For example, in figure 6.22, Symphony uses the function @VLOOKUP(*"Shelf 1",M81..P90,1*) to search for the value in column N corresponding to Shelf 1. Notice that the string argument is enclosed in double quotation marks in the @VLOOKUP statement.

Cue:
You can use negative offset numbers and numbers that exceed the number of columns in the lookup table to access other areas of the worksheet.

Fig. 6.21.

Using an offset number that exceeds the last column in the lookup table.

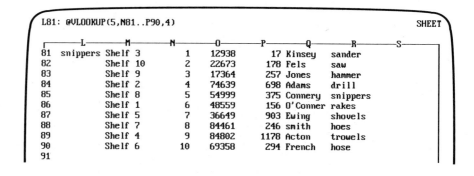

```
L81: @VLOOKUP(5,N81..P90,4)                                    SHEET
        L        M        N        O        P        Q        R        S
   81  snippers Shelf 3        1    12938       17 Kinsey   sander
   82           Shelf 10       2    22673      178 Fels     saw
   83           Shelf 9        3    17364      257 Jones    hammer
   84           Shelf 2        4    74639      698 Adams    drill
   85           Shelf 8        5    54999      375 Connery  snippers
   86           Shelf 1        6    48559      156 O'Conner rakes
   87           Shelf 5        7    36649      903 Ewing    shovels
   88           Shelf 7        8    84461      246 smith    hoes
   89           Shelf 4        9    84802     1178 Acton    trowels
   90           Shelf 6       10    69358      294 French   hose
   91
```

Fig. 6.22.

A string vertical lookup table.

```
L81: @VLOOKUP("Shelf 1",N81..P90,1)                           SHEET
        L        M        N        O        P        Q        R        S
   81       6 Shelf 3        1    12938       17 Kinsey   sander
   82         Shelf 10       2    22673      178 Fels     saw
   83         Shelf 9        3    17364      257 Jones    hammer
   84         Shelf 2        4    74639      698 Adams    drill
   85         Shelf 8        5    54999      375 Connery  snippers
   86         Shelf 1        6    48559      156 O'Conner rakes
   87         Shelf 5        7    36649      903 Ewing    shovels
   88         Shelf 7        8    84461      246 smith    hoes
   89         Shelf 4        9    84802     1178 Acton    trowels
   90         Shelf 6       10    69358      294 French   hose
   91
```

Reminder:

Use an offset value of 0 to return the position of the matched string in the comparison column.

If you use 0 as the offset number for the @VLOOKUP statement in figure 6.22, the value returned is 5. This number corresponds to the position of the matched string in the comparison column. The first entry (Shelf 3) is 0, the second entry (Shelf 10) is 1, and so on. If the search of the lookup table fails to produce a match, Symphony returns ERR.

The @HLOOKUP function is essentially the same as @VLOOKUP, except that @HLOOKUP operates on tables arranged across rows rather than down columns. The rules are the same as those for vertical tables. Look at an example of how the @HLOOKUP function works for a numeric lookup. (The same rules apply for a string lookup.) If you build the table in figure 6.23, the function @HLOOKUP(*5,L123..S125,1*) returns the value 567. The function @HLOOKUP(*8,L123..S125,1*) returns the value 890. And the function @HLOOKUP(*3,L123..S125,2*) returns the value 765.

A useful application for the @VLOOKUP and @HLOOKUP functions is the creation of tax tables that automatically retrieve the appropriate rate base on income. In fact, this application is the one for which the lookup function was originally developed. You also can use these functions for simple data management, such as handling inventory and employee lists, although these tasks can be performed better in Symphony with the database commands.

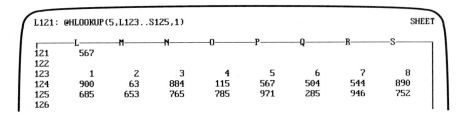

Fig. 6.23.
A numeric horizontal lookup table.

Retrieving Data from Specified Locations: @INDEX

The last data management function, @INDEX, is similar to the LOOKUP functions described in the previous section; however, @INDEX has some of its own unique features. The general form of the function is as follows:

@INDEX(*range,column_number,row_number*)

Like the LOOKUP functions, @INDEX works with a table of numbers. But unlike the LOOKUP functions, @INDEX does not use a test variable and a comparison column (or row). Instead, @INDEX requires you to indicate the column number and row number of the range from where you want to retrieve data. For example, if you use the function @INDEX(*L142..S145,3,2*) in figure 6.24, you get the value 2625.

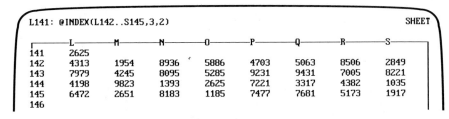

Fig. 6.24.
An example of @INDEX.

Notice that 0 corresponds to the first column, 1 corresponds to the second column, and so on. The same numbering scheme applies to rows. Therefore, using 3 for *column_number* and 2 for *row_number* indicates that you want the item from the fourth column, third row.

Although the behavior of the @VLOOKUP and @HLOOKUP functions may lead you to believe otherwise, with the @INDEX function you cannot use column and row numbers that fall outside *range*. Using negative numbers or numbers too large for the range causes Symphony to return the ERR message.

Reminder:

Use @INDEX when you know the exact position of a data item in a range of cells.

The @INDEX function is useful when you know the exact position of a data item in a range of cells and want to locate the item quickly. For instance, the @INDEX function works well for rate-quotation systems. Figure 6.25 shows an example of a system for quoting full-page magazine advertising rates.

Fig. 6.25.

Using @INDEX in a rate-quotation system.

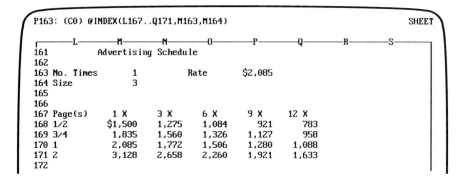

```
P163: (C0) @INDEX(L167..Q171,M163,M164)                          SHEET

       L       M       N       O       P       Q       R       S
161             Advertising Schedule
162
163 No. Times       1           Rate        $2,085
164 Size            3
165
166
167 Page(s)     1 X     3 X     6 X     9 X    12 X
168 1/2       $1,500   1,275   1,084     921     783
169 3/4        1,835   1,560   1,326   1,127     958
170 1          2,085   1,772   1,506   1,280   1,088
171 2          3,128   2,658   2,260   1,921   1,633
172
```

In this example, the function @INDEX(*L167..Q171,M163,M164*) returns a value of $2,085. This value corresponds to the amount in the first column and the second row of the index range. If you enter **6** in cell M163, the ERR message rather than a valid dollar amount appears.

Using Logical Functions

Symphony also includes logical functions. You can think of these as a subset of the mathematical functions. In all cases, Symphony analyzes logical functions as either TRUE or FALSE. If a logical function is TRUE, it has a numeric value of 1. If the logical function is FALSE, it has a numeric value of 0. The importance of a logical function's numeric value is clarified shortly.

Logical functions are advantageous because they enable you to build conditional tests into cells. These tests return different values depending on whether the tests are TRUE (1) or FALSE (0). Symphony's primary conditional function is @IF. Lotus has added several other logical functions, however, to increase the power of the program over earlier integrated packages (see table 6.1).

Creating Logical Statements: @IF

The general form of the @IF function is as follows:

@IF(*a,vtrue,vfalse*)

Table 6.1
Logical Functions

Function	Description
@IF(*cond,a,b*)	If *cond* is TRUE, then *a*; if *cond* is FALSE, then *b*
@ISERR(*cell reference*)	If *cell reference* contains ERR, then TRUE; otherwise, FALSE
@ISNA(*cell reference*)	If *cell reference* contains NA, then TRUE; otherwise, FALSE
@ISNUMBER(*cell reference*)	If *cell reference* contains a numeric value, then TRUE; otherwise, FALSE
@ISSTRING(*cell reference*)	If *cell reference* contains a string value, then TRUE; otherwise, FALSE
@TRUE	Returns a value of 1
@FALSE	Returns a value of 0

In this format, the first argument, *a*, is tested as TRUE or FALSE. If the result of the test is TRUE, @IF assigns the cell the value of the second argument, *vtrue*. If the result of the test is FALSE, @IF assigns the cell the value of the third argument, *vfalse*.

Reminder:

Use @IF to direct Symphony to do one thing if the condition is TRUE and another thing if the condition is FALSE.

Tip

@IF treats any nonzero number as TRUE. Although logical tests always return either 1 or 0, any number other than zero tests as TRUE. Thus, the formula @IF(–2,"Yes","No") evaluates –2 as TRUE and returns **Yes**.

Using Simple Logical Operators

In many instances, conditional functions require logical operators, which help to determine the relationship between two numbers or among several numbers. Following is a list of "simple" logical operators and their meanings:

Operator	Meaning
=	Equal
<	Less than
<=	Less than or equal to
>	Greater than
>=	Greater than or equal to
<>	Not equal

Simple logical operators have lower precedence than any mathematical operator, but all logical operators have equal precedence within their group.

As mentioned earlier, logical functions return either TRUE (1) or FALSE (0). *Conditional statements* follow the same line of reasoning. For example, the statement 5<3 is clearly FALSE, and the statement 16<27 is TRUE. Symphony's @IF function tests the conditional statement as either TRUE or FALSE, and then assigns a cell value based on the results of the test.

Following are examples of logical statements that use the @IF function, along with their English-language equivalents:

@IF(*B4>=450,B5,C7*)

If the value in cell B4 is greater than or equal to 450, then use the value in cell B5. Otherwise, use the value in cell C7.

@IF(*A3<A2,5,6*)

If the value in cell A3 is less than the value in cell A2, then assign the number 5. Otherwise, assign the number 6.

@IF(*G9<>B7,G5/9,G7*)

If the value in cell G9 is not equal to the value in cell B7, then use the value in cell G5 divided by 9. Otherwise, use the value in cell G7.

Reminder:

Surround string values with double quotation marks when you use them in logical functions.

@IF(*A9<>"January",45,"wrong entry"*)

If the value in cell A9 is not the string `January`, then assign number 45. Otherwise, assign the string `wrong entry`. Notice that if you enter a string value in cell A9, Symphony assigns either the *vtrue* or the *vfalse* argument. Note also that you must enter **"January"** with quotation marks in A9. If you enter a number in cell A9, or if the cell is left blank, Symphony returns the ERR indicator.

@IF(*@FALSE,"ok","not ok"*)

If FALSE (0), then assign `not ok`. Otherwise, assign `ok`. The value of this formula is always `not ok` because the value of @FALSE is always 0. This example emphasizes the numeric character of the @IF function.

Tip

Because @IF checks only for a nonzero numeric value, a formula like @IF(*A1,"Yes","No"*) returns `Yes` whenever cell A1 contains a numeric entry other than zero. Note, however, that entering a label (even a blank label) into A1 results in ERR. In the discussion of the @N and @S functions, you see how to correct this problem.

Using Complex Operators

Relationships get more complicated when another set of logical operators, the *complex operators*, is introduced:

Operator	Meaning
#NOT#	Not (logical)
#AND#	And (logical)
#OR#	Or (logical)

The complex logical operators have lower precedence than the simple logical operators. Among the complex operators, #AND# and #OR# have equal precedence; #NOT# has higher precedence. As you know, operators with higher precedence levels are evaluated first.

Reminder:
#NOT# has higher precedence than either #AND# or #OR#.

Using the complete set of logical operators, you can combine simple and complex operators to create the following @IF functions:

@IF(A1<>1#AND#G5="yes",E7,E6)

If the value in cell A1 is not equal to 1, *and* the value in cell G5 is **yes**, then use the value in cell E7. Otherwise, use the value in cell E6. The values in cells E6 and E7 can be either numbers or strings.

@IF(#NOT#(COST=50)#AND#A1=1,L10,K10)

If the amount entered in the cell named COST is *not* 50, *and* the value in cell A1 is equal to 1, then use the value in cell L10. Otherwise, use the value in cell K10.

Symphony's conditional functions are quite sophisticated. You can use the @IF function in a wide variety of instances to allow Symphony to make decisions. Figure 6.26 provides an example of how you can employ the @IF function.

Figure 6.26 shows a simple worksheet that summarizes a company's expenditures for the month of July 1990. Column A contains the date of each expenditure, and column B contains the amounts of the disbursements. Notice that column C has been labeled Code and that row 4 contains a sequence of numbers, beginning with 1 in column D and ending with 5 in column H. These numbers represent the various accounts to which the expenditures are charged. Now suppose that the following formulas are entered in the indicated cells:

D6	@IF($C6=D$4,$B6,0)
E6	@IF($C6=E$4,$B6,0)
F6	@IF($C6=F$4,$B6,0)

You can translate these formulas as: If the number in cell C6 (the code) equals the number in cell E4 (or cell F4) (the account), then enter the value in cell B6. Otherwise, enter 0.

Fig. 6.26.
A schedule of expenditures.

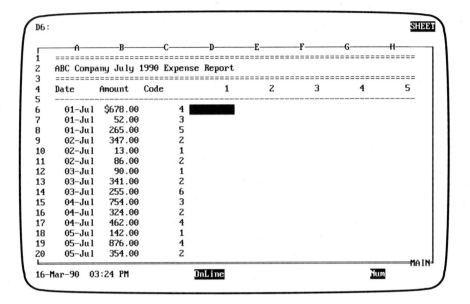

```
D6:                                                           SHEET
    ──A────────B────────C────────D────────E────────F────────G────────H──
1  ================================================================
2  ABC Company July 1990 Expense Report
3  ================================================================
4  Date      Amount   Code          1        2        3        4        5
5  ----------------------------------------------------------------
6  01-Jul    $678.00    4  ████████
7  01-Jul     52.00     3
8  01-Jul    265.00     5
9  02-Jul    347.00     2
10 02-Jul     13.00     1
11 02-Jul     86.00     2
12 03-Jul     90.00     1
13 03-Jul    341.00     2
14 03-Jul    255.00     6
15 04-Jul    754.00     3
16 04-Jul    324.00     2
17 04-Jul    462.00     4
18 05-Jul    142.00     1
19 05-Jul    876.00     4
20 05-Jul    354.00     2
                                                            ─MAIN─
   16-Mar-90  03:24 PM              OnLine                      Num
```

Assume that similar formulas exist in all the cells in range D6..H20. Suppose that you enter a code for each check recorded in column A. The code for each disbursement should be a number less than 6. With the proper codes entered, the result looks like figure 6.27.

Fig. 6.27.
Using @IF to check for matching accounts and codes.

```
D6: @IF($C6=D$4,$B6,0)                                       SHEET
    ──A────────B────────C────────D────────E────────F────────G────────H──
1  ================================================================
2  ABC Company July 1990 Expense Report
3  ================================================================
4  Date      Amount   Code          1        2        3        4        5
5  ----------------------------------------------------------------
6  01-Jul    $678.00    4    0.00     0.00     0.00   678.00     0.00
7  01-Jul     52.00     3    0.00     0.00    52.00     0.00     0.00
8  01-Jul    265.00     5    0.00     0.00     0.00     0.00   265.00
9  02-Jul    347.00     2    0.00   347.00     0.00     0.00     0.00
10 02-Jul     13.00     1   13.00     0.00     0.00     0.00     0.00
11 02-Jul     86.00     2    0.00    86.00     0.00     0.00     0.00
12 03-Jul     90.00     1   90.00     0.00     0.00     0.00     0.00
13 03-Jul    341.00     2    0.00   341.00     0.00     0.00     0.00
14 03-Jul    255.00     6    0.00     0.00     0.00     0.00     0.00
15 04-Jul    754.00     3    0.00     0.00   754.00     0.00     0.00
16 04-Jul    324.00     2    0.00   324.00     0.00     0.00     0.00
17 04-Jul    462.00     4    0.00     0.00     0.00   462.00     0.00
18 05-Jul    142.00     1  142.00     0.00     0.00     0.00     0.00
19 05-Jul    876.00     4    0.00     0.00     0.00   876.00     0.00
20 05-Jul    354.00     2    0.00   354.00     0.00     0.00     0.00
                                                            ─MAIN─
   16-Mar-90  03:27 PM              OnLine                      Num
```

Notice that in each cell, Symphony compares each code to the accounts located in row 4. In the cells where the code and account match, Symphony records the amount of the disbursement. In all the other cells, Symphony enters 0. This result is exactly what you can expect from the conditional tests used in the cells.

In a large worksheet with many formulas, you find that a large table of formulas like the one in figure 6.27 requires a long recalculation time. Chapter 17 shows you how to use the database statistical functions to summarize a series of entries without filling the worksheet with large tables of formulas.

Using Strings in Logical Functions

Strings create an additional level of complexity in Symphony's logical functions. When you use strings in conditional functions, you should know how Symphony reacts when you enter numbers or leave cells blank. The results can be quite different from those of similar numeric conditional tests. The cases that follow show some of the differences:

Cue:

Understand how Symphony treats numeric and string values differently.

In case 1, cell C1094 is left blank:

Function	Value Displayed On-Screen
@IF(*C1094="1"*, *"lambda"*, *"beta"*)	ERR
@IF(*C1094=1*, *"lambda"*, *"beta"*)	beta
@IF(*C1094=1#OR#C1094="1"*, *"lambda"*, *"beta"*)	ERR

In case 2, cell C1094 has the numeric value 1:

Function	Value Displayed On-Screen
@IF(*C1094="1"*, *"lambda"*, *"beta"*)	ERR
@IF(*C1094=1*, *"lambda"*, *"beta"*)	lambda
@IF(*C1094=1#OR#C1094="1"*, *"lambda"*, *"beta"*)	ERR

In case 3, cell C1094 has the string **1**:

Function	Value Displayed On-Screen
@IF(*C1094="1"*, *"lambda"*, *"beta"*)	beta
@IF(*C1094=1*, *"lambda"*, *"beta"*)	ERR
@IF(*C1094=1#OR#C1094="1"*, *"lambda"*, *"beta"*)	ERR

Some of these results may seem counterintuitive when you first look at them, particularly the final function in case 3. You might expect that Symphony would display **lambda** rather than the ERR message. These examples show, however, that you must have a good idea of what type of entry you are using in a logical function (numeric or string) before you use the entry. The discussion of the @ISSTRING, @ISNUMBER, and @CELL functions should help you evaluate entries. The discussion of the @S and @N functions can show you how to prevent the ERR result.

Using Error-Trapping Functions

Error-trapping functions test for and evoke NA and ERR messages in a worksheet. NA can be translated as **Not Available** and ERR as **Error**.

Using @NA and @ERR

If you have an instance in which you simply don't know what number to use for a value, but you don't want to leave the cell blank, you can use NA instead. Simply enter **@NA** in the cell. Symphony displays **NA** in that cell and in any other cell depending on that cell.

A problem you may run across, particularly when you set up templates for other people to use, is unacceptable values for cells. For example, suppose that you are developing a checkbook-balancing macro and want to make unacceptable those checks with values less than or equal to zero. One way to indicate nonacceptance of these kinds of checks is to use ERR to signal that fact. You might use the following version of the @IF formula:

@IF(*B9<=0,@ERR,B9*)

In simple English, this statement says that if the amount in cell B9 is less than or equal to zero, then display **ERR** on-screen; otherwise, display the amount. Notice that the @ERR function has been used to control the display in almost the same way as @NA.

Symphony also uses ERR as a signal when the program finds unacceptable numbers—for example, a division by zero or mistakenly deleted cells. ERR often shows up temporarily when you reorganize the cells in a worksheet. If errors persist, however, you may have to do some careful analysis to figure out why.

Just as for NA, Symphony displays **ERR** in any cells that depend on a cell with an ERR value. Sometimes many cells display **ERR** after you make only one or two small changes to a worksheet. To correct this problem, you must trace back down the chain of references to find the root of the problem.

Using @ISERR and @ISNA

@ISERR and @ISNA relate closely to the @ERR and @NA functions. @ISERR and @ISNA, commonly used with the @IF function, enable you to test a cell for the value ERR or NA.

Like the logical operators discussed earlier, the @ISERR and @ISNA functions are always either TRUE or FALSE. The function @ISERR(A1) is FALSE if cell A1 does not contain the value ERR, and TRUE if cell A1 is equal to ERR. Similarly, @ISNA(*A1*) is TRUE if A1 contains the value NA, and FALSE if the cell does not.

Tip

Although it may appear that @ISERR and @ISNA apply the same test as @IF(*A1=@ERR,1,0*) and @IF(*A1=@NA,1,0*), these two @IF formulas don't work. In both cases, the formulas evaluate to ERR, regardless of the value of cell A1. @ISERR and @ISNA are the only way you can check for ERR and NA.

You may want to use the @ISERR function frequently to keep ERR messages that result from division by zero from appearing in the worksheet. For example, at one time or another as you use Symphony, you will create a formula that divides a number by a cell reference, as in the following example:

23/A4

If A4 contains a value, the formula returns the value of the division. If A4 contains a label or a 0, or if A4 is blank, the function returns the value ERR. The ERR passes to other cells in the sheet, creating an unnecessary mess.

Using the following formula eliminates the ERR result:

@IF(*@ISERR(23/A4),0,23/A4*)

This function says that if the value of 23/A4 is ERR, then enter a 0 in this cell; otherwise, enter the value of the division 23/A4. The function effectively traps the ERR message and keeps it from displaying in the worksheet.

@ISNA works in much the same way. For example, the following formula tests cell A4 for the value NA:

@IF(*@ISNA(A4),0,A4*)

If the value of A4 is NA, the formula returns a 0. Otherwise, the formula returns the value in A4. You can use this type of formula to keep an NA message from spreading throughout a worksheet.

Cue:
Use @ISERR in an @IF formula to prevent an ERR result from propagating through a worksheet.

Determining the Aspect of a Cell: @ISSTRING and @ISNUMBER

Before you use the contents of a cell, you may want to test its *aspect*. One part of a cell's aspect is its type—whether the cell contains a number or a label or is empty. Other parts of a cell's aspect are its address (the row and column at which the cell resides), its label prefix (if any), the width of its column, and its format. Depending on the cell's aspect, you may want to use different methods to process the cell.

Symphony has several different functions for determining a cell's aspect. Which function you use depends on the particular situation. Symphony does, however, provide some redundancy in this area; usually, you can accomplish what you need to do in more than one way.

Two functions that determine the type of value stored in a cell are @ISSTRING and @ISNUMBER. Both of these functions are most often used with the @IF function, but you can use them with other functions as well.

You can use @ISNUMBER to verify whether a cell entry is a number. The general format of the function is as follows:

@ISNUMBER(*argument*)

If *argument* is a number, the numeric value of the function is 1 (TRUE). If *argument* is a string, including a blank (" ") string, the numeric value of the function is 0 (FALSE).

As a simple example, suppose that you want to test whether the value entered in cell B3 is a number. If the value is a number, you want to show the label **number** in the current cell; otherwise, you want to show the label **string**. To do this, use the following formula:

@IF(*@ISNUMBER(B3), "number", "string"*)

Reminder:

@ISNUMBER returns 1 (TRUE) if a number is in the referenced cell or if the referenced cell is blank.

With this function, you can be fairly certain that the appropriate label will appear in the current cell. But the @ISNUMBER function also gives blank cells a numeric value of 1. Obviously, the function is incomplete as it stands because it assigns the label **number** to the current cell if cell B3 is empty. Before the function is fully reliable, you must modify it to handle the case of blank cells.

At this point, consider using the @ISSTRING function. @ISSTRING works in nearly the same way as @ISNUMBER. @ISSTRING, however, determines whether a cell entry is a string value. The general format of the function is as follows:

@ISSTRING(*argument*)

Reminder:

@ISSTRING returns 1 (TRUE) if a string is in the referenced cell; if the referenced cell contains a number or blank, the function returns 0 (FALSE).

If *argument* is a string, then the value of the function is 1 (TRUE). If *argument* is a number or blank, however, the value of the function is 0 (FALSE). One nice feature of @ISSTRING is that it stops what Lotus calls the "ripple-through" effect of NA and ERR.

Returning to the earlier example that used @ISNUMBER, you can write a formula by using @ISSTRING to determine if B3 contains a string. Following is the formula:

@IF(*@ISSTRING(B3), "string", "number or blank"*)

The first step this formula performs is to test whether string data is in cell B3. If it is, the function assigns the label **string**. Otherwise, the formula assigns the label **number or blank**.

Notice that @ISNUMBER and @ISSTRING do not provide the means to determine the difference between blank cells and those that contain numeric entries. Another function, @CELL, *does* provide an accurate method of doing so.

Using Special Functions

These functions are included in a separate category because of their special power to give you detailed information about the contents and locations of cells (or ranges). The special functions include @CELL, @CELLPOINTER, @ROWS, @COLS, @@, @TRUE, @FALSE, and @APP.

Determining the Aspect of a Cell: @CELL

A more efficient way than @ISNUMBER or @ISSTRING to determine the aspect of a cell is to use the @CELL function. @CELL is one of the most comprehensive of Symphony's functions because it gives you many different options from which to choose. The general form of @CELL is as follows:

@CELL(*"string",range*)

The *string* is one of several words that indicates the aspect of the cell in which you are interested. Table 6.2 lists the values *string* can assume. The *range* represents a cell in the range format (such as A1..A1). If you use the single-cell format with @CELL, such as A1, Symphony returns ERR. If you specify a range larger than a single cell, Symphony evaluates the cell in the upper left corner of the range.

Tip

Symphony Releases 2.0 and later have a subtle but important change from earlier releases: @functions that required a range argument in earlier releases now automatically expand a single-cell entry such as A1 to the appropriate range entry A1..A1. The functions no longer return ERR if a single-cell argument is used.

Table 6.2 shows all the values the *string* argument can assume and the corresponding results from Symphony.

Table 6.2
@CELL String Arguments

String	Symphony Provides:
"address"	The address of the current cell expressed in absolute terms (for example, $G$19)
"contents"	The cell value
"row"	The row number (1 to 8192)
"col"	The column number (1 to 256)
"type"	The type of value stored in a cell: b Indicates a blank cell (even if the cell is formatted) v Indicates a number or numeric formula l Indicates a label or string formula
"prefix"	The label prefix of the current cell: ' Indicates a left-aligned label " Indicates a right-aligned label ^ Indicates a centered label | Indicates a special label such as a word processing format line or a page break blank Indicates a number, formula, or blank cell **Note:** A formula may be a label formula or a value formula.
"protect"	The protection status of the cell: 1 Indicates that the cell is protected 0 Indicates that the cell is unprotected
"width"	The column width of the column in which the cell resides (0 to 240) **Note:** Width may be different for each window.)
"format"	The numeric display format: G **G**eneral format F0 to F15 **F**ixed decimal (0 to 15 decimal places) P0 to P15 **P**unctuated (0 to 15 decimal places) (equivalent to 1-2-3's comma format) C0 to C15 **C**urrency (0 to 15 decimal places) S0 to S15 **S**cientific (0 to 15 decimal places) %0 to %15 **P**ercent (0 to 15 decimal places) D1 to D5 **D**ate (formats 1 to 5) T1 to T4 **T**ime (formats 1 to 4) L **L**iteral (equivalent to 1-2-3's **T**ext format) H **H**idden format

Following are some examples of how you can use the @CELL function:

@CELL(*"address", SALES*)

If the range named SALES is C187..E187, Symphony returns the absolute address $C$187. This feature provides a convenient way to list the upper left corner of a range's address in the worksheet. To list all the range names and their addresses, use the SHEET **R**ange **N**ame **T**able command.

@CELL(*"prefix", C195..C195*)

If the cell C195 contains the label `'Chicago`, Symphony returns ' (indicating left alignment). If cell C195 is blank, Symphony returns nothing; in other words, the current cell appears blank.

@CELL(*"format", A10*)

Symphony expands the second argument to A10..A10 and returns the format currently applied to cell A10.

@CELL(*"width", B12..B12*)

Symphony returns the width of column B in the current window, regardless of whether that width was set with the SHEET **W**idth command (for the individual column) or the SHEET **S**ettings **W**idth command (for the default column width).

@CELL(*"type", A1..A1*)

Symphony returns **b** if A1 is blank, **v** if A1 contains a number, or **l** if A1 contains a label. Notice that a cell that contains only a label prefix returns **l**, just as a cell with a 240-character label does.

Reminder:

Symphony returns the same "type" result for a cell that contains only a label prefix as it does for a cell with a long label.

Determining the Aspect of the Current Cell: @CELLPOINTER

The @CELLPOINTER function is similar to the @CELL function, except that @CELLPOINTER works with the current cell. The *current cell* is the cell where the cell pointer was located when the worksheet was last recalculated. The general format of the command is as follows:

@CELLPOINTER(*"string"*)

The strings you can use for this function are the same as those you use for @CELL (see table 6.2). For example, to determine the address of the current cell, you can enter in cell B22 **@CELLPOINTER("address")**. If recalculation is set to **A**utomatic, the value displayed in that cell is the absolute address $B$22. This same address remains until you make another entry elsewhere in the worksheet or press the Calc (F8) key. Either action recalculates the worksheet, changing the address that appears in cell B22 to reflect the position of the cell pointer when the worksheet recalculates. If recalculation is set to **M**anual, pressing Calc (F8) is the only action that causes the address to change.

Describing Ranges: @ROWS and @COLS

@ROWS and @COLS are two special functions that describe the dimensions of ranges. The general form of these commands is as follows:

@ROWS(*range*)

@COLS(*range*)

Suppose that you want to determine the number of columns in a range called EXPENSES and to display that value in the current cell. The function you enter is **@COLS(EXPENSES)**. Similarly, you can enter **@ROWS(EXPENSES)** to display the number of rows in the range.

Referring to Cells Indirectly: @@

The @@ function refers to the contents of one cell by way of another cell. The form of the function is as follows:

@@(*cell_address*)

The *cell_address* can be a single-cell address or a range name referring to a single cell. Thus, if cell B10 contains the label **A5**, and cell A5 contains the number 12000, the formula @@(B10) returns 12000.

Documenting Errors: @TRUE and @FALSE

Neither the @TRUE nor the @FALSE function requires an argument. The numeric value of @TRUE is 1; the numeric value of @FALSE is 0. In fact, the formula @TRUE*2 returns a value of 2 just as 1*2 does. Typically, the @TRUE and @FALSE functions are used with @IF and @CHOOSE, mainly for documentation purposes. For example, the function @IF(*B3<30,@TRUE,@FALSE*) is exactly equivalent to @IF(*B3<30,1,0*). The @TRUE and @FALSE functions provide better documentation than their numeric counterparts.

Determining whether an Add-In Program Is Attached: @APP

Symphony has a function, @APP, which has never been officially documented by Lotus Development Corporation. This function is used to determine if an add-in application is attached. The function takes the following form:

> @APP("*add_in*","*optional_message_if_attached*")

or

> @APP("*add_in*",*value_if_true*)

If the add-in program specified by *add_in* is attached, the function returns a TRUE value and displays the optional message. If the add-in is not attached, the function returns ERR. This function seems to be designed for use in a macro to determine whether a necessary add-in has been attached. The following macro, for example, checks to make sure that the MACROMGR.APP add-in is attached. If it is not the macro attaches the add-in:

> {IF @ISERR(@APP("MACROMGR",""))}{S}aaMACROMGR~Q

Notice that the optional message is not used because it would serve no purpose in the macro. You must, however, include a value for the function to return if the add-in is attached. That value can be a null—just two quotation marks together ("") as shown in the macro.

Although undocumented features are often changed or deleted by the manufacturer, you can feel relatively safe using @APP. Lotus Development Corporation recommends its use as the means of determining if add-ins are attached. Following is a list of some of the most common add-in programs used with Symphony; the string you use with @APP is given as well as a brief description of the program:

String	*Add-in Program*
ALLWAYS	ALLWAYS spreadsheet publishing
BASE	@BASE disk-based database manager
BASEFUNC	@DB functions for @BASE
BASEOPT	Options for the @BASE Option Pac
BASEOPTF	@NDX functions for @BASE Option Pac
BASEUTL	Utilities for @BASE
DOS	MS-DOS shell
INPUT	Range input
MACROMGR	Macro Manager
NETFILE	Network functions
OUTLINER	Text outliner
SPELLER	Spell checker
STAT	Statistical analysis
VIEWER	Lotus Magellan file viewer
VT100	VT100 terminal emulation

Using String Functions

Symphony has a variety of functions that give you significant power to manipulate strings. These string functions are especially useful when you perform database queries. When you use Symphony's string functions, however, be particularly careful not to mix data types. For instance, some functions produce strings, and other functions produce numeric results. You must be careful not to combine functions from these two different groups unless you have taken all the necessary precautions. The proper techniques for mixing data types are discussed throughout this section on string functions.

One other thing to consider about string functions is the numbering scheme used for the positions of characters in a label. These positions are numbered beginning with zero and continuing to a number that corresponds to the last character in the label. For example, the following illustration shows the position numbers for a long label:

```
                1111111111122222
      01234567890123456789901234
      'two chickens in every pot
```

Notice that the label prefix (') at the beginning of the label does not have a position number; the prefix is not considered part of the label. You cannot have a character in a negative position number. The importance of position numbers becomes clear in the next section.

Locating the Position of One String within Another: @FIND

One of the simplest string functions is @FIND. It is also one of the most convenient functions for explaining the use of position numbers in strings. You can use @FIND to locate the starting position of one string within another string. The general format of @FIND is as follows:

@FIND(*search_string,overall_string,start_number*)

Suppose that you want to find the position at which the string `every` occurs in the string `two chickens in every pot`. *search_string* is the string you want to locate. In the example, `every` is the search_string. *overall_string* is the target string to be searched. In the example, `two chickens in every pot` is the overall_string. Finally, *start_number* is the position number in *overall_string* where you want to start the search. Suppose that you want to start the search at position 6. If the overall_string you are searching is located in cell B5, the function you use is this:

@FIND(*"every",B5,6*)

The result of this example is the number 16, which is the starting position of the first (and only) occurrence of *every* in the overall_string. If the search_string *every* had not been found in the overall_string, Symphony would have returned ERR.

Notice that in this example the choice of a start_number of 6 had no bearing on the outcome of the function. You could just as easily have chosen 0, or any other number less than or equal to 16. If *every* appears more than once in the overall_string, however, you can use *start_number* to locate the search_string's occurrence elsewhere. Suppose that the following overall_string appears in cell B5:

    'two chickens in every pot, two cars in every garage

Also suppose that you want to locate all the occurrences of **every** in the overall_string. You can start with the function @FIND(*"every",B5,0*). Just as before, this formula returns a value of 16. You can then change the start-number by adding 1 to the result of the original formula (as in 1 + 16 = 17). The appropriate formula is then @FIND(*"every",B5,17*). This formula returns the number 39, which is the starting location of the second occurrence of *every*. Next, add 1 to the second result (1 + 39 = 40) and use @FIND(*"every",B5,40*). The result of this function is ERR. When you see the ERR message, you can be sure that you have found all the occurrences of the search_string.

One rule to remember about @FIND, and generally about strings, is that the maximum number of characters in a string is 240. Another rule is that Symphony truncates the start-number to a whole number if the number includes a decimal portion.

Remember:
The start_number *argument can be only whole numbers; Symphony truncates any decimals.*

You also should be aware that @FIND does not perform approximate searching as does the DOC **S**earch command. In the preceding example, if you use a search_string of **Every** rather than **every**, you get the ERR message and not a number value. See Chapter 9 for more information about the DOC **S**earch command.

Extracting One String from Another: @MID

Whereas @FIND helps you to locate one string within another, the @MID function lets you extract one string from another. This operation is called *substringing*. The general form of the function is as follows:

    @MID(*string,start_position,length*)

start_position is a number representing the character position in *string* where you want to start extracting characters. *length* indicates the number of characters you want to extract. For example, if you want to extract the first name from a label containing the full name **Laura Mann**, you can use @MID("Laura Mann",0,5). This function extracts the string starting in position 0 (the first character) and continuing for a length of five characters.

Suppose that you have a column containing a list of full names, and you want to extract the first and last names, putting them into separate columns. To accomplish this task, use the @MID and @FIND functions together. Because you know a blank space always separates the first and last names, you can use @FIND to locate the position of the blank in each full name. With this value, you can then set up the functions to extract the first and last names.

Suppose that cell A1 contains the full name `Gerald Frankel`. In cell B1, you place the following formula:

@MID(*A1,0,@FIND(" ",A1,0)*)

The value of this formula is `Gerald` because @FIND(*" ",A1,0*) returns a value of 6 for the *length* argument. Next, you place in column C the following formula:

@MID(*A1,@FIND(" ",A1,0)+1,99*)

In this formula, you are indicating that *start_position* is one character beyond the blank space. The *length* argument is specified as 99 characters. Obviously, using a length of 99 is overkill, but Symphony does not penalize you for this excess. The string that Symphony extracts is `Frankel`.

Now that you have seen how to use the @MID and @FIND functions to separate first and last names, you may want to try using these functions in a case with a name containing a middle initial.

Extracting Strings: @LEFT and @RIGHT

@LEFT and @RIGHT, special variations of the @MID function, are used to extract one string of characters from another, beginning at the leftmost or rightmost position in the underlying string. The general format of the functions is as follows:

@LEFT(*string,length*)

@RIGHT(*string,length*)

The *length* argument is the number of character positions that you want to extract from *string*. For example, if you are given the string `Cincinnati, Ohio 45243`, and you want to extract the ZIP code, you can use @RIGHT("Cincinnati, Ohio 45243",5).

@LEFT works the same way as @RIGHT, except that @LEFT extracts from the beginning of a string. For instance, you can extract the city in the previous example by using @LEFT(*"Cincinnati, Ohio 45243",10*).

Replacing Characters in a String: @REPLACE

The @REPLACE function removes a group of characters from a string and replaces the characters with another string. @REPLACE uses the same numbering scheme as @FIND. That is, @REPLACE numbers the character positions in a string starting with 0 and continuing to the end of the string (up to a maximum of 239). The general form of the command is as follows:

@REPLACE(*original_string,start_number,length,replacement_string*)

The *start_number* argument indicates the position where Symphony is to start removing characters in the *original_string*. *length* indicates how many characters to remove, and *replacement_string* contains the new characters that will replace the removed ones. For example, suppose that the string `Now is the time for all good men` appears in cell C1, and you want to replace *men* with *people*. The function to use is this:

@REPLACE(*C1,29,3,"people"*)

Instead of starting at 0 and counting up the 30 positions of the *start_number*, you may want to use the @FIND function. For instance, you can enter this formula:

@REPLACE(*C1,@FIND("men",C1,0),3,"people"*)

Cue:
Use @FIND to locate the starting position in a string rather than counting the characters.

This example is just one of many in which combining functions can save you much time and effort.

Finding the Length of a String: @LENGTH

The @LENGTH function simply returns the length of a string. The general form of the function is as follows:

@LENGTH(*string*)

For example, if cell E9 contains the string `Credit policy`, the value of @LENGTH(E9) is 13. Suppose that, in the same worksheet, cell J6 contains the following formula:

+E9&" "&"respondents"

The value of @LENGTH(J6) is 25.

A rule to remember about the @LENGTH function is that the length of numeric strings, as well as empty cells, is ERR. Empty strings (that is, cells that contain only a label prefix) have a length of 0.

Reminder:
If you use @LENGTH on numeric strings and empty cells, the result is ERR; empty strings have a length of 0.

Comparing Strings: @EXACT

The @EXACT function compares two strings. If the strings are alike, @EXACT returns a value of 1. If the strings are not alike, the function returns a value of 0. The general form of the function is as follows:

@EXACT(*string1,string2*)

The method of comparison for @EXACT is similar to the = operator you use in formulas. But whereas the = operator checks for an approximate match, the @EXACT function checks for an exact match. For example, if cell A2 contains the string `Marketing Function`, and cell B2 contains the string `marketing function`, the numeric value of A2=B2 is 1 because the two strings are an approximate match. Conversely, the numeric value of @EXACT(A2,B2) is 0 because the two functions are not an exact match.

You must remember one rule when you use @EXACT: You cannot use the function to compare nonstring arguments. For instance, if you are comparing two cells—A2, which is empty, and B2, which contains a valid string—the value of @EXACT(*A2,B2*) is ERR. In fact, if either argument is a nonstring value of any type (including numbers), Symphony returns the ERR message.

Converting Case: @LOWER, @UPPER, and @PROPER

Symphony offers three different functions for converting the case of a string value. First, @LOWER converts all the letters in a string to lowercase. If letters are already in lowercase, they remain so. For instance, if cell B3 contains the string `ALL iN GooD tiME`, the value of @LOWER(*B3*) is `all in good time`.

@UPPER, nearly the opposite of @LOWER, converts all the letters in a string to uppercase. For example, the value of @UPPER(*"ALL iN GooD tiME"*) is `ALL IN GOOD TIME`.

@PROPER capitalizes the first letter in each word of a label and converts all other letters in each word to lowercase. (*Words* are defined as groups of characters separated by blank spaces.) For example, the value of @PROPER(*"when IS tHE meeTING?"*) is `When Is The Meeting?`

As you might expect, @UPPER, @LOWER, and @PROPER do not work with nonstring values. For instance, if the cell referenced by these functions contains a number, Symphony returns ERR for each of these functions.

Repeating Labels: @REPEAT

@REPEAT repeats strings within a cell, in much the same way as the backslash (\) repeats characters. But @REPEAT has some distinct advantages over the backslash. The general form of the function is as follows:

@REPEAT(*string,number*)

The *number* argument indicates how many times you want to repeat *string* in a cell. For example, if you want to repeat the string C O G S three times, enter **@REPEAT("COGS",3)**. The resulting string is C O G S C O G S C O G S. @REPEAT follows Symphony's rule for long labels. That is, if the width of a column is 9 (the default column width), the string displays beyond the rightmost boundary of the column, provided no entry is in the cell to the right. The technique for repeating labels with the \ is different from that of @REPEAT. With \, Symphony fills the column exactly to the existing column width.

By using the @CELL and @LENGTH functions, you can set up a formula to fill a cell almost exactly. If A3 is the cell you want to fill by repeating the string C O G S, the first step is to enter **@CELL("width",A3..A3)** in an out-of-the-way cell, say K4. The next step is to enter **@LENGTH("COGS")** in another distant cell, like K5. Then enter **@REPEAT("COGS",K4/K5)** in cell A3. If the width of column A is 9 (the default column width), the label that appears in cell A3 is C O G S C O G S. Notice that because @REPEAT uses only the integer portion of the number argument, C O G S is repeated only twice rather than 2.25 times.

Eliminating Unwanted Blank Spaces: @TRIM

The @TRIM function trims unwanted blank spaces from a string. The spaces may occur at the beginning, end, or middle of a string. If more than one consecutive space occurs in the middle of a string, Symphony removes all but one of the blank spaces. For instance, if the string " When in the course of human · events " resides in cell A3, @TRIM(*A3*) appears as "When in the course of human events". Notice that the extra blank spaces have been removed. Notice also that the value of @LENGTH(A3) is 40, and the value of @LENGTH(*@TRIM(A3)*) is 34. (For trimming other characters besides blank spaces, see the following section on @CLEAN.

Removing Unwanted Characters: @CLEAN

Sometimes when you receive strings during a communications session, the strings arrive with nonprintable characters (ASCII codes below 32) interspersed throughout. The @CLEAN function removes the nonprintable characters from the strings. The general format of the function is as follows:

@CLEAN(*string*)

You also can use @CLEAN to remove the carriage-return characters from a string created in a DOC window. (A carriage-return symbol is the equivalent of an ASCII/LICS code 13.) Before you use in a concatenation formula or a function a string you created in a DOC window, it's a good practice to use @CLEAN first.

> **Tip**
>
> @CLEAN only removes characters below ASCII 32; it does not remove extra spaces (which are ASCII character 32). To completely clean up a string, you may have to use both @CLEAN and @TRIM.

Converting Strings to Numbers and Numbers to Strings

Two of the most important and powerful functions that Symphony offers are @STRING and @VALUE. The @STRING function converts a number to a string, and @VALUE changes a string to a number.

Converting Numbers to Strings: @STRING

You can use @STRING to override Symphony's automatic right-justification of numbers and to display a number justified to the left. The general form of the @STRING function is as follows:

@STRING(*number_to_convert,decimal_places*)

Because Symphony uses the fixed-decimal display format for the @STRING function, the *decimal_places* argument represents the number of places you want to display in the string. For example, if the *number_to_convert* argument is 9.482 and resides in cell J7, you can enter **@STRING(J7,2)** in the current cell. The result of this function is the string 9.48, displayed with left justification.

If the *number_to_convert* argument is 9.478 rather than 9.482, Symphony rounds the number to 9.48 and displays it as a left-justified label.

> **Tip**
>
> Although @STRING displays its results as though they were left-justified labels, if you edit the cell containing the @STRING formula and press the Calc (F8) key while still in EDIT mode, the formula converts to a numeric value instead of a string unless you manually add a label prefix before you press Enter. This is different from the action of most other string functions.

If you want to display a number in its string version with a percent sign or punctuated format, you can use the CONTENTS command from the Symphony Command Language. See Chapter 22 for more information on the CONTENTS command.

Converting Strings to Numbers: @VALUE

You may want to use the @VALUE function when you have been entering labels in a FORM window but later decide that you prefer to use the data as numbers. For example, suppose that you enter part numbers and their quantities, using Label as the default setting. (If you are not familiar with the FORM window at this point, see Chapter 17.) The information on part numbers works fine in the label format, but you want to change the format of the quantity data in order to sum different part quantities. You can convert the quantity data with @VALUE. The general form of the function is as follows:

@VALUE(*string*)

If cell K11 contains a database entry for the quantity data in the string format, you can enter @VALUE(*K11*) in an out-of-the-way cell in the worksheet, say Z11. If the string in cell K11 is **23**, then the number displayed in cell Z11 is **23**. You can now use the number in cell Z11 in any kind of numeric operation. For more examples of converting database entries, see Chapter 17.

Another nice feature of @VALUE is that besides converting strings that appear in the standard number format (for example, 23.445), you can also convert strings with fractions and with numbers displayed in scientific format. For example, if cell T10 contains the string **12 31/32**, @VALUE(*T10*) appears as **12.96875**. If cell T10 contains the string **12 54/32**, @VALUE still performs the appropriate conversion of the string to the number **13.6875**. Similarly, if a number is displayed as the string **1.37E+1**, @VALUE converts the string to the number **13.7**.

Reminder:
@VALUE converts string fractions into actual numbers.

You should remember a few rules when you use @VALUE. First, if you leave extra spaces in a string, Symphony does not object. The program, however, has trouble with some extra characters, although trailing percent signs and currency signs (such as $) that precede the string are okay. Experiment with different character signs to see how Symphony reacts. Finally, if you use numbers as the argument for @VALUE, Symphony simply returns the original number value.

Converting Numeric Values to String Values and Vice Versa: @N and @S

The ability to combine string and numeric arguments in one formula is sometimes useful. Ordinarily, Symphony does not allow you to combine such arguments; instead, the program returns an error. The way around this "error" problem is to use the @N or @S functions. The general form of these functions is as follows:

@N(*cell_range*)

@S(*cell_range*)

Although Symphony looks only at the upper left corner cell of the range argument, you must specify the argument as a range.

This process becomes particularly useful in a database report (see Chapter 17). You may want to use a formula to refer to a field that contains either a string value or nothing. If you use the formula +B20, and B20 is empty, the formula returns a 0. If you use the formula @S(*B20..B20*), however, Symphony evaluates that formula as a blank.

Similarly, you can use @N to give you either the cell's numeric value or 0 (if the cell contains a label, string formula, or nothing). Because both @N and @S require a range argument, Symphony automatically changes a single-cell argument into a range; that is, @N(*A1*) becomes @N(*A1..A1*).

Using Functions with the Lotus International Character Set

Reminder:

LICS is a character set created by Lotus; the code numbers may differ from ASCII code numbers.

Symphony offers a few special functions for interfacing with the Lotus International Character Set (LICS), what Lotus calls "an extension of the ASCII printable character set." (Be aware that the ASCII code number for a given character may not correspond to its LICS code number, although characters in the "normal" ASCII character set between 32 and 127 are the same.) You can best think of the LICS as a new character set created by Lotus and superimposed on top of the ASCII character set.

The complete set of LICS characters is listed at the back of the Symphony reference manual and includes everything from the copyright sign to the lowercase e with the grave accent (è). More characters are available than you will probably ever use, but you should know how to use them if the need ever arises.

Producing LICS Characters: @CHAR

You can use the @CHAR function to produce on-screen the LICS equivalent of a number between 0 and 255. The general form of the function is as follows:

> @CHAR(*number*)

Suppose that you want to make the cent sign (¢) appear on the screen. You can enter **@CHAR(162)** in a cell, and the cent sign appears. What is more, you can use a string formula to concatenate the cent sign to a number. For instance, you can enter the formula **+"12"&&@CHAR(162)** to produce the string **12¢**.

You should remember two simple rules when using @CHAR. First, if the numeric argument you are using is not between 1 and 255, Symphony returns the ERR message. Second, if the argument is not an integer, Symphony disregards the noninteger portion of the argument.

> ### Tip
>
> For most of the "international" or "extended" character-set symbols, the Symphony reference manual also lists compose sequences. Compose sequences are sets of keystrokes you can use to produce the desired character. The cent sign ¢, for example, can be produced by pressing the Compose (Alt-F1) key followed by the letter C and the vertical bar (|). You can use the Compose method of creating international characters to add them to labels or string formulas.

Using Nonprintable Characters in the LICS

Be aware that not all the LICS characters are printable, nor do they always show up on-screen. More specifically, LICS codes 1 through 31 are the problem. Because these codes include all the characters necessary for making boxes and arrows in Symphony, you may want to gain access to these characters. You can do so in one of two ways.

First, you can use the Edit (F2) key while you are in a SHEET window. Start with a SHEET window in a new worksheet. Use the **R**ange **F**ill command to enter the numbers 1 through 31, starting in cell B1 and moving down column B. Move to cell A1 and enter **@CHAR(B1)**; copy this formula down column A. Finally, use **R**ange **V**alues to convert the cells in column A to their actual string values. Even though the cells in column A appear blank, you can see the characters by moving the cell pointer to any cell in column A and pressing Edit (F2). Figure 6.28 shows how the screen should appear.

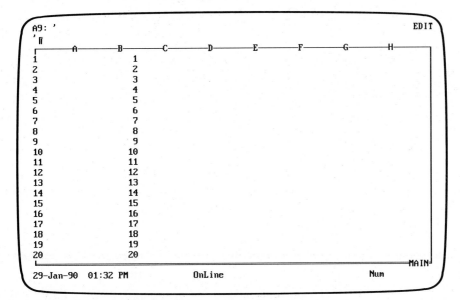

Fig. 6.28.

Viewing the nonprintable LICS characters.

Another way to see the nonprintable characters is to start with the SHEET window as it appears in figure 6.28 and change the window to a DOC window. In a DOC window, you can see all the nonprintable characters corresponding to ASCII/LICS codes 1 to 31. You can use these characters in a DOC window, but because they are nonprintable, only blanks appear when you try to print the characters. Be aware, however, that many of these characters are used as printer-control codes. Printing a Symphony range which contains these characters may produce unexpected results.

Finding the LICS Code Number: @CODE

Reminder:

@CHAR displays a code number as a LICS character; @CODE returns the code number of a LICS character.

The @CODE function is nearly the opposite of @CHAR. @CHAR takes a number between 0 and 255 and returns an ASCII/LICS character; @CODE goes the other way. That is, it examines an ASCII/LICS character and returns a number between 0 and 255. The general form of the function is as follows:

@CODE(*string*)

Suppose that you want to find the ASCII/LICS code number for the letter *a*. Enter **@CODE("a")** in a cell, and Symphony returns the number 97. If you enter **@CODE("aardvark")**, Symphony still returns 97, the code of the first character in the string.

If you specify a number as the argument for @CODE (expressed as a number and not a string), Symphony returns the ERR message.

Using Date and Time Functions

One of Symphony's most advanced features is its capability to manipulate dates and times. You can use this feature for such things as mortgage analysis, aging of accounts receivable, and time management.

Understanding Symphony's Serial-Numbering System

Reminder:

Symphony represents dates as serial numbers starting with January 1, 1900.

All aspects of Symphony's date-handling capability are based on the way Symphony represents any given date as a serial integer equal to the number of days from December 31, 1899, to the date in question. With this scheme, January 1, 1900, is represented by the number 1; January 2, 1900, is represented by the number 2; and so on. The maximum date that Symphony can handle is December 31, 2099, represented by the serial number 73050.

Symphony's time-handling capability is based on fractions of serial numbers. For instance, 8:00 A.M. is represented by the decimal fraction 0.333333 (or 1/3). Similarly, the decimal fraction for 10:00 P.M. is 0.916666. Symphony's serial-numbering system allows you to devise an overall number representing both date and time. The following chart shows several examples of dates and times, and the serial number that represents both:

Date	Time	Serial Number
January 3, 1900	01:00 A.M.	3.041666666
December 9, 1935	12:00 P.M.	13127.5
December 9, 1935	12:00 A.M.	13127
June 25, 1984	09:21 A.M.	30858.38958
December 31, 2099	11:00 P.M.	73050.95833

Note: Symphony uses the convention of calling noon 12:00 PM and midnight 12:00 AM. You can see this difference in the chart.

The serial-numbering system enables you to manipulate dates and times just as you would any other number in Symphony. For example, after setting the beginning date for a project and adding to that date the number of days that the project should take, you can easily determine the completion date. Working with time values is just as easy. For example, you can set up a complete schedule for the day by dividing it into hour increments.

Using Date Functions

Symphony's date functions include @DATE, @DATEVALUE, @DAY, @MONTH, @YEAR, and @NOW.

Converting a Date to an Integer: @DATE

Perhaps the most commonly used date function is @DATE. This function enables you to change a date to an integer that Symphony can interpret. The form of the @DATE function is as follows:

> @DATE(*year_number,month_number,day_number*)

Here are some examples showing how you can use the @DATE function:

- @DATE(*55,12,30*) =   20453
- @DATE(*12,1,1*) =   4384
- @DATE(*C7,C8,D10*) =   integer equivalent of the date represented by the cells C7, C8, and D10. If the cells contain the values 83, 12, and 25, respectively, the function has the value 30675.

Reminder:
Use @DATE to change a date into an integer that Symphony can interpret.

The numeric arguments have certain restrictions. *year_number* must be between 0 (indicating the year 1900) and 199 (the year 2099). *month_number* must be between 1 and 12. *day_number* must be one of the actual values for a given month (for example, 30 days for September and 31 days for December). Symphony truncates all but the integer portion of each numeric argument.

Once Symphony has interpreted a date as an integer, you can use the **F**ormat command to display the date in a more recognizable way (such as 06/26/90). For a discussion of Symphony's date and time formats, see the sections in this chapter entitled "Displaying Dates" and "Displaying Times." Chapter 5 discusses the formatting options in greater detail.

Converting a String to a Date: @DATEVALUE

Reminder:

@DATEVALUE accepts a date string and converts it to an integer.

@DATEVALUE is a variant of @DATE because, like @DATE, @DATEVALUE produces a serial number from the month, day, and year information you provide. But unlike @DATE, which expects numeric arguments, @DATEVALUE accepts a string as the argument. The general form of the function is as follows:

@DATEVALUE(*date_string*)

The *date_string* must be in any one of the available **D**ate formats—D1, D2, D3, D4, or D5. (See "Displaying Dates" later in this chapter.) If the string conforms to one of the formats, Symphony displays the appropriate serial integer. The following chart lists examples of the various date strings that @DATEVALUE accepts and the resulting integer.

Date Format	Function	Number
D1	@DATEVALUE("26-JUN-90")	33050
D2	@DATEVALUE("26-JUN")	33050
D3	@DATEVALUE("JUN-90")	33025
D4	@DATEVALUE("09/12/90")	33128
D5	@DATEVALUE("09/12")	33128

Notice that for the second example, Symphony supplies 90 as the year. Symphony uses the DOS system date to determine the missing year. In the third example, notice that Symphony defaults to the first day in June for the day value. You may prefer to enter the *date_string* in one of what Lotus calls the International date formats. (These formats are called D4 and D5 in Symphony. See the section entitled "Displaying Dates.")

Extracting the Day, Month, or Year

The functions @DAY, @MONTH, and @YEAR enable you to extract parts of a date in integer form. Consider these examples:

@DAY(*33206*) = 29

@MONTH(*33206*) = 11

@YEAR(*33206*) = 90

The three functions, taken together, are nearly the reverse of the @DATE function because they convert the integer format back into Gregorian format. You can use these functions for various time-related chores, such as aging accounts receivable and setting up a table for amortizing a loan.

Displaying Dates

The five date functions discussed thus far are extremely useful for entering dates in the worksheet in a form that Symphony can understand. But the results of these functions are integers that don't *look* like dates and are therefore hard to comprehend. For example, do you know the dates represented by the numbers 30124 and 32988?

The SHEET **F**ormat **D**ate command enables you to display these integers in one of the following five arrangements (Lotus calls them D1 through D5):

Number	Arrangement	Example
D1	DD-MMM-YY	26-Jun-90
D2	DD-MMM	26-Jun
D3	MMM-YY	Jun-90
D4	MM/DD/YY	06/26/90
D5	MM/DD	06/26

For all these examples, the integer displayed in the worksheet before formatting is 33206.

Notice that option D1 creates a string that is nine characters long—too long to be displayed in a column with the default width of nine. In general, you must expand to 10 or more characters any column containing dates formatted in the DD-MMM-YY format. Because you can display the other date formats in columns of normal width, you can frequently use these formats in place of the more detailed, but wider D1 format.

The default separation character for the International date formats (D4 and D5) is / (for example, 6/26/90). But you can also use periods or dashes as the separation characters. To specify that you want to use something other than the default setting for the International formats, however, you must modify one of the configuration settings. To modify the setting, use the SERVICES **C**onfiguration **O**ther **I**nternational **D**ate command; then you can select the format you like.

Suppose that you want to enter the *date_string* argument for the @DATEVALUE function in D4 (MM/DD/YY) format. If you enter **@DATEVALUE("6/26/90")**, Symphony displays the number **33206**. If you enter **@DATEVALUE("6-26-90")**, Symphony returns the ERR message. (Symphony does not expect the dash as the separation character unless you change the configuration settings.)

Returning Today's Date and Time: @NOW

The @NOW function returns today's date and time as an integer representing the number of days since December 31, 1899, and a fraction representing the time elapsed since 12:00 A.M.. This function takes advantage of an IBM PC's (and compatible's) timekeeping capability. If your computer has a clock that automatically supplies the date and time, or if you enter the date and time when prompted by DOS at the start of the day, the @NOW function gives you access to the system date and time in the current worksheet. For example, if you enter the date 6-26-90 in response to the DOS date prompt and 16:00 to the DOS time prompt (corresponding to 4:00 P.M.), the @NOW function has the value 33206.66.

Because the @NOW function depends on the PC DOS or MS-DOS system date and time, unless your machine has a system clock you must always remember to enter at least the date, and more preferably the date and time, in response to the operating-system prompt before you enter Symphony. (If you want to modify the operating system date and time in midsession, see the discussion on exiting to DOS in "Making Backup Copies of Files" in Chapter 7.)

Using Time Functions

As mentioned earlier in this chapter, time is expressed in fractions of serial numbers between 0 and 1. For example, 0.5 is equal to 12 hours (or 12:00 P.M.). Think of Symphony as a military timekeeper. That is, 10:00 P.M. in normal time is 22:00 in military time.

Symphony's timekeeping system may seem a little awkward at first, but you will get used to it quickly. Here are some general guidelines:

1 hour	=	0.041666
1 minute	=	0.000694
1 second	=	0.000011

Converting Time Values to Serial Numbers: @TIME

The @TIME function displays a serial number for a specified time of day. The general form of the function is as follows:

@TIME(*hour_number,minute_number,second_number*)

Here are some examples of how you can use @TIME:

@TIME(*3,12,30*) =   0.133680

@TIME(*23,0,0*) =   0.958333

@TIME(*C7,C8,D10*) =   integer equivalent of the time represented by cells C7, C8, and D10. If the cells contain the values 23, 12, and 59, respectively, the function has the value 0.967349.

The numeric arguments have certain restrictions. *hour_number* must be between 0 and 23. Both *minute_number* and *second_number* must be between 0 and 59. Symphony truncates all but the integer portion of each numeric argument.

Once Symphony has interpreted a time as a fraction of a serial number, you can use the **F**ormat command to display the time in a more recognizable way (for example, 10:42 P.M.). See the section entitled "Displaying Times" for a discussion of Symphony's time formats. Chapter 5 discusses the formatting options in greater detail.

Converting a String to a Time: @TIMEVALUE

Just like @DATEVALUE and @DATE, @TIMEVALUE is a variant of @TIME because @TIMEVALUE produces a serial number from the hour, minute, and second information you provide. Unlike @TIME, which uses numeric arguments, @TIMEVALUE uses a string argument. The general form of the function is as follows:

@TIMEVALUE(*time_string*)

The *time_string* must appear in one of the four time formats—T1 through T4. (See "Displaying Times" later in this chapter.) If the string conforms to one of the appropriate formats, Symphony displays the appropriate serial-number fraction. (If you then format the cell, Symphony displays the appropriate time of day.) The following chart shows some examples of the time strings that @TIMEVALUE accepts and the resulting serial number.

Time Format	Function	Number
T1	@TIMEVALUE("1:30:59 P.M.")	0.5631828704
T2	@TIMEVALUE("1:30 P.M.")	0.5625
T3	@TIMEVALUE("13:30:59")	0.5631828704
T4	@TIMEVALUE("13:30")	0.5625

Extracting the Second, Minute, or Hour

The @SECOND, @MINUTE, and @HOUR functions enable you to extract different units of time from a numeric time fraction. Consider these examples:

@SECOND(*30284.4432*) = 12

@MINUTE(*30284.4432*) = 38

@HOUR(*30284.4432*) = 10

Notice that the argument includes both an integer and a decimal portion. Although the integer portion is important for date functions, time functions disregard the integer. You can use @SECOND, @MINUTE, and @HOUR for various time-related chores, the most important of which is developing a time schedule.

Tip

Although the time functions ignore the integer portion of the date-time serial number, and the date functions ignore the fractional portion of the number, Symphony's operators do not. When comparing two date/time serial numbers, remember that Symphony records the serial numbers to six decimal places. Because 1 second is 0.000011, two serial numbers that are off by 0.1 second are considered nonmatching even though they display the same date and time using the date and time formats available. Use the @INT, @DAY, @MONTH, @YEAR, @HOUR, @MINUTE, or @SECOND functions to extract the portion of the serial number you need for an accurate comparison.

Displaying Times

The results of the time functions are serial-number fractions that don't look at all like the times you usually see. The SHEET **F**ormat **T**ime command enables you to display times in a more recognizable format. Lotus offers the following time formats, called T1 through T4:

Number	Arrangement	Example
T1	HH:MM:SS AM/PM	11:51:22 PM
T2	HH:MM AM/PM	11:51 PM
T3	HH:MM:SS (24 hours)	23:51:22
T4	HH:MM (24 hours)	23:51

For all these examples, the fractional number displayed in the worksheet before formatting is 0.994.

Notice that T1 creates a string 11 characters long and thus requires a column width of 12. For this reason, unless you need to display seconds, you may prefer the T2 format.

The International formats (T3 and T4) use the colon as the default separation character. But you can also use periods, commas, or other characters as separation characters. When you change the separation characters, you must modify one of the configuration settings, as you do for the date formats. To modify the setting, use the SERVICES **C**onfiguration **O**ther **I**nternational **T**ime command.

Cue:
Use the T2 format to display times in a format that fits in the default column width.

Performing Date and Time Arithmetic— General Comments

Notice that Symphony's date and time arithmetic capabilities incorporate both a set of functions and a set of formats. Don't be confused by this mix. The functions, like @DATEVALUE, enter dates or times in the worksheet; the formats display the functions in an understandable form. Although you can use the format without the function, or the function without the format, the two tools are not very meaningful when used apart.

In most cases, date and time arithmetic simply subtracts one number from another. By subtracting, you can easily determine the number of days between dates, or hours between times. For example, subtracting @DATE(*90,7,31*) from @DATE(*90,8,15*) results in the value 15 (days). Similarly, subtracting @TIME(*10,4,31*) from @TIME(*12,54,54*) results in a value of 0.11832175 (2 hours, 50 minutes, and 23 seconds).

You even can determine the number of minutes, hours, weeks, and years between two serial numbers by dividing the difference by an appropriate number. If you need only a rough idea, you can use the banker's convention of 7 days in a week, 30 days in a month, and 360 days in a year. If you want to be more exact, you can use the @MOD function for remainders. You can even build in odd-numbered months and leap years. Symphony's datekeeping and timekeeping allow you to simplify the analysis or make it as sophisticated as you like.

Besides using date and time functions in arithmetic calculations, you also can use them in logical expressions such as @IF(*@DATE(90,15,05)>B2,C3,D4*). In simple English this statement says: If the serial number equivalent to May 15, 1990, is greater than the value in cell B2, then assign the value in cell C3 to the current cell; otherwise, use the value in D4. You can use this kind of test to help keep track of investment portfolios or time performance.

Chapter Summary

In this chapter, you have seen examples of Symphony's SHEET functions at work. In the next chapter, you examine Symphony's file-handling commands. You will learn how to save and retrieve worksheet files and how to use the program's other, more sophisticated, file-management tools.

7

Managing Files

One of the commands you frequently use in Symphony is the SERVICES File command. Symphony files are similar to file folders in most offices. Each folder deals with one subject, and is easy to find, add to, delete, or modify. A Symphony file holds one worksheet, which includes the labels, values, and formulas you have entered into it, and also is easy to find, add to, delete, or modify.

Among other features, Symphony's file management system enables you to save worksheets; delete, retrieve, and combine files; and create links between files.

In this chapter, you learn how to do the following:

❑ Save files to disk

❑ Retrieve previously saved files from disk

❑ Extract and combine data from files

❑ Use passwords to protect files

❑ Erase files from computer memory or disk

❑ List files on disk

❑ Create links from a file in memory to a file on disk

Learning File Basics

Symphony stores its files on the hard disk, which is divided into directories (also called subdirectories). These directories help Symphony find the file you need quickly. For example, think of the hard disk as a four-drawer file cabinet. Each drawer is a directory that holds files on that directory's programs. When Symphony needs information on one of its programs, it looks in its directory and quickly finds the file.

In addition to worksheet files, Symphony contains several other file types, identified by their three-character extensions. These files include the following:

Extension	Type of File
.WR1	Worksheet
.PRN	Print (also known as ASCII or text)
.PIC	Graph
.CCF	Communications configuration
.CTF	Character-translation
.APP	Add-in program
.MLB	Macro library

Reminder:

Before you exit from the worksheet, or retrieve another file, or begin a new worksheet, save the file to disk to save your changes.

When you retrieve a worksheet file stored on disk, you are making a copy of the file and placing it in your computer's memory. The file stored on disk is unchanged. Placing a copy of your file in memory is how you make changes to the file. However, computer memory is only a temporary storage area. If you exit from Symphony, retrieve another file, or begin a new worksheet, you lose any changes you made to the file. You need to save the file to disk to save your changes.

If you save the file with the same name, the original file on disk is overwritten by the copy in memory. If you use a new name for the file in memory, your copy of the original file and the new file are saved on disk.

You can use any name from one to eight characters long to name your file. The rules for naming files are as follows:

Permitted

1. Letters (A – Z)
2. Numbers (0 – 9)
3. The ~ ! @ $ % ^ & [ ] - _ { } # ' characters

Not permitted

1. Blank spaces
2. The < > , . * characters

Symphony automatically adds the appropriate three-letter extension to the file name for you. You also can enter the file name in lower or uppercase, although Symphony automatically converts all characters to uppercase.

Tip

Name your files with names that have meaning to you. In this manner, you remember the purpose of your worksheet file. For example, if you work with budgets, you can name your 1990 budget file BUDGET90.

Using Symphony File Commands

In Chapters 4 and 5, you worked almost exclusively with the SHEET commands. However, to work with Symphony files, you use the SERVICES **F**ile commands. Recall from Chapter 2 that the SERVICES commands have a global orientation, and therefore can affect your entire application and Symphony itself. Also, the SERVICES command can be invoked from any environment.

When you select **F**ile from the SERVICES menu, the commands shown in figure 7.1 appear in Symphony's control panel:

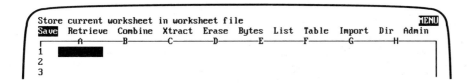

Fig. 7.1.
Symphony's SERVICES File menu.

Symphony's **F**ile commands enable you to perform the operations shown in table 7.1.

Table 7.1
Symphony's File Commands

Command	Use
Save	Save a file in memory to disk
Retrieve	Place a file from disk into memory
Combine	Copy, add, or subtract a cell or range from a file on disk to a file in memory
Xtract	Copy a cell or range from a file in memory to a file on disk
Erase	Erase a file on disk
Bytes	Check space available on current drive (in bytes)

Table 7.1 (continued)

Command	Use
List	Display a list of files on disk
Table	Place a table of files on disk to the worksheet in memory
Import	Place an ASCII file from disk to the worksheet in memory
Directory	Specify the directory Symphony should use
Admin	Update linking formulas

Saving Files

To save a file in your computer's memory to disk, use the SERVICES **F**ile **S**ave command. This command makes a permanent copy of the worksheet in memory, including its formats, range names, settings, and windows.

When you want to save a new file, but have other worksheet files on disk and need to know what they are before you save, Symphony supplies a list of these file names as shown in figure 7.2. To view these files, invoke the SERVICES **F**ile **S**ave command.

Fig. 7.2.

Displaying a list of previously saved file names.

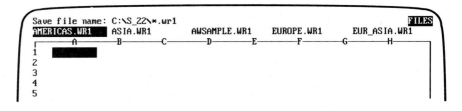

> ### Tip
> After you select SERVICES **F**ile **S**ave, if you press F10, Symphony displays a full–screen list of file names you can choose from. Move the cell pointer to the name you want to use for your file name, and press Enter. Symphony saves your file with that name.

You can select a file name by pressing the spacebar and using the left and right arrow keys; or by typing a file name, and pressing Enter. Remember, however, you overwrite the file on disk with the file in your computer's memory if you choose one of the file names Symphony furnishes.

> **Tip**
>
> You may need to work with the same file many times, but also need to keep previous versions of the file on disk. When this happens, name your files with consecutive names. You can tell which is the latest version of the file without losing any prior versions. For example, you can have a sales analysis in files SALES_01, SALES_02, and so forth.

If you are working with a previously saved file, and want to save it again, Symphony furnishes the file name as the default, as shown in figure 7.3.

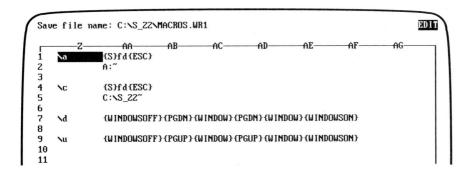

```
Save file name: C:\S_22\MACROS.WR1                                    EDIT
     Z         AA        AB        AC        AD        AE        AF        AG
 1  \a         {S}fd{ESC}
 2             A:~
 3
 4  \c         {S}fd{ESC}
 5             C:\S_22~
 6
 7  \d         {WINDOWSOFF}{PGDN}{WINDOW}{PGDN}{WINDOW}{WINDOWSON}
 8
 9  \u         {WINDOWSOFF}{PGUP}{WINDOW}{PGUP}{WINDOW}{WINDOWSON}
10
11
```

Fig. 7.3.
The default file name appears in Symphony's control panel when you save a previously saved file.

You can type a new name and press Enter, which creates a new file and does not overwrite the file on disk. However, if you press Enter, Symphony displays the following warning in the control panel:

> **A file with that name already exists -- replace it?**

If you choose Yes, the file in memory is assigned the same name as the one on disk, and is overwritten. If you choose No, the **File Save** operation is canceled. In this manner, Symphony prevents you from accidentally overwriting your previously saved files.

Retrieving Files

To use a previously saved file, use the File **R**etrieve command. When you invoke this command, Symphony makes a copy of the file on disk and places it into your computer's memory. If you have just started Symphony, or have a blank worksheet in memory, **File R**etrieve brings a copy of the disk file into memory. However, if you have a file currently in memory and invoke the **File R**etrieve command, the current file is replaced by the retrieved file. Be sure you have a copy of the file in memory saved to disk before you use the **File R**etrieve command, or all changes made since the last **File S**ave operation will be lost.

Reminder:
Make sure you save to disk a copy of the file in memory before you invoke the File Retrieve command, or you lose all changes since your last File Save operation.

Cue:

Press MENU F10 for a full-screen list of file names.

Similar to the **File Save** command, Symphony displays a list of five of the files on disk in the control panel. You select the file you need by typing its name, or pointing to it and pressing Enter. If you need to see more file names, use the left- and right-arrow keys to display the others. You can display all the file names at once by pressing F10, as shown in figure 7.4.

Fig. 7.4.

A full-screen list of file names.

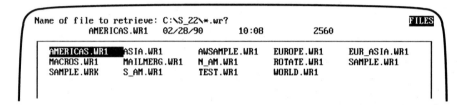

```
Name of file to retrieve: C:\S_22\*.wr?                           FILES
                AMERICAS.WR1   02/28/90      10:08         2560

AMERICAS.WR1   ASIA.WR1      AWSAMPLE.WR1   EUROPE.WR1   EUR_ASIA.WR1
MACROS.WR1     MAILMERG.WR1  N_AM.WR1       ROTATE.WR1   SAMPLE.WR1
SAMPLE.WRK     S_AM.WR1      TEST.WR1       WORLD.WR1
```

Symphony lists files on disk in alphabetical order, left to right. The second line of the control panel displays the file name highlighted by the cell pointer, the date and time the file was last saved, and its size in bytes. To select a file, point to the file and press Enter.

Tip

You can use Symphony 2.2's VIEWER add-in to select and retrieve a file. VIEWER enables you to see the contents of a file before placing it into memory, eliminating the need to retrieve a file to determine if it is the one you want. VIEWER is explained in Chapter 3.

Using Wild Cards To Retrieve Files

Whenever Symphony prompts you for a file name, you can include the asterisk (*) or the question mark (?) as wild cards in the file name. Wild cards are characters that enable you to make one file name match a number of files. Although you may use wild cards with many of the **File** commands, you will probably use these special characters most often with the **File Retrieve** command.

The ? matches any one character in the name (or no character if the ? is the last character in the file's eight-character name or three-character extension). The * matches any number of characters (or no character).

Reminder:

The asterisk wild card is helpful in finding file names quickly.

When you use wild cards in response to a file name prompt, Symphony lists only the files whose names match the wild card pattern. For example, if you type **SALES?** at the file name prompt, Symphony lists all file names that start with SALES, followed by any character, such as SALES_01, SALES_02, SALES_03, and so forth. If you type **SA***, Symphony lists all file names that start with SA, such as SALARY_1, SALES_01, SAMPLE, and so forth.

Retrieving a File Automatically

Symphony has the capability to automatically retrieve a file you specify from the Symphony subdirectory each time you invoke the program. This feature is useful when you create custom applications for others and want the user to work with a specific file.

To have Symphony automatically retrieve a file each time you start the program, select the SERVICES **C**onfiguration **A**uto command. Next, enter the name of the file to be retrieved, and press Enter. Finally, select **U**pdate to make the change permanent. The file you specified will now be the first file you see on-screen after you invoke Symphony. Remember, however, the specified file must be in the Symphony subdirectory so that the program can locate and place it into your computer's memory.

Reminder:
*Use the SERVICES Configuration **A**uto command to specify a file to be retrieved each time you invoke Symphony.*

Tip

Be careful how you use the SERVICES **C**onfiguration **A**uto command. Once you set this command, Symphony automatically retrieves the file you specify in the command. This feature may be dangerous if you also have an autoexecuting macro in the file that is not operating properly. You may inadvertently damage the file contents.

To stop Symphony from automatically retrieving a worksheet, use the DOS rename command to give it another name, or erase it entirely, or copy it to another directory and erase the original file. In all cases, Symphony cannot locate the file to retrieve it. Finally, make sure that your autoexecuting macro is fully debugged if you intend to use it in the file to be retrieved automatically.

Retrieving Files From Other Subdirectories

When you use the **F**ile **R**etrieve command, Symphony prompts you for a file name, provides you with a default file name, and lists the complete path, which includes the drive, directory and file name, such as `C:\SYMPHONY\SALES_01.WR1`. To retrieve or save a file in another directory without changing the current directory, press Esc twice to clear the path and then type a new path. You also can edit the existing path in the prompt. This capability is useful, for example, if you are upgrading from 1-2-3 and want to retrieve a worksheet from your 1-2-3 directory.

To use a file in another directory, invoke the **F**ile **R**etrieve command, and press the Backspace key until only `C:\` is displayed in Symphony's control panel, then press Enter. Symphony lists the other directories on the hard disk, as shown in figure 7.5.

Reminder:
Press Backspace to list all subdirectories; select a subdirectory to list all worksheet files in that subdirectory.

Fig. 7.5.

Hard disk directories from which you can retrieve files.

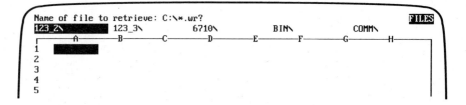

Now, point to the directory you want to retrieve the file from, and press Enter. If there are Symphony worksheet files in this directory, they display in the control panel, and you point to the file you need to retrieve it. If there are no files, type ***.wr?** and press Enter. Symphony displays all Symphony worksheet files in the directory for retrieval.

Tip

In the discussion above, if you type ***.w***, Symphony displays all Symphony *and* 1-2-3 files in the directory.

If you want to make this new directory the current directory, use the **F**ile **D**irectory command, which is discussed next.

Changing Directories

Symphony's **F**ile **D**irectory command enables you to use directories other than the default directory. To change to another directory, use the SERVICES **F**ile **D**irectory command. Press the Backspace key to delete the name of the default directory, type the name of the new directory, and press Enter.

You also can change the disk drive Symphony uses to retrieve and save files. For example, you may prefer to keep your Symphony worksheet files on the computer's drive A: to protect the data or save hard-disk space. To make another disk drive the current drive, press the Esc key, which clears the drive and directory in the **F**ile **D**irectory prompt. Type the letter of the disk drive, a colon (:), and press Enter. This change will be in effect until you change the directory again or exit Symphony.

To make another directory or drive the new default permanently, use the SERVICES **C**onfiguration **F**ile command. Press the Backspace key the number of times needed to clear the directory, type the new directory name, and press Enter. To change the disk drive, press the Esc key once, type the letter of the drive, a colon, and press Enter. In both cases, to make your changes permanent, invoke the SERVICES **C**onfiguration **U**pdate command.

Extracting and Combining Files

Symphony provides you with the capability to specify a range of the worksheet in memory and save it to another file on disk. This capability is useful, for example, if you have a large worksheet, and only want to print a report range. By printing only a small section of the original worksheet, you ensure that sufficient memory exists for Symphony, the file to be printed, and Allways, the spreadsheet publishing add-in.

Conversely, Symphony also enables you to combine files on disk with a file in your computer's memory. This capability is useful, for example, if you have created an income statement for your company by using Symphony, and have separate files for revenue, depreciation, taxes, and so forth.

When you save a worksheet range in memory to one on disk you are *extracting* a file; when you bring a file from disk into one in memory you are *combining* a file. Symphony's SERVICES **F**ile **X**tract and **F**ile **C**ombine commands, respectively, enable you to perform these operations. Both commands are explained in the following sections.

Extracting Ranges

Symphony's SERVICES **F**ile **X**tract command enables you to save a range from your worksheet in memory to another worksheet range on disk. This command is similar to the **F**ile **S**ave command, except that you are saving a range, and usually not the entire worksheet. Use this command to save a range or file before you make changes, to create smaller files that can be used in computers with less memory, to create a partial file for another user to work on, or to pass data to another file.

> **Reminder:**
> Use the SERVICES *File Xtract* command to save a range or file before you make changes.

The extracted range can be a single cell, multiple cells, or the entire application. The file created from an extracted range contains the cell contents of the range, including cell formats and protection status; range names in the file; file settings, such as column widths; and print, graph, and window settings.

To extract a range of your worksheet in memory to one on disk, invoke the SERVICES **F**ile **E**xtract command, and select either **F**ormulas or **V**alues. If you select **F**ormulas, cells in the extract range that contain formulas are copied into the extracted file as formulas. If you select **V**alues, cells containing formulas in the extract range from the worksheet in memory are converted to their current value, and these values are copied into the extracted file.

> **Reminder:**
> If the Calc indicator is on, press the F8 (Calc) key to calculate the worksheet before you use the *File Xtract Values* command.

Next, Symphony prompts you for a file name. You can point to an existing file name or type a new one, and press Enter. You may want to begin the name of the extract file with an *x*, such as XPRINT_1, to remind yourself of its purpose and that it is the extracted file.

Reminder:

To remind you of its purpose and that it is an extracted file, use a file name with an x such as XPRINT_1.

Now, specify the range you want to extract. You can type cell addresses, point and highlight the range, or use range names (including F10) to select the range. Finally, press Enter. If the range has been previously saved to disk, Symphony prompts you with the following message:

    A file with that name already exists -- replace it?

If you select Yes, Symphony writes over the file on disk with the contents of the extract range. If you select No, Symphony prompts you for another file name for the extract range.

The extracted range always begins in cell A1, no matter where the location of the range is in the original worksheet. For example, if you extract the contents of cells in row A10..G10 of the original worksheet, the cell contents move to row A1..G1 in the new worksheet.

Xtracting Formulas Techniques

Reminder:

Make sure you include cells, ranges, or range names the formulas depend on in the extract range, or Symphony cannot extract the formulas correctly.

When you extract formulas, make sure that you include cells, ranges, or range names the formulas depend on in the extract range, or Symphony cannot extract the formulas correctly. Also, be aware that when you extract formulas, the formulas adjust even if they are absolute. The formulas in the extracted files continue to be absolute; however, they have new addresses, because Symphony always places the extracted range in the new file beginning in cell A1.

Combining Files

Reminder:

Even absolute cell references adjust with the File Extract command.

Symphony's SERVICES **F**ile **C**ombine command enables you to retrieve a range from a worksheet on disk to the worksheet in memory. This command is similar to the **F**ile **R**etrieve command, except that you are retrieving a range, and not replacing the worksheet in memory with another from disk. Use this command when you want to copy or add data from a file on disk to a worksheet in memory.

To combine a file on disk with a file in memory, invoke the SERVICES **F**ile **C**ombine command. Symphony then provides you with the following options:

Option	Purpose
Copy	Brings a cell, range, named range, or worksheet from disk into memory. Cell contents from the disk file overwrite those in memory.
Add	Brings a cell, range, named range, or worksheet from disk into memory. Cell contents from the disk file are added to those in memory.

Option	Purpose
Subtract	Brings a cell, range, named range, or worksheet from disk into memory. Cell contents from the disk file are subtracted from those in memory.

You can use any of the **F**ile **C**ombine options with either an entire file (**E**ntire-File) or a range (**N**amed/**S**pecified-Range). The range can be a single cell or multiple cells.

For any of these options, place the cell pointer in the upper left corner of the area of the worksheet where you want the incoming data to be entered. For example, suppose that you want to add values from two separate files to the worksheet in figure 7.6. Because the values in both worksheets are stored in the same cells, you position the cell pointer in cell A1 before you use the **F**ile **C**ombine command.

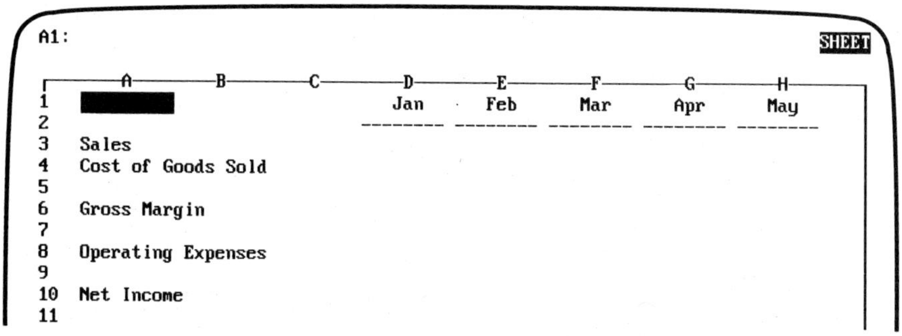

```
A1:                                                        SHEET
     A         B        C        D       E       F       G       H
 1   ████████                   Jan     Feb     Mar     Apr     May
 2                              -------- -------- -------- -------- --------
 3   Sales
 4   Cost of Goods Sold
 5
 6   Gross Margin
 7
 8   Operating Expenses
 9
 10  Net Income
 11
```

Fig. 7.6.
A worksheet before File Combine Copy.

Figure 7.7 displays the result of using the **F**ile **C**ombine **C**opy command with figure 7.6. The **F**ile **C**ombine **A**dd command is used with the worksheets in figures 7.7 and 7.8 to create the worksheet in figure 7.9.

Reminder:
File Combine Copy replaces cell entries, while Add and Subtract affect values accordingly.

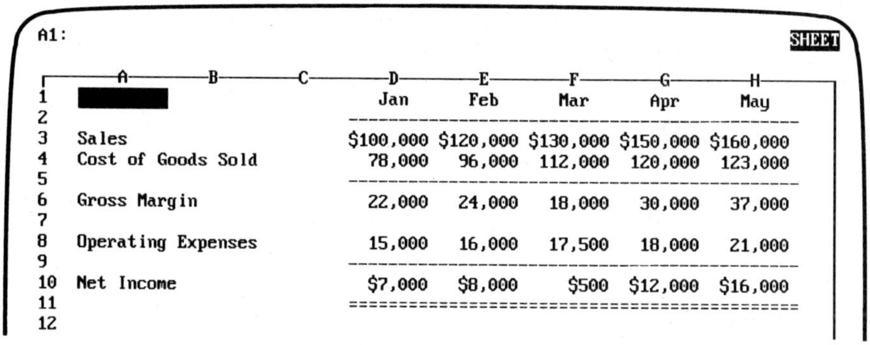

```
A1:                                                        SHEET
     A         B        C        D       E       F       G       H
 1   ████████                   Jan     Feb     Mar     Apr     May
 2                              ------------------------------------------
 3   Sales               $100,000 $120,000 $130,000 $150,000 $160,000
 4   Cost of Goods Sold    78,000   96,000  112,000  120,000  123,000
 5                              ------------------------------------------
 6   Gross Margin          22,000   24,000   18,000   30,000   37,000
 7
 8   Operating Expenses    15,000   16,000   17,500   18,000   21,000
 9                              ------------------------------------------
 10  Net Income            $7,000   $8,000     $500  $12,000  $16,000
 11                             ==========================================
 12
```

Fig. 7.7.
Results of File Combine Copy and figure 7.6.

Fig. 7.8.

A worksheet stored on disk.

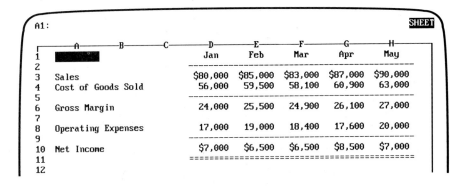

Fig. 7.9.

Results of File Combine Add and figures 7.7 and 7.8.

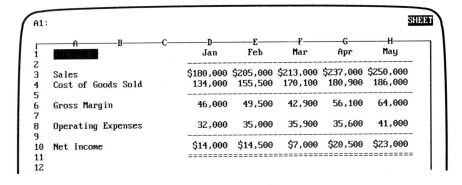

Tip

Use the SERVICES File Combine Subtract command to locate circular references in your worksheet. First, check the worksheet. If it is in manual recalculation, press the F8 key. Next, save the file to disk with the SERVICES File Save command, so that you have a permanent copy of the original file. Next, use the MENU Range Value command. The `Range to Copy FROM:` is the entire worksheet. The `Range to copy TO:` is cell A1. Now, save this version of the file to disk with a name that has meaning to you, such as VALUES. Next, invoke the SERVICES File Combine Subtract Entire–File command and specify VALUES. Cells with values other than zeros contain circular references.

Combining Formulas Techniques

Be careful when you use the **F**ile **C**ombine **C**opy command with formulas. All formulas, including those with absolute cell addresses, adjust automatically to their new location after you use the **F**ile **C**ombine **C**opy command. Make sure you include cells, ranges, and range names the formulas depend on, or the results will be wrong.

When you invoke the **F**ile **C**ombine **A**dd command with a range that includes formulas, Symphony converts formulas to values before adding them to the file in memory. Therefore, to ensure accurate results, be sure to press CALC (F8) before issuing the **F**ile **C**ombine **A**dd command if you have Symphony in manual recalculation mode. In this manner, you add your most up-to-date values to the worksheet in memory.

Transferring Files

Symphony provides you with two methods of transferring files internally and with other software programs. You can save and retrieve files in ASCII format by using both the SERVICES **P**rint **F**ile and SERVICES **F**ile **I**mport commands. Most software programs can create and use ASCII files. You also can use Symphony's **T**ranslate program to create or use files in another program's format.

Transferring ASCII Files

Use Symphony's SERVICES **F**ile **I**mport command to place a copy of a standard ASCII file from disk into the worksheet in memory. Symphony's .PRN files are one example of ASCII files, as are those produced by word processing and programming languages. ASCII stands for American Standard Code for Information Interchange, a data format most computers can recognize.

Think of the **F**ile **I**mport command as a special type of **F**ile **C**ombine command. You combine the data in ASCII format from disk into your worksheet in memory, beginning at the location of your cell pointer. Be sure to import the file into a blank area of the worksheet, otherwise existing cell entries will be overwritten. When you use the **F**ile **I**mport command, Symphony lists the .PRN files in the current directory. To list other ASCII files with other file extensions, such as .TXT, press Esc, type *.**TXT**, and press Enter.

Symphony prompts you for the type of ASCII file you want to import: **Text** or **Structured**.

Reminder:
*Even absolute cell references adjust with the **File Combine Copy** command.*

Caution:
*If you use the **File Combine Copy** command with formulas, be sure that you include the data referenced by the formulas.*

Reminder:
*Make sure that the Calc indicator is off before you save a file to be used in a **File Combine Add** or **S**ubtract operation.*

Reminder:
Make sure you import a file into a blank area of the worksheet, otherwise existing cell entries will be overwritten.

Importing Unstructured ASCII Files

The typical ASCII file contains lines of data, each line ending with a carriage return. Except for the carriage returns, these ASCII files have no structure. In this case, you use the **File Import Text** command to bring a copy of the ASCII file from disk into the worksheet in memory. You use the **Text** option most often with ASCII files created by word processing programs.

Figure 7.10 displays the result of importing a typical ASCII file into a worksheet in memory. Each line in the ASCII file becomes a long label in a cell, thus all the data is located in column A. If you want to manipulate the data with Symphony's commands and @functions, you need to separate and place the data in individual cells. To make the data usable, you invoke Symphony's MENU **Query Parse** command, discussed in Chapter 19.

Fig. 7.10.

An unstructured text file imported with the SERVICES File Import Text command.

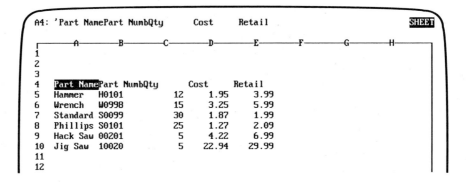

Importing Delimited ASCII Files

Some ASCII files are in a special format that enables them to be imported into separate cells without being parsed with Symphony's **Query Parse** command. This special format is called *delimited format*. A delimiter exists between each field, and labels are enclosed in quotation marks. A delimiter may be a space, comma, colon, or semicolon. If the labels are not enclosed in quotation marks, they are ignored, and only the numbers are imported.

To import a delimited file, use Symphony's **File Import Structured** command. Figure 7.11 is an example of a delimited file, and figure 7.12 displays the results after invoking the **File Import Structured** command and adjusting column widths.

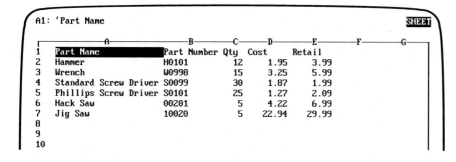

```
C:\INSET>type a:ascii.asc
"Part Name","Qty","Cost","Retail"
"Hammer","H0101",12,1,95,3.99
"Wrench","W0998",15,3.25,5.99
"Standard Screw Driver","S0099",30,1,87,1.99
"Phillips Screw Driver","S0101",25,1.27,2.09
"Hack Saw","00201",5,4.22,6.99
"Jig Saw","10020",5,22.94,29.99

C:\INSET>
```

Fig. 7.11.

A delimited ASCII file.

```
A1: 'Part Name                                                    SHEET
    ─────A─────────────B────C────D─────E──────────F─────────G───
 1  Part Name          Part Number Qty  Cost   Retail
 2  Hammer             H0101       12    1.95    3.99
 3  Wrench             W0998       15    3.25    5.99
 4  Standard Screw Driver S0099    30    1.87    1.99
 5  Phillips Screw Driver S0101    25    1.27    2.09
 6  Hack Saw           00201        5    4.22    6.99
 7  Jig Saw            10020        5   22.94   29.99
 8
 9
10
```

Fig. 7.12.

*The delimited ASCII file after invoking the SERVICES **F**ile **I**mport **S**tructured command and adjusting column widths.*

Transferring Files with Translate

Translate is a program separate from Symphony that is included with the Symphony software package. You use Translate to convert Symphony .WR1 files so they can be used by other software programs, and vice-versa.

To invoke Translate, type **trans** at your DOS prompt, or select **F**ile-Translate from the ACCESS menu. You can convert files to and from the following types of files:

Reminder:

Use the Translate program to use files created with another program.

Program name	File extension
1-2-3 1A	.WKS
1-2-3 2.0, 2.01, 2.2	.WK1
dBASE II, III	.DBF
DCA RFT format	.RFT
DIF	.DIF
MultiPlan SYLK	.SLK
Symphony 1.0	.WRK
Symphony 1.1, 1.2, 2.0, 2.2	.WR1
VisiCalc	.VC

To use Translate, select the format or program from which you want to translate with the up and down arrow keys and then press Enter; then choose the format or program to which you want to translate (see figures 7.13 and 7.14), using the same method. Note that dBASE III plus is not listed in figure 7.14, but is available by selecting dBASE III. Finally, choose the file you want to translate, type the name of the output file, and press Enter.

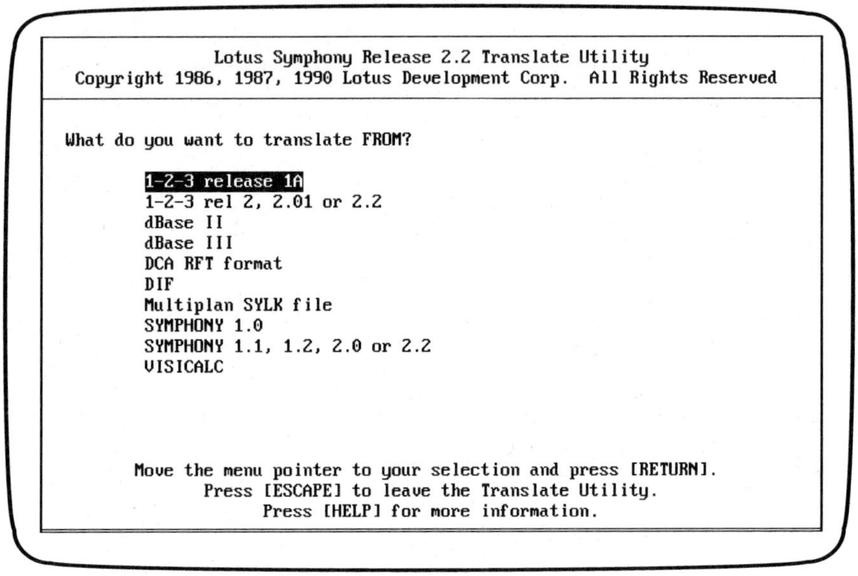

Fig. 7.13.

The menu of choices to translate from other programs to Symphony.

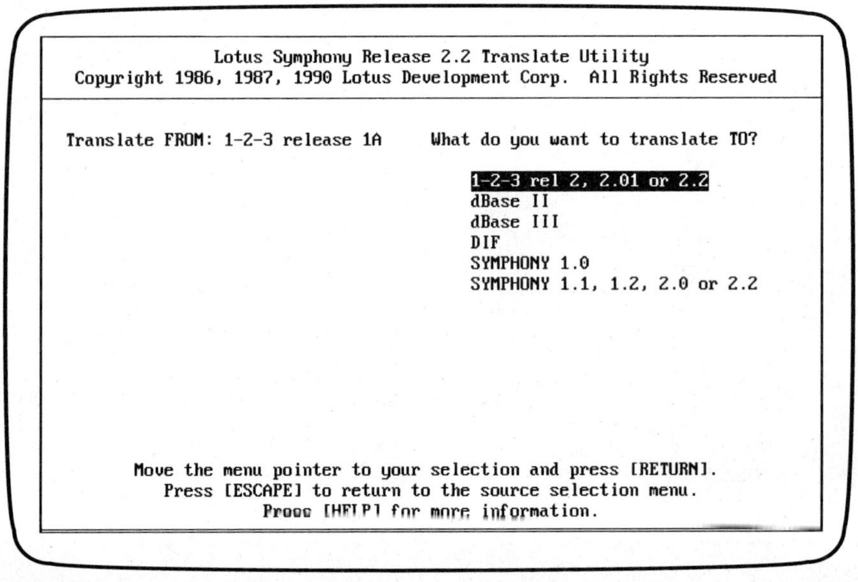

```
                    Lotus Symphony Release 2.2 Translate Utility
           Copyright 1986, 1987, 1990 Lotus Development Corp.  All Rights Reserved


         What do you want to translate FROM?

                     1-2-3 release 1A
                     1-2-3 rel 2, 2.01 or 2.2
                     dBase II
                     dBase III
                     DCA RFT format
                     DIF
                     Multiplan SYLK file
                     SYMPHONY 1.0
                     SYMPHONY 1.1, 1.2, 2.0 or 2.2
                     VISICALC




                 Move the menu pointer to your selection and press [RETURN].
                     Press [ESCAPE] to leave the Translate Utility.
                         Press [HELP] for more information.
```

Fig. 7.14.

The menu of choices to translate to other programs from Symphony.

```
                    Lotus Symphony Release 2.2 Translate Utility
           Copyright 1986, 1987, 1990 Lotus Development Corp.  All Rights Reserved


         Translate FROM: 1-2-3 release 1A        What do you want to translate TO?

                                                 1-2-3 rel 2, 2.01 or 2.2
                                                 dBase II
                                                 dBase III
                                                 DIF
                                                 SYMPHONY 1.0
                                                 SYMPHONY 1.1, 1.2, 2.0 or 2.2




                 Move the menu pointer to your selection and press [RETURN].
                  Press [ESCAPE] to return to the source selection menu.
                        Press [HELP] for more information.
```

When you translate to dBASE format, you can translate the entire file or a named range. In most cases, the file contains data in addition to the input range; therefore, make sure that you use the MENU **R**ange **N**ame **C**reate command to name the database input range. When you translate a file into a dBASE format, the range or entire file must consist only of a database input range.

Using 1-2-3 Files in Symphony

You can use 1-2-3 worksheet files directly with Symphony. This capability is convenient if you are upgrading from 1-2-3, or have colleagues that use 1-2-3.

To use a 1-2-3 worksheet with Symphony, use the SERVICES **F**ile **R**etrieve command. Next, press the Esc key, use the Backspace key to delete the directory, and type a new directory and file name. Symphony will retrieve the file as usual.

When you save the file, Symphony beeps and displays the message `File will be saved as .WR1`, informing you that the file will be saved in Symphony worksheet format. At this time, Symphony changes to EDIT mode, so you can specify where you want the file to be saved by typing the drive, directory, and name of the file. The original 1-2-3 worksheet will be left unchanged.

To use a 1-2-3 3.0 worksheet with Symphony, you need to use the DOS rename command and change the Release 3.0 file extension from .WK3 to .WK1 or .WR1. In addition, if the Release 3.0 file contains multiple worksheets, you need to translate each to single .WK1 worksheets with Release 3.0's Translate utility before they can be used by Symphony. In either case, formats and settings unique to 1-2-3 3.0 will be lost when you retrieve the worksheet file into Symphony.

Reminder:
You can use 1-2-3 1A, 2.0, 2.01, and 2.2 files directly with Symphony.

Reminder:
Formats and settings unique to 1-2-3 3.0 are lost when you retrieve the worksheet file into Symphony.

Other File Management Commands

Symphony provides you with the ability to remove files from disk, protect files, place a list of your disk-based files on the screen and worksheet, and check the amount of space left on the disk.

Erasing Files

To remove a file from disk, use Symphony's SERVICES **F**ile **E**rase command. Erasing unneeded files from the hard disk frees space for new files. Because the **F**ile **E**rase command removes a file from disk permanently, be sure to save important files and files you may need later to a diskette.

When you invoke the **F**ile **E**rase command, the menu in Symphony's control panel appears, as shown in figure 7.15.

Reminder:
Make sure you save important files and files you may need later before you use the File Erase command.

Fig. 7.15.
Symphony's File
Erase options.

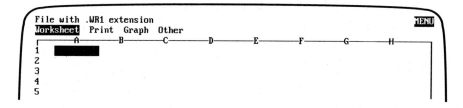

The menu helps you select the type of file you want to erase. Symphony displays the files in the control panel from the category you select, as follows:

Menu Choice	File Extension	Description
Worksheet	.WR1	Symphony worksheet files
Print	.PRN	ASCII or text files
Graph	.PIC	Symphony graph files
Other	(All)	All files in the Symphony directory

If you choose **W**orksheet, Symphony lists all files in the current directory that have .WR1 extension, and so forth, for print and graph files. If you select **A**ll, Symphony displays all files in the current directory.

Be aware that you can erase only one file at a time with the **File E**rase command. If you want to erase multiple files in one operation, you attach and invoke Symphony's DOS add-in. In this manner, with the DOS add-in and wild cards, you can erase similar files simultaneously.

Caution:

The File *Erase and* New *commands remove a file permanently from disk and memory, respectively.*

Finally, you should understand the difference between the SERVICES **File E**rase and SERVICES **N**ew command. **File E**rase removes a file you specify from disk, and the **N**ew command removes the file from your computer's memory. However, make sure that you have an exact copy of the file in memory saved on disk, because the **N**ew command replaces your file in memory with a blank Symphony worksheet.

Creating Lists and Tables of Files

Symphony provides you with two commands to help you keep track of files on disk. The **File L**ist command creates a list of files on screen, and the **File T**able command places a list of files in the worksheet. Both commands provide you with similar menu choices.

Reminder:

Create a list of files on-screen with the File List *command.*

To create a list of files on screen, use the SERVICES **File L**ist command. Symphony prompts you for the type of file you want listed, as shown in figure 7.16.

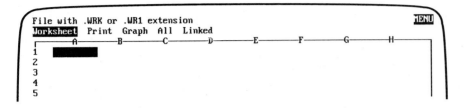

Fig. 7.16.
Symphony's File *List options.*

If you have the Macro Library Manager attached, an .MLB option also displays on the menu. After you select a file type, Symphony displays a full-screen list of the files, as shown in figure 7.17.

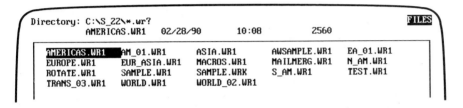

Fig. 7.17.
A list of files created with the SERVICES *File List* Worksheet *command.*

In addition to the list of files, Symphony displays the name, date, and time of the last save, and the size of the file in bytes where the cell pointer is located, in the second line of the control panel. To see similar information about any of the other files, move the cell pointer to that file.

The **File Table** command operates similarly to the **File List** command, only the information is placed in a specified location on the worksheet. The **File Table** command is convenient if you want to print out information about your files on a diskette.

To create a table of files, use the SERVICES **File Table** command. Symphony then prompts you for a directory. You can type in a new directory, or press Enter, which is the current directory (most of the time this will be your Symphony directory). Next, Symphony prompts you for the file type, similar to the **File List** command. After you select the file type, Symphony prompts you for a location in your worksheet for the table. Move the cell pointer to the upper left corner of the location for the table, in a blank area of the worksheet, as Symphony overwrites any cell entries with the file information. When you press enter, Symphony places the table in the worksheet, as shown in figure 7.18.

Symphony provides you with three characteristics about the files: the name of the file in the first column; the date (and time) the file was last saved; and the size in bytes of the file. In Figure 7.18, a column was inserted next to column B, and the cell entries in column B were copied to the new column C. The columns were widened appropriately, and column B and C were formatted as **Date 1** and **Time 1**, respectively.

Reminder:

When using the File Table *command, make sure that you move the cell pointer to a blank area of the worksheet, otherwise Symphony overwrites cell entries.*

Reminder:

Create a table of files in the current worksheet with the File Table *command.*

Fig. 7.18.

A table of file information.

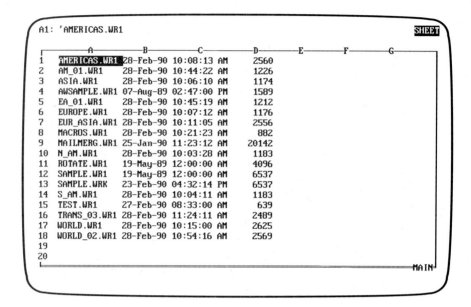

```
A1: 'AMERICAS.WR1                                              SHEET
         A         B          C            D      E     F     G
 1  AMERICAS.WR1 28-Feb-90 10:08:13 AM      2560
 2  AM_01.WR1    28-Feb-90 10:44:22 AM      1226
 3  ASIA.WR1     28-Feb-90 10:06:10 AM      1174
 4  AWSAMPLE.WR1 07-Aug-89 02:47:00 PM      1589
 5  EA_01.WR1    28-Feb-90 10:45:19 AM      1212
 6  EUROPE.WR1   28-Feb-90 10:07:12 AM      1176
 7  EUR_ASIA.WR1 28-Feb-90 10:11:05 AM      2556
 8  MACROS.WR1   28-Feb-90 10:21:23 AM       882
 9  MAILMERG.WR1 25-Jan-90 11:23:12 AM     20142
10  N_AM.WR1     28-Feb-90 10:03:28 AM      1183
11  ROTATE.WR1   19-May-89 12:00:00 AM      4096
12  SAMPLE.WR1   19-May-89 12:00:00 AM      6537
13  SAMPLE.WRK   23-Feb-90 04:32:14 PM      6537
14  S_AM.WR1     28-Feb-90 10:04:11 AM      1183
15  TEST.WR1     27-Feb-90 08:33:00 AM       639
16  TRANS_03.WR1 28-Feb-90 11:24:11 AM      2489
17  WORLD.WR1    28-Feb-90 10:15:00 AM      2625
18  WORLD_02.WR1 28-Feb-90 10:54:16 AM      2569
19
20
                                                            MAIN
```

Determining Disk Space in Bytes

Reminder:

Check the amount of remaining space of the current disk with the File Bytes command.

You can quickly check the amount of space remaining on the current disk with the **File B**ytes command. This command is useful if you are saving files to a diskette and need to monitor the amount of remaining disk space. When you invoke the SERVICES **File B**yte command, Symphony displays the information shown in figure 7.19.

Fig. 7.19.

Determining the number of bytes left on a disk.

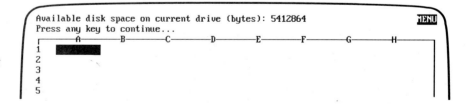

```
Available disk space on current drive (bytes): 5412864      MENU
Press any key to continue...
         A         B          C       D       E       F       G       H
 1
 2
 3
 4
 5
```

Press any key to return Symphony to SHEET mode.

Protecting Files

Reminder:

You can protect your worksheet files with the use of a password.

As part of Symphony's security system discussed in Chapter 1, Symphony provides you with the ability to protect the worksheet files with passwords. Once you password-protect a file, no one (including you) can retrieve the file without first supplying the password. This restriction applies to the **File** **R**etrieve, **F**ile **C**ombine, and Translate commands.

You password-protect a file during a **File S**ave or **File X**tract operation. After you invoke one of these commands, type the name of the file, press the space bar once, type **p**, and then press Enter. Symphony next prompts you for a password of 1 to 15 characters, with no spaces.

As you type the password, only small squares appear in Symphony's control panel, to keep your password confidential. When you finish typing the password, press Enter. Symphony prompts you to verify it by typing it again, as shown in figure 7.20.

```
Enter password: ████              Verify password: ████              EDIT
        A         B          C         D         E         F
1  WORLDWIDE INCOME STATEMENT  $(MILLIONS)
2                   QTR 1      QTR 2     QTR 3     QTR 4     TOTAL
3  Revenue
4     Americas      45         57        61        75        238
5     Eur_Asia      76         98        104       148       426
6                   ----------------------------------------------------
7  Tot Revenue      121        155       165       223       664
8                   ----------------------------------------------------
9  Expenses
10    Americas      33         46        48        52        179
11    Eur_Asia      49         68        73        73        263
12                  ----------------------------------------------------
13 Tot Expenses     82         114       121       125       442
14                  ----------------------------------------------------
15 Total Income     39         41        44        98        222
16                  ====================================================
17
```

Fig. 7.20.
Verifying a password.

After you press Enter, if both passwords are identical, the file is saved with a special format, and neither you nor anyone else can access the file without first supplying the password. If you try to retrieve a file with an incorrect password, Symphony beeps, flashes **ERROR**, and displays the message `Incorrect password` at the bottom of the screen. Press Esc to clear your screen and return to SHEET mode, invoke the **File R**etrieve command, and try again with the correct password.

Be aware that passwords are case-sensitive. The characters in the password may be all lowercase, all uppercase, or a combination of both. However, to retrieve a password-protected file, you must enter the correct password, and in the same case you assigned to the file.

When you save a file that has already been saved with a password, Symphony displays the message `[PASSWORD PROTECTED]` after the file name as shown in figure 7.21. To save the file with the same password, press Enter.

Cue:
Because passwords are case-sensitive and easily forgotten, you may want to write them down and store them in a safe place for emergency use.

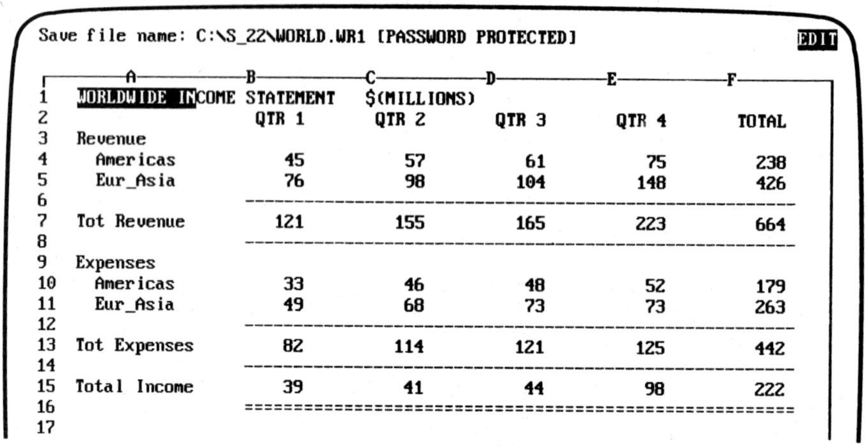

Fig. 7. 21.

Saving a password-protected file.

```
Save file name: C:\S_22\WORLD.WR1 [PASSWORD PROTECTED]                    EDIT
      A          B          C          D          E          F
 1  WORLDWIDE INCOME STATEMENT   $(MILLIONS)
 2                 QTR 1      QTR 2      QTR 3      QTR 4      TOTAL
 3  Revenue
 4     Americas     45         57         61         75         238
 5     Eur_Asia     76         98        104        148         426
 6              ----------------------------------------------------
 7  Tot Revenue    121        155        165        223         664
 8              ----------------------------------------------------
 9  Expenses
10     Americas     33         46         48         52         179
11     Eur_Asia     49         68         73         73         263
12              ----------------------------------------------------
13  Tot Expenses    82        114        121        125         442
14              ----------------------------------------------------
15  Total Income    39         41         44         98         222
16              ====================================================
17
```

To delete the password, press Backspace once to clear the [PASSWORD PROTECTED] message, and press Enter. To change the password, press Backspace once to clear the [PASSWORD PROTECTED] message, press your spacebar once, type **p**, and press Enter. Type your new password as before.

Chapter Summary

In this chapter, you learned another aspect of using Symphony—managing files. You learned how to save and retrieve files from disk, extract and combine data from files, and link files on disk. Also, you learned how to transfer and erase files, protect files, and find out information about your files. In Chapter 8, you get the opportunity through hands-on practice to try many Symphony SHEET environment features presented in earlier chapters.

8

Learning the SHEET Window: Hands-On Practice

In Chapters 1 through 7, you learned about Symphony's SERVICES commands and the SHEET environment. In this chapter, you have the opportunity to practice and develop your Symphony spreadsheet skills. You create, save, retrieve, and expand the simple worksheet application shown in figure 8.1.

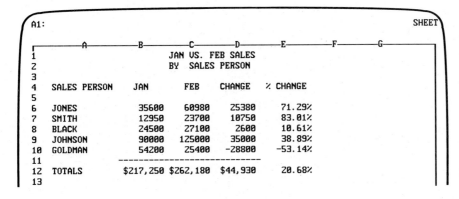

Fig. 8.1.
A sample worksheet model.

Take a few moments to analyze the model. The titles and headings are entered as labels. The JAN and FEB sales columns contain values, and the CHANGE and % CHANGE columns contain formulas. The TOTALS row also contains formulas.

Building the Model

As you build this model, you enter different types of data, activate several of the function keys, and use the SERVICES and SHEET menus. To create the SALES worksheet, begin by typing the labels, values, and formulas.

Entering Labels

Symphony automatically left-aligns labels in a cell and precedes each label with an apostrophe ('). To right-align a label as you enter it, precede the text with a quotation mark ("). To center the cell contents, type a caret (^) before you type the label data. If you want a character to repeat across the cell's column width, use the repeating label prefix (\). For example, type \- to create a dashed line in a cell.

To enter the initial label contents in the SALES worksheet, follow these steps. Remember that this book uses boldface type to indicate which keys you should press to execute a command.

1. Start the program by changing to the Symphony program directory and typing **symphony** at the DOS prompt.

2. A blank worksheet appears, and you are in SHEET mode.

3. Enter the labels as follows or refer to figure 8.2:

In cell:	Enter:
A1	JAN VS. FEB SALES
A2	BY SALES PERSON
A4	SALES PERSON
	Note: The label SALES PERSON extends into column B. Ignore this overlap for now. You fix it later.
A6	JONES
A7	SMITH
A8	BLACK
A9	JOHNSON
A10	GOLDMAN
A12	TOTALS
B4	^JAN
B11	\-
C4	^FEB
D4	"CHANGE
E4	"% CHANGE

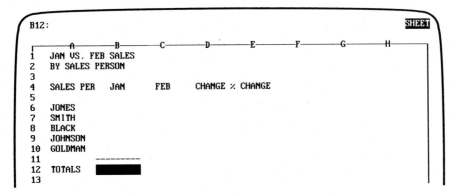

Fig. 8.2.
Labels for the sales worksheet model.

Compare your worksheet to figure 8.2. If you made a mistake as you typed the labels, position the cell pointer on the cell containing the error and retype the entry. (You use EDIT mode, the alternative method of correction, later in this chapter.) If you typed an entry into a cell that should be blank, place the cell pointer on the cell and remove the unwanted entry by using SHEET **E**rase.

The dashed line should extend across columns B through E. Follow these steps to copy the repeating label from cell B11 to C11..D11:

1. Place the cell pointer on cell B11.
2. Select SHEET **C**opy.
3. Press Enter to specify the FROM range as B11 (B11 is the location of the label you want to copy).
4. Move the cell pointer to cell C11 and type a period (.) to anchor the pointer at the beginning of the TO range.
5. Move the cell pointer to cell D11. The cells of the TO range should be highlighted on the screen. The TO range should read C11..E11. Press Enter to complete the command.

Column A needs to be wider than the other columns to accommodate the SALES PERSON label. Follow these steps to widen column A:

1. Place the cell pointer anywhere in column A.
2. Select SHEET **W**idth **S**et.
3. Enter **13** as the column width.

Save the worksheet by selecting SERVICES **F**ile **S**ave. Type **SALES** as the file name. (The file name can be up to eight characters long; no spaces are allowed.)

Remember to save your work periodically! Symphony does not automatically save for you.

Because you have saved the file, at this point you can do one of several things:

❏ Execute SERVICES **Exit Y**es to leave Symphony.

❏ Begin a new worksheet after invoking SERVICES **New Y**es.

❏ Select SERVICES **File R**etrieve to retrieve a different file.

❏ Continue working with the current SALES worksheet displayed on the screen.

Now, enter the values into the current model.

Entering Values

As you enter values, Symphony automatically lines them up on the right side of the cell. Although you cannot alter this alignment, you can change how the number is displayed: with commas, percent signs, dollar signs, and decimal places. You can change the overall format settings for the entire worksheet or for individual cells. (Refer to Chapter 5, "Formatting the Worksheet," for a complete explanation of the available options in Symphony.)

For this model, you establish **P**unctuated as the overall numeric format so that the numbers display commas. But two areas require special formatting. The last row of numbers (the totals) should have dollar signs, so you must individually format this range to **C**urrency. You also must format column E, the % CHANGE column, to **%** (percent) with **2** decimal places. Follow these steps to enter and format values:

1. Enter the following values in the indicated cells. Remember, do not type commas when entering the numbers; you add the commas with formatting.

In cell:	Enter:
B6	35600
B7	12950
B8	24500
B9	90000
B10	54200
C6	60980
C7	23700
C8	27100
C9	125000
C10	25400

2. Select SHEET **S**ettings **F**ormat **P**unctuated. Enter **0** for the number of decimals. Then select **Q**uit. Commas are automatically entered in the values you typed (see fig. 8.3).

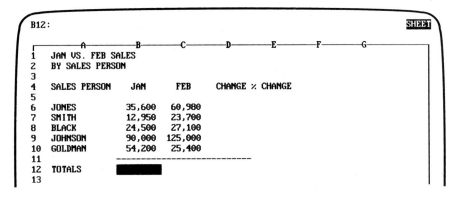

Fig. 8.3.
*Values formatted as
Punctuated with **0**
decimal places.*

3. To format the TOTALS row as **C**urrency, select SHEET **F**ormat **C**urrency. Enter **0** for the number of decimal places.

4. Specify the range B12..D12. When you enter the totals in this range, the numbers will display with dollar signs.

5. To format the % CHANGE column to **%** (percent), select SHEET **F**ormat **%** and enter **2**.

6. Specify E6..E12 as the range to format. When you enter the % CHANGE formulas in this range, the values will display with percent signs.

7. Resave the file with SERVICES **F**ile **S**ave **SALES Y**es.

The worksheet model now contains labels and values. To show the true power of an electronic spreadsheet compared to paper and pencil, you need to include one other type of input: formulas.

Entering and Copying Formulas

Symphony calculates formulas automatically; you only need to specify which mathematical operations are to be performed and which cell locations are to be involved in those operations. You create a formula either by typing each cell address and mathematical operator involved, or by typing the math operators and pointing to the cells. You also can use any of Symphony's built-in @functions. (See Chapter 6, "Using @Functions," for a detailed explanation of @functions.)

To complete the SALES worksheet, you need formulas to compute the following three items:

❏ The change between JAN and FEB sales (column D)

❏ The percentage change between JAN and FEB sales (column E)

❏ The totals (range B12..E12)

Follow these steps to enter the formula to calculate the change between JAN and FEB sales:

1. Enter **+C6-B6** in cell D6. The formula displays in the control panel, and the answer appears in the cell.

2. Select SHEET **C**opy.

3. Press Enter to specify cell D6 as the FROM range (the location of the formula you want to copy).

4. Move the cell pointer to cell D7 and type a period (.) to anchor the pointer at the top of the TO range.

5. Move the cell pointer to cell D10. The cells D7 through D10 should be highlighted on the screen, and the TO range should read D7..D10. Press Enter to complete the command. The screen should resemble figure 8.4.

Fig. 8.4.

The model after entering the CHANGE formula in column D.

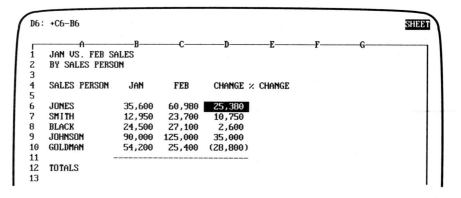

```
D6: +C6-B6                                                      SHEET
┌────────A─────────B────────C────────D────────E────────F────────G──────
1    JAN VS. FEB SALES
2    BY SALES PERSON
3
4    SALES PERSON    JAN      FEB      CHANGE % CHANGE
5
6    JONES          35,600   60,980   25,380
7    SMITH          12,950   23,700   10,750
8    BLACK          24,500   27,100    2,600
9    JOHNSON        90,000  125,000   35,000
10   GOLDMAN        54,200   25,400  (28,800)
11                         -------------------------
12   TOTALS
13
```

You used the typing method to enter the CHANGE formula. Some users prefer the "typing-only" method for entering relatively short formulas that contain only cells visible on the current screen. But as a general rule, a much easier way to enter formulas is the "type-and-point" method. When building formulas with the type-and-point method, you point to the cells rather than type the cell references. The following steps use this method to build the % CHANGE formula:

1. Place the cell pointer on cell E6.

2. Type **+** and press ← once to point to cell D6.

   Note: Do **not** press Enter as you create the formula; if you watch the control panel, you can see the formula being built.

3. Type a slash (/). The pointer returns to E6, the cell into which you are entering the formula. Press ← three times to point to cell B6

4. Press Enter to accept the final formula: +D6/B6.

5. Select SHEET **C**opy.

6. Press Enter to specify cell E6 as the FROM range (the location of the formula you want to copy).

7. Move the cell pointer to E7 and type a period (.) to anchor the pointer at the top of the TO range.

8. Move the cell pointer to E10. The cells E7 through E10 are highlighted on the screen, and the TO range should read E7..E10. Press Enter to complete the command. The screen should look like figure 8.5.

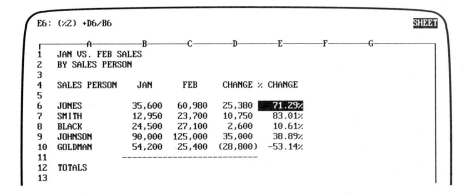

```
E6: (%2) +D6/B6                                                    SHEET
      ──A──────B──────C──────D──────E──────F──────G──
  1   JAN VS. FEB SALES
  2   BY SALES PERSON
  3
  4   SALES PERSON    JAN      FEB     CHANGE % CHANGE
  5
  6   JONES          35,600   60,980   25,380    71.29%
  7   SMITH          12,950   23,700   10,750    83.01%
  8   BLACK          24,500   27,100    2,600    10.61%
  9   JOHNSON        90,000  125,000   35,000    38.89%
 10   GOLDMAN        54,200   25,400  (28,800)  -53.14%
 11                         ─────────────────────────
 12   TOTALS
 13
```

Fig. 8.5.
The model after entering the % CHANGE formula in column E.

Use @SUM, one of Symphony's built-in @functions, to total the JAN column; then copy this formula across row 12. Follow these steps:

1. Enter the TOTALS formula **@SUM(B6..B10)** in cell B12.

2. Use SHEET **C**opy to copy FROM B12 TO C12..D12.

Also, copy the % CHANGE formula FROM E10 TO E12. The worksheet should look like figure 8.6.

```
E12: (%2) +D12/B12                                                SHEET
      ──A──────B──────C──────D──────E──────F──────G──
  1   JAN VS. FEB SALES
  2   BY SALES PERSON
  3
  4   SALES PERSON    JAN      FEB     CHANGE % CHANGE
  5
  6   JONES          35,600   60,980   25,380    71.29%
  7   SMITH          12,950   23,700   10,750    83.01%
  8   BLACK          24,500   27,100    2,600    10.61%
  9   JOHNSON        90,000  125,000   35,000    38.89%
 10   GOLDMAN        54,200   25,400  (28,800)  -53.14%
 11                         ─────────────────────────
 12   TOTALS       $217,250 $262,180  $44,930    20.68%
 13
```

Fig. 8.6.
The worksheet with all labels, values, and formulas entered.

Expanding the Model

This model was designed to compare sales in JAN and FEB, but works equally well for any two months in the year. You can expand the model by creating windows for different month combinations and then copying the model into these windows.

Creating Windows

One of Symphony's most powerful features is its capacity to keep separate information in different windows. You can switch quickly between windows by pressing Window (F6). The windows can be any size, and you can create as many as you need. Expand the sample model by creating two windows: one for January and February, and another for February and March. Follow these steps to create a window for January and February:

1. Select SERVICES **W**indow **C**reate.
2. Enter **JAN-FEB** as the window name.
3. Select SHEET as the window type.
4. Press Enter to select the entire screen as the window area.
5. Select **R**estrict **R**ange and specify A1..G20.
6. Select **Q**uit.

Notice the window name **JAN-FEB** at the bottom of the window. Now follow these steps to create a window for February and March:

1. Select SERVICES **W**indow **C**reate.
2. Enter **FEB-MAR** as the window name.
3. Select SHEET as the window type.
4. Press Enter to select the entire screen as the window area.
5. Select **R**estrict **R**ange and specify H1..O20.
6. Select **Q**uit.

Notice the window name **FEB-MAR** at the bottom of the window.

Copying between Windows

The Window (F6) key moves you from one window to the next. You can even use this key in the middle of the **C**opy command to copy information between windows. Follow these steps to copy the table from the JAN-FEB window to the FEB-MAR window:

1. Press Window (F6) until the JAN-FEB window is displayed. (Look at the window name at the bottom of the screen.)

2. Select SHEET **C**opy.

3. For the FROM range, indicate A1..E12; press Enter.

4. Press Window (F6) until you are in the FEB-MAR window.

5. The cell pointer should be in cell H1. Press Enter to complete the copy. Notice that the pointer then moves back to the JAN-FEB window.

6. Press Window (F6) until you reach the FEB-MAR window again.

Changing the Worksheet

Once you create the worksheet, you probably will want to make changes to it. Because you are using an electronic spreadsheet rather than a paper spreadsheet, making changes is a snap. You easily can move a cell or a range of cells, edit cells, and insert and delete rows and columns. Throw away your scissors and bottle of whiteout!

Moving Cells

In the model, the worksheet title would look better if it were centered above the entire table. Follow these steps to use the **M**ove command to rearrange the title:

1. Position the cell pointer on cell H1.

2. Select SHEET **M**ove.

3. Press ↓ to move to cell H2; the FROM range is now H1..H2. Press Enter.

4. Move the cell pointer to cell J1 and press Enter.

5. Repeat these steps to move the titles to cell C1 in the JAN-FEB window.

Using the Edit Key

Although you copied the JAN-FEB table to the FEB-MAR window, the table still contains references to January and February and data from those months. Revise the table so that it contains February and March headings. Use the Edit (F2) key to modify the cell contents as specified in these steps:

1. Press Window (F6) until you see the FEB-MAR window.

2. Place the cell pointer on cell J1.

3. Press Edit (F2) to display the contents of cell J1 in the control panel. Notice the **EDIT** mode indicator in the upper right corner of the screen.

4. Use ← or Ctrl-← to move the cursor to the *F* in *FEB*.

5. Press the Del key three times to remove *FEB*.

6. Type **MAR**. Notice how the characters are inserted.

7. Use ← to move the cursor to the *J* in *JAN*; delete this word with the Del key.

8. Type **FEB**.

9. Press Enter to exit EDIT mode.

10. Change the column headings from *JAN* and *FEB* to *FEB* and *MAR*. Simply type over the cell contents, remembering to first type the caret (^) to center the labels.

11. Use SHEET **W**idth **S**et to widen column H to 13.

Figure 8.7 shows how the FEB-MAR worksheet should look after you edit the labels.

Fig. 8.7.

Labels edited for the FEB-MAR window.

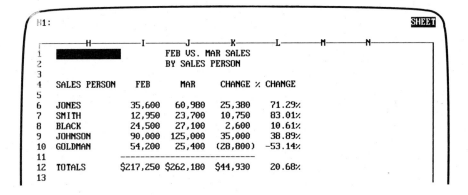

Inserting and Deleting Rows

Simple commands on the SHEET menu enable you to insert and delete easily any number of rows or columns. As long as you don't disturb an end point of a formula range, you can safely insert and delete without having to re-enter or edit a formula.

Follow these steps to add two new people to the FEB-MAR table by inserting two rows:

1. Place the cell pointer on cell H9.

2. Select SHEET **I**nsert **R**ow.

3. Press ↓ once to highlight the range H9..H10; press Enter to complete the row insertions.

4. Enter the following labels:

In cell:	Enter:
H9	THOMAS
H10	CARMAN

You enter the sales values for these people later, when you enter the February and March sales values for the rest of the sales people.

Follow these steps to delete the row containing the sales for SMITH:

1. Position the cell pointer on cell H7.

2. Select SHEET **D**elete **R**ow.

3. Press Enter to delete the current row.

The worksheet should look like figure 8.8.

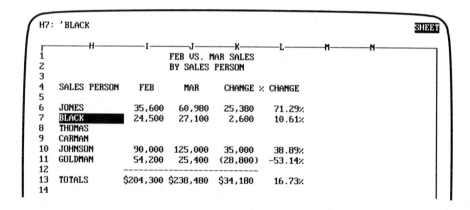

Fig. 8.8.
The FEB-MAR worksheet after inserting and deleting rows.

Protecting the Model

A great deal of time and effort goes into developing, testing, and entering data into a model. Although you have saved your file on disk, and you know that you should make a backup copy on another disk, you may want to consider using some additional protection measures available in Symphony.

You can build protection into a worksheet, preventing entry into some cells (cells containing formulas, for example) while permitting entry into others (such as input cells). When protection is enabled, you need not worry about accidentally typing over the formulas you worked so hard to create.

You also may want to password-protect the file so that no one else can retrieve the file without entering the correct password.

Preventing Accidental Overwrite

The only cells you need to change in the model worksheet are the monthly data figures. You should protect all other cells from accidental changes. Protecting a worksheet involves two steps: enabling global protection and unprotecting the cells you want to change.

Follow these steps to protect all cells in the worksheet except those in which you want to enter sales figures:

1. Select SERVICES **S**ettings **G**lobal-Protection **Y**es **Q**uit. This command protects all cells in the worksheet.

2. Select SHEET **R**ange **P**rotect **A**llow-Changes.

3. Specify the range of cells you want to be able to change: in this case, I6..J11. Unprotected cells appear brighter or in a different color on-screen. The **A** in these cells indicates the **A**llow-Changes protection status. Press Enter.

4. Enter the following values into the unprotected range (see fig. 8.9). Simply type over the existing data in these cells.

In cell:	Enter:
I6	60980
I7	27100
I8	35000
I9	45000
I10	125000
I11	25400
J6	75000
J7	26000
J8	35000
J9	45000
J10	150000
J11	26000

5. Try typing a value into a protected cell, such as K6. What happens? Press Esc to clear the error.

6. Turn off global protection by selecting SERVICES **S**ettings **G**lobal-Protection **N**o **Q**uit.

You also must copy the CHANGE and % CHANGE formulas into the inserted rows. You can copy both formulas at once by following these steps:

1. Position the cell pointer on cell K7.

2. Select SHEET **C**opy.

3. Press → once to highlight K7..L7 as the range to copy FROM; press Enter.

4. Indicate K8..K9 as the TO range and press Enter. The screen should resemble figure 8.10.

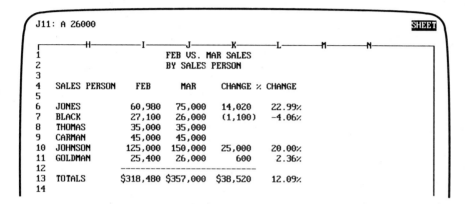

Fig. 8.9.

The changed values in the unprotected range (I6..J11).

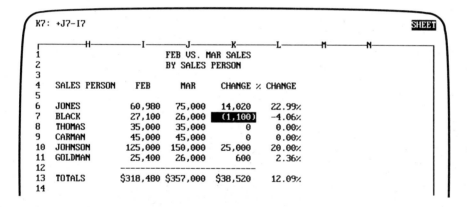

Fig. 8.10.

The model after copying the CHANGE and % CHANGE formulas into the inserted rows.

Password-Protecting the File

You can assign a password to a file by typing a **p** after the file name when you save the file. Keep in mind, however, that if *you* forget the password, you lock *yourself* out of the file, too!

Follow these steps to assign a password to the SALES file:

1. Select SERVICES **F**ile **S**ave.

2. Press the space bar and type **p**; press Enter.

3. Enter the password **test**. Blocks instead of characters appear on-screen as you type. Press Enter.

4. Verify the password by typing it a second time. Press Enter.

5. Select **Y**es to replace the file.

To see how password protection works, clear the screen and retrieve the file by following these steps:

1. Select SERVICES **N**ew **Y**es.

2. Select SERVICES **F**ile **R**etrieve.

3. Type **SALES** and press Enter.

4. Type the password **test**. Make sure that you type the password with the same combination of uppercase and lowercase characters you used when you specified the password initially. Press Enter.

Working with Large Worksheets

With a small worksheet, every change you make is instantly and automatically recalculated. When worksheets become large, however, you notice a delay in the time Symphony takes to recalculate the worksheet. You can deal with this problem in one of two ways. First, you can turn automatic recalculation off so that the worksheet recalculates only when you press the Calc (F8) key. Second, you can divide the large worksheet into several smaller ones by extracting ranges to new files.

Recalculating the Worksheet

Follow these steps to change the recalculation method to **M**anual. You then use the Calc (F8) key to recalculate the worksheet manually after you make some changes.

1. Select SHEET **S**ettings **R**ecalculation **M**ethod **M**anual **Q**uit.

2. Enter **74000** in cell J6. Notice the `Calc` indicator at the bottom of the screen (see fig. 8.11).

3. Enter **29000** in cell J7.

4. Press Calc (F8) to recalculate the worksheet. The `Calc` indicator disappears, and the formula results reflect the changes in the data.

5. Change back to automatic recalculation by selecting SHEET **S**ettings **R**ecalculation **M**ethod **A**utomatic **Q**uit.

```
 6   JONES        60,980   74,000    14,020    22.99%
 7   BLACK        27,100   29,000    (1,100)   -4.06%
 8   THOMAS       35,000   35,000         0     0.00%
 9   CARMAN       45,000   45,000         0     0.00%
10   JOHNSON     125,000  150,000    25,000    20.00%
11   GOLDMAN      25,400   26,000       600     2.36%
12                      ---------------------------
13   TOTALS     $318,480 $357,000   $38,520    12.09%
14
15
16
17
18
19
20
                                                      FEB-MAR
                            Calc
```

Fig. 8.11.
The Calc *indicator when recalculation is set to Manual.*

Extracting Ranges to Separate Files

The **F**ile **X**tract command copies sections of a worksheet into new files. With large applications, you may need to create smaller, separate files because of memory considerations. Follow these steps to put each two-month table in a separate file:

1. Select SERVICES **F**ile **X**tract **F**ormulas.

2. Enter **FEB-MAR** as the file name.

3. Indicate the range H1..L13 and press Enter.

4. Select SERVICES **N**ew **Y**es to clear the screen.

5. Select SERVICES **F**ile **R**etrieve and enter **FEB-MAR**. The screen should look like figure 8.12.

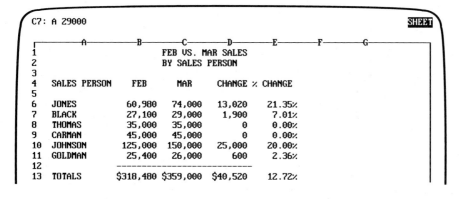

```
C7: A 29000                                          SHEET
      A         B        C        D        E      F      G
 1                   FEB VS. MAR SALES
 2                    BY SALES PERSON
 3
 4   SALES PERSON   FEB      MAR    CHANGE % CHANGE
 5
 6   JONES        60,980   74,000    13,020   21.35%
 7   BLACK        27,100   29,000     1,900    7.01%
 8   THOMAS       35,000   35,000         0    0.00%
 9   CARMAN       45,000   45,000         0    0.00%
10   JOHNSON     125,000  150,000    25,000   20.00%
11   GOLDMAN      25,400   26,000       600    2.36%
12                      ---------------------------
13   TOTALS     $318,480 $359,000   $40,520   12.72%
```

Fig. 8.12.
The FEB-MAR table extracted to a new file.

Chapter Summary

This chapter has provided you the opportunity to practice using Symphony's most important environment: the spreadsheet. You started building the model by entering labels, values, and formulas. You then expanded the model by creating windows for other versions of the worksheet. You changed the worksheet by editing, moving, inserting, and deleting. You also learned how to protect the model by password-protecting the file and by protecting sections of the worksheet so that you cannot inadvertently overwrite formulas or labels. Finally, you learned some tools for working with large worksheets: turning off automatic recalculation and extracting sections of the worksheet to smaller files.

In the following chapter, you learn how to master Symphony's word-processing environment.

Part III

Using the Symphony Word Processor

Working in a Symphony DOC Environment: Word Processing

Learning DOC Window: Hands-On Practice

Word Processing Add-Ins: Spelling Checker and Text Outliner

9

Working in a Symphony DOC Window: Word Processing

Learning to use Symphony's word processing environment is similar to learning to use the other program applications—spreadsheet, graphics, data management, and communications. The Symphony DOC environment shares a number of features with the other applications, including similarities in the display screen, the use of command menus, and the way Symphony stores text. Except for handling special format lines or print commands within the text, you don't need to master a new way of entering commands in Symphony's DOC window environment; the approach is the same as that for a SHEET, FORM, GRAPH, or COMM window.

What are the advantages of having a fully integrated software package that includes word processing? Once you begin to use Symphony's word processing feature—the Symphony DOC environment—you will find three major advantages to having this capability. The first is simply one of convenience. You do not have to access another program or change disks when you compose a letter or memo, or draft a report, or put a few notes together. Also, there is the handiness of learning one program but having five applications available at any time.

The second advantage to having word processing along with spreadsheet, data management, graphics, and communications is Symphony's capability to integrate word processing with the other applications. For instance, you can be working in a DOC window and at the same time have a SHEET or GRAPH window on the screen. You will find that this capability alone may make switching from a single word processing program to Symphony well worth it.

The third advantage to using Symphony's word processing capability is the simplification of many DOC operations through the use of macros, which are discussed in Chapter 21. That chapter shows you how to create macros for many moving, erasing, and copying operations. After learning Symphony's DOC environment and how to create Symphony macros interactively, you will be able to reduce many lengthy operations to one keystroke.

This chapter introduces you to Symphony's word processing capabilities so that you can make the DOC window environment a regular part of using the program. Included are the following topics:

❏ Creating a DOC window

❏ Viewing The DOC display

❏ Using The DOC function keys

❏ Getting started in a DOC window

❏ Entering text and moving the cursor

❏ Erasing and editing text

❏ Searching and replacing

❏ Formatting your document

❏ Integrating the DOC environment with other Symphony applications

Creating a DOC Window

You can use various methods to create a DOC window. First, if you work with a DOC window more frequently than other types of windows (SHEET, GRAPH, FORM, or COMM), then you can begin every work session with a DOC window by updating the SERVICES Configuration Window Type setting to DOC. To change the setting for the window type, retrieve the SERVICES menu by pressing Services (F9), select Configuration from the menu, and then choose Window. Next, select Type. When the five types of windows appear, select DOC. Finally, choose Update. The default window is then set to DOC. Every time you access the Symphony program or create a new worksheet with SERVICES New Yes, the window type will be DOC.

Reminder:

You can switch back and forth between a DOC window and the last used window by using Alt-F9.

If, however, you set the default window type to SHEET, GRAPH, FORM, or COMM, you can shift to a DOC window by pressing Type (Alt-F10) and selecting DOC. You also can use Alt-F9 to switch back and forth between a DOC window and the last used window. You can use one other procedure for setting the window type. Whenever you create a new window by using the Window Create command from the SERVICES menu, Symphony asks you to choose a window type. If the current window is not DOC, you can select it.

Viewing the DOC Display

When you enter the Symphony program for the first time, a SHEET window is the type of window to appear. Symphony has set the default setting for initial window type to SHEET. In the SHEET window, columns are represented by letters at the top, and rows are indicated by numbers down the left side. The SHEET window, which is bordered on all four sides, contains an indicator area in the top right and left corners. When you shift to a DOC window, either by pressing Alt-F10 or by creating a new window with the SERVICES **W**indow **C**reate command, the display remains much the same as for the SHEET window—still bordered on all four sides and containing indicators in the upper right and left corners.

In addition, DOC commands are displayed exactly as those for SHEET, GRAPH, FORM, and COMM (see fig. 9.1). When you retrieve the DOC command menu, it appears above the top line of the DOC border, and the explanation of the cursor-highlighted command appears above the menu line.

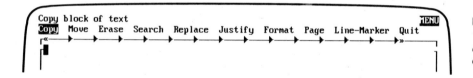

Copy block of text
Copy Move Erase Search Replace Justify Format Page Line-Marker Quit   MENU

Fig. 9.1.
The DOC commands displayed.

The DOC display screen, however, has some special features. First, the top line of the border indicates the left and right margins and all tab settings. The default setting (shown in the SERVICES **C**onfiguration settings sheet) for the left margin is 1 and for the right margin is 72. Tabs are set 5 spaces apart. The top line indicating margins and tabs is always displayed unless you change the border from **S**tandard to **L**ine or **N**one by selecting SERVICES **W**indow **S**ettings **B**orders.

Above the top line are three indicators: the cursor position (line, character, and page); the type of justification and spacing; and the mode indicator. An asterisk in the middle of the control panel indicates that the cursor is currently located on data that has been entered in another type of window.

If you are working in a DOC window and move the cursor to data that you have already entered in a SHEET environment, for example, Symphony displays the asterisk to remind you that DOC commands and operations and SHEET commands and operations are not interchangeable. For example, you cannot edit labels and numbers entered in a SHEET window by using the Backspace and Del keys as you are working in a DOC window. If you include special format lines (discussed later in this chapter) in your text, an asterisk appears when the cursor is positioned at these format lines, again telling you that you cannot change this text as you can other data.

Reminder:
DOC commands and operations and SHEET commands and operations are not inter-changeable.

One other indicator to note is the **Calc** indicator in the bottom right corner. **Calc** indicates that changes in the DOC window may affect calculations in spreadsheets created in other areas of your worksheet. If you do have spreadsheets in the worksheet, press Calc (F8) to recalculate cell values.

Using DOC Function Keys

Whenever you begin word processing operations in a DOC window, eight function keys are available, ranging from a key for justifying paragraphs to a key for jumping the cursor from one part of the text to another.

Two of these keys—Justify (F2) and Erase (F4)—perform the same operations as comparable commands from the DOC command menu. The following function keys have special uses for DOC operations:

Key	Function
Alt-F1 (Compose)	Used for creating special characters not included on the keyboard. To create a special character, press Alt-F1; then press the key(s) for the symbol. For example, to create a "less than or equal to" symbol, press Alt-F1 and then type **<=**.
Alt-F2 (Where)	Indicates in the lower left corner of the screen the page and line location of the cursor's current position. This information is also displayed at the top of the screen (for example, **Page 1,6**). The Where key is left over from earlier versions of Symphony, which did not display the page number at the top of the screen. This key is not too useful in Symphony releases greater than 2.0.
F2 (Justify)	Justifies paragraphs; completes the same operation as that of **J**ustify **P**aragraph from the DOC menu.
Alt-F3 (Split)	Divides a line of text or creates blank lines without leaving hard carriage returns.
F3 (Indent)	Indents a paragraph or section of text. (See the later sections on special formatting.)
Alt-F4 (Center)	Centers a line of text with respect to the margin settings for the line.
F4 (Erase)	Initiates the **E**rase command; completes the same operation as that of the **E**rase command from the DOC menu.
F5 (GoTo)	Used for jumping the cursor to another line on the same page, to a line on another page, or to a named line. (See the later section titled "The GoTo Key and Line-Marker Names.") When you press F5 and then Menu (F10), a list of all marked lines appears.

Getting Started in a DOC Window

What do you need to know as you begin using Symphony's word processor? You probably want to know how text is displayed, stored, and finally printed. You also need to know how to enter text on the screen and how to edit and change text.

Getting started in a DOC window requires that you understand the organization of the DOC command menu (fig. 9.2), the "accelerator" keys that are available, the kinds of special commands that are inserted within the text, and the different kinds of settings sheets that affect a DOC window.

```
Copy block of text                                              MENU
Copy  Move  Erase  Search  Replace  Justify  Format  Page  Line-Marker  Quit
```

Fig. 9.2.
Organization of the DOC command menu.

Using the DOC Command Menu

Using the DOC command menu requires the same operations as using the command menus for other windows. You simply press Menu (F10), move the cursor to the command, and complete the operations required by that command. The DOC commands fall into the following primary categories:

1. **C**opy, **M**ove, and **E**rase commands
2. **S**earch and **R**eplace commands
3. **F**ormat commands, including those for paragraph justification, spacing, margins, tabs, and operations connected with creating special "format lines," naming lines, and inserting page breaks

Using DOC Accelerator Keys

As an alternative to using the DOC command menu, you can use "accelerator" keys. For example, you can press Ctrl-C rather than select **C**opy from the DOC menu. Following is a list of the available accelerator keys:

Key	Description
Auto (Ctrl-J)	Turns auto-justification on/off
Begin (Ctrl-B)	Begins print attribute
Case (Ctrl-X)	Converts capitalization of characters
Copy (Ctrl-C)	Copies text
Delete Left (Ctrl-T)	Deletes text to start of line

Key	Description
Delete Line (Ctrl-D)	Deletes current line
Delete Right (Ctrl-Y)	Deletes text to end of line
Delete Word (Ctrl-Backspace)	Deletes previous word
Format (Ctrl-F)	Inserts format line
Merge (Ctrl-O)	Inserts merge character
Move (Ctrl-M)	Moves text
Next Page (Ctrl-PgDn)	Moves cursor to next page
Page (Ctrl-N)	Inserts page break
Paste (Ctrl-P)	Inserts last deleted text
Replace (Ctrl R)	Replaces text
Search (Ctrl-S)	Searches for text
Stop (Ctrl-E)	Ends print attribute
Top Page (Ctrl-PgUp)	Moves cursor to top of page

Using Print Attributes

You can place special print attributes (indicating boldface, italic, underlining, superscript, subscript, and combinations of these) within the text. For example, if you want Symphony to boldface a character, letter, or word, you enclose it within print attribute commands. Here are the steps to follow:

1. Signal the beginning of a special print attribute by pressing Ctrl-B. (B stands for "Begin Attribute.") The Print Attribute menu appears.

2. Select the appropriate print attribute from the menu. Following is a description of each option:

Attribute Option	Code
Boldface	B
Italic	I
Underline	U
Superscript	+
Subscript	-
Strike-through	X
Boldface italic	0 (Zero)
Boldface underline	1
Boldface italic underline	2

Attribute Option	Code
Italic underline	3
Boldface superscript	4
Italic superscript	5
Boldface subscript	6
Italic subscript	7
Boldface italic subscript	8
Boldface italic superscript	9
Include spaces in print attributes	S
Do not include spaces	Q

3. Signal the end of the print attribute by pressing Ctrl-E (for "End Attribute").

Before selecting these print attributes, make sure that your driver is set for the right printer(s). (See Appendix A's section on installing drivers.)

If you have a monochrome monitor, the attributed text appears either underlined or in low intensity. If you have a color monitor, the text appears in a different color. To identify which attribute has been selected, move the cursor anywhere within the attributed text and look in the control panel for the code. For example, a **U** displays in the control panel for underlined text, and a **B** appears for boldfaced text.

If you find you have selected the wrong attribute or later change your mind about a print attribute you selected, you can change the begin attribute. Place the cursor at the beginning of the attributed text, press Ctrl-B, and select the new attribute. Symphony automatically removes the old attribute.

To eliminate a print attribute entirely, perform the following steps:

1. Place the cursor at the beginning of the attributed text.
2. Press Erase (F4). The print attribute characters display on the screen.
3. Press Enter to erase the begin attribute character.
4. Place the cursor at the end of the attributed text.
5. Press Erase (F4).
6. Press Enter to erase the end attribute character.

Using Format Settings

The first step in using Symphony's DOC environment is to adjust special format settings. Besides inserting format lines in the text (discussed later in this chapter), Symphony provides two ways for controlling the format of a DOC environment: the default format settings stored in Symphony's configuration file (SYMPHONY.CNF), and the format settings that you can enter for each DOC window you create.

Format Settings in Symphony's Configuration File

The SERVICES **C**onfiguration **D**ocument setting establishes the default settings for tabs, justification, spacing, margins, display of hard spaces between words, display of carriage returns and hard tabs, and automatic justification of paragraphs. When you first enter Symphony, the following default settings are in operation:

Tab interval: 5

Justification: 1

Spacing: 1

Left margin: 1

Right margin: 72

Blanks visible: No

CRs visible: Yes

Auto-Justify: Yes

Hard-Tabs: Yes

Reminder:

If you do not update the sheet, the new settings that you enter are in effect only until you finish your current work session and exit from the program.

You can change any or all of these settings by selecting **C**onfiguration from the SERVICES menu, choosing **D**ocument, selecting each item to be changed, and then entering the new settings. Once you have changed the **C**onfiguration **D**ocument settings, you need to update the settings sheet by selecting **U**pdate from the **C**onfiguration menu. If you do not update the sheet, the new settings that you enter are in effect only until you finish your current work session and exit from the program.

The SERVICES **C**onfiguration **D**ocument settings are useful for storing format settings for frequently modified documents. You need to remember that **C**onfiguration **D**ocument settings control the format settings for the first DOC window that you create in any given file. You may therefore want to change the SERVICES **C**onfiguration **D**ocument settings to the kind of format you plan to use most often. For example, if you find that you frequently use the DOC environment for creating one-page memos, you may want to change the **C**onfiguration **D**ocument settings to the particular format required by the memos.

Format Settings in DOC Window

You can override **C**onfiguration **D**ocument settings, however, by using the **F**ormat **S**ettings command from the DOC menu. When you change **F**ormat

Settings, these settings control the format of any text you enter. Also, whenever you change **F**ormat **S**ettings in one DOC window and then create another DOC window, the second window inherits the format settings of the previous window unless you have deleted that window.

After you enter a DOC window, the next step is to determine whether you need to change format settings. As mentioned earlier, the top line of the border tells you where margins and tabs have been set. Above the top line in the control panel, Symphony indicates the type of justification and spacing. For example, **Left, Single** tells you that the window is set for left-justification and single-spacing.

Whenever you need to change format settings for the current DOC window, use the DOC **F**ormat **S**ettings command. This command enables you to enter settings for the current window and to save those settings along with the window. Suppose, for example, that you are creating a table, as shown in figure 9.3. In the window, you need a left margin of 15, a right margin of 60, and double-spacing. (Double- and triple-spacing do not appear on-screen, but they do appear in printed copy. See this chapter's section called "Setting Tabs, Spacing, and Margins.")

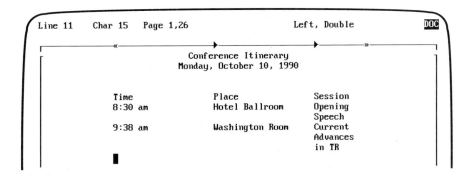

Fig. 9.3.
Creating a table in a DOC window.

In addition to checking the settings for margins, tabs, justification, and spacing before you begin to work in a DOC window, you also can check three other settings by retrieving the **F**ormat **S**ettings sheet from the DOC menu. (You also can change these three settings in the SERVICES **C**onfiguration **D**ocument settings.) The settings are the following:

❑ **B**lanks. If you select **Y**es, Symphony displays periods on the screen for every space. Because the default setting is **N**o, you need to change this setting only when you want spaces marked.

❑ **CR**s. Symphony displays hard carriage returns. **Y**es is the default setting.

❏ **A**uto-Justify. When **A**uto-Justify is set to **Y**es, which is the default setting, Symphony automatically justifies paragraphs after every editing change. If you select **N**o, paragraphs do not justify until you press Justify (F2) or select DOC **J**ustify. The Auto accelerator key (Ctrl-J) also turns automatic justification on and off.

Format Settings Guidelines

When you use the SERVICES **C**onfiguration **D**ocument settings, the DOC **F**ormat **S**ettings, and format lines, keep the following guidelines in mind:

❏ The **C**onfiguration **D**ocument settings provide the default settings; however, DOC **F**ormat **S**ettings can override **C**onfiguration **D**ocument settings.

❏ A DOC **F**ormat **S**ettings sheet is stored with each window you create, and the settings remain with that window until you change them.

❏ **B**lanks, **CR**s, and **A**uto-Justify settings override format lines.

Some examples can help clarify the relationships of the SERVICES **C**onfiguration **D**ocument settings, a DOC **F**ormat **S**ettings sheet, and format lines. You also can note the effect that creating different windows has on these three methods for adjusting format.

When you create the first DOC window for a worksheet, the DOC **F**ormat **S**ettings are inherited from the **C**onfiguration **D**ocument settings. Figure 9.4 shows the **C**onfiguration **D**ocument settings stored in the Symphony configuration file (SYMPHONY.CNF). The DOC **F**ormat **S**ettings for the DOC window, shown in figure 9.5, are the same as those in the **C**onfiguration **D**ocument settings.

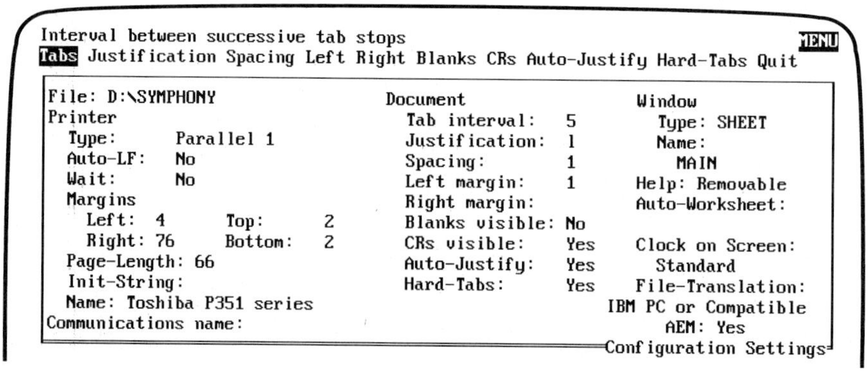

Fig. 9.4.

The SERVICES
Configuration
Document settings.

```
Interval between successive tab stops                               MENU
Tabs Justification Spacing Left Right Blanks CRs Auto-Justify Hard-Tabs Quit

File: D:\SYMPHONY                 Document              Window
Printer                            Tab interval:   5      Type: SHEET
  Type:       Parallel 1           Justification:  1      Name:
  Auto-LF:    No                   Spacing:        1        MAIN
  Wait:       No                   Left margin:    1      Help: Removable
  Margins                          Right margin:   1      Auto-Worksheet:
    Left:  4       Top:     2      Blanks visible: No
    Right: 76      Bottom:  2      CRs visible:    Yes    Clock on Screen:
  Page-Length: 66                  Auto-Justify:   Yes      Standard
  Init-String:                     Hard-Tabs:      Yes    File-Translation:
  Name: Toshiba P351 series                                IBM PC or Compatible
Communications name:                                       AEM: Yes
                                                     Configuration Settings
```

```
┌─────────────────────────────────────────────────────────────────────┐
│ Interval between successive tab stops                          MENU   │
│ Tabs  Justification  Spacing  Left  Right  Blanks  CRs  Auto-Justify  Quit │
│  ┌──────────────────────────────────────────────────────┐            │
│  │ Tab interval:     5                                    │           │
│  │ Justification:    1                                    │           │
│  │ Spacing:          1                                    │           │
│  │ Left margin:      1                                    │           │
│  │ Right margin:                                          │           │
│  │ Blanks visible:  No                                    │           │
│  │ CRs visible:     Yes                                   │           │
│  │ Auto-Justify:    Yes                                   │           │
│  └────────────────────────────Document Settings for window MAIN┘     │
└─────────────────────────────────────────────────────────────────────┘
```

Fig. 9.5.
The DOC Format Settings

Note that the right margin setting is initially left blank; Symphony automatically sets the right margin according to the size of the current window. When you create a second DOC window on the screen, that window inherits the DOC Format Settings from the first window. You can, however, change the settings in DOC Format Settings for the particular window in which you are working. In the example in figure 9.3, the DOC Format Settings have been changed to the following:

Tab interval: 17

Justification: 1 (1 = Left)

Spacing: 2

Left margin: 15

Right margin: 60

Blanks visible: No

CRs visible: Yes

Auto-Justify: No

You also can return to your original format settings by using the DOC Format Edit Current Reset command (see this chapter's section called "Creating, Editing, and Storing Format Lines"). If you decide that you don't need the format line at all, use the Erase command to delete the format line or the format line marker. Whenever you erase a named format line, the name is also deleted.

Reminder:
Whenever you erase a named format line, the name is also deleted.

Entering Text and Moving the Cursor

After you have made changes in the SERVICES Configuration Document settings and the DOC Format Settings, you are ready to begin entering text in the DOC window. Entering words from the keyboard is not much different from typing words on a typewriter keyboard, except for wordwrap and Insert/Overstrike modes.

Using Wordwrap

If you have used word processing programs before, you are probably familiar with wordwrap. In Symphony, as in other word processors, wordwrap is the capability of maintaining the right margin automatically and moving the cursor to the succeeding line. Whole words, then, are not divided but "wrapped around" to the next line. In other words, you do not have to press the carriage return to begin a new line. When wordwrap occurs, Symphony formats each line according to the controlling justification setting—**N**one, **L**eft, **E**ven, or **C**enter.

At times, you may want two words (or letters and numbers separated by spaces) to remain on the same line rather than have one word at the end of a line and the other word at the beginning of the next line. In this case, you can insert a "hard space" between the two words.

For example, you may want a trademark, product name, or company name, such as "J.P. McMurphy," to appear all on one line (see fig. 9.6). To have the entire name wrap around to the next line, take the following steps. Type **J.**, press Compose (Alt- F1), and then press the space bar twice. Symphony inserts a dot, indicating that a hard space is inserted. Next, type **P.**, press Compose, and again press the space bar twice. Symphony inserts another dot. Finally, type **McMurphy**. When margins are justified because of wordwrap, "J.P. McMurphy" remains on the same line.

Fig. 9.6.

Inserting hard spaces.

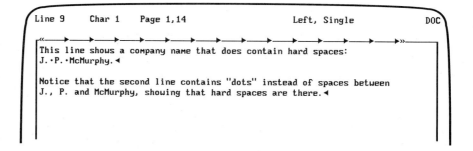

Using Insert and Overstrike Modes

The Insert mode is the default setting for entering characters from the keyboard. Whenever you enter characters in Insert mode, you can insert any character or a space to the immediate left of the cursor. Also, whenever the DOC environment is set in Insert mode, wordwrap is in effect.

The Overstrike mode is the opposite of the Insert mode. You turn on Overstrike by pressing the Ins key in the lower left corner of the numeric keyboard. In Overstrike mode, you can change characters or add spaces directly over the character or space where the cursor is positioned. Also, wordwrap is turned off in Overstrike mode. Whenever Overstrike mode is on, an **Ovr** indicator is displayed in the bottom right corner of your screen.

Using the Backspace key in both Insert and Overstrike modes erases the character to the left of the cursor. In Insert mode, however, characters to the right are shifted to the left when you press the Backspace key. In Overstrike mode, characters to the right remain in their original positions.

The real differences between entering text into a DOC window and typing text at a typewriter keyboard are noticeable when you use Symphony's word processor for performing many kinds of editing and formatting operations. These operations range from word-level changes, such as correcting spelling, to much larger changes, such as moving blocks of text or transferring text from other files.

Moving the Cursor in a DOC Window

An essential part of performing many editing and formatting operations is being able to move the cursor within a DOC window. You may find cursor movement to be quite convenient when you are working not only in DOC mode as you enter and change text, but also in POINT mode when you are completing such commands as **C**opy, **M**ove, and **E**rase.

Moving the cursor in a DOC window is similar to moving the cell pointer in a SHEET window; you use many of the same keys for both kinds of movements. You can use many more keys, however, to move the cursor in a DOC window.

The keys for moving the cursor in a DOC window include the following:

> The cursor keys: ←, →, ↑, ↓
> The PgUp and PgDn keys
> The Home key
> The End key
> The Ctrl key (used only in combination with others)
> The Scroll Lock key (used only in combination with others)
> The F2 key (used with the End key)
> The Alt + F2 keys (used with the End key)
> The Enter key (used with the End key)
> Any typed character (used with the End key)

Using these keys in a DOC window enables you to move the cursor from one character or space to another, from one word to another, from one line to another, from the beginning of the paragraph to the end (and vice versa), from one screen to another, and from the beginning of the window restrict range to the end (and vice versa). The sections that follow describe in detail each of these types of cursor movement.

Moving One Character or Space at a Time

You may at times want to move the cursor backward or forward one character or space, particularly when you need to correct a misspelling in a previous word on the current line. The keys listed here are used for moving from one character to another:

To move the cursor:	Use the following:
To preceding character	←
To next character	→
To any specific character	End, then specific character

You may find the last option especially convenient when you want to move forward to a specific spot in your text. Although using the **S**earch command is similar to using the End key and a specific character, the latter method saves you keystrokes. The **S**earch command requires six keystrokes, including one to return to DOC mode; the End key followed by a character requires only two.

Suppose that you want to move the cursor forward to a sentence that ends with a question mark. If you use **S**earch, you first retrieve the DOC menu by pressing Menu (F10) and then select **S**earch. Next, you type the character (in this case, a question mark), press Enter, and then indicate whether the search should be **F**orward or **B**ackward. Finally, after the cursor moves to the specific character, you select **Q**uit to move out of MENU mode and back to DOC mode. With the End key, you accomplish the same operation by pressing End and then pressing the Shift and question mark keys at the same time.

The End-key method is also convenient when you are highlighting a block for completing the **C**opy, **M**ove, or **E**rase commands. For example, suppose that you want to erase the beginning of the second sentence shown in figure 9.7A, erasing from `Although` to the comma after `character`. To erase this part of the sentence, first place your cursor at the beginning of the sentence, and then select the DOC **E**rase command or press Erase (F4). When the `Erase what block?` prompt appears, press End, then press the comma key (see fig. 9.7B), and finally press Enter.

Fig. 9.7A.

The cursor at the beginning of the block to erase.

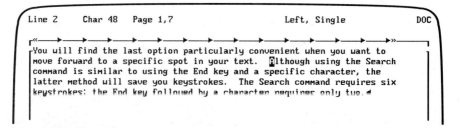

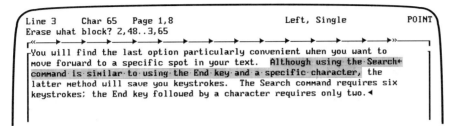

```
Line 3     Char 65    Page 1,8                Left, Single            POINT
Erase what block? 2,48..3,65
r«——▶——▶——▶——▶——▶——▶——▶——▶——▶——▶——▶»——
┌You will find the last option particularly convenient when you want to
│move forward to a specific spot in your text.  Although using the Search
│command is similar to using the End key and a specific character, the
│latter method will save you keystrokes.  The Search command requires six
│keystrokes; the End key followed by a character requires only two.◀
```

Fig. 9.7B.
The worksheet after pressing End and the comma key to highlight the block.

Search does, however, have several advantages over the End key. The Search command enables you to complete not only a forward, but also a backward search. The End key followed by a character operates only for forward movement. The Search command also can search for words or phrases, but the End key can search for only one character. (For more information on the Search command, see this chapter's section titled "Searching and Replacing.")

Reminder:
The Search command enables you to complete not only a forward, but also a backward search.

Moving From Word to Word

Moving the cursor from the beginning of one word to the beginning of the next or preceding word is convenient when you want to move quickly to the middle of a line or to edit a character at the beginning or end of a word. The following keys move the cursor from one word to another:

To move the cursor:	Use the following:
To the next word	Ctrl-→
To the preceding word	Ctrl-←

Moving From Line to Line

Two types of cursor movement from one line to another are available in Symphony. These include moving the cursor from one line of text to another and moving the cursor from one format line to another.

To move the cursor:	Use the following:
One line up	↑
One line down	↓
One format line up	End then Alt-F2
One format line down	End then F2

Moving To the Beginning or End of a Line

To move the cursor to the beginning or end of a line, use these keys:

To move the cursor:	Use the following:
To the beginning of a line	End then ←
To the end of a line	End then →

Moving To the Beginning or End of a Paragraph

To move the cursor to the beginning or end of a paragraph, use the following keys:

To move the cursor:	Use the following:
To the beginning of a paragraph	End then ↑
To the end of a paragraph	End then ↓

Moving the cursor to the beginning or end of a paragraph is especially useful when you want to copy, erase, or move a whole paragraph. Suppose that you want to erase a paragraph. First, place the cursor at either the beginning or the end of the paragraph. If you place the cursor at the beginning of the paragraph, next press Erase (F4). Symphony asks, `Erase what block?` Press the End key and the ↓ key to highlight the paragraph; and then press Enter.

Moving From Screen to Screen

Sometimes you may want to move quickly to the previous or next screen. One thing to keep in mind when you use the keys listed here is that Symphony moves the cursor exactly one screen. A previous or later screen does not overlap (see figs. 9.8A and 9.8B).

To move the cursor:	Use the following:
One window up	PgUp
One window down	PgDn

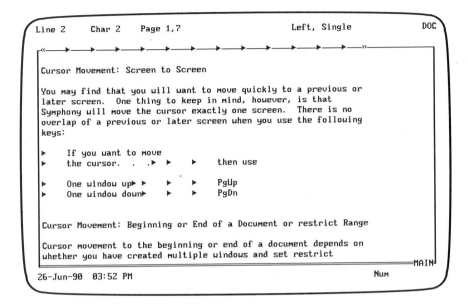

Fig. 9.8A.
A screen display.

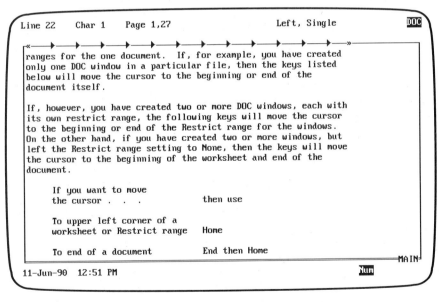

Fig. 9.8B.
The display after pressing PgDn.

Moving To the Beginning or End of a Document or Restrict Range

Cursor movement to the beginning or end of a document depends on whether you have created multiple windows and set restrict ranges for the document. If, for example, you have created only one DOC window in a particular file, then the keys listed after the next paragraph move the cursor to the beginning or end of the document itself.

If you have created two or more DOC windows, each with its own restrict range, these same keys move the cursor to the beginning or end of the restrict range for the window. On the other hand, if you have created two or more windows but left the restrict range setting to **N**one, then the keys move the cursor to the beginning of the worksheet and the end of the document.

To move the cursor:	*Use the following:*
To upper left corner of a worksheet or restrict range	Home
To end of a document or restrict range	End then Home

Moving To the Next Carriage Return

If you have hard carriage returns in your text, particularly in key places, such as at the ends of paragraphs or after headings, this method is useful for quickly moving the cursor to key spots in the text. For example, you may want to highlight an area of text when you are using the **C**opy, **M**ove, or **E**rase commands. To move the cursor to the next carriage return, press End and then press Enter.

Moving To the Top of a Page and Next Page

When working with multipage documents, you may often want to move from one page to the next or to the top of the current page. You can make those moves by using the following keys:

To move the cursor:	*Use the following:*
To first line of previous page	Ctrl-PgUp
To first line of next page	Ctrl-PgDn

To move to a specific page and line number, use GoTo (F5) as explained in the next section.

Moving To Specific Lines and Page Numbers

In addition to using the keys previously listed for moving the cursor from one part of your text to another, you also can use GoTo for jumping the cursor from one line to another or from one page to another. To move the cursor this way, first press GoTo (F5). Symphony asks, `Go to where?` In response, enter the line number to which you want to move the cursor. If your cursor is positioned at line 535 and you want to jump to line 555, type **555** and press Enter. You also can enter a page number when Symphony asks `Go to where?`, but you must still include a line number. For example, to move to the top of page 10, press GoTo (F5) and then enter **10,** a comma, and then the line number, for example 6, and then press Enter (six is the first line of printed text because of the top margin).

Using GoTo is particularly useful when you are comparing a printed copy of your text with the text on the screen. If, for example, you want to move the cursor to the middle of page 3, type **3,** a comma, and then the line number, which you determine by dividing the SERVICES **P**rint **S**ettings **P**age **L**ength setting in half. If the setting is 66, you type **3,33** at the prompt.

Moving To Named Lines

You also can use GoTo to move the cursor to lines you have named with the DOC **L**ine-Marker command. You may want to create a line marker and name for every key point in your document—each major heading of a chapter, for example (see fig. 9.9).

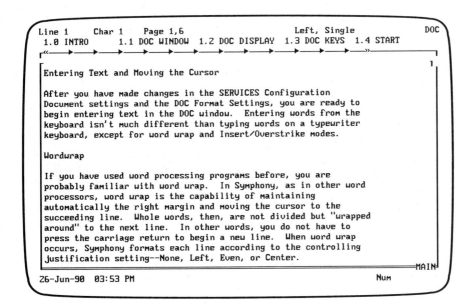

```
Line 1     Char 1    Page 1,6                    Left, Single          DOC
  1.0 INTRO       1.1 DOC WINDOW  1.2 DOC DISPLAY  1.3 DOC KEYS  1.4 START
┌─«──▶──▶──▶──▶──▶──▶──▶──▶──▶──»─┐
│                                                                   1 │
│ Entering Text and Moving the Cursor                                 │
│                                                                     │
│ After you have made changes in the SERVICES Configuration           │
│ Document settings and the DOC Format Settings, you are ready to     │
│ begin entering text in the DOC window.  Entering words from the     │
│ keyboard isn't much different than typing words on a typewriter     │
│ keyboard, except for word wrap and Insert/Overstrike modes.         │
│                                                                     │
│ Wordwrap                                                            │
│                                                                     │
│ If you have used word processing programs before, you are          │
│ probably familiar with word wrap.  In Symphony, as in other word    │
│ processors, word wrap is the capability of maintaining              │
│ automatically the right margin and moving the cursor to the         │
│ succeeding line.  Whole words, then, are not divided but "wrapped   │
│ around" to the next line.  In other words, you do not have to       │
│ press the carriage return to begin a new line.  When word wrap      │
│ occurs, Symphony formats each line according to the controlling     │
│ justification setting--None, Left, Even, or Center.            MAIN │
│ 26-Jun-90  03:53 PM                                    Num          │
```

Fig. 9.9.

Using line markers in a document.

Keeping a menu of line-marker names for key headings in a document has two applications. First, line-marker names enable you to move back and forth between sections by pressing GoTo and entering the name at the prompt (or pressing GoTo and F10, then moving the cursor to the name). Second, a menu of line-marker names can provide you with a key outline to your document (see fig. 9.10). If you create line-marker names for major headings of your text, you need to place numbers before the headings to keep them in their text order; otherwise, Symphony organizes all names alphabetically. (Symphony orders numbers between 1 and 9, including those with one or more decimal places.)

Fig. 9.10.

A menu of line marker names.

```
Line-marker name:                                              NAMES

  1.0 INTRO      1.1 DOC WINDOW 1.2 DOC DISPLAY1.3 DOC KEYS   1.4 START
  1.5 LINE/ATT   1.6 SETTINGS   1.7 ENTER/MOVE 1.8 WORD WRAP  1.9 INS/OVR
  2.0 CUR MOVE   2.1 ERASE/EDIT 2.2 MOVE       2.3 COPY       2.4 SEAR/REPL
  2.5 FORMAT     2.6 PAR JUSTIFY2.7 TAB/SP/MAR 2.8 PAGE L&B   2.9 INDENT
  3.0 FORM LINE  3.1 INTEGRATE
```

The following are guidelines for creating and using line-marker names:

1. Line-marker names can contain up to 15 characters.
2. Names can consist of any type of characters and can include spaces.
3. Symphony stores names either alphabetically or by number, with numbers taking precedence over letters.
4. You can display a menu of line-marker names by pressing GoTo, then pressing the DOC menu key.
5. You can display a complete list of line-marker names by pressing the DOC menu key after line-marker names appear in the control panel (see fig. 9.10).

As illustrated in figure 9.9, when you establish a line marker and create a name, Symphony stores each name. In some ways the DOC **L**ine-Marker command is like the SHEET **R**ange **N**ame command. Both allow you to create a name for a specific location on the worksheet and then use the name for moving the cursor to that location.

To create a line marker, place the cursor at the beginning of the line you want named. Next, select **L**ine-Marker from the DOC menu. When the options appear, choose **A**ssign if you are creating a line-marker name; select **R**emove if you want to delete a name.

When creating a name, you can either type a new name or move the cursor to a name that already exists. If you select an existing name, Symphony warns you that another line already has this name and asks whether you want to use the name here instead. If you select **Y**es, Symphony assigns that name to the line where the cursor is currently located. (See also the section in this chapter titled "Creating, Editing, and Storing Format Lines.")

Although range names have many other functions in spreadsheets, line-marker names are limited to these two primary functions:

1. Using line-marker names to find specific lines in your document; that is, pressing GoTo and then entering the line-marker name.

2. Using line-marker names to create a file of format lines, which you can store and then retrieve whenever you need to change a DOC window's format to a previously created format. If you store format lines in a separate file, you can use the SERVICES **F**ile **C**ombine command to add these format lines into your text.

Erasing and Editing Text

As you become accustomed to processing text, you may find yourself juggling many of the following tasks: (1) entering words, sentences, and paragraphs on-screen; (2) correcting misspellings and typographical errors and making other word-level corrections; (3) organizing your sentences, paragraphs, and sections; and (4) editing your text to improve its development and organization.

Symphony's DOC environment enables you to handle all four of these tasks easily and efficiently by combining the cursor-movement keys; the format settings; and the **E**rase, **M**ove, **C**opy, and **S**earch commands. This section describes the tools Symphony provides for completing different types of editing and erasing tasks.

Erasing and Editing Characters and Words

For the most part, simple editing consists of moving the cursor to a character or word and deleting, changing, or moving that character or word. To delete or change individual characters, use the cursor-movement keys, Backspace key, and Del key. The editing functions of the cursor keys and Backspace key depend on whether you are in Insert or Overstrike mode (see the earlier section titled "Insert and Overstrike Modes").

To move individual characters, you can use the **M**ove command from the DOC menu. In most cases, however, using the **M**ove command for this purpose requires as many, if not more, keystrokes than are required for simply deleting the character, moving the cursor (in the Insert mode) to the right of where you want the character moved, and retyping the character. If you find that you often have to correct letter reversals, such as reversing the *i* and *e* in the misspelled word *recieve*, then you can create a simple macro that reverses letters for you whenever you invoke the macro. (See Chapter 21 for an explanation of how to create this macro.) Or, simply make use of Symphony's Spelling checker add-in.

Erasing and Editing Lines, Sentences, Paragraphs, and Groups of Words

When you have to erase or edit segments of text larger than individual characters, use the **C**opy, **M**ove, and **E**rase commands from the DOC menu. These commands, combined with the various cursor-movement keys, make your job of changing and correcting text quite easy. You can use these cursor-movement keys to highlight the area you want erased, moved, or copied:

Use the following:	To highlight:
Space bar	A word
End →	A line
End, then the end punctuation of the sentence (. ? !)	A sentence (that doesn't contain these marks inside the sentence)
End ↓	A paragraph or portion of text from anywhere in a paragraph to the end of the paragraph
End, then Home	A section that ends with the end of your text or the end of the window's restrict range

Using the Erase Command and Key

When you need to erase a group of words; one or more lines, sentences, or paragraphs; or larger segments of text; the DOC **E**rase command and **E**rase (F4) make the procedure easy. **E**rase also enables you to delete format lines and print attributes from the text. When you use **E**rase, keep the following points in mind:

❏ Only the *last* block you erase can be restored with the Paste key (Ctrl-P). See the section in this chapter on "Unerasing Text."

❏ Because the **E**rase command can erase data outside the DOC window area in which you are working, be careful when you specify the block to be erased. To prevent erasing data accidentally, set a restrict range for your DOC window and make sure that the restrict range doesn't overlap data that you do not want changed.

❏ You can place the cursor at either the beginning or end of the block you want to erase.

❏ If **A**uto-Justify is turned on, Symphony automatically justifies paragraphs after you complete the **E**rase operation.

The procedure for erasing blocks of text requires four steps. First, position the cursor at the beginning or end of the block you want to erase. Second, initiate the **E**rase command by pressing Erase or selecting **E**rase from the DOC menu. Third, highlight the block you want to erase by moving the cursor to the end or back to the beginning of the block. (See the list in the preceding section for ways to highlight blocks.) Fourth, press Enter.

If you are erasing a format line, Symphony automatically highlights the whole line. You cannot erase, move, or copy only part of a format line.

Reminder:
You cannot erase, move, or copy only part of a format line.

Using Accelerator Keys for Deleting Text

Instead of pressing Erase (F4) and highlighting the area you want erased, you can use accelerator keys to delete words, lines, or parts of lines.

Use the following:	*To delete:*
Ctrl-Backspace	Word to left of cursor
Ctrl-D	Current line
Ctrl-T	From cursor to left end of line
Ctrl-Y	From cursor to right end of line

Unerasing Text

Because Symphony stores the last text you deleted in a temporary storage area called the "clipboard," you can retrieve accidentally deleted text. Paste accelerator (Ctrl-P) pastes the clipboard contents back into your document at the cursor location. You should remember two important points about unerasing text: (1) Symphony can restore only the most previously deleted text, and (2) text deleted with the Backspace or Del key is not stored in the clipboard and thus cannot be retrieved.

Reminder:
Text deleted with the Backspace or Del key is not restored in the clipboard and cannot be retrieved.

Moving Text within the Same File

The **M**ove command from the DOC menu enables you to move characters, words, sentences, or larger blocks of text to any area within the DOC window's restrict range if a restrict range is set, or within the worksheet if the restrict range is set to **N**one. Be careful, however, when you are using the **M**ove command, because it can affect data in other windows.

Follow these guidelines when using **M**ove:

❏ The area where you are moving TO must be within the DOC window's restrict range. If, for example, you are moving 20 lines of text to the end of your present text located at line 590, and you have set your restrict range at 600, the message `Not enough room in the Restrict range` appears. To correct this problem, change SERVICES **W**indow **S**ettings **R**estrict.

❏ Whenever you move text to an area within other text, Symphony moves all existing text down. Symphony also automatically justifies the text, if DOC **F**ormat **S**ettings **A**uto-Justify is set to **Y**es. Otherwise, you must justify the text by pressing Justify (F2) or using the DOC **J**ustify command.

❏ Using the **M**ove command can affect data entered in other types of windows on the same worksheet. For example, a spreadsheet entered below the DOC window area can be affected by **M**ove if you do not restrict the range for the DOC window.

❏ When you use the DOC **M**ove command, it does not overwrite other data, as does the SHEET **M**ove command.

With these guidelines in mind, you may find that using the **M**ove command is fairly easy. To move any portion of text, you must position the cursor at the beginning of the text you want moved (see fig. 9.11A). Then select **M**ove from the DOC menu or press **M**ove accelerator (Ctrl-M). When `Move FROM what block?` appears, indicate the area to be moved by highlighting it with the cursor (see fig. 9.11B).

After you indicate the move FROM area, press Enter. Next, indicate where to move TO by moving the cursor to the place you want the text to begin. Then press Enter. If DOC **F**ormat **S**ettings **A**uto-Justify is set to **N**o, you may need to justify the paragraph by pressing Justify or selecting **J**ustify from the DOC menu (see fig. 9.11C).

Fig. 9.11A.

The cursor at the beginning of the block to move.

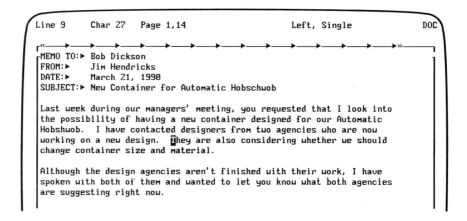

```
Line 9      Char 27    Page 1,14                 Left, Single          DOC

MEMO TO:▶ Bob Dickson
FROM:▶    Jim Hendricks
DATE:▶    March 21, 1990
SUBJECT:▶ New Container for Automatic Hobschwob

Last week during our managers' meeting, you requested that I look into
the possibility of having a new container designed for our Automatic
Hobshwob.  I have contacted designers from two agencies who are now
working on a new design.  They are also considering whether we should
change container size and material.

Although the design agencies aren't finished with their work, I have
spoken with both of them and wanted to let you know what both agencies
are suggesting right now.
```

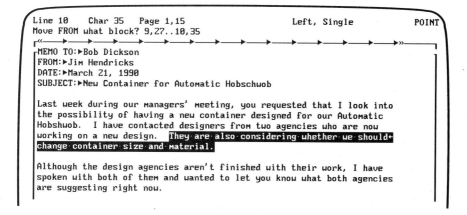

Fig. 9.11B.
The worksheet after highlighting the block.

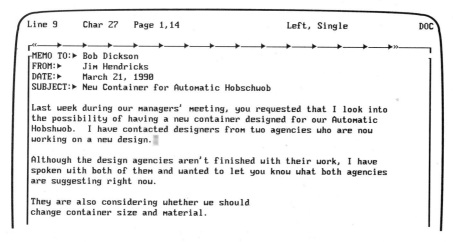

Fig. 9.11C.
The worksheet after moving the text.

If you want to move text to an area in another DOC window, when the **Move TO where?** prompt appears, press Window (F6). You may need to press the Window key several times until the window to where you want the text moved appears. Once the cursor is positioned in the correct window, move the cursor to the place where the text should begin. Press Enter to complete the move operation.

Another way of moving text is to DOC **E**rase it from the original location, place the cursor where you want to move the text, and then paste it with Paste accelerator (Ctrl-P). Just be careful that you don't erase any additional text before pasting the text you want restored; as you may recall, only the last deleted text is stored in the clipboard.

Copying Text within the Same File

Copy, the first command on the DOC menu, enables you to copy characters, words, lines, or larger blocks of text to another blank area of the worksheet. Following are a few guidelines for using the **C**opy command:

❏ The area to which you are copying must be within the DOC window's restrict range, and the restrict range should be large enough to accommodate the copied text. When you execute the Copy execute the **C**opy command, text following the copied portion moves down; enough room should be available within the restrict range for the text to move down.

❏ After you copy text to another part of the window, Symphony automatically justifies the text and all the following paragraphs if DOC **F**ormat **S**ettings **A**uto-Justify is set to **Y**es. Otherwise, you must justify the text by pressing Justify (F2) or selecting the DOC **J**ustify command.

❏ Using the **C**opy command can affect data entered in other types of windows on the same worksheet. For example, a spreadsheet entered below the DOC window area can be affected by **C**opy if you do not restrict the range for the DOC window.

❏ When you use the DOC **C**opy command, it does not overwrite other data, as does the SHEET **C**opy command.

To copy any portion of text, position the cursor at the beginning of the text to be copied. Then select **C**opy from the DOC menu or press Copy accelerator (Ctrl-C). When `Copy FROM what block?` appears, indicate the area to be copied by moving the cursor (see fig. 9.12A).

After you indicate the copy FROM area, next indicate where to copy TO by moving the cursor to the place you want the copied text to begin (see fig. 9.12B). Then press Enter. If DOC **F**ormat **S**ettings **A**uto-Justify is set to **N**o, you may need to justify the paragraph by pressing Justify or by selecting **J**ustify from the DOC menu (see fig. 9.12C).

If you need additional copies of the same text, you can paste them in with Paste accelerator (Ctrl-P), because copied text is stored in the clipboard. After you make your first copy with the **C**opy command, place the cursor where you want the next copy to go, and press Ctrl-P. Continue until you have made all the copies you need.

If you want to copy to an area in another DOC window, when the `Copy TO where?` prompt appears, press Window (F6). You may need to press the Window key a few times until the window in which you want the text to be copied appears. Once the cursor is in the correct window, move the cursor to the place where the copied text should begin. Press Enter to complete the copy operation.

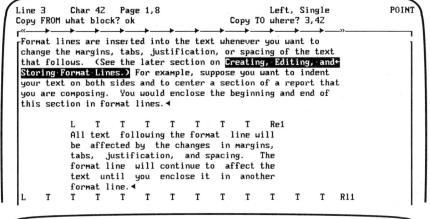

Fig. 9.12A.
Highlighting the block to be copied.

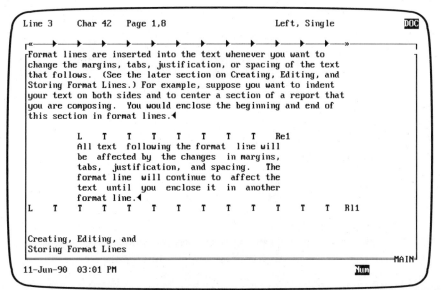

Fig. 9.12B.
The cursor at the spot where the text is to be copied.

Fig. 9.12C.
The worksheet after copying the text.

Copying Text from One File to Another

In addition to copying text from one area to another within the same window or from one window to another, you also can copy text to other files. You may want to copy text from an existing file to another existing file. Or you may want to copy text from an existing file to a new file.

For copying text from one file to another existing file, follow the first procedure described here. Suppose, for example, that you are writing a letter to a client to promote a new product your company is introducing (see fig. 9.13A). As you begin writing the letter, you realize that a paragraph from text in another file will fit well into your letter.

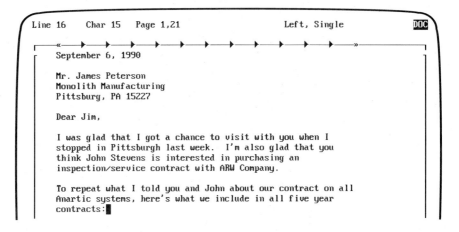

Fig. 9.13A.
A sample letter.

Follow these steps for copying the paragraph into your letter:

1. Using SERVICES **F**ile **S**ave, save the current worksheet that contains the beginning of the letter to the client.

2. Using SERVICES **F**ile **R**etrieve, retrieve the file that contains the paragraph you want to copy into the letter.

3. When the worksheet for the second file appears, move your cursor to the paragraph you want to copy (see fig. 9.13B).

4. Switch from a DOC to a SHEET window by pressing Type (Alt-F10) and selecting SHEET.

5. Retrieve the SHEET command menu, select **R**ange, and then select **N**ame **C**reate (see Chapter 4's section called "Creating Range Names").

6. Enter a range name for the paragraph when the `Range name:` prompt appears.

7. Indicate the range for the paragraph you want to copy. Notice that in SHEET mode, word processing text appears as long labels originating in column A (see fig. 9.13C).

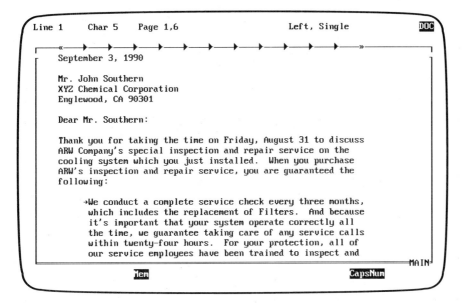

Fig. 9.13B.

Placing the cursor at the beginning of the text to copy.

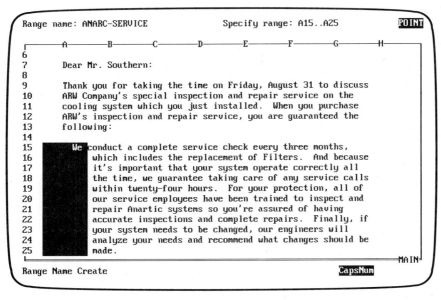

Fig. 9.13C.

Text as long labels in SHEET mode.

8. Using SERVICES **F**ile **S**ave, save the file with the same name it had when you retrieved it.

9. Using SERVICES **F**ile **R**etrieve, retrieve the file containing the letter into which you want to copy the paragraph.

10. Place the cursor at the beginning of where you want to copy the paragraph. Make sure enough blank space is below the cursor to accommodate the paragraph. Otherwise, the paragraph will overwrite existing text (see fig. 9.13D).

Fig. 9.13D.

The cursor at the spot where the text is to be copied.

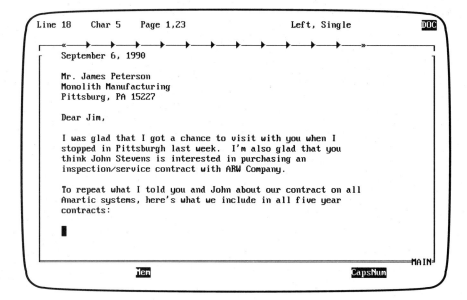

```
Line 18     Char 5     Page 1,23                 Left, Single          DOC

 «────►──►──►──►──►──►──►──►──►──►──»
    September 6, 1990

    Mr. James Peterson
    Monolith Manufacturing
    Pittsburg, PA 15227

    Dear Jim,

    I was glad that I got a chance to visit with you when I
    stopped in Pittsburgh last week.  I'm also glad that you
    think John Stevens is interested in purchasing an
    inspection/service contract with ARW Company.

    To repeat what I told you and John about our contract on all
    Anartic systems, here's what we include in all five year
    contracts:

    █

                                                              MAIN
               Mem                              CapsNum
```

11. Select SERVICES **F**ile **C**ombine **C**opy **N**amed-Area and type in the range name for the paragraph.

12. Next, indicate whether you want to preserve line markers in the paragraph text.

13. Select the file where the paragraph is stored and press Enter.

The paragraph should now be copied into your letter (see fig. 9.13E).

If you find that you frequently copy a particular section of text from one file to another, you may want to create a separate file for that special section of text. Copying a section of text involves using the SERVICES **F**ile **X**tract command and requires the following steps:

1. To copy a section of text, retrieve the file containing the text you want to copy (use SERVICES **F**ile **R**etrieve) and place the cursor at the beginning of that text.

2. Select the **F**ile **X**tract command from the SERVICES menu.

3. If you are not extracting any spreadsheet data, press Enter at the **Preserve Formulas** prompt.

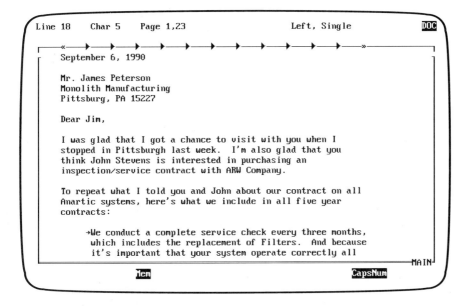

```
Line 18    Char 5    Page 1,23              Left, Single          DOC

   «——▶——▶——▶——▶——▶——▶——▶——▶——▶——▶——»
  September 6, 1990

  Mr. James Peterson
  Monolith Manufacturing
  Pittsburg, PA 15227

  Dear Jim,

  I was glad that I got a chance to visit with you when I
  stopped in Pittsburgh last week.  I'm also glad that you
  think John Stevens is interested in purchasing an
  inspection/service contract with ARW Company.

  To repeat what I told you and John about our contract on all
  Anartic systems, here's what we include in all five year
  contracts:

       →We conduct a complete service check every three months,
       which includes the replacement of Filters.  And because
       it's important that your system operate correctly all
                                                          MAIN

            Mem                                   CapsNum
```

Fig. 9.13E.
The worksheet after copying the paragraph into the letter.

4. When the `Xtract file name:` prompt appears, enter a name for the new file to which you want the text copied.

5. Indicate the range of the text you want copied and press Enter.

Your section of text is then copied into the new file. (If you don't supply an extension, Symphony uses WR1.) Whenever you want to copy this text into another document, use the SERVICES **F**ile **C**ombine command described earlier in this section. If you are copying the entire file into your current file, select SERVICES **F**ile **C**ombine **C**opy and then **E**ntire-File rather than **N**amed-Area. As with many Symphony word processing operations, you also can create macros for the copy operations described in this section (see Chapter 21).

Moving Text to a Document in Another File

To move text to a document in another file, use the procedure described in the previous section—with one additional step. After you copy a block from one file to another, you can then delete the original block.

Searching and Replacing

One distinguishing feature of word processing programs is their search-and-replace capabilities. Programs differ in their speed for completing search-and-replace operations, in the options available for performing these operations, and in the ease of using them. In most respects, Symphony's search-and-replace capabilities compare favorably to similar capabilities of many sophisticated word processing programs.

Symphony, for example, provides both forward and backward search, performs search-and-replace operations quickly, and makes using search-and-replace operations quite easy. **S**earch and **R**eplace are separate commands located in Symphony's DOC menu. You can invoke these commands with the accelerator keys (Ctrl-S and Ctrl-R) as well.

You can search for and replace the following types of strings entered in a DOC window:

❑ A single character, including those characters in the Lotus International Character set, such as *a, 4, &, ***

❑ A cluster of characters (for example, prefixes and suffixes such as *ed*), with no cluster containing more than 50 characters and spaces

❑ A single word

❑ Groups of words and characters, with no group containing more than a total of 50 characters and spaces

❑ Symphony's word processing symbols, such as carriage returns, spaces, tabs, and page breaks

You can search for and replace the following word processing symbols (note that you must enclose each symbol in backslashes):

Special symbol:	Symphony finds:
\~\	A carriage return character
\^\	A tab character
\:\	A page break character
\-\	A space, tab, or hard space
\\\	A backslash character

For example, if you want to add a tab at the beginning of each paragraph, you can search for \~\ (a carriage return, which precedes each paragraph) and replace it with \~\\^\ (a carriage return and a tab).

You also can use wild cards in the search-and-replacement string if you don't know what character appears in a single character position. For example, if you type **Sm\?\th** as the search string, Symphony finds Smith, Smythe, or Smathers. (Note that, as with the word processing symbols, you must enclose each wild card in backslashes.) The basic wild card is \?\, which finds any character in the indicated position, but additional wild cards are available to narrow down the search to either a letter or number:

Wild Card string:	Symphony finds:
\?\	Any character
\&\	Any letter or number
\a\	Any letter
\A\	Any uppercase letter
\#\	Any number

When the string to be searched for is composed of words, the search is affected by whether you enter the words in upper- or lowercase.

If you search for:	Symphony finds:
1. All lowercase	Any combination of upper- and lowercase letters
Example: tutorial program	tutorial program Tutorial Program Tutorial program
2. Initial letter capitalized	Initial letter capitalized, but other letters can be either uppercase or lowercase
Example: Tutorial Program	Tutorial Program
3. All uppercase	Only all uppercase
Example: TUTORIAL PROGRAM	TUTORIAL PROGRAM

When you are searching once for a single character and you are performing a forward search, use End and then type the character. If, however, you want to search for more than one occurrence, or if you want to search backward for a single character, you need to use the DOC **S**earch command. Although the **S**earch command performs both forward and backward searches, the **R**eplace command searches for and replaces a string only by working forward through the text. To overcome this limitation, you can create a simple macro that automatically moves the cursor to the beginning of your document and initiates the **R**eplace command. (See Chapter 21 for more information on creating macros.)

Using the Search Command

If you follow the guidelines provided in the previous discussion, you may find the **S**earch command quite easy to use. To begin the search, retrieve the DOC menu and select **S**earch, or press Search accelerator (Ctrl-S). When the prompt **Search for what?** appears, enter the string you want Symphony to find and press Enter. Symphony then provides the following options for searching the text:

> **F**orward   **B**ackward   **Q**uit

Select either of the first two options to initiate the document search. When Symphony finds the first occurrence of the string, the cursor highlights the string. At this point, you have two options. You can continue the search by selecting either **F**orward or **B**ackward, or you can select **Q**uit. When you select **Q**uit, the cursor remains at the string's location so that you can edit, move, or delete the string. If you press Ctrl-Break before you select **Q**uit, the cursor moves back to where it was when you initiated the **S**earch command.

If Symphony cannot find the string in the direction you indicated, **String not found** displays in the bottom left corner of your screen. You can then select **F**orward or **B**ackward to begin the search in the opposite direction, or choose **Q**uit to move from MENU mode back to DOC mode.

Using the Replace Command

To use the **R**eplace command, you must either retrieve the DOC menu and select **R**eplace, or press Replace accelerator (Ctrl-R). When the prompt **Replace what?** appears, enter the string you want Symphony to replace and press Enter. Symphony then asks, **Replace it with what?** Enter the replacement string and press Enter.

At this point, Symphony begins the search for the first occurrence of the string, conducting a forward search from the cursor to the end of the document. If Symphony does not find the string, the program displays **String not found** in the bottom left corner of the screen and returns you to the **Replace what?** prompt. But if Symphony finds the first occurrence of the string, the following menu appears:

> **O**nce   **C**ontinue   **S**kip   **A**ll-Remaining   **Q**uit

If you select **O**nce, Symphony replaces the string and returns to DOC mode. If you select **C**ontinue, Symphony replaces the string and searches for the next occurrence of the string. When the next occurrence is found, Symphony again waits for you to respond by selecting any of the items from the menu. If you select **S**kip, Symphony skips over the string and searches for the next occurrence. When you select **A**ll-Remaining, Symphony finds and replaces every occurrence of the string, beginning at the cursor's position and finishing at the end of the document. After completing the search-and-replace operation, Symphony displays `No more occurrences found`. Select **Q**uit from the menu to return to DOC mode.

Formatting Your Document

For text entered in Symphony's DOC window, you can set the format in three ways. First, you can control format through the SERVICES **C**onfiguration **D**ocument settings. Second, you can control format through **F**ormat **S**ettings in the DOC menu. Third, you can control format by creating format lines within the DOC window.

The three formatting methods, including the effects they have on one another, were discussed earlier in the section titled "Format Settings." This section describes the different kinds of format commands and how they affect text as it appears on the screen and as it is printed.

Setting Paragraph Justification

You can set and regulate paragraph justification in a number of ways. The **J**ustification setting, in both the SERVICES **C**onfiguration **D**ocument and the DOC **F**ormat **S**ettings menus, controls paragraph justification within each window. Remember that **F**ormat **S**ettings override **C**onfiguration **D**ocument settings. In the DOC window in a worksheet, however, format settings are inherited from the **C**onfiguration **D**ocument settings of the SERVICES menu. Whatever **J**ustification setting is in effect in a format line or **F**ormat **S**ettings controls automatic justification when turned on, and controls the changes made when you invoke Justify (F2) and the DOC **J**ustify command.

Using Justification Settings

You can control justification with the DOC **F**ormat **S**ettings **J**ustification command or with the **J**ustification setting for a format line. DOC **F**ormat **S**ettings **J**ustification can be determined by either SERVICES **C**onfiguration **D**ocument **J**ustification, by the DOC **F**ormat **S**ettings **J**ustification of a previously created DOC window, or by you.

The **J**ustification setting for a format line, on the other hand, is determined by you if you are creating a new format line or editing one. Also, the **J**ustification setting for a format line can be determined by DOC **F**ormat **S**ettings **J**ustification whenever you choose to reset a format line to the DOC **F**ormat **S**ettings. In any case, when you want to change justification, you are given the following four options:

None   **L**eft   **E**ven   **C**enter

Whatever option is set in DOC **F**ormat **S**ettings **J**ustification controls justification for your DOC window unless you create a format line within the text. If you do, the format line overrides **F**ormat **S**ettings **J**ustification. Keep in mind the differences between DOC **F**ormat **S**ettings and format lines.

If you change DOC **F**ormat **S**ettings **J**ustification after you have entered text, the setting affects all text except that preceded by a format line. For example, the DOC **F**ormat **S**ettings **J**ustification setting for the text shown in figure 9.14 is **L**eft. All paragraphs in the text have the same format, so no format lines are entered. If you change DOC **F**ormat **S**ettings **J**ustification to **E**ven, the justification automatically changes throughout the text (see fig. 9.15).

If, however, the original text contains a format line, as in figure 9.16, changing DOC **F**ormat **S**ettings **J**ustification affects all text except the text after the format line (see fig. 9.17).

Reminder:

*When you set either the DOC **F**ormat **Settings** Justification or the format line at **None**, text no longer wordwraps as you type.*

When you set either the DOC **F**ormat **S**ettings **J**ustification or the format line at **N**one, text no longer wordwraps as you type. Automatic justification, the **J**ustify key, and the **J**ustify command are turned off. When all three are inactive, entering text on the screen is like entering text at a typewriter. You can continue typing to the right-margin limit. In a Symphony DOC window, this limit is a total of 240 characters and spaces.

With the **J**ustification **N**one setting, you control the carriage return and can thus format the section of text however you want. But if you change the **J**ustification setting from **N**one to **L**eft, **E**ven, or **C**enter, then all text, except text following format lines, is changed.

Fig. 9.14.

*Text formatted with DOC **F**ormat **Settings** Justification **Left**.*

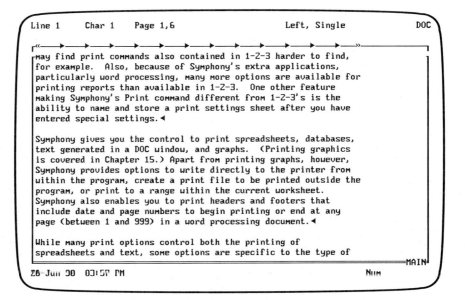

```
Line 1     Char 1     Page 1,6                    Left, Single        DOC
┌─»─────►─────►─────►─────►─────►─────►─────►─────►─────»─┐
│┌may find print commands also contained in 1-2-3 harder to find,
│for example.  Also, because of Symphony's extra applications,
│particularly word processing, many more options are available for
│printing reports than available in 1-2-3.  One other feature
│making Symphony's Print command different from 1-2-3's is the
│ability to name and store a print settings sheet after you have
│entered special settings. ◄
│
│Symphony gives you the control to print spreadsheets, databases,
│text generated in a DOC window, and graphs.  (Printing graphics
│is covered in Chapter 15.) Apart from printing graphs, however,
│Symphony provides options to write directly to the printer from
│within the program, create a print file to be printed outside the
│program, or print to a range within the current worksheet.
│Symphony also enables you to print headers and footers that
│include date and page numbers to begin printing or end at any
│page (between 1 and 999) in a word processing document. ◄
│
│While many print options control both the printing of
│spreadsheets and text, some options are specific to the type of
│                                                              ═MAIN═
│28-Jun-90  03:57 PM                                   Num
└─
```

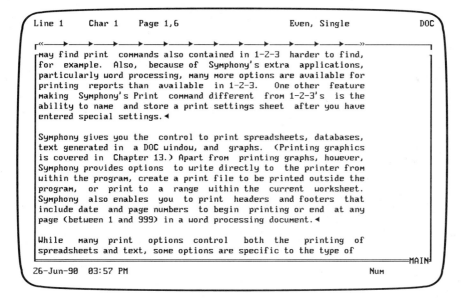

Fig. 9.15.
*The settings changed to **Even**.*

```
Line 1     Char 1     Page 1,6                    Even, Single              DOC
┌«──▶──▶──▶──▶──▶──▶──▶──▶──▶──▶──▶──»─────────────────────────────────┐
│may find print  commands also contained in 1-2-3  harder to find,     │
│for  example.  Also,  because of  Symphony's extra  applications,      │
│particularly word processing, many more options are available for     │
│printing  reports than  available  in 1-2-3.   One other  feature     │
│making  Symphony's Print  command different  from 1-2-3's is the       │
│ability to name  and store a print settings sheet  after you have     │
│entered special settings.◀                                            │
│                                                                      │
│Symphony gives you the  control to print spreadsheets, databases,     │
│text generated in  a DOC window, and  graphs.  (Printing graphics      │
│is covered in  Chapter 13.) Apart from  printing graphs, however,      │
│Symphony provides options  to write directly to  the printer from     │
│within the program, create a print file to be printed outside the     │
│program,  or print to  a range within the  current worksheet.         │
│Symphony  also enables  you  to print  headers  and footers  that     │
│include date  and page numbers  to begin  printing or end  at any     │
│page (between 1 and 999) in a word processing document.◀              │
│                                                                      │
│While  many print  options control  both the  printing of            │
│spreadsheets and text, some options are specific to the type of      │
│                                                                    ═MAIN╛
26-Jun-90  03:57 PM                                          Num
```

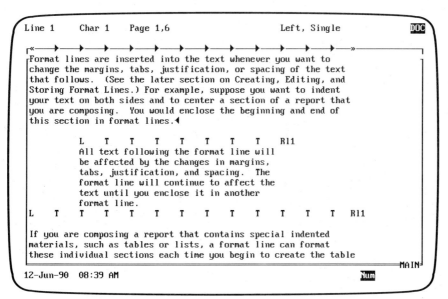

Fig. 9.16.
Adding a format line.

```
Line 1     Char 1     Page 1,6                    Left, Single             DOC
┌«──▶──▶──▶──▶──▶──▶──▶──▶──▶──▶──»────────────────────────────────────┐
│Format lines are inserted into the text whenever you want to          │
│change the margins, tabs, justification, or spacing of the text       │
│that follows.  (See the later section on Creating, Editing, and       │
│Storing Format Lines.) For example, suppose you want to indent        │
│your text on both sides and to center a section of a report that      │
│you are composing.  You would enclose the beginning and end of        │
│this section in format lines.◀                                        │
│                                                                      │
│          L    T    T    T    T    T    T    R11                      │
│          All text following the format line will                     │
│          be affected by the changes in margins,                      │
│          tabs, justification, and spacing.  The                      │
│          format line will continue to affect the                     │
│          text until you enclose it in another                        │
│          format line.                                                │
│L    T    T    T    T    T    T    T    T    T    T    R11            │
│                                                                      │
│If you are composing a report that contains special indented          │
│materials, such as tables or lists, a format line can format          │
│these individual sections each time you begin to create the table     │
│                                                                    ═MAIN╛
12-Jun-90  08:39 AM                                          Num
```

Left is the default setting in SERVICES **C**onfiguration **D**ocument **J**ustification. When **J**ustification is set to **L**eft in DOC **F**ormat **S**ettings or in a format line, text is left-justified against either the default margin (1) or your margin setting. When the **J**ustification setting is **L**eft, lines on the right are ragged (see fig. 9.18).

Fig. 9.17.

Unaffected format line setting.

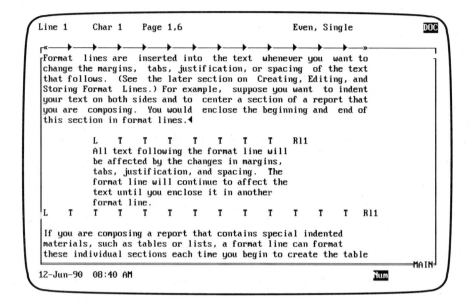

Fig. 9.18.

Left-justified text with ragged-right margin.

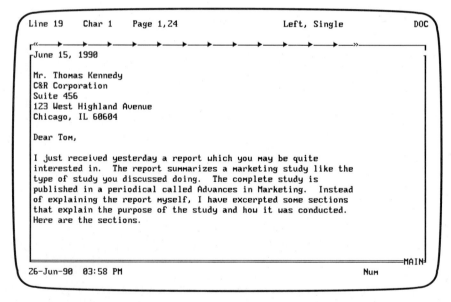

When you use the **J**ustification **E**ven setting, Symphony justifies text along both the left and right margins (see fig. 9.19). To justify the text on both sides, Symphony enters extra spaces within each line. In documents where the lines are short, **E**ven justification may leave a number of large spaces within the text (see fig. 9.20).

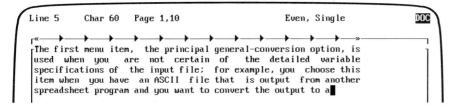

Fig. 9.19.
Even-justified text.

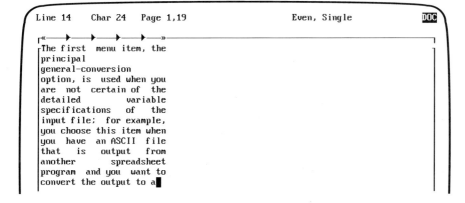

Fig. 9.20.
Even-justified text with short lines.

Center, which is the last option for **J**ustification, centers every line of text according to the left and right margins controlling the section of the document (see fig. 9.21).

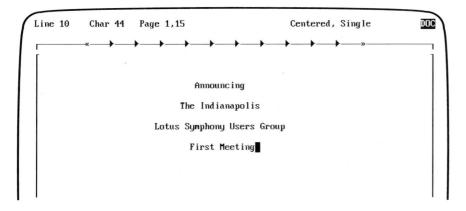

Fig. 9.21.
*The **Justification** Center setting.*

While the **J**ustification command controls the paragraph alignment, the **A**uto-Justify command determines whether the paragraphs are automatically or manually refitted into the margins after you make editing changes.

Using Automatic Justification

You can set paragraph justification to automatic or manual. The default setting is automatic, set with SERVICES **C**onfiguration **D**ocument **A**uto-Justify **Y**es. The **A**uto-Justify setting in **F**ormat **S**ettings of the DOC menu inherits the default setting. You can override the SERVICES **C**onfiguration **D**ocument **A**uto-Justify setting by changing the setting in DOC **F**ormat **S**ettings or by pressing Auto accelerator (Ctrl-J).

Whenever DOC **F**ormat **S**ettings **A**uto-Justify is set to **Y**es, paragraphs are automatically justified when you disturb the original justification by using any of the word processing commands (for example, **C**opy, **E**rase, **M**ove, or **R**eplace) or by inserting or deleting text. Paragraphs are justified according to the margin settings and justification settings that control margins—either DOC **F**ormat **S**ettings or a format line. If you change the margins or justification manually for any part of your text, the **A**uto-Justify setting can affect that text, changing it to the margins and justification controlling the text around that portion.

Using the Justify Command and Key

As mentioned earlier, the Justify key, **J**ustify command, and **A**uto-Justify command operate according to the justification setting controlling a section of text. If you have turned off auto-justification, you must justify paragraphs or larger units of text by using Justify (F2) or the **J**ustify command from the DOC menu. Suppose that you want to erase the second sentence of the paragraph shown in figure 9.22A. If auto-justification is turned off, then after you erase the sentence, you need to press Justify (see fig. 9.22B).

Fig. 9.22A.

Erasing text with auto-justification turned off.

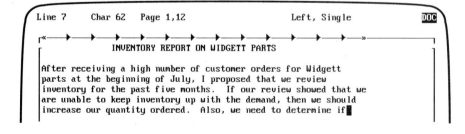

Fig. 9.22B.

The worksheet after text is erased.

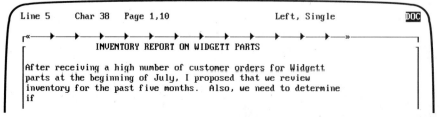

The **J**ustify command in the DOC menu is different from the Justify key in one respect. When you select DOC **J**ustify, you have two choices: **P**aragraph and **A**ll-Remaining. Selecting **P**aragraph performs the same operations that are performed by the Justify key. Selecting **A**ll-Remaining justifies not only the paragraph where the cursor is located but all following paragraphs to the end of the document.

Cue:
*To justify all paragraphs in your document, select DOC **J**ustify **A**ll-Remaining.*

Setting Tabs, Spacing, and Margins

As with justification, you can regulate the tab, spacing, and margin settings by entering new settings in the **C**onfiguration **D**ocument settings of the SERVICES menu, in the **F**ormat **S**ettings of the DOC menu, or in a format line. For all three types of settings, the options for changing tabs, spacing, and margins are the same. Also, the effect of one type of setting on another (for example, the effect of DOC **F**ormat **S**ettings on SERVICES **C**onfiguration **D**ocument settings) is the same as that mentioned earlier for **J**ustification.

If you want to modify the tab setting, you can change the default setting of 5 (SERVICES **C**onfiguration **D**ocument **T**abs), change the tab setting for a specific DOC window (DOC **F**ormat **S**ettings **T**abs), or change the tab setting for a section of text by creating a format line (DOC **F**ormat **C**reate or **E**dit). With the SERVICES **C**onfiguration **D**ocument **T**abs command or the DOC **F**ormat **S**ettings **T**abs command, you can set the interval between tab stops to any number between 1 and 240, whereas with the DOC **F**ormat **C**reate or **E**dit command, you can set tab stops wherever you like. (See the section in this chapter on "Creating, Editing, and Storing Format Lines" for specific information on setting and clearing tabs in a format line.)

Tab settings are indicated in the top line of the standard border of a DOC window by right arrows positioned between the left and right margin indicators. In a format line, a tab setting is indicated with a T.

The default setting for spacing is 1 (single). You can, however, change spacing to double or triple in the SERVICES **C**onfiguration **D**ocument **S**pacing settings, in the DOC **F**ormat **S**ettings **S**pacing command, or in a format line. Whenever you change from single-spacing to double- or triple-spacing, Symphony does not display either double- or triple-spacing on the screen, but the correct spacing is apparent when you print the document (see figs. 9.23A and 9.23B). Spacing is one of the few settings that control print format but not the screen display.

Reminder:
Spacing is one of the few settings that control print format but not the screen display.

Even though double- or triple-spacing does not appear on the screen, Symphony still counts your lines according to the spacing you set. The page and line number in the control panel reflect the accurate printed page and line number of the cursor position. If double-spacing is set, the line number increments by two as you move the cursor down a line on your screen (for example, from **Page 1,6** to **6Page 1,8**). The control panel also indicates the spacing with **Single, Double**, or **Triple**.

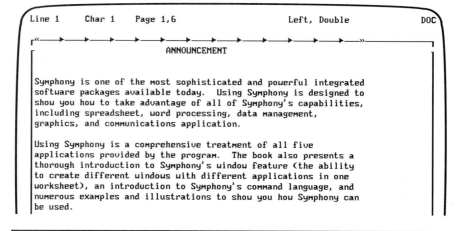

Fig. 9.23A.
How double-spacing appears on-screen.

Fig. 9.23B.
Printed document with double-spacing.

The margin settings, indicated as **L**eft and **R**ight on the command menus of SERVICES **C**onfiguration **D**ocument and DOC **F**ormat **S**ettings, are displayed in the top line of the standard DOC border as two less-than and two greater-than signs (<< and >>). In a format line, margins are indicated by the L and R indicators on each side of the line (see fig. 9.24).

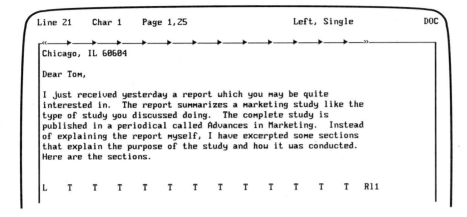

```
Line 21    Char 1    Page 1,25                 Left, Single          DOC

 «      ►    ►    ►    ►    ►    ►    ►    ►    ►    ►    ►  »
 Chicago, IL 60604

 Dear Tom,

 I just received yesterday a report which you may be quite
 interested in.  The report summarizes a marketing study like the
 type of study you discussed doing.  The complete study is
 published in a periodical called Advances in Marketing.  Instead
 of explaining the report myself, I have excerpted some sections
 that explain the purpose of the study and how it was conducted.
 Here are the sections.


 L   T    T    T    T    T    T    T    T    T    T    T  R11
```

Fig. 9.24.

Margins indicated on top border line and format lines.

If you want to set margins in either SERVICES **C**onfiguration **D**ocument or DOC **F**ormat **S**ettings, select **L**eft or **R**ight from the appropriate menu. When you are changing the left margin, Symphony displays the prompt `Default Left Margin:`. At this prompt, enter a figure between 1 and 240. To change the right margin, select **R**ight. Two other options then appear: **S**et and **R**eset. Use **S**et when you want to enter a right margin between 1 and 240. Use **R**eset when you want the right margin adjusted to the width of the DOC window in which you are working.

Reminder:

When you want the right margin adjusted to the width of the DOC window in which you are working, use either SERVICES Configuration Document Right or DOC Format Settings Right.

See the section in this chapter titled "Creating, Editing, and Storing Format Lines" for instructions on setting left and right margins in a format line.

The left margin on your screen may be different from the left margin on printed pages. Here's how left margin settings for screen and print affect one another. If you have set the left margin for text on the screen to 1 and the left margin print setting to 4, Symphony prints a left margin of 5. In other words, Symphony adds the DOC left margin setting to the left margin setting for print (see Chapter 12 for an explanation of print commands).

Controlling Page Length and Page Breaks

Two settings in the SERVICE menu are available for controlling the number of lines of text for each printed page. First, the default value for page length is set in SERVICES **C**onfiguration **P**rinter **P**age-Length. This page-length setting is stored in Symphony's configuration file (SYMPHONY.CNF). Second, you can change page length for any document you are creating by changing SERVICES **P**rint **S**ettings **P**age Length.

SERVICES **P**rint **S**ettings **P**age Length overrides SERVICES **C**onfiguration **P**rinter **P**age-Length for the particular window in which you are working. If you do not change SERVICES **P**rint **S**ettings **P**age Length, the page-length setting is inherited from either SERVICES **C**onfiguration or the SERVICES **P**rint **S**ettings created for another window in the same worksheet.

In the control panel, Symphony displays the page and line number where the cursor is positioned (see fig. 9.25). The page and line numbers are determined by the setting in SERVICES **P**rint **S**ettings **P**age **L**ength. Consider the example shown in figure 9.25. If the setting for SERVICES **P**rint **S**ettings **P**age **L**ength is 66, Symphony displays **Page 12,51** in the control panel. If you change the setting to 33, however, Symphony then displays **Page 29,23**.

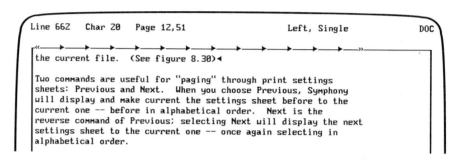

Fig. 9.25.

Page and line number displayed in control panel.

Reminder:

*If you want to control where a page ends and a new one begins, use the DOC **Page** command.*

When you print text entered in a DOC window, Symphony automatically ends one page and begins another according to the page-length setting in SERVICES **P**rint **S**ettings **P**age **L**ength. But if you want to control where a page ends and a new one begins, use the DOC **P**age command.

Suppose, for example, that you want to keep on separate pages certain sections of a report, as in figure 9.26. To break the page between the two sections, place the cursor on the line where you want the break to occur and select **P**age from the DOC menu. Alternatively, you can use Page accelerator (Ctrl-N). Symphony then places a marker (::) in the left margin to indicate that the page will break at that line. If you want to change a page break, simply erase the break by using Erase (F4) or the DOC **E**rase command.

Indenting Sections and Varying Format within the Text

If you are composing a letter, memo, or report in which the format is consistent—that is, the text contains all paragraphs of the same margins, spacing, and so on—then setting the format is easy. But if your document contains sections of text that vary from the regular format (for example, with indented paragraphs, tables, or lists), you can simplify your job by using Symphony's Indent (F3) and format lines.

You may want at times to indent a section of text underneath another section, as shown in figure 9.27. To indent this way, use Indent (F3). To indent a whole section, you need to change from Insert to Overstrike mode if you are not already in that mode. Next, move the cursor to the space where you want each line of indented text to begin. Press the Indent key, then type the section of text. When you finish typing, press Justify (F2) or use the **J**ustify command to justify the section of text.

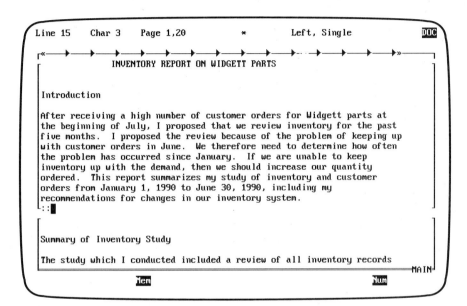

Fig. 9.26.
Inserting a page-break marker

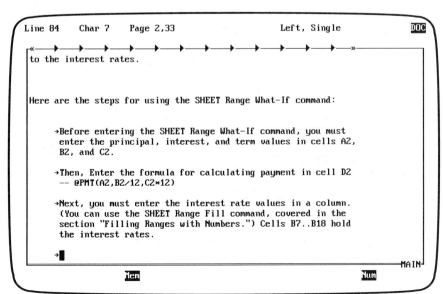

Fig. 9.27.
Indenting sections of text.

The Indent key is also useful whenever you want to include an itemized list containing items that are preceded by numbers, letters, or bullets (see fig. 9.28). Follow the steps discussed in the previous paragraph, with one variation. Instead of pressing Indent before you begin typing a section of text, first type the number, letter, or bullet and then press Indent. Repeat this procedure for each item in your list.

Fig. 9.28.

Using the Indent key to create an indented list.

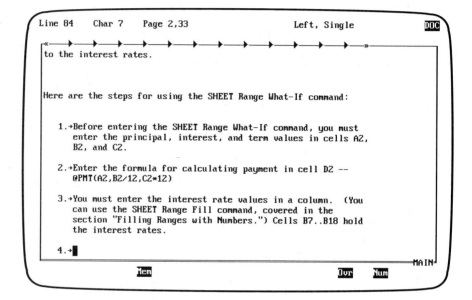

Here are the steps for using the SHEET Range What-If command:

1. Before entering the SHEET Range What-If command, you must enter the principal, interest, and term values in cells A2, B2, and C2.

2. Enter the formula for calculating payment in cell D2 -- @PMT(A2,B2/12,C2*12)

3. You must enter the interest rate values in a column. (You can use the SHEET Range Fill command, covered in the section "Filling Ranges with Numbers.") Cells B7..B18 hold the interest rates.

4.

Creating, Editing, and Storing Format Lines

If you find that you repeatedly change the format in the documents you write, then you can create, name, and store format lines for changing the format whenever you want. As mentioned earlier, format lines enable you to change the format settings in a DOC window as you are entering text on the screen. Format lines are particularly useful, for example, whenever you want to indent a block of text or create special lists or tables. Keeping a file of format lines makes it possible for you to retrieve special formats without having to re-create these lines each time. This section describes how to create, name, store, retrieve, and edit format lines.

You can create format lines in your text wherever you want to change margins, tabs, paragraph justification, or spacing. For example, if you want to indent on both the left and right a section of quoted text, you can use a format line to set off the text, as shown in figure 9.29.

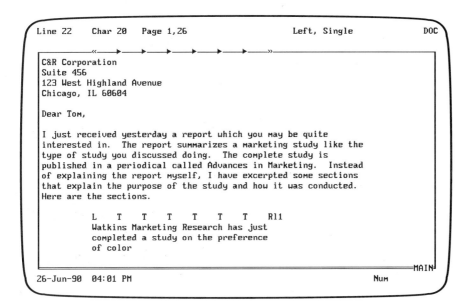

Fig. 9.29.

Inserting a format line to indent a section of text.

To create a format line, retrieve the DOC menu and select **F**ormat, then choose **C**reate, or use accelerator , Ctrl-F. Symphony asks, `Where should format line(s) be inserted?` Move the cursor to the line just before the line where the newly formatted text is to begin, and press Enter. On this preceding line, Symphony then places a format line with the same settings as those controlling the text preceding the format line. For example, if you are creating a format line for the first time in the DOC window, the format line inherits the settings controlling that window. In figure 9.30, the format line settings duplicate the margin and tab settings indicated in the top line of the border and the justification and spacing settings indicated in the control panel.

After displaying a format line on the screen, Symphony provides a menu for changing, naming, and storing format lines; using them; or removing the name of a format line (see fig. 9.31).

To change a format line, select either **M**argins/Tabs, **J**ustification, or **S**pacing. When you choose **M**argins/Tabs, for example, the control panel clears, and your next step is to change margins and tabs on the format line.

Think of editing a format line as editing text in a document. You insert and delete the **L** (left margin), **T** (tab), and **R** (right margin) symbols and insert and delete spaces until the format line is just as you want it. To set the left margin, delete the existing **L** and insert an **L** where you want the left margin to be. To shorten the right margin, place the cursor on **R** and backspace to the appropriate location. To lengthen the right margin, make sure that Insert mode is on, place the cursor on the **R**, and insert spaces until the **R** is in the desired spot.

Fig. 9.30.

A format line inheriting the settings for the window.

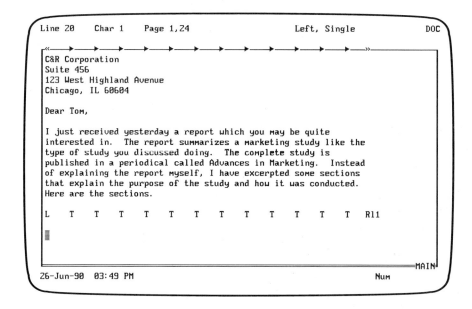

```
Line 20    Char 1    Page 1,24                    Left, Single         DOC
«————————————————————————————————————————————»
C&R Corporation
Suite 456
123 West Highland Avenue
Chicago, IL 60604

Dear Tom,

I just received yesterday a report which you may be quite
interested in.  The report summarizes a marketing study like the
type of study you discussed doing.  The complete study is
published in a periodical called Advances in Marketing.  Instead
of explaining the report myself, I have excerpted some sections
that explain the purpose of the study and how it was conducted.
Here are the sections.

L    T    T    T    T    T    T    T    T    T    T    R11


▮
                                                            MAIN
26-Jun-90  03:49 PM                                          Num
```

Fig. 9.31.

The format line menu.

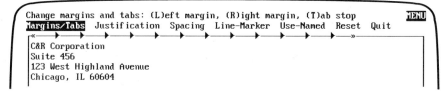

```
Change margins and tabs: (L)eft margin, (R)ight margin, (T)ab stop    MENU
Margins/Tabs  Justification  Spacing  Line-Marker  Use-Named  Reset  Quit
«————————————————————————————————————————————»
C&R Corporation
Suite 456
123 West Highland Avenue
Chicago, IL 60604
```

Reminder:

You should work in the Overstrike mode when setting and clearing tabs in a format line, so that the right margin is not affected by the insertions and deletions you may make.

It is best to work in Overstrike mode when setting and clearing tabs in a format line, so that the right margin is not affected by the insertions and deletions you may make. To set a specific tab stop, position the cursor in the format line at the place where you want the tab stop and type a **T**. To clear a tab stop, place the cursor on the tab to clear and press the space bar (Overstrike mode must be on).

After you have changed margin and tab settings, press Enter. The format line menu appears again. At this point, you can make other changes (such as paragraph justification or spacing), assign a name to the format line, or exit from the menu.

If you want to change justification or spacing, simply select one of those choices from the menu and enter the appropriate setting. Symphony indicates justification by displaying the first letter of the type of justification (**n** := None, **l** := Left, **e** := Even, **c** := Center) after the **R** (right margin) indicator. Spacing is indicated directly after justification (**1** := Single, **2** := Double, **3** := Triple).

Once you have entered all settings for the format line, you have two options. First, you can exit from the DOC menu and return to the text by choosing **Q**uit. Second, you can create a name for the format line. When you create a name, the format line settings are stored with that name and can be retrieved and reused whenever you need them.

To create a name and store the format line, select **L**ine-Marker from the format line menu. When Symphony displays two options (**A**ssign and **R**emove), choose **A**ssign and enter a name when the `Name to assign:` prompt appears. At this point, the format line settings are stored with the line's assigned name. Finally, select **Q**uit to exit from the menu and go back to DOC mode.

After you have named a format line, you can reuse the line when needed. Just select **F**ormat from the DOC menu, then **U**se-Named. Symphony asks, `Where should format line(s) be inserted?` Move the cursor to the place where you want the line(s). Afterward, press Enter. Symphony displays the name of your format line with an @ sign preceding it. All named format lines are displayed this way when you reuse them.

In addition to creating and naming format lines, you also can edit either a named format line or one that is currently in the DOC window but not named. To edit either type, select **F**ormat **E**dit, then either **C**urrent or **N**amed. Whenever you edit either type of format line, you can change any of the format settings (**M**argins/Tabs, **J**ustification, or **S**pacing) or have Symphony change the format line to the DOC window's default format settings. To change a format line to the window's default format settings, select **R**eset.

Integrating Symphony's DOC Window with Other Types of Windows

One advantage of Symphony's word processing feature, as mentioned earlier, is the capability to integrate word processing with the applications of spreadsheet, data management, graphics, and communications. Here's an example of how you can integrate a DOC window with a SHEET, FORM, and GRAPH window.

In figure 9.32, you can see four separate windows created on the screen. The first is a FORM window containing the data form. The second window, a SHEET window, displays the database created from form entries. The third window, GRAPH, is the graphics representation of one part of the database—column D, "Working Capital." Finally, notice the long rectangular DOC window at the bottom of the screen.

What's the connection of the DOC window to the others? From the text in the DOC window, you can see that the user is beginning to write a report summarizing important conclusions from the data entered and presented in other windows. Having both a SHEET and a GRAPH window at hand helps you analyze and organize text. In addition, you can make a report more effective by combining either a database or graphics into the text. To combine a database or part of the data into the text, you can use the SERVICES **F**ile **C**ombine command at the point in the document where the database is to appear. To integrate a graph, you can print a copy of the graph and then insert it into the printed copy of your report.

Fig. 9.32.

Integrating four different windows.

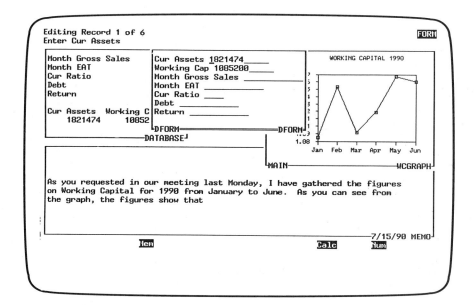

```
 Editing Record 1 of 6                                              FORM
 Enter Cur Assets

 Month Gross Sales    Cur Assets 1821474_____         WORKING CAPITAL 1990
 Month EAT            Working Cap 1085200_____
 Cur Ratio            Month Gross Sales _____      7
 Debt                 Month EAT _____       6
 Return               Cur Ratio ____              5
                      Debt _____          4
 Cur Assets  Working C Return _____         3
    1821474    10852                              2
                     ⌐DFORM══════════DFORM─┐      1
                 ─DATABASE┘                     1.08
                                                     Jan Feb Mar Apr May Jun
                                        └MAIN─               ─WCGRAPH┘

 As you requested in our meeting last Monday, I have gathered the figures
 on Working Capital for 1990 from January to June.  As you can see from
 the graph, the figures show that

                                                        ─7/15/90 MEMO┘
            Mem                              Calc
                                             Num
```

Chapter Summary

This chapter has introduced you to the power Symphony offers in its word processing capabilities. You have learned how to create a DOC window, how to enter and edit text in your document, how to move, copy, and erase blocks of text, and how to use Symphony's search-and-replace operations. This chapter also explained formatting a document with the appropriate paragraph justification, tabs, spacing, margins, page length, and format lines. In the next chapter, you can get some hands-on practice for working in a DOC window.

10

Learning DOC Window: Hands-On Practice

In Symphony's DOC environment, you can type letters, memos, reports, and other word-processed documents. Because Symphony is an integrated program, you can even switch modes in the middle of a report and type a spreadsheet table using SHEET mode's extensive calculation capabilities.

In this chapter, you practice many of the word processing functions discussed in Chapter 8. You type a memo, make corrections, format the document, and make other, more extensive changes to the document. This memo also will include a simple spreadsheet. Figure 10.1 shows the memo you create.

Creating a Document

Creating a document involves two basic steps: typing the text and making corrections. If you have been using a typewriter or a spreadsheet program to type your documents, you may find that Symphony's word processor saves you time in all areas of document creation.

Typing Text

One convenient feature in word processing is automatic wordwrap. Words automatically wrap to the next line when you reach the right margin. The only time you need to press Enter is when you want to finish a paragraph, leave a blank line, or end a short line.

Fig. 10.1.

The final version of the DOC memo.

```
                           MEMORANDUM

        DATE:      December 8, 1987
        TO:        Joe Manager
        FROM:      Bill Boss
        SUBJECT:   November Sales


        The November  sales figures for your  division just arrived.
        (Because of  our new Symphony  program, we were able  to get
        the totals in record time!)  It looks like most sales people
        in your division had a  fairly good month.  Sales for Jones,
        Black, and Johnson were  up from last  month.  I'm  not too
        surprised that Goldman's sales were down because his October
        sales were at such an extraordinary level ($125,000) that it
        would  have  been  hard  to  top.  I  am worried  about Smith,
        however.  His  sales have been steadily  decreasing over the
        year.  Please call to set  up an appointment to discuss this
        issue.

        Here  is  a  summary of  the November  sales figures  for the
        sales people in your division:

                      JONES     $75,000
                      SMITH      23,000
                      BLACK      52,000
                      JOHNSON    59,000
                      GOLDMAN    85,000
                                ---------
                      TOTAL    $294,000

        Remind your sales people about  the following issues as soon
        as possible:

            The  retail  price  of product  line  A  will
            increase  by  10%.  All  other  prices  will
            remain the same until further notice.

            Beginning in January, quotas will increase by
            15% over this year's quotas.

            Because  of cash  flow  problems, no  bonuses
            will be given this year.

        Keep up the good work, Joe.  Talk to you soon.  Don't forget
        to call me about that appointment.
```

In this portion of the exercise, you type the first half of the memo (see fig. 10.2), by performing the following steps:

1. Load the Symphony program. A blank worksheet displays.

2. Press Type (Alt-F10) to display the TYPE menu.

3. Select **DOC**. The word processing window appears, with the default format line at the top.

4. Type the memo shown in figure 10.2. (The arrow-shaped symbols in the document are tab and carriage-return symbols. Press Tab when you see an arrow pointing to the right, and

Enter when the arrow points to the left.) Don't worry about making typing mistakes; you can correct them later. If you prefer, you can correct with the Backspace key as you type. Remember, press Enter only to perform the following functions:

❏ end a short line of text

❏ create a blank line

❏ end a paragraph

5. Select SERVICES **F**ile **S**ave.

6. Enter **MEMO**.

Note: The document remains on-screen after you save it.

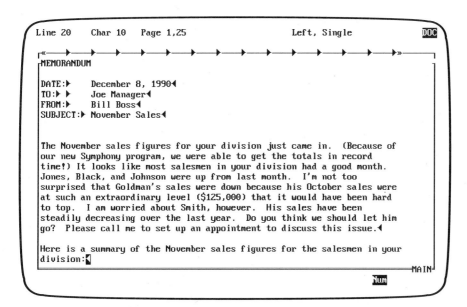

Fig. 10.2.
Typing a memo in DOC mode.

Moving the Cursor

Before you can correct your mistakes in the memo, you need to know how to move the cursor. First, however, you should probably learn how *NOT* to move the cursor: Never use the space bar or the Tab or Enter keys to move the cursor because you will insert spaces or symbols into the document. The basic cursor-movement keys are the arrow keys. When you have a long document, however, the arrow keys get tiresome; so Symphony offers many different, faster ways to move the cursor. (For a detailed description of these commands, refer to Chapter 9's section called "Moving the Cursor in a DOC

Window.") You practice a few of these shortcuts in your document. Practice moving the cursor by performing the following steps:

1. Use the arrow keys to move the cursor into the first paragraph of the memo.

2. Press Ctrl-→ several times to move the cursor a word at a time to the right.

3. Press Ctrl-← to move the cursor left one word.

4. Press Ctrl-Home to move to the beginning of the line.

5. Press Ctrl-End to move to the end of the line.

6. Press End then Home to move to the end of the document.

7. Press Home to move the cursor to the beginning of the document.

8. Press Ctrl-S to move the cursor to a specific word in the document. Type **Smith** and press Enter.

9. Select **F**orward. The cursor moves to the first occurrence of **Smith**. This occurrence is the one you wanted (and the only one in the document, for that matter!).

10. Select **Q**uit.

11. Press Ctrl-X. Ctrl-X changes the case of the current character. The uppercase **S** in Smith becomes lowercase. Move the cursor back to **S** and press Ctrl-X again to return it to uppercase.

Correcting Mistakes

You can correct typing mistakes by: (1) deleting, (2) inserting, and (3) overstriking. Symphony offers an abundance of ways to delete text. The Del key deletes single characters. If you have more than a few characters to remove, you can delete a section of text with Erase (F4) or the DOC **E**rase command. Accelerator keys are available for deleting words, lines, and parts of lines.

The Insert key toggles you between Insert and Overstrike modes. By default, all text is inserted. If you want to type over text (for example, if you transposed two characters), you can temporarily switch to Overstrike mode by pressing Ins. Pressing Ins again turns Insert mode back on.

If auto-justify is on (the default setting), paragraphs automatically adjust to the margins when you insert and delete text. If auto-justify is off, you must press Justify (F2) to realign each paragraph manually after you make editing changes. You also can press Ctrl-J to turn auto-justify on and off.

Overstrike the phrase `came in` with the word `arrived`.

1. Position the cursor on the `c` in `came in`, in the first sentence of the first paragraph.
2. Press the Ins key to turn on Overstrike mode. The `Ovr` indicator displays at the bottom of the screen.
3. Type **arrived.**
4. Press the Ins key to turn off Overstrike mode.

Insert several words and phrases in the paragraph.

1. Position the cursor on the `g` in `good month`, at the end of the third line in the first paragraph.
2. Make sure Insert mode is on. (The `Ovr` indicator should *not* display at the bottom of the screen.)
3. Type **fairly** followed by a space. The text is pushed to the right, and the paragraph realigns automatically.

   Note: If auto-justify is off, you need to press Justify (F2) to realign the paragraph after inserting text.
4. Position the cursor on the `J` in `Jones`, in the fourth line of the first paragraph.
5. Type **Sales for** followed by a space.

Delete several words by using three of the deletion methods: the Del key, the Erase key (F4), and an accelerator key.

1. Position the cursor on the word `me` in the last sentence of the first paragraph.
2. Press the Del key three times.

   Note: If auto-justify is off, you need to press Justify (F2) to realign the paragraph after deleting text.
3. Position the cursor on the beginning of the sentence `Do you think we should let him go?`.
4. Press Erase (F4).
5. Press → until the entire sentence (including the two spaces after the question mark) is highlighted. (See fig. 10.3.)
6. Press Enter.
7. Position the cursor on the space after the word `last` in `last year`, in next to the last sentence in the first paragraph.
8. Press Ctrl-Backspace to delete the word `last`. The paragraph realigns automatically.

Use the previous techniques to correct any other mistakes you may have made. Your document should now look similar to figure 10.4.

Fig. 10.3.

A highlighted block to erase.

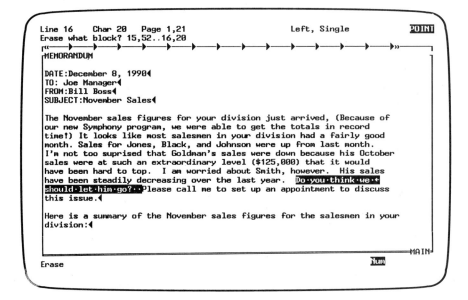

Fig. 10.4.

After making deletions and corrections.

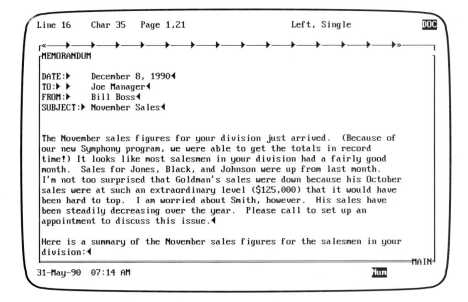

If you accidentally delete text, you can restore it with the Paste accelerator key (Ctrl-P). Experiment by deleting some text and then pasting it back into the document.

1. Position the cursor anywhere on the first line of the paragraph.

2. Press Ctrl-D to delete the current line.

3. With the cursor in the same location, press Ctrl-P to paste it back.

4. Place the cursor in the middle of the line.

5. Press Ctrl-Y to delete from the cursor to the end of the line.

6. Undelete the text by pressing Ctrl-P.

7. Press Ctrl-T to delete from the cursor to the beginning of the line.

8. Undelete with Ctrl-P.

Formatting the Document

Symphony offers many features to enhance your document so that it is much more than just words on the page. You can automatically center lines, boldface and underline text, right-justify the margins, and change the margin settings.

Changing the Format Settings

Format settings control the margins, tabs, line spacing, and justification of the entire document. You also can format individual sections by creating special format lines. You will insert a format line later in this chapter, but for now just change the document's overall margin and justification settings.

The default right margin is 72. This margin is too wide for your memo. Set a new right margin for the document by performing the following steps:

1. The cursor can be anywhere in the document.

2. Select DOC **F**ormat **S**ettings.

3. Select **R**ight **S**et to set the right margin.

4. Type **60** and press enter. The **F**ormat **S**ettings menu redisplays.

   Note: You will not see the effect of your margin change until you exit the menu.

Now change the justification of the document by performing the following steps:

1. Select **J**ustification **E**ven.

2. Select **Q**uit to see the formatting changes. Notice that the text reformatted itself to the new right margin. The right margin is smooth because you changed justification from left to even. (See fig. 10.5.)

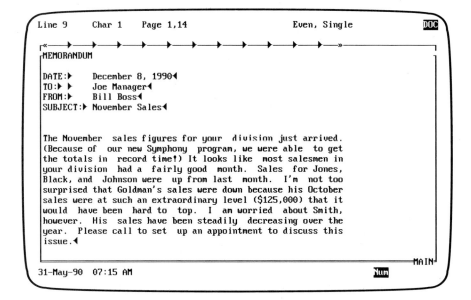

To center a title on a typewriter you had to go to the center of the page and backspace once for every two characters in the title. In Symphony, you type the title at the left margin and press Center (Alt-F4).

1. Position the cursor anywhere on the word MEMORANDUM.

2. Press Alt-F4. The title is centered.

Using Print Attributes

Besides centering, another way to make text stand out is with print attributes: boldface, underline, italic, and so on. You must place a "begin attribute" command where the print attribute should begin and an "end attribute" command at the end. The attributes are actually codes embedded in the text that instruct the printer how to print the text. On the screen, the attributed text appears in a different color or shading, depending on your monitor. The attribute codes are only visible when you use the **E**rase command or switch to SHEET mode.

Boldface the word MEMORANDUM by performing the following steps:

1. Position the cursor at the beginning of the word MEMORANDUM.

2. Press Ctrl-B to begin an attribute. The attribute menu displays in the control panel.

3. Select **B** for Bold.

Note: "Begin bold" attribute symbols were inserted into the text, although you cannot see them. The text after the cursor should be shaded or colored differently, indicating boldfaced text.

4. Position the cursor after the word **MEMORANDUM** (on the carriage-return symbol).

5. Press Ctrl-E to end the attribute. Only the word **MEMORANDUM** should be shaded differently now.

Boldface the memo headings (DATE:, TO:, FROM:, and SUBJECT:) by performing the following steps:

1. Position the cursor on the beginning of the word **DATE:**.

2. Press Ctrl-B to begin the attribute. The attribute menu displays in the control panel.

3. Select **B**

4. Position the cursor after the colon.

5. Press Ctrl-E to end the attribute.

6. Repeat steps 1 through 5 to boldface TO:, FROM:, and SUBJECT:.

Underlining text involves the same method, except you choose the **U** (underline) attribute. Underline several words in the first paragraph by performing the following steps:

1. Position the cursor on the **e** in the word **extraordinary**, in the seventh line of the first paragraph.

2. Press Ctrl-B to begin the attribute.

3. Select **U**

4. Position the cursor on the space after the word.

5. Press Ctrl-E to end the attribute.

6. Repeat steps 1 through 5 to underline the word **worried**, in the eighth line of the first paragraph.

If you decide you no longer want the text underlined or boldfaced, you can remove the attributes. You must use Erase (F4) or the DOC **E**rase command to delete the attributes, because the codes display only when you choose this command. The Del key does not work. Remove the attributes by performing the following steps:

1. Position the cursor at the beginning of the word **worried**.

2. Press Erase (F4). Notice the attributes before and after each word that has an attribute assigned (see fig. 10.6.).

3. Because the begin attribute codes are already highlighted, press Enter. The underlining is removed.

Fig. 10.6.
The print attributes displayed.

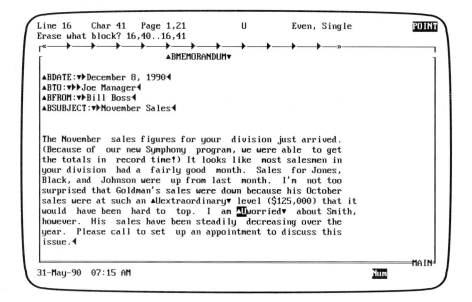

```
Line 16    Char 41   Page 1,21        U          Even, Single        POINT
Erase what block? 16,40..16,41
▶«———▶———▶———▶———▶———▶———▶———▶———▶———▶———▶———»▶
                        ▲BMEMORANDUM▼

▲BDATE:▼▶December 8, 1990◀
▲BTO:▼▶▶Joe Manager◀
▲BFROM:▼▶Bill Boss◀
▲BSUBJECT:▼▶November Sales◀


The November  sales figures for your  division just arrived.
(Because of  our new Symphony  program, we were able  to get
the totals in  record time!) It looks like  most salesmen in
your division  had a  fairly good  month. Sales  for Jones,
Black, and  Johnson were  up from last  month. I'm  not too
surprised that Goldman's sales were down because his October
sales were at such an ▲Uextraordinary▼ level ($125,000) that it
would  have been  hard to  top.  I  am ▲U worried▼  about Smith,
however.  His  sales have been steadily  decreasing over the
year.  Please call to set  up an appointment to discuss this
issue.◀
                                                          ┌MAIN┐

31-May-90  07:15 AM                                       Num
```

Note: Even though the underlining effect is removed, you should still clean up your text and remove the end attribute code.

4. Position the cursor after the word **worried**.

5. Press Erase (F4). Notice the end attribute code.

6. Press Enter. The end attribute code is removed.

When printed, your document should look like figure 10.7.

Fig. 10.7.
The printed result.

```
                          MEMORANDUM
          DATE:      December 8, 1987
          TO:        Joe Manager
          FROM:      Bill Boss
          SUBJECT:   November Sales


          The November  sales figures for your  division just arrived.
          (Because of  our new Symphony  program, we were able  to get
          the totals in  record time!) It looks like  most salesmen in
          your division  had a  fairly good  month. Sales  for Jones,
          Black, and  Johnson were  up from last  month. I'm  not too
          surprised that Goldman's sales were down because his October
          sales were at such an extraordinary level ($125,000) that it
          would  have been  hard to  top.  I  am worried  about Smith,
          however.  His  sales have been steadily  decreasing over the
          year.  Please call to set  up an appointment to discuss this
          issue.

          Here  is a  summary of  the November  sales figures  for the
          salesmen in your division:
```

Including a Spreadsheet in a Document

By switching to SHEET mode, you can type a spreadsheet table in any word processing document—it is that easy. SHEET mode offers several advantages over DOC mode for table typing. First, the columns are already established in the spreadsheet. In DOC mode, you would have to calculate where to set the tab stops and then set each tab. Second, the spreadsheet can total your columns and rows for you.

See Chapters 3, 4, 5, and 8 for additional information on using a SHEET window.

Entering Labels, Values, and Formulas

If the data was already typed in this or another spreadsheet, you can copy it into the document. In this exercise, however, you need to enter the labels and values yourself. First, you must switch to SHEET mode.

1. Press Switch (Alt-F9) to switch to the last mode you were in (SHEET).

   Note: You also can use Type (Alt-F10) and select a SHEET window.

2. Type the following labels so that your spreadsheet looks like figure 10.8:

In cell:	Enter:
C24	**JONES**
C25	**SMITH**
C26	**BLACK**
C27	**JOHNSON**
C28	**GOLDMAN**
C30	**TOTAL**

3. In cell D29 type \-

4. Type the following values:

In cell:	Enter:
D24	**75000**
D25	**23000**
D26	**52000**
D27	**59000**
D28	**85000**

Fig. 10.8.

Entering labels in SHEET mode.

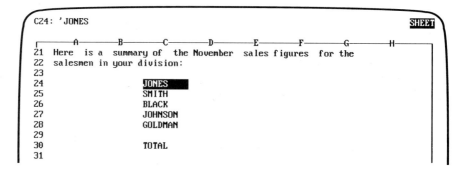

Compare your spreadsheet to figure 10.9. If you made a mistake as you typed the cell contents, position the cell pointer on the cell containing the error and then either retype the entry or use Edit (F2). If you typed an entry into a cell that should be blank, place the cell pointer on this cell and remove the unwanted entry by using SHEET **E**rase.

Fig. 10.9.

Adding the sales figures.

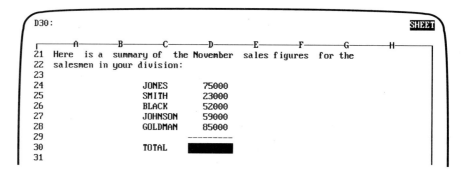

This basic spreadsheet requires only one formula: the total. Keep in mind, however, that your formulas can get as complex as needed.

1. Position the cell pointer on cell D30.
2. Enter **@SUM(D24.D28)**. The total (294000) appears in the cell.

Formatting the Spreadsheet

By default, Symphony doesn't punctuate the numbers. Change the overall format settings to **P**unctuated, and then format the top and bottom numbers in the column to **C**urrency. Figure 10.10 displays the formatted spreadsheet.

1. Select SHEET **S**ettings **F**ormat **P**unctuated.
2. Enter **0** for the number of decimals. Select **Q**uit. All numbers now have commas.

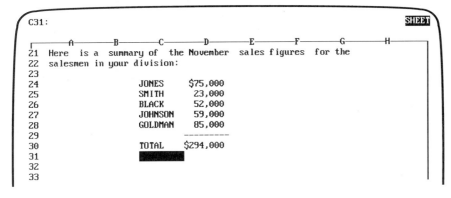

Fig. 10.10.

The formatted spreadsheet.

3. Select SHEET **F**ormat **C**urrency. Enter **0** for the number of decimals.

4. Type **D24** as the range to format and press Enter. The top number in the column now has a dollar sign.

5. Select SHEET **F**ormat **C**urrency. Enter **0** for the number of decimals.

6. Type **D30** as the range to format and press Enter. The total now has a dollar sign also.

The table is now finished; you can switch back to the DOC window. If you later need to change any of the labels or values you entered in the spreadsheet, you *must* switch back to SHEET mode. Symphony does not permit spreadsheet changes in DOC mode.

Creating Additional Editing and Formatting

In this final exercise, you finish typing the memo. Part of the memo is indented from the left and right margins, so you need to create a new format line for this text. After this exercise, you also add two more editing functions to your repertoire: **M**ove and **R**eplace.

Inserting Format Lines

Each document can have any number of format lines, which control the settings for sections of text. The format lines appear in the document on the screen but do not print. You can change the margins and tabs in an inserted format line by using your regular editing keys (arrow keys, Backspace, Del, Ins, and so on).

Type the rest of the memo and then insert a new format line for the indented paragraphs by performing the following steps:

1. Press Switch (Alt-F9) to switch back to DOC mode, if you haven't done so already.

2. Starting two lines below the table, type the text displayed in figure 10.11A.

Fig. 10.11A.

Typing the rest of the memo.

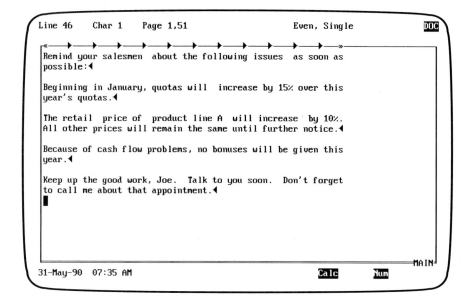

```
Line 46    Char 1    Page 1,51                Even, Single              DOC
«────►───►───►───►───►───►───►───►───►───►──»
Remind your salesmen  about the following issues  as soon as
possible:◄

Beginning in January, quotas will  increase by 15% over this
year's quotas.◄

The retail  price of  product line A  will increase ' by 10%.
All other prices will remain the same until further notice.◄

Because of cash flow problems, no bonuses will be given this
year.◄

Keep up the good work, Joe.  Talk to you soon.  Don't forget
to call me about that appointment.◄
█
                                                              MAIN
31-May-90  07:35 AM                         Calc        Num
```

3. Place the cursor on the **B** in **Beginning**, in the second paragraph after the spreadsheet.

4. Select DOC **F**ormat **C**reate.

   Note: You also can use the Format accelerator key (Ctrl-F) to insert a format line.

5. Press Tab to anchor the range so that you can highlight.

6. Press the ↓ to highlight three paragraphs, as shown in figure 10.11B. Press Enter. Format lines are inserted above and below the three paragraphs.

7. Select **M**argins/Tabs. The cursor moves into the format line.

8. The cursor should be on the left margin symbol (**L**). Press the space bar five times to move the left margin over five spaces.

9. Move the cursor to the right margin symbol (**R**).

10. Press the Backspace key until the right margin is at character number 50 (look in the control panel for the **Char 50** display).

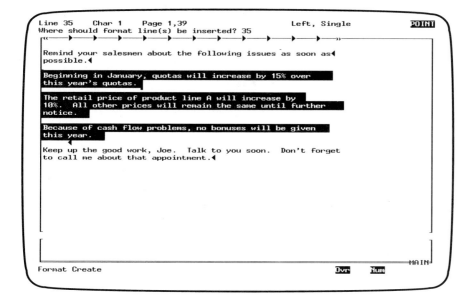

Fig. 10.11B.
The text to be reformatted.

11. Press Enter when you are finished editing the format line.

12. Select **Q**uit to see the effect of your format changes. Your document should look similar to figure 10.11C.

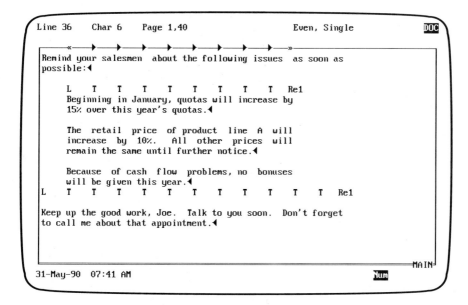

Fig. 10.11C.
New format lines.

Moving Text

Another common part of the editing process is cutting and pasting. When you need to reorganize text, use Symphony's **M**ove command.

Move one of the indented paragraphs by performing the following steps:

1. Position the cursor at the beginning (`Char 1`) of the first indented paragraph.
2. Select DOC **M**ove or use the Move accelerator key (Ctrl-M). Symphony asks, `Move FROM what block?`
3. Press the ↓ twice to highlight the paragraph and the blank line after the paragraph.
4. Press Enter. Symphony asks, `Move TO where?`
5. Move the cursor to the beginning (`Char 1`) of the last indented paragraph (`Because of cash flow problems...`).
6. Press Enter. The paragraph is deleted from the original location and inserted into the new spot. Your document should resemble figure 10.12.

   Note: If you did not place the cursor at character 1, you may have extra spaces at the beginning of the paragraph. Use the Del key to remove them.

Fig. 10.12.
After rearranging paragraphs.

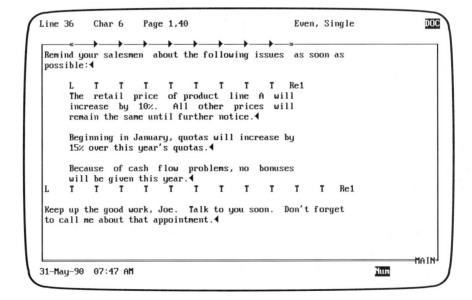

```
Line 36     Char 6     Page 1,40                    Even, Single          DOC
    «————▶——▶——▶——▶——▶——▶——▶—»
Remind your salesmen  about the following issues  as soon as
possible:◀

        L    T    T    T    T    T    T    T    T   Re1
        The  retail  price  of product  line  A  will
        increase  by  10%.   All  other  prices  will
        remain the same until further notice.◀

        Beginning in January, quotas will increase by
        15% over this year's quotas.◀

        Because  of cash  flow  problems, no  bonuses
        will be given this year.◀
    L    T    T    T    T    T    T    T    T    T   Re1

Keep up the good work, Joe.  Talk to you soon.  Don't forget
to call me about that appointment.◀


                                                              MAIN
31-May-90  07:47 AM                                      Num
```

Replacing Text

If you find that you have consistently used the wrong word or phrase throughout a document, you can use Symphony's **R**eplace command to make the corrections for you.

Use **R**eplace to replace `salesmen` with `sales people`.

1. Press Home to move the cursor to the top of the document.

   Note: The **R**eplace command only searches forward from the cursor position, so you should place the cursor at the top of the document before invoking the command.

2. Select DOC **R**eplace or use the Replace accelerator key (Ctrl-R) to begin the replacement operation. Symphony prompts you to enter the word to replace.

   Note: The last word you searched for (Smith) displays. You can type over this word.

3. Enter **salesmen**. Symphony then prompts you for the replacement text.

4. Enter **sales people.** Symphony displays the **R**eplace menu and finds the first occurrence of `salesmen`.

5. Select **C**ontinue to replace the first occurrence and continue the search. Symphony finds the second occurrence of `salesmen`.

6. Select **C**ontinue until the message `No more occurrences found` appears.

7. Press Esc to cancel the message.

Continue does a discretionary replace; this option stops at each occurrence of the word or phrase and gives you a chance to Skip it. If you want to replace all occurrences of the word automatically, select **A**ll-Remaining rather than **C**ontinue.

The final printed document appears in figure 10.13.

Chapter Summary

In this hands-on practice chapter, you learned the most commonly used features in word processing. You typed a memo, corrected mistakes, enhanced the document with print attributes, formatted the document with new margins and justification, performed an electronic cut-and-paste operation, and used Symphony's search-and-replace feature. You also typed a table in the middle of the document by using Symphony's SHEET mode. This step is what integration is all about.

Fig. 10.13.

The final printed document.

```
                        MEMORANDUM

   DATE:      December 8, 1987
   TO:        Joe Manager
   FROM:      Bill Boss
   SUBJECT:   November Sales


   The November  sales figures for your  division just arrived.
   (Because of  our new Symphony  program, we were able  to get
   the totals in record time!)  It looks like most sales people
   in your division had a  fairly good month.  Sales for Jones,
   Black, and  Johnson were  up from last  month.  I'm  not too
   surprised that Goldman's sales were down because his October
   sales were at such an extraordinary level ($125,000) that it
   would  have  been  hard  to  top.   I  am worried  about Smith,
   however.   His  sales have been steadily  decreasing over the
   year.  Please call to set  up an appointment to discuss this
   issue.

   Here  is a  summary of  the November  sales figures  for the
   sales people in your division:


                  JONES     $75,000
                  SMITH      23,000
                  BLACK      52,000
                  JOHNSON    59,000
                  GOLDMAN    85,000
                            ---------
                  TOTAL     $294,000


   Remind your sales people about  the following issues as soon
   as possible:

        The  retail  price  of product  line  A  will
        increase  by  10%.   All  other  prices  will
        remain the same until further notice.

        Beginning in January, quotas will increase by
        15% over this year's quotas.

        Because  of cash  flow  problems, no  bonuses
        will be given this year.

   Keep up the good work, Joe.  Talk to you soon.  Don't forget
   to call me about that appointment.
```

11

Word-Processing Add-Ins: Spelling Checker and Text Outliner

Add-in applications are outside programs that you can attach to Symphony so that the commands of add-ins become part of the Symphony program. In other words, add-in applications enable you to extend Symphony's basic functions. Generally you attach the application only when you need to use a special function and then detach the application when you are finished.

> **Tip**
> The word processing add-ins, unlike add-ins that add @functions, can be detached after use. Detaching add-ins frees up memory, which enables you to attach and use other add-ins.

Symphony releases 2.0 and later include two word processing add-in applications: a spelling checker and a text outliner. Spelling Checker locates misspelled words and typing errors so that you can correct them. Text Outliner enables you to create outlines and tables of contents and organize the structure of your documents. In this chapter, you learn how to do the following:

❏ Spell-check a document
❏ Correct mistakes
❏ Create an auxiliary dictionary
❏ Create, edit, and print an outline
❏ Create a document by using an outline

333

Spelling Checker

The Spelling Checker add-in checks for typing and spelling mistakes in your word processing files, which enables you to produce more professional-looking documents. But Spelling Checker does more than just find misspelled words. Checker also locates repeated words (for example, when you accidentally type the same word twice in a row), and makes sure that each sentence begins with a capital letter.

After you issue the command to begin spell-checking, Spelling Checker checks each word in the document against the 80,000 words in the application's standard dictionary. If the word is not in the dictionary, or appears to be the start of a new sentence and is not capitalized, or is repeated, Spelling Checker highlights the word so that you can decide whether the word needs correction. At this point, Spelling Checker gives you the following options:

❏ If the word is misspelled, you can edit the word yourself or choose from a list of possible correct spellings. If the word is correctly spelled but is just an unusual word or proper noun, you can bypass it and proceed to the next word, or you can add the word to an auxiliary dictionary. Auxiliary dictionaries are covered later in this chapter.

❏ If the word appears to start a sentence but is not capitalized, you can choose to have Spelling Checker capitalize it, or bypass it and proceed to the next word, or quit checking.

❏ If the word is repeated, you can choose to erase it, or bypass it and proceed to the next word, or quit checking.

❏ You can check the entire document, a selected portion of the document, or even a single word. Be aware, however, that if Symphony's DOC **F**ormat **S**ettings **A**uto-Justify setting is set to the default of **Y**es, Symphony re-justifies the document from the start of the spell-check range to the end of the document even if no errors are found. Thus checking even a single word near the beginning of a long document can take considerable time.

Attaching and Invoking the Speller

Reminder:

To use Spelling Checker, your computer must have at least 640K of conventional memory.

Before you can use the Spelling Checker, you must first attach it. The Spelling Checker program, when attached, takes an extra 137K of memory. Thus, to use Spelling Checker, your computer must have at least 640K of conventional memory. If you are using other memory-resident programs or have attached other applications, you may not have enough memory to attach Spelling Checker. If you get an insufficient memory message, you have to detach your other applications or remove your memory-resident programs.

Because Spelling Checker requires so much memory, you may not want to load the application automatically when you load Symphony. If you have the spare memory, however, it may be more convenient not to have to attach the application every time you want to spell-check. To determine which applications you want to autoload, use the SERVICES **A**pplication **A**ttach command and select **SPELLER.APP** from the list of applications by moving the cursor to **SPELLER.APP** and pressing Enter. The Spelling Checker copyright screen appears, and eventually the **A**pplication menu reappears in the control panel. Select **Q**uit.

To invoke the Spelling Checker, select DOC **V**erify. You may be tempted to choose **I**nvoke from the **A**pplication menu to begin the spell-checking, but if you do, you get the message `Select Verify from the DOC menu`.

Once you have finished spell-checking a document, you may want to detach the application to free up memory for other applications or files. If you edit and spell-check other documents, you can leave Spelling Checker attached. With Symphony 2.2's Advanced Expanded Memory feature, you should be able to work on large files with Spelling Checker attached. If you receive a `Memory Full` message, however, you should detach Spelling Checker. To detach the application, Select the SERVICES **A**pplication **D**etach command and choose **SPELLER.APP.**

Spell-Checking a Document

After you have attached Spelling Checker, you are ready to begin spell-checking a document. If the document is not already on your screen, retrieve the file you want to check. Place the cursor at the beginning of the document, or if you want to check just part of the document, place the cursor at the beginning of the area you want to check. Press the DOC Menu key (F10) and notice the new menu option that appears: **V**erify. Select this option and the **V**erify menu displays, as shown in the control panel of figure 11.1.

At this point, you should make sure that the spell-check settings are correct. Select **S**ettings to view the Spelling Checker settings sheet shown in figure 11.2.

Setting Spell-Check Options

By selecting DOC **V**erify **S**ettings **O**ptions, you can change several spelling defaults: **A**utocorrect, **S**entence, and **H**yphens.

Setting **A**utocorrect to **Y**es tells Spelling Checker to automatically correct all occurrences of a misspelled word. In other words, if you consistently misspelled a word throughout the document, Spelling Checker stops at the first misspelling so that you can indicate how you want it corrected, and then Spelling Checker automatically corrects any other words misspelled the same way. If **A**utocorrect is set to **N**o (the default), Spelling Checker stops at each spelling error.

Cue:
By using Autocorrect Yes, you can use Spelling Checker to automatically correct all words misspelled the same way.

Fig. 11.1.
The Verify menu.

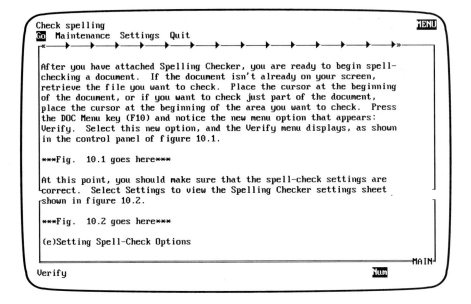

```
Check spelling                                                    MENU
GO  Maintenance  Settings  Quit

    After you have attached Spelling Checker, you are ready to begin spell-
    checking a document.  If the document isn't already on your screen,
    retrieve the file you want to check.  Place the cursor at the beginning
    of the document, or if you want to check just part of the document,
    place the cursor at the beginning of the area you want to check.  Press
    the DOC Menu key (F10) and notice the new menu option that appears:
    Verify.  Select this new option, and the Verify menu displays, as shown
    in the control panel of figure 10.1.

    ***Fig.  10.1 goes here***

    At this point, you should make sure that the spell-check settings are
    correct.  Select Settings to view the Spelling Checker settings sheet
    shown in figure 10.2.

    ***Fig.  10.2 goes here***

    (e)Setting Spell-Check Options

                                                                  MAIN
Verify                                                            Num
```

Fig. 11.2.
The Spelling Checker settings sheet.

```
Maintain Spelling Checker configuration files (.SCF)              MENU
Name  Dictionaries  Options  Quit

    Dictionaries:
      Standard: C:\SYM22\AMERICAN.LEX
      Aux 1:    C:\SYM22\PERSONAL.DCT
      Aux 2:
      Aux 3:
      Aux 4:
      Aux 5:
      Aux 6:
    Options:
      Autocorrect: No     Sentence: Yes     Hyphens: Yes
                               Spelling Checker settings: C:\SYM22\SPELLER.SCF
```

You should be aware that the autocorrect option requires additional memory because all the words you correct are stored in memory. If you run out of memory during spell-checking, you see the message `Cannot add more words for autocorrection`. You can continue spell-checking by pressing Esc, but any new misspelled words are not autocorrected. If you quit the session, you clear the memory of all words recorded for automatic correction, and you can then start spell-checking from where you stopped.

The next checking option is **S**entence. With a **Y**es setting (the default), Spelling Checker ensures that each sentence begins with a capital letter. If the application finds a sentence that begins with a lowercase letter, the following options appear in the control panel:

Capitalize **R**esume **Q**uit

You then choose **C**apitalize to have Spelling Checker capitalize the letter, or **R**esume to leave the letter lowercase. Spell Checker assumes that any word (except for the first word in the spell check range) that follows a period is the start of a new sentence.

The last option on the Spelling Checker settings sheet is **H**yphens. This option determines whether Spelling Checker considers a hyphenated word as one word or two. With a **Y**es setting (the default), Spelling Checker looks in the dictionary for two words; the letters before the hyphen are considered one word, and the letters after the hyphen are another. With a **N**o setting, Spelling Checker searches the dictionary for the entire hyphenated word.

Any settings you change remain in effect only while Spelling Checker is attached. Read the section called "Settings Sheets" later in this chapter to see how to store these settings permanently once you have changed them.

Reminder:

Spell checker assumes that any word (except for the first word in the spell-check range) that follows a period is the start of a new sentence.

Correcting Mistakes

To begin the spell-check, select DOC **V**erify **G**o. Spelling Checker asks you for a spell-check range, and you must highlight the text you want to spell-check. You can check the entire document, a designated range, or a word. To check from the cursor to the end of the document, press End and then Home to highlight quickly the rest of the text. (If the cursor is not at the correct starting point, you must first press Esc to unanchor the range; then you position the cursor and reanchor by pressing Tab. Then you can highlight the text.)

After you indicate the spell-check range, the correction menu appears, as shown in figure 11.3. You choose the appropriate option on the correction menu, depending on whether the word is misspelled or simply not in the dictionary.

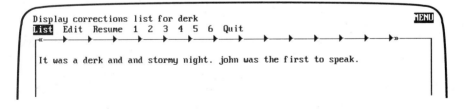

Fig. 11.3.
The correction menu.

Use the first two options, **L**ist and **E**dit, to correct a misspelled word. If you are unsure of the correct spelling, choose **L**ist. Spelling Checker gives you a list of possible correct spellings (see fig. 11.4). If one of the suggestions is correct, you can highlight it with the pointer and press Enter. Spelling Checker then corrects the word in the document. When the **A**utocorrect option in the settings sheet is set to **Y**es, all identical misspellings are also corrected.

Fig. 11.4.

After selecting List.

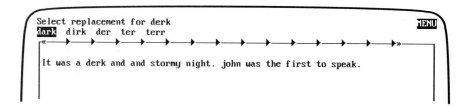

```
Select replacement for derk                                    MENU
derk  dirk  der  ter  terr

It was a derk and and stormy night. john was the first to speak.
```

Spelling Checker does not always list the spelling you are looking for. Press Esc to clear the list and display the correction menu if you do not see the correct spelling listed. Occasionally, Spelling Checker cannot find any possible corrections for the word and thus displays the message **No correction words found**. You must then find an old-fashioned dictionary and look up the correct spelling yourself.

When the mistake is merely a typo and you know the correct spelling, choose the **E**dit option. This option displays the misspelled word in the control panel and takes you into EDIT mode. You can use all your regular edit keys (arrows, Del, Backspace) to correct the word. When you press Enter, the misspelled word in your document is replaced by the corrected word. Again, when the **A**utocorrect option is set to **Y**es, all repeated misspellings are corrected as well.

Cue:

To speed spell-checking, put as many of your business-specific words as possible into your auxiliary dictionary.

Often the words that Spelling Checker finds are not actually misspelled; they are words specific to your type of business or company (proper nouns, acronyms, technical terms, and so on). If Spelling Checker highlights one of these words and you rarely use it in any of your documents, choose **R**esume. This option skips over the word and takes you to the next misspelling. On the other hand, if you use the word frequently (your name, for instance), you can add the word to an auxiliary dictionary. The more words you add to auxiliary dictionaries, the faster spell-checking works in the future, because Spelling Checker never again stops at a word you have added to the auxiliary dictionary.

To add a word to the personal dictionary (the auxiliary dictionary that is automatically created for you), choose option **1** on the correction menu. If you have created other auxiliary dictionaries, choose the appropriate number from **2** through **6**. If you have not created and set any auxiliary dictionaries, the message **not defined in settings sheet** is displayed when you select a number.

Note that each possible variation of a word (singular, plural, different verb tenses, lowercase, all uppercase, and capitalized) is considered a different word and must be added separately to the dictionary.

The last option on the correction menu is **Q**uit. Use this option to exit the verification process before it is complete.

> **Tip**
>
> The **Q**uit option prevents Symphony from re-justifying the text to the end of the document. This option can save considerable time when you are editing a long document.

Besides the correction menu just discussed, you may have several other menus displayed during the spell-checking process. When Spelling Checker encounters a double word (as in *I read the the* book), the menu shown in the control panel of figure 11.5 appears.

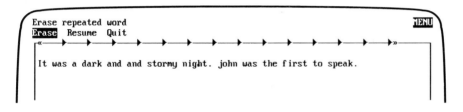

Fig. 11.5.
When Spelling Checker finds a double word.

If you typed the word twice in error, choose **E**rase, and Spelling Checker eliminates one of the words. Choose **R**esume to leave both words in the document. **Q**uit cancels the spell-checking process.

The capitalization menu is another menu you may use during spell-checking. As mentioned earlier, with the **S**entence option set to **Y**es, Spelling Checker looks for sentences that do not begin with a capital letter. When Spelling Checker finds such a sentence, the program displays the following options:

   Capitalize **R**esume **Q**uit

Choose **C**apitalize (as shown in figure 11.6) to have Spelling Checker capitalize the letter, or **R**esume to leave the letter lowercase. **Q**uit exits the spell-checking process.

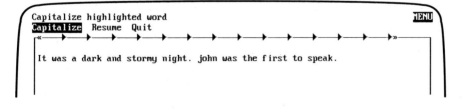

Fig. 11.6.
When Spelling checker finds a non-capitalized word at the beginning of a sentence.

Using Auxiliary Dictionaries

One auxiliary dictionary, PERSONAL.DCT, is included with the program and is automatically specified on the Spelling Checker settings sheet next to **Aux 1**.

You can use this dictionary for adding all the words you commonly use that are not in Spelling Checker's standard dictionary (AMERICAN.LEX). Or you may find it more convenient to store your words in separate auxiliary dictionaries.

The Spelling Checker has room for up to six auxiliary dictionaries. Each department in a company may want to create its own auxiliary dictionary, and the company itself can have a dictionary of names and acronyms used companywide. In a large company, one person should create the dictionary of special words and then distribute it to the people who need it.

Creating an Auxiliary Dictionary

To add words to an auxiliary dictionary, you must first define the dictionary on the Spelling Checker settings sheet. If you want an auxiliary dictionary (in addition to PERSONAL.DCT), use the DOC **V**erify **S**ettings **D**ictionaries **S**et command. Choose a number from **2** to **6** and then give the dictionary a name (SALES, for example). Spelling Checker tells you that this file is a new file and asks if you want to create it. Choose **Y**es, and Spelling Checker gives the file a .DCT extension (SALES.DCT, for example). This new name appears on the settings sheet, as in figure 11.7. The dictionary's full path name is also specified on the settings sheet.

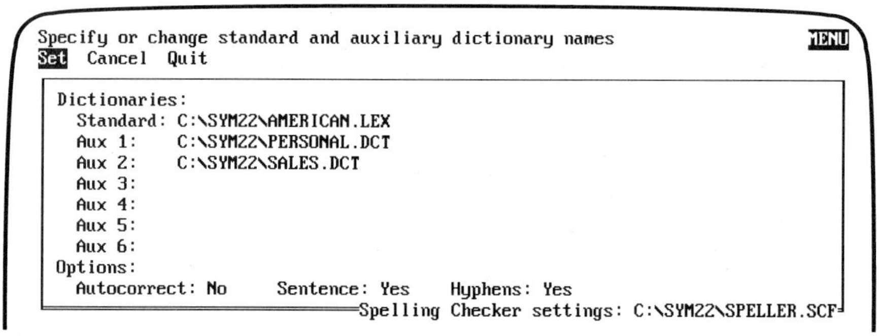

Fig. 11.7.

Adding another auxiliary dictionary.

```
 Specify or change standard and auxiliary dictionary names              MENU
 Set  Cancel  Quit
 ┌──────────────────────────────────────────────────────────────────────┐
 │ Dictionaries:                                                          │
 │   Standard: C:\SYM22\AMERICAN.LEX                                      │
 │   Aux 1:    C:\SYM22\PERSONAL.DCT                                      │
 │   Aux 2:    C:\SYM22\SALES.DCT                                         │
 │   Aux 3:                                                               │
 │   Aux 4:                                                               │
 │   Aux 5:                                                               │
 │   Aux 6:                                                               │
 │ Options:                                                               │
 │   Autocorrect: No      Sentence: Yes     Hyphens: Yes                  │
 └──────────────────────────────Spelling Checker settings: C:\SYM22\SPELLER.SCF┘
```

Tip

Symphony normally looks for the standard dictionary, AMERICAN.LEX, and the first auxiliary dictionary, PERSONAL.DCT, in the Symphony program directory. Additional auxiliary dictionaries, however, are stored in your files directory (SERVICES **C**onfiguration **F**ile) unless you specify otherwise.

The auxiliary dictionary names you define remain in the settings sheet only as long as Spelling Checker is attached. Thus, you must use the **Dictionaries Set** command to activate an auxiliary dictionary each time you want to add words to it. PERSONAL.DCT, however, is automatically defined. If you want your auxiliary dictionaries to be set automatically when you use Spelling Checker, you can save the settings. See the section titled "Settings Sheets" later in this chapter for further details.

After the dictionary is listed on the settings sheet, you can add words to the dictionary in three ways. The first method—adding words during spell-checking—was discussed in the previous section on the correction menu. The following two sections discuss the alternative methods for adding words.

Using the Maintenance Menu

By using the **Maintenance Add** command, you can add words to an auxiliary dictionary by typing them one at a time. Before you can add words to an auxiliary dictionary, however, you must define and list the dictionary in the settings sheet, as explained in the previous section.

To add a word with the **Maintenance** command, select DOC **Verify Maintenance Add**. Select the dictionary to which you want to add the word. Choose **1** to add the word to the PERSONAL dictionary, or select the appropriate previously defined dictionary. To see the dictionary name associated with each number, you can highlight the number and read the description, as shown in figure 11.8. After choosing the dictionary, type the word you want to add.

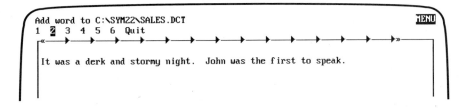

```
Add word to C:\SYM22\SALES.DCT                                    MENU
1 2 3 4 5 6 Quit
«»

It was a derk and stormy night.  John was the first to speak.
```

Fig. 11.8.
Adding words to an auxiliary dictionary.

The **Maintenance** command also gives you options to **Delete** and **Modify** words in your auxiliary dictionaries. These two options are important in case you accidentally add a misspelled word. To remove a word from an auxiliary dictionary, select DOC **Verify Maintenance Delete**. Select the dictionary from which you want to remove the word and then type the word.

Use the **Modify** command when you want to correct a word you have added to the dictionary. The **Modify** option saves you from having to delete and then add the word. After you select DOC **Verify Maintenance Modify** and choose the right dictionary, Spelling Checker asks for the `Current word` and the `Replacement word`. The program assumes that you want to edit the word, so after you provide the current word, Spelling Checker automatically fills in the same word for the replacement word and puts you in EDIT mode.

Looking at an Auxiliary Dictionary

> **Tip**
>
> Although using the Maintenance command is an expedient way to add, delete, and modify words, the command does not enable you to determine whether other words are misspelled. You may want to make it a practice to regularly view your dictionaries by using the Symphony spreadsheet.

The problem with the **M**aintenance command is that it does not show you the dictionary, so you may not discover that the dictionary contains misspelled words. Or maybe you know that you added a misspelled word, but you do not remember exactly how you misspelled it. None of the **M**aintenance commands provide a list from which you can look up words.

Because the auxiliary dictionaries are stored in a standard text format called ASCII, however, and Symphony can import this type of file, you can look at your auxiliary dictionaries in the spreadsheet.

Reminder:

Before you edit your auxiliary dictionaries, it is wise to make a backup copy of the file.

Before you edit your auxiliary dictionaries, it is wise to make a backup copy of the file. Exit to DOS and copy the file to a floppy disk. For example, go to the drive/directory where your PERSONAL.DCT is located and then copy it to drive A: **COPY PERSONAL.DCT A:**

To look at your PERSONAL.DCT (make sure that you have added some words to it first, because the default file is empty), clear the screen by selecting SERVICES **N**ew **Y**es. Then retrieve an ASCII file by using the SERVICES **F**ile **I**mport **T**ext command. Choose PERSONAL.DCT (or whichever dictionary file you want to view), and the words appear down column A, one word in each cell (see fig. 11.9).

Reminder:

Words in auxiliary dictionaries must always remain in ASCII alphabetized order. Words beginning with upper-case letters appear before words beginning with lowercase letters.

If all you want to do is look at this list to help you correct mistakes with the DOC **V**erify **M**aintenance command, you can print the list and use it as a reference guide. You also can correct the mistakes right in the spreadsheet. Use the SHEET **D**elete **R**ow command to remove words, and SHEET **I**nsert **R**ow to add new words. Use the Edit key (F2) to modify misspelled words. As you insert words, make sure that the list remains alphabetical and that all the words beginning with uppercase letters are alphabetized before the lowercase words (see fig.11.9). The dictionary does not work properly if the words are not alphabetized in this manner.

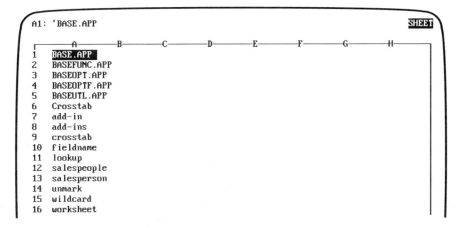

```
A1:  'BASE.APP                                                    SHEET
    ┌──A────────B────────C────────D────────E────────F────────G────────H────
  1  BASE.APP
  2  BASEFUNC.APP
  3  BASEOPT.APP
  4  BASEOPTF.APP
  5  BASEUTL.APP
  6  Crosstab
  7  add-in
  8  add-ins
  9  crosstab
 10  fieldname
 11  lookup
 12  salespeople
 13  salesperson
 14  unmark
 15  wildcard
 16  worksheet
```

Fig. 11.9.
A dictionary file.

To save the dictionary when you are finished with modifications, print the dictionary to a file, by following these steps:

Reminder:
You cannot use the File Save command to save a dictionary file. File Save creates a worksheet file, not an ASCII file.

1. Switch to a DOC window so that you do not have to specify a source range when you print.

2. Select SERVICES **P**rint **S**ettings **D**estination **F**ile.

3. Enter the name of your auxiliary dictionary (for example, PERSONAL.DCT).

4. Select **D**estination **E**rase **Y**es to erase the old auxiliary dictionary file (otherwise Symphony appends your corrected list to the end of the existing PERSONAL.DCT file).

5. Select **M**argins **N**o-Margins.

6. Select **Q**uit **G**o **Q**uit. The dictionary is printed to the file.

Note that you must use the previous steps, not the **F**ile **S**ave command, to save the dictionary file. **F**ile **S**ave creates a worksheet file, not an ASCII file.

Settings Sheets

If you want to permanently change the default for your spell-check options (**A**utocorrect, **S**entence, **H**yphens), or have auxiliary dictionaries automatically defined in the settings sheet, you need to save the sheet to a Spelling Checker configuration file. The **N**ame command on the **V**erify **S**ettings menu provides an option to **S**ave configuration files. The default file is called SPELLER.SCF, which is the configuration file that is automatically pulled up when you attach Spelling Checker. Though you can have multiple configuration files, you may probably only need this one. Thus, when you want to save changes to your Spelling Checker settings sheet, save the changes to SPELLER.SCF. Symphony warns you that the file already exists and asks if you want to replace the file. Select **Y**es.

Reminder:
When you want to save changes to your Spelling Checker settings sheet, save the changes to SPELLER.SCF.

Reminder:

If you have several different auxiliary dictionaries, you may want to create separate configuration files for various combinations of the dictionaries.

If you have several different auxiliary dictionaries, you may want to create separate configuration files for various combinations of the dictionaries. Then you can choose the appropriate configuration for each document you check. Use the **N**ame **S**ave command and enter a name to identify the file. Spelling Checker automatically assigns the file extension .SCF. For example, if you name the configuration file SALES, the complete file name is SALES.SCF.

To use other Spelling Checker configuration files that you have previously saved, select the **N**ame **R**etrieve command and enter the appropriate file name. The settings sheet then appears with the name in the lower right corner of the sheet. When you spell-check a document, Spelling Checker uses the options and dictionaries listed in the settings sheet.

To return to the default Spelling Checker settings, select **N**ame **D**efault-Settings. The settings are changed only while Spelling Checker is attached.

The **N**ame **E**rase command deletes Spelling Checker configuration files that you have previously saved.

Spell-Checking a Spreadsheet

Reminder:

Select Format Justification None when you spell-check your words so that each word remains on a separate line instead of jumbled together.

In addition to spell-checking documents, Spelling Checker also checks spreadsheets—with one major limitation. Spelling Checker checks only the words entered into the first column of the window. Retrieve the spreadsheet you want to spell-check, and switch to a DOC window. The words that appear in a brighter intensity on your screen are the only ones Spelling Checker considers. Select DOC **F**ormat **J**ustification **N**one so that each word remains on a separate line. If you do not select this option, the lines jumble together. Once you take these steps, you are ready to begin spell-checking the same way you do with documents.

None of the cells in the spell-check range can be protected. If they are, Symphony displays the message `Cannot check protected cells`. You should then disable protection with the SERVICES **S**ettings **G**lobal-Protection **N**o command.

Using Text Outliner

Text Outliner helps you structure and refine documents; helps you create outlines and tables of contents; and simplifies restructuring when you make major revisions in a document.

Most often the reason for creating an outline is to provide a structure for writing a document. Consequently, the Text Outliner can help you create a more organized document. You can also use outlines to help organize your thoughts for lectures and speeches. For example, you can use an outline as a "cheat sheet" when giving a speech, or give the outline to the audience to let the listeners know what topics you will be discussing.

You may be thinking that you can type outlines just fine in DOC mode so why use Text Outliner? Basically, Text Outliner automates the process of creating and modifying an outline. By using Text Outliner, you do not have to do any tabbing or numbering; the outline format is created automatically. Also, in a word processor you have to create two separate documents (the outline and the body text), and after creating the outline you have to retype your outline headings into the text manually. With Text Outliner however, you type the outline headings once, and you can view the outline with headings only (no text) or with the headings integrated into the text.

Additionally, if you need to reorganize the outline or document, the outlining features make it a much easier process. Working in the OUTLN window, you can quickly move, copy, and delete entire sections (headings, subheadings, and associated text). In a DOC window, you have to highlight large blocks of text and do a lot of scrolling to accomplish the same thing.

With Text Outliner, you can make global changes to your headings. For example, you can specify print attributes (such as boldface) for all your headings with a single command. You also can change the amount of indentation in the outline levels by pressing a single key. You can't make these kinds of global changes in DOC mode.

Attaching and Invoking the Outliner

Before you can use Text Outliner to create or modify an outline, you must first attach the Outliner add-in application. By attaching the Outliner, you have a sixth window type available (see fig. 11.10), and when you select OUTLN, the Menu key offers a whole set of new commands (see fig. 11.11).

Cue:

You can cut hours off your projects by using Text Outliner, because it automates the process of creating and modifying an outline.

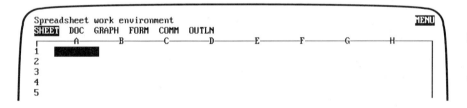

Fig. 11.10.

The TYPE menu with Text Outliner attached.

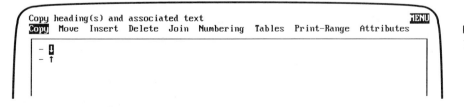

Fig. 11.11.

The OUTLN menu.

Attaching Text Outliner is similar to attaching Spelling Checker. Use the SERVICES **A**pplication **A**ttach command and select **OUTLINER.APP** from the list of applications. The Text Outliner copyright screen appears, and eventually the **A**pplication menu reappears in the control panel. Select **Q**uit. You do not invoke the Outliner application with SERVICES **A**pplication **I**nvoke. If you try, Symphony displays the message `Press [TYPE] and select OUTLN`.

If you retrieve an outline file without first attaching Text Outliner, you may get the message `(must Attach OUTLINER)` in the middle of the screen. This message indicates that you saved the file while in the OUTLN window, and because OUTLN is not a valid window type until you attach Text Outliner, Symphony cannot display the outline in an OUTLN window. (You can look at the spreadsheet or document version of the outline in a SHEET or DOC window without attaching Text Outliner, but the text will not look much like an outline.) After you attach Text Outliner, the error message disappears, and the outline displays.

If you use Text Outliner every day, you can have Symphony automatically attach the add-in each time you load Symphony. Use the SERVICES **C**onfiguration **O**ther **A**pplication **S**et command to attach the application automatically.

Reminder:

To create an outline or use any of the Text Outliner commands, you must be in an outline window.

To create an outline or use any of the Text Outliner commands, you must be in an outline window. Press the Type key (Alt-F10) and select OUTLN. Note that the OUTLN window type is only offered when Text Outliner is attached.

After you have finished using Text Outliner, you can detach it to free up memory for other applications or files. Use the SERVICES **A**pplication **D**etach command and select **OUTLINER.APP**, or select SERVICES **A**pplication **C**lear to clear all applications.

The Text Outliner application, like all Symphony add-ins, automatically detaches itself when you exit Symphony, unless you have configured Symphony to attach Text Outliner automatically every time you load Symphony.

Creating an Outline

The OUTLN window displays several special symbols, as you can see in figure 11.12. The ↓ indicates the top of the outline, while the ↑ indicates the bottom. The minus sign (–) indicates that the heading has no subheadings beneath it. The plus sign (+) tells you that the heading does have subheadings.

To create entries in your outline, you invoke the **I**nsert command from the main OUTLN menu.

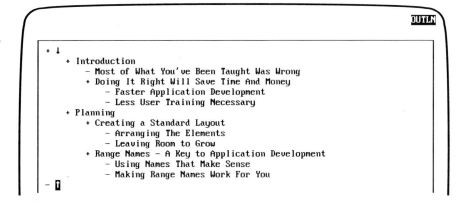

Fig. 11.12.
The OUTLN window.

Inserting Headings

Text Outliner offers two ways to insert headings into an outline: with the OUTLN **I**nsert command or with the Ins key. The Ins key requires fewer keystrokes, so you may probably use this method most of the time.

When you select the **I**nsert command from the OUTLN menu or by pressing the Ins key, the heading level menu displays:

Same-Level   **L**ower-Level   **H**igher-Level   **Q**uit

Figures 11.13, 11.14, and 11.15 show how the heading **Macros** appears after it is inserted at different levels. If you select **S**ame-Level, the new heading is given the same level of indentation as the heading **Making Range Names Work For You** (see fig. 11.13).

Lower-Level makes the new heading a subheading of the currently highlighted heading and indents the new heading four spaces from the previous heading. (You can adjust the number of spaces in the indentation. The procedure for changing the number is discussed in the section on "Changing Indentation" later in this chapter). **Macros** was inserted at a **L**ower-Level in figure 11.14.

Higher-Level makes the new heading one level higher than the currently highlighted heading and places the new heading four spaces to the left of the previous heading (see fig. 11.15).

After you have indicated the heading level, type the text for the heading. Text Outliner automatically places you in EDIT mode, so you can use your edit keys to correct mistakes (see the section titled "Editing Headings" later in this chapter for additional information). Press Enter when you are finished typing the heading. The heading level menu reappears so that you can continue adding headings to your outline.

Fig. 11.13.

Inserting a Same-Level heading.

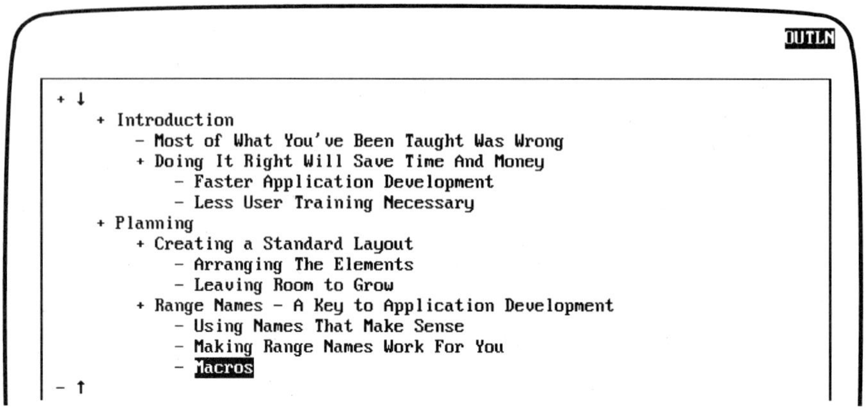

```
                                                              OUTLN
    + ↓
        + Introduction
            – Most of What You've Been Taught Was Wrong
            + Doing It Right Will Save Time And Money
                – Faster Application Development
                – Less User Training Necessary
        + Planning
            + Creating a Standard Layout
                – Arranging The Elements
                – Leaving Room to Grow
            + Range Names – A Key to Application Development
                – Using Names That Make Sense
                – Making Range Names Work For You
                – Macros
    – ↑
```

Fig. 11.14.

Inserting a Lower-Level heading.

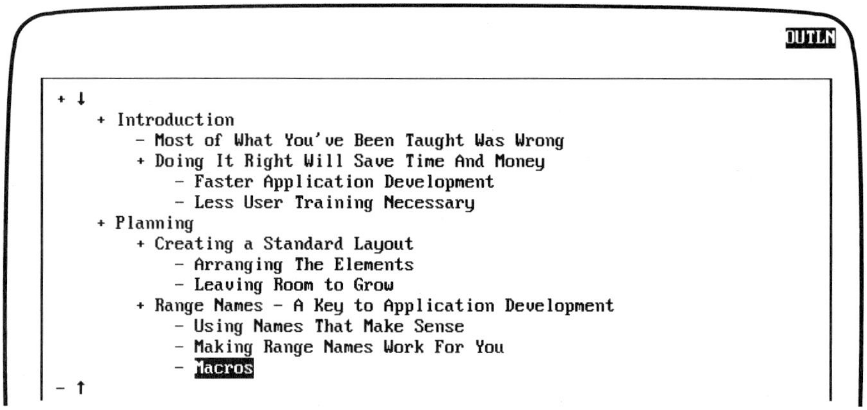

```
                                                              OUTLN
    + ↓
        + Introduction
            – Most of What You've Been Taught Was Wrong
            + Doing It Right Will Save Time And Money
                – Faster Application Development
                – Less User Training Necessary
        + Planning
            + Creating a Standard Layout
                – Arranging The Elements
                – Leaving Room to Grow
            + Range Names – A Key to Application Development
                – Using Names That Make Sense
                – Making Range Names Work For You
                – Macros
    – ↑
```

Fig. 11.15.

Inserting a Higher-Level heading.

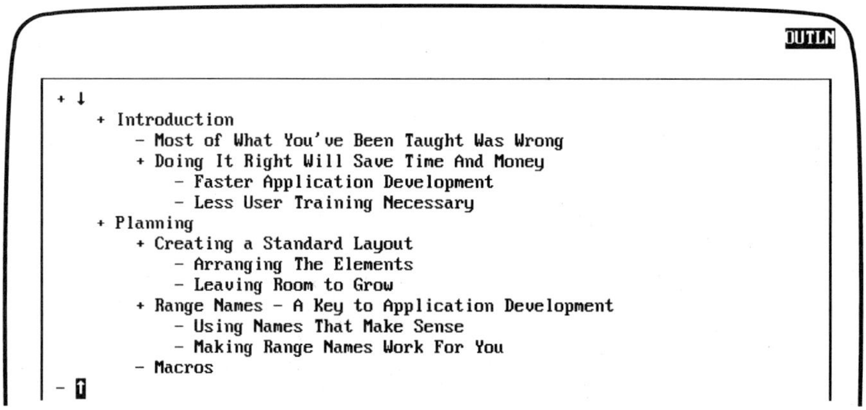

```
                                                              OUTLN
    + ↓
        + Introduction
            – Most of What You've Been Taught Was Wrong
            + Doing It Right Will Save Time And Money
                – Faster Application Development
                – Less User Training Necessary
        + Planning
            + Creating a Standard Layout
                – Arranging The Elements
                – Leaving Room to Grow
            + Range Names – A Key to Application Development
                – Using Names That Make Sense
                – Making Range Names Work For You
            – Macros
    – ▮
```

Select **Q**uit when you are finished inserting outline entries. If you accidentally exit the **I**nsert command, simply position the cursor immediately above the point where you want to insert another entry and press the Ins key again. See the section titled "Inserting Additional Headings" later in this chapter for information on inserting headings in an existing outline.

Note that **H**igher-Level moves the heading back only a single level. If you need to move back two levels, select **H**igher-Level and make a blank entry, which you can delete later. (A minus sign appears with no heading next to it.) Then choose **H**igher-Level again and type your heading. Refer to the section on "Deleting Headings" later in this chapter to see how to remove the blank heading.

If you accidentally indicate the wrong level, use the **M**ove command to move the heading to the correct level.

Moving around in an Outline

Moving around in an outline is quite different from moving around in a document. First of all, in OUTLN mode, you do not have a single-character cursor as you do in DOC mode. Instead, you have a pointer, similar to SHEET mode's cell pointer, except that the OUTLN pointer's length varies according to the length of the heading.

Your cursor-movement keys also work differently in OUTLN mode, as shown in the following list:

Key	Moves pointer to the
↑	Previous heading at the same level
↓	Next heading at the same level
←	Previous heading, regardless of level
→	Next heading, regardless of level
Ctrl-←	Previous heading at higher level
Ctrl-→	Next heading at higher level
Home	Top of the outline
End	Bottom of the outline

The PgUp and PgDn keys work the same way as they do in DOC mode without regard to outline level. In OUTLN mode, the GoTo key (F5) does not move to a page or a line number; instead, this key switches you to DOC mode with a single keystroke.

Displaying Outline Numbers

By default the outline is not numbered, but by pressing the Tab key you can get two different types of numbering systems. Press the Tab key once, and each level in the outline is numbered sequentially (1, 2, 3,...). See figure 11.16 for an example of sequential numbering.

Press the Tab key a second time, and multilevel (absolute) numbering displays (1, 1.1, 1.2, 1.2.1,...). See figure 11.17 for an example of multilevel numbering.

Fig. 11.16.

An example of sequential numbering.

```
                                                              OUTLN
   + ↓
       + 1 Introduction
          - 1 Most of What You've Been Taught Was Wrong
          + 2 Doing It Right Will Save Time And Money
             - 1 Faster Application Development
             - 2 Less User Training Necessary
       + 2 Planning
          + 1 Creating a Standard Layout
             - 1 Arranging The Elements
             - 2 Leaving Room to Grow
          + 2 Range Names - A Key to Application Development
             - 1 Using Names That Make Sense
             - 2 Making Range Names Work For You
       + 3 Macros
          - 1 Modular Macros
          - 2 A Standard Suite
   - ↑
```

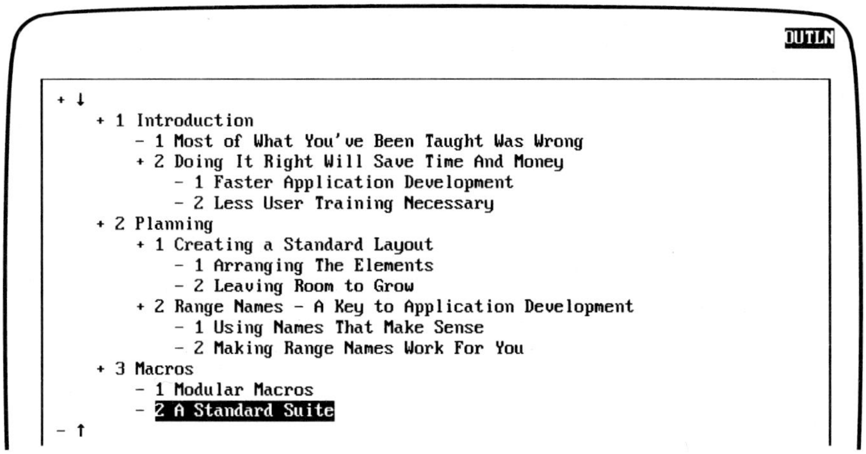

Fig. 11.17.

An example of multilevel numbering.

```
                                                              OUTLN
   + ↓
       + 1 Introduction
          - 1.1 Most of What You've Been Taught Was Wrong
          + 1.2 Doing It Right Will Save Time And Money
             - 1.2.1 Faster Application Development
             - 1.2.2 Less User Training Necessary
       + 2 Planning
          + 2.1 Creating a Standard Layout
             - 2.1.1 Arranging The Elements
             - 2.1.2 Leaving Room to Grow
          + 2.2 Range Names - A Key to Application Development
             - 2.2.1 Using Names That Make Sense
             - 2.2.2 Making Range Names Work For You
       + 3 Macros
          - 3.1 Modular Macros
          - 3.2 A Standard Suite
   - ↑
```

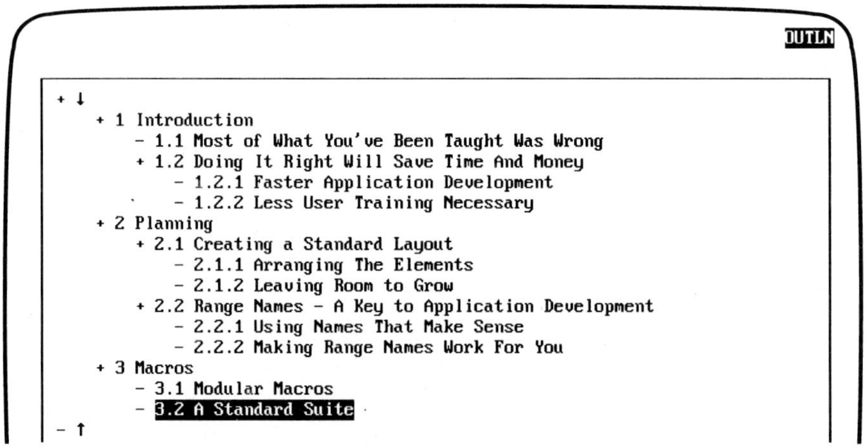

Press the Tab key a third time, and the default outline (no numbering) displays. Unfortunately, Text Outliner does not offer a Roman numeral system (I, A, 1, a).

You must be in OUTLN mode when you press the Tab key. If you are in the middle of inserting entries, you are in EDIT mode, and the Tab key has no effect.

Reminder:
If you are in the EDIT mode and press the Tab key, the key does not work. You must be in the OUTLN mode.

Hiding and Exposing Headings

Sometimes when you create a long outline with many subheadings, you lose sight of what your major topics are. If this situation occurs, you may want to hide the subheadings so that you can view just the major headings. Text Outliner offers the following keys to hide temporarily and expose subheadings:

Key	Description
– (on numeric keypad)	Hides all subheadings of highlighted heading
+ (on numeric keypad)	Exposes all subheadings one level under highlighted heading
* (on numeric keypad)	Exposes all subheadings at all levels under highlighted heading

After you have hidden headings, you can look at the special symbols to the left of the headings to determine which headings are hidden. Remember, the minus sign (–) indicates that a heading does not have any subheadings, and the plus sign (+) indicates that subheadings exist. If a heading has a + next to it, but you do not see any subheadings, you can deduce that the subheadings are hidden. For example, in figure 11.18, the `Introduction` and `planning` headings have hidden subheadings, but the `Macros` heading does not.

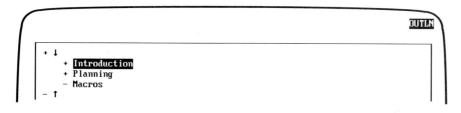

Fig. 11.18.
Hidden subheadings.

The quickest way to display just your major headings is to press Home to go to the top of your outline, and then press minus (–) to hide all the headings. Then press plus (+) to expose the headings one level under the current heading, as shown in figure 11.18.

If you have selectively hidden certain subheadings and want to expose them all, you can go to each heading and press plus (+) to expose its subheadings.

A faster way, however, is to go to the top of the outline and press the asterisk (*) to expose all the headings.

Printing an Outline

You cannot directly print your outline as it appears in an OUTLN window. If you do try to print, when you specify a SERVICES **P**rint **S**ettings **S**ource **R**ange, you immediately see that something is wrong. You are switched into SHEET mode, and the outline is triple-spaced with multilevel numbering, a bunch of special codes, and no indentation at the different levels. You can print this version of the outline, but it may not look much like an outline.

Caution:

When you specify the destination range, make sure that you indicate an empty part of the spreadsheet. Otherwise, the outline copies over and replaces any cells containing data.

You can print an exact copy of the outline, however, as you see it in the OUTLN window. The **T**ables **O**utline command on the OUTLN menu makes a duplicate of your outline in another part of the spreadsheet so that you can specify this range as the **S**ource. To create this copy, select OUTLN **T**ables **O**utline. You are automatically switched into SHEET mode, and Text Outliner asks you for a destination range. Be sure to indicate an empty part of the spreadsheet. Otherwise, the outline copies over and replaces any cells containing data. Make sure that you *DO NOT* specify the area containing the spreadsheet version of your outline.

After you copy the outline to the spreadsheet (see fig. 11.19), you can use the SERVICES **P**rint command to print the outline. Specify the copy you just made as the **S**ource **R**ange.

Fig. 11.19.

After copying an outline to a spreadsheet.

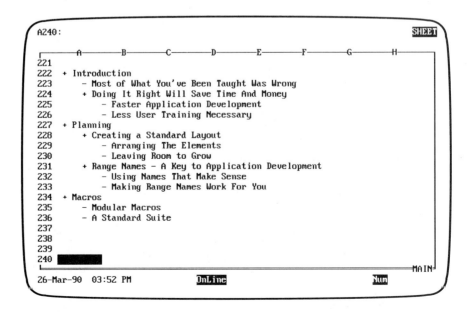

If the outline is part of a document (see the section on "Using an Outline To Create a Document" later in this chapter), you may find the **T**ables **O**utline command useful for printing only the outline (no text).

Modifying an Outline

One of the benefits of creating outlines in Text Outliner rather than in a word processor is Text Outliner's capacity to manipulate headings and subheadings rather than individual characters. For example, if you want to move a section, you do not need to highlight all the text and subheadings that belong with that section. You highlight just the heading and Text Outliner automatically highlights the entire section. Unfortunately, although you can adjust the highlight to add additional sections at the same level, you cannot adjust it to move only part of the current section. If you want to move just a portion of a section you'll have to leave the menu, move the cursor to a lower level within the section, and select OUTLN **M**ove again. The same applies for deleting and copying.

Reminder:
When you want to move a section, highlight just the heading and Text Outliner automatically highlights the entire section.

In Text Outliner, you can format headings as a group rather than one by one. With the OUTLN **A**ttributes command, you can specify the print attributes either for all levels, for a specific level, or for an individual heading. You can also change the amount of indentation in the outline levels by pressing a single key. In a DOC window, you cannot make global changes like these.

Editing Headings

If you make a mistake in one of your outline entries after you have entered it, you can use the Edit key (F2) to correct it. If you are in the middle of inserting an entry, you are automatically in EDIT mode and consequently do not need to press the Edit key. Editing a heading in an OUTLN window is almost identical to editing a spreadsheet cell in a SHEET window. Use the pointer to highlight the heading you want to edit, and press F2. You then get a single-character cursor rather than a rectangular pointer. Use the right- and left-arrow keys to move the cursor, and take advantage of the following editing keys:

Key	Function
Del	Deletes character at cursor
Backspace	Deletes character to left of cursor
Home	Moves to beginning of heading
End	Moves to end of heading
Esc (once)	Clears entry
Esc (twice)	Restores original entry

Characters are automatically inserted to the left as you type. And you cannot overtype characters as you can in DOC mode.

Inserting Additional Headings

To insert a heading after the outline has been created, place the pointer above where you want the new heading to appear. This positioning may not be what you expect, because data is inserted above the cursor in DOC and SHEET modes. In OUTLN mode, though, headings are inserted below the pointer. For example, to insert the heading `Their Own Window` between the headings `Modular Macros` and `A Standard Suite`, as shown in figure 11.20, you place the pointer on `Modular Macros`.

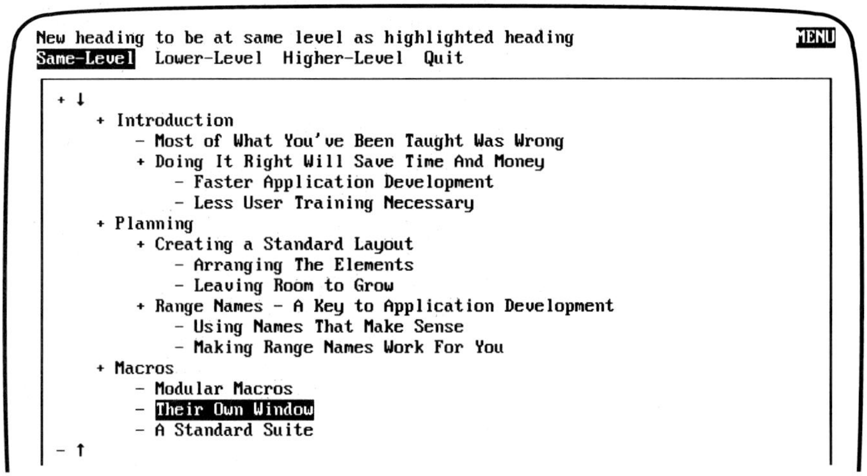

Fig. 11.20.

Inserting a new heading.

```
New heading to be at same level as highlighted heading        MENU
Same-Level  Lower-Level  Higher-Level  Quit

  ← ↓
      + Introduction
          - Most of What You've Been Taught Was Wrong
          + Doing It Right Will Save Time And Money
              - Faster Application Development
              - Less User Training Necessary
      + Planning
          + Creating a Standard Layout
              - Arranging The Elements
              - Leaving Room to Grow
          + Range Names - A Key to Application Development
              - Using Names That Make Sense
              - Making Range Names Work For You
      + Macros
          - Modular Macros
          - Their Own Window
          - A Standard Suite
  - ↑
```

After you have placed the pointer in the proper location, use the OUTLN **I**nsert command or the Ins key. You must then choose the heading level: **S**ame-Level, **L**ower-Level (a subheading), or **H**igher- Level (one level higher). Next, type the heading text and press Enter. If you are finished adding headings, choose **Q**uit. Otherwise, select the heading level for the next insert and then continue.

If the outline was numbered, it dynamically renumbers as you insert new entries.

Reminder:

You cannot delete a heading without also deleting its subheadings and all text that falls under both the headings and subheadings.

Removing Headings

To remove a heading, use the OUTLN **D**elete command or the Del key. First, place the pointer on the heading you want to remove. Press the Del key or choose OUTLN **D**elete. The message `Delete what?` appears in the control panel. The heading and all its subheadings (if any) are highlighted. This highlighting should tell you that you cannot delete a heading without also deleting its subheadings. Furthermore, if any text falls under the heading or subheadings in the document, this text also is deleted. Make sure that you want to delete all this material! Fortunately, Text Outliner asks you to confirm your intent to delete heading(s) and associated text, as shown in figure 11.21. If all you want to do is remove a heading, and not the text, you may want to use the **J**oin command (see the next section).

```
 Delete heading(s) and associated text?                          MENU
 No  Yes
 ┌──────────────────────────────────────────────────────────┐
 │ + ↓                                                        │
 │       + Introduction                                       │
 │           - Most of What You've Been Taught Was Wrong      │
 │           + Doing It Right Will Save Time And Money        │
 │               - Faster Application Development             │
 │               - Less User Training Necessary              │
 │       + Planning                                           │
 │           + Creating a Standard Layout                     │
 │               - Arranging The Elements                     │
 │               - Leaving Room to Grow                       │
 │           + Range Names - A Key to Application Development  │
 │               - Using Names That Make Sense                │
 │               - Making Range Names Work For You            │
 │       + Macros                                             │
 │           - Modular Macros                                 │
 │           - Their Own Window                               │
 │           - A Standard Suite                               │
 │ - ↑                                                        │
 └──────────────────────────────────────────────────────────┘
```

Fig. 11.21.
Deleting headings.

If you have hidden any subheadings with the minus key (–), the hidden headings are also deleted, even though they are not displayed. You may want to go to the top of the outline and press the asterisk (*) to expose all headings before you delete anything. With all headings displayed, you see exactly what headings and subheadings you are deleting. You also may want to save your file before you delete, because the **D**elete command is so convenient that it borders on being dangerous.

You also can delete more than one heading at a time. By default, Text Outliner highlights the single heading on which your pointer rests (and any subheadings), but you can use your arrow keys to highlight additional entries.

If the outline was numbered, it dynamically renumbers as you delete entries.

Merging Outline Sections

The OUTLN **J**oin command merges together two adjoining sections. In effect, **J**oin deletes the heading and moves its subheadings and associated text to the previous heading. So rather than move the subheadings and then delete the main heading, you can use **J**oin to do it in one step.

The **J**oin command does have its limitations. You can join sections only at the same or higher level. This concept is best explained by example. Refer to figure 11.22 (which also shows multilevel dynamic numbering). You can join the headings `Introduction` and `Most of What You've Been Taught Was Wrong`, because `Introduction` is at a higher level. But Text Outliner does not let you join `planning with Most of What You've Been Taught Was Wrong`, because the heading before `planning` is at a lower level. If you attempt to perform this operation, you get the message `Target must be at same or higher level`.

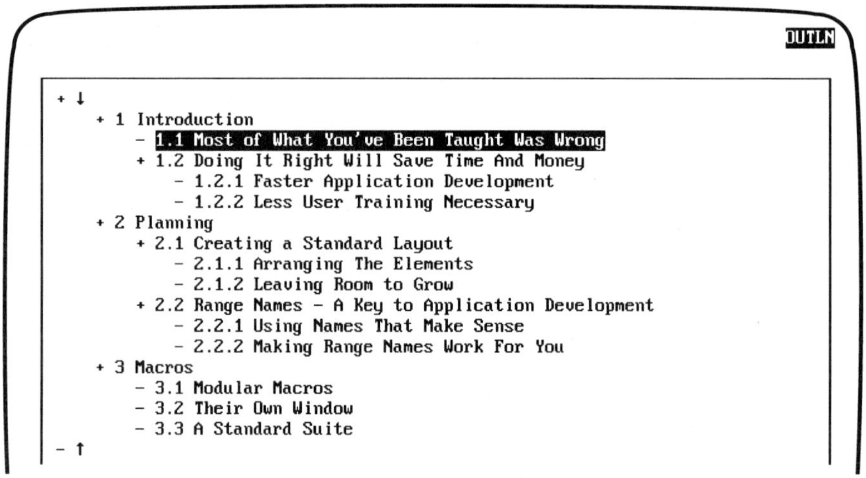

Fig. 11.22.

Before joining *Most of What You've Been Taught Was Wrong to Introduction.*

```
                                                              OUTLN

    + ↓
        + 1 Introduction
            - 1.1 Most of What You've Been Taught Was Wrong
            + 1.2 Doing It Right Will Save Time And Money
                - 1.2.1 Faster Application Development
                - 1.2.2 Less User Training Necessary
        + 2 Planning
            + 2.1 Creating a Standard Layout
                - 2.1.1 Arranging The Elements
                - 2.1.2 Leaving Room to Grow
            + 2.2 Range Names - A Key to Application Development
                - 2.2.1 Using Names That Make Sense
                - 2.2.2 Making Range Names Work For You
        + 3 Macros
            - 3.1 Modular Macros
            - 3.2 Their Own Window
            - 3.3 A Standard Suite
    - ↑
```

To merge two sections, select OUTLN **J**oin. Text Outliner asks, `Merge what section with preceding section?`. Move the pointer to the section you want to merge. Text Outliner highlights not only the section you point to, but also the preceding section. You are asked to confirm your intention. As you can see in figure 11.23, all the text and subheadings of the second section are added onto the first section, and the heading for the second section (`Most of What You've Been Taught Was Wrong`) is deleted. If you had previously hidden any of the headings in the merged section, the **J**oin operation automatically exposes these subheadings.

If the outline was numbered as in this example, it dynamically renumbers after you use the **J**oin command. Notice that the section `Doing It Right Will Save Time And Money` changed from number 1.2 to 1.1.

Copying Outline Sections

Use the **C**opy command to copy a section of your outline to another location in the outline. This command copies the heading(s) you highlight, any

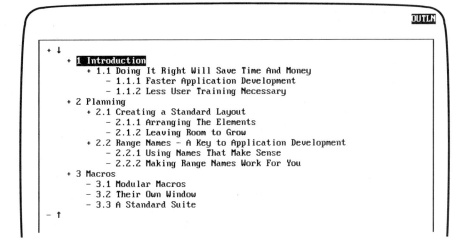

Fig. 11.23.
After using the Join command.

subheadings (including ones you may have previously hidden), and any accompanying text that exists in the DOC window.

Select OUTLN **C**opy, and Text Outliner asks, `Copy what?` Highlight the heading or headings you want to duplicate and press Enter. Text Outliner then asks, `Copy after what heading?` As with the **I**nsert command, the entries are inserted after the pointer. Place the pointer on the line above where you want the copy to go, and then press Enter. The heading level menu displays in the control panel. Note that you are asked to choose the level with respect to the highlighted heading, not the level at which the headings were previously. Choose the appropriate level, and the section copies.

Reminder:
When copying text, make sure that you place the pointer on the line above where you want the copy to go, and then press Enter.

If the outline was numbered, it dynamically renumbers after you use the **C**opy command.

Moving Outline Sections

The **M**ove command has two purposes in Text Outliner. First, **M**ove reorganizes your outline if you want to restructure it. Second, you can use the command to change the level of a heading. (See the next section, "Changing Levels.") The **M**ove command relocates the heading(s) you highlight, any subheadings you may have previously hidden, and accompanying text in the DOC window.

Select OUTLN **M**ove, and Text Outliner asks, `Move what?` Highlight the heading or headings you want to move and then press Enter. Text Outliner asks, `Move after what heading?` As with the **I**nsert and **C**opy commands, the entries are inserted after the pointer. Place the pointer on the line above where you want the section to be moved and press Enter. The heading level menu displays in the control panel. Note that you are asked to choose the level with respect to the highlighted heading, not the level at which the headings were previously. Choose the appropriate level, and the section moves.

If the outline was numbered, it dynamically renumbers after you use the **M**ove command.

Changing Levels

Because the **M**ove command asks you to specify what level you want the heading to have in its new location, you can use this command to change a heading's level without actually relocating the heading. Suppose that you want the heading `Macros` in figure 11.24 to be a subheading of `planning`. Select OUTLN **M**ove. Text Outliner asks, `Move what?` Highlight `Macros` and press Enter. Text Outliner asks, `Move after what heading?` Place the pointer on the preceding line, which keeps the heading in the same position in the outline, and press Enter. The heading level menu displays in the control panel. You want the heading to be at a higher level than the target heading (`Making Range Names Work For You`), so select **H**igher-Level. The section moves to the right—changes level. The outline now looks like figure 11.25.

Fig. 11.24.

Before changing heading levels.

```
                                                              OUTLN
    + ↓
      + 1 Introduction
        + 1.1 Doing It Right Will Save Time And Money
          - 1.1.1 Faster Application Development
          - 1.1.2 Less User Training Necessary
      + 2 Planning
        + 2.1 Creating a Standard Layout
          - 2.1.1 Arranging The Elements
          - 2.1.2 Leaving Room to Grow
        + 2.2 Range Names - A Key to Application Development
          - 2.2.1 Using Names That Make Sense
          - 2.2.2 Making Range Names Work For You
      + 3 Macros
          - 3.1 Modular Macros
          - 3.2 Their Own Window
          - 3.3 A Standard Suite
    - ↑
```

Take a look at a slightly more complicated example. Suppose that you want the subheading `Their Own Window` to be a major heading, and you want the heading below it (`A Standard Suite`) to be a subheading of `Their Own Window`, not of `planning`. Figure 11.26 illustrates how you want to restructure the outline.

You may think that all you have to do is move `Their Own Window` to a higher level. But figure 11.27 shows the results of this move. The subheadings still "belong" to the heading `Macros`, so they stay put, and the new major heading (`Their Own Window`) moves after the subheading `A Standard Suite`. Consequently, you must perform a second move operation to move the subheading. Highlight the subheading `A Standard Suite` and move it after `Their Own Window`, specifying a **L**ower-Level. Now the outline looks like figure 11.26.

```
                                                          OUTLN
 + ↓
     + 1 Introduction
         + 1.1 Doing It Right Will Save Time And Money
             - 1.1.1 Faster Application Development
             - 1.1.2 Less User Training Necessary
     + 2 Planning
         + 2.1 Creating a Standard Layout
             - 2.1.1 Arranging The Elements
             - 2.1.2 Leaving Room to Grow
         + 2.2 Range Names - A Key to Application Development
             - 2.2.1 Using Names That Make Sense
             - 2.2.2 Making Range Names Work For You
         + 2.3 Macros
             - 2.3.1 Modular Macros
             - 2.3.2 Their Own Window
             - 2.3.3 A Standard Suite
 - ↑
```

Fig. 11.25.
*Moving Macros
to a new level.*

```
                                                          OUTLN
 + ↓
     + 1 Introduction
         + 1.1 Doing It Right Will Save Time And Money
             - 1.1.1 Faster Application Development
             - 1.1.2 Less User Training Necessary
     + 2 Planning
         + 2.1 Creating a Standard Layout
             - 2.1.1 Arranging The Elements
             - 2.1.2 Leaving Room to Grow
         + 2.2 Range Names - A Key to Application Development
             - 2.2.1 Using Names That Make Sense
             - 2.2.2 Making Range Names Work For You
         + 2.3 Macros
             - 2.3.1 Modular Macros
         + 2.4 Their Own Window
             - 2.4.1 A Standard Suite
 - ↑
```

Fig. 11.26.
*Changing Their
Own Window to
a major heading*

```
                                                          OUTLN
 + ↓
     + 1 Introduction
         + 1.1 Doing It Right Will Save Time And Money
             - 1.1.1 Faster Application Development
             - 1.1.2 Less User Training Necessary
     + 2 Planning
         + 2.1 Creating a Standard Layout
             - 2.1.1 Arranging The Elements
             - 2.1.2 Leaving Room to Grow
         + 2.2 Range Names - A Key to Application Development
             - 2.2.1 Using Names That Make Sense
             - 2.2.2 Making Range Names Work For You
         + 2.3 Macros
             - 2.3.1 Modular Macros
             - 2.3.2 Their Own Window
             - 2.3.3 A Standard Suite
     - 2.4 Their Own Window
```

Fig. 11.27.
*The first step of the
move.*

Formatting an Outline

Reminder:

Text Outliner's Attribute command enables you to format headings as a group rather than one by one.

If you were creating an outline in DOC mode, without using Text Outliner, you would have to format each of your headings individually with the appropriate print attribute (such as boldface or underlined). You would have to press Ctrl-B and specify an attribute before each heading, and then press Ctrl-E after each heading. With the Text Outliner's **A**ttribute command, however, you can format headings as a group rather than one by one, allowing you to format all your headings quickly and consistently. Furthermore, you can indicate the print attributes for all levels, for all headings at a certain level, or for an individual heading.

By indicating special print attributes for your headings, you can easily discern them from the document text, and from each other, when you print the document or outline. To format your headings, select OUTLN **A**ttributes. The following menu displays in the control panel:

Global **L**evel **S**ingle

To format all the headings with the same print attribute, choose **G**lobal. To assign a special format for all the headings at a particular level, select **L**evel. Choose **S**ingle to set the attributes for only one heading.

If you choose **L**evel, Text Outliner asks, `Attributes for what level?` Place the pointer on any heading in the level you want to format, and then press Enter. If you choose **S**ingle, Text Outliner asks, `Attribute for what heading?` Point to the appropriate heading and press Enter.

After you choose one of the three options, you see the attribute menu. This menu is similar to the menu you get in DOC mode when you press Ctrl-B, except that the OUTLN version has two additional choices: **N**on-Printing and **C**lear. If you choose **N**on-Printing, the heading(s) do not print in the document, although they do print in the outline. (The section titled "Outlining an Existing Document" later in this chapter discusses when you may want to use this nonprinting feature.) If you no longer want any attributes for the heading(s), select **C**lear to remove the attributes.

Changing Indentation

By default, each level in the outline is indented four spaces from the previous level. But you are one keystroke away from changing the amount of indentation: you can type a number from 1 to 9 to control the indentation. For example, if you want each level indented 9 spaces from the preceding level, type 9. You instantly see the effect of the new indentation in your outline. Figure 11.28 shows a 9-space indentation.

Reminder:

You must be in OUTLN mode when type the numbers to change indentation.

You must be in OUTLN mode when you type the number. If you are inserting entries (that is, you are in EDIT mode), you cannot change the indentation.

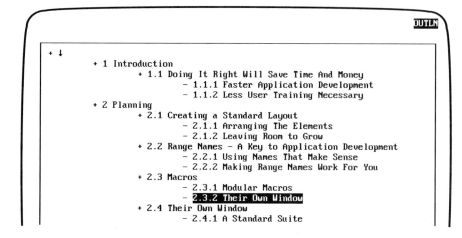

Fig. 11.28.
Nine-space indentation.

Using an Outline To Create a Document

So far, this section of the chapter has concentrated on creating and modifying outlines. Creating the outline, however, is just the first step. Most often the reason for creating an outline is to provide you with a structure for writing a document. This section discusses how to use the outline to help you write and edit a document effectively.

Switching between OUTLN and DOC

When you want to type text into your outline, you need to switch to DOC mode. The quickest way to go to DOC mode is to press the GoTo key (F5). The GoTo key in OUTLN mode switches to DOC mode in one keystroke. You can also press the Type key (Alt-F10) and select DOC, or press the Switch key (Alt-F9) if the last mode you were in was DOC. To switch back from DOC to OUTLN, use the Switch or Type keys.

When you switch to DOC mode, the cursor is placed underneath the heading on which the pointer rested in OUTLN mode. Similarly, when you switch back to OUTLN mode, the pointer is placed at the heading under which the cursor was located. Thus, you can use the outline to move quickly to different sections of a long document. If you are working in your document and want to move to a distant section, switch to OUTLN, move the pointer to the section to which you want to go, and then switch back to DOC. Your cursor will be underneath the desired heading. It's much faster to move the pointer in a compact outline than to scroll in the document.

Using Outline in the DOC Window

When you switch from OUTLN to DOC, your outline headings are surrounded by codes, as shown in figure 11.29. The codes are described here:

Code	Description
{B}	Section-begin marker
{E}	Section-end marker
{-B}	Section-begin marker (hidden section in the outline)
{N}	Nonprinting heading

Fig.11.29.

The outline in the DOC window.

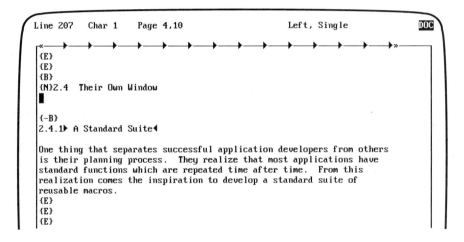

```
 Line 207    Char 1    Page 4,10                    Left, Single          DOC

 «————▶——▶——▶——▶——▶——▶——▶——▶——▶——▶——▶——▶»
 {E}
 {E}
 {B}
 {N}2.4   Their Own Window
 █

 {-B}
 2.4.1▶ A Standard Suite◀

 One thing that separates successful application developers from others
 is their planning process.  They realize that most applications have
 standard functions which are repeated time after time.  From this
 realization comes the inspiration to develop a standard suite of
 reusable macros.
 {E}
 {E}
 {E}
```

The section-begin marker, {B} or {-B}, appears on the line above each section. The section-end marker, {E}, appears after any subheadings or document text. If the heading does not have any subordinate headings, the section-end marker appears three lines under the heading. You should type the text associated with the heading above the end marker.

If you place the cursor on a line containing a marker, the control panel displays an asterisk. The asterisk indicates that you cannot edit the line in DOC mode. If you try to type anything on this line, Symphony beeps and displays at the bottom of the screen the message `Cannot alter this area of the document`. Because in DOC mode you cannot edit the lines containing begin or end markers, you do not need to worry about deleting them accidentally.

These special symbols do not print, nor do they leave blank lines when you print the document. To confirm this fact, look at the page and line number in the control panel as you move the cursor from a line containing a section marker to the line below it. You see that the line number does not change. You can also switch to SHEET mode and move the cursor to a cell containing a section marker; you'll see that it is a label with the vertical bar (|) prefix, meaning a non-printing label.

The {N} symbol preceding a heading indicates that this heading will not be included in the printed document. You cannot edit nonprinting headings, as indicated by the asterisk in the control panel.

You can edit your headings (except for nonprinting headings) while in a DOC window, and the headings automatically change in the OUTLN window. If you completely erase a heading, the first line of text displays in the outline as a heading. If the line is blank, the following message appears where the heading formerly was in the OUTLN window: `[No heading on line below section-begin marker]`. To correct this error, switch back to DOC mode and type the heading on the line directly underneath the section-begin marker. The heading may no longer be at the right level, so you may have to use the **M**ove command to adjust the level. (See the section on "Changing Levels," covered earlier in this chapter.)

The headings are automatically numbered in DOC mode, regardless of whether the outline is numbered in OUTLN mode. If you do not want the numbers in the document headings, you can remove them, as explained in the next section.

Removing Outline Numbers

By default, the headings in DOC mode are numbered with the multilevel system (1, 1.1, 1.1.1). In most cases, you probably don't want numbered headings in the document. You may then want to remove the numbering in the document before you print. Switch to the OUTLN window and select OUTLN **N**umbering **D**elete-Numbers. In addition to removing outline numbers in the DOC window, this command removes the numbering and indentation in the OUTLN window, as shown in figure 11.30. To restore numbering and indentation, use the OUTLN Numbering Renumber command.

Because the indentation is eliminated from the outline, you may not want to use this command while working in the OUTLN window. You probably will issue the **D**elete-Numbers command before printing and then restore the numbering and indentation with the **R**enumber command the next time you work with the outline.

If you have turned off the numbering in your document, you may lose track of where you are in terms of your outline. When Text Outliner is attached, you have several additional commands available to you in DOC mode. One of these commands, **F**ormat **L**ocation, tells you which outline section your cursor is in. The current section (for example, Section 5.4) displays in the lower left corner of the screen until you move the cursor. The **F**ormat **L**ocation command saves you from switching to OUTLN mode, turning numbering back on to see where you are, then switching back to DOC mode.

Cue:

To help you keep track of your location in the outline, keep the numbering on in the document.

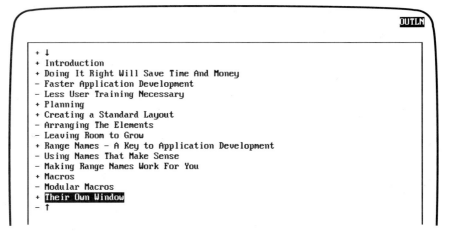

Fig. 11.30.
The results of selecting OUTLN Numbering Delete-Numbers.

Outlining an Existing Document

Cue:

You can improve the structure and organization of existing documents by outlining them.

If you type all or part of a document before creating an outline, it is not too late to outline the document. But why would you want to outline an existing document? First, an outline shows you the document's structure at a glance. Sometimes when writing you get lost in what you are saying and lose track of the document's organization. The outline may lead you to reorganize some of the sections.

This line of thought leads directly to the second reason for outlining an existing document: If you do need to reorganize the document, the outlining features make the process much easier. Working in the OUTLN window, you can quickly move, copy, and delete entire sections (headings, subheadings, and associated text).

To create an outline for existing text, you make the outline entries in DOC mode, not OUTLN mode. When Text Outliner is attached, an additional command appears on the DOC **F**ormat menu: **O**utline-Section. With this command, you can indicate the heading and the text to be included with the heading.

Select DOC **F**ormat **O**utline-Section. Highlight the text to be included in this section (including any subsections) and press Enter. Text Outliner asks you to **Enter heading for this section**. Type the heading and press Enter. The new heading appears, and the begin- and end-section markers are inserted in the appropriate places in the document (see fig. 11.31). Repeat this procedure for each section.

Reminder:

Frequently switch back and forth between DOC and OUTLN mode to ensure that you are structuring the outline properly.

If you switch to OUTLN mode, you can see the outline you are creating in DOC mode. Switch back and forth between DOC and OUTLN mode frequently so that you can make sure that you are indicating the correct range for each section and, hence, structuring the outline properly.

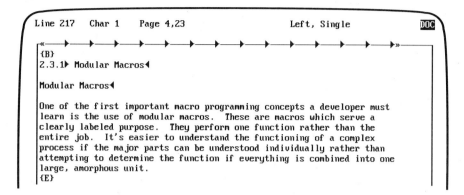

```
Line 217   Char 1    Page 4,23              Left, Single        DOC

«————————————————————————————————————————————————»
{B}
2.3.1▶ Modular Macros◀

Modular Macros◀

One of the first important macro programming concepts a developer must
learn is the use of modular macros.  These are macros which serve a
clearly labeled purpose.  They perform one function rather than the
entire job.  It's easier to understand the functioning of a complex
process if the major parts can be understood individually rather than
attempting to determine the function if everything is combined into one
large, amorphous unit.
{E}
```

Fig. 11.31.
Inserting headings in an existing document.

When an existing document contains already-typed section titles, you either need to delete the titles or specify the outline headings as nonprinting (OUTLN **A**ttributes **G**lobal **N**on-Printing).

Printing an Outlined Document

In a DOC window, Symphony prints all the text by default. So to print the entire document, make sure that you are in DOC mode and then issue the SERVICES **P**rint **G**o command. Symphony prints your entire document along with the headings and section numbers. If you do not want the section numbers to print, use the OUTLN **N**umbering **D**elete-Numbers command before printing. Any headings specified as **N**on-Printing with the OUTLN **A**ttributes command do not print at all.

If you want to print a part of the document, select SERVICES **P**rint **S**ettings **S**ource **R**ange and then highlight the appropriate part of the text. An alternative (and faster) way of specifying certain sections to print, though, is Text Outliner's **P**rint-Range command. With this command, you only have to highlight the outline heading(s) of the text that you want to print, as illustrated in figure 11.32. This command makes it convenient to print certain sections of a long document selectively.

Cue:
*By using **P**rint-Range, you can quickly and selectively print certain sections of a long document.*

If you save the document with a **P**rint-Range specified, this **S**ource **R**ange is permanently stored in the **P**rint settings sheet. The next time you issue the **P**rint command, this range prints. To return to the default setting of the entire document, issue the SERVICES **P**rint **S**ettings **S**ource **C**ancel command.

Creating a Table of Contents

Another reason for outlining a document is to have Text Outliner create a table of contents for the document. The OUTLN **T**ables **T**able-of-Contents command generates a table of contents containing headings, section numbers, indentation, blank lines between level changes, leader dots, and page numbers. Figure 11.33 is an example of a table of contents generated by Text 32 Outliner. The table is stored in the spreadsheet and can be printed separately.

Fig. 11.32.

Highlighting a range to print.

```
Print what range (includes document text)?                          POINT

  + ↓
    + 1 Introduction
        + 1.1 Doing It Right Will Save Time And Money
            - 1.1.1 Faster Application Development
            - 1.1.2 Less User Training Necessary
    + 2 Planning
        + 2.1 Creating a Standard Layout
            - 2.1.1 Arranging The Elements
            - 2.1.2 Leaving Room to Grow
        + 2.2 Range Names - A Key to Application Development
            - 2.2.1 Using Names That Make Sense
            - 2.2.2 Making Range Names Work For You
        + 2.3 Macros
            - 2.3.1 Modular Macros
        + 2.4 Their Own Window
  - ↑
```

Fig. 11.33.

A table of contents.

```
I1: '1 Introduction ...................................................  SHEET
    ┌─────I──────J──────K──────L──────M──────N──────O──────P──
 1  1 Introduction ....................................................  1
 2
 3      1.1 Doing It Right Will Save Time And Money ...................  1
 4
 5          1.1.1 Faster Application Development .......................  1
 6          1.1.2 Less User Training Necessary ........................  2
 7
 8  2 Planning .........................................................  2
 9
10      2.1 Creating a Standard Layout ................................  2
11
12          2.1.1 Arranging The Elements ..............................  2
13          2.1.2 Leaving Room to Grow ................................  3
14
15      2.2 Range Names - A Key to Application Development ............  3
16
17          2.2.1 Using Names That Make Sense .........................  3
18          2.2.2 Making Range Names Work For You .....................  3
19
20      2.3 Macros .....................................................  3
    └────────────────────────────────────────────────────────MAIN─
    27-Mar-90  10:37 AM              OnLine                      Num
```

To create a table of contents, select OUTLN **T**ables **T**able-of-Contents. Text Outliner then asks you to enter several parameters. The first prompt is **Enter width**. The number you enter here determines where the page number is placed in the table. If you accept the default (72), Text Outliner places the page number 72 characters from the left margin of the table.

The second prompt is **Enter indentation**. Regardless of the indentation used in your outline, you can specify a different indentation for the table of contents. You can specify a 1- to 9-space indentation.

Text Outliner next asks you to **Enter number of heading levels to include in table**. The default is 32, or all, heading levels. If you only want your major headings in the table of contents, you can specify 1 or 2 heading levels.

Text Outliner then switches you into SHEET mode and asks you for a destination range. Make sure you indicate an empty part of the spreadsheet; otherwise, the table of contents copies over and replaces any cells containing data. After you copy the table of contents to the spreadsheet, you can use the SERVICES **P**rint command to print the table. Specify the table that Text Outliner just created as the **S**ource **R**ange.

You can edit the table of contents before you print. Switch to DOC mode and turn off justification with the DOC **F**ormat **S**ettings **J**ustification **N**one command. If you do not turn off justification, the lines of the table wrap together, leaving you with a jumbled mess that no longer resembles a table of contents!

Caution:
If you edit the table of contents before you print, make sure that you switch to DOC mode and turn off justification.

Whenever you revise your document, keep in mind that the table of contents may no longer be accurate. If you have made significant revisions, you need to generate a new table of contents. Do not forget to erase the old table before creating the new one.

Reminder:
If you make significant changes in the document, you need to generate a new table of contents.

If you do not want section numbering in the table of contents, turn off numbering with the OUTLN **N**umbering **D**elete-Numbers command before you generate the table. Bear in mind that this command also turns off indentation, so the different levels in the table will not be indented, and blank lines will not appear between section-level changes.

Chapter Summary

By using the Spelling Checker and Text Outliner add-in applications, you can add power to Symphony's word processing. With Spelling Checker, you can reduce the number of typing and spelling mistakes in your documents and spreadsheets, enabling you to produce more professional-looking documents. Text Outliner enables you to create outlines and tables of contents for your documents. Furthermore, you may probably find that your long documents are easier to revise and organize with Text Outliner.

Part IV

Creating Symphony Reports and Graphs

Printing Spreadsheets and Word
Processing Documents

Using Allways: The Spreadsheet
Publisher

Creating and Displaying Graphs

Printing Graphs

Creating and Printing Graphs:
Hands-On Practice

12

Printing Spreadsheets and Word Processing Documents

Symphony's printing capabilities enable you to print customized spreadsheets, word processing documents, graphs, and databases. This chapter shows you how to print spreadsheets and word processing documents. Graph printing requires special processing and is handled in Symphony's companion program, PrintGraph. Graph printing is discussed in Chapters 15 and 16, and database printing is covered in Chapter 18.

In this chapter you learn how to do the following:

- ❏ Print to a file and a range
- ❏ Print reports
- ❏ Set print options, headers, and footers
- ❏ Set margins and page lengths
- ❏ Print cell formulas

Except when printing graphs, Symphony options enable you to write directly to the printer from within the program; to write to a remote printer by using a local area network and a logical device name; to create a print file to be printed outside the program; and to print to a range within the current worksheet. Symphony also enables you to print headers and footers that include dates and page numbers, and to begin or end printing at any page (between 1 and 999) in a word processing document or spreadsheet.

A local area network (or LAN), is a collection of computers connected by adapters and cables making it possible for multiple users to share common hardware, software and data files. A logical device name is a naming convention used by a program to identify a specific printer on the network.

371

Although many print options control the printing of both spreadsheets and text, some options specify the type of application. For example, the SERVICES **P**rint menu provides options for printing spreadsheets **A**s-Displayed or as **C**ell-Formulas. Also, you can tell Symphony to reprint column and row headings for each page of a spreadsheet you print. Special print options related to printing documents include regulating underlined, boldface, superscript, and subscript characters in text.

Learning SERVICES Configuration Printer and SERVICES Print

Before you can get Symphony to work with your printer, you must select and access the proper printer driver. (See Appendix A for more information on setting drivers.) The printer driver provides a **C**onfiguration **P**rinter **S**ettings sheet that contains default settings for the printer, and a **P**rint **S**ettings sheet that defines settings for the print output. All that remains is to specify what is to be printed.

Besides the default settings, Symphony enables you to customize the printer configuration and the print output appearance. Before you can customize, you must modify the SERVICES **C**onfiguration **P**rinter settings (see fig. 12.1), and the SERVICES **P**rint **S**ettings (see fig. 12.2).

The SERVICES **C**onfiguration **P**rinter holds the default settings for single sheet versus continuous feed and for margins, page length, and initialization string. These settings are inherited by the first **P**rint **S**ettings sheet in a worksheet. For example, if your **C**onfiguration **P**rinter setting for the left margin is 5 and for the right margin is 65, the first **P**rint **S**ettings sheet you retrieve in a worksheet displays these margins. In addition, **C**onfiguration **P**rinter contains settings for printer type (parallel or serial) and automatic line feed, which are necessary settings for sending output directly to the printer.

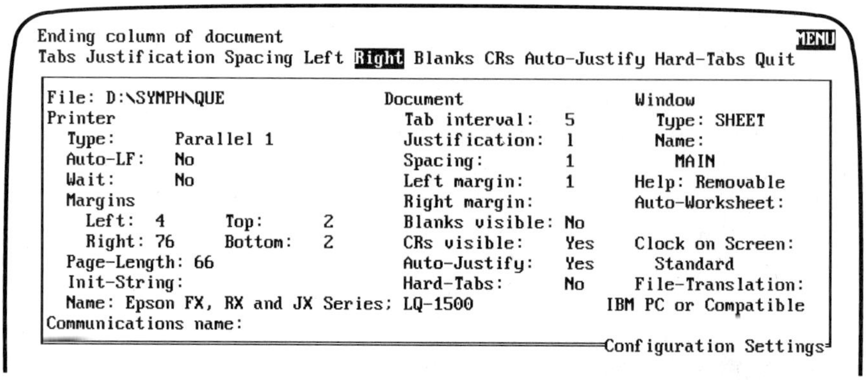

Fig. 12.1.
SERVICES Configuration Printer settings.

```
Ending column of document                                                MENU
Tabs Justification Spacing Left Right Blanks CRs Auto-Justify Hard-Tabs Quit
┌─────────────────────────────────────────────────────────────────────────┐
│ File: D:\SYMPH\QUE              Document              Window               │
│ Printer                          Tab interval:   5     Type: SHEET        │
│   Type:      Parallel 1          Justification:  1     Name:              │
│   Auto-LF:   No                  Spacing:        1       MAIN             │
│   Wait:      No                  Left margin:    1     Help: Removable    │
│   Margins                        Right margin:         Auto-Worksheet:    │
│     Left:  4        Top:     2   Blanks visible: No                       │
│     Right: 76       Bottom:  2   CRs visible:    Yes   Clock on Screen:   │
│   Page-Length: 66                Auto-Justify:   Yes     Standard         │
│   Init-String:                   Hard-Tabs:      No    File-Translation:  │
│   Name: Epson FX, RX and JX Series; LQ-1500           IBM PC or Compatible│
│ Communications name:                                                      │
│                                               └Configuration Settings┘    │
└───────────────────────────────────────────────────────────────────────── │
```

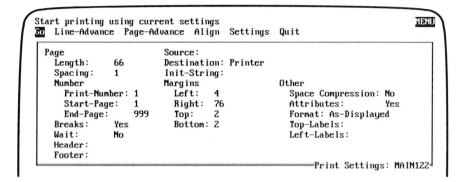

Fig. 12.2.
SERVICES Print Settings.

You can, however, change the **C**onfiguration **P**rinter settings and update the Symphony configuration file to include new settings. Eight choices are available for parallel or serial interface between Symphony and a printer (**C**onfiguration **P**rinter **T**ype). You also can choose a printer name from the printers you selected during the Install program (**C**onfiguration **P**rinter **N**ame). This feature is helpful if you have more than one printer attached to your system. Settings also are available for having either Symphony or your printer automatically advance the paper at the end of each line (**C**onfiguration **P**rinter **A**uto-LF). When you determine which **C**onfiguration **P**rinter settings to change and how to change them, consult the manual that comes with your printer.

Reminder:
Configuration Printer Name enables you to choose a printer name, which is a helpful feature if you have more than one printer attached to your system.

Through SERVICES **C**onfiguration **P**rinter, you also can regulate whether the printer continuously loads paper after finishing a page or waits (**C**onfiguration **P**rinter **W**ait). SERVICES **C**onfiguration **P**rinter contains settings for left, right, top, and bottom margins (SERVICES **C**onfiguration **P**rinter **M**argins) and page length (SERVICES **C**onfiguration **P**rinter **P**age-Length). Finally, print type and size are controlled by the setting in SERVICES **C**onfiguration **P**rinter **I**nit-String (see the section on "Sending an Initialization String to the Printer," later in this chapter).

As figure 12.2 shows, SERVICES **P**rint has many types of options, including selections that regulate the format for printing spreadsheets, and the naming and use of print settings sheets.

Using the Print Menu

The examples in this chapter explain many of the SERVICES **P**rint menu options (see fig. 12.2). A general introduction to the types of commands that are available may help you understand Symphony's print capabilities. Print commands fall into the following categories:

1. Commands for indicating what should be printed, stored in a print file, or entered into a range in the worksheet (**S**ettings **S**ource).

2. Commands for having source data printed directly, stored in a print file, or entered into a range in the worksheet (**S**ettings **D**estination).

3. Commands regulating page format:

   a. Number of lines per page (**S**ettings **P**age **L**ength).

   b. Spaces between lines in spreadsheets or databases (**S**ettings **P**age **S**pacing).

   c. Headers on each page (**S**ettings **P**age **H**eader).

   d. Footers on each page (**S**ettings **P**age **F**ooter).

   e. Margins (**S**ettings **M**argins).

   f. Boldface, underlining, superscript, and subscript (**S**ettings **O**ther **A**ttributes).

   g. Printing of spreadsheet data—as displayed on-screen versus displayed with cell formulas (**S**ettings **O**ther **F**ormat).

   h. Printing of worksheet labels (**S**ettings **O**ther **T**op-Labels, **S**ettings **O**ther **L**eft-Labels, and **S**ettings **O**ther **N**o-Labels).

   i. Numbers printed on each page (**S**ettings **P**age **N**umber).

4. Commands controlling printer operations:

   a. Page breaks (**S**ettings **P**age **B**reaks).

   b. Paper feed (**S**ettings **P**age **W**ait).

   c. Print size and type (**S**ettings **I**nit-String).

5. Commands for creating, naming, using, resetting, and deleting print settings sheets:

   a. Creating and naming print settings sheets (**S**ettings **N**ame **C**reate).

   b. Using print settings sheets (**S**ettings **N**ame **U**se, **S**ettings **N**ame **P**revious, and **S**ettings **N**ame **N**ext).

   c. Deleting print settings sheets (**S**ettings **N**ame **D**elete, **S**ettings **N**ame **R**eset, and **S**ettings **N**ame **I**nitial-Settings).

Reminder:

*To keep from accidentally printing the same data twice, use the **Q**uit option to exit the SERVICES **P**rint menu.*

The SERVICES **P**rint menu is one of Symphony's "sticky" menus. To stay out of trouble, you must exit **P**rint through the **Q**uit option. Whenever you perform a function from this menu, the program returns to exactly where you were before you made your selection. Be careful not to press Enter again at this point unless you want to execute the same function twice. It is disconcerting to return from printing the worksheet with the **G**o function, only to press Enter again accidentally and print the file a second time. To interrupt a print operation, press Ctrl-Break and then Esc to clear the ERROR message.

Whenever you print to a printer, a print file, or a range in a worksheet, you must press SERVICES **P**rint **G**o to begin printing. When you create a print file (when the **D**estination is a **F**ile), the operation is not completed until you exit the **P**rint menu by either choosing **Q**uit or pressing Esc.

Determining When and How To Print

Before you print a file you must decide what data you want to print (**S**ource). This feature is an option when printing in the DOC mode, but is required for printing spreadsheets. In the DOC mode, the print range is automatically provided by Symphony. The next step is to decide where you want that data to be printed (**D**estination).

Specifying the Source

To print data from the SHEET environment you must specify a source. The source defines the location in the worksheet of the data you want to print. The SERVICES **S**ource menu offers three choices: **R**ange, **D**atabase, and **C**ancel. For the most part, you will be printing from a range in the worksheet. Specify the range by using the directional arrows and pointing to the upper-left and lower-right corners of the range to be printed.

To print from the DOC environment you need not define a range. Symphony assumes that you want to print the entire document displayed on-screen. If you want to print only part of a document, use the **S**ource setting to designate what part of the document you want to print. If you do not specify a source and you are printing from a restricted DOC window, Symphony assumes that the **S**ource **R**ange is the same as the **W**indow **R**estrict **R**ange and prints all characters that appear in the **W**indow **R**estrict **R**ange.

Reminder:
You must specify a source when printing from a restricted DOC window, or Symphony will print all characters that appear in the Window Restrict Range.

Specifying a Destination

Besides specifying the source, you also must specify the destination. SERVICES **P**rint **S**ettings **D**estination tells Symphony where you want the data sent. The choice you may be using most often is the printer. However, Symphony also enables you to "print" the data to a range in the current worksheet or to a disk file. The **P**rint **S**ettings **D**estination menu contains the following options: **P**rinter, **F**ile, **R**ange, **E**rase, and **C**ancel.

Printing to a Printer

The **P**rinter option takes the specified source and prints it to the printer. This option is the default setting. If you do not alter the destination, all data is printed to the printer. The printer listed in the default field is taken from the choices that you made when you installed Symphony and also by any settings you specified with the SERVICES **C**onfiguration **P**rint command.

Printing to a Logical Device

With Symphony's networking capabilities, you can print by using a printer somewhere else on that network. To do so, you have to know the logical device name of the printer you want to use, plus select the appropriate printer during the Symphony install. You tell Symphony the logical device you want to use by invoking SERVICES **C**onfiguration **P**rinter **T**ype. Make certain that the **D**estination is set to printer. Now use the **P**rint menu options (**P**rint **A**lign **G**o) to write the files you want to print on the logical device.

The only limit to the number of files you can print is the amount of system memory available. To print multiple files, use the **P**rint **P**age-Advance and **P**rint **L**ine-Advance commands to separate the files with page breaks or blank lines. After selecting the files you want to print, select **Q**uit from the **P**rint menu. **Q**uit tells Symphony to close the connection to the logical device and print your work on the selected machine.

Printing to a File

The next option is **F**ile. This option enables you to print data to a special disk file called a print file. This file has the default file extension of PRN. You can print to a file if you want to work with the file in another software program, or if the system you are working on does not have a printer, or if your printer is not working, or if you want to create a file whose output you can send over data communications lines.

Reminder:

Once you print to a PRN file, you will not be able to retrieve it under SERVICES File Retrieve.

Print files are a special kind of DOS file. They contain actual data instead of program instructions usually contained in a Symphony file. For this reason, once you choose to print to a PRN file you will not be able to retrieve it under SERVICES **F**ile **R**etrieve. You can load this type of file into the worksheet with SERVICES **F**ile **I**mport (see Chapter 7).

When you do create a print file, make sure that you change the margin settings in the print settings sheet with SERVICES **P**rint **S**ettings **M**argin **N**o-Margins. This command eliminates margins and page breaks and sets single-spacing. Also note that if you print repeatedly to the same print file, Symphony appends your report or text to the end of the file. If you want to replace the existing file, you need to erase it (SERVICES **P**rint **S**ettings **D**estination **E**rase) before you print.

Printing to a Range

The **R**ange option makes it possible to print one range of the current worksheet into another range in the worksheet. "Printing" data to a range in the worksheet is particularly valuable when you want to import SHEET data into a DOC window. For example, when you transfer spreadsheet data into the DOC window of a worksheet with the SERVICES **P**rint **S**ettings **D**estination **R**ange command, you can edit the data or use DOC commands on the data as you would with data originally entered in the DOC mode.

Printing to a range in the worksheet is different from using the SHEET **C**opy command. With SHEET **C**opy, you can copy a spreadsheet or parts of a spreadsheet into a DOC window. But even though the spreadsheet section is copied into a DOC area, you cannot use the Del or Backspace key to change the entries.

Before you print to a range in the worksheet, make sure that the destination range is empty. To erase the current range, select **P**rint **S**ettings **D**estination **E**rase. The destination range should be large enough to accommodate the header, footer, and top and bottom margins. If the range is not large enough, an error message displays.

Symphony offers an alternative to creating a print file if your printer is not working or if you do not want to print immediately: you can name and store print settings and then retrieve those settings later when you want to print a spreadsheet or word processing text. Being able to save print settings alleviates having to reset print commands and also enables you to use a print settings sheet for other documents or spreadsheets. (See the section titled "Naming, Using, and Deleting Print Settings Sheets" later in this chapter.)

Printing Data: a Few Examples

Shown here to help you understand Symphony's print capabilities are three examples of data and how you can print them. The first example is a spreadsheet (Mom's Root Beer Company Cash-Flow Projection) that is printed with the minimum number of print options. In this case, the spreadsheet is printed much as it appears on-screen, without any of the special options. Figure 12.3 shows a portion of the screen display of the spreadsheet.

The second example of a data printout (Inventory Report on Cattuna) has been created in a DOC window; again, the data is to be printed much as it appears on-screen. Although the double-spacing feature is specified, the screen display remains single spaced (see fig. 12.4).

The third example (The Cattuna Distributing Inventory, figure 12.5), shows how to use the special options for printing spreadsheets.

For the first sample, called Mom's Root Beer Report, you may be more interested in the figures on the cash-flow projection for the next 10 years than in the format of the printed page. The only thing special you may do when printing this data is print all 12 columns on one standard 8 1/2-by-11-inch page.

Whether you decide to print the data immediately or create a print file and print it later, you begin either operation by selecting **P**rint from the SERVICES menu.

Fig. 12.3.

An example: Mom's Root Beer Company Cash-Flow Projection.

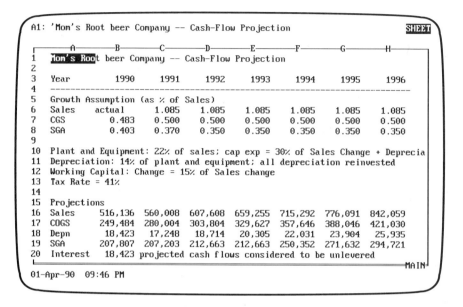

```
A1: 'Mom's Root beer Company -- Cash-Flow Projection          SHEET

      ┌───A────────B────────C────────D────────E────────F────────G────────H───
    1  Mom's Root beer Company -- Cash-Flow Projection
    2
    3  Year          1990     1991     1992     1993     1994     1995     1996
    4  ─────────────────────────────────────────────────────────────────────
    5  Growth Assumption (as % of Sales)
    6  Sales    actual      1.085    1.085    1.085    1.085    1.085    1.085
    7  CGS          0.483    0.500    0.500    0.500    0.500    0.500    0.500
    8  SGA          0.403    0.370    0.350    0.350    0.350    0.350    0.350
    9
   10  Plant and Equipment: 22% of sales; cap exp = 30% of Sales Change + Deprecia
   11  Depreciation: 14% of plant and equipment; all depreciation reinvested
   12  Working Capital: Change = 15% of Sales change
   13  Tax Rate = 41%
   14
   15  Projections
   16  Sales    516,136  560,008  607,608  659,255  715,292  776,091  842,059
   17  COGS     249,484  280,004  303,804  329,627  357,646  388,046  421,030
   18  Depn      18,423   17,248   18,714   20,305   22,031   23,904   25,935
   19  SGA      207,807  207,203  212,663  212,663  250,352  271,632  294,721
   20  Interest  18,423 projected cash flows considered to be unlevered
      └────────────────────────────────────────────────────────────────MAIN┘

   01-Apr-90  09:46 PM
```

Fig. 12.4.

An example: Inventory report on Cattuna.

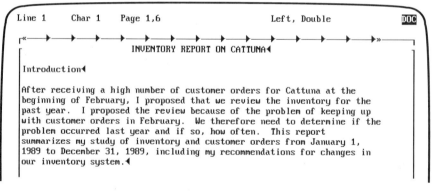

```
Line 1     Char 1     Page 1,6              Left, Double         DOC

┌«───►───►───►───►───►───►───►───►───►───►───►───►───►»──┐
│                  INVENTORY REPORT ON CATTUNA◄          │
│                                                        │
│  Introduction◄                                         │
│                                                        │
│  After receiving a high number of customer orders for Cattuna at the    │
│  beginning of February, I proposed that we review the inventory for the │
│  past year.  I proposed the review because of the problem of keeping up  │
│  with customer orders in February.  We therefore need to determine if the│
│  problem occurred last year and if so, how often.  This report          │
│  summarizes my study of inventory and customer orders from January 1,   │
│  1989 to December 31, 1989, including my recommendations for changes in  │
│  our inventory system.◄                                │
```

Designating a Print Range

Reminder:

Choose Database whenever the source is data specified in the database settings sheet.

One of the first steps in printing any data is to designate a range of cells to be printed. As indicated earlier, the command used to designate a range is SERVICES **P**rint **S**ettings **S**ource **R**ange. In addition to **R**ange, Symphony provides another option for indicating the source of the print output: **D**atabase. You choose **D**atabase whenever the source is data specified in the database settings sheet (see Chapter 17).

In the first and second print examples, setting the range requires selecting SERVICES **P**rint **S**ettings **S**ource **R**ange. If the source range begins with the upper left corner of the window's restrict range and ends with the lower right corner of the restrict range, first move the cursor to the upper left corner. Then select SERVICES **P**rint **S**ettings **S**ource **R**ange. Symphony prompts you for the

```
A1:  'Month                                                    SHEET
┌─────────────A─────────────B──────C──────D──────E──────F──────┐
1  Month                    Jan    Feb    Apr    May    June
2  =============================================================
3  Beginning Inventory       43     51     60    472     30
4  Past Demand for Month     28     16     10     12     20
5  Ending Inventory          15     35     42     30     10
6  Quantity Ordered          36      0      0      0     36
7  Setup Costs ($10 per order) $10.00  $0.00  $0.00  $0.00 $10.00
8  Inventory Costs ($.2/unit) $3.00  $7.00  $8.40  $6.00  $2.00
9  Shortage Costs ($1/unit)  $0.00  $0.00  $0.00  $0.00  $0.00
10 Total Costs for Month    $13.00  $7.00 $14.80  $6.00 $12.00
11 Cum Cost from Last Month  $0.00 $13.00 $20.00 $43.20 $49.20
12 Cumulative Costs to Date $13.00 $20.00 $34.80 $49.20 $61.20
13
14
15 Order Qunatity Input Cell ->    36
16 Order Point Input Cell ---->    28
17
18                         Order   Cumulative    Order   Cumulativ
19                         Quant   Cost          Quant   Cost
20                         ----------------      -----------------
└──────────────────────────────────────────────────────────MAIN┘
01-Apr-90  09:47 PM
```

Fig. 12.5.
An example: The Cattuna Distributing Inventory.

Range to be printed:. Press the Tab key followed by the End key, then the Home key. The cursor highlights the complete restrict range. This sequence also is useful for pointing to a print range when the range is the entire sheet. You can temporarily prevent columns from being printed by using the SHEET **W**idth **H**ide command.

In the third print example, setting the print range is more complicated. Printing the spreadsheet part of this document requires setting multiple ranges to print the inventory on two 8 1/2-by-11-inch pages. You must designate and print these ranges one at a time.

Because a print file has been created for this third example, the ranges will be appended one after the other in the file. Symphony enables you control the format of each range that is written. This feature is helpful when you want to control the printing of each part of the inventory. Each time a range is designated and print options are changed, you must select **G**o from the SERVICES **P**rint menu in order to send the range to the print file. **G**o also is required to send a range to the printer. To exit the Print menu, choose **Q**uit or press Esc.

Reminder:
Each time a range is designated and print options are changed, you must select Go from the SERVICES Print menu.

Setting Print Options

Besides designating print ranges, the only other data-printing task that requires any kind of detailed explanation is setting print options. Several print options will be designated for the Cattuna Distributing Inventory, whereas only a few options will be used for Mom's Root Beer Report (to get everything on one page) and the Inventory Report on Cattuna.

Special print options are available for both spreadsheets and text. The options for spreadsheets include the following:

❏ Spacing

❏ Printing column and row labels along the top and left on every page

❏ Printing **C**ell-Formulas rather than cell entries **A**s-Displayed

For DOC text, special print options include printing special print attributes: underlined, boldface, superscript, or subscript characters. The DOC **F**ormat **S**ettings **S**pacing command controls spacing for printing text created in a DOC window.

Setting Headers and Footers

For the third example, the first step after designating a print range is to set the header and footer options. These options allow you to specify up to 240 characters of text in each of three positions—left, center, and right—in the header and footer. Realistically, you should use only enough text to fit on an 8 1/2-inch-wide page, unless printing with wide paper.

You can enter all the text yourself, but Symphony has special characters that control page numbers, the current date, and the location where text is printed in the header and footer lines. These special characters are as follows:

This character automatically prints page numbers, starting with the number entered in SERVICES **P**rint **S**ettings **P**age **N**umber. If you use **P**rint **A**lign, the page number is reset to the number in SERVICES **P**rint **S**ettings **N**umber.

@ This character automatically includes the current date in the form 06/01/90 and takes the date from what you entered when you loaded DOS—that is, the current date.

| Headers and footers have three separate segments: left-justified, centered, and right-justified. Use this character to separate one segment from another. Notice the following examples of entries for header or footer lines:

What you type:

Cattuna Distributing Co. Inventory | | | page #
| Cattuna Distributing Co. Inventory, page #
Cattuna Distributing Co. Inventory, @, page # |

What appears on the page:

Cattuna Distributing Co. Inventory   page 1
            Cattuna Distributing Co. Inventory, page 1
      Cattuna Distributing Co. Inventory, 07/24/88, page 1

Reminder:
*For the header and footer options to work, you must set SERVICES **Print** Settings **Page** Breaks to **Yes**.*

You can use these symbols (@ | #) in either headers or footers. Also, the date appears in the format for month, day, and year (MM/DD/YY). Figures 12.14A and 12.14B at the end of this chapter show how the header and footer options are set up with the special characters for the third report. For the header and footer options to work, you must set SERVICES **P**rint **S**ettings **P**age **B**reaks to **Y**es. Otherwise, Symphony ignores your header and footer entries.

You should note two things about headers and footers. First, Symphony always places two blank lines below the header and two above the footer line. Second, if you use the # special character for page numbers, and if you want to print data a second time, you must reset the page-number counter by selecting SERVICES **P**rint **A**lign. Otherwise, the page counter picks up where it left off.

You cannot change headers or footers in the middle of a report. If you want to print different headers and footers in different sections of a printout, you must create a separate print settings sheet, enter the new header or footer, and set **P**rint **S**ettings **P**age **N**umber **S**tart-Page to the number of the first page of the new section.

Setting Margins

Margin settings that control the size of text margins as the text is printed are located in the following three settings sheets:

1. SERVICES **C**onfiguration **P**rinter **M**argins, which contains default margin settings.
2. SERVICES **P**rint **S**ettings **Ma**rgins, which contains the specific margin settings you enter for a specific print output.
3. DOC **F**ormat **S**ettings **L**eft, which affects the left margin of text entered in a DOC window.

Note that when printing the left margins of text created in a DOC environment, Symphony adds the margin settings in DOC **F**ormat **S**ettings **L**eft to those in SERVICES **P**rint **S**ettings **M**argins **L**eft.

If you are retrieving the print settings sheet (SERVICES **P**rint **S**ettings) for the first time in a worksheet, you may notice that the sheet contains the margin settings stored in SERVICES **C**onfiguration **P**rinter **M**argins.

When setting your margins for data entered in a SHEET or DOC window, you can either use those provided by SERVICES **C**onfiguration **P**rinter **M**argins or enter new margin settings. The SERVICES **P**rint **S**ettings **M**argins option overrides SERVICES **C**onfiguration **P**rinter. The default margin settings (from the edge of the paper) stored in SERVICES **C**onfiguration **P**rinter **M**argins are as follows:

Left 4
Right 76
Top 2
Bottom 2

You can change right and left margin settings to settings between 0 and 240, and top and bottom margin settings to settings between 0 and 16. Whenever you change margin settings in SERVICES **C**onfiguration **P**rinter **M**argins, you can update the Symphony configuration file to these new settings by selecting **U**pdate from the SERVICES **C**onfiguration menu.

Reminder:

Margin settings can change depending on whether you are printing a spread-sheet or text from a DOC window.

The SERVICES **P**rint **S**ettings **M**argins command operates on both spreadsheets and text entered in a word processing window. The same margin settings can result in different margins, however, depending on whether you are printing a spreadsheet or text from a DOC window.

For the first example, Mom's Root Beer Report, you want to fit everything on an 8 1/2-by-11-inch page. But the worksheet contains 12 active columns of data, which, when combined, form a total worksheet width of 108 characters. The only way to fit everything on one page is to use compressed print on a dot-matrix printer. You can get up to 136 characters on a line with this type of print. With five characters for the left margin and a worksheet width of 108, you can just stay under the limit of 136. You should set the right margin at 136 and send an **I**nit-String to the printer to use compressed print (see the section on "Sending an Initialization String to the Printer").

Reminder:

You can let the printer print up to 80 columns on one page with either pica or elite type, then continue to another page with what is left over.

An alternative to the compressed print is to use the current defaults. You can let the printer print up to 80 columns on one page with either pica or elite type, then continue to another page with what is left over. This solution is not an ideal one, but it is the only other choice.

For the second example, the Inventory Report on Cattuna, you want a left margin of 5 and a right margin of 72. As you recall, for text from a DOC window, Symphony adds the left margin settings from DOC **F**ormat **S**ettings **L**eft to the left margin settings in SERVICES **P**rint **S**ettings **M**argins. The original setting in DOC **F**ormat **S**ettings for the left margin is 4; the setting in SERVICES **P**rint **S**ettings **M**argins is 1. Symphony therefore prints a left margin of 5.

For the third example, the Cattuna Distributing Inventory, the top and bottom margins are set at 8. These margin settings, which are the distance from the top of the page to the header and from the bottom of the page to the footer, should give you a good appearance. The left margin is set at 4 for this report, and the right margin at 76. You may have to try several different combinations to get the setup you want.

Repeating Labels on Multipage Printouts

Reminder:

Symphony enables you to print column and row headings on a multipage printout.

Symphony enables you to print column and row headings on a multipage printout, such as the spreadsheet in the third example. If, for example, you want to print a comparative income statement that has several columns of monthly figures carrying beyond the first page, you can have the row headings that usually occur in the first column of the first page repeated on each page. SERVICES **P**rint **S**ettings **O**ther **T**op-Labels is the option you can use to repeat column labels. SERVICES **P**rint **S**ettings **O**ther **L**eft-Labels repeats row labels.

You also can use SERVICES **P**rint **S**ettings **O**ther **T**op-Labels or **L**eft-Labels whenever you want to extract part of a database and have the correct column and row headings printed with it. For example, suppose that you want to print only one section from a database, such as the one shown in figure 12.6, which extends from column A to column J.

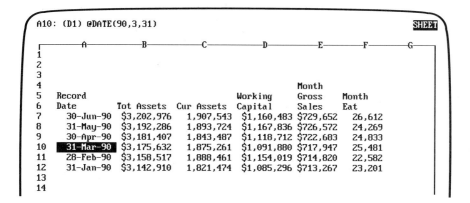

Fig. 12.6.
A sample database.

If you want to print only the range from A10..J12 and also print labels with the range, you would follow this procedure: Select SERVICES **P**rint **S**ettings **S**ource **R**ange and indicate the range of the database that you want to print. In this case, enter A10..J12. After indicating the range, select **D**estination **P**rinter and make any necessary page or margin changes.

To have labels printed, select SERVICES **P**rint **S**ettings **O**ther **T**op-Labels. To indicate which labels should be your top labels, enter the row range or highlight the row where column headings are located. In figure 12.6, for example, you highlight A4..J6. To indicate which labels should be your left labels, select SERVICES **P**rint **S**ettings **O**ther **L**eft-Labels and specify the column of labels you want printed. You are now ready to begin printing, unless you first want to name the settings sheet you just created so that you can use it again. The printed database range is shown in figure 12.7.

Record			Working	Month Gross-	Month		Debt to	Return	
Date	Tot Assets	Cur Assets	Capital	Sales	EAT	Cur Ratio	Equity	On Assets	DSO
31-Mar-88	$3,175,632	1,875,261	$1,091,880	$717,947	25,481	2.54	0.54	0.10	54
29-Feb-88	$3,158,517	1,888,461	$1,154,019	$714,820	22,582	2.39	0.55	0.09	55
31-Jan-88	$3,142,910	1,821,474	$1,085,296	$713,267	23,201	2.57	0.55	0.09	57

Fig. 12.7.
A printed portion of the database.

When you are using the SERVICES **P**rint **S**ettings **O**ther **T**op-Labels and **L**eft-Labels commands to print labels on consecutive pages after the first page, be careful that you do not include the column and row labels when you set the **S**ource **R**ange. If you set the **S**ource **R**ange to include column and row borders and also enter a range in **T**op-Labels and **L**eft-Labels, Symphony prints the labels twice on the first page (see fig. 12.8).

Fig. 12.8.
Labels printed twice.

			Common
Balance Sheet	Balance Sheet		
Assets	Assets		31-Jul-88	Size
Cash	Cash		$275,000	8%
Marketable Securities	Marketable Securities		35,000	1%
Accounts Receivable	Accounts Receivable	1,256,000		
Allowance for Doubtful Accounts	Allowance for Doubtful Accounts	8,000		
Net Accounts Receivable	Net Accounts Receivable		1,248,000	39%
Inventory	Inventory		359,000	11%
Prepaid Expenses	Prepaid Expenses		70,000	2%
Other	Other		23,000	1%
Total Current Assets	Total Current Assets		2,010,000	62%
Property, Plant, and Equipment	Property, Plant, and Equipment	956,700		
Accumulated Depreciation	Accumulated Depreciation	123,700		
Net Property, Plant, and Equipmen	Net Property, Plant, and Equipment		833,000	26%
Investment-Long-Term	Investment-Long-Term		396,000	12%
Total Noncurrent Assets	Total Noncurrent Assets		1,229,000	38%
Total Assets	Total Assets		$3,239,000	100%

Reminder:
*To avoid printing labels twice on the first page, do not include the column and row labels in the **S**ource **R**ange when using SERVICES **P**rint **S**ettings **O**ther Top-Labels or Left-Labels.*

Sending an Initialization String to the Printer

You can regulate both the print size and type through the **I**nit-String (initialization string) commands. Two separate **I**nit-String settings are available: one in SERVICES **C**onfiguration **P**rinter and one in SERVICES **P**rint **S**ettings. The SERVICES **C**onfiguration **P**rinter **I**nit-String is stored in Symphony's configuration file (.CNF) and controls SERVICES **P**rint **S**ettings **I**nit-String, unless you change the SERVICES **P**rint **S**ettings **I**nit-String.

The **I**nit-String option sends a string of up to 39 characters to the printer every time you select **G**o from the SERVICES **P**rint menu. All printers are different, so you must look carefully at your printer's manual to see what is required for your printer. The string is composed of backslashes (\) followed by the decimal equivalent of special characters in ASCII code.

You can change the print size and type by selecting SERVICES **P**rint **S**ettings **I**nit-String. After you select this command, Symphony asks you to enter the printer-control sequence (see fig. 12.9). At the printer-control sequence prompt, you should enter the special control code(s) for your printer. (Again, consult your printer's manual.)

Like the other SERVICES **P**rint **S**ettings commands, the **I**nit-String is a temporary override of the SERVICES **C**onfiguration **P**rinter setting, unless you name the settings sheet. If you name the settings sheet, it is saved for you to use again. (For a more-detailed look at this option, refer to the Symphony Reference Manual, and your printer manual.) If you do not expect to use your printer's special features and just want regular printing, then don't worry about the **I**nit-String command.

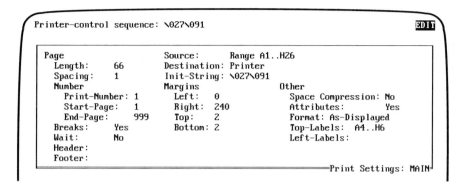

```
Printer-control sequence: \027\091                          EDIT

Page                      Source:      Range A1..H26
  Length:      66         Destination: Printer
  Spacing:      1         Init-String: \027\091
  Number                  Margins                 Other
    Print-Number: 1         Left:    0              Space Compression: No
    Start-Page:   1         Right:  240            Attributes:        Yes
    End-Page:   999         Top:      2            Format: As-Displayed
  Breaks:      Yes         Bottom:   2            Top-Labels:  A4..H6
  Wait:         No                                Left-Labels:
  Header:
  Footer:
                                              Print Settings: MAIN
```

Fig. 12.9.
Entering the printer-control sequence for Init-String.

Setting the Page Length

The SERVICES **C**onfiguration **P**rinter setting for the number of lines printed on one page is 66. You can change this number temporarily or store a new page length in a named print settings sheet. You can set page length to any number between one and 100 with SERVICES **P**rint **S**ettings **P**age Length. This option is helpful when you use special forms, paper, or type sizes. Because standard 8 1/2-by-11-inch paper has been used for the three examples in this chapter, however, this option defaults to 66 in all three examples.

Printing Cell Formulas

Symphony enables you to print cell contents in more than one way. For the sample reports in this chapter, the contents are printed just as they are displayed on-screen (except for spacing in the second example); also printed is a one-line-per-cell listing of the cell formulas for the Mom's Root Beer Report.

The command SERVICES **P**rint **S**ettings **O**ther **F**ormat controls the way cell formulas are printed. When you enter this command, you are given the following choices:

As-Displayed   **C**ell-Formulas

The **C**ell-Formulas option creates the one-line-per-cell listing of the contents of a worksheet. This option is convenient for debugging and also can be useful for re-creating formulas in other worksheets. Figure 12.10 shows the **C**ell-Formulas listing of Mom's Root Beer Report.

The **A**s-Displayed option reverses the **C**ell-Formulas option. **A**s-Displayed returns to printing the format as it appears on-screen.

Reminder:
Cell-Formulas is a convenient option for debugging and re-creating formulas in other worksheets.

Fig. 12.10.

A partial Cell-Formulas listing for Mom's Root Beer Report.

```
A1: 'Mom's Root beer Company -- Cash-Flow Projection     S7: (F3) 0.5
A3: 'Year                                                T7: (F3) 0.5
B3: 1988                                                 U7: (F3) 0.5
C3: 1989                                                 V7: (F3) 0.5
D3: 1990                                                 A8: ' SGA
E3: 1991                                                 B8: (F3) +B19/B16
F3: 1992                                                 C8: (F3) 0.37
G3: 1993                                                 D8: (F3) 0.35
H3: 1988                                                 E8: (F3) 0.35
I3: 1989                                                 F8: (F3) 0.35
J3: 1990                                                 G8: (F3) 0.35
K3: 1991                                                 H8: (F3) 0.35
L3: 1992                                                 I8: (F3) 0.35
M3: 1993                                                 J8: (F3) 0.35
N3: 1994                                                 K8: (F3) 0.35
O3: 1995                                                 L8: (F3) 0.35
P3: 1996                                                 M8: (F3) 0.35
Q3: 1997                                                 N8: (F3) 0.35
R3: 1998                                                 O8: (F3) 0.35
S3: 1999                                                 P8: (F3) 0.35
T3: 2000                                                 Q8: (F3) 0.35
U3: 2001                                                 R8: (F3) 0.35
V3: 2002                                                 S8: (F3) 0.35
A4: \-                                                   T8: (F3) 0.35
B4: \-                                                   U8: (F3) 0.35
C4: \-                                                   V8: (F3) 0.35
D4: \-                                                   A10: 'Plant and Equipment: 22% of sales; cap exp = 30% of Sales Change + Depreciation
E4: \-                                                   A11: 'Depreciation: 14% of plant and equipment; all depreciation reinvested
F4: \-                                                   A12: 'Working Capital: Change = 15% of Sales change
G4: \-                                                   A13: 'Tax Rate = 41%
H4: \-                                                   A15: 'Projections
I4: \-                                                   A16: ' Sales
J4: \-                                                   B16: (P0) 516136
K4: \-                                                   C16: (P0) +B16*C6
L4: \-                                                   D16: (P0) +C16*D6
M4: \-                                                   E16: (P0) +D16*E6
N4: \-                                                   F16: (P0) +E16*F6
O4: \-                                                   G16: (P0) +F16*G6
P4: \-                                                   H16: (P0) +G16*H6
Q4: \-                                                   I16: (P0) +H16*I6
R4: \-                                                   J16: (P0) +I16*J6
S4: \-                                                   K16: (P0) +J16*K6
T4: \-                                                   L16: (P0) +K16*L6
U4: \-                                                   M16: (P0) +L16*M6
V4: \-                                                   N16: (P0) +M16*N6
A5: 'Growth Assumptions (as % of Sales)                  O16: (P0) +N16*O6
A6: ' Sales                                              P16: (P0) +O16*P6
B6: (F3) "actual                                         Q16: (P0) +P16*Q6
C6: (F3) 1.085                                           R16: (P0) +Q16*R6
D6: (F3) 1.085                                           S16: (P0) +R16*S6
E6: (F3) 1.085                                           T16: (P0) +S16*T6
F6: (F3) 1.085                                           U16: (P0) +T16*U6
G6: (F3) 1.085                                           V16: (P0) +U16*V6
H6: (F3) 1.085                                           A17: ' COGS
I6: (F3) 1.085                                           B17: (P0) 249284
J6: (F3) 1.085                                           C17: (P0) +C16*C7
K6: (F3) 1.085                                           D17: (P0) +D16*D7
L6: (F3) 1.085                                           E17: (P0) +E16*E7
M6: (F3) 1.085                                           F17: (P0) +F16*F7
N6: (F3) 1.085                                           G17: (P0) +G16*G7
O6: (F3) 1.085                                           H17: (P0) +H16*H7
P6: (F3) 1.085                                           I17: (P0) +I16*I7
Q6: (F3) 1.085                                           J17: (P0) +J16*J7
R6: (F3) 1.085                                           K17: (P0) +K16*K7
S6: (F3) 1.085                                           L17: (P0) +L16*L7
T6: (F3) 1.085                                           M17: (P0) +M16*M7
U6: (F3) 1.085                                           N17: (P0) +N16*N7
V6: (F3) 1.085                                           O17: (P0) +O16*O7
A7: ' CGS                                                P17: (P0) +P16*P7
B7: (F3) +B17/B16                                        Q17: (P0) +Q16*Q7
C7: (F3) 0.5                                             R17: (P0) +R16*R7
D7: (F3) 0.5                                             S17: (P0) +S16*S7
E7: (F3) 0.5                                             T17: (P0) +T16*T7
F7: (F3) 0.5                                             U17: (P0) +U16*U7
G7: (F3) 0.5                                             V17: (P0) +V16*V7
H7: (F3) 0.5                                             A18: ' Depn
I7: (F3) 0.5                                             B18: (P0) 18423
J7: (F3) 0.5                                             C18: (P0) +C16*0.22*0.14
K7: (F3) 0.5                                             D18: (P0) +D16*0.22*0.14
L7: (F3) 0.5                                             E18: (P0) +E16*0.22*0.14
M7: (F3) 0.5                                             F18: (P0) +F16*0.22*0.14
N7: (F3) 0.5                                             G18: (P0) +G16*0.22*0.14
O7: (F3) 0.5                                             H18: (P0) +H16*0.22*0.14
P7: (F3) 0.5                                             I18: (P0) +I16*0.22*0.14
Q7: (F3) 0.5                                             J18: (P0) +J16*0.22*0.14
R7: (F3) 0.5                                             K18: (P0) +K16*0.22*0.14
```

Naming, Using, and Deleting Print Settings Sheets

As mentioned several times throughout this book, one of Symphony's advantages is the program's capability to name (and thus save) settings sheets. When you name settings sheets, you can retrieve them and reuse the settings in the worksheet. You can save settings sheets, however, only if you save the file in which they were created.

Reminder:
You can save settings sheets only if you save the file in which they were created.

SERVICES **P**rint **S**ettings can enter the print settings for two different documents at the same time. After you have finished printing the first document, retrieve the named settings sheet, align or advance paper if needed, and then select **G**o to begin printing the next document.

Here is how you use the options provided by named print settings sheets. After entering all the settings—margins, headers, footers, and so on—select SERVICES **P**rint **S**ettings **N**ame. When you select **N**ame, the following menu appears:

> **U**se **C**reate **D**elete **P**revious **N**ext **I**nitial-Settings **R**eset **Q**uit

From the **N**ame menu, choose **C**reate. When Symphony asks for the `Name for new Print settings sheet:`, enter a name, preferably one that will remind you of the document for which the name was created.

Before exiting from the file, you need to save the file by using the SERVICES **F**ile **S**ave command; having saved the file, you also retain the print settings sheet. Whenever you decide to use the print settings sheet again, select SERVICES **P**rint **S**ettings **N**ame **U**se. A list of named print settings sheets displays in the control panel of your screen. If you want to see a complete listing of print settings sheets, press the SERVICES key (F9), and Symphony displays a complete listing of sheets for the current file (see fig. 12.11).

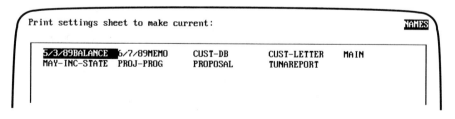

Fig. 12.11.
A list of print settings sheet for the current file.

Two commands are useful for "paging" through named print settings sheets: **P**revious and **N**ext. When you choose **P**revious, Symphony displays and makes current the settings sheet previous to the current one. (The sheets are in alphabetical order by name.) The **N**ext command is the reverse of **P**revious; this option displays the settings sheet following the current one.

You not only can create, use, and cycle through print settings sheets, but also you can edit and delete them. One command is available for changing the print

Reminder:

To erase all named print settings sheets in a particular file, use SERVICES Print Settings Name Reset.

settings sheet currently on the screen back to the default settings in SERVICES **C**onfiguration **P**rinter. To delete a single settings sheet, use the SERVICES **P**rint **S**ettings **N**ame **D**elete command. If, however, you want to erase all named print settings sheets in a particular file, select SERVICES **P**rint **S**ettings **N**ame **R**eset. After you use this command, print settings from SERVICES **C**onfiguration **P**rinter are in effect.

Controlling the Printer

Symphony makes it possible for you to control the printer. In fact, Symphony provides so much control that you hardly ever have to touch the printer except to turn it on just before printing and turn it off when you are done.

The ability to control the printer is important in printing the Cattuna Inventory. Between some of the different sections and text to be printed for this report, you need to space down several lines. The SERVICES **P**rint **L**ine-Advance command makes the printer skip a line each time you enter the command. In this example, the command will be used several times in a row to skip between some of the sections.

The SERVICES **P**rint **P**age-Advance command causes the printer to advance the paper to the top of a new page each time you enter the command. When you use **P**age-Advance at the end of a printing session, Symphony prints the footer on the next page. If you **Q**uit from the SERVICES **P**rint menu before issuing the **P**age-Advance command, the last footer does not print.

Reminder:

Use the SERVICES Print Align command, which automatically aligns the paper in the printer.

Finally, when you start printing this report, you need a way to signal to the printer where the top of the page is. The command used to align the page is SERVICES **P**rint **A**lign. Again, this command saves you from having to touch the printer control buttons.

You must enter the SERVICES **P**rint **G**o command to start the printer. This command also enables you to send a range to a print file (SERVICES **P**rint **S**ettings **D**estination **F**ile) and to a worksheet (SERVICES **P**rint **S**ettings **D**estination **R**ange).

If you want to interrupt the printing of a report in midstream, simply press Ctrl-Break simultaneously. The print buffer may take some time to clear, depending on the buffer's size, but Symphony eventually returns you to the worksheet. Press Esc to clear the ERROR message displayed in the MODE indicator.

Now that you understand how to set print options, you may want to take a closer look at the three examples.

Examining the Printed Results

In figures 12.12A, 12.12B, 12.13A, 12.13B, 12.14A, and 12.14B, you can see the SERVICES **P**rint **S**ettings sheet and the final printed copy of each of the three reports. Each example requires different commands for printing, which are listed subsequently.

```
Overall page settings                                          MENU
Page  Source  Destination  Init-String  Margins  Other  Name  Quit

  Page                    Source:      Range A1..L30
    Length:     66        Destination: Printer
    Spacing:    1         Init-String: \027\091
    Number                Margins                Other
      Print-Number: 1       Left:    4             Space Compression: No
      Start-Page:   1       Right:   240           Attributes:        Yes
      End-Page:     999     Top:     2             Format: As-Displayed
    Breaks:     Yes       Bottom:  2             Top-Labels:
    Wait:       No                               Left-Labels:
    Header:
    Footer:
                                              Print Settings: ROOTBEER
```

Fig. 12.12A.

The print settings sheet for Mom's Root Beer Report.

```
Mom's Root beer Company -- Cash-Flow Projection

Year        1988      1989      1990      1991      1992      1993      1988      1989      1990      1991      1992
...................................................................................................................
Growth Assumptions (as % of Sales)
Sales     actual     1.085     1.085     1.085     1.085     1.085     1.085     1.085     1.085     1.085     1.085
CGS        0.483     0.500     0.500     0.500     0.500     0.500     0.500     0.500     0.500     0.500     0.500
SGA        0.403     0.370     0.350     0.350     0.350     0.350     0.350     0.350     0.350     0.350     0.350

Plant and Equipment: 22% of sales; cap exp = 30% of Sales Change + Depreciation
Depreciation: 14% of plant and equipment; all depreciation reinvested
Working Capital: Change = 15% of Sales change
Tax Rate = 41%

Projections
Sales     516,136   560,008   607,608   659,255   715,292   776,091   842,059   913,634   991,293 1,075,553 1,166,975
COGS      249,284   280,004   303,804   329,627   357,646   388,046   421,030   456,817   495,647   537,776   583,487
Depn       18,423    17,248    18,714    20,305    22,031    23,904    25,935    28,140    30,532    33,127    35,943
SGA       207,807   207,203   212,663   230,739   250,352   271,632   294,721   319,772   346,953   376,444   408,441
Interest   18,423 projected cash flows considered to be unlevered
EBT        22,199    55,553    72,427    78,583    85,263    92,510   100,373   108,905   118,162   128,206   139,103
Tax         9,724    22,777    29,695    32,219    34,958    37,929    41,153    44,651    48,446    52,564    57,032
EAT        12,475    32,776    42,732    46,364    50,305    54,581    59,220    64,254    69,716    75,641    82,071

Cash Flow  30,898    50,024    61,446    66,669    72,336    78,485    85,156    92,394   100,247   108,769   118,014

Cap Expend 64,757    30,410    32,995    35,799    38,842    42,144    45,726    49,612    53,829    58,405    63,369
Work Cap              6,581     7,140     7,747     8,405     9,120     9,895    10,736    11,649    12,639    13,713

Net CF               13,034    21,312    23,123    25,089    27,221    29,535    32,045    34,769    37,725    40,931
```

Fig. 12.12B.

The printed result.

```
Change print settings                                          MENU
Go  Line-Advance  Page-Advance  Align  Settings  Quit

  Page                    Source:      Range A19..IV50
    Length:     66        Destination: Printer
    Spacing:    1         Init-String:
    Number                Margins                Other
      Print-Number: 1       Left:    1             Space Compression: No
      Start-Page:   1       Right:   76            Attributes:        Yes
      End-Page:     999     Top:     2             Format: As-Displayed
    Breaks:     Yes       Bottom:  2             Top-Labels:
    Wait:       No                               Left-Labels:
    Header:
    Footer: !#
                                              Print Settings: TUNAREPORT
```

Fig. 12.13A.

The print settings sheet for Inventory Report for the Cattuna.

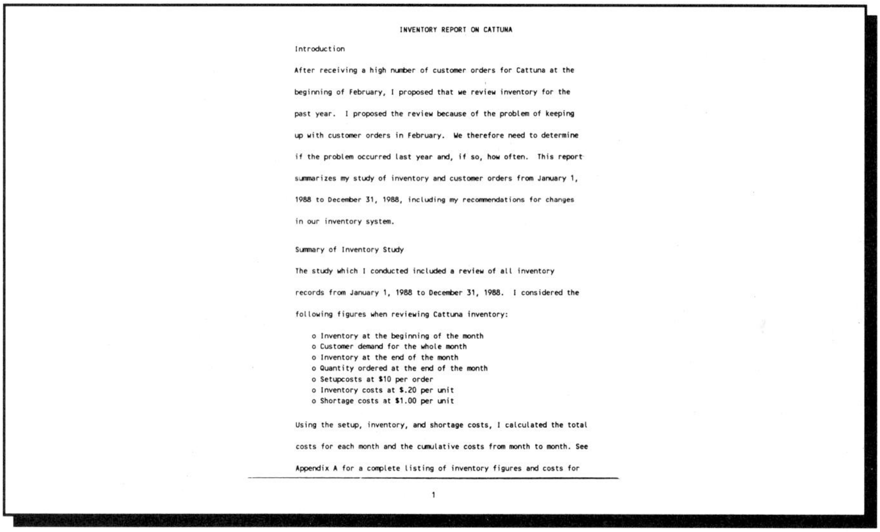

Fig. 12.13B.

The printed result.

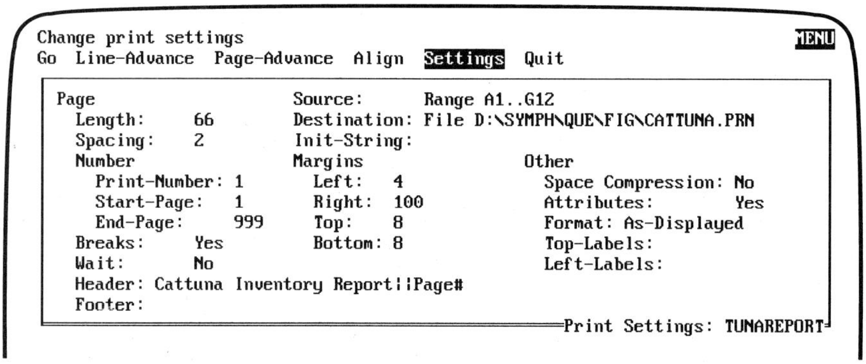

```
                              INVENTORY REPORT ON CATTUNA

                     Introduction

                     After receiving a high number of customer orders for Cattuna at the

                     beginning of February, I proposed that we review inventory for the

                     past year.  I proposed the review because of the problem of keeping

                     up with customer orders in February.  We therefore need to determine

                     if the problem occurred last year and, if so, how often.  This report

                     summarizes my study of inventory and customer orders from January 1,

                     1988 to December 31, 1988, including my recommendations for changes

                     in our inventory system.

                     Summary of Inventory Study

                     The study which I conducted included a review of all inventory

                     records from January 1, 1988 to December 31, 1988.  I considered the

                     following figures when reviewing Cattuna inventory:

                         o Inventory at the beginning of the month
                         o Customer demand for the whole month
                         o Inventory at the end of the month
                         o Quantity ordered at the end of the month
                         o Setupcosts at $10 per order
                         o Inventory costs at $.20 per unit
                         o Shortage costs at $1.00 per unit

                     Using the setup, inventory, and shortage costs, I calculated the total

                     costs for each month and the cumulative costs from month to month. See

                     Appendix A for a complete listing of inventory figures and costs for

                                              1
```

Fig. 12.14A.

The print settings sheet for the Cuttuna Distributing Inventory.

```
Change print settings                                                    MENU
 Go  Line-Advance  Page-Advance  Align  Settings  Quit

 Page                      Source:       Range A1..G12
   Length:      66         Destination: File D:\SYMPH\QUE\FIG\CATTUNA.PRN
   Spacing:      2         Init-String:
 Number                    Margins                 Other
   Print-Number: 1           Left:    4              Space Compression: No
   Start-Page:   1           Right:  100             Attributes:       Yes
   End-Page:   999           Top:      8             Format: As-Displayed
 Breaks:     Yes             Bottom: 8               Top-Labels:
 Wait:       No                                      Left-Labels:
 Header: Cattuna Inventory Report||Page#
 Footer:
                                             Print Settings: TUNAREPORT
```

Fig. 12.14B.

The printed result.

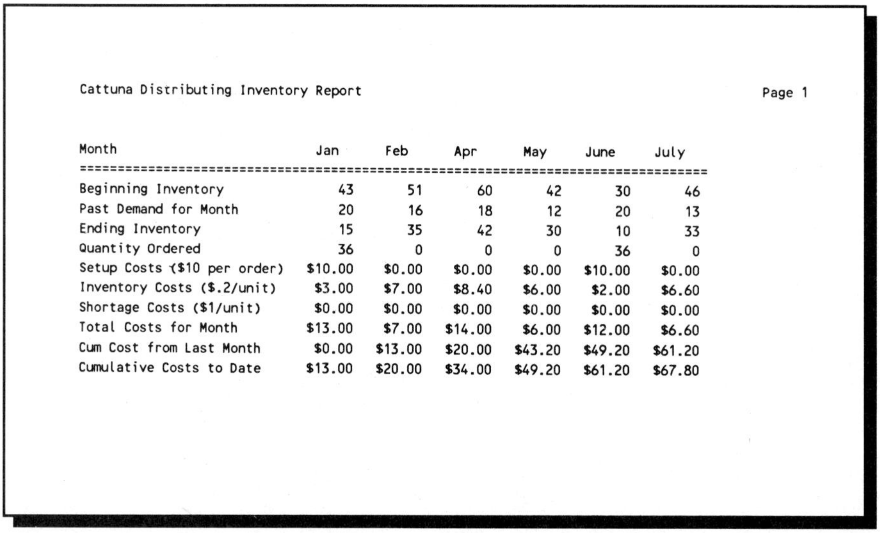

```
Cattuna Distributing Inventory Report                              Page 1


Month                       Jan     Feb     Apr     May    June    July
=======================================================================
Beginning Inventory          43      51      60      42      30      46
Past Demand for Month        20      16      18      12      20      13
Ending Inventory             15      35      42      30      10      33
Quantity Ordered             36       0       0       0      36       0
Setup Costs ($10 per order) $10.00  $0.00   $0.00   $0.00  $10.00  $0.00
Inventory Costs ($.2/unit)   $3.00  $7.00   $8.40   $6.00   $2.00  $6.60
Shortage Costs ($1/unit)     $0.00  $0.00   $0.00   $0.00   $0.00  $0.00
Total Costs for Month       $13.00  $7.00  $14.00   $6.00  $12.00  $6.60
Cum Cost from Last Month     $0.00 $13.00  $20.00  $43.20  $49.20 $61.20
Cumulative Costs to Date    $13.00 $20.00  $34.00  $49.20  $61.20 $67.80
```

To print the Mom's Root Beer Company Cash-Flow Projection (figs. 12.12A and 12.12B), you enter the following commands:

1. SERVICES **P**rint **S**ettings **S**ource **R**ange **A1..L30** and press Enter.
2. SERVICES **P**rint **S**ettings **I**nit-String **\O19** and press Enter.
3. SERVICES **P**rint **S**ettings **M**argins **R**ight **136** and press Enter.
4. SERVICES **P**rint **S**ettings **M**argins **Q**uit.
5. SERVICES **P**rint **S**ettings **Q**uit.
6. SERVICES **P**rint **G**o.

The only special entries made in the **P**rint commands for the Mom's Root Beer Report are **I**nit-String and **M**argins. Otherwise, printing this report merely requires setting the range and selecting **G**o when you are ready to begin printing.

To print the Inventory Report on Cattuna (figs. 12.13A and 12.13B), you enter the following commands:

1. SERVICES **P**rint **S**ettings **P**age **F**ooter |# and press Enter.
2. SERVICES **P**rint **S**ettings **P**age **Q**uit.
3. SERVICES **P**rint **S**ettings **S**ource **R**ange, press End Home keys and press Enter.
4. SERVICES **P**rint **S**ettings **M**argins **L**eft **1** and press Enter.
5. SERVICES **P**rint **S**ettings **M**argins **Q**uit.
6. SERVICES **P**rint **S**ettings **Q**uit.
7. SERVICES **P**rint **G**o.

The only special entry for printing the Inventory Report is the footer entry |#. Through this entry, the page number is centered and printed at the bottom of the first page (see fig. 12.13B).

If you compare figure 12.4 (the Inventory Report as it appears on-screen) with figure 12.13B (the printed copy), you see a difference in spacing. The on-screen report appears with single-spacing (except for the extra spaces added manually after the first paragraph). The report, however, is printed with double-spacing. Double- and triple-spacing settings do not affect the text on-screen. If DOC **F**ormat **S**ettings **S**pacing or a format line is set with double-or triple-spacing, these settings control the spacing during printing.

In addition, for any text created in a DOC window, spacing in the printed copy is controlled by DOC **F**ormat **S**ettings **S**pacing or a format line rather than SERVICES **P**rint **S**ettings **P**age **S**pacing. Keep in mind that if you want your document printed with double- or triple-spacing, enter the setting in DOC **F**ormat **S**ettings **S**pacing. Also keep in mind that the spacing you add manually to your document is also added to the spacing setting, as shown by the extra spacing after the first paragraph in figure 12.13B.

Reminder:
The spacing you add manually to your document also is added to the spacing setting.

To print the Cattuna Distributing Inventory (figs. 12.14A and 12.14B), you would enter the following commands:

1. SERVICES **P**rint **S**ettings **P**age **S**pacing **2**.
2. SERVICES **P**rint **S**ettings **P**age **H**eader **Cattuna Distributing Inventory Report | | Page#** and press Enter.
3. SERVICES **P**rint Settings **P**age **Q**uit.
4. SERVICES **P**rint **S**ettings **S**ource **R**ange **A1..G12** and press Enter.
5. SERVICES **P**rint **S**ettings **D**estination **F**ile **Cattuna**, and press Enter.
6. SERVICES **P**rint **S**ettings **M**argins **T**op **8** and press Enter.
7. SERVICES **P**rint **S**ettings **M**argins **B**ottom **8 Q**uit **Q**uit.
8. SERVICES **P**rint **G**o.

This third example requires six special options, as indicated by the previous list of commands. First, to make the sheet easy to read, you must change spacing from single to double. Second, you enter a header identifying the report on the left side and the page number on the right. Third, if you want to use this report in another software program, you can create a print file. Finally, to center the report evenly on the page, you change the top and bottom margins to eight.

Chapter Summary

This chapter showed you how to print data by using Symphony's SERVICES **P**rint command. Included were the major print operations that you will need when you begin printing spreadsheets and word processing documents. Symphony's print capabilities, however, extend beyond what is discussed in this chapter. For example, Symphony also can print database reports, labels, and form letters. These operations require integrating the print functions with Symphony's data-management capabilities (Symphony's FORM window). In Chapter 17, "Managing Data," you will find a discussion of the special print functions connected with using Symphony's FORM window.

13

Using Allways: The Spreadsheet Publisher

Allways is an add-in application that formats and prints Symphony spreadsheets. Allways gives Symphony the following capabilities:

❑ Up to eight fonts in a printout

❑ Graphs in the same printout as worksheet data

❑ Color printing if you have a color printer

❑ Enclosed cells in boxes, or outlined ranges

❑ Double underlines, and adjustments in row height and column width

❑ Shading of worksheet areas

❑ Editing in the worksheet without returning to Symphony

This chapter shows you how to prepare professional-looking financial reports that include both numeric data and graphs on the same page, how to produce business forms, and how to print large amounts of data on one piece of paper by using a small font.

To use Allways, your computer needs 640K of conventional memory and 1M of available disk space for the Allways drivers. Also, the Allways Setup program must be run to select the equipment you want to use with Allways. Allways does not use the display and printer drivers that come with Symphony. Setup copies the Allways program files and defines the type of equipment you are using to display and print your work. Setup program instructions are described in Appendix A.

Allways produces a what-you-see-is-what-you-get (WYSIWYG) display that resembles the printed output. To see all the formatting changes you make with Allways, your computer should be equipped with a graphics display adapter and screen display card.

Installing Allways

To install Allways you must run the Symphony 2.2 Setup program, which copies the Allways files to your Symphony 2.2 directory. Once this is done you are ready to begin the Allways Setup (See Appendix A).

Attaching Allways

Before you can use Allways, it must be *attached*, or loaded, into memory. To attach Allways to Symphony, select SERVICES **A**pplication **A**ttach. Next select **ALLWAYS.APP** from the application add-ins that appear on-screen. Press Enter, and Allways is loaded into memory.

To eliminate the numerous steps involved when attaching Allways, use the following macro: {SERVICES}aaALLWAYS~q

If you use Allways frequently, you may want the program to be attached automatically whenever Symphony is loaded. To automate this feature, start Symphony and select SERVICES **C**onfiguration **O**ther **A**pplication **S**et, as shown in figure 13.1.

Fig. 13.1.

*Selecting SERVICES **C**onfiguration **O**ther **A**pplication **S**et in Symphony.*

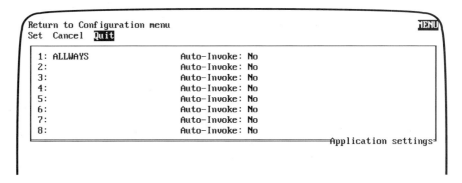

```
Return to Configuration menu                                        MENU
Set  Cancel  Quit
    1: ALLWAYS                   Auto-Invoke: No
    2:                           Auto-Invoke: No
    3:                           Auto-Invoke: No
    4:                           Auto-Invoke: No
    5:                           Auto-Invoke: No
    6:                           Auto-Invoke: No
    7:                           Auto-Invoke: No
    8:                           Auto-Invoke: No
                                              Application settings
```

Select a number from 1 to 8 to specify an add-in number for Allways (you can attach as many as eight add-ins to Symphony). Select **ALLWAYS.APP** from the list of application add-ins, and then press Enter. Make sure that you **Q**uit this menu and then select **U**pdate to write this information to the **C**onfiguration file.

Working with Allways

Because Allways is an add-in for use with Symphony, the worksheet and screen display may remind you of the Symphony SHEET environment. Allways gives you the same three screen divide areas found in the Symphony SHEET: the worksheet, the control panel and the status line.

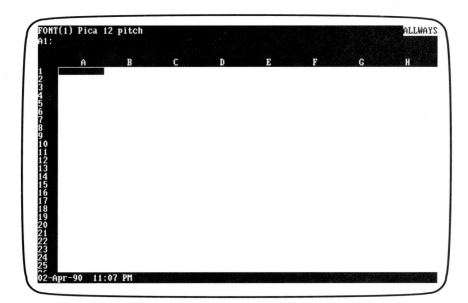

Changing the Worksheet

Formatting changes made to your spreadsheet appear in the worksheet area. Row numbers appear in the left border of the worksheet and column letters show in the top border below the control panel, as shown in figure 13.2.

```
FONT(1) Pica 12 pitch                                    ALLWAYS
A1:
         A       B       C       D       E       F       G       H
1
2
3
4
5
6
7
8
9
10
11
12
13
14
15
16
17
18
19
20
21
22
23
24
25
02-Apr-90  11:07 PM
```

Fig. 13.2.
A blank Allways worksheet.

Using the Control Panel

The control panel contains three lines of information to tell you what Allways is doing. The first line displays the format of the current cell: font, color, data, boldface, underline, and lines or shading. The far right of this line shows the mode you are in. When you invoke Allways, the mode shows **ALLWAYS**. The mode indicator changes to reflect the different operations you perform.

The MODE indicator and related modes include the following:

Allways Modes Indicating Current Window

Mode Indicator	Description
ALLWAYS	You are in the Allways mode and ready to select a command
EDIT	You have pressed EDIT (F2) to change an entry
ERROR	An error message is displaying in Allways. Press ESC or RETURN to clear the message

Allways Modes Indicating Current Window—(continued)

Mode Indicator	Description
FILES	You are being asked to specify a file
HELP	Allways is displaying a HELP screen after you pressed HELP (F1)
MENU	Allways is displaying a menu of commands
POINT	You are being asked to specify a range
WAIT	A command or process is completing in Allways
WARN	A warning message is being displayed

The second line, unless you press MENU (F10) or / (slash), contains the address and contents of the current cell. When you press F10 or /, the second line contains information about the highlighted menu item in the third line.

When you press MENU (F10) or / (slash), this line displays the Allways main menu.

Using the Status Line

The date-and-time indicator (providing it is configured to display in Symphony), and the status indicators that show when you use certain keys, appear at the bottom of the screen. The list of indicators includes the following:

Indicator	Meaning
ANC	The cell pointer has anchored to highlight a range before selecting a command
CALC	Formulas in the worksheet need to be recalculated; press CALC (F8)
CAPS	CAPS LOCK key is on
CIRC	A circular reference, a formula that refers to itself, is contained in the worksheet
END	The END key is on
LINK	A formula referencing another file is contained in the worksheet
NUM	The NUM LOCK key is on
OVR	The INS key is on, invoking the overstrike mode
SCROLL	The SCROLL LOCK key is on

Using Graphics- and Text-Display Modes

Allways displays your work in one of two modes: graphics or text.

The advantage of using the graphics mode, provided your computer has a graphics monitor and display card, is the capability to make on-screen data resemble the final printout. Also, when you make a formatting change you see its effect immediately on-screen.

Be careful when using the graphics mode. Some fonts cut characters off at the right edges of columns. When this happens, you can show the full characters by widening the column with the Allways **W**orksheet **C**olumn command.

Caution:
In the graphics mode, some fonts cut off characters at the right edges of columns.

The Allways text mode gives you a spreadsheet that appears as it does in Symphony. You can't see the effect of the formats you select (you must refer to the first line of the control panel to see the format of the current cell); however, your printouts look the same as if they had been developed on a graphics screen.

To change modes, access the **D**isplay **M**ode command or press DISPLAY (F6).

Using Allways Keys

Besides using the same keys that you use in Symphony to move around the worksheet, Allways provides additional function keys as follows:

Key	Function
CALC (F8)	ALLWAYS mode: Recalculates all formulas in a worksheet. NOTE: Recalculation must be set to manual.
DISPLAY (F6)	ALLWAYS mode: Switches between graphics mode and text mode for screen display.
EDIT (F2)	ALLWAYS mode: Displays contents of current cell in control panel so you can edit the entry, and puts Allways in EDIT mode.
ENLARGE (Alt-F4)	ALLWAYS mode: Enlarges the display. You may continue to press ENLARGE (Alt-F4) to enlarge cells up to 140% of their normal size.
GOTO (F5)	ALLWAYS mode: Moves the cell pointer directly to the cell or named range specified.
GRAPH (F7)	ALLWAYS mode: Lets you see the actual graphs on the screen by turning on the graph display. May be used to toggle back and forth between hatched boxes and graph displays. *NOTE:* Your screen must be in graphics mode for you to see the actual graphs when you use GRAPH (F7).

Key	Function
HELP (F1)	Displays the Allways Help screen.
MENU (F10)	ALLWAYS mode: Displays the Allways main menu. POINT mode: Displays a menu of named ranges in the worksheet. FILES mode: Displays a menu of file names.
REDUCE (F4)	ALLWAYS mode: Reduces the display. If you continue to press this key, you can reduce cells down to 60% of their normal size.

Working with Accelerator Keys

Accelerator keys are combinations of Alt and letter or number keys that reduce the keystrokes required for many formatting tasks. These key combinations may be used as command shortcuts.

Reminder:

Accelerator keys do not prompt for a range; you must define the cell or range before you use the accelerator key.

Accelerator keys do not prompt for a range; you must define the cell or range before you use the accelerator key.

To use the accelerator keys, press and hold down Alt, then press the number or letter key for the task you want to perform (letters may be upper or lower case).

The accelerator keys are as follows:

Key	Function
ALT-B	Boldface: Set/Clear
ALT-G	Grid lines: On/Off
ALT-L	Lines: Outline/All/None
ALT-S	Shading: Light/Dark/Solid/None
ALT-U	Underline: Single/Double/None
ALT-1	Set Font 1
ALT-2	Set Font 2
ALT-3	Set Font 3
ALT-4	Set Font 4
ALT-5	Set Font 5
ALT-6	Set Font 6
ALT-7	Set Font 7
ALT-8	Set Font 8

Using the ALLWAYS Menu

Allways contains a series of menu commands that work much like Symphony menus. To call up the ALLWAYS menu, use either MENU (F10) or / (slash).

Commands are selected either by moving the menu pointer to the command and pressing Enter, or by pressing the first character of the command. If you need to select a command from a submenu, or select an item from a list, or respond to a prompt to complete a command, you can select the item by using the up and down arrows to highlight the item you want, or by typing the number shown to the left of the item you want and pressing Enter, as shown in figure 13.3.

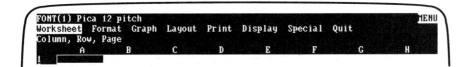

Fig. 13.3.

The Allways menu commands.

Specifying A Range

Some Allways commands require that you specify a range. Although specifying an Allways range is similar to specifying a Symphony range, Allways gives you an additional feature: you can select the range first and then proceed with the command. No matter which method you select, you must specify a range by typing the range address, or by using a range name created in Symphony, or by highlighting the range, as shown in figure 13.4.

Reminder:

Allways enables you to select the range first and then proceed with the command.

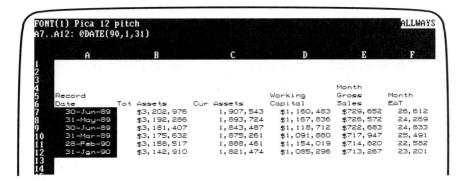

Fig. 13.4.

A highlighted range.

Working in the Edit Mode

Allways enables you to edit in the worksheet without returning to Symphony by using EDIT (F2). The EDIT mode in Allways is similar to the EDIT mode in Symphony SHEET environment. Position the cell pointer on the cell you want to edit and press EDIT (F2). The contents of the cell appear in the second line of the control panel. Make the modifications you want and then press Enter.

Using the Allways Help System

Allways comes equipped with a series of Help screens that you can access by using HELP (F1). Although Symphony and Allways Help systems work much the same, Allways does not provide direct help for error messages. If you get an error message in Allways you must write down the error message, press ESC or Enter to clear the error message from the screen, press HELP (F1), select the **E**rror **M**essage **I**ndex from the **H**elp **I**ndex, and then look up the error message, correct the error, and proceed.

Saving And Retrieving Formats

As long as Allways is attached, you need not do anything special to save or retrieve the formats you create. Allways does these automatically.

Allways retrieves your formats when you retrieve a spreadsheet by using Symphony's SERVICES **F**ile **R**etrieve. Also, Allways automatically saves your formatting changes when you save a worksheet by using Symphony's SERVICES **F**ile **S**ave. The formats created with Allways should be thought of as part of the worksheet. Formats are saved in separate files with the extension ALL.

Caution:

If you end Symphony without saving the worksheet, all changes and formats that you made are lost.

Note: Formatting changes you make in Allways do not become permanent until you save the worksheet. If you end Symphony without saving the worksheet, changes that you made with Allways (as well as changes that you made to the worksheet itself) are lost. Also, if you detach Allways without first saving the worksheet, all changes are lost.

Synchronizing Allways Formats

Frequently when using the Symphony worksheet you make modifications that change the appearance or location of the data in the cells. To keep its formats synchronized with the cells to which they apply, Allways must be attached to Symphony. If Allways is not attached, the changes you make to a formatted worksheet may result in a mismatch between the cells of your worksheet and their corresponding Allways formats.

Returning To Symphony

When you complete the formatting you want with Allways, you may want to return to Symphony. This move can be made by using MENU (F10) and selecting **Q**uit from the control panel menu options; or by hitting ESC.

Allways remains in memory until you **D**etach it through the SERVICES menu. Do not detach Allways without first saving the worksheet and all changes. If you later want to modify the worksheet, you should make sure that Allways is attached to synchronize these changes.

Using Worksheet Commands

Using the worksheet commands enables you to divide large worksheets into pages, and adjust column width and row height. You also can fine-tune spacing between lines of data, create page breaks on large worksheets, and produce thick horizontal or vertical lines.

Adjusting the Worksheet Column

You can adjust the width of any column or restore the width of columns to the width used in Symphony by pressing either **W**orksheet **C**olumn **R**eset or **W**orksheet **C**olumn **S**et-Width, as shown in figure 13.5. These selections perform the following functions:

❏ **R**eset takes a column or range of columns and returns them to their Symphony widths

❏ **S**et-Width enables you to designate the width of the column either by using the arrow keys or typing in a number value (including up to two decimal places) from 0 to 240. You also can use Ctrl-left arrow or Ctrl-right arrow to move one-tenth of a character at a time.

Using Worksheet Page

Worksheet **P**age enables you to manually insert row and column page breaks. Row page breaks occur when the print range is too long for the paper, and column page breaks occur when the print range is too wide for the paper.

If you decide not to insert manual page breaks, Allways proceeds vertically, just like Symphony, to compensate for a print range that exceeds both the width and length of the page. Allways begins by first printing the page in the top left of the print range, then the one below it, and so on. After it reaches the bottom of the print range, Allways moves to the top of the print range again, starts with the next column page break to the right, and works its way down again.

Fig. 13.5.
Worksheet Column width.

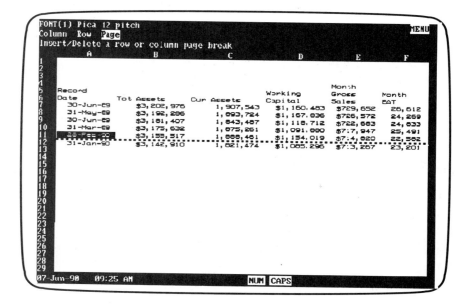

The page break shows as a dashed line that extends the full length or width of the worksheet, as shown in figure 13.6. If you do not insert page breaks, Allways calculates its own page breaks when the print range has reached the limit.

Fig. 13.6.
The ALLWAYS page break.

Adjusting the Worksheet Row

Allways automatically adjusts the height of each row to accommodate the largest font used in that row. Although the Allways row heights may change, the Symphony row heights are unaffected. You can change row heights in Symphony only by developing complex setup strings. Allways offers the **W**orkshop **R**ow **S**et-Height command, however, which enables you to manually set the height of a single row or a range of rows, as shown in figure 13.7. To use this command for several consecutive rows, set the range by anchoring it with the period then using the cursor arrows to define the range, and then select the desired height. Row height dimensions range from 0 to 255 points. This feature defines the type size and is adjusted to accommodate various font sizes.

You may want to let Allways handle the height of the rows to ensure that data is not lost. With height set to automatic, Allways adjusts the height to accommodate the size of the character. If you adjust the height manually, you might cut off parts of characters by miscalculating the point size required. Also, you may want to experiment with this command to fine-tune the spacing between lines of data or to create special effects such as shade or black bars of varying heights.

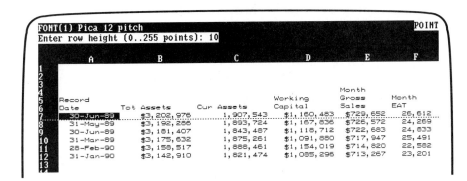

Fig. 13.7.
Worksheet Row Height.

Using Format Commands

The **F**ormat commands enable you to change the appearance of your worksheet by performing any of the following actions:

❏ Replace one font with another

❏ Save commonly used groups of fonts for use with more than one worksheet

❏ Alter the visual effect of the worksheet by using boldface and underlining

❏ Draw boxes around information

❏ Create contrast and backdrops through the use of shading

❏ Print text and numbers in color, if you have a color printer

❏ Create thick vertical or horizontal lines by adding solid black shading and then reducing the column or row.

To gain a better understanding of **F**ormat command capabilities, you should know the following terms:

Term	Description
Typeface	The overall design of the printed characters. Some common typefaces are Courier and Times
Point	A unit of measurement to determine the height of a character
Font	A typeface in a particular point size
Pitch	The number of characters that occupy an inch horizontally. The pitch is used to measure width of characters on a dot-matrix printer.
Font set	A group of eight fonts available for use with the worksheet. You control the contents of a font set by selecting any of the fonts supported by your printer or supplied by Allways.
Default font	The font used throughout the worksheet except in cells you have formatted with another font. The default font is font 1.
Font library	A file that contains a font set that you have saved. You may use this font set with other worksheets.

To further enhance your knowledge of the capabilities of these format commands, take a closer look at each menu option.

Format Bold

The **F**ormat **B**old command enables you to add boldface to cells to make the data contained in those cells stand out. This command may be invoked from the **F**ormat menu, as shown in figure 13.8, or by using the Alt-B function key. Alt-B can be used as a toggle key to add or remove the boldface.

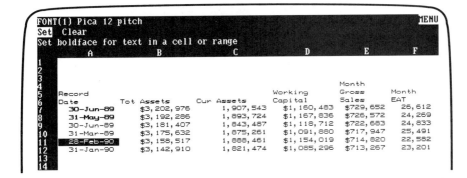

Fig. 13.8.
*The Format **Bold**
command.*

Format Color

The **Format** **C**olor command has seven colors that can be used on text and numbers, provided you have a printer that supports this feature. You can select Red-on-neg to have Allways print negative numbers in red, or black if positive. Or, if you want to make data disappear, select White and "white out" the data you want to eliminate. A formatted color range with underlining also uses the specified color to underline.

To access the **Format** **C**olor option, press MENU (F10), select **Format** **C**olor, select the color you want as shown in figure 13.9, specify the range, and then press Enter.

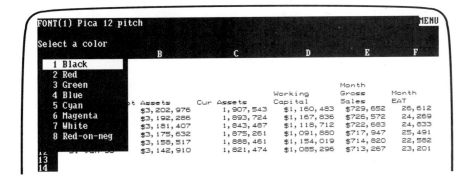

Fig. 13.9.
*The Format **Color***

Format Fonts

Most of Allways' formatting effects are produced through the use of different text fonts. A *font* consists of a *typeface* (for example, Times), a *point size*, and sometimes an *attribute* (such as bold or italic). Each worksheet can use as many as eight different fonts (how many you use is limited only by the amount of your printer memory), which are stored in a *font set*. To access fonts, select **Format** **F**ont, and the font set appears, numbered 1 to 8. Appearing with the set is a

Reminder:
Changes you make to the font set apply to the current worksheet only; different worksheets have different font sets.

command menu that enables you to replace fonts in the font set, or work with font libraries, or change default font sets. Remember that changes you make to the font set apply to the current worksheet only; different worksheets have different font sets. Font sets can be saved on a disk and then retrieved for use with any worksheet.

Format Font Default

The Allways default font set consists of Times and Triumvirate typefaces in various point sizes. The default font set is used automatically whenever you begin formatting a new worksheet. If you want to create your own font set to replace the default font, you can do so through the **F**ormat **F**ont **D**efault command. After you access the command, select either **R**estore, which replaces the current font set with the default font set, or **U**pdate, which saves the current font set as the default font set.

If you design your worksheet with the original default font set, then decide to create a new default font set, select **U**pdate to replace the old set, then select **R**estore to modify the existing worksheet to reflect the new font.

Format Font Library

If you change fonts frequently, you may want to save font sets for use with other worksheet files. Font sets can be named and saved in a font library to be used again in any worksheet. To save the current font set in a library, select **F**ormat **F**ont **L**ibrary **S**ave. Allways prompts you for a file name. Type a file name of up to eight characters and press Enter; Allways saves the file and adds the extensions AFS (Allways Font Set).

When you want to use a font library, select **F**ormat **F**ont **L**ibrary **R**etrieve. Allways shows a list of library files that have the AFS extension. Highlight the file you want and press Enter.

Format Font Replace

Reminder:

When you replace fonts, Allways automatically changes any worksheet cells formatted with that particular font.

At times you may want to replace fonts. Because you are limited to eight fonts per worksheet, however, you must use one of the fonts in the default font set; you cannot add fonts to the set.

To replace one of the fonts in the current set with a font not currently shown, select **F**ormat **F**ont. Use the cursor keys to highlight the font you want to replace. Select **R**eplace. Allways displays a list of all the fonts your printer can produce, as shown in figure 13.10. Highlight the desired font in that list and press Enter. Allways then shows a list of point sizes that can be used in the new font. Highlight the desired point size and press Enter.

When you replace fonts, Allways automatically changes any worksheet cells formatted with that particular font number.

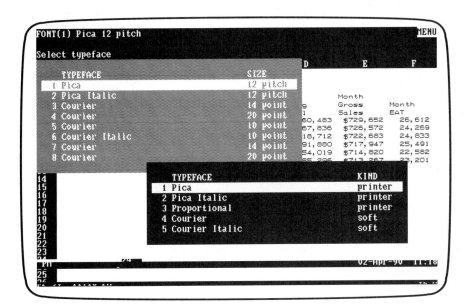

Fig. 13.10.

Format Font
Replace

Format Font Use

The **F**ormat **F**ont **U**se command enables you to format cells in a font of your choice. Although **U**se does not replace the font in the font set, as **R**eplace does, the command enables you to select a range of cells and choose a font from the font set to use in the specified range only. The Alt-1 to Alt-8 keys may be used to apply fonts to a cell or a highlighted range.

Format Lines

You can make your worksheet look more professional by adding horizontal or vertical lines and creating boxes. Allways enables you to box cells, outline ranges, create lines along any of the four edges of a cell, and create patterns in ranges by using lines, as shown in figure 13.11. Be careful when placing lines in cells. One cell's left edge is another cell's right edge.

Fig. 13.11.

Format Lines

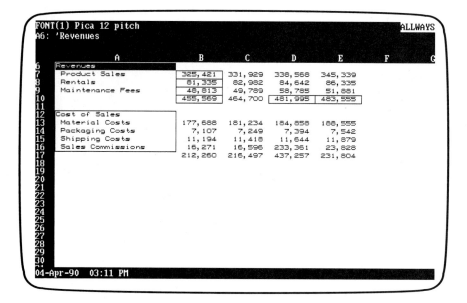

The **F**ormat **L**ines menu contains the following options:

Option	Function
Outline	Outlines a range
Left	Draws a vertical line along the left edge of each cell in a range
Right	Draws a vertical line along the right edge of each cell in a range
Top	Draws a horizontal line along the top edge of each cell in a range
Bottom	Draws a horizontal line along the bottom edge of each cell in a range
All	Draws a box around each cell in a range
Clear	Removes lines of any type

If you have outlined a range, using the Alt-L combination removes the outline and draws a box around each cell in the range. Using Alt-L again clears all the lines.

You can change the weight of lines in several ways. To change the darkness of lines before you print, execute **L**ayout **O**ptions **L**ine-Weight and choose **N**ormal, **L**ight, or **H**eavy. You may not notice any difference in line weight on the screen, but the printout should reflect any changes you make.

Format Reset

If you do not like the current worksheet format, or you want to see the worksheet in the original format, select the **F**ormat **R**eset command. **R**eset cancels all formatting made during the current session and returns to the default format, in the color black, with no boldface, underlining, lines, or shading.

Format Shade

This menu option enables you to create contrast on the worksheet by using light, dark, or solid black shading, as shown in figure 13.12. This feature is available through the **F**ormat **S**hade command, or by using the Alt-S key combination to cycle through the shading choices. The first time you press Alt-S, the range is lightly shaded. The second time, the range is dark; and the third time, it is shaded solid. Press Alt-S once more and all shading is cleared. If you want to use the menu to remove shading, choose **F**ormat **S**hade **C**lear.

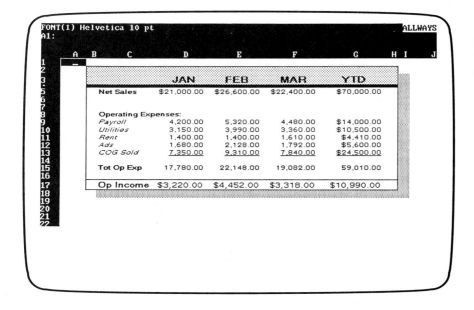

Fig. 13.12.
Three shades on one worksheet.

Format Underline

With this menu option you can use two types of underlining: single and double, as shown in figure 13.13.

You can use the menu option or Alt-U key combination to use this feature. The first time you press Alt-U, the range is single underlined. The second time, it is double underlined; the third time, underlining is canceled. You also can invoke the **F**ormat **U**nderline **C**lear command to cancel underlining. Underlining may not be used for blank cells or spaces.

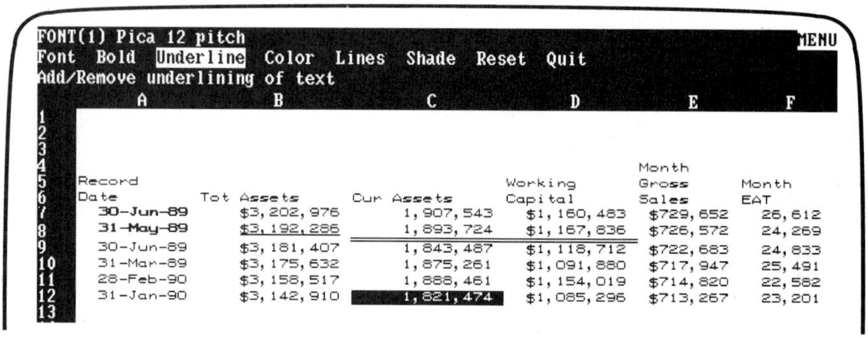

Fig. 13.13.

Two types of underlining.

```
FONT(1) Pica 12 pitch                                            MENU
Font  Bold  Underline  Color  Lines  Shade  Reset  Quit
Add/Remove underlining of text
          A           B            C           D          E         F
1
2
3
4                                            Month
5  Record                        Working    Gross     Month
6  Date        Tot Assets   Cur Assets   Capital    Sales     EAT
7    30-Jun-89   $3,202,976   1,907,543   $1,160,483  $729,652  26,612
8    31-May-89   $3,192,286   1,893,724   $1,167,836  $726,572  24,269
9    30-Jun-89   $3,181,407   1,843,487   $1,118,712  $722,683  24,833
10   31-Mar-89   $3,175,632   1,875,261   $1,091,880  $717,947  25,491
11   28-Feb-90   $3,158,517   1,888,461   $1,154,019  $714,820  22,582
12   31-Jan-90   $3,142,910   1,821,474   $1,085,296  $713,267  23,201
13
```

Using Graph Commands

The Allways GRAPH option enables you to include graphs in the worksheet along with the spreadsheet data, to print worksheets and graphs together, to display graphs as is or in the hatched-box environment, to turn the graph display on or off, and to enhance the appearance of graphs.

Reminder:

When you change a graph saved to a PIC file, you must re-save the modified graph to the same PIC file.

The graphs you use with Allways work with a PIC file created by Symphony. To save graphs in Allways, you must first create the graphs in Symphony and then use Symphony's SHEET **G**raph **I**mage-Save command or GRAPH **I**mage-Save command. When you change a graph saved to a PIC file, you must re-save the modified graph to the same PIC file.

You can use graphs created in Symphony in the following Allways environments:

❏ **G**raph **A**dd: This option enables you to include a graph in the worksheet. When you access this option through the **G**raph **A**dd command, you see a list of PIC files in the current directory, as shown in figure 13.14. Select the graph you want, specify the range where you want it to appear, and then press Enter.

Notice how Allways fits the graph into the designated range. When you want to resize a graph, use the **G**raph **S**ettings **R**ange command and Allways automatically sizes the graph to fit into the specified range.

❏ **G**raph **F**onts-Directory: This option enables you to specify the directory containing the FNT files included in the PrintGraph program. Allways uses the FNT files to display and print graphs. You need to use this option only if the font files are in a directory other than the Symphony directory.

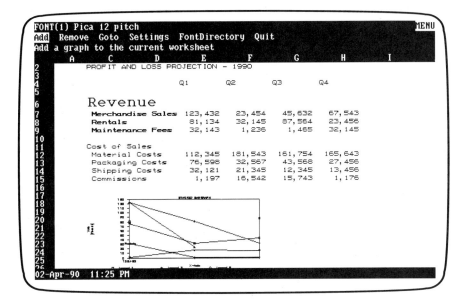

Fig. 13.14.
The Graph Add command.

❑ **G**raph **G**oto: This option helps you find graphs quickly in any size worksheet. When you access this command, select the graph you want from the list that appears and press Enter, as shown in figure 13.15.

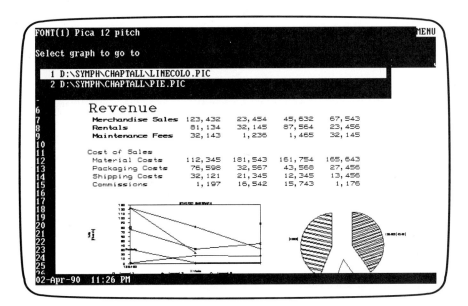

Fig. 13.15.
The Graph Goto command.

❏ **G**raph **R**emove: This option enables you to remove a graph from the worksheet without affecting the PIC file on disk, as shown in figure 13.16.

Fig. 13.16.
The Graph Remove command.

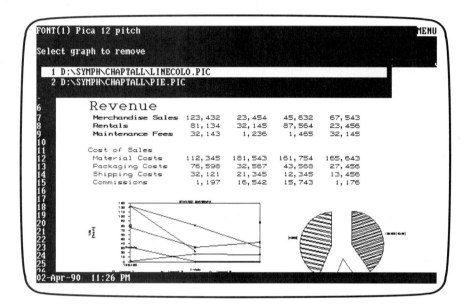

❏ **G**raph **S**ettings: Allways automatically assigns to each graph you add to the worksheet, a settings sheet that contains position and print information for that graph. This settings sheet, as shown in figure 13.17, contains **G**raph **S**ettings **C**olors commands that perform the following tasks:

Graph **S**ettings **C**olors:	Sets colors for graph data ranges
Graph **S**ettings **D**efault:	Restores or updates the default graph settings
Graph **S**ettings **F**onts:	Sets the fonts to be used for text in graphs
Graph **S**ettings **M**argins:	Sets margins for the graph
Graph **S**ettings **P**IC-File:	Replaces a graph in the worksheet with a different graph file
Graph **S**ettings **Q**uit:	Returns the program to ALLWAYS mode
Graph **S**ettings **R**ange:	Moves the graph to a different range or changes its size
Graph **S**ettings **S**cale:	Sets the scaling factor for fonts

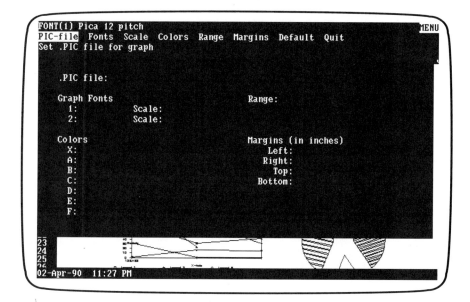

Fig. 13.17.
*The GRAPH
Settings menu.*

Using Layout Commands

Allways layout commands enable you to control the appearance of the printed page, print a header at the top or a footer at the bottom of each page, repeat a border on each page, print grid lines between each row and column, change the thickness of lines created with **F**ormat **L**ines, and save frequently used layouts for use with several worksheets.

Using Layout Borders

You can create top, bottom, and left borders on each page of your document by using the **L**AYOUT **B**orders command. When the option list appears, as shown in figure 13.18, select the option you want, define the range, press Enter, and the borders you specified are placed on a single page or each page of a multiple-page printout.

Remember that when you select the range for any of the borders, the entire row or column is selected. You may not enter data at the range line. The only data that may be accepted for these borders is the data already in the worksheet.

Reminder:
*When you select
the range for any of
the borders, the
entire row or
column is selected.*

Using Layout Default

Every new worksheet contains a default page layout of 8 1/2 inches by 11 inches, margins of one inch, a normal line weight, and no grid lines. Other page layout settings are blank.

Fig. 13.18.
The Layout menu.

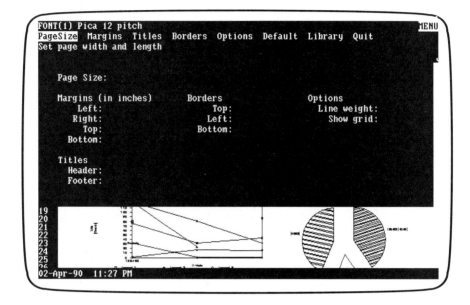

You can create your own default page layout by using the **L**ayout **D**efault option and modifying the settings. If you want to alter the default layout for a particular worksheet, do not select **L**ayout **D**efault **U**pdate. That command changes the default settings permanently to those of the current worksheet. Instead, make your changes, finish the worksheet, then use **L**ayout **D**efault **R**estore, as shown in figure 13.19, to return layout settings to the default values.

Fig. 13.19.
The Layout Default Restore option.

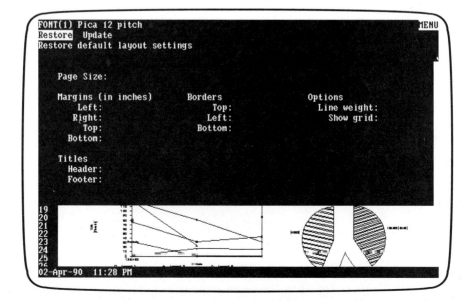

Using Layout Library

Layout Library enables you to create a library of page layouts on disk. Individual page layouts are useful when you want to create several different reports from the same worksheet. Instead of redefining a page layout each time you create a report, you can retrieve the appropriate layout from the Layout Library.

The following commands are available in the Layout Library menu:

Command	Function
Erase	Deletes a page layout library file from disk
Retrieve	Retrieves a page layout library file from disk for use with the current worksheet
Save	Saves the current page layout in a library file on disk

Using Layout Library Erase

Use Layout Library Erase to delete a page layout library file that you previously saved. Library files use the file extension ALS. When you select this menu option, a list of ALS files in the current directory displays. You select the file you want to delete and press Enter. If you need to delete a file from another directory, press ESC to clear the file names, edit the driver and/or directory, and then press Enter.

Using Layout Library Retrieve

Layout Library Retrieve enables you to retrieve a previously saved page layout and make it current.

Using Layout Library Save

Layout Library Save enables you to name the current page layout and save it in a library file on disk, as shown in figure 13.20.

Setting Layout Margins

To position a spreadsheet on a page, you may need to modify the margins. Unless you have changed the default page layout, the margins are set to one inch. To change margins, select Layout Margins, and a submenu appears with settings for Left, Right, Top, and Bottom. Type in the number of inches you want (you can include up to two decimal places) and press Enter.

Fig. 13.20.
*Layout Library
Save*

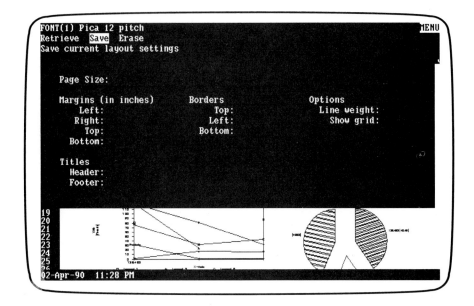

Using Layout Options

The **L**ayout **O**ptions enable you to turn the worksheet grid on and off, and set the thickness of lines you add to the worksheet with **F**ormat **L**ines.

Using Layout Options Grid

You can enclose every cell in the worksheet and the printout with grid lines by using the **L**ayout **O**ptions **G**rid command. However, you cannot change the line weight of grid lines. Once the lines are turned on they are present throughout the worksheet. To partially enclose worksheet data with lines, use the **F**ormat **L**ines **A**ll command.

You access the **G**rid command as stated previously, or by pressing Alt-G. Press Alt-G once to turn the grid lines on and twice to turn them off.

Using Layout Options Line-Weight

Layout **O**ptions Line-Weight changes the weight of lines created with **F**ormat **L**ines. You cannot use the command to change the thickness of individual lines; however, you can customize the thickness of individual lines by using **F**ormat **S**hade **S**olid, **W**orksheet **C**olumn **S**et-Width, and **W**orksheet **R**ow **S**et-Height.

Although some printers may not respond to line-weight variation, laser printers and high-density dot-matrix printers provide sufficient resolution to make it worth your while to vary line weights.

Using Layout PageSize

The PageSize option enables you to modify the page size to accommodate the worksheet. You must tell Allways the page size so that it can position your printout properly. You can specify the page size or physical dimensions of the paper you are printing on.

Page size dimensions are limited only by your printer. Generally, you use the standard 8 1/2-by-11-inch setting. However, a custom option also is available that enables you to type in the paper's width and length in inches (you can include up to two decimal places).

Using Layout Titles

The **L**ayout **T**itles command enables you to create headers and footers in your documents. A header is a line of text that appears at the top of each printed page; a footer is a line of text that appears at the bottom of each page.

To create headers and footers, follow these guidelines:

❏ Unless you modify print margin settings and page size, headers and footers each can be 240 characters long (including spaces).

❏ To divide a header or footer into separate segments for the right, left, and center portions of each line, use the split vertical bar (|). Allways left-aligns text before a split vertical bar, centers text after the first split vertical bar, and right-aligns text after the second split vertical bar. Unless the split vertical bar is used, Allways left-aligns the entire header or footer.

❏ The # symbol may be used in a header or footer to include a page number on every page of the printout. The symbol also can be combined with text for additional description.

❏ The @ symbol may be included anywhere in the header or footer to include the current date on every page of the printout. Allways uses the date supplied by your computer's internal clock (see fig. 13.21).

Note: Headers take three lines at the top of the page, and footers take three lines at the bottom. In both places, one line is for the text and two lines separate the text from the worksheet. Headers and footers are always printed in font 1 (the default font).

Using Print Commands

Allways provides several features that enable you to control the printing process. You can select a printer driver and interface, specify the number of copies to print, print a selection of pages, and specify printer-specific options.

Fig. 13.21.

The header and footer menu screen.

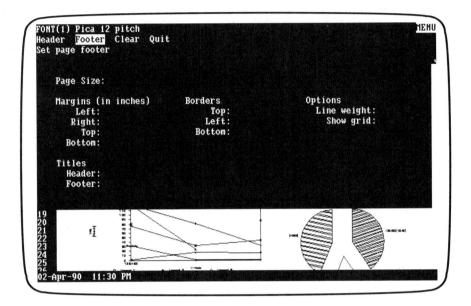

To use the print options more effectively, you may want to learn the following terms:

Term	Function
Orientation	Defines the way data appears on the page. Some printers support portrait orientation (data runs vertically on the page); others support landscape orientation (data runs horizontally on the page).
Page Break	Breaks the data into column or row pages to adjust when the data is too wide or too long for the paper. Allways displays page breaks in the worksheet as dashed lines.
Printer Driver	A file containing the software needed to run your printer. Drivers are selected during the Setup program.
Interface or port	Defines the way your printer is connected to the computer. You may have either a serial or parallel interface and each computer may have more than one interface of either type.
Resolution	Represents the number of dots per inch in which the printer can produce graphics. The greater the number of dots per inch, the higher the resolution and the better the quality. However, the higher the resolution, the more time it takes to print the graphics.
Bin	Represents the paper feed options on certain printers.

Using Print Configuration

This feature enables you to select different printers and interfaces and change configuration settings without leaving Allways. Once you change your configuration, the new settings remain in effect until you change them again. No matter what type of printer you have, the **C**onfiguration menu will contain **P**rinter **I**nterface and **Q**uit menu options. Other options display in the menu depending on the type of printer (see figs. 13.22 and 13.23).

Configuration settings are accessible through the **P**rint **C**onfiguration option.

Print Configuration Bin

Some printers have more than one sheet-feeding option, such as multiple paper trays or manual feed. If your printer offers these features, Allways displays the BIN command option. When you select BIN, a menu of bin options displays. You can then select the appropriate option you need to access the paper for your printer.

Print Configuration Cartridge

The **P**rint **C**onfiguration **C**artridge controls printers that support font cartridges or font cards. The display of this option depends on the type of printer you have and whether or not it supports this feature.

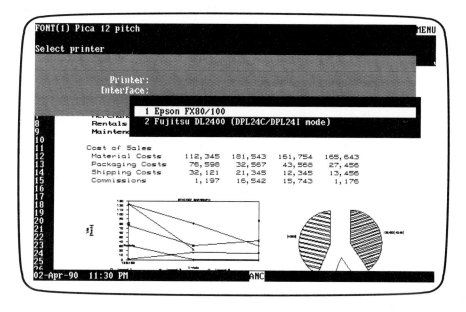

Fig. 13.22.
The printer selection.

Fig. 13.23.
The interface selection.

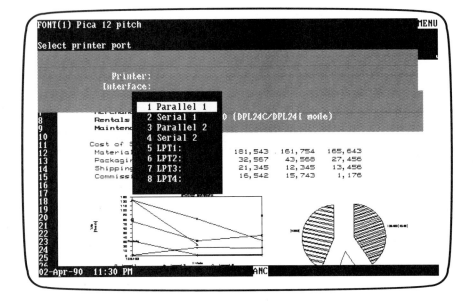

Print Configuration Interface

Interface means the way the printer is connected to the computer. The default interface is Parallel 1, which is the most common configuration. With this command, you can change the specified interface (port). The interface may be serial or parallel and the computer may have more than one interface of either type.

When you access this feature through **P**rint **C**onfiguration **I**nterface, a list of interface options displays.

Note: When you select a serial interface, you must set the baud rate for your printer by using the operating system's **M**ode command. Using this mode can be troublesome because each time you set the **M**ode command, you must exit Symphony. For this reason, you may want to consider entering the **M**ode command in your AUTOEXEC.BAT file. Refer to the operating system manual for your computer to obtain more information about the **M**ode command.

Print Configuration Orientation

This command shows whether your printer supports portrait or landscape orientation for your printout. **P**ortrait prints the worksheet down the length of the page (vertically), and **L**andscape prints the worksheet across the width of the page (horizontally).

Print Configuration Printer

If you selected more than one printer driver during Setup, you have the capability to switch printers. To switch, access the **P**rint **C**onfiguration **P**rinter command and select a printer driver from the list that displays.

Print Configuration Resolution

Some printers enable you to adjust the resolution for graphics. Adjustments are made through the **P**rint **C**onfiguration command.

Resolution affects only certain aspects of printing. For example, the LaserJet printer resolution modification affects only the printing of graphs and grid lines because the soft fonts are printed by downloading them, rather than by using the LaserJet graphics mode.

Cue:
A general rule is that the higher the resolution the better the quality.

Print File

If you want to postpone printing the output to a printer, use the **P**rint **F**ile option. This option enables you to save your output to an encoded file on disk, with the file extension ENC.

When you are ready to print the encoded file on a printer, you must end the Symphony session and use the operating system copy command with the /B switch. This file contains certain printer codes and if the /B switch is not used the codes may be misinterpreted as end-of-file marks and the printout may be prematurely terminated.

Encoded files created by Allways are binary files that other programs cannot read. Encoded files are used to postpone printing and not to promote their use with other programs.

Print Go

After you select a print range, use the **P**rint **G**o command to start the print job. If you forget to select a range, Allways prompts you for one. The Ctrl-Break keys may be used to stop printing .

Print Range

Before you can send data to the printer, you must specify the data you want to print by defining the print range. Access this command through MENU (F10) and select **P**rint **R**ange. The menu options are **S**et and **C**lear. Use **S**et and then specify the range you want to print. The print range is defined with dashed lines that outline the boundaries and vertical and horizontal page breaks, as shown in figure 13.24. These lines remain on the screen until they are removed with the **P**rint **R**ange **C**lear command. The print range is saved as part of the format file in the ALL file extension.

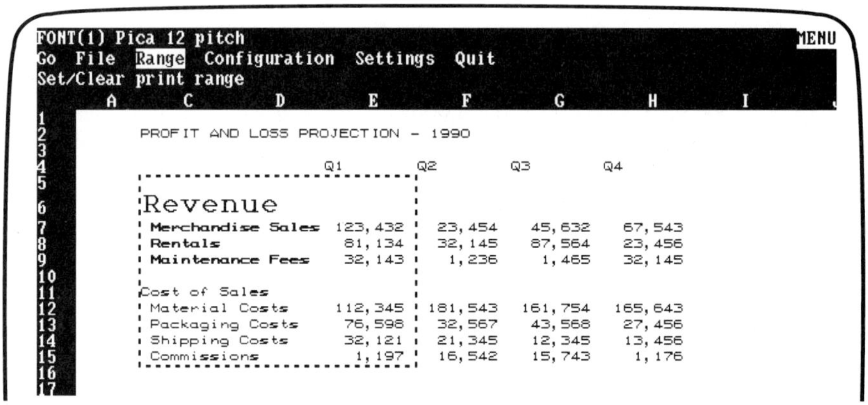

Fig. 13.24.

The defined print range.

```
FONT(1) Pica 12 pitch                                              MENU
Go  File  Range  Configuration  Settings  Quit
Set/Clear print range
        A      C        D        E        F        G        H        I
1
2        PROFIT AND LOSS PROJECTION - 1990
3
4                        Q1          Q2        Q3        Q4
5       ----------------------------------
6       :Revenue                          :
7       : Merchandise Sales  123,432 :  23,454    45,632    67,543
8       : Rentals             81,134 :  32,145    87,564    23,456
9       : Maintenance Fees    32,143 :   1,236     1,465    32,145
10      :                                :
11      :Cost of Sales                   :
12      : Material Costs     112,345 : 181,543   161,754   165,643
13      : Packaging Costs     76,598 :  32,567    43,568    27,456
14      : Shipping Costs      32,121 :  21,345    12,345    13,456
15      : Commissions          1,197 :  16,542    15,743     1,176
16      ----------------------------------
17
```

Print Settings

The **P**rint **S**ettings command enables you to determine which pages to print, the page numbering for headers and footers, the number of copies to print, and whether a pause should be used to permit changing of the paper manually before each page. The **P**rint **S**ettings affect the current Allways session; they are not saved as part of the format file in the ALL extension file.

The Print Settings consist of the following options:

Option	Function
Begin	Enables you to specify the page number at which to begin printing. At times you may want to print only one page of a 10-page worksheet.
Copies	Enables you to select the number of copies of the worksheet page you want to print.
First	Enables you to specify the first page you want printed.
End	Enables you to determine the last page you want printed.
Quit	Returns the program to the Allways mode.
Reset	Ignores modifications made to the **P**rint **S**ettings and returns to the default settings.
Wait	Enables you to determine whether the printer pauses for a paper change before printing each page, or restores continuous printing.

Use **P**rint **S**ettings to gain access to these options, as shown in figure 13.25.

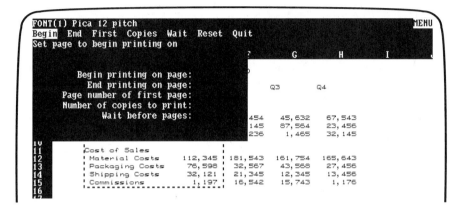

Fig. 13.25.
The Print Settings menu.

Using Display Commands

Allways contains a set of display commands that governs the worksheet screen display. Although these commands affect the presentation of the worksheet on-screen, they have no effect on the printouts. Display commands achieve the following affects:

❏ Reduce the worksheet or look at very small fonts to get an overall picture. (Display Zoom)

❏ Vary the colors on a color monitor (Display Colors)

❏ Display graphs on the screen as part of the worksheet (Display Graphs)

Figure 13.26 shows the display menu options.

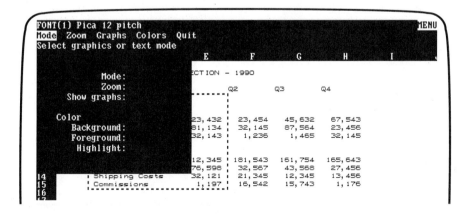

Fig. 13.26.
The display menu options.

Using Display Mode

The **D**isplay **M**ode command offers two choices: **G**raphics and **T**ext. You cannot format in the graphics mode unless you have a graphics monitor and display card. Without the monitor and card, you are restricted to text mode when formatting worksheets. Whether you select the text mode because of the hardware you have, or by preference, formatting changes are not viewed on the screen in text mode. You access **D**isplay **M**ode through the menu option, or by using F6 to switch between graphics and text mode.

If you select the **G**raphics command the screen display closely resembles your final printed output. This feature is better known as WYSIWYG (What You See Is What You Get). All format changes are seen immediately on-screen, as shown in figure 13.27.

Fig. 13.27.

*An example of the
Graphics mode.*

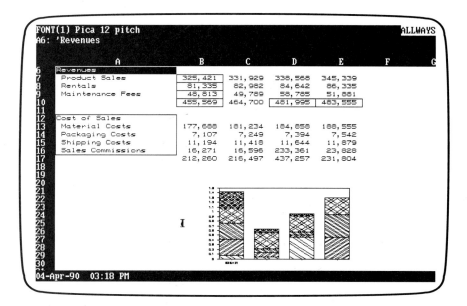

Selecting the **T**ext mode displays the worksheet the same as in Symphony. Allways formats cannot be viewed on-screen. A record of the specified Allways formats is recorded in the first line of the control panel. The printouts look as if you had developed them on the graphics screen, as shown in figure 13.28.

Using Display Zoom

The **D**isplay **Z**oom command enables you to enlarge or reduce the worksheet display size. The capability to vary size is useful, for example, when you use very small fonts and must enlarge the display, or when you need an overall picture of a large area of the worksheet and must reduce the display.

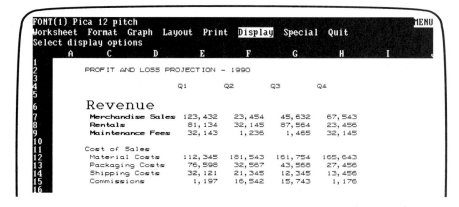

Fig. 13.28.

An example of **Text** *mode.*

Access the **D**isplay **Z**oom command through the control panel menu, or by using F4 (to reduce), or Alt-F4 (to enlarge). If you invoke **Z**oom through the control panel, the size selection does not change the screen display until you use the **Q**uit menu selection. However, using the function keys provides an "on-the-spot" change in the screen display.

The **D**isplay **Z**oom offers the following options:

Option	Function
Tiny	Reduces cells to 60% of their normal size
Small	Reduces cells to 84% of their normal size
Normal	Displays cells the same size as in the Symphony worksheet (normal size)
Large	Enlarges cells to 120% of their normal size
Huge	Enlarges cells to 140% of their normal size

Using Display Graphs

The **D**isplay **G**raphs command enables you to choose between seeing the actual graph on the screen or a hatched box that indicates the range in which the graph is positioned. This command is accessed through the control panel menu, or by pressing F7, as shown in figures 13.29 and 13.30.

Although displaying a hatched box gives a faster response time as you are working with Allways, you may want to display the graph so that you can examine it before you print it. For this reason you may want to take advantage of F7 and use it to toggle between the graph display and the hatched box display on the screen.

Fig. 13.29.

An example of the Graphs mode.

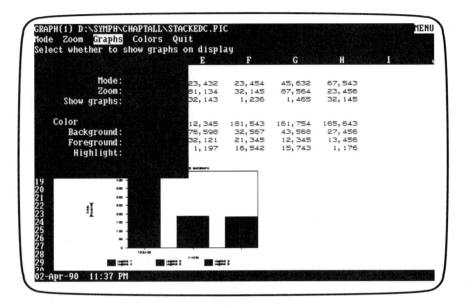

Fig. 13.30.

An example of the hatched box mode.

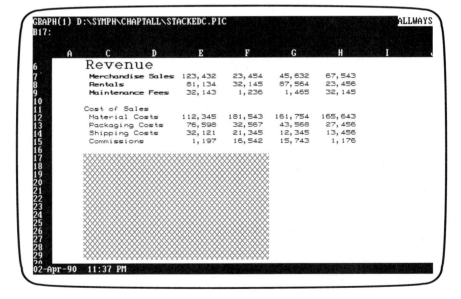

The **D**isplay **G**raphs command behaves differently if you select the **D**isplay **T**ext mode command. In **T**ext mode, the display of graphs is represented as a series of G characters throughout the range in which the graph is positioned, as shown in figure 13.31.

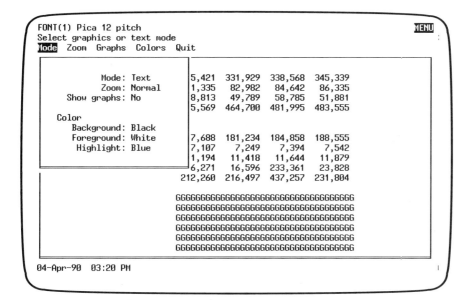

Fig. 13.31.
An example of the G character display.

Using Display Colors

The **D**isplay **C**olors command controls the colors Allways uses to display items on-screen if you have a color monitor. Also, you may change these colors by using this command, as shown in figure 13.32. Once you change the colors, they remain in effect for future Allways sessions.

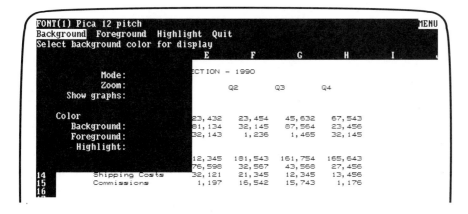

Fig. 13.32.
Displaying the color menu options.

The **D**isplay **C**olors command options consist of the following:

Option	Function
Background	From a number of dark colors, selects the color for the screen background
Foreground	From a number of light tones, selects the color for the worksheet area
Highlight	Selects the color of the cell pointer
Quit	Returns you to the previous menu

Selecting **B**ackground, **F**oreground or **H**ighlight presents you with a list of colors from which you are expected to select the color of your choice, as shown in figure 13.33.

Fig. 13.33.
A list of
Background colors.

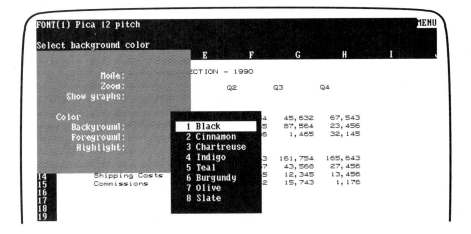

Using Display Quit

The **D**isplay **Q**uit command is used to return the program to the Allways mode.

Using Special Commands

When the standard formatting commands cannot meet your needs, Allways provides special formatting commands that enable you to make large-scale changes easily. These special commands enable you to perform the following functions:

❑ Create a format and then import it into other worksheets

❑ Copy a special format for use in multiple sections of the worksheet

❏ Justify text in accordance with the fonts and column widths you are using

❏ Move the format of one cell to another

Remember that cell formats include font, boldface, underlining, lines, color, and shading.

Using Special Copy

This command enables you to copy the format of a cell or range to another section of the worksheet. The command copies only the format, not the data. You cannot copy graphs with the special copy command.

To access this command use MENU (F10) and select the **S**pecial **C**opy option. You can copy the format of a single cell to a range, or you can duplicate formats throughout a range by defining a source range that includes either a single column, or a single row or both, and then specifying a target range that includes multiple columns or rows.

Using Special Import

This command enables you to import the format of one worksheet into another worksheet. No matter the format of the current worksheet, **S**pecial **I**mport removes that format and replaces it with the format you import.

You access **S**pecial **I**mport through MENU (F10). Remember, cell formats you import appear in exactly the same location on the current worksheet as they appear in the worksheet they are imported from. If the two worksheets are not identical, the cell formats may appear in unexpected places.

Reminder:
Cell formats you import appear in exactly the same location on the current worksheet as they appear in the worksheet they are imported from.

Using Special Justify

The **S**pecial **J**ustify command enables you to justify text to accommodate the fonts and column widths you are using. By specifying a range for justification, you enable Allways to take the labels in the left-most column of that range and rewrap them so that no label extends beyond the right-most column of the range when the worksheet is printed. You get a warning message if the range you specify is not large enough to fit the text you want to justify. You access this command through MENU (F10).

Using Special Move

The **S**pecial **M**ove command, accessed through MENU (F10), enables you to move the format of one cell or range to another. This feature differs from copying a format. Copying a format results in the "moving" of formats from the source range to the exact range in the destination range.

When formats are moved from one range to another, the destination range adopts the formats of the source range and the source range formats are reset. A good example of this is when the formats of one column are moved to the left and two rows up. The destination range is always the same dimension as the source range.

Chapter Summary

This chapter introduced you to the Allways add-in application package that comes with Symphony. You learned that,although Allways is not a full-featured desktop publishing program, it can perform many desktop publishing tasks to enhance the printing of Symphony graphs, worksheets, documents and database reports. You learned that you can customize reports to meet specific requirements by using Allways fonts, borders, lines, and shading options. Finally, you learned that Allways provides enhanced printing capabilities without having to leave Symphony to use another program to obtain similar results.

14

Creating and Displaying Graphs

Symphony's graphics are integrated with the spreadsheet for quick and easy use. For example, to make a graph of your work, you take the data you entered in the spreadsheet and use the graphics commands to create a picture of the data. GRAPH and SHEET mode are so unified, that when you change a number in the spreadsheet, the graph automatically reflects the change.

Although Symphony has a good set of graphics commands, the program is not as powerful as some dedicated graphics packages. However, if you need graphics principally for analytic purposes rather than for presentations, Symphony may have all the power you need. Also, you may find that graphs help you spot trends and interpret your data better than tables of figures.

Tip

During the Install program, you can indicate that you want to display graphs and text at the same time.

Accessing SHEET and GRAPH Windows

Symphony can display graphs and text at the same time on the same screen. If you select the Shared mode of display when you create your driver set, Symphony can show a graph in one window and text in another (see Appendix A for more information on setting up drivers). In fact, Symphony does not restrict the number of windows you can create; you can show as many different graph or text windows as you can fit on the screen at any one time.

You access all of Symphony's graphing capabilities by using the **G**raph command within the SHEET environment, or you can set up a separate GRAPH window specifically designed to display graphs. The GRAPH window has all the capabilities of a SHEET window. What's the difference then? When do you want to use a SHEET window for graphing, and when is a GRAPH window more appropriate?

The difference between a SHEET window and a GRAPH window is how long a graph remains displayed on the screen. When you are in a SHEET window, you choose **P**review from the main **G**raph menu to display a graph on the screen. The main **G**raph menu includes these options:

> **P**review **1**st-Settings **2**nd-Settings **I**mage-Save **Q**uit

By selecting **P**review, you can display a graph temporarily. The graph remains displayed only until you press any key. Then you see the spreadsheet, and the main **G**raph menu reappears in the control panel.

On the other hand, when you are in a GRAPH window, the current graph displays automatically in the window. You can use the **A**ttach option to display other graphs on the screen. The GRAPH window menu includes these options:

> **A**ttach **1**st-Settings **2**nd-Settings **I**mage-Save

When you select **A**ttach, any graph that you name remains displayed in the window indefinitely. The only way you can eliminate the graph from the window is to attach another graph or delete the graph name (see "Deleting Graph Settings," later in this chapter).

Otherwise, all the commands in the **G**raph menu of the SHEET environment are exactly the same as those in the main menu of the GRAPH environment. You can even pass settings back and forth between the two environments. For example, you can create a pie chart in the SHEET environment and give those settings a name, such as SALESPIE. You can then use the same settings to display SALESPIE in a GRAPH window. Because the settings are shared by the two windows, any changes you make in one environment are also made in the other.

Most of the examples in this chapter show commands that are available for graphing in both SHEET and GRAPH windows. The section titled "More on GRAPH Windows" (later in this chapter), however, includes several examples in which you need to choose the GRAPH environment.

Using Symphony Settings

Symphony's graph feature offers so many options that they do not fit on one settings sheet. Consequently, the settings have been divided into two sheets, called **1**st-Settings and **2**nd-Settings.

You can get from the **2**nd-Settings command menu to the **1**st-Settings menu by choosing **Q**uit from the **2**nd-Settings menu to return to the main **G**raph menu. You can then select **1**st-Settings. An easier way is available, though. Symphony offers a **S**witch option as the first selection in both the **1**st- and **2**nd-Settings command menus. **S**witch enables you to switch back and forth between the two graph settings sheets without having to return to the main **G**raph menu.

Learning the Types of Graphs

Regardless of the environment, SHEET or GRAPH, Symphony offers six basic types of graphs:

Bar

Stacked-Bar

Line

Pie

XY

High-Low-Close-Open

Creating Simple Bar Graphs

Suppose that you have created a simple worksheet containing data about store openings over the past five years for the three biggest retailers in the United States, as shown in figure 14.1. You can create many interesting graphs that help make the data more understandable. For example, you can build a bar chart to illustrate the data on Sears alone. This graph is shown in figure 14.2.

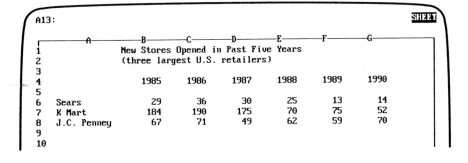

Fig. 14.1.

Sample worksheet data.

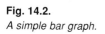

Fig. 14.2.
A simple bar graph.

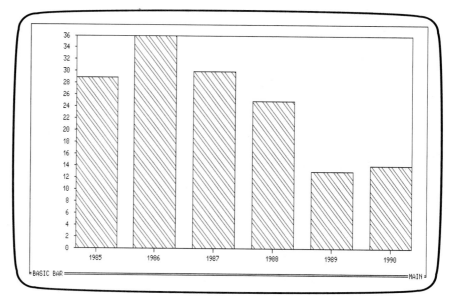

Making a Bar Graph in a SHEET Window

Bar graphs are used to compare different sets of data. A typical bar graph has vertical bars that show value by the height of the bar. To create a bar graph, start in a SHEET window that has the spreadsheet you want to graph and select SHEET **G**raph.

Selecting the Type of Graph

After you select **G**raph, then **1**st-Settings, you must choose the type of graph you want to produce. Figure 14.3 shows the **1**st-Settings menu and settings sheet. Note that the default graph type is **Line**.

Select **T**ype from the **1**st-Settings menu. The following menu then appears:

    Line **B**ar **S**tacked-Bar **X**Y **P**ie **H**igh-Low-Close-Open

Because you are creating a bar graph, choose **B**ar from this menu. Notice that Symphony automatically returns you to the **1**st-Settings menu and settings sheet.

```
Switch to 2nd-Settings                                                   MENU
Switch  Type  Range  Hue  Format  Data-Labels  Legend  Cancel  Name  Quit

      Type:     Line

   Range                Hue  Format  Data-Labels        Legend

   X                    1
   A                    2    Both
   B                    3    Both
   C                    4    Both
   D                    5    Both
   E                    6    Both
   F                    7    Both
                                              Graph 1st-Settings: MAIN
```

Fig. 14.3.

The 1st-Settings menu and settings sheet.

Specifying Data Ranges

Now that you have told Symphony what type of graph to create, you must give the ranges of data you want to use in the graph. You begin this process by selecting **R**ange from the **1**st-Settings menu. Selecting **R**ange brings up the following menu:

X A B C D E F Quit

The appropriate range for the simple bar graph is **A**. After you choose this option, Symphony prompts for a range definition.

You can define the range with cell references or a range name. In this example, the coordinates are B6..G6 (the Sears data in fig. 14.1). Remember that you can enter this reference by typing the cell coordinates from the keyboard or by using the POINT mode. (If you are in the GRAPH environment when you want to designate a range, Symphony temporarily shifts to the SHEET environment.)

The bar graph in the example requires only one range, but Symphony enables you to specify as many as six data ranges per graph. The letters **B** through **F** on the **R**ange menu represent the other ranges. Later in this chapter, you add the K Mart and J.C. Penney data to the graph.

This graph also needs labels along the **X**-axis to define the data items you are plotting. You add these labels by selecting **X** from the **1**st-Settings **R**ange menu and pointing to the appropriate range of labels in the worksheet. In this example, the labels are in the range B4..G4 (see fig. 14.1). Symphony uses the contents of the cells in the indicated range as the **X**-axis labels. (The values in the range B4..G4 are stored as numbers; however, Symphony uses them as labels in this instance.)

Each of the data ranges for the sample graph consists of a partial row of data, but the data range also can be a partial column. The graphs in this chapter include examples of both vertical and horizontal data ranges. Remember, however, that the range must be a continuous set of cells. The ranges A2..A6, D3..F3, and F14..F30 are legal ranges; but the ranges A2,A4,D7 and E5,E8,F17,L4 are not.

Viewing the Graph

The final step in producing the graph is to choose **P**review from the main **G**raph menu. The results of selecting this command depend on your hardware and how you configured it during installation. (For more on installing the system, see Appendix A.) If you have a nongraphics screen, nothing happens; all you get is a beep. But don't worry; although you can't see the graph on the display, it still exists in your computer's memory. You can use the PrintGraph program (see the next chapter) to print your graph.

If you have a graphics card and either a black-and-white or color monitor, the bar graph displays on the screen after you enter **P**review. Notice that in both cases, the temporary GRAPH window, which is created by your selecting **P**review, replaces the SHEET window on the screen. (This change always happens when you are in the SHEET environment regardless of whether you selected Shared or Toggle mode during installation.) You can return to the worksheet by pressing any key.

Finally, if you are fortunate enough to have a dual monitor system with both a graphics monitor and a monochrome display (and you selected the Dual mode during installation), the bar chart appears on the graphics monitor, and the worksheet remains on the monochrome display. If your graphics monitor can display color, you can format the graph to take advantage of that capability, too. You must have a color printer, however, in order to print the graph in color.

Adding Titles

Although the picture created so far has graphics appeal, the graph does not offer much information. To complete the graph, you must add titles. For example, you can enter titles for the graph itself and for the X and Y axes. You first access the SHEET **G**raph **2**nd-Settings command menu. Figure 14.4 shows this command menu in the control panel above the **G**raph **2**nd-Settings sheet.

You then select **T**itles from the **2**nd-Settings command menu. The **G**raph **2**nd-Settings **T**itles command produces the following choices:

    First **S**econd **X**-axis **Y**-axis **Q**uit

```
Switch to 1st-Settings                                        MENU
Switch  Titles  Y-Scale  X-Scale  Other  Name  Quit
  Titles                                    Type: Bar
    First:                      X-Axis:
    Second:                     Y-Axis:
  Y-Scale                  X-Scale              Other
    Type      Automatic      Type    Automatic   Grid:   None
    Lower:                    Lower:              Hide:   No
    Upper:                    Upper:              Color:  No
    Format:   G              Format: G           Skip:   1
    Exponent: Automatic      Exponent: Automatic Origin: 0
    Width:    9                                  Aspect: 1
                                       Graph 2nd-Settings: BASIC BAR
```

Fig. 14.4.

The 2nd-Settings menu and settings sheet.

The **T**itles command enables you to assign a main title and subtitle to appear at the top of the graph (the **F**irst and **S**econd options) and also titles for the X and Y axes (the **X**-axis and **Y**-axis options). Figure 14.5 shows the original bar graph with the titles added. To enter the **X**-axis title for this sample graph, select **X**-axis and simply type **Year** and then press Enter. Then choose **Y**-axis and type **Number of Stores** and press Enter.

Cue:

You can assign four graph titles: two at the top, one on the X-axis, and one on the Y-axis.

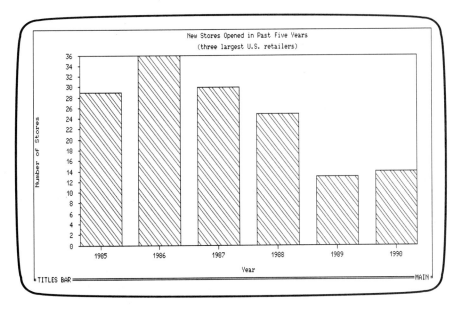

Fig. 14.5.

A bar graph with titles added.

Note the graph titles at the top of figure 14.5. These titles were entered using the **F**irst and **S**econd options. **F**irst was used for the main title, "New Stores Opened in Past Five Years," and **S**econd for the subtitle below it, "(three largest U.S. retailers)."

You usually enter these titles by typing the title from the keyboard. In this case, however, we used the special backslash (\) feature available with the **T**itles command. This feature enables you to enter the contents of cells. To use the contents of a cell for a title, place a backslash (\) before the cell address when Symphony asks you for a title. For example, enter **\B1** for **F**irst and **\B2** for **S**econd. Notice that these selections appear in the **2**nd-Settings sheet (see fig. 14.6).

Fig. 14.6.

*Using cell references to enter the **F**irst and **S**econd titles.*

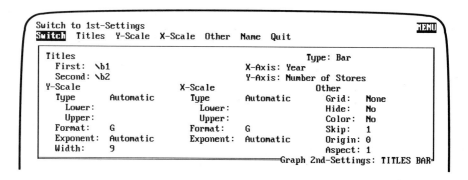

```
Switch to 1st-Settings                                              MENU
Switch  Titles  Y-Scale  X-Scale  Other  Name  Quit
┌──────────────────────────────────────────────────────────────────┐
│ Titles                                    Type: Bar               │
│   First:  \b1                      X-Axis: Year                   │
│   Second: \b2                      Y-Axis: Number of Stores       │
│ Y-Scale                 X-Scale                 Other             │
│   Type      Automatic     Type      Automatic     Grid:   None    │
│     Lower:                  Lower:                 Hide:   No      │
│     Upper:                  Upper:                 Color:  No      │
│   Format:   G             Format:   G             Skip:   1       │
│   Exponent: Automatic     Exponent: Automatic     Origin: 0       │
│   Width:    9                                     Aspect: 1       │
└──────────────────────────────────Graph 2nd-Settings: TITLES BAR──┘
```

Reminder:

A Symphony graph title can be no longer than 39 characters.

You also can use a range name for a title or label. To do so, enter the range name rather than the cell reference after the backslash. Incidentally, a Symphony graph title can be no longer than 39 characters.

You should be aware of two particulars of Symphony's graph titles. First, Symphony always disregards label prefixes when setting up titles, so the program automatically centers the **F**irst and **S**econd graph titles when displaying the graph. Second, the **F**irst and **S**econd titles look very much alike in size and intensity on the screen, but the PrintGraph program prints the **F**irst title much larger than the **S**econd. (This capability is explained in the following chapter.)

Changing the Automatic Scale Settings

Symphony automatically sets the scale (upper and lower limits) of the **Y**-axis according to the range you designate. This feature is extremely convenient. Symphony uses a scale that shows all the data points in the graph with the graph filling as much of the window as possible. If Symphony did not automatically set the scale, creating graphs would be much more cumbersome.

Sometimes you may want to change the scale that Symphony has chosen for a graph. For example, you may want to focus attention on a certain range of values, such as those surrounding a target goal, or you may want to create a series of graphs that all have the same scale.

Overriding Automatic Scaling

You can override Symphony's automatic scaling in several ways. The commands for overriding automatic scaling are accessed through the **2nd**-Settings **Y**-Scale and **X**-Scale commands. Suppose that you have selected **2nd**-Settings **Y**-Scale. The following menu appears:

Type **F**ormat **E**xponent **W**idth **Q**uit

The **T**ype option selects the kind of scale overriding that you want. Symphony usually uses linear scales, but you also can set logarithmic scales. The options that appear once you have selected **T**ype are as follows:

Manual-Linear **A**utomatic-Linear **L**ogarithmic

The **M**anual-Linear option manually overrides Symphony's automatic scaling in a linear fashion. With **M**anual-Linear, you must manually set the lower and upper boundaries of the scale. **L**ogarithmic, on the other hand, enables you to override Symphony's automatic linear scaling in a logarithmic fashion; however, Symphony still sets the upper and lower boundaries on its own. (See "Advanced Graphics Options" at the end of this chapter for more information on logarithmic scaling.)

Cue:
Use the Manual-Linear option to change the scale of the Y-axis.

When you choose **M**anual-Linear, Symphony requests upper and lower boundaries for the scale limits. Figure 14.7 shows how this function works. This figure uses the same data as figure 14.5, except that the scale has been changed to show an upper limit of 60 and a lower limit of -60.

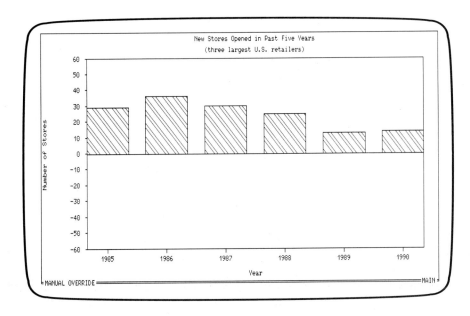

Fig. 14.7.
Manually overriding Symphony's automatic scaling.

If you decide that you want to eliminate the manual overrides you have set up, you can select the **A**utomatic-Linear option to reset the scaling to automatic.

Formatting Numbers

The **F**ormat option of the **2**nd-Settings **X**- and **Y**-Scale commands enables you to change the way the numbers on the **X**-axis and **Y**-axis are displayed. The alternatives under this option are the same as those for the SHEET **F**ormat command. You can specify that the numbers be displayed with a fixed number of digits, with a $ or embedded comma, or as a percentage with an appended % sign. For example, figure 14.8 shows the same graph as figure 14.7, except that in figure 14.8 the scale has been assigned the **F**ixed **2** format.

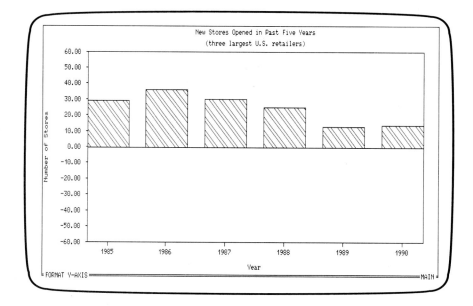

Fig. 14.8.

*The **Y**-axis labels formatted to **F**ixed 2.*

Changing to Nonzero Origin

When you use the **M**anual-Linear option, Symphony always ignores a positive lower limit or a negative upper limit on the **Y**-axis scale; this feature ensures that zero (the origin) is always on the scale. Symphony offers another option, however, that enables you to change a graph's origin. This option is accessed through the **2**nd-**S**ettings **O**ther **O**rigin command. For example, you can change the origin of the graph in figure 14.5 from 0 to 10. Figure 14.9 shows how the graph changes. Note that to display the data, you must reset the graph to **A**utomatic-Linear.

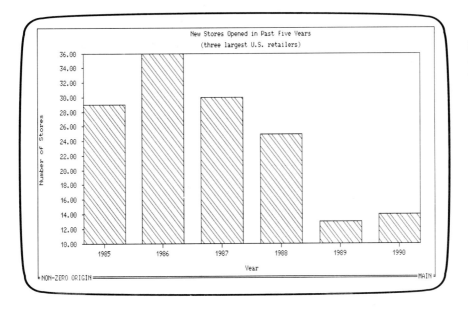

Fig. 14.9.
A graph with a nonzero origin.

Using Other Scale Options

Several other scale options also format graphs. These options include logarithmic scaling, controlling the width of **Y**-axis scale numbers, and controlling Symphony's scaling messages. These options are best applied to more complex graphs and therefore are discussed in "Advanced Graphics Options" at the end of this chapter.

Saving and Recalling Graph Settings

Only one set of graph settings can be the *current* graph settings. Before you can build a new set of graph settings sheets, you must store the old ones.

By invoking the **N**ame option from either the **1**st- or **2**nd-Settings command menu, you can instruct Symphony to remember the parameters stored in the current graph settings sheets. The **N**ame command gives you these options:

    Use **C**reate **D**elete **P**revious **N**ext **I**nitial-Settings **R**eset **Q**uit

With the **C**reate option, you can create a 15-character name for the current settings. All the settings in both the **1**st- and **2**nd-**S**ettings sheets—the data range settings, graph titles, and axis titles—are saved under this name. For example, you can name your current graph BASIC BAR. The new name appears in the lower right corner of both the **1**st- and **2**nd-Settings sheets; when you save the Symphony file, the name is saved as part of the spreadsheet.

Reminder:
*By invoking the **N**ame option from either the lst- or 2nd-Settings command menu, you can instruct Symphony to remember the parameters stored in the current graph settings sheet.*

You can recall a named set of **1**st- and **2**nd-Settings sheets at any time by issuing the **N**ame **U**se command. When you issue this command, Symphony presents a list of all the named sets of graph settings stored in the current worksheet (the *settings catalog*). You can select the set you want by typing the name from the keyboard or pointing to the name in the list. Symphony then retrieves the **1**st- and **2**nd-Settings sheets of the named set and makes them the current set. To see this graph in SHEET mode, choose SHEET **G**raph **P**review.

If you save a file without naming the current graph settings, Symphony still keeps your current graph settings.

Using Graph Settings Catalogs

You can create several different graph settings sheets for a single file, even for a single window. The entire group of settings in a worksheet file is called a catalog. The **N**ame **C**reate and **N**ame **U**se commands make it easy to create and use a catalog of settings sheets. For example, the settings sheets for all the various graphs in this chapter are contained in a single catalog. After each settings sheet was created, it was attached to a GRAPH window, and a picture of the graph was taken.

Two other options available in the **N**ame menu help you select settings sheets from a catalog. These commands are **P**revious and **N**ext. When you select **P**revious, Symphony automatically selects the settings sheet that alphabetically precedes the current settings sheet in the catalog. For example, suppose that you had the following catalog of settings names:

POOR SCALES	OVERRIDE
MAIN TEXT	LOGARITHMIC
X-AXIS LABELS	MANUAL
BASIC BAR	MANY PARTS
FORMAT Y-AXIS	NONZERO ORIGIN

If the current settings name is BASIC BAR and you select **P**revious, Symphony shifts the current settings to X-AXIS LABELS. If the current settings name is POOR SCALES when you choose **P**revious, however, Symphony uses the last entry in the list, NONZERO ORIGIN. The **N**ext option works just the opposite from **P**revious.

Deleting Graph Settings

To delete a single settings name from the worksheet, use the **1**st-or **2**nd-Settings **N**ame **D**elete command. As with the **N**ame **C**reate command, Symphony prompts you with a list of all the settings names in the current worksheet file. You can point to the name you want to delete, or type the name from the keyboard.

To delete all the settings names, you can issue **N**ame **R**eset. This command automatically deletes all the settings names in the catalog. Be careful. When you delete the settings names, all the settings for all the graphs in the current file are lost. A "Yes/No" confirmation step in the **N**ame **R**eset command gives you a second chance if you accidentally type **R** for **R**eset. After you enter **Y**es, however, all the settings for all the graphs are gone.

You must remember two rules in regard to deleting graph names. First, you cannot delete the current settings name. For example, suppose that FORMAT Y-AXIS is the current graph settings name. You must make another settings name current before you can delete FORMAT Y-AXIS.

A second thing to remember about deleting settings names in Symphony is that the program provides no barrier to deleting a settings name that is attached to a GRAPH window. The GRAPH window then simply appears blank on the screen, and the settings for the GRAPH window are reset to the default configuration settings.

Resetting All the Current Graph Settings

Instead of deleting a settings name, you can completely reset all the settings associated with that name by using the **N**ame **I**nitial-Settings command. When you select the **I**nitial-Settings option, Symphony resets the current settings sheet to the default settings. For example, suppose that you have created what you thought were the correct settings for a graph of revenue projections and named the settings PROJECT REVENUE. Suppose also that you later discover that the settings in PROJECT REVENUE are all wrong. You can go through a detailed sequence of making current another settings name, deleting PROJECT REVENUE with the **N**ame **D**elete command, and finally re-creating PROJECT REVENUE with **N**ame **C**reate. A much easier way to reset all the settings for PROJECT REVENUE, however, is to use the **I**nitial-Settings command while the name is still current.

Resetting a Portion of the Current Graph Settings

Besides resetting all the current settings for a particular name, you also can delete selected settings with the **1**st-Settings **C**ancel command. In fact, you can delete all or just a portion of the **1**st-Settings with this command. Settings that you can delete include range addresses, formats, data labels, legends, and hues (colors or patterns). For example, suppose that you have the **1**st-Settings sheet that appears in figure 14.10. Notice all of the settings for the A range (**R**ange, **H**ue, **D**ata-Labels, and **L**egend).

To delete only the range addresses from the A row, select **C**ancel from the **1**st-Settings menu. The following options then appear:

Entire-Row **R**ange **F**ormat **D**ata-Labels **L**egend **H**ue

Fig. 14.10.

An example of a 1st-Settings sheet.

```
 Switch to 2nd-Settings                                         MENU
 Switch  Type  Range  Hue  Format  Data-Labels  Legend  Cancel  Name  Quit

      Type:      Bar

   Range                 Hue  Format  Data-Labels        Legend

   X B4..G4              1
   A B6..G6              5            A B6..G6            \a6
   B                     3
   C                     4
   D                     5
   E                     6
   F                     7
                                          Graph 1st-Settings: RANGE CANCEL
```

Select **R**ange, which produces the following menu:

> **G**raph **X A B C D E F Q**uit

To cancel the A range, select **A**. The **1**st-Settings sheet then appears as shown in figure 14.11. Notice that this cancellation does not affect the other A range settings (**H**ue, **D**ata-Labels, **L**egend).

Fig. 14.11.

After canceling the A-range addresses.

```
 For A range                                                    MENU
 Graph  X  A  B  C  D  E  F  Quit

      Type:      Bar

   Range                 Hue  Format  Data-Labels        Legend

   X B4..G4              1
   A                     5            A B6..G6            \a6
   B                     3
   C                     4
   D                     5
   E                     6
   F                     7
                                          Graph 1st-Settings: RANGE CANCEL
```

If you want to delete all the entries for the A range (**H**ue, **F**ormat, **D**ata-Labels, and **L**egends), select the **1**st-Settings **C**ancel **E**ntire-Row **A** command. The **1**st-Settings sheet then looks like figure 14.12.

To delete all the settings for the entire graph, select **1**st-Settings **C**ancel **E**ntire-Row **G**raph. Symphony resets all the settings in the **1**st-Settings sheet to the default settings.

```
For A range                                          MENU
Graph  X  🔲  B  C  D  E  F  Quit
    ┌──────────────────────────────────────────────────────┐
    │    Type:      Bar                                     │
    │                                                      │
    │   Range              Hue  Format  Data-Labels    Legend │
    │                                                      │
    │   X B4..G4            1                              │
    │   A                   2                              │
    │   B                   3                              │
    │   C                   4                              │
    │   D                   5                              │
    │   E                   6                              │
    │   F                   7                              │
    └──────────────────────────Graph 1st-Settings: RANGE CANCEL┘
```

Saving Graphs for Printing

As mentioned earlier, the main Symphony program does not have the capability of printing graphs. You must use the PrintGraph program or Allways add-in for this task. Before you can print a graph with PrintGraph or Allways, however, you must save the graph. The **I**mage-Save option from the GRAPH menu or SHEET **G**raph menu saves the current graph settings, including all the selected formatting options. All saved graph files have the extension PIC.

Once you have created a PIC file, you can no longer access it from Symphony. The PIC file is accessible only from PrintGraph or Allways. If you want to re-create the graph on-screen from within Symphony, you must give the settings a name in the current worksheet file. See the next chapter for detailed information on using PrintGraph or see Chapter 13 for printing graphs in Allways.

Reminder:

The main Symphony program cannot print graphs. You must use the PrintGraph program or Allways add-in for this task.

Reminder:

Once you create a PIC file, you no longer can access it from Symphony. Such files are accessible only through PrintGraph or Allways.

Creating a More Complex Bar Graph

Increasing the complexity of the bar graph shown in figure 14.5 may help you understand more about Symphony's graph capabilities. You can build a more complex bar graph by including the data for the two other major U.S. retailers, K Mart and J. C. Penney, with the Sears data you have already graphed.

This chart adds to the settings in the basic bar graph you have been working on. If you want to keep the original bar graph, create a new graph name before you continue with this section. From either settings menus (**1**st-Settings or **2**nd-Settings) choose **N**ame **C**reate and enter COMPLEX BAR.

Adding More Data Ranges

After you create a new settings name, your next step is to specify two additional data ranges. You must first access the **1**st-Settings **R**ange menu. Because you have already created one data range, the next set of data goes into the B range. To enter the data range, select **B** from the **R**ange menu and indicate the range B7..G7 (see fig. 14.1). To enter the third data set, select **C** and indicate the location of the data: B8..G8. If you are in a SHEET window, use **G**raph **P**review to draw the graph. The graph then appears as shown in figure 14.13.

Fig. 14.13.

A bar graph with three data ranges.

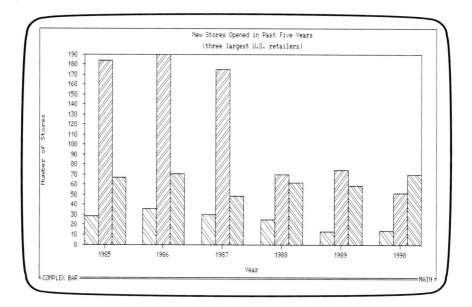

For an additional challenge, you may try creating a special graph window. To do so, use the SERVICES **W**indow **C**reate command and enter a window name; you may want to use MY GRAPH for the name. You can then call up the GRAPH menu by selecting the Menu key (F10). Finally, use the **A**ttach option from the GRAPH menu to attach the settings to the window.

Using Legends

Reminder:

Legends are necessary whenever the graph contains more than one set of data.

Whenever you have more than one set of data on a graph, you need some method to distinguish one set from another. Symphony has several ways to help you distinguish data sets. Line graphs provide different symbols to mark the different data points. Bar charts use different patterns of crosshatches. If your display is on a color monitor, Symphony can also use color to make the distinction.

Even with the different patterns of color or crosshatches, legends to label the patterns are necessary. At the bottom of figure 14.14, below the **X**-axis, are three different legends corresponding to the three different ranges of data already graphed. You enter these legends with the **1**st-Settings **L**egend command. After you have selected this option, you type the actual legend text. For example, you can enter **Sears** for legend A. Or, as with titles, you can enter legends with a backslash (\) and a cell reference or range name. For example, you can enter \A6 for **1**st-Settings **L**egend **A**, \A7 for **B**, and \A8 for **C**. The legends in the settings sheet shown in figure 14.15 were entered with this method. The corresponding graph is shown in figure 14.14.

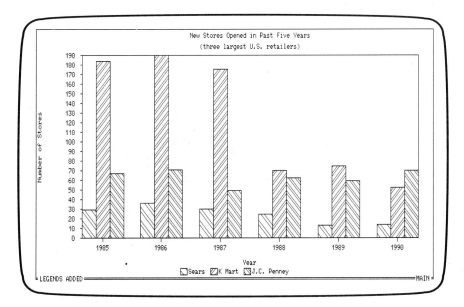

Fig. 14.14.
A bar graph with legends.

Fig. 14.15.
Using cell references to enter legends.

Controlling Bar Graph Crosshatches

Notice the different crosshatches within the bars in figure 14.14. The earlier bar graphs in this chapter also contained crosshatches, but because only one set of data was included, only one pattern of crosshatches appeared. Because the graph in figure 14.14 has several sets of data, the contrast between crosshatches is much greater. Crosshatching makes it easy to distinguish among different data sets when they are graphed in black and white. Normally, Symphony controls the crosshatches for you.

Although most of the time you may want Symphony to control the crosshatching, the program does allow you to select patterns yourself. Symphony offers seven different crosshatching patterns with a numbering scheme of 1 through 7. Figure 14.16 shows the patterns and their respective numbers.

Fig. 14.16.

Available bar graph crosshatching patterns.

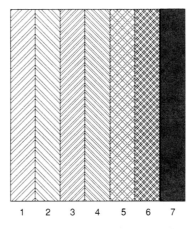

Suppose that you prefer the patterns numbered 5 through 7. To change the patterns for the data sets, use the **1**st-Settings **H**ue command. If you want to change the patterns for data set A to pattern 5, choose **A 5**; to change data set B to pattern 6, use **H**ue **B 6**; and so on. Figures 14.17 and 14.18 show the **1**st-Settings sheet and associated bar graph with these selected patterns.

On the **1**st-Settings sheet, the **H**ue for range X is 1. Changing the **H**ue selection for range X has no effect when you are displaying a graph in black and white. When you are using color, though, the **H**ue selection enables you to change the color of the labels below the **X**-axis.

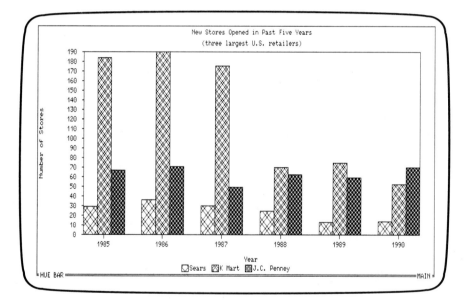

Fig. 14.17.
The 1st-Settings sheet after changing the crosshatching patterns.

Fig. 14.18.
The resulting bar graph.

Displaying the Graph in Color

If you have a color monitor, you can instruct Symphony to display graphics in color. The capability to produce colors is one of the nicest features of the program. Just what colors Symphony uses depends on your hardware. If you have a Color Graphics Adapter (CGA), Symphony can display graphics in only three different colors (white, red, and blue). These colors are not to be confused, however, with the large selection of colors the program can use for printing graphs if you have the appropriate printer or plotter. (Printing graphs and the additional colors available are covered in the following chapter.)

To display in color the graph from figure 14.18, select **C**olor **Y**es from the **2**nd-Settings **O**ther menu. You can then set the bars and lines for the data and label ranges to different colors. Symphony offers the following hues for computers with CGA monitors:

Hue Number	Actual Color	EGA/VGA
1	White	White
2	Red	Yellow
3	Blue	Purple
4	White	Blue
5	Red	Red
6	Blue	Light Blue
7	White	Chartreuse (yellow/green)

The list of colors available for a CGA monitor is obviously somewhat limited, and the colors for your particular machine may be different. Computers with Enhanced Graphic Adapters (EGA) can have up to seven different colors. You should consult your dealer if you have any questions about what colors Symphony can produce on your machine.

Changing Colors in Bar Graphs

If you don't like the colors that Symphony chooses for the different ranges, you can change the hues. For example, suppose that you prefer the outside scales and numbers to be red and the bars to be blue for data range A, white for B, and red for C. Use the **1**st-Settings **H**ue command to make the appropriate changes. To select red for the outside scales and numbers, choose **1**st-Settings **H**ue **X 2**; to have blue for range A, use **1**st-Settings **H**ue **A 3**.

You can also use the **H**ue option to control the crosshatches. Whether Symphony uses colors or crosshatches for filling in the bars in a bar graph depends on whether you have invoked color. Unfortunately, on bar graphs, you cannot have colors and crosshatches at the same time. (You can with pie charts; see the section titled "Pie Chart Crosshatches," later in this chapter.)

Using Stacked-Bar Graphs

A slight variation of the basic bar graph is the stacked-bar graph. Stacked-bar graphs are frequently used to compare different sets of data while showing the components and total of each data set. In these graphs, the totals are created by stacking the component data items one on another.

In figure 14.19, you can see the total number of store openings for the three largest U.S. retailers. This graph uses the same settings as the COMPLEX BAR graph you created earlier except it is a stacked-bar instead of a basic bar. All you have to do to create this graph is choose **S**tacked-Bar on the **T**ype menu. **P**review draws the graph in the SHEET environment.

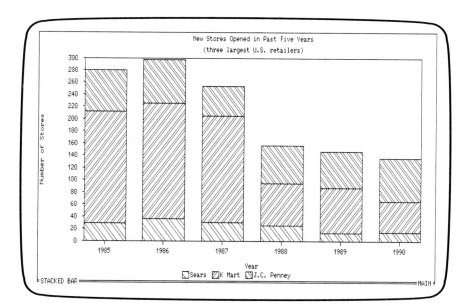

Fig. 14.19.
A stacked-bar graph.

Using Line Graphs

Symphony also offers line graphs, which are particularly useful for showing time-series data but are by no means restricted to this use. Consider the data on European Foreign Currency that appears in figure 14.20. These data list the month-end exchange rates for French francs and West German deutsche marks. (These data are fictitous.)

Create a line graph of the French franc plotted against time. Since **L i n e** is the default graph type, you don't need to specify the **T**ype setting. Select **1**st-Settings **R**ange **A** and specify the A range, C8..C19. The next step is to enter the range of dates in column B as the **X** range. As with the bar graphs shown earlier, you enter **X**-axis labels by selecting the **X** option from the **1**st-Settings **R**ange menu. In this example, use the range B8..B19.

As always, the graph is drawn with **P**review when you are in the SHEET environment and is automatically displayed when you are in the GRAPH environment. Figure 14.21 illustrates this line graph.

Fig. 14.20.

Sample exchange rate data.

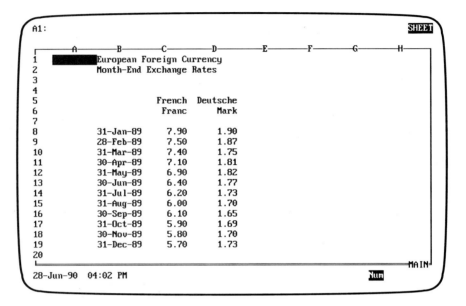

Fig. 14.21.

A line graph drawn from the French franc data.

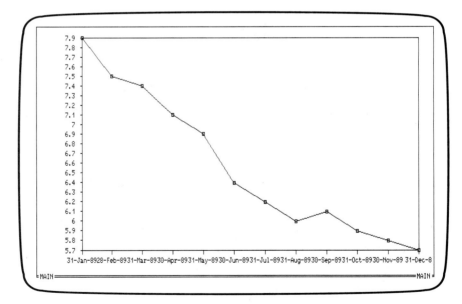

Skipping Labels

Using the entire set of data labels in column B causes a minor problem—the graph simply does not have enough room to display all the labels without overlapping them. This problem can occur any time you have many X labels or unusually long ones.

Symphony offers two solutions. One option is to reformat the dates in a shorter form (for instance, format D2—DD/MMM). If you prefer not to change the format, however, you can use the **2**nd-Settings **O**ther **S**kip command to skip every nth X label when the graph is displayed. After you enter the command, Symphony prompts you for the skipping factor. In most cases, as in the example shown in figure 14.22, skipping every other label (specifying a factor of **2**) is sufficient to clean up the graph. On some graphs, however, it may be necessary to choose a much larger factor. Symphony has the capability to skip as many as 8,192 X labels.

Cue:

*When the X-axis labels overlap, specify a skipping factor with the **2**nd-Settings **O**ther **S**kip command.*

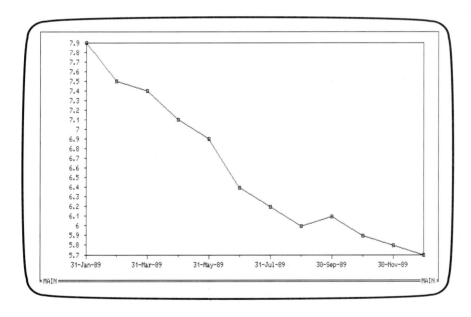

Fig. 14.22.

*After specifying a skipping factor of **2**.*

Finishing the Graph

Once again, titles have been added to the graph (see fig. 14.23). To add these titles, select **T**itles from the **2**nd-Settings menu and enter the titles shown for **F**irst, **S**econd, and **Y**-axis.

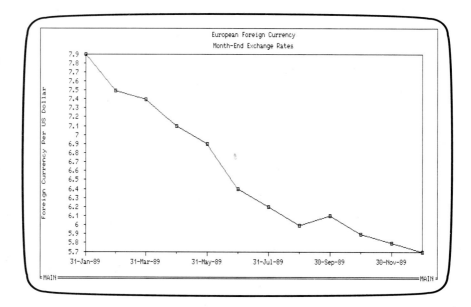

Fig. 14.23.

The line graph with titles.

Now, add the exchange rates for deutsche marks. Create a B range that specifies the data in range D8..D19. Also specify the Legend for the A range as \C6 and the B range as \D6. Figure 14.24 illustrates the new graph.

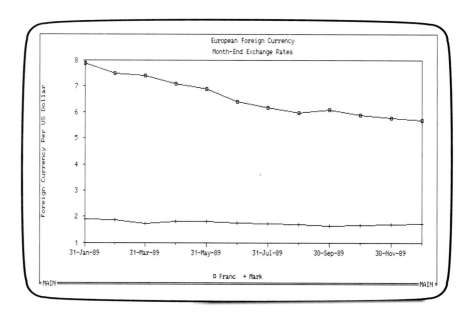

Fig. 14.24.

A line graph with two data ranges.

Controlling Lines and Symbols

Notice the different symbols (box and plus) at the points of intersection on the graph. So far, you have seen only one of the four ways of displaying a line graph. The command that controls the lines and symbols at the points of intersection on a line graph is **1**st-Settings Format **A** through **F**. After you choose one of the ranges from A through F, Symphony provides the following options:

> **L**ines **S**ymbols **B**oth **N**either

Lines signals Symphony to connect the different data points with straight lines and no symbols. Figure 14.25 shows the graph from figure 14.24 with lines only for both ranges.

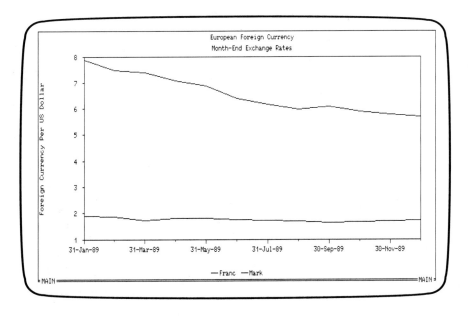

Fig. 14.25.

A line graph with lines but no symbols.

The **S**ymbols option tells Symphony to leave out the straight lines and use different graphic symbols for each data range. The symbols are as follows:

A □	D ▷
B +	E x
C ◇	F ▽

Figure 14.26 shows the graph with symbols but no lines. Although you can use this format with line charts, it is more commonly used with XY plots.

The third choice, **B**oth, is the default used in figures 14.21 through 14.24 to produce both lines and symbols. Because it is difficult to tell one data set from another without using both lines and symbols, **B**oth is the preferred option in most cases.

Fig. 14.26.

A line graph with symbols but no lines.

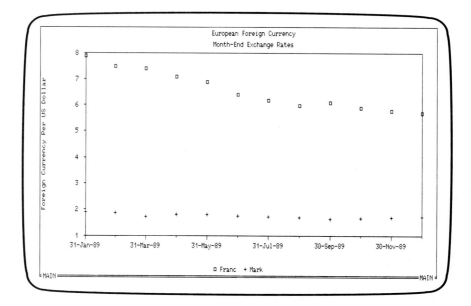

The **N**either option suppresses both lines and symbols. You may wonder how points of intersection can be shown if neither lines nor symbols appear on the graph. The answer is through **D**ata-Labels.

Using Data-Labels

Cue:

Use the Data-Labels option to label each data point with its exact value.

Symphony's **D**ata-Labels command uses data from a SHEET window as labels in a graph. These labels are placed in the graph near the data points. The **D**ata-Labels option is a part of the **G**raph **1**st-Settings menu. After you choose **1**st-Settings **D**ata-Labels, the following menu appears:

A B C D E F Quit

Notice that the options here correspond to the data range options; one set of data labels exists for each set of data. In general, you may want to use the same coordinates to define the data labels and the data range. After you indicate the range containing the data labels, Symphony gives you the choice of placing the data labels above or below the data point, centered on the data point, or to the left or right of the data point.

The data labels can be numbers or text. In most cases, you may want to use numbers as data labels. You can use text to briefly explain why a data point is particularly high or low. If you use text, be sure to keep the strings short to avoid cluttering the graph.

Figures 14.27 and 14.28 show the **1**st-Settings sheet and sample line graph with data labels and without symbols or lines. You can use data labels in a line chart that includes lines and symbols, as well as in a graph that contains no lines or symbols. In fact, in line charts with multiple data sets, you need lines or symbols to differentiate the various data sets. Otherwise, the graph looks like a jumble of numbers as shown in figure 14.28.

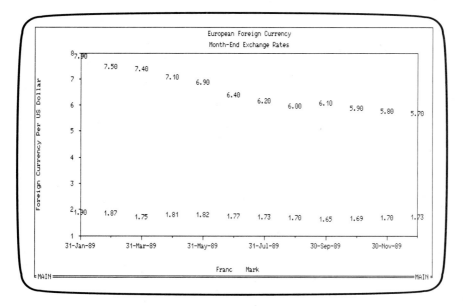

Fig. 14.27.
A 1st-Settings sheet with data labels and without symbols or lines.

Fig. 14.28.
A line graph with data labels and two data sets.

If you are not using lines or symbols (on a line graph), you may want to center the data labels on the data points. Otherwise, you will want to choose one of the other options to avoid cluttering the graph.

Data labels also work with bar graphs. In bar graphs, the labels are centered above each bar. As with line charts, data labels in bar graphs can be helpful in identifying the numeric value associated with each data point.

Sometimes it is easy to get confused about the difference among the X-axis titles, the X labels, and the data labels. An X-axis title usually describes the units of measure used on the X-axis (like dollars or years). X labels distinguish the different data points (for example, 1987 and 1988 data). Data labels describe individual data items.

Adding Grids

Cue:

Use grids to increase readability of individual data points.

Symphony offers still another option for formatting graphs: **G**rid. The command to create a grid is **2**nd-Settings **O**ther **G**rid. The submenu under this command offers the following choices:

    Horizontal **V**ertical **B**oth **N**one

The first choice creates a horizontal grid that extends from each tick-mark on the Y-axis scale. This type of grid is shown in figure 14.29. A vertical grid has vertical lines extending from each label on the X-axis. The **B**oth choice causes both types of grids to display. The last choice, **N**one, eliminates all grids from the current graph settings.

Horizontal grids are probably the most common.

Fig. 14.29.

A horizontal grid.

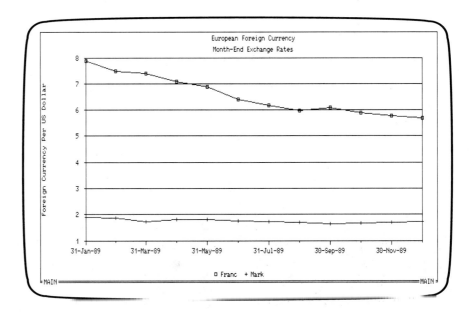

Using Pie Charts

Pie charts, another of Symphony's graph types, show relationships within a single set of data items. Each data item is a slice of the pie, and the entire pie represents the sum of the slices.

In many ways, a pie chart is the simplest of Symphony's graphs. Only one data range can be represented by a pie chart, so only the **1**st-Settings **R**ange **A** option is needed to define a pie. Because a pie chart has no axes, you cannot use the X- and Y-axis titles. Similarly, grids, scales, and data labels are not used with pie charts.

Reminder:
Only one data range can be represented by a pie chart.

One convenient way to show the advantages as well as the limitations of a pie chart is to add data to figure 14.1. As you can see in figure 14.30, the additional data are simply the regions and their respective store openings for the year 1990.

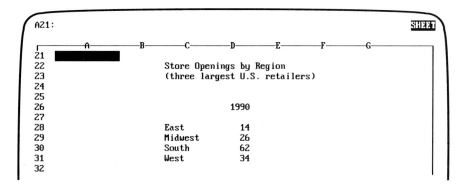

```
A21:                                                              SHEET
┌─────────A────────B────────C────────D────────E────────F────────G──────┐
21 ███████████████
22                        Store Openings by Region
23                        (three largest U.S. retailers)
24
25
26                                  1990
27
28                        East         14
29                        Midwest      26
30                        South        62
31                        West         34
32
```

Fig. 14.30.
Sample data for a pie chart.

To create a pie chart from the data in figure 14.30, first select **P**ie from the **1**st-Settings **T**ype menu. Next, indicate D28..D31 as the A range. Because pie charts do not have an X- or a Y-axis, Symphony adopts the convention of using the X-range as the captions for the slices of the pie. Here you designate C28..C31 as the X label range. Figure 14.31 shows the resulting graph.

In this pie chart, you should notice the number of slices in the pie and the percentages next to the labels. The number of slices in the pie corresponds to the number of data items in the A range—in this case, four. The most important limitation on the number of data items used in a pie chart is that the labels tend to get bunched up if you use too many items. Each situation is different, but you may need to collect some of the smaller slices into an "Other" category if you have too many data items.

Fig. 14.31.

The pie graph based on the data in figure 14.30.

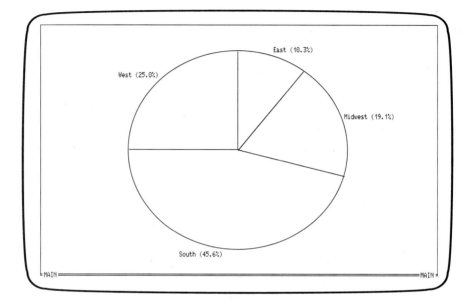

The point of a pie chart is to show the relationship of each data item to the whole. Symphony automatically calculates the percentage of each slice and places this percentage next to the appropriate label. It would be nice, however, if you also displayed the value of each data item next to the percentage. Although the basic Symphony program does not offer this feature, you can use an add-on package such as Allways, Freelance Plus®, or Graphwriter II.

Understanding The Aspect Ratio

The aspect ratio is the ratio of height to width in a graph. For most graph types, changing the aspect ratio slightly has no adverse visual effect. When you change the aspect ratio in a pie chart, however, the pie may be noticeably *not* round. In fact, even with the same aspect ratio, some computers may show a round pie chart, but others may show the same pie as an ellipse. Therefore, Symphony offers a special command to control the aspect ratio of pie charts: **2**nd-Settings **O**ther **A**spect. If you find that your pie charts do not look round, you may want to use this command.

Setting Up Pie Chart Crosshatches

Symphony also gives you the choice of using crosshatches in pie charts. Pie charts have the same number of crosshatching patterns as bar charts, but the patterns themselves are different. Figure 14.32 shows Symphony's pie chart crosshatching patterns.

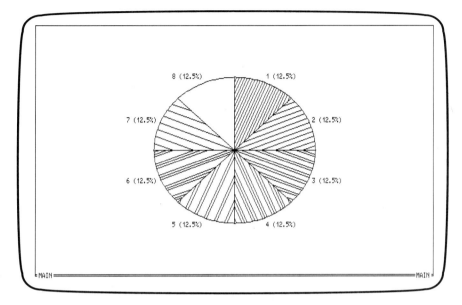

Fig. 14.32.
Available pie chart crosshatching patterns.

When setting up crosshatching patterns for a bar chart, you use the **H**ue choice from the **1**st-Settings menu. With pie charts, you must set up a special range of values containing hatching pattern numbers. (Lotus also calls them "hue" numbers.) You then assign the range of pattern numbers to the B range of the pie chart. Because pie charts do not use the B range for assigning other data, this range is free for pattern numbers.

Reminder:
To add patterns to a pie chart, specify a B-range.

For example, suppose that you want to assign pattern 1 to the first slice of the pie chart. Then, starting at the top of the pie chart and moving clockwise, pattern 2 is assigned to slice 2; pattern 3 to slice 3; and so on. To get the proper crosshatching patterns, you must place the pattern numbers in the worksheet (as they appear in the range F28..F31 in fig. 14.33) and assign them to the B range. If you set **C**olor to **N**o, using the **2**nd-Settings **O**ther command, the pie chart then appears as illustrated in figure 14.34.

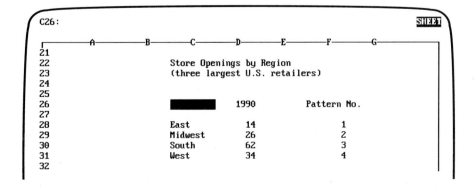

Fig. 14.33.
Placing the crosshatching patterns in the worksheet.

Fig. 14.34.

The pie chart after specifying crosshatching patterns.

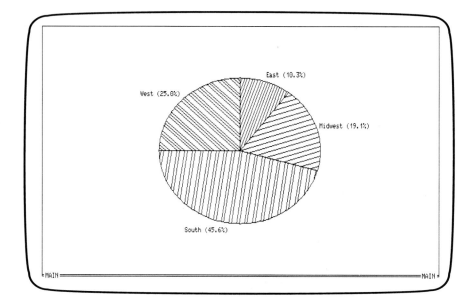

Using Color in Pie Charts

Unlike a bar graph, you can use both color and crosshatches in a pie chart; but whenever you use color in a pie chart, Symphony automatically draws all slices with the same crosshatch pattern. When you use color, the values you code in the B range control the color of the slices but not their crosshatch patterns.

For example, suppose that you want to reproduce in color the pie chart shown in figure 14.34. If you have a Color Graphics Adapter, you assign the colors just as you do for bar charts.

B-Range Value	Actual Color	EGA/VGA
0 or blank	No color, no crosshatches	Same
1	White	Same
2	Red	Yellow
3	Blue	Purple
4	White	Blue
5	Red	Red
6	Blue	Light Blue
7	White	Green

Notice that a B-range value of 0 causes Symphony to omit both color and crosshatches.

You can choose from seven different colors if you have a computer with an Enhanced Graphics Adapter.

Symphony draws the labels, titles, and percentages, using the **H**ue designated for the X range. The slices are outlined with the **H**ue specified in the A range. Remember that the **1**st-Settings **H**ue numbers have no bearing on the colors in a pie chart; the values in the B range determine the color.

Reminder:

Remember that the 1st-Settings Hue numbers have no bearing on the colors in a pie chart; the values in the B range determine the color.

Making Exploded Pie Charts

Exploded pie charts enable you to draw emphasis to one or more slices in a pie chart. By adding a value of 100 to the normal B-range value, you can have Symphony set a slice apart from the others. For example, suppose that you want to produce the graph shown in figure 14.34 but with the slice for the West Coast region exploded. The spreadsheet in figure 14.35 shows how you must change the B range, and figure 14.36 shows the exploded pie chart.

You can explode more than one slice in a pie chart. Simply add 100 to each B-range pattern number that you want to explode.

Cue:

By adding a value of 100 to the normal B-range value, you can have Symphony set a slice apart from the others.

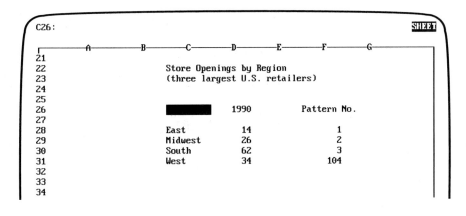

Fig. 14.35.
Adding 100 to the West region's B-range value.

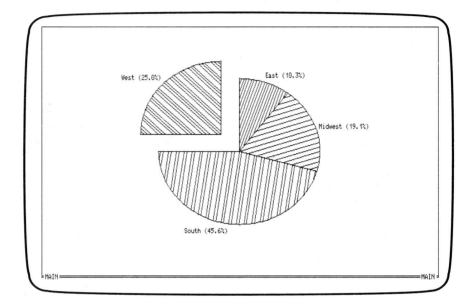

Fig. 14.36.

The pie chart with the West slice exploded.

Creating XY Graphs

Symphony also offers XY graphs, which are sometimes called scatter plots. In an XY graph, two or more data items from the same data range can share the same X value. Obviously, this arrangement is not possible with a line chart. XY graphs are not used to show time series data. Instead, XY graphs help to illustrate the relationships between different attributes of data items, such as age and income or educational achievements and salary.

In an XY graph, the X labels become more than simple labels on the graph. They are, in fact, the X-axis scale, which means that an XY graph requires as a minimum of information an X range and an A range.

In every other respect, an XY plot is like a line graph. In fact, you can think of a line graph as a specialized type of XY graph. For an example of an XY graph, look at the data in figure 14.37 and the resulting graph in figure 14.38. (The X range is C6..C19, and the A range is E6..E19 in these figures.)

Reminder:

Typically, XY graphs are displayed with a Symbols-only format.

Note that titles have been added to this graph and that the format has been set to show only symbols rather than both lines and symbols. To set this format, select the **F**ormat option from the **1**st-Settings menu, choose **A**, and specify **S**ymbols. Typically, XY graphs are displayed with this format. You can display the graph, however, using any format you choose. If you format an XY graph to include lines between the data points, be sure that at least one of the data sets is sorted in ascending or descending order. Otherwise, the lines that connect the data points cross one another and make the graph difficult to read.

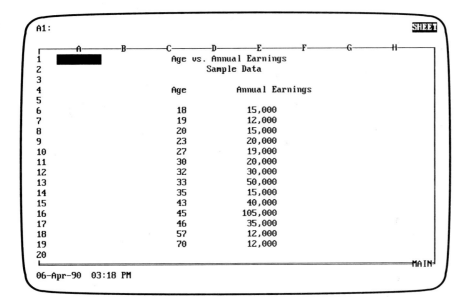

Fig. 14.37.
Sample data for an XY graph.

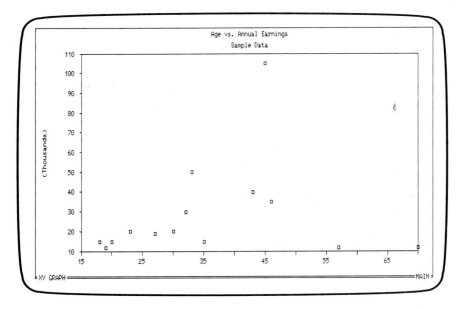

Fig. 14.38.
An XY graph.

Frequently, scatter plots also include a line, called the *regression line*, which is an approximation of the trend suggested by the data in the graph. Unfortunately, Symphony cannot produce an XY graph with a regression line.

Making High-Low-Close-Open Charts

Finally, Symphony offers high-low-close-open graphs. This type of graph is most often used for illustrating the daily price movements of stocks. But you can also track temperatures or financial data that experience price fluctuations.

When setting up the high-low-close-open graph, you should think of it as a special kind of bar graph. For example, to create a bar graph of just the high prices for a series of days, you enter those values as the A range and enter the graph **T**ype as **B**ar. To change the bars to lines, you simply change the graph **T**ype to **H**igh-Low-Close-Open. Figure 14.39 shows some typical stock quotation data, and figure 14.40 illustrates the graph you produce by designating the A range as D6..D15. Specify the X range as C6..C15.

Fig. 14.39.

Sample stock quotation data.

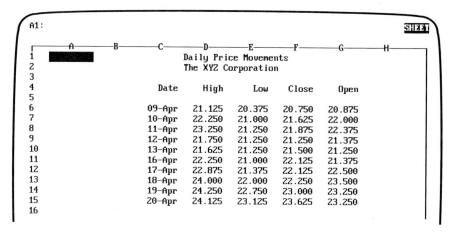

This type of chart, however, is really no more useful than a bar chart of the same data. To add more information to the graph, you must designate a B range. Once again, if the graph were a bar chart, including a B range would simply add another series of bars to the graph. But because the **T**ype is **H**igh-Low-Close-Open, adding a B range has a different effect. Both the high and low prices for each day are combined into a single vertical line.

By adding a third and fourth range to the graph (the C and D ranges), you combine the closing and opening price information into the graph. An example of a high-low-close-open chart is shown in figure 14.41. The closing prices are represented by the right tick marks and the opening prices by the left tick marks on the vertical lines in the graph.

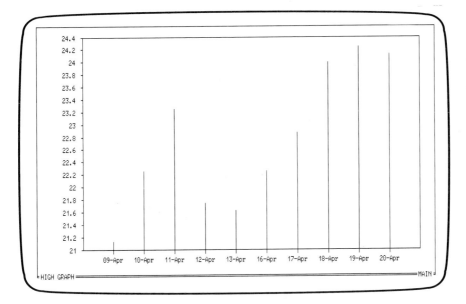

Fig. 14.40.
After designating D6..D15 as the A range.

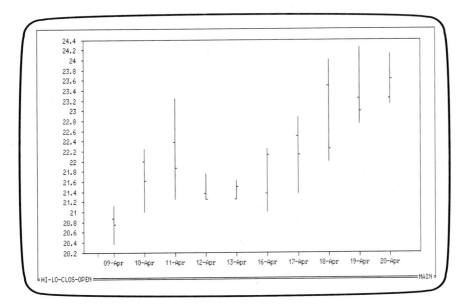

Fig. 14.41.
The high-low-close-open chart.

A good technique to remember when organizing the data for a high-low-close-open chart is to arrange the data in parallel columns in the same sequence as the graph name: high, low, close, open. This method helps to prevent confusion when you must designate ranges for the graph.

Using Advanced Graphics Topics

Symphony has several advanced options relating to GRAPH windows and also some special command options.

Learning More About GRAPH Windows

When you start out with a new file, attaching graph settings to a GRAPH window is fairly simple. You usually have only one graph settings name and one GRAPH window. After you have several graph settings names and GRAPH windows, however, matching the proper settings name with the proper window can be a problem.

Using Current Graph Settings

A typical method for creating graphs is to start in the SHEET environment with the **G**raph command. Then, after you have all the settings and have decided that you want to **A**ttach the settings to a GRAPH window, the first step is to create the new GRAPH window. Interestingly enough, when you create a new graph window, Symphony automatically attaches the current settings to the new window. Although this automatic feature saves work in many cases, it can also create problems in other situations.

For example, suppose that you have created all the graph settings for a pie chart and named the settings PIE1. You then decide that you want to create a second pie chart, PIE2, which is the same as PIE1 but uses color. The first step you take to create the new PIE2 graph settings is to use the **1**st- or **2**nd-Settings **N**ame command to create the new name, PIE2. (If you do not create the new name before modifying the current settings, all the changes are made to the PIE1 settings.) You can then make changes to the current settings; these changes will apply to PIE2.

Now, suppose that you want to **A**ttach the named settings to GRAPH windows. If you start by creating a new GRAPH window to display the PIE1 settings, Symphony automatically attaches the current settings to the new window. Because the current settings are those for PIE2, the new window shows those settings immediately. This feature can be confusing. After you attach the PIE1 settings to the new GRAPH window, though, the window appears as you originally intended. Note. You must always remember the name of the current graph settings. If you are not careful, you may wind up using the wrong graph settings.

Changing from One GRAPH Window to Another

When you are changing from one GRAPH window to another, the current graph settings travel with you. Even though the new window usually has named graph settings of its own, those settings do not appear in the **1**st- and **2**nd-Settings sheets unless you issue the **N**ame **U**se command.

A frequent mistake is to change windows and immediately start altering graph settings. Again, be careful not to make changes to the wrong graph settings.

Reminder:

A frequent mistake is to change windows and immediately start altering graph settings. Be careful not to make changes to the wrong graph settings.

Deleting a GRAPH Window

As you may recall, Symphony does not allow you to delete the current named graph settings. But the program provides no barriers to deleting the current GRAPH window. If you do delete the current GRAPH window, the next most recently accessed window appears on the screen.

Unfortunately, Symphony does not have a **W**indow **R**ename option. Therefore, the best technique for renaming a GRAPH window is to start from the original graph window and create a new window with the appropriate name. If you start from the original window, Symphony uses all its settings when you create the new window. You can then delete the old window, using the SERVICES **W**indow **D**elete command.

Using "What If" Graphing

Symphony's graphics can be an integral part of "what if" analysis. You can use graphics extensively to fine-tune projections, budgets, or projects. You'll be amazed at how graphics helps you understand the impact of changes in your data on the results of your models.

If you select the Shared mode of display when you create your driver set, you can use windowing to perform outstanding "what if" analysis (see Appendix A for more information on setting up drivers). For example, you can set up one window to display spreadsheet data and another window with a related graph; you can then display both windows simultaneously on the screen. When you make a change in the data, the GRAPH window immediately reflects the change. You can even show multiple GRAPH windows on the screen at once. Figure 14.42 shows SHEET and GRAPH windows that appear simultaneously on-screen (see Chapter 2 for more information on windows).

In figure 14.42 the value for 1990 is $190,311. If you increase the value for 1990 by 200,000, the change is immediately reflected in the graph (see fig. 14.43).

Keep in mind that using graphs is a good way to verify the reasonableness of your data. You may be surprised at how much help a simple graph can be for checking your work.

Reminder:

Using graphs is a good way to verify the reasonableness of your data.

Fig. 14.42.

A SHEET and a GRAPH window on-screen simultaneously.

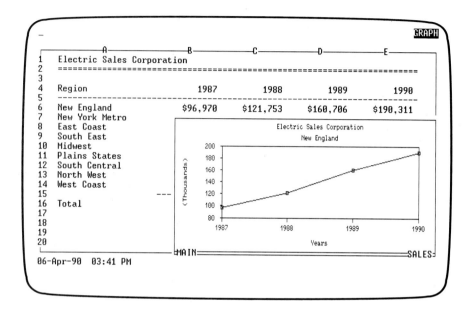

Fig. 14.43.

Changes to the worksheet reflected in the graph.

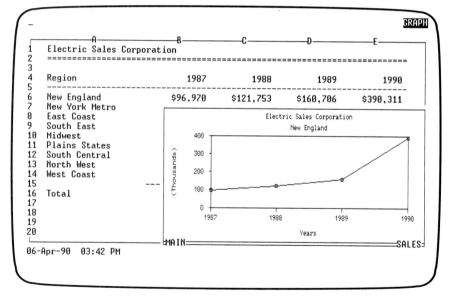

Pressing The Draw Key

GRAPH windows have only one special key associated with them—the Draw key (Alt F8). Pressing the Draw key causes Symphony to redraw automatically all the windows that appear on the screen, GRAPH windows included.

> **Tip**
>
> By turning off the **A**uto-Display you can prevent distracting screen-redrawing when changing a spreadsheet.

The Draw key is normally used with the **A**uto-Display option of the SERVICES **W**indow **S**ettings command. If you set a GRAPH window's **A**uto-Display to **N**o, Symphony does not redisplay that window unless you press Draw (or unless that window is made the current window). For example, suppose that you have the windows appearing on the screen as shown in figure 14.42, and you want to change the data as shown in figure 14.43. If you have set the **A**uto-Display option to **N**o for the GRAPH window on the right side of the screen, when you make the change in the data for the SHEET window on the left, the GRAPH window does not redraw. If you press the Draw key, however, the updated GRAPH window reappears on the right just as in figure 14.43.

Learning Special Command Options

Symphony offers several other special command options. Most of these options involve controlling Symphony's numeric scaling. But some relate to Symphony's capability to hide certain parts of a graph.

Using Logarithmic Scale Override

The advantage of logarithmic scaling is that it enables you to compare very large and very small numbers in a reasonable fashion. Sometimes when you use linear scaling in Symphony, extremely large numbers in a range can dwarf their smaller companion numbers. For example, suppose that you want to create a bar graph of the number of parts produced on a new production process during the first eight months of 1990. Figure 14.44 shows how the graph may appear.

Cue:

The advantage of logarithmic scaling is that it enables you to compare very large and very small numbers in a reasonable fashion.

Because of the relatively large number of parts produced in August (11 million), the smaller quantities for January through April (80 to 10,000) cannot be seen. Figure 14.45 shows the same numbers graphed with the **2**nd-Settings **Y**-Scale **T**ype command set to **L**ogarithmic.

Note that Symphony creates evenly spaced tick marks along the Y-axis; however, the numbers that are assigned to the marks are not evenly distributed numerically. Each tick mark corresponds to a power of 10. For example, the first tick mark corresponds to $10^1=10$, the second mark to $10^2=100$, the third to $10^3=1,000$, and so on. The **2**nd-Settings **Y**-Scale **T**ype **A**utomatic-Linear command resets the Y-axis to automatic linear scaling.

Fig. 14.44.

Problems with linear scaling.

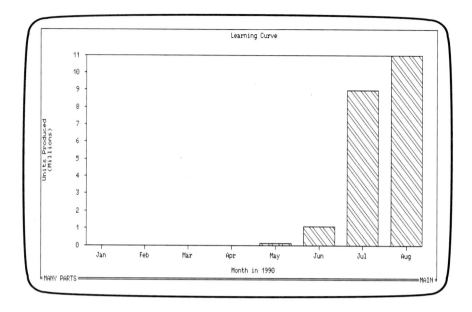

Fig. 14.45.

After issuing 2nd-Settings Y-scale Type Logarithmic.

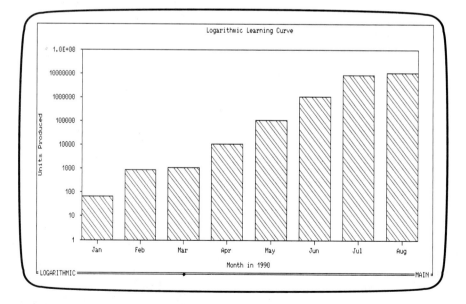

Reminder:

Change the width of the Y-Scale if numbers appear in scientific notation or if asterisks display.

Changing the Y-Axis Scale Width

Notice in figure 14.45 that the largest Y-axis scale number appears in Symphony's scientific format as 1.0E+08. Because the default width of Symphony's scale numbers is nine characters, Symphony is incapable of displaying 100,000,000 (the fixed format equivalent of 1.0E+08). Therefore, Symphony opts for the scientific format. If you want the 100 million scale number to appear in its full fixed format, you can use the **W**idth option of the **2**nd-Settings **Y**-Scale command to change the width to 10 or greater. Conversely, if you set the width to less than nine characters, Symphony shows asterisks. Note: **W**idth is not an option for the **2**nd-Settings **X**-Scale command.

Controlling Symphony's Automatic Scaling Labels

Anyone who graphs very large numbers may experience problems with the program's automatic scaling labels. (Scaling labels are the messages that appear next to the X- and Y-axis labels when the values being graphed are in the thousands or greater.) For example, when you graph numbers in the billions, Symphony uses a scaling factor label of (**Times 1E9**) rather than (**Billions**).

If you don't like the automatic scaling labels that Symphony offers, you can select your own—up to a point. The technique is to specify manually an exponent (power of ten) representing the number of zeros to be truncated when a range is graphed.

For example, suppose that you have the graph in figure 14.46, and you want to change the scaling message from (**Times 1E9**) to something more readable. By using the **M**anual option of the **2**nd-Settings **Y**-Scale **E**xponent command, you can get Symphony to display (**Millions**) by selecting an exponent of 6 (see fig. 14.47). Although Symphony does not show the label (**Billions**), (**Millions**) certainly beats (**Times 1E9**).

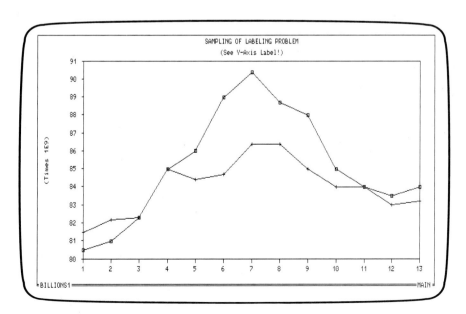

Fig. 14.46.

An example of automatic scaling labels on the Y-axis.

Fig. 14.47.
*After changing the scaling message with **2**nd-Settings **Y**-Scale **E**xponent **M**anual.*

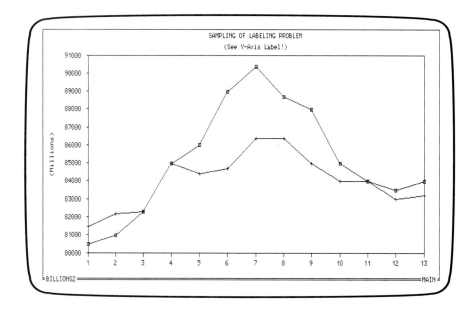

Hiding Parts of a Graph

Symphony enables you to hide all the different elements of a graph that reside outside the box containing the graph. These elements include titles, scale numbers, exponents, and legends. When you select the **H**ide option from the **2**nd-Settings **O**ther command menu, the box portion of the graph occupies the entire window. You can also hide the X- and Y-axis scale numbers by selecting the **H**idden option from the **2**nd-Settings **X**- or **Y**-Scale **F**ormat **O**ther command.

Chapter Summary

Symphony's windowing feature adds a new dimension to the term business graphics. To get a good feel for Symphony's power, you should start working with graphics at the earliest possible point in your introduction to Symphony. The more you work with Symphony's graphics, the more you realize the benefits of the program's integration. The next chapter augments your graphics knowledge by describing Symphony's PrintGraph program for printing graphs.

15

Printing Graphs

As discussed in Chapter 14, you cannot print a graph with the SERVICES **P**rint command; you must use the separate PrintGraph program. Printing a graph requires several steps. First, you must use the **I**mage-Save command on the GRAPH menu to create a special picture file. Then you exit Symphony and load the PrintGraph program. Finally, you select the picture file you want to print and issue the **G**o command to begin printing.

Lotus deviated from its customary all-in-one style because of size. By making PrintGraph a separate program, Lotus decreased the total size of the main program. Unfortunately, this move also limited interactive capability in printing graphs in Symphony.

Still, the PrintGraph program has many strengths; for one, it is easy to use. The menus and command structure are similar to Symphony's main program. The PrintGraph program also enables you to batch process, which means that the program can print several graphs consecutively. Finally, PrintGraph produces high-resolution output on graphics printers and plotters, makes enlargements and reductions, enables rotations, and offers several colors and font types.

Even though Symphony enables you to show graphs and text on the screen simultaneously, you cannot print graphs and text in the same operation unless you use Allways (see Chapter 13).

Accessing the PrintGraph Program

Most often you will probably use PrintGraph immediately after a Symphony session. Before leaving Symphony, make sure that you have saved the graph file by using the Image-Save option from either the SHEET **G**raph or the GRAPH menu (as explained in the previous chapter). Then use the SERVICES **E**xit command to leave Symphony. If you get the ACCESS SYSTEM menu when you exit Symphony, choose the **P**rintGraph option. Otherwise, if you get your system prompt, you can type **access** to display the ACCESS SYSTEM menu or type **pgraph** to directly load PrintGraph.

If you have sufficient RAM, you also can enter the PrintGraph program through the SERVICES DOS command. The advantage of this technique is that you do not have to reload Symphony after leaving PrintGraph; you can go directly back into Symphony by typing **exit** after the system prompt. Be careful, though. Always save your files before trying this technique.

To use this method, you must first attach the DOS.APP file (as explained in Chapter 7). Next, you should check how much RAM is available by using the SERVICES **S**ettings command. If you have approximately 256K left (a conservative estimate), you should be able to run PrintGraph simultaneously with Symphony. You may, however, need more RAM to print several graphs at one time. Once you have left Symphony (using the SERVICES DOS command), type **pgraph** at the system prompt. At this point the PrintGraph program is loaded into memory.

Configuring PrintGraph

To configure PrintGraph, you must first select the appropriate driver set during installation (see Appendix A). The graphics devices you have access to when you run PrintGraph depend entirely on the devices you select during installation. If you do not select any graphics device during installation, you cannot run PrintGraph.

The Install program enables you to select more than one graphics device. (For example, you may have a plotter and a printer.) After you choose one graphics device, you are asked if you have another graphics printer. Each time you answer **Y**es to this question, you can choose another printer. The only restriction is that a device must be supported by Symphony. If your printer or plotter is not on the list of Symphony-supported graphics devices, you may want to call Lotus Development to see whether a device driver has been released for your printer or plotter.

The second stage of configuring PrintGraph occurs after you are in the program; you need to indicate your particular hardware setup. Figure 15.1 shows an example of the PrintGraph screen when you are running the program for the first time.

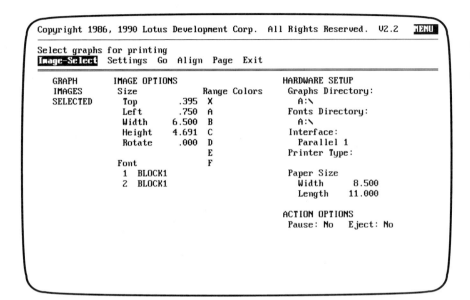

Fig. 15.1.
*The PrintGraph
screen.*

Choosing a Printer

After you are in the program, you need to choose a device to print the graphs—even though you selected a printer during installation. This seemingly redundant step is required for two reasons: you may have selected more than one graphics printer in the Install program; and, because most printers can print in different modes (for example, high and low quality) you must select which mode you want to use.

To select a printer, choose **S**ettings from the main PrintGraph menu, and then choose **H**ardware. The **H**ardware menu includes these options:

Graphs-Directory **F**onts-Directory **I**nterface **P**rinter **S**ize-Paper **Q**uit

Select **P**rinter. After you have made this choice, a menu of the graphics devices you selected during installation appears on the screen (see fig. 15.2). With some printers you may have several choices. For example, in figure 15.2 notice that the Epson RX-80 has choices for high and low density. High density produces the best print quality but takes much longer to print than low density. You may want to choose low density for your rough drafts and switch to high density for your final output.

To select a printer, move the cursor to the appropriate line and press the space bar. This action marks the selected printer with a # symbol. When you press Enter, PrintGraph returns to the hardware settings menu.

Cue:
Choose a low-density printer for a quick, rough-draft graph. Then switch to high-density for your final output.

Fig. 15.2.

A menu of graphics devices.

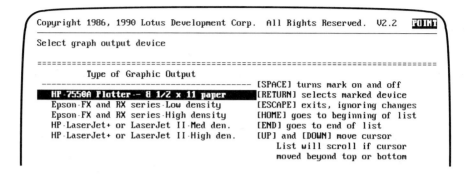

```
Copyright 1986, 1990 Lotus Development Corp.  All Rights Reserved.  V2.2  POINT

Select graph output device

===============================================================================
       Type of Graphic Output
--------------------------------------------  [SPACE] turns mark on and off
  HP-7550A Plotter -- 8 1/2 x 11 paper        [RETURN] selects marked device
  Epson-FX and RX series-Low density          [ESCAPE] exits, ignoring changes
  Epson-FX and RX series-High density         [HOME] goes to beginning of list
  HP-LaserJet+ or LaserJet II-Med den.        [END] goes to end of list
  HP-LaserJet+ or LaserJet II-High den.       [UP] and [DOWN] move cursor
                                                 List will scroll if cursor
                                                 moved beyond top or bottom
```

Selecting Graph and Font Directories

When you configure PrintGraph to your hardware, you must also indicate the directories for the graph and font files. The information you supply for the **G**raphs-Directory and **F**onts-Directory tells PrintGraph which directories to search for the graph (.PIC) and font (.FNT) files. A:\ is the default drive and directory for the graph and font files. If you have a hard disk and have stored all your graph and font files in a subdirectory (for example, C:\SYM22), you must change these default settings. On systems with two floppy disk drives, change the graph directory to B:\ where your data files (worksheets, graphs, and so forth) are stored.

Specifying an Interface Card

The **I**nterface option of the **H**ardware menu specifies either a parallel or a serial interface card for your system. You are given eight choices:

1. A parallel interface—the default.
2. A serial interface (RS-232-C-compatible). You must specify a baud rate (see following paragraphs).
3. A second parallel interface.
4. A second serial interface (RS-232-C-compatible). You must specify a baud rate (see following paragraphs).
5-8. One of four possible remote devices, LPT1 through LPT4.

If you specify a serial interface, you must select a baud rate, which determines the speed at which data is transferred. Because each printer has its own requirements, you need to consult your printer's manual for the appropriate rate. Many printers accept more than one baud rate, so a general guideline is to choose the fastest baud rate that the printer accepts without corrupting the data. The available baud rates appear in table 15.1.

Table 15.1
Available Baud Rates

Setting	Baud
1	110
2	150
3	300
4	600
5	1,200
6	2,400
7	4,800
8	9,600
9	19,200

Configurations to Save and Reset

To save the hardware settings, select **S**ave from the **S**ettings menu. The saved settings are then active for subsequent PrintGraph sessions. PrintGraph saves the settings in a file called PGRAPH.CNF, which is read each time PrintGraph is loaded. Another option in the **S**ettings menu, **R**eset, provides a function almost the opposite of **S**ave. **R**eset cancels all the settings made during the current session and returns to the options that were present when PrintGraph was loaded or the options that were saved during the current session, whichever occurred last.

Reminder:

Once you have configured PrintGraph, be sure to save the new settings.

Specifying Image Settings

Besides settings for your hardware configuration, other settings affect the way graphs appear on the printed page. These **I**mage settings apply to all the graphs printed in a batch. All the **I**mage settings are saved when you update the CNF file. If you want different **I**mage settings for different graphs, you must select and print the graphs one at a time.

To specify the **I**mage settings, select **I**mage from the **S**ettings menu. The following choices are then displayed:

    Size **F**ont **R**ange-Colors **Q**uit

Adjusting Graph Size and Orientation

The **S**ize option in the **I**mage menu enables you to adjust the sizes of graphs and to decide where they will be printed on a page. This option also enables you to rotate the axes by as much as 360 degrees. The menu for the **S**ize option gives you the following choices:

> Full Half Manual Quit

Full means that the graph will occupy an entire page, and **H**alf indicates that the graph will take up a half-page. PrintGraph automatically handles all the spacing and margins for both these choices unless you specify **M**anual.

Selecting **M**anual produces these options:

> Left Top Width Height Rotation Quit

Use **L**eft, **T**op, **W**idth, and **H**eight to adjust the respective margins. **R**otation adjusts the number of counterclockwise degrees of rotation. You must choose a number between 0 and 360. A setting of 0 degrees causes no rotation—the X-axis prints as it normally appears on-screen. A setting of 180 degrees prints the graph upside down, and 90 or 270 degrees prints the graph sideways.

Interestingly enough, if you choose the **F**ull option, Symphony automatically prints graphs rotated 90 degrees. Thus the X-axis of a bar graph runs along the long edge of an 8 1/2-by-11-inch page. If you choose the **H**alf option, Symphony considers the degree of rotation 0; the X-axis of a bar graph runs along the short edge of a sheet of paper so that you can fit two graphs on a single page.

Reminder:

To avoid distortion, maintain the 1 to 1.385 width-height ratio.

You need to experiment to get the results you want from **R**otation. When you select **H**alf, the default settings for **W**idth and **H**eight are 6.500 and 4.691, respectively. This setting gives a width-height ratio of approximately 1 (X-axis) to 1.385 (Y-axis). If you change the ratio, distortion can, and often does, occur when PrintGraph fits a rotated graph into the specified height and width. Distortion in bar and line graphs is usually not a problem. Distorted pie charts, however, probably will look like ellipses rather than pies. When you change the settings for height and width, the best way to avoid distortion is to maintain the 1 to 1.385 ratio.

Choosing Fonts

Symphony can print in different character types (fonts) on any graphics printer or plotter. The **F**ont option offers you 11 different character types (see fig. 15.3) from which you can choose. The number after the font name indicates the density—how dark the printed characters will be. The fonts followed by a 2 are identical to the fonts with the same names followed by a 1, but the number 2 fonts are darker.

Tip

Not all fonts are suitable for serious business graphs. You may find the Italic and Script fonts difficult to read.

This is BLOCK1 type

This is BLOCK2 type

This is BOLD type

This is FORUM type

This is ITALIC1 type

This is ITALIC2 type

This is LOTUS type

This is ROMAN1 type

This is ROMAN2 type

This is SCRIPT1 type

This is SCRIPT2 type

Fig. 15.3.
Fonts available for printing graphs.

You can set the first line of text, the graph title, in one font, and the remaining text in another. If you specify only one font, PrintGraph uses this font for all the text in the graph.

An example is the exploded pie chart of retail-store openings from the previous chapter; a dark Block typeface is used for the first graph title and a lighter Block for the other lines. To get these fonts, you specify BLOCK2 for **Font 1** (the first line of the title), and BLOCK1 for **Font 2**. If another font had not been chosen for **Font 2**, it would have automatically taken on the same value as **Font 1**.

Once you specify the fonts for a graph, they appear in the settings sheet. Figure 15.4 shows a settings sheet in which ITALIC2 was specified for **Font 1**, and ITALIC1 for **Font 2**.

Fig. 15.4.

A settings sheet to print a graph in ITALIC2 and ITALIC1 fonts.

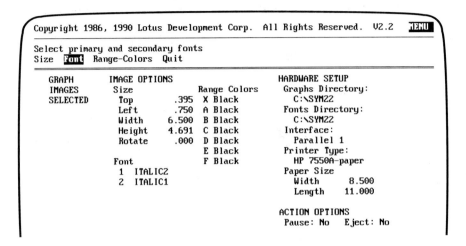

```
Copyright 1986, 1990 Lotus Development Corp.  All Rights Reserved.  V2.2   MENU

Select primary and secondary fonts
Size  Font  Range-Colors  Quit

   GRAPH        IMAGE OPTIONS                    HARDWARE SETUP
   IMAGES        Size            Range Colors    Graphs Directory:
   SELECTED       Top       .395  X Black          C:\SYM22
                  Left      .750  A Black        Fonts Directory:
                  Width    6.500  B Black          C:\SYM22
                  Height   4.691  C Black        Interface:
                  Rotate    .000  D Black          Parallel 1
                                  E Black        Printer Type:
                  Font            F Black          HP 7550A-paper
                   1  ITALIC2                    Paper Size
                   2  ITALIC1                      Width     8.500
                                                   Length   11.000

                                                ACTION OPTIONS
                                                  Pause: No   Eject: No
```

Choosing Range-Colors

If you have a color-printing device, you can select **R**ange-Colors from the **I**mage menu. This option sets the colors for printing or plotting different parts of graphs. If the device you are using does not support color graphics (most printers do not), of course, you have no choice of colors.

PrintGraph assigns a default color of black to every data range and to the grid, axes, and scales. You may assign any color to any data range, however, or you may assign the same color to more than one data range.

When you select **R**ange-Colors, PrintGraph asks you to assign colors to the data ranges. Each time you specify a range letter (**X** or **A** through **F**), Printgraph displays a list of colors from which you can choose. The colors you use in PrintGraph do not have to be the same colors you use in the main Symphony program. In fact, you don't have to have a color monitor to print color graphs. On the other hand, if the graphics printer you specified does not print in color, your only choice is black.

After you have assigned colors to the ranges, the screen looks similar to figure 15.5.

You may save the color settings by means of the **S**ave option from the **S**ettings menu. This choice saves **R**ange-Colors settings (and all other image and hardware settings) to PGRAPH.CNF so that the settings are automatically used in the next PrintGraph session.

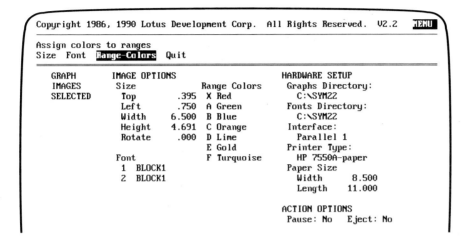

Fig. 15.5.
The screen after you assign colors.

Choosing Page Size

You specify the dimensions of the paper your graphics printer uses by selecting **S**ettings **H**ardware **S**ize-Paper. The default settings are 8 1/2 inches wide and 11 inches long.

Selecting Files for Printing

Once you have configured PrintGraph, you can return to the main PrintGraph menu and choose **I**mage-Select. After your initial use of PrintGraph, **I**mage-Select will probably be the first step every time you use the program. This option gives you a list of all the PIC files in your Graphs Directory. These are the files you created with the **I**mage-Save command. A typical list of graph files is shown in figure 15.6.

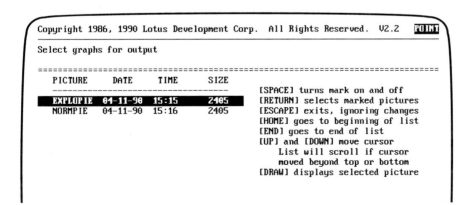

Fig. 15.6.
A sample list of graph files.

> **Tip**
> If no files are listed when you chose **I**mage-Select, check to make sure that the correct Graphs Directory is listed in the settings sheet.

The directions for selecting files appear on the right side of the display. To select a graph file to print, use the up and down arrow keys to position the cursor at the appropriate entry; then press the space bar. Pressing the space bar places a # next to the graph name to indicate that the graph has been selected for printing. Press Enter to return to the main PrintGraph menu.

DRAW
ALT-F8

You can select as many graphs as you want before you press Enter. A # appears next to each graph you select. If you can't remember which graph is contained in a particular PIC file, you can press Draw (Alt-F8) to view the graph. You may notice that the graph looks slightly different than it did in Symphony because PrintGraph displays the graph titles and labels in the relative sizing in which they will print.

Working with Batch Printing

If you have selected multiple graphs with the **I**mage-Select command, you need to consider how the sheets of paper will be fed into and ejected from the printer. Two settings control page handling: **P**ause and **E**ject. These options are on the **S**ettings **A**ction menu.

If you want each graph printed on a separate page, choose **E**ject **Y**es. This option issues a form-feed command to your printer after each printed graph. By default, this option is set to **N**o.

Reminder:
If your graphics device accepts only single sheets of paper, make sure you tell PrintGraph to pause between pages.

If you have a graphics device that accepts only single sheets of paper, such as the HP 7470A plotter, you must tell PrintGraph to pause between pages by choosing **P**ause **Y**es from the **A**ction menu. Many graphics devices, such as the HP plotter, are smart enough to know when you have room to print the next graph. If you do have room, the device prints. Otherwise, it pauses for you to load another piece of paper.

If, on the other hand, you have a graphics device that accepts continuous-form paper, such as the IBM Color Graphics Printer, you can have graphs printed continuously and unattended. **N**o is the default setting for the **P**ause option.

Printing and Exiting

Caution:
Do not choose **A***lign unless the paper is at the top of the page in the printer.*

Usually, you want to choose the **A**lign selection in the main PrintGraph menu before you print. This option is similar to the one in Symphony's **P**rint menu; it sets the program's built-in, top-of-page marker. When you choose the **A**lign option, PrintGraph assumes that the paper is correctly aligned in the printer with the top of the form in the right place.

Note: Many printers have controls that enable you to feed the paper a line or a page at a time. PrintGraph does not recognize these controls. If you use the printer control to form-feed the paper and do not use the **A**lign command, PrintGraph will be off when it next issues a form-feed command.

To print a graph, you must select **G**o from the main PrintGraph menu. After you have done so, PrintGraph begins printing. If you are printing several graphs on a slow dot matrix printer, you may as well have lunch while it prints, because PrintGraph's high-resolution printing takes a long time. Printing the graph shown in figure 15.7 on an Epson RX-80 in high-density mode, took about 10 minutes. Printing the same graph with an HP LaserJet Series II in high-density mode required less than two minutes.

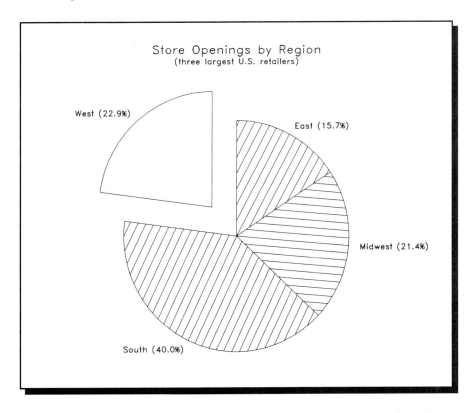

Fig. 15. 7.
A pie chart printed on an HP LaserJet.

The **P**age selection in the main PrintGraph menu advances the paper to the top of the next page. You need to use this option if you have not turned on the **E**ject option. The **P**age option also form-feeds the last page at the end of a printing session.

To exit from PrintGraph choose **E**xit from the main PrintGraph menu. After you select **E**xit, you are returned to the ACCESS SYSTEM or to DOS, depending on which way you entered PrintGraph.

Chapter Summary

This chapter showed you how to use the PrintGraph program to produce high-resolution, presentation-quality graphs. PrintGraph is a separate program from Symphony, an arrangement that deviates slightly from Lotus's integrated approach; but, the results produced by the PrintGraph program are outstanding, and the program is easy to use.

The next chapter offers you a chance to practice your newfound skills in creating and printing graphs with Symphony and PrintGraph.

16

Creating and Printing Graphs: Hands-On Practice

Symphony's graphing capabilities integrate directly with the SHEET environment: your graphs are based on the data in your spreadsheets. The printing of graphs, however, is accomplished through the separate PrintGraph program or Allways add-in.

In this chapter, you learn how to perform the following functions:

❑ Create and print graphs
❑ Store and recall graphs
❑ Work with graphs in a SHEET window
❑ Revise graphs in a GRAPH window

If you want to review a concept in greater detail as you work through the practice exercises in this chapter, refer to Chapter 14, "Creating and Displaying Graphs," and Chapter 15, "Printing Graphs."

Creating Graphs

For the graphs in this practice chapter, you use data from the SALES spreadsheet you developed in Chapter 8, "Learning SHEET Window: Hands-On Practice." You create two graphs: a bar graph displaying January versus February sales; and a pie chart of the January sales data.

Creating a Bar Graph

For the sales bar graph, place the salespeople's names along the X-axis, and use the January and February sales as the two data ranges. Begin by retrieving the SALES spreadsheet you built in Chapter 8. (If you have not created this spreadsheet, you need to do so before proceeding.)

1. Select SERVICES **F**ile **R**etrieve.
2. Type **SALES** and press Enter, or point to the file named SALES and press Enter.

Because you are creating a bar graph of the sales data for January and February, name this graph JAN/FEB-BAR.

1. Press F6 until the JAN-FEB window displays (the lower right corner of the screen displays the window name).
2. Select SHEET **G**raph **1**st-Settings **N**ame **C**reate.
3. Enter **JAN/FEB-BAR**.

Specify the ranges for this bar graph.

1. Select **T**ype **B**ar.
2. Select **R**ange **X**.
3. Enter **A6..A10**. (This range includes the salespeople's names, which will go along the X-axis.)
4. Select **A** for the first data range.
5. Enter **B6..B10** (the January data).
6. Select **B** for the second data range.
7. Enter **C6..C10** (the February data).
8. Select **Q**uit **Q**uit **P**review to display the graph. (It should match fig. 16.1.) Notice the graph's name, JAN/FEB-BAR, in the left corner of the window.

Without legends, you don't know which data range is January and which is February. Also, the graph is incomplete without titles.

1. Press any key to return to the **G**raph menu.
2. Select **1**st-Settings **L**egend.
3. Select **A** for the first data range legend.
4. Enter **JAN**.
5. Select **B** for the second data range legend.

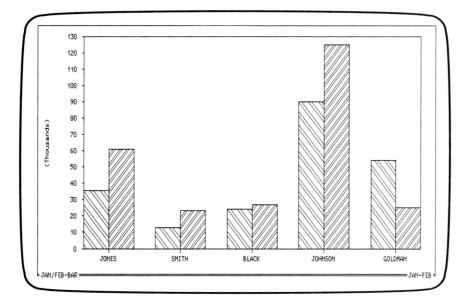

Fig. 16.1.
*A bar graph with
two data ranges.*

6. Enter **FEB**.

7. Select **Q**uit **S**witch to go to the **2**nd-Settings sheet, where the **T**itles option is located.

8. Select **T**itles.

9. Select **F**irst.

10. Enter **\C1** to use the contents of cell C1 (`JAN VS. FEB SALES`) as the graph's top title.

11. Select **S**econd.

12. Enter **\C2** to use the contents of cell C2 (`BY SALES PERSON`) as the second title.

13. Select **X**-axis.

14. Enter **SALES PERSON**.

15. Select **Y**-axis.

16. Enter **SALES VOLUME**.

17. Select **Q**uit **Q**uit **P**review. Your graph should resemble figure 16.2.

18. Press any key to display the **G**raph menu.

19. Save and replace the file. (Select SERVICES **F**ile **S**ave, press Enter to accept the name SALES, and select **Y**es to replace.)

Fig. 16.2.

The bar graph after adding titles and a legend.

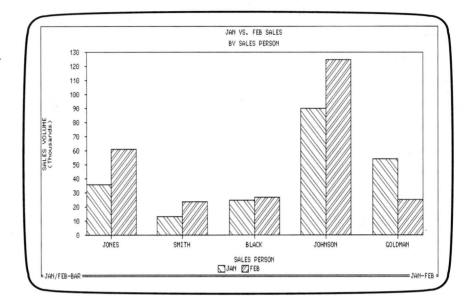

Creating a Pie Chart

Due to the nature of a pie chart, you can graph only one set of data: the A range. In its most basic form, the pie chart is simply a circle divided into sections of different sizes. By adding a B data range, however, you can indicate cross-hatching patterns for each segment and even explode one or more pieces of the pie.

The pie chart you are going to create displays the January data. Name this new graph before creating the settings.

1. Select SHEET **G**raph **1**st-Settings **N**ame **C**reate.

2. Enter **JAN-PIE**.

The B range from the bar graph you just created does not apply to this graph, so you must cancel this range.

1. Select **C**ancel **E**ntire-Row **B**.

2. Select **Q**uit.

Specify a title for the pie chart.

1. Select **T**ype **P**ie.

2. Select **S**witch to go to the **2**nd-Settings sheet.

3. Select **T**itles **F**irst.

4. Press Esc to remove the top title that is left over from the bar graph.

5. Enter **JANUARY SALES**.

6. Select **Q**uit **Q**uit **P**review. Your graph should look similar to figure 16.3.

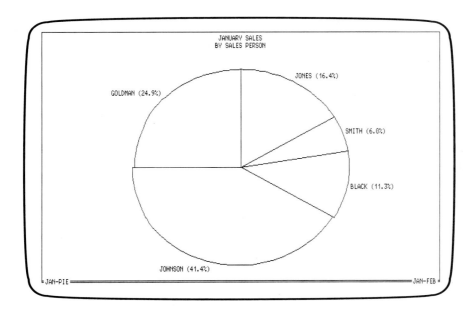

Fig. 16.3.
*A pie chart of
January sales.*

What a dull graph! Create a B range to specify shading patterns for the different pieces of the pie. You need to return to SHEET mode to enter this range.

1. Press any key to display the **G**raph menu; select **Q**uit to go to SHEET mode.

2. In cells F6..F10, enter the numbers 1 through 5 to specify a different pattern for each section (see fig.16.4).

3. Select SHEET **G**raph **1**st-Settings **R**ange.

4. Select **B** for the second data range.

5. Enter **F6..F10** (the range of shade values).

6. Select **Q**uit **Q**uit **P**review. The graph now should look like figure 16.5.

Now the graph is much more attractive. You can further enhance a pie chart by exploding one of its sections. To explode one of the segments, you add 100 to the slice's shade value. Return to the spreadsheet and change one of the shade values.

1. Press any key to display the **G**raph menu, and select **Q**uit to go to SHEET mode.

Fig. 16.4.
Entering crosshatch pattern numbers in column F.

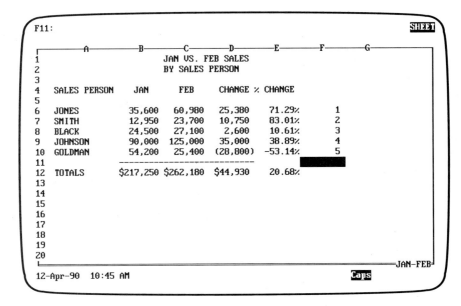

Fig. 16.5.
After using the B range to specify crosshatch patterns.

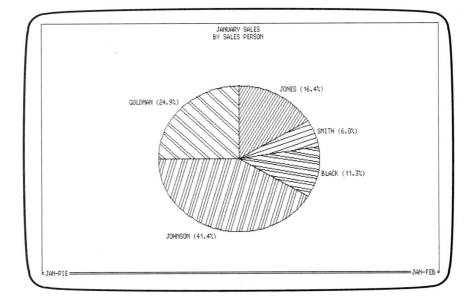

2. In cell F7, enter **102**.

3. Select SHEET **G**raph **P**review. Figure 16.6 shows the exploded pie chart.

4. Save and replace the file.

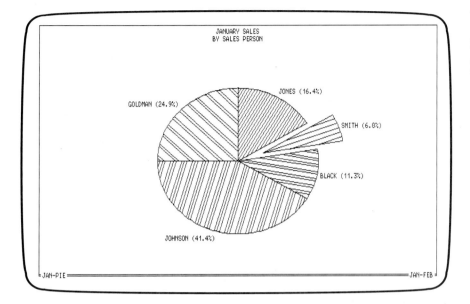

Fig. 16.6.
*An exploded pie
chart.*

Working with Named Graphs

Once you have created and named your graphs, you may want to display them
so that you can view them and make changes. You can use two ways to call up
the various graphs you have named, depending on which window type you are
using. In a SHEET window, you recall a named graph by selecting the **N**ame **U**se
command. Then you must choose **P**review to see the graph. If you are working
in a GRAPH window, the **A**ttach command recalls the specified graph settings
and automatically displays the graph.

Using a Graph

To work with the bar graph you created earlier, you first need to **U**se it.

1. Select SHEET **G**raph **1**st-Settings **N**ame **U**se. A list of named
   graphs appears.

2. Select the name **JAN/FEB-BAR** from the list.

3. Select **Q**uit **P**review to view the bar graph of January and
   February data. Your graph should look just like the one in
   figure 16.2.

4. Press any key to display the **G**raph menu.

The fact that each graph has two settings sheets (**1**st-Settings and **2**nd-Settings) gives you an idea of how many options are available. One option changes the format of the numbers on the Y-axis. Another changes the crosshatching patterns, or "hue," of the bars.

1. Select **2**nd-Settings **Y**-Scale **F**ormat **C**urrency.
2. Enter **0** for the number of decimal places.
3. Select **Q**uit **S**witch to move to the **1**st-Settings sheet.
4. Select **H**ue.
5. Select **A** for the first data range.
6. Select **7** to choose pattern **7**.
7. Select **B** for the second data range.
8. Select **1** to choose pattern **1**.
9. Quit from the submenus and **P**review these changes (see fig. 16.7.) Notice the dollar signs next to the numbers on the Y-axis, and the different shading patterns of the bars.

Fig. 16.7.

After formatting the Y-scale and changing the bar crosshatch patterns.

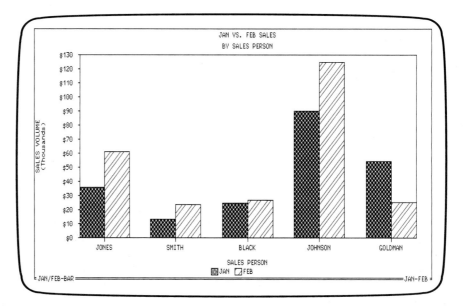

You also can change the spreadsheet data and quickly see the modifications reflected in your graphs. Correct an error in the January data and then view the revised JAN-PIE graph.

1. Select **1**st-Settings **N**ame **U**se.
2. Select **JAN-PIE**.

3. **P**review the graph and notice that SMITH has 6 percent (6.0%) of the January sales.

4. Go to SHEET mode.

5. In B7, enter **20000**.

6. Select SHEET **G**raph **P**review. The graph in figure 16.8 appears.

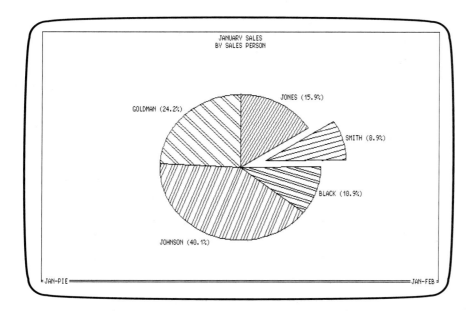

Fig. 16.8.
Reflecting changes made to the spreadsheet data.

Note that the graph automatically redrew and recalculated the percentages. Smith now has a larger slice of the pie.

Attaching a Graph

Another way to work with graphs in Symphony is through a GRAPH window. When you are in GRAPH mode, the graph currently attached to the window is automatically displayed. (No **P**review command exists.)

Both the JAN/FEB-BAR graph and the JAN-PIE graph belong to the JAN-FEB window, so you attach each of these graphs to this window.

1. Go to SHEET mode.

2. Press Alt-F10 to display the TYPE menu.

3. Select GRAPH as the window type. (The JAN-PIE graph automatically displays because it was the last graph you used in this window.)

4. Select GRAPH **A**ttach. A list of graph names appears.

5. Select **JAN/FEB-BAR** from the list.

The JAN/FEB-BAR bar chart automatically displays in the window. Change this graph to a stacked-bar graph.

1. Select GRAPH **1**st-Settings **T**ype **S**tacked-Bar.

2. Select **Q**uit, and the new graph displays. (See fig. 16.9.)

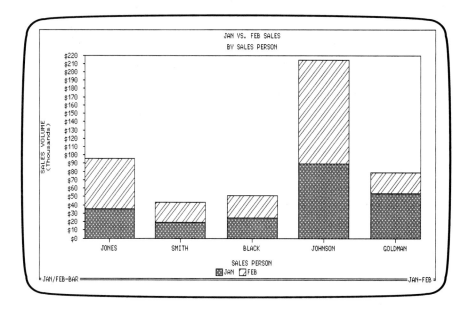

Fig. 16.9.
A stacked-bar graph.

The Y-scale contains too many increments. Change the Y-scale to have a different upper limit (for example, 300,000).

1. Select GRAPH **2**nd-Settings **Y**-Scale **T**ype **M**anual-Linear.

2. Press Enter to keep the lower limit at 0.

3. Enter **300000** for the upper limit.

4. Select **Q**uit **Q**uit to view the new graph.

Now attach JAN-PIE so that you can change that graph.

1. Select GRAPH **A**ttach.

2. Select **JAN-PIE**.

JAN-PIE displays. Change the aspect ratio of the pie so that the circle is wider.

1. Select GRAPH **2**nd-Settings **O**ther **A**spect.

2. Enter **.5**.

3. Select Quit to view the new graph, which should resemble figure 16.10.

4. Change the aspect ratio back to its default value (1).

5. Save and replace the file.

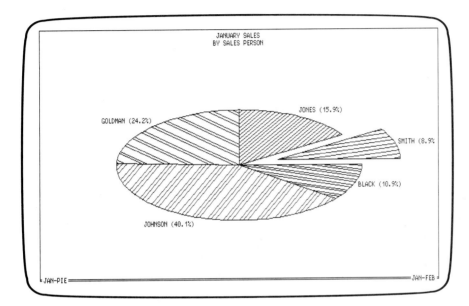

Fig. 16.10.
After changing the aspect ratio of the pie chart.

Printing Graphs

Once you have created your graphs and are satisfied with how they look on-screen, you may want to print them. To print graphs, you must access a utility program outside the main Symphony program. This program is called PrintGraph. Because PrintGraph is separate from Symphony, before you exit Symphony you must save each of the graphs you want to print.

Saving Graphs for Printing

The **I**mage-Save command on the **G**raph menu is the option you use to save graphs for printing. This command stores the graph in a file with a PIC extension.

First, save the JAN-PIE graph for printing. (Make sure this graph is the current one.)

1. Change the window type back to SHEET.

2. Select SHEET **G**raph **I**mage-Save.

3. Enter **PIE** as the graph file name. (Symphony stores the file under PIE.PIC.)

Save the JAN-FEB/BAR graph for printing.

1. Select **1**st-Settings **N**ame **U**se.
2. Select **JAN/FEB-BAR**.
3. Select **Q**uit **I**mage-Save.
4. Enter **BAR** as the graph file name. (Symphony stores the file under BAR.PIC.)

Using Default PrintGraph Settings

Once you are in the PrintGraph program, you need only a few keystrokes to produce a default half-size graph displaying block style print. You will print the PIE graph with the default settings.

Before you begin this practice session, make sure that the PrintGraph hardware setup (**P**rinter, **I**nterface, **F**onts-Directory, **G**raphs-Directory, and **S**ize-Paper) is appropriate for your equipment. See Chapter 15's section on the "Configuration of PrintGraph" for information on hardware setup.

To print the PIE graph, first make sure that your file is saved and that you have image-saved each of the graphs you want to print. Then use the following command sequences:

1. **E**xit from Symphony.
2. If the ACCESS SYSTEM menu displays, select PrintGraph. Or, if the DOS prompt (C > or A >) appears, make sure that the PrintGraph program is in the current directory or drive and enter **pgraph**.
3. Choose **I**mage-Select from the main PrintGraph menu.
4. Position the highlighted bar on P I E and press Enter. (This step marks [with a # symbol] the highlighted file name. The main PrintGraph menu redisplays.)
5. Check the printer, making sure that it is on-line and that the print head is at the top edge of the paper.
6. Select **A**lign to ensure that Symphony recognizes the current top-of-page.
7. Select **G**o and wait for the half-size graph to print.
8. Select **P**age from the main PrintGraph menu to advance the paper to the top of the next page.
9. Check the output, which should match figure 16.11.

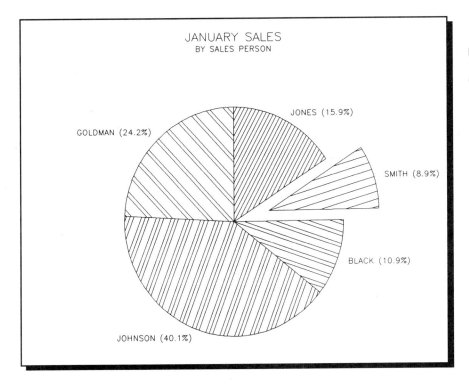

Fig. 16.11.
The printed pie chart.

Changing PrintGraph Settings

You use the main PrintGraph menu's **S**ettings option to alter print options. Most of the **S**ettings options deal with establishing a specific print environment (location of files, type of printer, and so on) and are not illustrated here. In this final practice session, you use two options (**F**ont and **S**ize) to change the default graph's image and produce a full-size graph with two font styles.

To produce this full-size stacked-bar graph, use the following command sequences:

1. Choose **I**mage-Select from the main PrintGraph menu.
2. Position the highlighted bar on **PIE** and press the space bar to unselect this file.
3. Position the highlighted bar on **BAR** and press Enter.
4. Select **S**ettings **I**mage **S**ize **F**ull.
5. Select **Q**uit to exit the **S**ize submenu.
6. Select **F**ont **1** to access a list of Symphony font styles.
7. Position the highlighted bar on **FORUM** and press the space bar to specify this print style for the top center title. Press Enter.

8. Select **F**ont **2**.

9. Position the highlighted bar on **LOTUS** and press the space bar to specify the print style for the remaining descriptive text. Press Enter.

10. Select **Q**uit **Q**uit to exit the submenus.

11. Select **A**lign **G**o and wait while the graph prints.

12. Select **P**age to eject the page from the printer.

13. Check the printed full-size graph to be sure that it matches figure 16.12.

14. Select **E**xit.

Chapter Summary

This chapter has given you a chance to practice creating and working with graphs in Symphony's SHEET and GRAPH windows. You also practiced printing these graphs with the separate PrintGraph program. Review the detailed graphing information in Chapters 14 and 15, and check this book's troubleshooting section for additional tips.

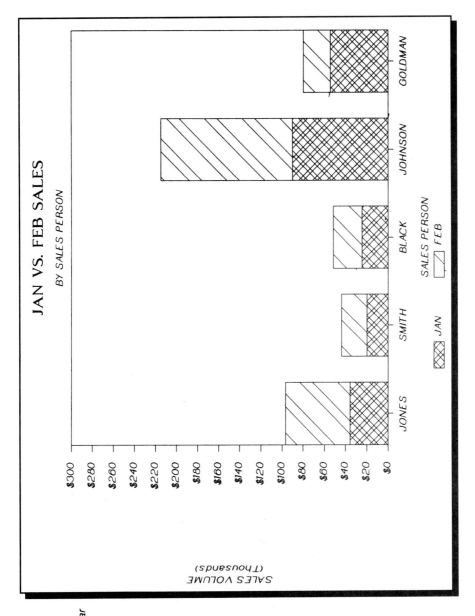

Fig. 16.12.
The stacked-bar chart printout.

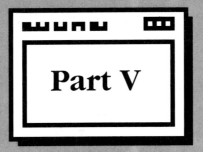

Part V

Managing Data with Symphony

Managing Data

Managing Data: Hands-On Practice

17

Managing Data

Data management involves all the commands and procedures for creating and manipulating a database. With Release 2.2, Symphony now offers two different forms of database management: the traditional in-RAM database it has always supported, and the @BASE add-in database manager, which uses on-disk dBASE-compatible files. Each form has advantages in certain situations. This chapter examines both forms and discusses their strengths. Because the two forms are distinct, the chapter is divided into two major sections. The first part of the chapter looks at Symphony's traditional in-RAM database manager; the second part covers the @BASE add-in.

Symphony's traditional in-RAM database-management environment includes three distinct areas: the FORM window, the database commands in the SHEET environment, and database statistical functions. You use a FORM window to set up and manipulate individual records. You use the SHEET commands to work with groups of records. Finally, you use database statistical functions to determine statistics about groups of records within a database.

These three areas are closely interrelated. For example, you can create a database of all your customers' names and addresses by means of a special form set up in a FORM window. Once the database is created, you can then use the database commands in the SHEET environment to extract the names of customers who operate in a specific location. (Many of the settings used in the FORM window can also be used in the SHEET window.) Finally, you can use database statistical functions to determine the number of customer names you've extracted and their average monthly orders from your company.

Reminder:

You can use the in-RAM database manager to hide everything but the input form, thus simplifying data entry.

Symphony's in-RAM data-management program has many strengths. First, you can create forms and add or modify records easily. Second, when you are using a FORM window, you can hide everything in the database except the input form. Therefore, you can set up a data-entry environment for someone who does not know, or care to know, Symphony. Third, Symphony's in-RAM data management is fast. Because all the operations are RAM-based, you can manipulate rapidly almost any information you want. Finally, the data management is integrated; you can use data-management techniques in all of Symphony's working environments—SHEET, DOC, GRAPH, FORM, and COMM.

Although Symphony's in-RAM data-management environment is strong in several respects, it is weak in others. Most notably, like everything else in Symphony, the fact that it is RAM-based places strict limitations on the size and the kinds of applications for which you can use data management.

Modifying an existing database was quite difficult in earlier releases of Symphony. You had to insert and delete columns, create and delete range names, and modify all the different database ranges manually. Fortunately, in Symphony 2.0 and later, you can easily move, insert, and delete fields with **F**ield, a FORM menu option.

Another drawback is that Symphony's data management is hard to learn. It is probably one of the most complex operations in the program. As you soon see, many special rules apply. But you may find that you need to know only some of those rules to accomplish what you want.

The structure of the first part of this chapter follows the three natural divisions inherent in Symphony's data management: the use of FORM windows, SHEET database commands, and database statistical functions. Also included is a section on printing database reports. This topic is a particularly good one with which to end a discussion of the in-RAM database environment because it incorporates many different aspects of Symphony's data-management capability.

The second part of this chapter deals with the @BASE database-management environment. @BASE has two distinct areas: the BASE window and the @DB functions used in the SHEET window. You use the BASE window to set up and manipulate records. You use @DB functions in the SHEET window to manipulate records or determine statistics about groups of records within a database.

These two areas are closely interrelated. For example, you can create a database of customers' names and addresses by using a special form you set up in the BASE window. Once the database is created, you can use the database commands in the BASE window to extract to the SHEET window all the customers in a specific location. Finally, you can use the database statistical functions to determine the number of customer names you've extracted and their average monthly orders from your company.

Like its in-RAM program, Symphony's @BASE program also has many strengths. First, you can create forms to add or modify records easily. Second, you can use the BASE window to look at records in a database with either the input form or the browse screen. Third, you can work with databases in @BASE that are too large for Symphony's in-RAM database manager.

Creating a new @BASE database or modifying an existing one is easy. Like the in-RAM database manager, @BASE has commands that assist you. @BASE, however, has additional commands that make the task of modifying a database even easier.

Although @BASE is strong overall, it has some weaknesses. Most notably, the @DB functions can produce unexpected results unless you incorporate them into macros. Another drawback is that @BASE does not offer a direct way to print a database report. You must either import @BASE records into a SHEET window or use the @BASE functions in a SHEET or DOC window to produce reports.

Reminder:
@BASE can handle database files that are too large for the in-RAM database manager.

Calling All 1-2-3 Users

If you are an experienced 1-2-3 user, you have a distinct advantage in learning Symphony's data management—provided you keep an open mind. Many of the important techniques are the same in both programs, but Symphony has added several new techniques. Most of them are associated with Symphony's FORM window, so mastering this window requires patience.

Cue:
If you know how to manage data in 1-2-3, you're more than halfway to learning how to manage data in Symphony.

The structure of the FORM environment may seem rigid at first, and lacking some of the flexibility and user control so appealing in 1-2-3. Once you get to know the FORM environment, however, you can learn to use it to your advantage. For example, the FORM window has several special ranges. Some are new, others may look familiar, and all have special locations that Symphony automatically chooses. After you learn the rules for these special ranges, however, you don't have to stick to Symphony's locations. You can put the special ranges anywhere you want.

You can use Symphony's data management in a way remarkably similar to 1-2-3's data management if you want. Symphony has all the capabilities of 1-2-3, but you miss the full power of Symphony's data management if you limit yourself to 1-2-3's methods. Symphony can handle many routine chores for you (setting up database ranges, criterion ranges, and output ranges, for instance). You will learn quickly when to let Symphony do the work for you and when to do it yourself.

If you are an experienced 1-2-3 user, you may want to go directly to the section titled "Using the FORM Window to Create Databases." You can expect the FORM window to be different from what you are used to. By the time you come to the SHEET commands and the database statistical functions, however, you will feel at home. Give special attention to the ranges used in the SHEET environment and the locations of the **Q**uery commands in the menu structure, but database statistical functions should require only a cursory review. Finally, pay close attention to the information about printing database reports, particularly if you intend to print form letters or mailing lists.

Keep in mind that Symphony has more severe RAM limitations than 1-2-3. Because the main Symphony program requires approximately 320K of RAM, you have only about 320K left for applications and add-ins. (This figure assumes that you have 640K on your computer and no expanded memory.)

Understanding Database Fundamentals

A *database* is a collection of related pieces of information. In its simplest form, a database is a list that can contain any kind of information, from addresses to tax-deductible expenses.

Reminder:

A database is a range of cells that spans at least one column and at least two rows.

In Symphony, a database is a range of cells that spans at least one column and at least two rows. This basic definition alone contains nothing that sets a database apart from any other group of cells. But because a database is actually a list, another important aspect is its method of organization. Just as a list must be properly organized before you can gain information from it, a database must be properly organized also. Remembering the underlying similarity between a database and any other group of cells in Symphony can help you learn about the different commands presented in this chapter. You will begin to see many other instances where you can use these commands in what might be considered nondatabase applications.

Understanding the Organization of a Database

Reminder:

Databases are made up of records; records are made up of fields; fields have field names.

As mentioned previously, an important aspect of a database is the way it is organized. This organization relies heavily on the composition of the database itself. To understand this composition, you need certain general definitions. First, databases are made up of records. Each record corresponds to an item in a list. In Symphony, a *record* is a row of cells within a database. Second, records are made up of fields. In Symphony, a *field* is a single cell (or column) within a record. Finally, you use *field names* at the tops of columns to identify fields; field names are required for nearly every database operation. Figure 17.1 shows a simple database.

In figure 17.1, the second record resides in row 4. The name that is highlighted, `Cotter, James F.`, is one of the four fields for that record. The field name for the items in column A is NAME.

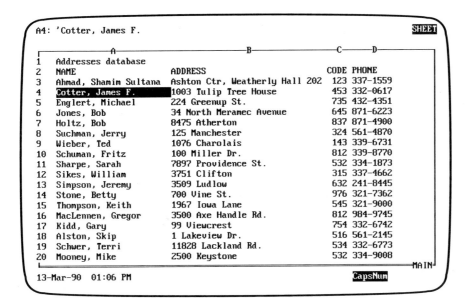

Fig. 17.1.
A sample database.

Knowing What You Can Do with a Database

If the database in figure 17.1 were your database, what would you use it for? You might want to sort it by last name to get an alphabetical list. You might also want to query the database for a name or group of names. For example, you could search out the street address for a particular person or select all the people in the database with the same telephone exchange. Sorting and querying are the chief methods used in Symphony to get meaningful information from a database. Symphony offers several ways to sort and query, depending on whether you are in a SHEET or a FORM window.

Using the FORM Window to Create Databases

One of the nicest features of creating a database in a Symphony FORM window is the amount of work the program does for you behind the scenes. In a FORM window, you rarely see the entire database; yet Symphony constantly keeps track of it. You can browse through a database, looking at one record at a time, or you can view the records with a special form that you build with Symphony's help.

Reminder:
Although you rarely see the entire database in a FORM window, Symphony keeps track of it all.

To gain a better understanding of Symphony's FORM window, suppose that you are a manufacturer of special accessory chips for the semiconductor market and you want to build a "Customer Priority" database for one of your best-selling but difficult-to-manufacture computer chips. Because demand is far higher than you can supply, you want the database to be the foundation for a priority system that allocates chips as fairly as possible but at the same time maximizes your profit.

Building a Simple Input Form

While planning the database, you decide that you want to use Symphony's forms capability, and you also decide that the database should contain the following fields to hold the indicated type of data:

Field Name	Type	Length	Example Value
ORDER NUMBER	Label	7 characters	PO1435
CUSTOMER NAME	Label	21 characters	Amdek Corporation
PHONE	Label	13 characters	312-364-1180
PRIORITY	Number	2 decimal	1
ENTRY DATE	Serial number	10 decimal	7/23/88
PROMISE DATE	Serial number	10 decimal	8/23/88
AMOUNT	Number	8 decimal	23000

Tip

With Symphony, you can use field names up to 15 characters in length and include spaces and other special characters. However, if you want to convert an in-RAM database to an @BASE on-disk database, the @BASE field-name rules are more restrictive. The rules for naming @BASE fields are as follows:

1. Field names cannot be longer than 10 characters.

2. Field names can contain letters, numbers, and the underscore character but must begin with a letter.

3. Field names cannot contain spaces.

4. Field names must be unique.

If you follow these rules when you name fields in the in-RAM database, converting the database to the @BASE environment later will be much easier.

The simplest way to build an input form for a database is to use the FORM **G**enerate command. Before you can use this command, however, use either a SHEET or DOC window to enter the field names. Figure 17.2 shows how to enter the field names for the Priority database in a SHEET window.

Reminder:
*Use a SHEET or DOC window to enter field names and then use FORM **G**enerate to build an input form.*

```
A1: 'ORDER NUMBER                                              SHEET
┌─────A───────B───────C───────D───────E───────F───────G───────H────┐
1    ORDER NUMBER
2    CUSTOMER NAME :L:21
3    PHONE:L:13
4    PRIORITY :N:2
5    ENTRY DATE :D:10
6    PROMISE DATE :D:10
7    AMOUNT:N:8
8
```

Fig. 17.2.
Entering field names in a SHEET window.

Notice that the field names are entered in a single column. You also can enter the names across a row. In a SHEET window, Symphony does not care which way you choose, as long as you place the field names in consecutive cells. Nonconsecutive cells lead to blank columns in the database and waste space (and can also cause problems if you later decide to convert the in-RAM database to an @BASE database).

Tip

To conserve memory (a major consideration with an in-RAM database), erase the field names *you entered* in the SHEET or DOC window *after* Symphony uses them to generate the database. Delete the row or rows occupied by the field names to move the rest of the database ranges as high as possible in the worksheet. Save the file and retrieve it to recover the memory freed by this process.

Immediately after each field name, for all but the field ORDER NUMBER, is a letter followed by a colon and a number. The letters and numbers are used to indicate the field type and the field length, respectively. When you issue the FORM **G**enerate command, Symphony uses this information to set up the database. If you do not specify a type or length, as is the case with ORDER NUMBER, Symphony uses the default settings.

The choices you have for the field type are **L** (label), **N** (number), **D** (date), **T** (time), or **C** (computed). The label and number choices tell Symphony whether you want to store entries for those fields as labels or numbers. Symphony uses its special serial-numbering scheme to store date and time values. Therefore, if you enter a date in any of the valid date formats (D1 through D5), Symphony converts the entry to a serial number. If you select a computed field type, Symphony calculates the value based on a formula you supply. (Computed fields are treated in more depth in "Using Advanced FORM Features" later in this chapter.)

Specifying a field length tells Symphony how wide the columns in the database should be. For example, if you choose a length of 10 for the ENTRY DATE field, Symphony uses a column width of 10 for that field in the database.

Reminder:

When you enter field names in a DOC window, you must enter them down a column.

Figure 17.3 shows how to enter field names in a DOC window. When you use a DOC window, you must enter field names down a column. Before you enter the field names, issue the DOC **F**ormat **S**ettings **J**ustification **N**one command to prevent Symphony from putting two or more field names on the same line. (When you customize the input form later in this chapter, you can combine field names on the same line.)

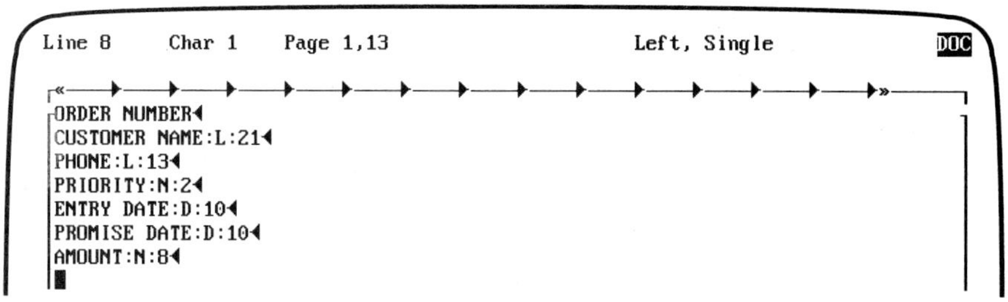

Fig. 17.3.

Entering field names in a DOC window.

```
Line 8      Char 1     Page 1,13                    Left, Single        DOC
┌«──▶───▶───▶───▶───▶───▶───▶───▶───▶───▶───▶───▶──▶»──┐
┌ORDER NUMBER◀                                          ┐
│CUSTOMER NAME:L:21◀
│PHONE:L:13◀
│PRIORITY:N:2◀
│ENTRY DATE:D:10◀
│PROMISE DATE:D:10◀
│AMOUNT:N:8◀
▌
```

Using the FORM Generate Command

To use the input form you created, change to a FORM window. When you do so, Symphony displays a blank screen with the message `No Definition range defined` at the top. Disregard the message this first time; it soon disappears. To initiate the FORM **G**enerate command, press the Menu (F10) key to display the main FORM window menu:

> **A**ttach **C**riteria **I**nitialize **R**ecord-Sort **G**enerate **F**ield **S**ettings

When you select **G**enerate, Symphony displays the following menu options:

> **L**abel **N**umber **D**ate **T**ime **C**omputed

These choices define the default field type. If you choose **N**umber, for example, you tell Symphony that any field name without an accompanying field-type indicator should be a number field. In this example, choose **L**abel for the default field type.

Next, Symphony asks you for a default field length. The length you choose is the value Symphony uses when a field-length number is not explicitly declared. Enter **7**, which is the default length you want for the ORDER NUMBER field. (You already explicitly declared the lengths for all the other fields when you entered the field names in the input form.)

After you have selected a length, Symphony asks you for a database name. The name you choose should be descriptive, because it is used to establish a series of range names. For this database, enter **priority**.

Finally, Symphony asks you for a field-names range. So that you can choose the range, Symphony temporarily shifts to the SHEET environment. Specify the proper range. In this case, enter the range **A1..A7**, which is the column of field names shown in figure 17.2.

After you enter the field-names range, Symphony generates several database ranges (described later in this chapter) and then shifts to an input form, provided you have entered the field-name information correctly. Figures 17.4A and 17.4B show how the input form appears in both FORM and SHEET mode.

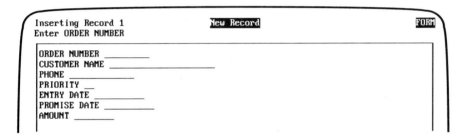

Fig. 17.4A.

The input form in FORM mode.

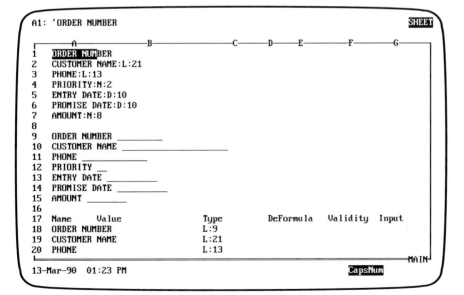

Fig. 17.4B.

The input form in SHEET mode.

Reminder:

Symphony uses the field lengths you specify in the input form to determine column width and the number of underscores in the input form.

As mentioned earlier, Symphony uses the lengths you specify to determine the individual column widths in the database. As shown in figure 17.4B, however, Symphony also uses the field lengths to determine the number of underscores that follow the field names in the input form.

In figure 17.4B, notice that the field names you entered are in the range A1..A7. Symphony used this information to generate the database. The entry form is in the range A9..A15. The database definition range starts in cell A17 (Symphony adds the column headings in row 17). Later in this chapter you learn how to customize the database using these ranges.

Entering a Record

When the input form has been generated, you can start entering records. To enter the order number for the first input record, simply start typing. For example, type **PO1435** and press Enter. When you press Enter, the cursor moves to the second field in the input form, the CUSTOMER NAME. For this field, type **Amdek Corporation** and press Enter. Continue this process until you have entered the last value for the last field in the record. To insert the record in the database, press the Ins (Insert) key. After you press Ins, Symphony enters the current record in the database and erases the data from the input form so that you can enter another record.

Following is a guide to important keys for entering and revising data records in an input form displayed in a FORM window:

Key	Activity
PgDn	Moves sequentially to the next record in the database. When you are entering or editing data, adds the record to the database and displays the next record or a new blank record.
PgUp	Moves sequentially to the previous record in the database. When you are entering or editing data, adds the record to the database and displays the previous record.
Enter (or Tab)	Moves the cursor to the next field in the record.
Home	Adds the current record to the database and moves to the first record in the database. If you are not entering or editing data, displays the first record.
End	Adds the current record to the database and moves to the last record in the database. If you are not entering or editing data, displays the last record. End followed by PgDn positions you at the end of the database and generates a blank form ready for input.

Key	Activity
GoTo (F5)	Jumps directly to a record if you enter the record number.
Edit (F2)	Enables you to revise an existing entry. After you press Edit to activate the field, you then can use the edit keys, such as Backspace, Esc, and Del, in the same manner as in SHEET mode (see Chapter 2).
Esc	Clears the current field if pressed once. If pressed twice, clears all fields and restores their original values. If pressed three times, removes the current entry and returns to the previous record.
Backspace	Clears the current field.
Begin typing	Causes Symphony to erase the current entry; enables you to enter a new entry when you are editing a field.
Ins	Adds the current record to the database and displays a new blank form during data entry. When you are editing data, adds the current record to the database, leaving the record in the form with the cursor at the first field.
Del	Deletes the current record from the database during editing of data. You must respond to a Yes/No confirmation prompt.
↑	Moves the cursor to the previous field above or to the left of the current cell.
↓	Moves the cursor to the next field below or to the right of the current cell.
→	Moves the cursor to the next field.
←	Moves the cursor to the previous field during entry of new data.
Ctrl-→	Moves the cursor to the first field in the form.
Ctrl-←	Moves the cursor to the last field in the form.

Reminder:

Press Esc once to clear the current field, twice to return fields to their original values, and three times to return to the previous record.

When you enter a record in a database by pressing the Ins key, Symphony places a copy of the record in a special database area located in the rows below the input form. The exact location of that area is not important for now. What is important is that when you use a FORM window, Symphony automatically does much of the work that you would otherwise have to do yourself.

Reminder:

Symphony does much of the work in entering a record into the database for you.

When you enter a date in the example input form, Symphony automatically changes the date to the D1 display format. For example, figure 17.5 shows how the screen appears just after you enter the ENTRY DATE in D4 (Full

International) format but before you press Enter. Figure 17.6 shows what happens after you press Enter. Just as with the @DATEVALUE function, you can enter the date in a FORM window in any one of the valid date formats: D1 through D5. (You cannot, however, use a formula or a function in an input form.) Later you learn how to change the date to any display format you want.

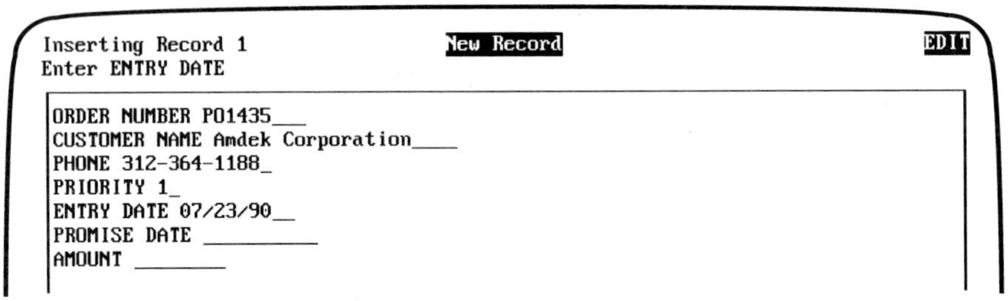

Fig. 17.5.

After entering the entry date but before pressing Enter.

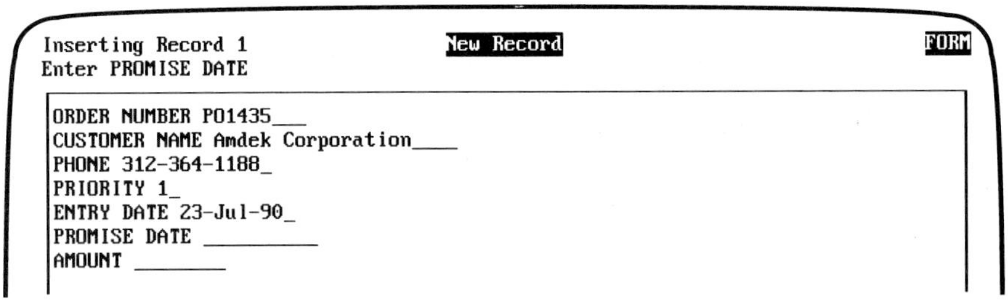

```
 ┌─────────────────────────────────────────────────────────────────┐
 │ Inserting Record 1                    ▐New Record▌         EDIT  │
 │ Enter ENTRY DATE                                                 │
 │  ┌──────────────────────────────────────────────────────────────┤
 │  │ORDER NUMBER PO1435___                                         │
 │  │CUSTOMER NAME Amdek Corporation____                            │
 │  │PHONE 312-364-1188_                                            │
 │  │PRIORITY 1_                                                    │
 │  │ENTRY DATE 07/23/90__                                          │
 │  │PROMISE DATE _____                                        │
 │  │AMOUNT _____                                                │
```

Fig. 17.6.

After pressing Enter (the date is formatted as D1).

```
 ┌─────────────────────────────────────────────────────────────────┐
 │ Inserting Record 1                    ▐New Record▌         FORM  │
 │ Enter PROMISE DATE                                               │
 │  ┌──────────────────────────────────────────────────────────────┤
 │  │ORDER NUMBER PO1435___                                         │
 │  │CUSTOMER NAME Amdek Corporation____                            │
 │  │PHONE 312-364-1188_                                            │
 │  │PRIORITY 1_                                                    │
 │  │ENTRY DATE 23-Jul-90_                                          │
 │  │PROMISE DATE _____                                        │
 │  │AMOUNT _____                                                │
```

Modifying the Current Record before Insertion

Sometimes you discover a mistake before you insert a record. You have several ways to modify the entry. Suppose that you discover an error immediately after entering an order number, and you want to go back and change it. One way is to press ↑, which returns you to the ORDER NUMBER field, and start typing. The old entry immediately disappears and clears the way for the new entry. Another method is to use the Edit (F2) key. Move the cursor to the ORDER NUMBER field and press Edit (F2); you can then use the Backspace, Esc, and Del keys just as you do in EDIT mode in a SHEET window (see Chapter 2 for more on the Edit key). Another alternative is to use the Backspace key. When you press Backspace, Symphony erases the field where the cursor is and moves the cursor to the next field. You then can position the cursor and make the correct entry. If you press the Esc key twice, all fields are cleared and their previous values are restored.

Modifying Previous Records

If you have already pressed the Ins key when you find an error in a record, you must make that record current again before you can modify it. One way to make the record current is to use the PgUp key to browse through the records, one by one in the input form, until you reach the one you want to modify. Another way is to use the GoTo (F5) key. If you can remember the number of the incorrect record, simply press GoTo (F5) and type the record number. Symphony immediately displays that record in an input form.

Undoing Changes to a Record

If you change a record that was previously inserted in the database, and then decide you don't like the changes you made, you can always recall the original copy of the record. Simply press the Esc key twice. The first time you press Esc, Symphony clears the field where the cursor resides and restores the original value of the field. The second time you press Esc, Symphony restores the entire original record.

Adding New Records

If, after making the initial entries to the database, you decide to add more records, first use the End key to go to the last record in the database. Then press the PgDn key. Symphony displays a **New Record** indicator at the top of the screen and a blank entry form below.

Reminder:

To add new records to an existing database, press End PgDn.

> **Tip**
>
> Symphony does not enable you to add new records between or before existing records. As you learn later in this chapter, you can re-sort the database into the proper order after you add the new record.

Adding new records is similar to making changes in existing records. Simply enter the value you want in a field and press Enter. When you press Enter, Symphony shifts the cursor down to the next field in the input form. After entering the last field, press the Ins key to enter the new record in the database. You can add as many new records as you want up to the practical limitations of RAM. Be sure to press Ins once for each record after you enter all the fields for that record.

Deleting Records

Deleting records is the easiest operation in a FORM window. Simply use the GoTo, PgUp, or PgDn key to make current the record you want to delete. Then press the Del key. Symphony asks if you are sure you want to delete this record. Answer **Y**es, and Symphony erases the record from the database and displays the next record in the form.

Tip

If you delete all the database records, Symphony readjusts the ranges named by the field names. If you must delete all the records, take some precautions. Deleting all the range names causes the range names for each field to refer to the field-name row (instead of to the first row of the database). If this happens, some @functions don't adjust properly. Although the database still works, database reports may produce incorrect results.

If you delete all the records in the database, switch to a SHEET window and press the GoTo (F5) key. Enter the name of the database range (this is the name of the database followed by _DB). Press the Menu (F10) key, select **R**ange **N**ame **L**abels **D**own, highlight all the field names, and press Enter. This action adjusts the range names back to their original state.

Sorting the Database

Suppose that you have entered several records in the Priority database and you want to sort the database by priority number. To sort the database, you must first select the FORM **S**ettings option. Figure 17.7 shows a copy of the FORM settings sheet with the **S**ettings menu in the control panel.

Fig. 17.7.

The FORM settings sheet and Settings menu.

```
Database, Criterion, Output ranges                                    MENU
Basic  Form  Underscores  Sort-Keys  Report  One-Record  Name  Cancel  Quit

Basic Ranges                          Report Ranges
   Database:      PRIORITY_DB            Main:         PRIORITY_MA
   Criterion:     PRIORITY_CR            Above:        PRIORITY_AB
   Output:             •                 Below:
Form Ranges                             Type          Single
   Entry:         PRIORITY_EN            Entry list:
   Definition:    PRIORITY_DF            Input cell:
Underscores:      Yes                  One-Record:     No
Sort-Keys
   1st-Key:              2nd-Key:                3rd-Key:
     Order:                Order:                  Order:
                                             Database Settings: PRIORITY
```

The next step in a sort is to select the **S**ort-Keys option from the **S**ettings menu. When you choose **S**ort-Keys, Symphony displays three options:

    1st-Key **2**nd-Key **3**rd-Key

To sort the database by priority number, choose **1**st-Key. Symphony shifts temporarily to the SHEET environment so that you can select the proper field. Figure 17.8 shows the database range A34..G53 (corresponding to the PRIORITY_DB range name in the settings sheet in fig. 17.7). This range is the same one that would appear if you selected **B**asic **D**atabase from the **S**ettings menu.

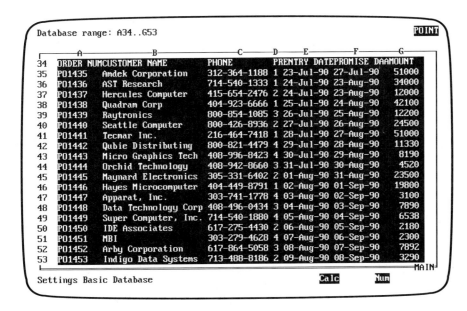

Fig. 17.8.
The database range.

Note: Symphony uses the field length you specified to set the column widths in the SHEET window. Because the field names are labels placed in the top row of the database range, field names longer than the field length appear truncated in the SHEET window. In figure 17.8, for example, the field name ORDER NUMBER in column A is truncated to ORDER NUM, PRIORITY in column D is truncated to PR, and PROMISE DATE in column F is truncated to PROMISE DA.

When Symphony shows you the database range, simply point to any item in the PRIORITY field (column D) to designate the primary sort key. For example, you can point to cell D35. After you point to the **1**st-Key, Symphony asks whether you want to sort in **A**scending or **D**escending order. Because you want the priority numbers to appear in ascending order, type **A** (for **A**scending).

Tip

If you point to the first row below the field names when you specify a sort key, Symphony shows the field name instead of an address for the sort key in the settings sheet. The field names make it easier to remember what the current sort keys are.

Reminder:

*After a sort, the input form reappears; use **S**ettings **B**asic **D**atabase to display the database and check the sort.*

After you set up the **1**st-Key, press Menu (F10) to return to the main FORM menu and then issue the **R**ecord-Sort command. Symphony asks whether you want to sort **A**ll the records or only the **U**nique records. (If you select **U**nique, Symphony removes all duplicate records.) After you select **A**ll or **U**nique, Symphony rearranges the data according to priority number and returns you to the entry database form. Figures 17.9A and 17.9B show the settings sheet and the newly sorted database. The database appears only after you use the **S**ettings **B**asic **D**atabase command.

Note: The entry form in the FORM window also goes by the names *database form* and *input form*, depending on the function it performs.

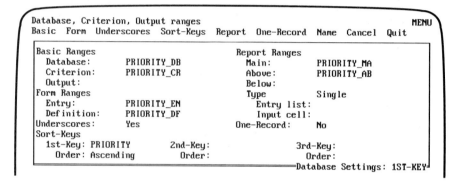

Fig. 17.9A.

The settings sheet showing the 1st-Key sort as the PRIORITY field.

```
Database, Criterion, Output ranges                                    MENU
Basic  Form  Underscores  Sort-Keys  Report  One-Record  Name  Cancel  Quit
 ┌──────────────────────────────────────────────────────────────────────┐
 │Basic Ranges                          Report Ranges                     │
 │  Database:        PRIORITY_DB          Main:        PRIORITY_MA         │
 │  Criterion:       PRIORITY_CR          Above:       PRIORITY_AB         │
 │  Output:                               Below:                          │
 │Form Ranges                             Type         Single             │
 │  Entry:           PRIORITY_EN            Entry list:                    │
 │  Definition:      PRIORITY_DF            Input cell:                    │
 │Underscores:       Yes                  One-Record:   No                 │
 │Sort-Keys                                                               │
 │  1st-Key: PRIORITY       2nd-Key:              3rd-Key:                │
 │    Order: Ascending        Order:                Order:                │
 │                                            ═══Database Settings: 1ST-KEY│
 └──────────────────────────────────────────────────────────────────────┘
```

Fig. 17.9B.

The database sorted on the PRIORITY field.

```
Database range: A34..G53                                            POINT
  ┌───A──────────B──────────────C──────────D────E────────F───────G──────┐
34│ORDER NCUSTOMER NAME         PHONE        PRENTRY DATEPROMISE DAAMOUNT │
35│P01438 Quadram Corp          404-923-6666 1 25-Jul-90 24-Aug-90  42100 │
36│P01441 Tecmar Inc.           216-464-7418 1 28-Jul-90 24-Aug-90  51000 │
37│P01435 Amdek Corporation     312-364-1188 1 23-Jul-90 22-Aug-90  23000 │
38│P01436 AST Research          714-540-1333 1 24-Jul-90 23-Aug-90  34000 │
39│P01446 Hayes Microcomputer   404-449-8791 1 02-Aug-90 24-Aug-90  19800 │
40│P01440 Seattle Computer      800-426-8936 2 27-Jul-90 24-Aug-90  24500 │
41│P01453 Indigo Data Systems   713-488-8186 2 09-Aug-90 24-Aug-90   3290 │
42│P01450 IDE Associates        617-275-4430 2 06-Aug-90 24-Aug-90   2180 │
43│P01445 Maynard Electronics   305-331-6402 2 01-Aug-90 24-Aug-90  23500 │
44│P01437 Hercules Computer     415-654-2476 2 24-Jul-90 23-Aug-90  12000 │
45│P01444 Orchid Technology     408-942-8660 3 31-Jul-90 24-Aug-90   4520 │
46│P01452 Arby Corporation      617-864-5058 3 08-Aug-90 24-Aug-90   7892 │
47│P01439 Raytronics            800-854-1085 3 26-Jul-90 24-Aug-90  12200 │
48│P01448 Data Technology Corp  408-496-0434 3 04-Aug-90 24-Aug-90   7890 │
49│P01442 Qubie Distributing    800-821-4479 4 29-Jul-90 24-Aug-90  11330 │
50│P01443 Micro Graphics Tech   408-996-8423 4 30-Jul-90 24-Aug-90   8190 │
51│P01451 MBI                   303-279-4628 4 07-Aug-90 24-Aug-90   2300 │
52│P01449 Super Computer, Inc.  714-540-1880 4 05-Aug-90 24-Aug-90   6530 │
53│P01447 Apparat, Inc.         303-741-1778 4 03-Aug-90 24-Aug-90   3100 │
  └──────────────────────────────────────────────────────────────MAIN────┘
Settings Basic Database                              Calc        Num
```

Notice that the priority numbers appear in ascending order, but you have no way to tell the relative priorities within a group. For example, five purchase-order numbers have priority 1, but no priorities are apparent within that group. If you want to prioritize within each group, you can use the dollar amount of the order (or some other field) as the **2**nd-Key (see fig. 17.10A). Figure 17.10B shows what happens when you select cell G35 as the **2**nd-Key with **D**escending order and re-sort the database with the **R**ecord-Sort command. You can specify up to three different sort keys.

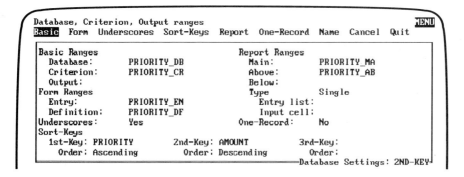

Fig. 17.10A.
The settings sheet showing the 2nd-Key sort as the AMOUNT field.

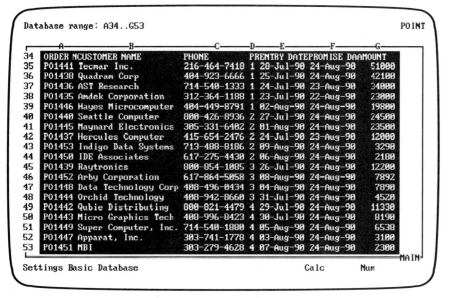

Fig. 17.10B.
The database sorted on the PRIORITY field and then on the AMOUNT field.

Besides using the **S**ettings **B**asic **D**atabase command to see the entire sorted database, you can also browse through the individual records one at a time to check their order. As soon as you leave the FORM **S**ettings menu, the FORM window appears with the database form so that you can look at one record at a time. Remember that when you re-sort the database, the first record to appear is the record at the *end* of the sorting order.

Although you use the FORM window to look at individual records, and the SHEET window to view several records at once, the two windows have a great deal in common when it comes to database operations. For example, the SHEET **Q**uery **R**ecord-Sort command is almost the same as the FORM **R**ecord-Sort command. The differences between the SHEET and FORM database commands are presented later in this chapter.

Working with FORM Settings Sheets

Just as with other types of settings sheets (including GRAPH, DOC, and COMM), you can name and save FORM settings sheets.

Naming Settings Sheets

Cue:

Save a settings sheet with FORM Settings Name Create so that you can use those settings at a later time.

The settings sheet that appears in figure 17.9A was stored under the name 1ST-KEY; the sheet figure 17.10A was stored under 2ND-KEY. (If you look at the right corners of both figures, you can see the names of the settings sheets.) To save a group of settings under a name, you use the FORM **S**ettings **N**ame command to display the following menu:

    Use **C**reate **D**elete **P**revious **N**ext **I**nitial-Settings **R**eset **Q**uit

Use the **C**reate option to name a settings sheet. Use the **U**se option to recall one of the settings you named previously so that you can modify it.

By default, Symphony assigns the name of the database to the settings sheet. If you want to assign a different name to the settings sheet, you can use up to 15 characters of any type.

Attaching Settings Sheets

To use a settings sheet with the current database, you must attach the settings sheet. For example, if you want to go back and forth in the Priority database between sorting by order number and sorting by priority number, you may want to create two different settings sheets: ORDER NUMBER, which contains a sort key (**S**ort-Keys **1**st-Key) from column A; and PRIORITY, which has a sort key from column D. Depending on how you want the database sorted at any given time, use the FORM **A**ttach command to attach the appropriate settings sheet to the database; re-sort the database using this settings sheet.

Note: When you select FORM **S**ettings **N**ame **U**se, you specify a database to create or modify. When you select FORM **A**ttach, you actually make a settings sheet available to Symphony to use with the database.

Creating a Catalog of Settings Sheets

The FORM **S**ettings **N**ame menu offers the **P**revious and **N**ext options. These options enable you to browse sequentially through a catalog of settings sheets and select the one you want. Be careful, though. Just because you have made a settings sheet current by using the **N**ext or **P**revious command, don't assume that Symphony will automatically use that settings sheet the next time you perform a **R**ecord-Sort or other database operation. You must attach the settings name to the database before Symphony can use the settings.

Reminder:
After you make a settings sheet current, you must attach it to the database before Symphony can use it to perform a sort.

Searching for Records

In addition to sorting a database, Symphony's FORM environment makes searching for records easy. You can search for records individually or in groups. For example, suppose that you are given the Priority database sorted by priority number and amount, and you want to find the record for order number PO1452.

To find a record in the database, you must enter selection criteria. The criteria can be numbers, labels, or formulas. To enter selection criteria, choose FORM **C**riteria. Symphony displays the following options:

>   **U**se   **I**gnore   **E**dit

To enter selection criteria and to modify criteria, select **E**dit. Symphony displays a blank input form with the message `Editing Criterion Record 1 of 1` at the top of the screen. (Symphony lets you enter as many as four different criterion records.) To specify the database record for PO1452, enter that order number in the ORDER NUMBER field. Figure 17.11 shows the input form just after you enter the order number.

```
Editing Criterion Record 1 of 1                          EDIT
Enter ORDER NUMBER

 ORDER NUMBER PO1452___
 CUSTOMER NAME _____
 PHONE _____
 PRIORITY __
 ENTRY DATE _____
 PROMISE DATE _____
 AMOUNT _____
```

Fig. 17.11.
Entering an order number in a criterion record.

Next, press PgUp to return to the database. Choose FORM **C**riteria **U**se to have Symphony use the selection criteria you established. Symphony selects the record that matches the specified criteria (see fig. 17.12).

Fig. 17.12.

The selected record.

```
┌─────────────────────────────────────────────────────────────────────┐
│ Editing Record 12 of 19 (1 Match)                               FORM │
│ Enter ORDER NUMBER                                                    │
│  ┌──────────────────────────────────────────────────────────────┐    │
│  │ ORDER NUMBER PO1452_                                          │    │
│  │ CUSTOMER NAME Arby Corporation_____                          │    │
│  │ PHONE 617-864-5058_                                          │    │
│  │ PRIORITY 3_                                                  │    │
│  │ ENTRY DATE 28-Jul-90_                                        │    │
│  │ PROMISE DATE 27-Aug-90_                                      │    │
│  │ AMOUNT 7892____                                             │    │
│  └──────────────────────────────────────────────────────────────┘    │
│                                                                       │
└─────────────────────────────────────────────────────────────────────┘
```

Once you have seen the record for PO1452, and you want to move to another task, choose FORM **C**riteria **I**gnore. This command returns you to the database, but the criteria you have set up remain in the criterion record. If you want to reinvoke the criteria later, simply select FORM **C**riteria **U**se again. As you see in "Printing Database Reports" later in this chapter, Symphony does not ignore criteria when printing a database report even if you select **C**riteria **I**gnore.

Using Formulas in Criteria

Besides choosing individual records, you can also set up criteria to select a group of records. Suppose, for example, that you want to select all records in the database whose amount is greater than $10,000. To enter this criteria, select FORM **C**riteria **E**dit. Because the criteria for the purchase order still reside in the input form, you must first delete the purchase-order number from the ORDER NUMBER field. To do so, enter a blank space or press Backspace while the cursor is in the ORDER NUMBER field. Next, move to the AMOUNT field and enter the formula **+?>10000**. This entry may not look like a formula, but it has special meaning in a criterion record.

Reminder:

Use a question mark in a formula in a criterion record when you want Symphony to use one of the special range names it established.

The question mark in the formula indicates to Symphony that you want the program to supply a cell address. Symphony uses one of the special range names that the program sets up when you issue the **G**enerate command. Look back at figures 17.7 and 17.8; they show you the range name (PRIORITY_DB) and the database range for the Priority database. When setting up the database, Symphony uses the field-name headings as range names for the cells directly below (see row 34 of fig. 17.8). In other words, cell A35 is named ORDER NUMBER, cell B35 is CUSTOMER NAME, and so on. Therefore, when you use a question mark in a criterion formula, Symphony substitutes the appropriate range name for the cell where you enter the formula. (In this case, Symphony substitutes AMOUNT for the question mark because you entered the formula in the AMOUNT field.)

Because you are entering a formula, be sure to precede the question mark with a plus (+) sign. Otherwise, the formula does not work correctly.

After you enter the criteria for records with an amount greater than $10,000, press PgUp and select FORM **C**riteria **U**se; Symphony returns 10 records that meet the criteria. Figure 17.13 shows the first of the 10 records that match the criteria. The message at the top of the screen indicates which record is in the input form. You can use the Home, End, PgUp, and PgDn keys to browse through the records that match the selection criteria. Use the FORM **C**riteria **I**gnore command to return to the entire database.

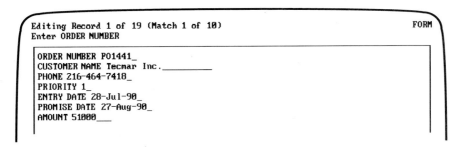

```
Editing Record 1 of 19 (Match 1 of 10)                    FORM
Enter ORDER NUMBER

   ORDER NUMBER PO1441_
   CUSTOMER NAME Tecmar Inc._____
   PHONE 216-464-7418_
   PRIORITY 1_
   ENTRY DATE 28-Jul-90_
   PROMISE DATE 27-Aug-90_
   AMOUNT 51000___
```

Fig. 17.13.
The first of 10 selected records.

Now suppose that you want to select all the records in the database whose amount is greater than $10,000 *and* whose priority number is 2 or below. Use FORM **C**riteria **E**dit to edit the criterion record you have constructed. Next, move to the PRIORITY field and enter the formula **+?<=2**. Don't be concerned if you don't see the entire formula. You can verify it by using the Edit (F2) key even though PRIORITY is a two-position field. Because you still want every record whose amount is greater than $10,000, leave the original +AMOUNT>10000 formula in the AMOUNT field.

Reminder:
Put multiple criteria in one criterion record if you want all the criteria met in a search.

By combining the two formulas in the same criterion record, you are telling Symphony that you want to combine these two criteria with the AND operator. In other words, for a record to filter through the criteria you have set up, the record must pass *both* tests. Figure 17.14 shows the second record that meets the new criteria.

```
Editing Record 2 of 19 (Match 2 of 8)                     FORM
Enter ORDER NUMBER

   ORDER NUMBER PO1438_
   CUSTOMER NAME Quadram Corp_____
   PHONE 404-923-6666_
   PRIORITY 1_
   ENTRY DATE 25-Jul-90_
   PROMISE DATE 24-Aug-90_
   AMOUNT 42100___
```

Fig. 17.14.
A record meeting the AND criteria.

Suppose, on the other hand, that you want all the records that have a priority of 2 or below *or* have an amount greater than $10,000. To combine criteria with OR, place them in different criterion records. Keep the original formula in the first criterion record (+AMOUNT>10000) and delete the criterion formula for the PRIORITY field. Then select **C**riterion **E**dit and press PgDn to add another criterion record. After placing the +?<=2 formula in the PRIORITY field of the second record, press PgUp twice to return to the database. Finally, invoke the **C**riteria **U**se command to initiate the search. This time you get 12 records that match the criteria.

Adding a Criterion Range

As mentioned earlier, Symphony allows you to construct up to four criterion records, which can give you fairly complex criteria. At times, however, you may want to step outside Symphony's structure. For example, you may want to add additional criterion records (more than Symphony's basic four). To do so, you must know where Symphony stores the criterion range. If you use the FORM **S**ettings **B**asic **C**riterion command, Symphony displays the criterion range. Figure 17.15 shows the criterion range for the OR example explained in the preceding section. Notice that each formula appears as a **1** in the figure, and that the two formulas appear on different lines. Criteria combined with OR reside on different lines in a criterion range; criteria combined with AND reside on the same line. The value of a formula is always true or false (1 or 0). These formulas appear as **1**s because both their values are true for the records to which they currently refer. If you shift to the SHEET environment and use the SHEET **F**ormat **O**ther **L**iteral display format on these formulas, they display in their normal form.

When you use the **G**enerate command, Symphony automatically sets up the criterion range and names it based on the name of the database. The name of the criterion range in this example is PRIORITY_CR. When you first use the **G**enerate command, the criterion range consists of the field names and one blank row (A29..G30 in the example). As you add criterion records, however, the range grows. Because you added two criterion records in the current example, the criterion range is three rows deep (A29..G31). Symphony automatically keeps track of the criterion range, the database range (A18..H24), and several other important ranges. This feature is one of the most convenient elements of building a database in the FORM environment.

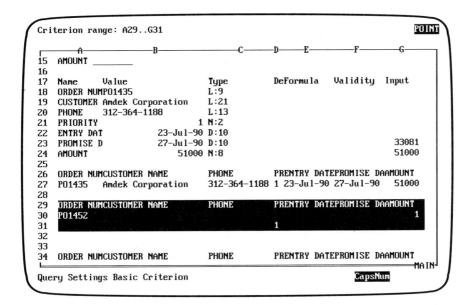

Fig. 17.15.
The criterion range.

Symphony automatically sets up the FORM window to allow enough space for four criterion records. But what if you want five? For example, suppose that you want to select all the records for the following customer names:

> Quadram Corp
> Indigo Data Systems
> Seattle Computer
> AST Research Inc.
> Orchid Technology

To select the records for Quadram Corp, simply place that name in the CUSTOMER NAME field of a criterion record. To use all five names, however, you need five criterion records.

If you want to add another record to the criterion range, first shift to the SHEET environment. Move the cursor to the criterion range by pressing GoTo (F5) and entering **PRIORITY_CR**. The cursor appears at the top left corner of the criterion range. The easiest way to add a criterion record is to use SHEET **I**nsert **R**ows to insert a blank row below the field-name headings in the criterion range. Because this method inserts a row in the middle of the range, the criterion range automatically expands. Figure 17.16 shows the new criterion range.

Reminder:

Shift to the SHEET environment and use Insert Rows to insert a new criterion record in the criterion range.

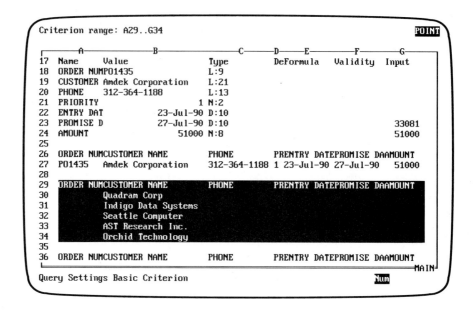

Fig. 17.16.

After inserting a row in the criterion range.

When you make the appropriate change to the criterion range, Symphony instantly recognizes five criterion records.

Tip

With Symphony, you also can use the #OR# operator to combine criteria in a single criterion record. Instead of adding an extra row to the criterion range, you can place the following formula in an existing criterion record:

+CUSTOMER NAME="Quadram Corp"#OR#CUSTOMER NAME="Indigo Data Systems"

You can place criterion formulas in any of the criterion fields. For example, you can put the #OR# formula just shown in the PHONE field. When you place a criterion formula in a field that has nothing to do with the formula (a customer-name formula in a PHONE field, for example), you cannot use ? to designate the field name. Instead you must type the field name (or a cell address from that field) in the formula.

Searching for Approximate Matches

Reminder:

Symphony does not recognize any difference between uppercase and lowercase letters when searching for labels.

Symphony uses approximate matching when evaluating the labels in a record. (The DOC **S**earch command uses approximate matching also.) For example, suppose that you want to find all the records in the Priority database whose CUSTOMER NAME field begins with *A*. When you enter the formula **@LEFT(?,1)="A"** in the CUSTOMER NAME field of the first criterion record, Symphony returns four database records. If you type the formula with a lowercase *a*, **@LEFT(?,1)="a"**, Symphony returns the same results because the program does not recognize the difference between lowercase and uppercase letters when matching labels.

Using Wild Cards in Criterion Records

Symphony also has wild-card provisions for matching labels. The characters ?, *, and ~ have special meanings when used in criterion records.

The ? character instructs Symphony to accept any character in that position (just as the character does in DOS). For example, if you want to find the record for order number PO1452 but suspect that you typed a zero rather than a capital O for the second character when you entered the record, you can use the label P?1452.

The * character tells Symphony to accept all characters that follow the *. Suppose that you want to select the records in the Priority database whose CUSTOMER NAME begins with *A*. You can enter **A*** or **a***. Be forewarned: Symphony does not recognize the * character when you put characters after it. For example, *dek* is an invalid use of the wild-card character.

Caution:
*Symphony does not recognize any character that you type after the * wild-card character.*

When placed at the beginning of a label, the ~ character indicates that all the values except those that follow it are to be selected. For example, if you want all the records in the Priority database *except* those that begin with the letter *A*, you can enter **~A*** in the first criterion record.

Although the ~ character works well for labels, it doesn't work for formulas and numbers. To get the same results with a number or a formula, you must use either the <> or the #NOT# logical operator. For example, if you want to select all the records in the Priority database except those whose priority number is 4, enter **+?<>4**. (Notice that the ? character is not used as the label wild card in this case; it is used to refer to the PRIORITY field.) Alternatively, you can enter the formula **#NOT#?=4**. Both formulas give the same results.

Caution:
You cannot use the ~ character with numbers or formulas.

Modifying and Deleting Records While Searching

Suppose that while you are searching a database, you find a record that requires modification. You can stop the search by using the FORM **C**riteria **I**gnore command and return to the database to edit the record. This method is not desirable because you have to find the record again before you can modify it. A better technique is to modify the record on the spot.

When you are in a FORM window, you can modify any record. If you modify the record to the point where it no longer fits the criteria, Symphony no longer lets you see the record during the search operation (unless you change the selection criteria). If, on the other hand, you perform a search in a SHEET window using the **Q**uery command, you cannot modify records.

Besides modifying records while searching in a FORM window, you also can delete records. Just press the Del key to delete the displayed record. Symphony asks for confirmation before deleting the record.

Under no circumstances can you add a record while you are in the middle of a search operation in a FORM window. This statement holds even if one of the records that conforms to the search criteria is the last record in the database. (Recall that under normal circumstances, you must move to the last record in the database before adding a record.)

Using Advanced FORM Features

Now that you are familiar with the basics of creating a standard input form and entering a simple database, you are ready to learn some of the more-advanced features of Symphony's FORM window. For example, up to this point, Symphony has automatically handled the layout of input forms and has entered all the important ranges with little help from you. You now learn how to create customized input forms and make other modifications to a database to better suit your personal data-management needs.

Creating Special Input Forms

Suppose that you decide to create a special input form for entering additional records in the Priority database. To begin with, you decide to place two fields on the same line in the input form. Assume that you want to put the PHONE field on the same line as the CUSTOMER NAME field. To do so, you can use the FORM **F**ield **M**ove command.

Reminder:

Select FORM Field Move to move one field to the same line as another field.

After you choose FORM **F**ield **M**ove, Symphony displays the `Select field to move` prompt. Position the cursor on the field you want to move (PHONE in this example) and press Enter. Next, Symphony asks you to select the new position for the field. Move the cursor to the appropriate position—in this case, several spaces after the CUSTOMER NAME field—and press Enter. Symphony warns you that any data to the right or below the database ranges may move; select **Y**es to proceed.

The field moves, but you are left with a blank line in the original PHONE field position (see fig. 17.17). To get rid of this blank line, you must be familiar with another special range created when Symphony generated the database: the entry range.

Modifying the Entry Range

Symphony creates the entry range when you issue the **G**enerate command. Figure 17.18 shows the entry range for the Priority database.

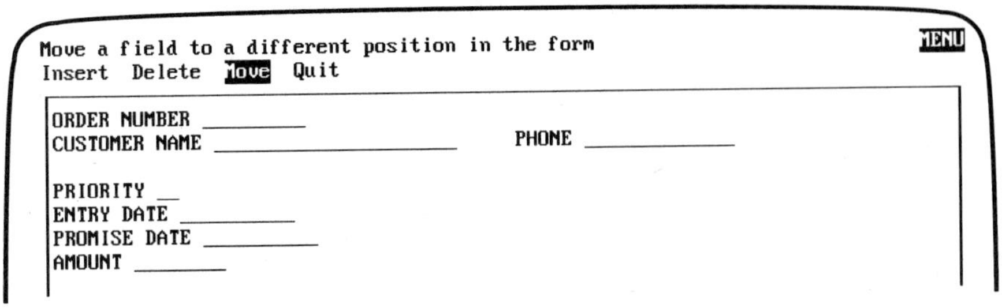

```
┌────────────────────────────────────────────────────────────────┐
 Move a field to a different position in the form          MENU
 Insert  Delete  Move  Quit
 ┌──────────────────────────────────────────────────────────────┐
 │ ORDER NUMBER _____                                        │
 │ CUSTOMER NAME _____     PHONE _____      │
 │                                                              │
 │ PRIORITY __                                                  │
 │ ENTRY DATE _____                                        │
 │ PROMISE DATE _____                                       │
 │ AMOUNT _____                                               │
 └──────────────────────────────────────────────────────────────┘
```

Fig. 17.17.

The input form after moving the PHONE field.

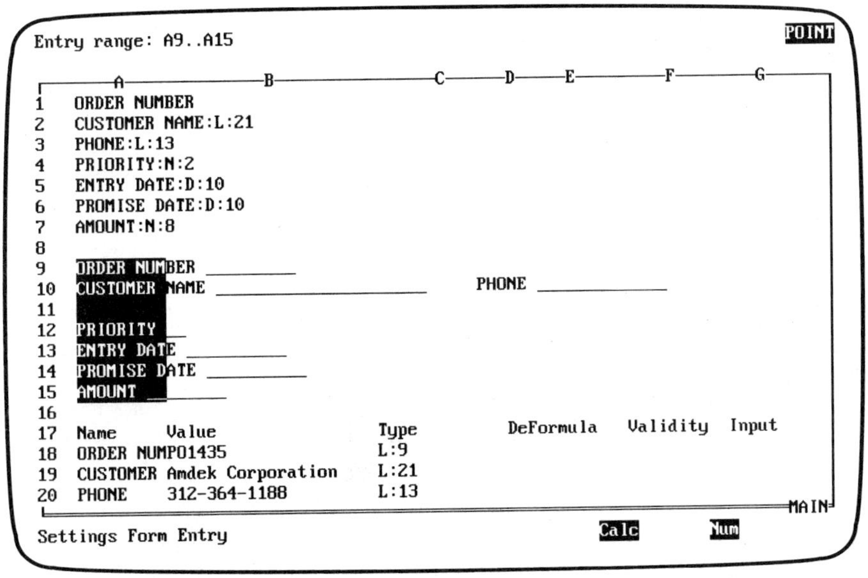

```
┌────────────────────────────────────────────────────────────────┐
 Entry range: A9..A15                                      POINT
 ┌─A────────────B───────────C────D───E──────F───────G──────────┐
 1    ORDER NUMBER
 2    CUSTOMER NAME:L:21
 3    PHONE:L:13
 4    PRIORITY:N:2
 5    ENTRY DATE:D:10
 6    PROMISE DATE:D:10
 7    AMOUNT:N:8
 8
 9    ORDER NUMBER _____
 10   CUSTOMER NAME _____     PHONE _____
 11
 12   PRIORITY __
 13   ENTRY DATE _____
 14   PROMISE DATE _____
 15   AMOUNT _____
 16
 17   Name     Value             Type      DeFormula  Validity  Input
 18   ORDER NUMP01435            L:9
 19   CUSTOMER Amdek Corporation L:21
 20   PHONE    312-364-1188      L:13
 └──────────────────────────────────────────────────────MAIN┘
 Settings Form Entry                       Calc       Num
└────────────────────────────────────────────────────────────────┘
```

Fig. 17.18.

The entry range.

The entry range (A9..A15) contains a column of label entries, the same labels that appear in the input form when you enter data. If you want to remove the blank line, you must modify the entry range. First, press Type (Alt-F10) to change to the DOC environment. (You can change to the SHEET environment and use the SHEET **D**elete **R**ows command, but the procedure is easier in the DOC environment.) Make sure that DOC **F**ormat **S**ettings **J**ustification is set to **N**one so that Symphony does not try to justify the entry range.

After you change to the DOC environment, move the cursor to the entry range— to the blank line between CUSTOMER NAME and PRIORITY. Use the Del key to remove the blank line. Figure 17.19 shows the entry range after the change.

The address of the entry range is stored in the settings sheet under the name PRIORITY_EN. (Symphony assigned this name when you used the **G**enerate command.) If you issue the FORM **S**ettings **F**orm **E**ntry command, Symphony highlights the PRIORITY_EN range. You should not have to change this setting.

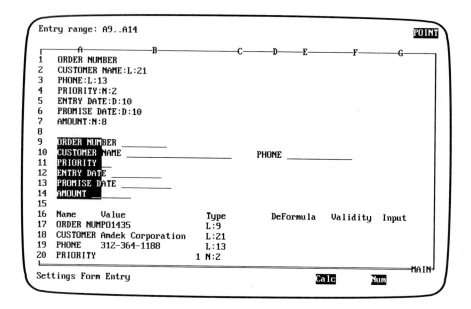

Fig. 17.19.

The entry range after deleting the blank line.

The FORM **F**ield **M**ove command automatically repositions the fields in the entry and definition ranges, but not in the database, criterion, and report ranges. (The definition and report ranges are discussed later in the chapter.) If you want to move the field in these other ranges, you must use the SHEET **M**ove command. Keep in mind, however, that SHEET **M**ove does not insert; you will probably have to make the move in several steps so that you don't overwrite data.

Changing the position of the PHONE field in the input form does not affect the way Symphony enters records in the database. In fact, you can put several field names on the same line. Symphony processes them sequentially from left to right as though they were all on separate lines.

Changing Underscores

Reminder:

Increase the width of the field by adding underscores to the input form in the DOC environment.

Suppose that you want to modify the input form to allow longer entries by increasing the size of the CUSTOMER NAME field from 21 to 30 characters. To do so, simply shift to the DOC environment, position the cursor on the CUSTOMER NAME label, and add 9 underscore characters to the 21 already there. Incidentally, you can stop underscores from appearing at all in the input form by selecting FORM **S**ettings **U**nderscores **N**o.

Tip

The entry range is contained in one column as a series of long labels, regardless of how many fields are on a line. Although Symphony automatically places the field names to the left of the underscore characters, the field names aren't necessary for proper operation of the input form. In fact, Symphony ignores everything in the input form except the underscores. Because this is so, you can include user instructions or other helpful notes on the input form.

Modifying the Definition Range

If you prefer not to change the input form, but you still want it to handle longer customer names, Symphony offers the scrolling-characters technique. To use this technique, you have to know how to change the definition range. The definition range for the Priority database (PRIORITY_DF: A17..H23) appears in figure 17.20.

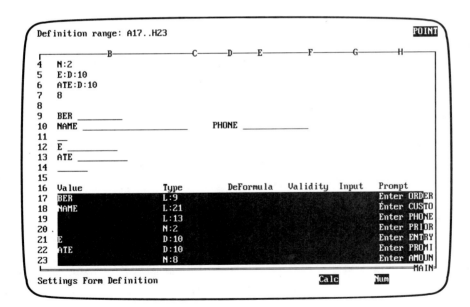

Fig. 17.20.
The definition range.

The definition range, which is the most comprehensive range in the FORM work environment, contains fields for checking the type of entries made and their validity; that is, whether they fall within a certain range of values. The definition range is also where you control the format for displaying entries and other customization.

To change the number of characters you can enter in the CUSTOMER NAME field without changing the input form, switch to the SHEET environment. Next, move the cursor to the Type field in the definition range. The Type field that defines the CUSTOMER NAME field in the Priority database is cell C18 in figure 17.20. (Find the correct cell by looking at the entries in the Name column, the first column in the definition range.) Notice that the Type field is where Symphony stores the type and length information you provided when you created the database. Change the value in cell C18 from L:21 (for label, 21 characters long) to L:30. When you switch back to the FORM environment, you can now enter labels up to 30 characters long in the CUSTOMER NAME field. Because the input form does not have enough visible room to display a 30-character string, however, Symphony begins scrolling when you reach the 21st character.

The FORM window scrolling feature also works for number entries. Be forewarned, however, that because Symphony can store numbers with as many as 15 decimal places, the scrolling feature is practical only up to that point. When you get beyond 15 places, Symphony automatically shifts to the scientific format.

Another mistake to watch out for is eliminating the definition-range address in the settings sheet when you rearrange the input form. To access the definition range in the settings sheet, use FORM **S**ettings **F**orm **D**efinition. Normally, if you have eliminated the definition-range address, the entry in the settings sheet is blank. You must restore the correct value in order for the FORM window to work properly.

Note: The definition range starts in the row below the row with the labels Name, Value, Type, Default, Formula, Validity, Input, and Prompt. The range extends to the right over eight columns and down as far as the last field name. If you have to restore the correct address values for the definition range, be sure to highlight this entire area but don't include the row with the column labels.

Creating Defaults

Now that you are familiar with the basic concept of the definition range, you are ready to make more modifications to the input form. Suppose, for example, that you want to set up the current date as the default entry date in the input form. As the default, the current date shows up every time you create a new record. You then have the option of keeping the current date or overriding it with another date.

To set up a default in the input form, you must make the proper entry in the Default field of the definition range. Although the label in cell D16 of figure 17.20 is truncated (it reads **D e**), the label indicates the Default column. To have the current date display as the default in the ENTRY DATE field, enter the formula **@INT(@NOW)** in cell D21, the cell corresponding to the ENTRY DATE field in the Default column. The formula @INT(@NOW) takes the integer portion of the current date-and-time serial number, as explained in Chapter 6. Figure 17.21 shows the input form with the new ENTRY DATE default.

```
Inserting Record 20              New Record                    FORM
Enter ORDER NUMBER

  ORDER NUMBER _____
  CUSTOMER NAME _____    PHONE _____
  PRIORITY __
  ENTRY DATE 13-Mar-90_
  PROMISE DATE _____
  AMOUNT _____
```

Fig. 17.21.
The input form with the entry date default.

You also can enter labels or numbers as defaults. For example, to have the priority number default to the highest priority, you can enter the number **1** in cell D20 of the definition range.

No matter what default you use (formula, label, or number), you should always make sure that your entry is the correct type for that database field. Although Symphony performs a validity check on the default value, the program does not check whether the default is the correct entry type. If you are not careful, you may wind up with character data in a number field, or vice versa.

Computing Fields

Suppose that, as a company policy, you always assign a promise date that is 30 days after the entry date. Therefore, after you enter the entry date, you want Symphony to compute the promise date. Symphony lets you define a computed field when you first create the database. That time is the best time to define a computed field, but if you decide later that you want to enter one, change the type designation in the Type column of the definition range to C (for computed).

To complete the change, enter the formula **+B21+30** in cell E22. Column E is labeled Formula in figure 17.20. Whenever you enter a formula for computing a field or transforming a field, always enter the formula in the Formula column of the definition range. Notice that the formula refers to a value in column B, the Value column. Symphony uses the Value column as a temporary holding place for the current record before writing it to the database. (Symphony also places the result of the formula in the Value column.) Make the formulas for computed fields refer to the appropriate cells in the Value column. Figure 17.22 shows the input form after PROMISE DATE is computed from ENTRY DATE.

Reminder:
Make formulas for computed fields refer to cells in the Value column of the definition range.

Fig. 17.22.

The promise date computed from the entry date.

```
Editing Record 20 of 20                                    FORM
Enter ORDER NUMBER
  ORDER NUMBER _____
  CUSTOMER NAME _____        PHONE _____
  PRIORITY __
  ENTRY DATE 13-Mar-90_
  PROMISE DATE 12-Apr-90_
  AMOUNT _____
```

When you use the input form, notice that the cursor jumps past a computed field. Because the field is computed from the values in other fields of the same record, you cannot enter a value manually. Therefore, when you designate a field as the computed type, be sure that you will not want to change the field manually.

You should also avoid the mistake of trying to compute fields from other records in the database. The difficulty of creating general formulas for this purpose is beyond the scope of the beginner. You can refer to *values* outside the definition range but not to *formulas* outside the definition range. Symphony does not recalculate formulas outside the definition range during database operation.

Tip

Because Symphony bypasses computed fields when using the input form, you can use computed fields as a way to skip certain entries in a large input form. A database with fields for each month's sales, for example, can be made to allow only the current month's sales field to be used. Just change the other fields' types to computed and enter a formula that makes their value equal to the entry in the Value column. In the Priority database, for example, you can prevent modification of entries in the CUSTOMER NAME field by placing the formula +B18 in cell E18 of the definition range and changing cell C18 of the definition range to C:21. You must change C18 back to L:21 and erase the formula in E18 when you want to allow new entries or modifications to existing entries in the CUSTOMER NAME field.

Transforming Fields

Reminder:

You can modify transformed fields; you cannot modify computed fields.

Besides computing fields, you also can transform them. The main difference between the two methods is that you can manually modify transformed fields but not computed fields.

Suppose, for example, that you always enter order numbers beginning with the letters *PO*. Rather than enter the entire order number yourself, you want to type only the number portion and have Symphony enter the initial string for you. To arrange this setup, type the formula **+"PO"&G17** in cell E17 of the definition form for the Priority database. (***Note:*** Do not be concerned if ERR is generated before you can enter data.) Cell E17 resides in the Formula column, the same column you use to enter a formula for a computed field. But this time the formula refers to a cell in the Input column. Figure 17.23 shows the Input column in the definition range.

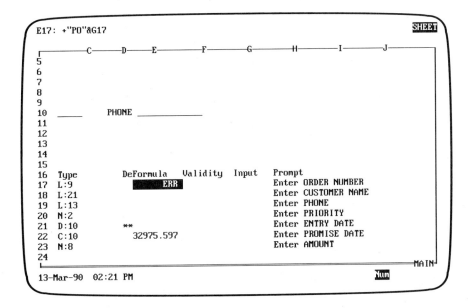

Fig. 17.23.
The Input column in the definition range.

Entries from the input form are stored temporarily in the Input column. You never actually see values in the Input column; however, any formula that transforms an entry must refer to this column.

Figure 17.24 shows the input form after an order number is entered but before Enter is pressed. Figure 17.25 shows the input form after Enter is pressed.

Reminder:
Make formulas for transformed fields refer to cells in the Input column of the definition range.

```
 Inserting Record 20        New Record              EDIT
 Enter ORDER NUMBER

  ORDER NUMBER 1469_____
  CUSTOMER NAME _____        PHONE _____
  PRIORITY __
  ENTRY DATE 13-Mar-90_
  PROMISE DATE 12-Apr-90_
  AMOUNT _____
```

Fig. 17.24.
After entering the order number but before pressing Enter.

Fig. 17.25.

After pressing Enter.

```
Inserting Record 20                New Record                      FORM
Enter CUSTOMER NAME

ORDER NUMBER PO1469___
CUSTOMER NAME _____        PHONE _____
PRIORITY __
ENTRY DATE 13-Mar-90_
PROMISE DATE 12-Apr-90_
AMOUNT _____
```

As another example of transforming an entry, assume that you want to enter customer phone numbers without having to enter the hyphens. To do so, you can enter the following formula in cell E19 of the definition range:

@LEFT(G19,3)&"-"&@MID(G19,3,3)&"-"&@RIGHT(G19,4)

Just as default and computed entries, transformed entries are stored in the Value column (column B) until the record is placed in the database.

Performing Edit Checks

Symphony offers some simple edit checks that depend on the field-type indicators you use when creating a database. For example, if you indicate that a field is a date field (with a D field-type indicator), you must enter the date in one of the valid date formats, or Symphony beeps at you. Similarly, you must enter time in one of the valid time formats.

Incidentally, Symphony automatically uses the D1 format for displaying dates in the input form, the database range, and the Value column of the definition range. Times are displayed in the T1 format. If you want to modify the way in which a date or time is displayed, change the format in the Value column of the definition range. Any change you make is reflected in the input form.

Symphony also checks for valid numbers and labels when you use N and L field-type indicators. For example, because the PRIORITY field in the example database is designated as a two-character field, you must enter a number between 0 and 99. When a field is a label field, however, Symphony accepts just about any entry. About the only edit check that Symphony provides for a label field is to test its length.

Reminder:

Place formulas that do validity checks in the Validity column of the definition range; make the formulas refer to the Value column.

Performing Value Checks

Besides the simple edit checks that Symphony provides through field-type indicators, you also can validate inputs by using formulas. For example, suppose that you want to disallow priority numbers greater than 4 in the Priority database. You can enter the formula **+B20<=4** in cell F20 of the definition range. Column F is the Validity column; the formula refers to a cell in the Value column. Value-checking formulas must always be written this way. If you need to check for several conditions, combine the formulas with #AND#, #OR#, or #NOT#. If you want to ensure that all priority numbers are between 0 and 4, for example, enter the formula **+B20>=0#AND#B20<=4** in cell F20 of the definition range.

You need to remember two rules when you use value-checking formulas. First, make sure that any default values you use pass the check; Symphony does not check default values. Second, value-checking formulas test the value in the Value column, not the values actually input.

Here's an example showing the importance of this second rule. Suppose that you want to build a formula to check the four right-hand digits of the order number in the Priority database and also use another formula to enter the *PO* portion of the order number. The formula to transform the order number is +"PO"&G17. This formula refers to a cell in the Input column; Symphony places the result of the formula in the Value column. Because the value-checking formula tests the value in the Value column, you must use a formula that works with the transformed order number. The following is such a formula:

@IF(@ISERR(@VALUE(@RIGHT(B17,4))),@FALSE,@TRUE)

This formula converts the four right-hand digits of the order number from characters to numbers. The formula then tests for an ERR message indicating that the conversion has not taken place. If the conversion does take place, no ERR message is produced, and the value of the function is 1. Otherwise, the value of the function is 0. If the validity check fails, Symphony beeps, flashes **ERROR**, and displays the message `Invalid field entry`. Press Esc or Enter to clear the error. The invalid entry is not placed in the field; instead, Symphony keeps the cursor in the field and waits for you to continue. You then can make a valid entry in the field or move to another field without making an entry in the current field.

Changing Prompts

In column H of figure 17.23, you can see the prompts that Symphony displays in the control panel when you enter data in the input form. Symphony automatically supplies these prompts when you generate the database.

Suppose that you want to change the prompt for the priority number from `Enter Priority` to `Priority?`. Simply enter the new label in cell H20 of the definition range, and Symphony uses the new prompt for the next record you enter.

Reminder:

Change the Prompt column of the definition range to change the prompt that appears in the control panel.

Changing Formats

You can change the format of the AMOUNT field in the Priority database to the **Currency 0** format. Move the cursor to cell B23 in the definition range (the Value column) and change the format there. A simple way is to switch to the SHEET environment and use the SHEET **F**ormat command. Symphony then displays in the new currency format the amounts entered in the input form.

Changing the display format in the input form does not change the format in the records stored in the database range (PRIORITY_DB). Because most of the time you see the records only as they appear in the input form, however, you don't really care how they appear in the database range. If you do want to format the database range, use the SHEET **F**ormat command and indicate the column of values in the database range that you want to format.

Adding a Field to the Database

No matter how well you have thought out and planned your database, it's likely you will need to add a field at a later date. Symphony 2.0 added the FORM **F**ield **I**nsert command which makes this type of structural change easy. (Earlier releases of Symphony required that you insert the field manually into the database, criterion, entry, report, and definition ranges.)

In the customer database you have been building in this chapter, assume that you want to add a COMMENT field after the AMOUNT field. Select FORM **F**ield **I**nsert. Symphony asks you to supply a series of items. Enter **COMMENT** in response to the `Specify field name:` prompt, select **L**abel for the field type, and enter **20** for the field length. When prompted `Select position for field`, put the cursor under AMOUNT and press Enter. Symphony warns you that any data to the right or below the database ranges may move; select **Y**es to proceed.

Symphony automatically inserts the new field in the input form and all other database ranges (criterion, report, definition, and database).

Deleting a Field

Reminder:

When you use FORM Field Delete, also use SHEET Delete Rows or switch to DOC mode and press Del to delete the blank row from the entry and definition ranges.

The FORM **F**ield command also has an option to **D**elete a field. After you select the field to delete (choose COMMENT for this example), Symphony asks you to confirm the deletion by answering **Y**es or **N**o. As with moving a field, deleting a field leaves a blank line in the input form. Because in this example you deleted the COMMENT field from the end of the form, you do not notice the blank line. If the blank line were in the middle of the form, however, you would want to delete it in SHEET or DOC mode. (See "Modifying the Entry Range" earlier in this chapter for details.)

The FORM **F**ield **D**elete command deletes the field from the entry and definition ranges but not from the database, criterion, and report ranges. You must remove these columns yourself with the SHEET **E**rase or **M**ove command. You also may have to adjust column widths with SHEET **W**idth **S**et.

Using Multiple Input Forms

When you create an entry form, the **G**enerate command automatically attaches the form to the database. You can activate different input forms for the same database with the FORM **A**ttach command. For example, you can use two different input forms when you want to keep certain fields confidential in a database. You also need to use the **A**ttach command when you create more than one database settings sheet and you want to switch to these alternate settings. Just remember, though, that the entry form and the definition range must match.

Note: The *entry range* is the input form viewed in the SHEET or DOC window. The *input form* is the entry range viewed in the FORM window. These terms refer to the same thing in different windows.

Using the SHEET Database Commands

As mentioned earlier, SHEET database commands are used to manipulate groups of database records. For database operations in the SHEET environment, use, if possible, the settings automatically created in the FORM environment so that you don't have to re-create the settings yourself. You always have the option of creating or modifying the settings in the SHEET environment, however. Determining when to use Symphony's automatic capabilities and when to use your own is an acquired art. As you become more familiar with Symphony, you should find this choice increasingly easier to make.

Reminder:
You can use the SHEET commands to manipulate a database; but keep the FORM settings specified when the database was created.

A good time to use the SHEET environment is after you have built a database with Symphony's FORM environment. For example, suppose that you want to make a copy of all the records whose PRIORITY field has the value 4. Symphony's SHEET commands give you a way to accomplish this task.

The main command for performing database operations in the SHEET environment is the **Q**uery command. (*Query* is just another word for *search*.) The simplest **Q**uery command option is **R**ecord-Sort.

Using the SHEET Query Record-Sort Command

The only difference between FORM **R**ecord-Sort and SHEET **Q**uery **R**ecord-Sort is that in the SHEET window you may have to specify the range to be sorted. As in the FORM window, the range to be sorted is called the database range. You must enter in the **Q**uery settings sheet the cell addresses of the database range (use SHEET **Q**uery **S**ettings **B**asic **D**atabase to locate that range). Fortunately, if the database was generated in the FORM window, the database range should already be designated correctly. If you have to specify the range to be sorted, remember to include the field-name headings for a sort operation. If you forget to include the field names in the database range, Symphony still performs the sort but leaves the first record exactly where it is: first.

Using the SHEET Query Settings Command

You can invoke the settings sheet for the SHEET **Q**uery commands by selecting SHEET **Q**uery **S**ettings. The settings sheet is the same one that appears in the FORM window; in fact, the settings that are currently attached to the FORM window also reside in the SHEET **Q**uery settings sheet. If you make a change in the FORM settings sheet, the same change is immediately reflected in the SHEET **Q**uery settings sheet, and vice versa. Figure 17.26 shows the **Q**uery settings sheet for the Priority database. Notice that the sheet appears exactly as it did in the FORM window (see fig. 17.10A).

Fig. 17.26.

The Query settings sheet.

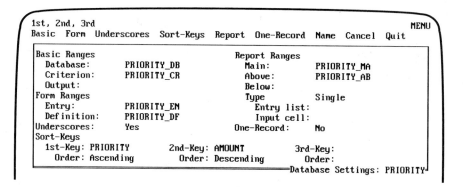

If you use 1-2-3, you know that you can use the Query key to repeat a database operation using the current settings. Symphony does not offer a Query key. With Symphony's settings sheets (and the way the **Q**uery menu is set up), a Query key is not necessary. Just by issuing one of the commands in the menu, you invoke a database operation using the latest settings.

Before you can execute the SHEET **Q**uery commands, you must set up the following three ranges:

1. The criterion range specifying the search criteria

2. The database range to be searched

3. The output range where Symphony will write the output in the worksheet (not required for the **F**ind or **D**elete commands)

The criterion and database ranges are automatically specified in the database settings sheet when you generate the database in the FORM window. You have to enter the specific search criteria into a criterion range in the SHEET environment. (See "Searching with Query Find" later in this chapter for an example of how this is done.) You must specify an output range when you want to use the SHEET **Q**uery **E**xtract and SHEET **Q**uery **U**nique commands

All you need to specify for the output range is a single row containing the names of the fields you want copied; you do not have to include all the field names. You can specify a larger area for the output range, but Symphony only requires a range that includes the field names.

Reminder:

The output range is a single row containing the names of the fields you want copied.

Understanding the Ways to Search for Records

Besides **R**ecord-Sort and **S**ettings, the SHEET **Q**uery menu also lists a series of other subcommands. Here are these commands and their functions:

Command	Function
Find	Moves down through a database, locating the cursor at records that match given criteria (similar to issuing FORM **C**riteria **U**se and then browsing through the resulting records)
Extract	Creates copies in a specified area of the worksheet of all or some of the fields in certain records that match given criteria
Unique	Similar to **E**xtract, but recognizes that some of the records in the database may be duplicates; includes only unique records in the output range
Delete	Deletes all the records in a database that match given criteria and shifts the remaining records to fill in the gaps

Searching with Query Find

Suppose that you want to find in the Priority database all the records with a priority of 4. First, make sure that the database range has been appropriately specified. To check the database range, use SHEET **S**ettings **B**asic **D**atabase to verify the range A34..G53.

Next, enter the selection criteria. Recall that the FORM window offers a **C**riteria command for entering and invoking criteria. The SHEET window does not have such a command. Instead, you must manually enter the criteria in a criterion range. For the current example, enter the number **4** in cell D29. Then make sure that the criterion range is designated as A28..G29 in the **Q**uery settings sheet. Figure 17.27 shows the highlighted criterion range.

Now that the appropriate ranges have been specified, you can issue the SHEET **Q**uery **F**ind command. Figure 17.28 shows what happens when you do. The cursor highlights the first record that conforms to the search criteria. Press ↓ to move to the next record that conforms to the criteria. If you continue to press

Reminder:

In the SHEET environment, you must manually enter a criterion range and designate it in the Query settings sheet.

↓, you can browse through the records that conform to the search criteria. Use ↑ to move in the opposite direction and go to the previous record that conforms to the criteria. The Home and End keys take you to the first and last records that fit the search criteria. To end the Find operation and return to the **Q**uery menu, you can press either Enter or Esc.

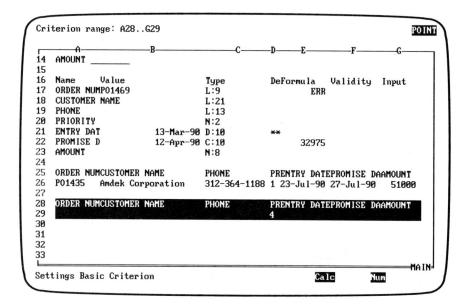

Fig. 17.27.
The criterion range.

Fig. 17.28.
Finding the first record that meets the selection criteria.

When you manually enter criteria in the criterion range (see fig. 17.27), you must place numbers and labels below the appropriate field name. The same is not true for formulas. Formulas are written using relative addressing with reference to the first row (the field names) of the database. In formulas, the addresses are important, not what field names they fall under.

Reminder:
The cell addresses in a formula must be specified; it doesn't matter under which field name a formula falls.

Note: You cannot use the ? character to have Symphony automatically supply the address for you in the SHEET window. Recall that you *can* use this wild-card character to refer to an address in the FORM window.

Suppose that you want to search the Priority database for every record in which the customer name begins with any letter after the letter *L*. The following criterion ranges are equivalent (the field names in the criterion range are displayed in a special typeface; the formula in question appears in standard type):

```
Customer Name            Priority
@LEFT(CUSTOMER NAME,1)>"L"
Customer Name            Priority
                         @LEFT(CUSTOMER NAME,1)>"L"
```

Notice that the range name CUSTOMER NAME is used in the examples instead of cell address B35. When you build a database in the FORM window, Symphony automatically creates range names for the first records directly below the field-name headings; you should use these names to your advantage in the SHEET environment.

Cue:
In the FORM window, Symphony assigns the field names as range names to the first record; use these range names in the SHEET window.

Searching with Query Extract

Suppose that you want to create copies of all the records in the Priority database in which the promise date occurs after August 24, 1990. The command you use to perform this kind of operation is SHEET **Q**uery **E**xtract. Figure 17.29 shows the results. As you can see, the **E**xtract operation copies to the specified output range (in this case, the area below the field names) all the records that conform to the selection criteria.

In figure 17.29, the output range was set up manually because Symphony does not use an output range in a FORM window. To create an output range, use the SHEET **C**opy command to copy the field-name row from the database range. When you specify the output range in the SHEET **Q**uery **S**ettings **B**asic **O**utput settings sheet, you only have to enter the row containing the field names (A55..G55 in fig. 17.29). After specifying the output range and entering the appropriate criteria in the criterion range, you can extract the records.

Reminder:
Use SHEET Copy to copy the field-names row from the database range to the location of the output range.

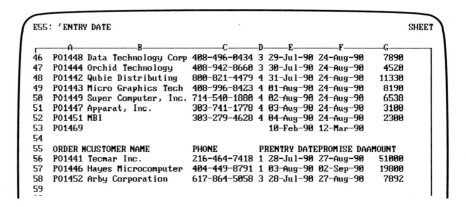

Fig. 17.29.

Extracting records that meet the selection criteria.

The advantage of the **E**xtract option is that it allows you to do detailed analysis on a database. You can use **Q**uery **E**xtract to pull data from one or more records in a database and perform special processing on the subset. You must be careful, however, to designate the database and criterion ranges properly.

Tip

Specifying the output range using just the row containing the field names causes Symphony to erase everything below the output range to the bottom of the worksheet. You can limit the area used by the output range by specifying an exact number of rows for the output range; if you do, however, make sure that the specified range is large enough to hold all the extracted records.

The theoretical maximum number of records in a database is about 8,000, but the actual limit is much lower than that. If you are performing an **E**xtract operation on a large database, the output range will probably take up quite a bit of room. The room the output range takes up further restricts the space you can devote to the database.

Always consider the requirements for the output range and how they may limit the kind of **E**xtract you can perform. With a fairly small database, you have no limitation. The larger a database gets, however, the more you should keep an eye on the amount of RAM available. A frequent check of the SERVICES **S**ettings command can tell you how much RAM is left and allow you to gauge the kinds of **E**xtract operations possible with the available RAM. As you see when you learn about the @BASE add-in database manager, one of the largest advantages @BASE has over the in-RAM database manager is its ability to handle much larger databases.

Searching with Query Unique

Another type of search, which uses a variation of the **Q**uery command, selects all the unique records in a database. **Q**uery **U**nique can copy all the unique records from a database to a separate part of the worksheet. A popular way to use this command is to focus on specific fields in a database. To show how this operation works, suppose that you want to get a listing of all the companies represented in a customer database (see fig. 17.30); notice that all the records have a NAME and a COMPANY field.

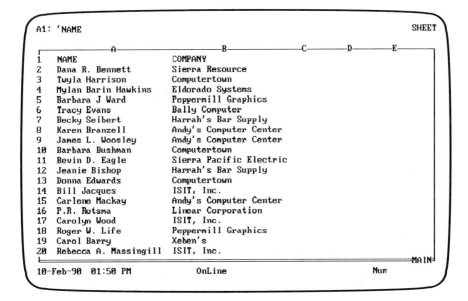

```
A1: 'NAME                                                        SHEET
┌────────A────────────────────B──────────C──────D──────E────────┐
│ 1  NAME                  COMPANY                                 │
│ 2  Dana R. Bennett       Sierra Resource                        │
│ 3  Twyla Harrison        Computertown                           │
│ 4  Mylan Barin Hawkins   Eldorado Systems                       │
│ 5  Barbara J Ward        Peppermill Graphics                    │
│ 6  Tracy Evans           Bally Computer                         │
│ 7  Becky Seibert         Harrah's Bar Supply                    │
│ 8  Karen Branzell        Andy's Computer Center                 │
│ 9  James L. Woosley      Andy's Computer Center                 │
│ 10 Barbara Bushman       Computertown                           │
│ 11 Bevin D. Eagle        Sierra Pacific Electric                │
│ 12 Jeanie Bishop         Harrah's Bar Supply                    │
│ 13 Donna Edwards         Computertown                           │
│ 14 Bill Jacques          ISIT, Inc.                             │
│ 15 Carlene Mackay        Andy's Computer Center                 │
│ 16 P.R. Rotsma           Linear Corporation                     │
│ 17 Carolyn Wood          ISIT, Inc.                             │
│ 18 Roger W. Life         Peppermill Graphics                    │
│ 19 Carol Barry           Xeben's                                │
│ 20 Rebecca A. Massingill ISIT, Inc.                             │
│                                                       ═══MAIN═══┘
│ 10-Feb-90  01:50 PM          OnLine                 Num         │
```

Fig. 17.30.

A sample customer database.

As you can see, several companies are listed more than once in the database. To avoid copying duplicate records to the output range, use **Q**uery **U**nique. The **U**nique option is set up like the **E**xtract option, but the results can be quite different. Figure 17.31 shows how the **E**xtract and **U**nique options work on the same criterion range (C22..C23).

Reminder:

Query Unique extracts records without duplicating the field specified in the criterion range.

In this example, the criterion range has only one field name in it (COMPANY), and the cell below the field name has been deliberately left blank. For the **E**xtract operation, this setup allows all the records in the database to meet the criterion. Therefore, the results of the **E**xtract show copies of the company fields from every record in the database. The **U**nique operation, however, eliminates all the duplicate listings of the companies. The result of the **U**nique operation is a list of the individual companies in the customer database. This list can then be used as the Entry list for multipass database reports.

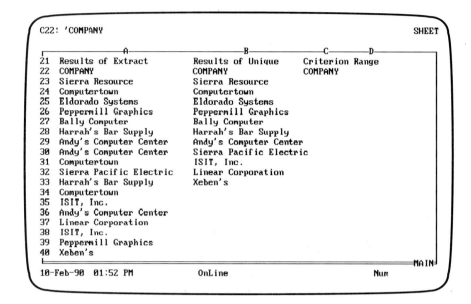

Fig. 17.31.

Comparing Query Extract to Query Unique.

Searching with Query Delete

The last method used to search records is **Query Delete**, which removes unwanted records from a database. (This option is similar to the FORM **Record-Sort Unique** operation, except that SHEET **Query Delete** does not sort the database.) Figure 17.32 shows a portion of an Overdue Accounts database. Suppose that you want to purge all the paid accounts from the Overdue Accounts database, but only after you verify that the accounts have been paid.

Cue:

Use Query Extract to verify the records specified by the criterion range before you use Query Delete.

First, extract all the paid records to verify their accuracy. To do so, use SHEET **Query Extract** with the criterion range shown in figure 17.33. This figure also shows the results of the **Extract**. After you perform the **Extract** operation and review the results, use the same criterion range to perform the **Delete** operation.

After a confirmation step, the database appears as shown in figure 17.34. Notice that **Query Delete** removes the records that meet the criteria and closes up the gaps left in the database. Like **Query Find**, **Query Delete** does not require an output range.

When you use **Query Delete**, make sure that you are deleting the correct records. The precautionary step of extracting them first is a good idea. This way you can verify that you have set up the right criterion range. Once you delete the records, they are gone from RAM. If you make a mistake with **Query Delete**, *do not save the file after the deletion.* You can regain the original database by bringing the file back from storage with the SERVICES **File Retrieve** command and writing over the current worksheet.

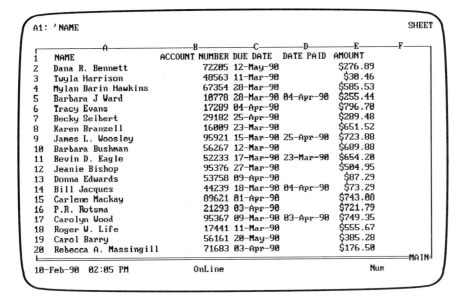

Fig. 17.32.
An Overdue Accounts database.

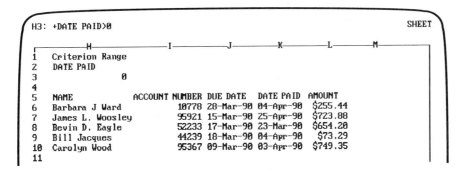

Fig. 17.33.
The criterion range and results of the Extract.

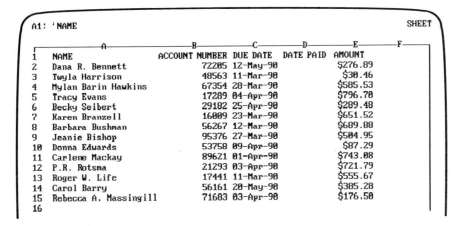

Fig. 17.34.
After deleting the extracted records.

Using the Query Parse Command

The final option offered in the **Q**uery menu is **P**arse. Although you may find other uses for the command, **Q**uery **P**arse is principally designed to take data received during a communications session and convert it to a usable form. Because the use of **Q**uery **P**arse is so intimately connected with the COMM environment, **Q**uery **P**arse is covered in Chapter 19.

Using Database Statistical Functions

Symphony's database statistical functions are similar to the standard statistical functions discussed in Chapter 6, but the database functions have been modified to manipulate database fields. Like the standard statistical functions, the database statistical functions perform in one simple statement what would otherwise take several statements to accomplish. Because of their efficiency and ease of application, you should take advantage of Symphony's database functions. The functions include the following:

Function	Description
@DCOUNT	Gives the number of items in a list
@DSUM	Sums the values of all the items in a list
@DAVG	Gives the average value of all the items in a list
@DMIN	Gives the minimum of all the items in a list
@DMAX	Gives the maximum of all the items in a list
@DSTD	Gives the standard deviation of all the items in a list
@DVAR	Gives the variance of all the items in a list

The general form of these functions is as follows:

@DFUNC(*database_range,offset,criterion_range*)

Reminder:

An offset *of 0 refers to the first column in the database; an* offset *of 1 means the second column; and so on.*

The *database_range* and *criterion_range* arguments are the same as those used by the SHEET **Q**uery commands and all the commands in the FORM window. You can use the standard settings for the database and criterion ranges (the ones in the database settings sheet used to produce the database), or you can specify different ranges. As usual, *database_range* defines the database to be scanned; *criterion_range* specifies which records to select from the database. *offset* can be either 0 or a positive integer and indicates which field to select from the database records. An *offset* of 0 means the first column; 1 means the second column; and so on.

An example that uses the database statistical functions involves computing the mean, variance, and standard deviation of the average interest rates offered by money market funds for a given week. If you are unfamiliar with the concepts of mean, variance, and standard deviation, refer to Chapter 6, where these concepts are explained.

Figure 17.35 shows a Money Market Returns database and the results of the various database statistical functions. The functions to find the maximum and minimum rates of return are included also.

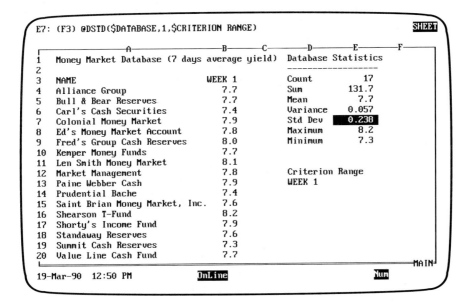

Fig. 17.35.

Results of using database statistical functions on a Money Market Returns database.

The equations and their related statistics are as follows:

Statistic	Formula
Count	@DCOUNT(A3..B20,1,D13..D14)
Sum	@DSUM(A3..B20,1,D13..D14)
Mean	@DAVG(A3..B20,1,D13..D14)
Variance	@DVAR(A3..B20,1,D13..D14)
Standard Dev.	@DSTD(A3..B20,1,D13..D14)
Maximum	@DMAX(A3..B20,1,D13..D14)
Minimum	@DMIN(A3..B20,1,D13..D14)

The results, as seen in figure 17.35, indicate that the mean return for the week for the 17 different money market funds is an annual percentage rate of 7.7 (cell E5). The variance is approximately 0.057 (cell E6), yielding a standard deviation of approximately 0.238 (cell E7). This standard-deviation figure indicates that about 68 percent of the money market funds are returning an annual rate of between 7.46 percent and 7.94 percent. The following formulas explain the principle of standard deviation based on the mean:

One standard deviation below mean = 7.7 − 0.238 = 7.46

One standard deviation above mean = 7.7 + 0.238 = 7.94

Summit Cash Reserves returns the lowest rate at 7.3 percent. The 7.3 value comes from the @DMIN function used in cell E9. This value approaches two standard deviations below the mean, computed as follows:

Two standard deviations below mean = 7.7 − (2 x 0.238) = 7.22

Because approximately 95 percent of the population falls within plus or minus two standard deviations of the mean, Summit Cash Reserves is close to being in the lower 2.5 percent of the population of money market funds for that week. (5 percent is divided by 2 because the population is assumed to be normal.)

Conversely, the Shearson T-Fund returns the highest rate: 8.2 percent. The @DMAX function determines the highest rate (cell E8), which is just over two standard deviations above the mean of the highest 2.5 percent of the population.

Obviously, the database statistical functions can tell you a great deal about the database as a whole and how to interpret different values in it. These functions are also quite useful for printing database reports.

Printing Database Reports

Symphony has a special feature for printing database reports. You can print advanced database reports, like mailing lists and form letters, or something as simple as a listing of the database as it appears in the worksheet. Depending on the criteria that you set up, the database report can include all or separate portions of a database; you can use SERVICES **P**rint **S**ettings to direct the report to the printer, a file, or a range within the worksheet.

In the first example, you see how to use the database-reporting feature to print the entire Priority database to the printer. In the second example, you see how to print a portion of the database and direct it to a range within the current worksheet. In the final example, you see how to print groups of database records, with each group placed on a separate page. The last example also shows you how to use database statistical functions with the reporting feature.

Printing the Entire Database

Reminder:

Symphony sets up the above and main report ranges when you issue FORM Generate.

To print the entire Priority database, you must be familiar with two report ranges: the above and main ranges. Symphony sets up both ranges automatically when you use the FORM **G**enerate command to create the database.

Specifying the Above Report Range

To access the above range (and all the other report ranges), select FORM
Settings **R**eport. The following menu appears:

> **M**ain **A**bove **B**elow **T**ype **Q**uit

Figure 17.36A shows the FORM settings sheet; figure 17.36B highlights the
above range for the Priority database. As you can see, the above range contains
the same field-name headings as the database and criterion ranges. Symphony
uses these field names for the column headings of the report. However,
Symphony prints at the top of the database report any text you put in the above
range. Use the SHEET **M**ove and **I**nsert commands to create an above range that
is deeper than one line. To create report titles, expand the above range to
include the text you want printed at the top of the first page of the report.

Reminder:

*Include in the
above range any
text you want to
appear at the top of
the first page of the
report.*

```
Database, Criterion, Output ranges                              MENU
Basic  Form  Underscores  Sort-Keys  Report  One-Record  Name  Cancel  Quit
┌──────────────────────────────────────────────────────────────────────┐
│ Basic Ranges                      Report Ranges                        │
│   Database:      PRIORITY_DB         Main:       PRIORITY_MA            │
│   Criterion:     PRIORITY_CR         Above:      PRIORITY_AB            │
│   Output:                            Below:                             │
│ Form Ranges                          Type        Single                │
│   Entry:         PRIORITY_EN           Entry list:                      │
│   Definition:    PRIORITY_DF           Input cell:                      │
│ Underscores:     Yes                 One-Record:  No                    │
│ Sort-Keys                                                               │
│   1st-Key:              2nd-Key:              3rd-Key:                  │
│     Order:                Order:                Order:                  │
│                                       ═══════════Database Settings: PRIORITY
└──────────────────────────────────────────────────────────────────────┘
```

Fig. 17.36A.

*The FORM settings
sheet.*

```
Above report range: A25..G25                                   POINT
┌──────────────────────────────────────────────────────────────────────┐
│ ──A────────B─────────C────D────E────────F────────G──                  │
│ 6   PROMISE DATE:D:10                                                   │
│ 7   AMOUNT:N:8                                                          │
│ 8                                                                       │
│ 9   ORDER NUMBER _____                                               │
│ 10  CUSTOMER NAME _____     PHONE _____               │
│ 11  PRIORITY __                                                         │
│ 12  ENTRY DATE _____                                               │
│ 13  PROMISE DATE _____                                             │
│ 14  AMOUNT _____                                                     │
│ 15                                                                      │
│ 16  Name      Value           Type        DeFormula  Validity  Input   │
│ 17  ORDER NUMP01469           L:9              ERR                      │
│ 18  CUSTOMER NAME             L:21                                      │
│ 19  PHONE                     L:13                                      │
│ 20  PRIORITY                  N:2                                       │
│ 21  ENTRY DAT    13-Mar-90    D:10        **                            │
│ 22  PROMISE D    12-Apr-90    C:10            32975                     │
│ 23  AMOUNT                    N:8                                       │
│ 24                                                                      │
│ 25  ORDER NUMCUSTOMER NAME       PHONE     PRENTRY DATEPROMISE DAAMOUNT │
│                                                         ═══════════MAIN │
└──────────────────────────────────────────────────────────────────────┘
Settings Report Above                              Calc  CapsNum
```

Fig. 17.36B.

*The above range
highlighted.*

Specifying the Main Report Range

The main range is contained in the single row directly below the above range in the worksheet (A27..G27); in the Priority database, the main range is called PRIORITY_MA. This range contains the cells to be printed once for each record in the database report. If you locate the cursor on the values in the range, you can see that they refer to the fields in the first record of the database range. For example, cell A27 contains +ORDER NUMBER.

Specifying the Report Criteria

The final step before you use the SERVICES **P**rint command is to enter selection criteria in the criterion range. (Use the FORM **C**riteria **E**dit command to enter selection criteria in a FORM window.) To print all the records in the database, make sure that you use the **C**riteria **E**dit command to delete any criterion records from the criterion range.

Directing the Report to the Printer

To direct a report to the printer, select the SERVICES **P**rint **S**ettings command. The **S**ource setting should be **D**atabase. When you select **D**atabase, you must tell Symphony which FORM settings sheet to use. For this example, suppose that the name of the settings sheet shown in figure 17.36A is PRIORITY. Figure 17.37 shows the **P**rint settings sheet with **S**ource set to **D**atabase PRIORITY.

Fig. 17.37.

*The **P**rint settings sheet with **S**ource set to **D**atabase PRIORITY.*

```
Start printing using current settings                        MENU
Go  Line-Advance  Page-Advance  Align  Settings  Quit

 Page                       Source:      Database PRIORITY
   Length:      66          Destination: Printer
   Spacing:     1           Init-String:
 Number                     Margins                  Other
   Print-Number: 1            Left:    4               Space Compression: No
   Start-Page:   1            Right:   76              Attributes:      Yes
   End-Page:     999          Top:     2               Format: As-Displayed
 Breaks:       Yes          Bottom:  2               Top-Labels:
 Wait:         No                                    Left-Labels:
 Header:
 Footer:
                                              Print Settings: MAIN
```

After the settings sheets are filled out, select SERVICES **P**rint **G**o. Symphony produces the database report, a portion of which appears in figure 17.38.

```
ORDER NCUSTOMER NAME      PHONE       PRENTRY DATEPROMISE DAAMOUNT
PO1441 Tecmar Inc.        216-464-7418 1 28-Jul-90 27-Aug-90   51000
PO1438 Quadram Corp       404-923-6666 1 25-Jul-90 24-Aug-90   42100
PO1436 AST Research       714-540-1333 1 24-Jul-90 23-Aug-90   34000
PO1435 Amdek Corporation  312-364-1188 1 23-Jul-90 22-Aug-90   23000
PO1446 Hayes Microcomputer 404-449-8791 1 03-Aug-90 02-Sep-90  19800
PO1440 Seattle Computer   800-426-8936 2 04-Aug-90 24-Aug-90   24500
PO1445 Maynard Electronics 305-331-6402 2 05-Aug-90 24-Aug-90  23500
PO1437 Hercules Computer  415-654-2476 2 24-Jul-90 23-Aug-90   12000
PO1453 Indigo Data Systems 713-488-8186 2 25-Jul-90 24-Aug-90   3290
PO1450 IDE Associates     617-275-4430 2 26-Jul-90 24-Aug-90    2180
PO1439 Raytronics         800-854-1085 3 27-Jul-90 24-Aug-90   12200
PO1452 Arby Corporation   617-864-5058 3 28-Jul-90 27-Aug-90    7892
PO1448 Data Technology Corp 408-496-0434 3 29-Jul-90 24-Aug-90  7890
PO1444 Orchid Technology  408-942-8660 3 30-Jul-90 24-Aug-90    4520
PO1442 Qubie Distributing 800-821-4479 4 31-Jul-90 24-Aug-90   11330
PO1443 Micro Graphics Tech 408-996-8423 4 01-Aug-90 24-Aug-90   8190
PO1449 Super Computer, Inc. 714-540-1880 4 02-Aug-90 24-Aug-90  6538
PO1447 Apparat, Inc.      303-741-1778 4 03-Aug-90 24-Aug-90    3100
PO1451 MBI                303-279-4628 4 04-Aug-90 24-Aug-90    2300
PO1469                  0            0 0 10-Feb-90 12-Mar-90       0
```

Fig. 17.38.
The printed database report.

Notice that the column widths in the report appear just as they do in the database. To change the column widths in the printed report, change the column widths of the database. An alternative is to direct the report to a range in the worksheet with the column widths you like, and then print directly from that range. This procedure is described in the following section.

Reminder:
To change the column widths of the report, change the column widths of the database.

Printing a Portion of a Database to a Range

If you want to print just a portion of a database, you must modify the criterion range to select only the records you want. Suppose that you want to print all the records in the database whose AMOUNT field is greater than $10,000. Use FORM **C**riteria **E**dit to enter **+?>10000** in the AMOUNT field of the criterion range. Press PgUp and issue FORM **C**riteria **U**se to get the appropriate records.

Once you enter the selection criteria, suppose that you want to direct the output to a range rather than the printer. In this case, set SERVICES **P**rint **S**ettings **D**estination to **R**ange and enter an appropriate range. Figure 17.39 shows how the worksheet appears when the database report has been directed to a range. Notice that the results are long labels.

Creating Database Subtotals

Symphony gives you a way to create subtotals by using the database report feature with the database statistical function @DSUM. Suppose that you want to create a report with a separate page presenting each group of records for each priority in the Priority database. You also want the total dollar amount for each priority.

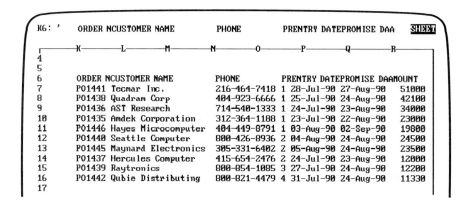

Fig. 17.39.

Printing the database to a range.

Specifying Multiple Passes

Up to this point, the two database report examples have required only a single pass through the database. Therefore, the FORM **S**ettings **R**eport **T**ype command has been left at **S**ingle, the default setting. When you want to produce subtotals (or any other database statistics), however, you must set the report type to **M**ultiple. (Familiarity with the SHEET **R**ange **W**hat-**I**f command is helpful for understanding this example; see Chapter 4 for a discussion of this command.)

Before you can set the report type to **M**ultiple, you must switch to the SHEET environment and build a small table of input values (what Symphony calls an *Entry list*) in an out-of-the-way area of the worksheet. The Entry list contains the list of values you want to substitute into the criterion range. Symphony substitutes the values in the Entry list into the criterion range to produce subtotals for each priority. You can use the SHEET **R**ange **F**ill command to enter the values in cells C1..C4 in figure 17.40.

Note: The values you place in the Entry list are the same values you would place one at a time in the criterion range to produce individual reports. By placing them in the Entry list and setting the report type to **M**ultiple, you tell Symphony to produce each report automatically.

When you issue the FORM **S**ettings **R**eport **T**ype **M**ultiple command, Symphony asks for the address of the Entry list you created. For this example, enter **C1..C4**. Symphony then asks for an input cell, that is, the cell where you want Symphony to substitute the values in the Entry list. You want Symphony to substitute the values into the PRIORITY column of the criterion range, so enter cell **D32**.

At this point, you have almost all the settings for producing separate report pages. But you still need to enter the @DSUM function for printing subtotals. To enter the @DSUM function in the proper location, you need to know about the below range.

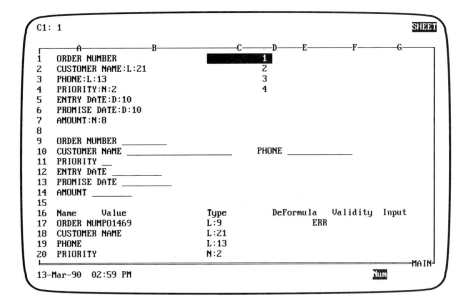

Fig. 17.40.

Creating an Entry list (C1..C4).

Specifying the Below Report Range

The below range, the final settings report range, is used to enter information at the end of a report. When you create a database with the **G**enerate command, Symphony automatically provides enough room to enter a below range that is one row deep. Symphony does not, however, set up the address of this range; you must do that.

Reminder:

Use the below range to specify information to be printed at the end of the report.

Before you enter the address of the below range, first decide how you want the bottom of the report to look. As you did for the above range, you can use the SHEET **M**ove and **I**nsert commands to create a below range deeper than one row. Suppose that you want a series of hyphens across the bottom of the report, with the subtotals below the hyphens. Figure 17.41 shows how the below range (A27..G29) must appear in this case.

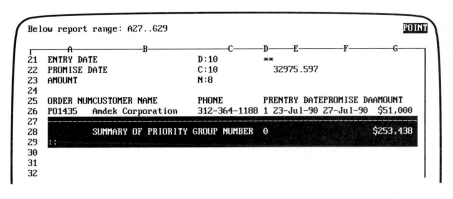

Fig. 17.41.

A sample below range.

The @DSUM function appears in cell G28. The actual formula in that cell is as follows:

@DSUM(*PRIORITY_DB,6,PRIORITY_CR*)

The formula in cell D28 is +D32 (the PRIORITY column of the criterion range that was specified as the input cell). Notice that the third line of the below range contains the page-marker characters (::). To enter the marker in the below range, shift to the DOC environment and issue the **P**age command or enter the page marker directly in the FORM window by adding the label I:: to cell A29. Symphony will send a form-feed command to the printer after printing the report for each PRIORITY group.

Once you set the print ranges (above, main, below, and entry), issue the SERVICES **P**rint command. The **S**ource for the reports is again **D**atabase, but this time the **D**estination is a **F**ile called **MULTIPAS.PRN**. Figure 17.42 shows how the first two pages of the report appear when you print MULTIPAS.PRN.

Fig. 17.42.

Printing separate pages with database subtotals.

```
Order nCustomer name        Phone        PrEntry datePromise daAmount
P01441 Tecmar Inc.          216-464-7418 1 28-Jul-90 27-Aug-90  $51,000
P01438 Quadram Corp         404-923-6666 1 25-Jul-90 24-Aug-90  $42,100
P01436 AST Research         714-540-1333 1 24-Jul-90 23-Aug-90  $34,000
P01435 Amdek Corporation    312-364-1188 1 23-Jul-90 22-Aug-90  $23,000
P01446 Hayes Microcomputer  404-449-8791 1 03-Aug-90 02-Sep-90  $19,800
-----------------------------------------------------------------------
       Summary of Priority Group Number  1                     $169,900
```

```
Order nCustomer name        Phone        PrEntry datePromise daAmount
P01440 Seattle Computer     800-426-8936 2 04-Aug-90 24-Aug-90  $24,500
P01445 Maynard Electronics  305-331-6402 2 05-Aug-90 24-Aug-90  $23,500
P01437 Hercules Computer    415-654-2476 2 24-Jul-90 23-Aug-90  $12,000
-----------------------------------------------------------------------
       Summary of Priority Group Number  2                      $60,000
```

Notice that the AMOUNT field in the report appears in the **C**urrency **0** format. To control the format of the display, simply change the format of the cells in the main range. If you do, you may have to widen the AMOUNT column. If you see asterisks in the cell, select SHEET **W**idth **S**et and specify a wider column.

Printing Mailing Labels

Printing mailing labels is simple once you are familiar with the basics of generating database reports. A good database for showing how to print mailing labels is the database of names and addresses shown in figure 17.43.

```
A1: 'FIRST                                                      SHEET
    ┌──────A────────B────────C────────────────D────────E───F─
  1  FIRST         LAST      ADDRESS              CITY       STAZIP
  2  Shamim SultanaAhmad     Ashton Ctr, Weatherly HaReno    NV 89502
  3  James F.      Cotter    1003 Tulip Tree House Pewaukee  WI 53072
  4  Michael       Englert   224 Greenup St.      Reno       NV 89509
  5  Bob           Jones     34 North Meramec Avenue Excelsior MN 55331
  6  Bob           Holtz     8475 Atherton        Tonka Bay  MN 55331
  7  Jerry         Suchman   125 Manchester       Miles City MT 59301
  8  Ted           Wieber    1076 Charolais       Phoenix    AZ 85027
  9  Fritz         Schuman   100 Miller Dr.       Brooklyn CenterMN 55429
 10  Sarah         Sharpe    7897 Providence St.  Waconia    MN 55387
 11  William       Sikes     3751 Clifton         Reno       NV 89512
 12  Jeremy        Simpson   3509 Ludlow          Howard Beach NY 11414
 13  Betty         Stone     700 Vine St.         Eden Prairie MN 55344
 14  Keith         Thompson  1967 Iowa Lane       Mt Vernon  NH 03057
 15  Gregor        MacLennen 3500 Axe Handle Rd.  Scobey     MT 59263
 16  Gary          Kidd      99 Viewcrest         St Charles MO 63303
 17  Skip          Alston    1 Lakeview Dr.       Reno       NV 89509
 18  Terri         Schwer    11828 Lackland Rd.   Ballwin    MO 63011
 19  Mike          Mooney    2500 Keystone        Roseville  MN 55113
 20
    └──────────────────────────────────────────────────MAIN┘
 19-Mar-90  01:58 PM         OnLine                   CapsNum
```

Fig. 17.43.

A mailing-label database of names and addresses.

To print mailing labels, you must change the position and contents of the main range. The first step is to shift to the SHEET environment and go to an out-of-the-way area of the worksheet. Then enter the following formulas in three consecutive cells down a column, for example in K1..K3:

+FIRST&" "&LAST

+ADDRESS

+CITY&", "&STATE&" "&ZIP

As an alternative, instead of entering the preceding formulas in the SHEET environment, you can shift to a DOC window and enter these lines:

&FIRST& &LAST&

&ADDRESS&

&CITY&, &STATE& &ZIP&

The DOC structure is more in keeping with standard mail-merging conventions in which each field name is enclosed by ampersands and automatically concatenated.

The next step is to cancel the current report ranges from the settings sheet, because the above and below ranges are not needed. Switch back to the FORM window and select **S**ettings **C**ancel **R**eport. Issue the FORM **S**ettings **R**eport **M**ain command to designate the main range. To print one-inch labels, you must include three blank lines below cell K3 (assuming that your printer prints six lines per inch and you have one-inch mailing labels). Therefore, specify a main

Reminder:

Change the organization of the main range when you want to print mailing labels.

range of **K1..K6**. Then designate SERVICES **P**rint **S**ettings **S**ource as **D**atabase and **D**estination as **P**rinter. Be sure to set SERVICES **P**rint **S**ettings **P**age **B**reaks to **N**o; otherwise you waste labels at the top and bottom of each page. Figure 17.44 shows the results of this operation.

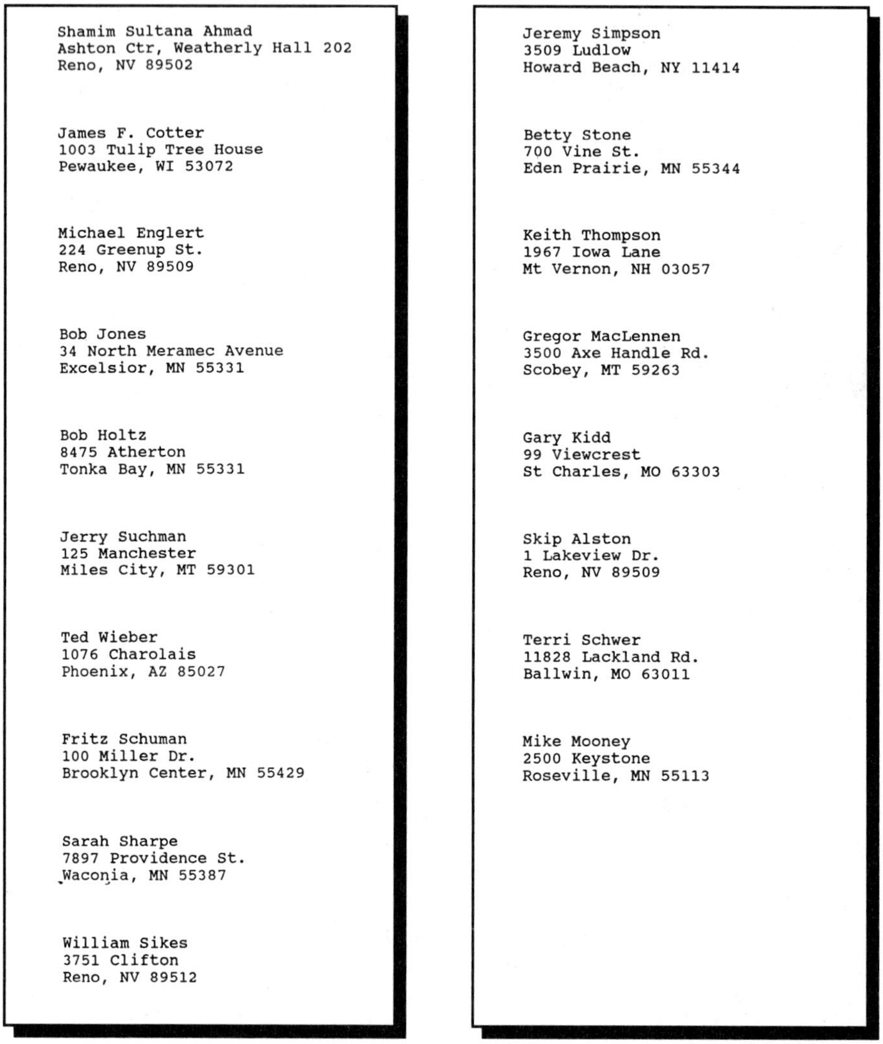

Fig. 17.44.
Printing mailing labels.

```
Shamim Sultana Ahmad
Ashton Ctr, Weatherly Hall 202
Reno, NV 89502


James F. Cotter
1003 Tulip Tree House
Pewaukee, WI 53072


Michael Englert
224 Greenup St.
Reno, NV 89509


Bob Jones
34 North Meramec Avenue
Excelsior, MN 55331


Bob Holtz
8475 Atherton
Tonka Bay, MN 55331


Jerry Suchman
125 Manchester
Miles City, MT 59301


Ted Wieber
1076 Charolais
Phoenix, AZ 85027


Fritz Schuman
100 Miller Dr.
Brooklyn Center, MN 55429


Sarah Sharpe
7897 Providence St.
Waconia, MN 55387


William Sikes
3751 Clifton
Reno, NV 89512
```

```
Jeremy Simpson
3509 Ludlow
Howard Beach, NY 11414


Betty Stone
700 Vine St.
Eden Prairie, MN 55344


Keith Thompson
1967 Iowa Lane
Mt Vernon, NH 03057


Gregor MacLennen
3500 Axe Handle Rd.
Scobey, MT 59263


Gary Kidd
99 Viewcrest
St Charles, MO 63303


Skip Alston
1 Lakeview Dr.
Reno, NV 89509


Terri Schwer
11828 Lackland Rd.
Ballwin, MO 63011


Mike Mooney
2500 Keystone
Roseville, MN 55113
```

As a simple exercise to test your understanding of printing database reports, see if you can figure out how to print mailing labels by ZIP code. *Hint:* You'll have to use the **M**ultiple pass option.

Printing a Form Letter

A final demonstration of Symphony's capability to print database reports is the form letter. Suppose that you want to send a letter to all the customers in the Priority database whose records have been entered on or after August 4, 1990. An example of the letter follows:

Dear IDE Associates:
We are pleased to receive your order and have entered it as
PO1450. Please use this number when you contact us about the
status of your order. As promised, you should receive
your chips on
 09/07/90
If the status of your order changes, we will phone you at
617-275-4430. Please inform us if this number is not the
correct number.
Sincerely,
Tom Perkins

The first step in producing this form letter is to enter the contents in an out-of-the-way area of the worksheet (or create a DOC window). To produce the preceding letter, move the cursor down to cell A200, switch to the DOC environment, and type the letter. Where you need variable information from the database, type the relevant field name enclosed by ampersands (&). Here is how the form letter should look:

Reminder:
To include variable information in a form letter, surround the relevant field name with ampersands.

Dear &CUSTOMER NAME&:
We are pleased to receive your order and have entered it as
&ORDER NUMBER&. Please use this number when you contact us about the
status of your order. As promised, you should receive
your chips on
 &PROMISE DATE&
If the status of your order changes, we will phone you at
&PHONE&. Please inform us if this number is not the
correct number.
Sincerely,
Tom Perkins
 |::

Notice the page break (|::) at the end of the letter, which ensures that each letter is printed on a new page. In the DOC window you see only the ::; the page break appears as |:: only when the cursor is on the cell containing the page break and the window type is SHEET.

After entering the contents of the letter, you must designate the selection criteria for the records whose entry date is on or after August 4, 1990. Figure 17.45 shows the criterion range (A28..G29) and the formula in the ENTRY DATE column. Symphony uses this criterion range as you print the form letter to extract the matching records from the database; you don't have to use **Q**uery **E**xtract before printing.

Fig. 17.45.

The ENTRY DATE formula in the criterion range.

```
E29:  +ENTRY DATE>=@DATE(90,8,4)                                          SHEET
┌────────A────────B──────────────────C──────D────E──────────F──────────G──
│25  ORDER NCUSTOMER NAME          PHONE         PRENTRY DATEPROMISE DAAMOUNT
│26  P01441 Tecmar  Inc.           216-464-7418 1 28-Jul-90 27-Aug-90  $51,000
│27
│28  ORDER NCUSTOMER NAME          PHONE         PRENTRY DATEPROMISE DAAMOUNT
│29                                                        ████████0
│30
│31
│32
│33  ORDER NCUSTOMER NAME          PHONE         PRENTRY DATEPROMISE DAAMOUNT
│34  P01441 Tecmar  Inc.           216-464-7418 1 28-Jul-90 27-Aug-90    51000
│35  P01438 Quadram Corp           404-923-6666 1 25-Jul-90 24-Aug-90    42100
│36  P01436 AST Research           714-540-1333 1 24-Jul-90 23-Aug-90    34000
│37  P01435 Amdek Corporation      312-364-1188 1 23-Jul-90 22-Aug-90    23000
│38  P01446 Hayes Microcomputer    404-449-8791 1 03-Aug-90 02-Sep-90    19000
│39  P01440 Seattle Computer       800-426-8936 2 04-Aug-90 24-Aug-90    24500
│40  P01445 Maynard Electronics    305-331-6402 2 05-Aug-90 24-Aug-90    23500
│41  P01437 Hercules Computer      415-654-2476 2 24-Jul-90 23-Aug-90    12000
│42  P01453 Indigo Data Systems    713-488-8186 2 25-Jul-90 24-Aug-90     3290
│43  P01450 IDE Associates         617-275-4430 2 26-Jul-90 24-Aug-90     2180
│44  P01439 Raytronics             800-854-1085 3 27-Jul-90 24-Aug-90    12200
└──────────────────────────────────────────────────────────────────MAIN─
  10-Feb-90  03:18 PM              OnLine                         Num
```

The final step before using the SERVICES **P**rint command is to designate the main range. The main range is the range of the letter itself, A200..I216 for this example. This choice allows for the longest lines in the letter. If you choose a range that is narrower, say A200..C216, the lines are truncated when you print the letter.

Reminder:

When printing a letter, specify a main range wide enough to accommodate all the characters in the longest line of the letter.

Figure 17.46 shows the FORM settings sheet for printing the letter. Notice that the above and below ranges are left blank in this example.

Fig. 17.46.

The settings sheet for printing the sample form letter.

```
Define ranges for database report                                        MENU
Basic  Form  Underscores  Sort-Keys  Report  One-Record  Name  Cancel  Quit
Basic Ranges                            Report Ranges
  Database:        PRIORITY_DB            Main:        A200..I216
  Criterion:       PRIORITY_CR            Above:
  Output:                                 Below:
Form Ranges                               Type         Single
  Entry:           PRIORITY_EM              Entry list:
  Definition:      PRIORITY_DF              Input cell:
Underscores:       Yes                   One-Record:    No
Sort-Keys
  1st-Key:                    2nd-Key:                  3rd-Key:
  Order:                      Order;                    Order:
                                                ─Database Settings: PRIORITY
```

If you want to send the letter directly to the printer, select SERVICES **S**ettings **P**rint **D**estination **P**rinter and **S**ource **D**atabase.

Using the @BASE Add-In Database Manager

With Symphony 2.2, Lotus Development has added a powerful new add-in database manager that uses dBASE-compatible database files on disk. Unlike the in-RAM database manager included in Symphony, @BASE can work with databases as large as your disk space. The @BASE add-in also offers increased sorting capabilities; because the add-in works with existing Symphony features, it gives you more flexibility than most stand-alone database products.

Reminder:
The @BASE add-in can work with files as large as can fit on your disk.

Attaching @BASE

The @BASE add-in consists of three parts:

Part of Add-in	Features Contained In
BASE.APP	The basic add-in
BASEFUNC.APP window	The new @functions you can use in the SHEET
BASEUTL.APP	The @BASE utility commands

Although the basic BASE.APP add-in is required before you can use either of the other two, it's important that you load the three in the proper order. BASEFUNC.APP, like all other add-ins that add @functions, cannot be detached without exiting from Symphony. It also prevents any memory from being freed if another add-in that was attached earlier is detached. It's important, therefore, to make sure that BASEFUNC.APP is attached before any other add-ins. As soon as you attach these add-ins, they are ready to use. Some add-in programs like ALLWAYS must be installed before they can be attached.

When you use the @BASE add-in, attach BASEFUNC.APP, then BASE.APP, and finally BASEUTL.APP. To attach the entire @BASE add-in, press the Services (F9) key and select **A**pplication **A**ttach. Then highlight BASEFUNC.APP and press Enter. Select **A**ttach again, highlight BASE.APP, and press Enter. Finally, select **A**ttach, highlight BASEUTL.APP, press Enter, and select **Q**uit.

Reminder:
Attach the parts of the @BASE add-in in the following order: BASEFUNC.APP, BASE.APP, and BASEUTL.APP.

To call attention to how different the @BASE database manager is from Symphony's in-RAM database manager, an additional window, called BASE, is added when you attach @BASE. To begin using the BASE window, switch the window type by pressing Type (Alt-F10) and selecting BASE. The @BASE main

Reminder:
Return to the @BASE main screen before using the Services key.

screen appears (see fig. 17.47). Remember that you must always return to this screen before you can switch to another window type or use Symphony's Services (F9) key for any other operation.

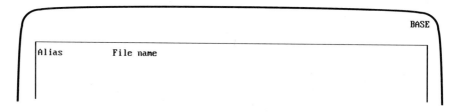

Fig. 17.47.
The @BASE main screen.

Understanding the @BASE Menu

The @BASE main menu (see fig. 17.48) appears when you press the Menu (F10) key. The commands available are divided into five groups. The **F**ile command presents a submenu of the commands you use to open, close, modify, or create database files. The **D**ata command is used to work with the records contained in the files. The **C**riteria command is similar to the FORM **C**riteria command described earlier in this chapter. The **S**ettings command is used to modify @BASE's global settings. The **U**tility command lets you convert existing Symphony databases into @BASE databases and copy the special @BASE functions within the SHEET environment.

Fig. 17.48.
The @BASE main menu.

Table 17.1 shows a breakdown of the @BASE menu options.

Table 17.1
The @BASE Menu Commands

Command	Description
File	@BASE commands that manipulate database files.
Open	Opens an @BASE database file for use.
Close	Closes an open @BASE database file.
Use	Presents the **S**et and **C**ancel options for the default file.
Define	Creates a new @BASE database file.

Command	*Description*
Modify	Redefines, adds, or deletes fields in an existing database file.
Extract	Creates a new database file from an open database file by using some or all fields and records.
Field-Rename	Renames one or more fields in a database file.
Post	Updates all open database files on disk without closing them.
Data	@BASE commands which manipulate the data contained in database files.
Browse	Displays a database file in a browse table containing all or selected fields. Records may be edited in the browse table.
Form	Displays a database file one record at a time in an entry form. Records may be edited or entered in the form.
Replace	Replaces data in specified fields for all active records in a mass update.
Crosstab	Generates a crosstab report in the worksheet. You can select a count or a sum report for items matching the current criteria.
Sort	Sorts the records in a database file. Sorting levels can include up to 256 fields. Sorted records are written to a disk file.
Transfer	Includes commands for copying records. See the **Utility** commands for additional database-translation commands.
Copy	Copies selected records from one database file to another.
Import	Copies records from a database file to a Symphony worksheet.
Export	Copies records from a Symphony worksheet to an existing @BASE database file.
Label-Import	Copies field names from a database file to a Symphony worksheet.
Delete	Includes commands to mark and delete records.
Mark	Marks all active records for deletion. Active records are those matching the currently active criteria.
Unmark	Removes the deletion mark from all active records.

Table 17.1—(continued)

Command	Description
Pack	Deletes all marked records from the database file.
Delete-All	Deletes all records (both marked and unmarked) from the database file. Creates a new, empty database containing the identical structure.
Criteria	Commands relating to record-selection criteria.
Prompt	Creates record-selection criteria using prompts.
Edit	Creates record-selection criteria or edits the active criteria.
Save	Saves the active criteria as a label in the worksheet.
Retrieve	Retrieves record-selection criteria stored in the worksheet.
Cancel	Cancels the active criteria.
Settings	Commands for setting the @BASE global configuration.
Deleted	Options for handling records marked as deleted.
Skip-Deleted	Ignores records marked for deletion when performing database operations.
Use-Deleted	Uses records marked for deletion when performing database operations.
Year	Options for the number of digits in the year number.
2-digit	Uses 2 digits for the year number. For example, 1990 appears as **90**.
4-digit	Uses 4 digits for the year number. For example, 1990 appears as **1990**.
Blanks	Options specifying the handling of blank fields.
Zeros	Treats blank numeric, date, and logical fields as zeros in calculations.
NA	Treats blank numeric, date, and logical fields as NA in calculations.
File-Directory	Sets the directory where @BASE database files are stored.
Update	Saves the current global settings in an @BASE configuration file.
Quit	Returns to the main @BASE menu.

Command	Description
Utility	Additional utility functions.
File	Options to handle files.
Translate	Creates an @BASE database from an existing Symphony database.
Import	Sets the type of external data file.
ASCII	Appends records in a fixed-length ASCII file to an @BASE database.
Delimited	Appends records in a delimited ASCII file to an @BASE database.
Status	Displays information about an @BASE database.
Delete	Deletes a closed database file from disk.
Criteria-Copy	Copies @DB formulas within a worksheet, automatically adjusting references. Symphony's Copy command does not correct cell references in @DB functions.

The best way to gain a better understanding of the difference between the @BASE add-in database manager and the in-RAM database manager is to create a new database in the BASE window.

Suppose that you own a computer consulting group and have a number of contacts at various companies. You want to maintain a database that enables you to call up information about the customer's company when you enter the customer's name. Because you may have several contacts for each company, you want to save time by entering each company's information only once. To do this, you create two databases; one with company information, and one with customer information. To relate the two databases to each other, you include one common piece of information in each database: the company name. This is where the term *relational database* arose: from the ability to relate information in one file to information in other files.

Reminder:
A relational database enables you to relate information in one file to information in other files.

Defining an @BASE Database

Switch to the BASE window and press Menu (F10). Select **F**ile **D**efine and type **offices** for the database name. Press Enter. @BASE prompts you for the next piece of information. For example, type **Company** and press Enter (because @BASE creates dBASE-compatible database files, you can use a maximum of 10 characters for field names). @BASE prompts you for the field type. Select

Reminder:
Field names in an @BASE database cannot be more than 10 characters long.

Character and press Enter. Specify **26** for the field length. Typing the following field information, pressing Enter after each entry:

Field Name	Type	Length
Company	Char	26
Address	Char	22
City	Char	17
State	Char	2
ZIP	Char	6
Phone	Char	9

Your screen should look like figure 17.49 (@BASE provided the column headings in the first row). Press the Esc key twice and select **S**ave. You are asked for the database alias. Accept **OFFICES** by pressing Enter; the database definition is saved. This is one of the major differences between Symphony's two database managers: @BASE automatically saves your work if you leave Symphony, the in-RAM database manager does not.

Fig. 17.49.

Defining an @BASE database.

```
Enter field name:                                         FIELD

 Name        Type       Length    Decimals
 COMPANY     Char         26
 ADDRESS     Char         22
 CITY        Char         17
 STATE       Char          2
 ZIP         Char          6
 PHONE       Char          9
```

Using the @BASE Entry Form

The @BASE entry form looks similar to the entry form you generate with the FORM **G**enerate command. If you compare figures 17.4A and 17.50, you won't see too much difference. You will notice some major differences when you *use* the form, however.

When @BASE creates its entry form, it places each field name below the preceding one, regardless of the number of pages required. Although both the in-RAM and @BASE database managers accept up to 256 fields, showing that many fields on one screen is difficult. If the combination of field names and data-entry underscores is too large to fit on one screen, the in-RAM database manager displays the message **Form too large to fit in window.** @BASE, on the other hand, simply scrolls the fields up or down through the window to fit them all in.

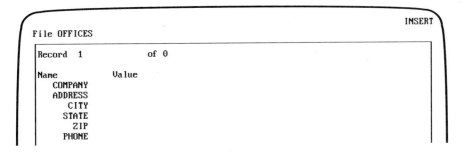

Fig. 17.50.
The @BASE entry form before any data has been entered.

Another major difference between the two databases is that you can customize the entry form generated by the FORM **G**enerate command but you cannot modify the one created by @BASE. It's not possible, for example, to place two fields on one line in an @BASE entry form as you can in an in-RAM entry form.

Reminder:
You cannot customize an @BASE entry form as you can an in-RAM entry form.

In addition, you cannot define computed fields or transformed fields in an @BASE entry form. In an example earlier in this chapter, you set up a transformed field in an in-RAM database that added the letters *PO* to an order number so that *1469* became *PO1469* in the database. @BASE does not allow you to define fields to be calculated or transformed.

One effect of these differences is the very real need to plan ahead when designing an @BASE database. Because you must move through fields sequentially (no jumping around the entry form), make sure that you place the most commonly used fields first. If you have a database with 200 fields, for example, you must move through the first 199 fields before you can enter data in field 200. There is a bright side to this, however; unlike the entry form used by the in-RAM database manager, the @BASE entry form leaves the cursor in the same field as you move from record to record. Thus, once you move to field 200 in record 1, the cursor stays in field 200 when you move to records 2, 3, and so on.

Reminder:
You must move sequentially through fields in an entry form.

Adding Data to an @BASE Database

When the entry form is displayed, you're ready to start entering records into the Offices database. Press Menu (F10), select **D**ata **F**orm, and accept **OFFICES**. Notice that the screen shows **Record 1 of 0**, indicating that you're adding a new record beyond the existing ones. Just start typing your entries. For example, type **Access Systems** and press Enter to add the first company. When you press Enter, the cursor moves down to the second field, ADDRESS, and waits for your entry. For this field, type PO Box 70023 and press Enter. Continue in this way until you have entered text for the CITY, STATE, ZIP, and PHONE fields. The screen should look like figure 17.51. To add this record to the database, press the Ins key. The screen now shows **Record 2 of 1** to indicate that the database now has one record and you're working on another new record.

Fig. 17.51.

The entry form after typing data for the first record.

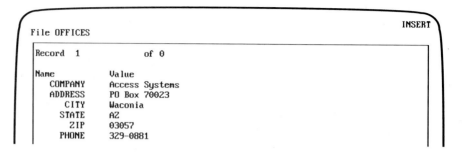

```
                                                              INSERT
File OFFICES

Record  1              of 0

Name        Value
  COMPANY   Access Systems
  ADDRESS   PO Box 70023
     CITY   Waconia
    STATE   AZ
      ZIP   03057
    PHONE   329-0881
```

Following is a guide to important keys for entering or revising data records in an @BASE entry form:

Key	Activity
PgDn	Moves sequentially to the next record in the database. When you are editing data, adds the record to the database and displays the next record.
PgUp	Moves sequentially to the previous record in the database. When you are editing data, adds the record to the database and displays the previous record.
Enter	Adds data you've typed to the current field and moves the cursor to the next field.
Home	Adds the current record to the database and displays the first record in the database if you are editing data. Otherwise, just displays the first record.
End	Adds the current record to the database and displays the last record in the database.
GoTo (F5)	Jumps directly to a record if you enter the record number.
Edit (F2)	Activates the field if you want to revise an existing entry. You can then use the edit keys, such as Backspace, Esc, and Del, in the same manner as in SHEET mode (see Chapter 2).
Esc	Clears the current field if pressed once while you are editing an entry in a field. Press twice to restore the previous value. Press three times to return to the @BASE menu. Deletes the new record and returns to the previous record if pressed once while you are adding a new record. Press twice to return to the @BASE menu. In other situations, returns you to the @BASE menu.

Reminder:

Press Esc once to clear the current field, twice to restore the previous value, and three times to return to the @BASE menu if you are editing an existing record.

Key	Activity
Backspace	If you are editing an entry in a field, removes the character preceding the cursor.
Begin typing	Erases the current entry during editing of a field so that you can type a new entry.
Ins	Adds the current record to the database and displays a new blank form during data entry. When you are editing data, adds the current record to the database, jumps to the end of the database, and displays a new blank form.
Del	Marks the current record for deletion from the database during editing of data. Press Del again to remove the mark. Records are not physically deleted until a BASE **D**ata **D**elete **P**ack command is issued.
↑	Moves the cursor to the previous field in an entry form.
↓	Moves the cursor to the next field in an entry form.

Browsing through an @BASE Database

Once you add all the records to the database, you may want to examine the records in a tabular form. Return to the @BASE menu, select **D**ata **B**rowse, accept **OFFICES**, and select **A**ll. Because @BASE attempts to show the complete information for each field in the record, you can see only the first two fields of information (see fig. 17.52A). With the browse screen, however, you can move around and see the other fields. Press → twice to move the cursor to the right two cells; you now can see the rest of the fields (see fig. 17.52B).

```
                                                    BROWSE
  File COMP

  Record   COMPANY                    ADDRESS
  1        Access Systems             PO Box 70023
  2        Andre Computer Center      401 S Virginia
  3        Computertown               445 Apple Street
  4        Computing Reserves, Inc.   1105 Terminal Way
  5        ITIS, Inc.                 126 Mount Rose
  6        Last Computer Consultants  PO Box 3417
  7        Linear Corporation         4914 S Virginia
  8        Peppermill Graphics        345 N Virginia Street
  9        System Computing Services  250 N Virginia Street
  10       Valley Electronics         PO Box 11007
  11       Xeboc Disk Repair          4600 Kietzke Lane
```

Fig. 17.52A.

The browse screen showing the first two fields of the Offices database.

Fig. 17.52B.

The browse screen showing the remaining fields of the Offices database.

```
                                                                    BROWSE
  File COMP

  Record    ADDRESS              CITY              STATE  ZIP    PHONE
  1         PO Box 70023         Waconia           AZ     03057  329-0881
  2         401 S Virginia       Tonka Bay         CA     11414  348-2770
  3         445 Apple Street     St Charles        IA     52722  348-3000
  4         1105 Terminal Way    Scobey            IL     53072  356-3300
  5         126 Mount Rose       Roseville         KA     55113  358-6900
  6         PO Box 3417          Richmond Heights  MN     55331  689-4011
  7         4914 S Virginia      Reno              MO     55343  784-3366
  8         345 N Virginia Street Prior Lake       MT     55344  785-2222
  9         250 N Virginia Street Phoenix          NH     55372  786-3232
  10        PO Box 11007         Pewaukee          NV     55387  786-3663
  11        4600 Kietzke Lane    Mt. Prospect      NY     55406  786-5700
```

Reminder:

You can edit the database in the browse screen; just move the cursor to the text you want to change and type over it.

While in the browse screen, you can edit the information in any of the fields. Just move the cursor to the data you want to change and type over it. You cannot move the cursor beyond the existing fields or records, however. To add a new record, press the Ins key to make the entry form appear. The screen shows a message indicating that you're adding a record to the end of the database. Once you finish browsing through the database, press the Esc key once to return to the @BASE menu; press Esc again to return to the @BASE screen. Remember: you cannot use Symphony's Services (F9) key, the Switch (Alt-F9) key, or the Type (Alt-F10) key unless you return to the @BASE screen.

Creating a Relational Database

You are now ready to explore a major advantage that the @BASE database manager offers over the in-RAM database manager: the capacity to create relational databases. In the example being developed in the preceding sections, you need two database files, one containing the company names, addresses, and so on, and the other containing names of customers working at those companies. Instead of typing company information for each customer, you can use a common field—the company name—to relate the two database files.

The second database contains just three fields, LAST_NAME, FIRST_NAME, and COMPANY. To create this database, use another of the @BASE capabilities. Instead of defining a new database and entering the data using the entry form, you may want to convert an existing Symphony database to an @BASE database.

Converting an Existing Symphony Database to @BASE

Suppose that you have the Symphony database shown in figure 17.53. This database contains customer names and their companies. Instead of retyping the database in the @BASE environment, you decide to convert it.

```
LAST_NAME       FIRST_NAME   COMPANY
Anton           Mylan        Valley Electronics
Aubol           Jacqueln     Linear Corporation
Brown           Larry        ITIS, Inc.
Bruesch         Carlene      Linear Corporation
Chamberlain     Tom          Peppermill Graphics
Chapweske       Raynell      Andre Computer Center
Choate          Gordon       Computing Reserves, Inc.
Danz            Debra        Access Systems
Delin           Carolyn      System Computing Services
Dennis          Sally        Last Computer Consultants
Diacumakos      Harry        ITIS, Inc.
Flagg           Monique      System Computing Services
Gaudette        Bevin        ITIS, Inc.
Holt            P.R.         Xeboc Disk Repair
Jones           Karen        Xeboc Disk Repair
Kidd            Barbara      Andre Computer Center
Kuc             Rebecca      Computertown
Maclennan       Roger        Computing Reserves, Inc.
Markowitz       Carolyn      Valley Electronics
McKinnies       Sally        ITIS, Inc.
Mills           Linda        Last Computer Consultants
Miquelon        Bill         Last Computer Consultants
Mooney          Barbara      Computertown
Olson           Tracy        System Computing Services
Orlikowski      John         Valley Electronics
Saevig          Ernest       Computertown
Schaubach       James        Peppermill Graphics
Stene           Michael      Peppermill Graphics
Stokes          Jack         Last Computer Consultants
Sunstrom        Donna        Andre Computer Center
Thompson        Martha       Linear Corporation
Wallace         Twyla        Valley Electronics
White           Stacy        Linear Corporation
Whiting         Carol        Peppermill Graphics
Wieber          Becky        Computing Reserves, Inc.
Willeford       Jeanie       System Computing Services
Wood            Ann          Access Systems
```

Fig. 17.53.

An existing Symphony database.

To convert an existing Symphony database to an @BASE database, follow these rules:

❏ The existing Symphony database must be in memory. @BASE does not make the conversion until you load the database file into memory.

❏ Field names cannot be longer than 10 characters and must start with a letter. Any character other than letters, numbers, and the underscore is considered invalid and produces an error. Don't include any spaces in field names.

❏ No blank columns can appear in the existing database.

❏ @BASE determines the field types by looking at the entries in the first record:

If the cell is blank, contains a label or a string formula, and is unformatted, that column translates as a character field.

If the cell is formatted with a date format, that column translates as a date field.

If the cell is formatted with a time format, that column translates as a numeric field.

If the cell is formatted with a numeric format, that column translates as a numeric field regardless of contents.

Hidden columns translate as character fields.

❏ Field lengths are determined by the following:

Character fields use the column width or the length of the longest field entry, whichever is greater.

Time fields are converted to numeric fields and assigned a length of 7.

Date fields have a length of 8.

Other numeric fields use the column width from the Symphony database as their length in the @BASE database.

Hidden columns in the Symphony database have a length of 9 in the @BASE database.

To begin the conversion process, first load the existing database. Check it against the preceding rules and make any necessary changes. Change to the BASE window, press Menu (F10), and select **Utility File Translate**. Symphony shifts back to the SHEET window so that you can highlight the existing database range. If the worksheet contains a database settings sheet, Symphony highlights the current database range. If the highlighted range is correct, press Enter to accept the highlighted range; otherwise, highlight the correct database range and press Enter. Symphony next asks for the new database name. In this example, supply the name **CONTACTS**. Symphony next offers **CONTACTS** as the database alias; press Enter to accept this alias.

The @BASE field definition screen appears (see fig. 17.54). If any of @BASE's guesses for field types, lengths, or number of decimal places is incorrect, move the cursor to the incorrect information, press Edit (F2), and make the correction. Make sure that this information is correct; it is used to translate the existing database. Once you verify the field definitions, press Esc and select **S**ave to proceed with the conversion. The new @BASE database is written to disk, and the @BASE menu reappears.

```
                                                              FIELD
    Name              Type      Length    Decimals
    LAST_NAME         Char        13
    FIRST_NAME        Char        12
    COMPANY           Char        27
```

Fig. 17.54.
The field definition screen.

Understanding Utility File Translate and Data Transfer Export

Some @BASE menu selections may appear slightly confusing. For example, consider the difference between **U**tility **F**ile **T**ranslate and **D**ata **T**ransfer **E**xport. Both appear to copy Symphony in-RAM databases to @BASE databases. You used **U**tility **F**ile **T**ranslate in the preceding example because no @BASE database existed and you wanted to create one automatically. You use **D**ata **T**ransfer **E**xport, on the other hand, to *add* records from a Symphony database to an existing @BASE database; this command does not create a new @BASE database.

Reminder:
Utility File Translate creates a new @BASE database; Data Transfer Export adds records to an existing @BASE database.

Using Two Database Files as One

Now that you have the two database files CONTACTS and OFFICES, it's time to see how they can be related. First, however, consider a few facts about Symphony and @BASE. If you want to use the @BASE @DB functions in the Symphony SHEET window, you must attach the BASEFUNC.APP add-in. You must open a database before you can use any of the @DB functions except @DBOPEN. In addition, the @DB functions don't always calculate properly using Symphony's natural-order recalculation. For this example, assume that you still have the BASEFUNC.APP add-in attached; this section examines ways around the other two considerations.

Suppose that you want to have Symphony supply the company name, address, and so on when you enter a customer's name. Because the company information is in the OFFICES database and the customer names are in the CONTACTS database, you must use @DB functions to "connect" the databases. @DB functions can enable you to look up information in OFFICES by relating it to information found in CONTACTS. Figure 17.55 shows a sample form where the customer's first name is typed in cell B1 and the last name in cell B2. Formulas in cells B4 through B9 bring in information from OFFICES database.

Fig. 17.55.

The customer information form.

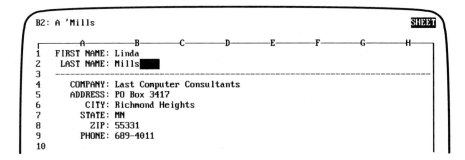

```
B2: A 'Mills                                                    SHEET
   ┌────A────────B────────C────────D────────E────────F────────G────────H──────
 1 │ FIRST NAME: Linda
 2 │  LAST NAME: Mills█
 3 │----------------------------------------------------------------------------
 4 │     COMPANY: Last Computer Consultants
 5 │    ADDRESS: PO Box 3417
 6 │       CITY: Richmond Heights
 7 │      STATE: MN
 8 │        ZIP: 55331
 9 │      PHONE: 689-4011
10 │
```

Following are the formulas that appear in cells B4 through B9 of the customer information form. To create this form, type the labels in column A (COMPANY, ADDRESS, and so on) and then enter the formulas in the indicated cells in column B:

Cell	Formula •
B4	@DBFLD("CONTACTS","COMPANY",@DBFIRST ("CONTACTS","FIRST_NAME=B1.AND.LAST_NAME=B2"))
B5	@DBFLD("OFFICES","ADDRESS",@DBFIRST ("OFFICES","COMPANY=B4"))
B6	@DBFLD("OFFICES","CITY",@DBFIRST ("OFFICES","COMPANY=B4"))
B7	@DBFLD("OFFICES","STATE",@DBFIRST ("OFFICES","COMPANY=B4"))
B8	@DBFLD("OFFICES","ZIP",@DBFIRST ("OFFICES","COMPANY=B4"))
B9	@DBFLD("OFFICES","PHONE",@DBFIRST ("OFFICES","COMPANY=B4"))

Note: @BASE uses dots or pound signs (#) around the operators AND, OR, and NOT. Although #AND# and .AND. are equivalent, this chapter uses the dot convention for the @BASE operators.

Be sure to type each formula starting in cell B4 and proceeding down to B9. Once all the formulas are entered, type the first and last name of a customer from the CONTACTS database in cells B1 and B2.

Opening Databases and Understanding the ERR Message

If your screen looks like the one in figure 17.56 after you type the formulas, @BASE is telling you that the database files haven't been opened.

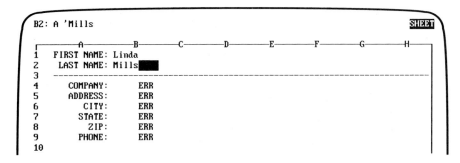

B2: A 'Mills   SHEET

```
        A        B         C       D       E      F      G      H
  1  FIRST NAME: Linda
  2   LAST NAME: Mills
  3  ---------------------------------------------------------------
  4      COMPANY:       ERR
  5      ADDRESS:       ERR
  6         CITY:       ERR
  7        STATE:       ERR
  8          ZIP:       ERR
  9        PHONE:       ERR
 10
```

Fig. 17.56.
*The customer
information form as
it appears if the
database files
aren't open.*

You can open database files in two ways. You can switch to the BASE window and use the **F**ile **O**pen command, or you can use the @DBOPEN function. Because you're working in the SHEET window, using @DBOPEN makes sense. Enter these two formulas in cells B10 and B11 of the customer information form:

Reminder:
*Open databases in
@BASE with BASE
File **O**pen or
@DBOPEN.*

> @DBOPEN*("CONTACTS")*
>
> @DBOPEN*("OFFICES")*

Both cells show a value of 1, indicating that the two database files have been opened. Cells B4 through B9 still show ERR, however, indicating that something is still wrong. Press the Calc (F8) key a few times, and all of the formulas show correct results.

Symphony normally tries to recalculate formulas according to a "natural order" in which every formula is ranked according to its dependencies. The @DB functions, however, seem to recalculate in the order in which they were entered into the worksheet. That is, if you entered the formula in cell B5 before you entered the one in B4, B5 recalculates before B4. Because you added the formulas in B10 and B11 after you entered the formulas that depend on them (B4 through B9), the @DBOPEN formulas open the databases after B4 through B9 have already tried to access the databases. The second time you press Calc (F8), the databases have been opened, and the formulas in B4 through B9 work properly.

Unfortunately, even if you enter all formulas in the correct order and everything seems to be working correctly, you can develop problems later. When you edit an @DB formula, Symphony moves it to the end of the recalculation list. To see this, place the cursor on cell B4 and press the Edit (F2) key. Without making any changes press Enter. Because the results in B5 through B9 depend on the result of B4, you must press Calc (F8) twice to make sure that you have accurate information.

For users who have grown accustomed to having Symphony handle recalculation details, having to press Calc (F8) several times in @BASE can be a real trap. You must be extra careful to make sure that you have accurate results. Perhaps a future release will make the @DB functions recalculate in the same manner as all other Symphony functions.

Until a future release solves the problem, one way you can ensure correct results is to set the recalculation method to **R**ow-by-Row and make sure that each formula is below any others which must be calculated first. Although this may be practical in a small worksheet, it soon becomes difficult to manage as the worksheet becomes more complex.

A second method to ensure that the @DB formulas are calculated in the proper order is to use the macro {RECALC *range*} and {RECALCCOL *range*} commands. This method, too, has drawbacks: if you forget to use the macro and rely on the Calc key, the results may be incorrect once again.

A third method is to set SHEET **S**ettings **R**ecalculation **I**teration to a number higher than the default of 1. Chapter 4 discusses the use of this command with circular references; the same principles apply here. Of course, this method has a drawback too: in very large worksheets, each recalculation pass can take considerable time. Use caution when you specify the number of iterations.

Using the New @DB Functions

When you use @BASE, Symphony gains 20 new @functions. These functions are divided into three groups: statistical, logical, and file manipulation. You use the @DB functions in the SHEET window—not in the BASE window.

Like all other Symphony functions, each of the new function names is preceded by the @ sign. Any arguments are contained within parentheses and are separated by either commas or semicolons. No spaces are allowed except within an argument enclosed in quotation marks. Arguments that are literal strings must be enclosed in quotation marks, or Symphony assumes that the argument is the range name of a cell that contains the argument.

Reminder:

Symphony does not adjust cell references contained within quotation marks in an @DB function.

Because many of the @DB functions use criteria arguments contained within quotation marks, the Symphony **C**opy command does not adjust the references properly. For example, consider the formula contained in cell B5 of the preceding example:

@DBFLD*("OFFICES","ADDRESS",@DBFIRST("OFFICES","COMPANY=B4"))*

This formula contains the criteria argument *"COMPANY=B4"* which indicates that cell B4 contains the value to be compared with the value found in the COMPANY field in the OFFICES database file. Because this argument is contained within quotation marks, Symphony does not adjust it while copying it to another cell. If you copied this formula from B5 to C5 with SHEET **C**opy, the formula remains unchanged.

If you want the criteria reference to be adjusted when you copy the formula, use the BASE **U**tility **C**riteria-Copy command. To try this command, switch to the BASE window and select BASE **U**tility **C**riteria-Copy. Symphony switches back to the SHEET window and prompts you to specify the cell to copy. Specify B5, press Enter, and select C5 as the output range. Leave the menu and switch back to the SHEET window. Compare the formulas in cells B5 and C5 to see how the references were adjusted. **C**riteria-**C**opy adjusts cell references within quotation marks for @DB functions, although the absolute-reference dollar signs ($B$5, for example) still keep a cell reference absolute.

Using the Statistical @DB Functions

Five of the new @DB statistical functions are similar to the database statistical functions discussed earlier in this chapter. You can use the @BASE functions in the same way you use their in-RAM database counterparts:

@BASE Statistical Function	Database Statistical Function
@DBCNT(*alias,criteria*)	@DCOUNT
@DBSUM(*alias,fieldname,criteria*)	@DSUM
@DBAVG(*alias,fieldname,criteria*)	@DAVG
@DBMAX(*alias,fieldname,criteria*)	@DMAX
@DBMIN(*alias,fieldname,criteria*)	@DMIN

In these @DB functions, *alias* is the database alias name, *fieldname* is the name of the database field, and *criteria* is any optional selection criteria. All these arguments must be in quotation marks unless the argument is given as a cell or range address containing the argument string.

The @DBRECS function is similar to @DBCNT, except that it returns the count of all records contained within the database instead of just those that are currently active. The in-RAM @DVAR and @DSTD database statistical functions are not duplicated by @BASE functions.

Reminder:
@DBRECS returns the count of all records contained within the database.

Using the Logical @DB Functions

@BASE contains three functions called logical @DB functions. These functions provide information about the status of an individual database record.

Logical @DB Function	Description
@DBISACT(*alias,recno,criteria*)	Determines if the record is active, that is, if it matches any optional, active criteria and is not marked for deletion (unless BASE **S**ettings **D**eleted **U**se-Deleted has been invoked).

Logical @DB Function	Description
@DBISDEL(*alias, recno*)	Determines if the record is marked for deletion. No criteria or @BASE settings affect this function.
@DBISNA(*alias, fieldname, recno*)	Returns a value of 1 if the specified field in the specified record is empty. Returns 0 if it contains an entry. Returns ERR if the database is not open or if the record or field do not exist.

In these @DB functions, *recno* is the number of the record, and *criteria* is optional. *alias* is the database alias name and *fieldname* is the name of the desired field; these two arguments must be enclosed in quotation marks unless a range name or range address is used.

Using File Manipulation @DB Functions

@BASE provides 11 functions called file manipulation functions. Of these, 10 are used to open and close database files, add or delete records, find specific records, and read or write field information.

File Manipulation @DB Function	Description
@DBOPEN(*database, alias, criteria, access_type, codepage*)	

Opens a closed database file. Returns 1 if the file was closed and was opened successfully; otherwise returns 0. The *alias* argument is optional.

The optional *access_type* can be one of the following:

Exclusive or E (default)
Primary or P
Read-Only or R

The optional *codepage* argument is the IBM PC codepage for ASCII-to-LICS file translation.

@DBCLOSE(*alias*)

Closes an open database file. Returns 1 if the file was open and was closed successfully; otherwise returns 0.

@DBDEL(*alias, recno, del_flag*)

Either marks or unmarks a record for deletion. To mark, use @TRUE as the *del_flag*; to unmark, use @FALSE as *del_flag*.

File Manipulation @DB Function   Description

@DBFIRST(*alias,criteria*)

Returns the record number of the first record that matches either the currently active criteria or the criteria specified as the optional *criteria* argument.

@DBLAST(*alias,criteria*)

Returns the record number of the last record that matches either the currently active criteria or the criteria specified as the optional *criteria* argument.

@DBNEXT(*alias,criteria,next_flag*)

Returns the record number of the next record that matches either the currently active criteria or the criteria specified as the optional *criteria* argument. If the optional *next_flag* argument is @TRUE, the function looks only at the next physical record. If *next_flag* is @FALSE, the function searches to the end of the database for matches.

@DBPREV(*alias,criteria,prev_flag*)

Returns the record number of the next previous record that matches either the currently active criteria or the criteria specified as the optional *criteria* argument. If the optional *prev_flag* argument is @TRUE, the function looks only at the next previous physical record. If *prev_flag* is @FALSE, the function searches to the beginning of the database for matches.

@DBAPP(*alias,fieldname1,value1,fieldname2,value2...*)

Appends a new record to the end of a currently open database file. This record can be blank or you can specify values for fields with the optional *fieldname* and *value* arguments. Enclose the *fieldname* and *value* arguments in quotation marks.

@DBFLD(*alias,fieldname,recno*)

Returns the contents of the specified field in the specified record.

@DBUPD(*alias,fieldname,recno,value*)

Updates the *value* of a specified field within the specified record.

The last @DB function doesn't really fit the definition of a file manipulation function because it doesn't affect any database files at all. @DBMAIN simply tests to see whether the @BASE main menu is currently being displayed. The only use for this function is within a macro because the @DB functions are used

Reminder:
Use @DBMAIN in a macro to determine whether the @BASE main menu is currently being displayed.

in the SHEET window and the @BASE menu can display only in the BASE window.

Most of the @DB functions, in fact, were clearly designed for use in advanced applications development using the Symphony Command Language (macros). When you use @DB functions in macros, many of the problems associated with the @DB functions—primarily the recalculation problem—disappear. Although Chapters 21 and 22 cover Symphony macros in depth, the following sections use a simple example to show how to use @DB functions in macros.

Using @DB Functions with Macros

In a previous example, you saw that because the @DB functions don't calculate in "natural" order, their use in a worksheet can be troublesome. Symphony macros, on the other hand, make controlling the order of calculation easy. Suppose that you want to automate the relational-database example to ensure that correct information is always displayed. Recall that several conditions can prevent you from seeing the correct information in figures 17.55 and 17.56. With macros, you can trap these error conditions and make sure that misleading information isn't displayed.

Figure 17.57 looks similar to figure 17.55 except that cells B4 through B9 no longer contain formulas. Figure 17.58 shows the macro, \N, which places the data in the cells in the customer information form. Following is an explanation of the macro.

Fig. 17.57.

A customer information form that uses a macro.

```
B4: 'Last Computer Consultants                                        SHEET
 ┌──────A───────B───────C───────D───────E───────F───────G───────H──────
 1   First name: JACK
 2   Last Name: STOKES
 3  ─────────────────────────────────────────────────────────────────────
 4       Company: Last Computer Consultants
 5       Address: PO Box 3417
 6          City: Richmond Heights
 7         State: MN
 8           ZIP: 55331
 9         Phone: 689-4011
10
```

```
A27: '{LET B4,@dbfld("CONTACTS","COMPANY",@dbfirst("CONTACTS","FIRST_NAME    EDIT
ld("CONTACTS","COMPANY",@dbfirst("CONTACTS","FIRST_NAME=B1.AND.LAST_NAME=B2"))}
      A        B        C        D        E        F        G        H
21  \N
22  {GETLABEL "First name? ",B1}
23  {GETLABEL "Last Name? ",B2}
24  {LET F4,@DBOPEN("CONTACTS")}
25  {LET F4,@DBOPEN("OFFICES")}
26  {IF #NOT#@dbfirst("CONTACTS","FIRST_NAME=B1.AND.LAST_NAME=B2")}{BRANCH \N}
27  {LET B4,@dbfld("CONTACTS","COMPANY",@dbfirst("CONTACTS","FIRST_NAME=B1.AND.
28  {LET B5,@dbfld("OFFICES","ADDRESS",@dbfirst("OFFICES","COMPANY=B4"))}
29  {LET B6,@dbfld("OFFICES","CITY",@dbfirst("OFFICES","COMPANY=B4"))}
30  {LET B7,@dbfld("OFFICES","STATE",@dbfirst("OFFICES","COMPANY=B4"))}
31  {LET B8,@dbfld("OFFICES","ZIP",@dbfirst("OFFICES","COMPANY=B4"))}
32  {LET B9,@dbfld("OFFICES","PHONE",@dbfirst("OFFICES","COMPANY=B4"))}
33  {LET F4,@DBCLOSE("CONTACTS")}
34  {LET F4,@DBCLOSE("OFFICES")}
35  {DRAW}{BRANCH \N}
36
```

Fig. 17.58.
The macro for the customer information form.

Cell	Description of Macro Line
A21	The macro name, \N, is placed in the cell immediately above the macro code. SHEET **R**ange **N**ame **L**abel **D**own is used to assign the range name to the macro beginning in A22. Naming the macro \N means that you can invoke the macro by pressing Alt-N.
A22	Displays the **First Name?** prompt and places the answer in cell B1.
A23	Displays the **Last Name?** prompt and places the answer in cell B2.
A24	Opens the @BASE database file CONTACTS.DBF and places the result (1 or 0) in cell F4. None of the optional arguments are specified with the @DBOPEN function, so the file is opened with the alias CONTACTS, no active criteria, exclusive access, and no codepage support. The value placed in F4 is ignored.
A25	Opens the @BASE database file OFFICES.DBF in the same manner as CONTACTS.DBF was opened.
A26	Checks to see that a valid first and last name were entered. Because @DBFIRST returns 0 if a record matching the criteria is not found, adding the #NOT# logical operator causes the macro to branch back to the beginning of the \N macro if the complete name doesn't produce a match with one of the records in CONTACTS.
A27	Places in cell B4 the company name from the matching record in OFFICES. Notice that this @DB formula is exactly the same formula that was in cell B4 in figure 17.55. Because the macro executes instructions sequentially, you can be sure that cell B4 will contain accurate company information before the @DB formulas in cells A28 through A32 are executed.

Cell	Description of Macro Line
A28	Places the company's address in cell B5 using the @DB formula from cell B5 of figure 17.55.
A29	Places the company's city in cell B6 using the @DB formula from cell B6 of figure 17.55.
A30	Places the company's state in cell B7 using the @DB formula from cell B7 of figure 17.55.
A31	Places the company's ZIP in cell B8 using the @DB formula from cell B8 of figure 17.55.
A32	Places the company's phone number in cell B9 using the @DB formula from cell B9 of figure 17.55.
A33	Closes the CONTACTS.DBF file and places the result code in cell F4.
A34	Closes the OFFICES.DBF file and places the result code in cell F4.
A35	Redraws the screen and branches back to restart the macro.

Reminder:

Place @DB functions in a macro to ensure that formulas are calculated in the proper order.

By using @DB functions in macros, you can ensure that database files are opened before they are needed. You also ensure that each formula containing an @DB function is calculated in the proper sequence. As a final housekeeping chore, you make certain that the database files are closed after you use them.

Using Macros for a More Complex Example

Suppose that your database contains two people with the same first and last names. The macro in figure 17.58 finds the first record that matches the name and report the information for that person. But what if the second (or third) match is really the one you want? It would be quite difficult to modify the formulas in figure 17.55 to account for this situation. With macros, on the other hand, you easily can check for multiple record matches and then ask the user which one is correct.

Figure 17.59 shows one way to modify the macro shown in figure 17.58 so that the macro asks for the company name if two or more names are found to match the user's entry. @DBCNT is used to determine how many records match the user's entry. Notice that cell A26 has been modified to use the @DBCNT function as well. Because @DBCNT returns the number of records that match a given set of criteria, you can use the function to determine whether any records match, as is done in cell A26, or whether multiple records match, as is done in cell A28.

The \N macro in figure 17.59 works just like the one in figure 17.58 except that cell A28 was added. This extra line checks to see how many records match the first name in cell B1 and the last name in cell B2. If more than one match occurs, the routine WHICH_ONE is called. WHICH_ONE prompts the user to supply

```
A27: '{LET B4,@DBFLD("CONTACTS","COMPANY",@DBFIRST("CONTACTS","FIRST_NAME    EDIT
LD("CONTACTS","COMPANY",@DBFIRST("CONTACTS","FIRST_NAME=B1.AND.LAST_NAME=B2"))}_
┌───────A───────B───────C───────D───────E───────F───────G───────H──
21    \n
22    {GETLABEL "First Name? ",B1}
23    {GETLABEL "Last Name? ",B2}
24    {LET F4,@DBOPEN("CONTACTS")}
25    {LET F4,@DBOPEN("OFFICES")}
26    {IF @DBCNT("CONTACTS","FIRST_NAME=B1.AND.LAST_NAME=B2")=0}{BRANCH \n}
27    {LET B4,@DBFLD("CONTACTS","COMPANY",@DBFIRST("CONTACTS","FIRST_NAME=B1.AND.
28    {IF @DBCNT("CONTACTS","FIRST_NAME=B1.AND.LAST_NAME=B2")>1}{WHICH_ONE}
29    {LET B5,@DBFLD("OFFICES","ADDRESS",@DBFIRST("OFFICES","COMPANY=B4"))}
30    {LET B6,@DBFLD("OFFICES","CITY",@DBFIRST("OFFICES","COMPANY=B4"))}
31    {LET B7,@DBFLD("OFFICES","STATE",@DBFIRST("OFFICES","COMPANY=B4"))}
32    {LET B8,@DBFLD("OFFICES","ZIP",@DBFIRST("OFFICES","COMPANY=B4"))}
33    {LET B9,@DBFLD("OFFICES","PHONE",@DBFIRST("OFFICES","COMPANY=B4"))}
34    {LET F4,@DBCLOSE("CONTACTS")}
35    {LET F4,@DBCLOSE("OFFICES")}
36    {DRAW}{BRANCH \n}
37
38    WHICH_ONE
39    {GETLABEL "More than one match. Which company do you want? ",B4}
40    {IF @DBCNT("OFFICES","COMPANY=B4")=0}{BEEP}{BRANCH WHICH_ONE}
41
42
43
44
45
46
47
48
49
└────────────────────────────────────────────────────────────────MAIN─
03-Apr-90  00:34 AM                                            Num
```

Fig. 17.59.

A modified macro that requests the company name if more than one match is found.

the correct company name. The answer is placed in cell B4; cell A40 verifies that a valid name was entered. If a valid name was not entered, the computer beeps and loops back to ask for the company name again.

As an exercise in determining how well you understand macros, consider how you can modify WHICH_ONE to verify that the user entered a company name that matches one of the selected customer records. You may want to modify the macro to display a list of the company names from which the user can select.

Understanding When Macros are Disadvantageous

Although the @DB functions clearly work very well in macros, some @BASE operations are best handled manually. Sorting a database, for example, is a task which is difficult at best using macros. Suppose that you want to know which customers work for each company. To get this information, you would probably sort the CONTACTS database by company, then last name, and finally first name.

Reminder:

Some @BASE operations are best performed manually; macros don't work well in all situations.

To perform this sort, start by switching to the BASE window. If the CONTACTS database does not appear on-screen, you must open it before sorting. Once you verify that CONTACTS is open, select BASE **D**ata **S**ort. See what happens if you try to enter the field name **COMPANY**. Unlike most of Symphony's operations, the BASE **S**ort command does not allow you to type the field information; you have to point to the correct field by moving the cursor and pressing Enter. Although you can use a macro to move the cursor and select the fields for the sort keys, this approach requires careful planning. In this case, to select ascending sorts based on company, last name, and first name, you must move the cursor down two, press Enter, press A for **A**scending, move the cursor up two, press Enter, press A, move down one, press Enter, and press A. You then press Esc, O for **O**verwrite, and finally E for **E**xecute. Figure 17.60 shows the screen after you select the fields for sorting.

Once the database has been sorted, verify the new sort order by using BASE **D**ata **B**rowse **A**ll. Figure 17.61 shows the browse window after the database has been sorted.

Although the CONTACTS database has only three fields, most of your databases will probably be much larger. Because the @DB file manipulation functions @DBFIRST, @DBNEXT, @DBPREV, and @DBLAST find records based on their physical position in the database, it's often important to sort a database before producing reports. Just as you sorted CONTACTS.DBF to make it easier to see which customers worked for the various companies, you often have to access database records in a particular order. With a large number of fields, however, it can be difficult to devise a macro that properly sorts the database. A solution is available, however, in an optional add-in called the Option Pac.

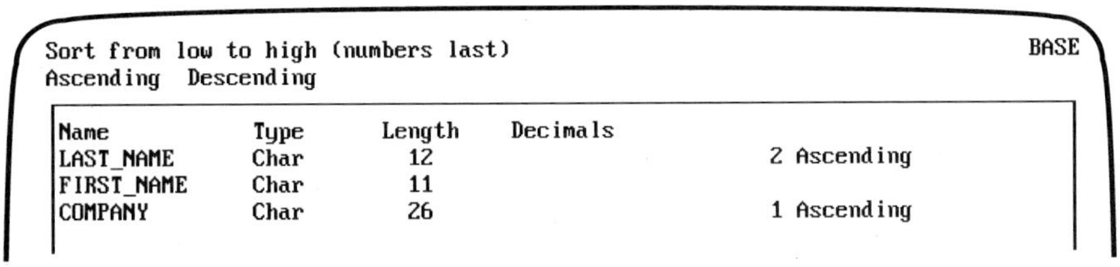

Fig. 17.60.

Sorting the CONTACTS database.

```
Sort from low to high (numbers last)                              BASE
Ascending  Descending

Name          Type      Length    Decimals
LAST_NAME     Char      12                              2 Ascending
FIRST_NAME    Char      11
COMPANY       Char      26                              1 Ascending
```

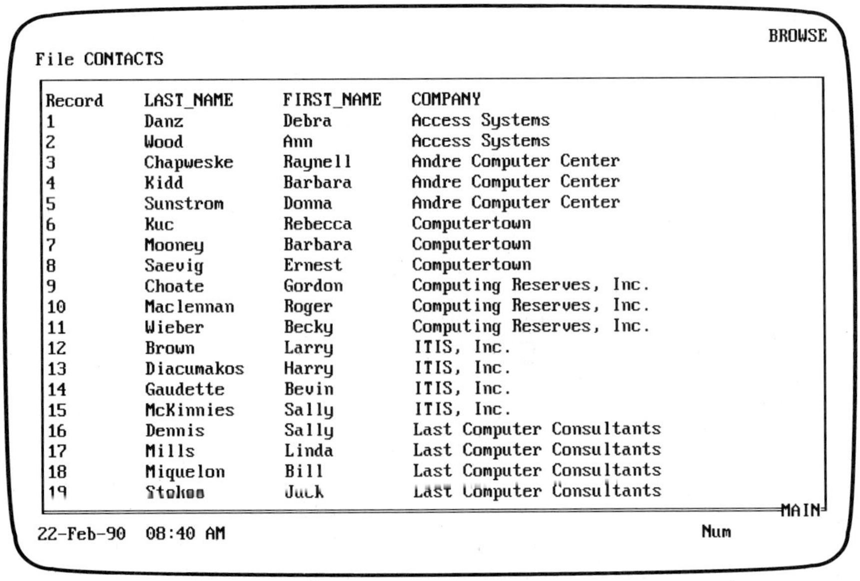

Fig. 17.61.

The browse screen after sorting the CONTACTS database.

```
                                                               BROWSE
File CONTACTS

Record  LAST_NAME    FIRST_NAME   COMPANY
1       Danz         Debra        Access Systems
2       Wood         Ann          Access Systems
3       Chapweske    Raynell      Andre Computer Center
4       Kidd         Barbara      Andre Computer Center
5       Sunstrom     Donna        Andre Computer Center
6       Kuc          Rebecca      Computertown
7       Mooney       Barbara      Computertown
8       Saevig       Ernest       Computertown
9       Choate       Gordon       Computing Reserves, Inc.
10      Maclennan    Roger        Computing Reserves, Inc.
11      Wieber       Becky        Computing Reserves, Inc.
12      Brown        Larry        ITIS, Inc.
13      Diacumakos   Harry        ITIS, Inc.
14      Gaudette     Bevin        ITIS, Inc.
15      McKinnies    Sally        ITIS, Inc.
16      Dennis       Sally        Last Computer Consultants
17      Mills        Linda        Last Computer Consultants
18      Miquelon     Bill         Last Computer Consultants
19      Stokes       Jack         Last Computer Consultants
                                                               MAIN

22-Feb-90   08:40 AM                                    Num
```

Using the @BASE Option Pac

Personics Corporation, the developers of the @BASE add-in, have developed an enhancement package for less than $100 that works with @BASE. This package, called the @BASE Option Pac, adds several important features that make the Symphony/@BASE combination a powerful relational database manager. The features available with the Option Pac are listed in the following chart:

Feature	Purpose
Indexing	Adds considerable speed to record lookups by maintaining a small index file (like the index of a book) that permits direct access to records. Without indexing, @BASE must read an entire database file, starting at the beginning, to find a desired record. Indexing also removes the need to sort the database because index files are automatically sorted; new records added to the end of the database automatically appear in the desired sequence.
File Joining	Allows creation of true relational databases where data redundancy is eliminated. One record in one file can provide the necessary information for several related records in another file.
Computed Fields	Eliminates the need for complex macros to calculate values based on other field values. This feature also reduces disk-storage requirements because computed fields are not stored as separate fields in the database file.
View Files	Provides an automatic means of performing database setups. View files maintain the definitions of joined files and computed fields and keep track of which database files must be opened. Opening a view file automatically performs the steps required to set up these conditions.
@NDX Functions	Provides new @functions that work with index files and indexed records. These functions let you incorporate the advantages of indexing in macro-driven applications.

Reminder:

The optional @BASE Option Pac provides enhancements to the basic @BASE package.

The Option Pac adds many powerful features to @BASE. Further information is available from Personics Corporation:

> Personics Corporation
> 63 Great Road
> Maynard, MA 01754
> (800) 445-3311

Additional information about each of the Option Pac features is provided in the following sections.

Using the Indexing Capability of Option Pac

The indexing capability provides several benefits including much faster record lookups and automatic record sorting. Lookups are much faster because a small index file contains information showing the exact location of each record. Instead of searching through all database records, Symphony can go directly to the desired record.

One problem common to both the in-RAM and @BASE database managers is that when you add new records to the database, you must append them to the end of the database. Your carefully sorted address file may suddenly have Andersen's record added right after Wilson's. Adding new records becomes a two-step process: first you add the record, then you re-sort the database. With indexing, you simply add the new record.

Another strong advantage of indexing appears when you want to view a database sorted by using a different sort key. Instead of viewing a database sorted by last name, you may want to see the database sorted by current sales (the field names CUR_SALES). Using either the in-RAM or the standard @BASE database manager, you have a multi-step process: first specify the CUR_SALES field as the new sort key and then re-sort the database. With an indexed database, you specify CUR_SALES as the index and the database instantly appears as if it had been re-sorted using CUR_SALES.

Using the Joining Capability of Option Pac

The joining capabilities provided by Option Pac give @BASE true relational database capabilities. Although figures 17.57 and 17.58 show one method of relating one database file to another, the Option Pac method of joining database files is much easier to use and greatly simplifies database application development. In Chapter 18, you follow an example of how to join database files using Option Pac.

Using the Computed Field Capability of Option Pac

The Symphony in-RAM database manager offers a computed field type not available in @BASE. Option Pac makes the computed field type available to the @BASE user. One advantage of Option Pac's computed field type is that although the definition of the computed field is stored with the database, the computed value is not. This storage method saves disk space. Symphony's in-RAM database computed fields are stored in the database; they use disk space when you save the file and memory when you load it.

Using the View Files Capability of Option Pac

Database views enable you to define conditions for relational databases, such as which files must be open, how files are joined, and any computed fields. If you save a view file, you can retrieve it later to reestablish all the conditions. View files save time; you don't have to redo all the steps like opening each database, setting up the joined fields, and redefining the computed fields.

Using the @Functions in Option Pac

The Option Pac also adds several new @functions that relate to indexed files and view files. These new @functions can be combined with existing @BASE @DB functions and the Symphony Command Language to provide a very powerful database-management product.

The @functions included with the Option Pac fall into several groups. The following chart lists the @functions and provides a brief description of each:

Function	Description
File Management	
@NDXOPEN	Opens an index file.
@NDXCLOSE	Closes an index file.
@VIEWOPEN	Opens a view file.
Statistical	
@NDXAVG	Returns the average of the specified field for records matching the index.
@NDXCNT	Returns the number of records that match the index.
@NDXMAX	Returns the maximum field value for matching records.

Function	Description
@NDXMIN	Returns the minimum field value for matching records.
@NDXSUM	Returns the sum of field values for matching records.

File Manipulation

@NDXFIRST	Returns the first record that matches the index.
@NDXLAST	Returns the last record that matches the index.
@NDXNEXT	Returns the next record that matches the index.
@NDXPREV	Returns the next previous record that matches the index.

Index Manipulation

@NDXSELECT	Selects the primary index.
@NDXPAD	Constructs an index.

Chapter Summary

In this chapter, you have seen how to use Symphony's FORM window, database commands in the SHEET environment, and database statistical functions. You have seen a demonstration of Symphony's special report-generating capabilities, which are a part of the FORM environment. You also have seen how to use the @BASE add-in database manager and have had the opportunity to compare the capabilities of both. You've seen how to convert a database from one database manager to the other and have seen an example of how to use macros to manipulate a database. In Chapter 18, you practice many of the database operations introduced in this chapter. Chapter 18 also provides more examples using Symphony's @BASE add-in database manager. Chapter 22 presents some examples of how to use the Symphony Command Language to help build input forms and perform other FORM window operations.

18

Managing Data: Hands-On Practice

Chapter 17 led you through the many different aspects of Symphony's data management: creating and modifying a database, sorting, searching, using database statistical functions, and producing reports. This hands-on practice chapter concentrates on data-management basics to get you up and running quickly. In the first part of the chapter, you use Symphony's in-RAM database manager and the FORM environment to generate a database, enter data, sort the data, locate records according to different search criteria, and produce simple reports.

In the second part of the chapter, you use the @BASE add-in to create an on-disk version of the same database you create in the first part of the chapter. You have the opportunity to compare the two database environments and see how they differ. You also practice using some of the @DB functions and some simple macros to manipulate the @BASE database. Finally, you look at the optional @BASE Option Pac to see how it enhances the @BASE add-in.

Creating the In-RAM Database

The database you create in the first part of this chapter tracks information about sales people for a company with regional sales divisions.

You use the FORM window to create a database. But you must first type the field names, types, and lengths in a SHEET or DOC window. To begin creating the database you use for this practice session, follow these steps:

1. Load the Symphony program. A blank worksheet displays, and you are in SHEET mode.

2. Refer to figure 18.1 and enter the following labels:

In Cell:	Enter:
A1	LAST_NAME:L:15
A2	FIRST_NAME:L:15
A3	DIV:L:4
A4	CUR_SALES:N:12
A5	QUOTA:C:12

Fig. 18.1.

Typing the field names for the input form.

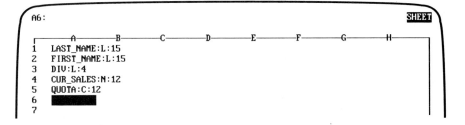

Tip

Use field names that follow the rules for @BASE field names when you create a Symphony in-RAM database. Converting the in-RAM database to an @BASE database is easier when the field names are valid in @BASE.

Once you enter the field names in the worksheet, switch to the FORM environment to generate the database and all the special database ranges. Follow these steps to generate the database:

1. Press the Type (Alt-F10) key and select FORM.

   Note: The message `No Definition range defined` appears in the control panel. Disregard this message; it disappears as soon as you generate the database.

2. Select FORM **G**enerate.

3. Choose **L**abel as the default field type. (In this example, the choice you make here doesn't really matter, because you specified the field types for each field in the SHEET environment.)

4. Press Enter to accept the default field length. Again, the choice you make here doesn't matter, because you already indicated the specific lengths.

5. Enter **SALES** as the name for the database settings sheet.

6. Specify the field-name range as **A1..A5**. Symphony instantly creates and displays the input form.

As soon as you generate an input form, you can begin entering data. Enter one record into the database by following these instructions:

1. Type **Peterson** in the LAST_NAME field and press Enter.

2. Enter **Stewart** in the FIRST_NAME field.

3. Enter **NE** (for Northeast) in the DIV field.

4. Enter **310000** in the CUR_SALES field. The screen should look like figure 18.2.

   Note: The cursor skipped past the QUOTA field and went back to the LAST_NAME field because you designated the QUOTA field as computed (C). You enter the formula for this computed field in "Entering Formulas," later in this chapter.

5. Press the Ins key to insert the record. A blank data-entry form appears.

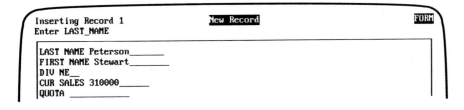

Fig. 18.2.
Entering a new record.

Saving the file after you generate the database is a good idea. Follow these steps to save the file:

1. Select SERVICES **F**ile **S**ave.

2. Enter **SALES** as the file name.

Viewing the Database Ranges

Symphony created several special database ranges in the worksheet when you issued the **G**enerate command. Examine these ranges by following these steps:

1. Press the Switch (Alt-F9) key to return to SHEET mode. Look at everything Symphony created with the **G**enerate command: the entry range, the definition range, the report ranges, the criterion range, and the database range.

2. Press Switch (Alt-F9) to switch back to FORM mode.

3. Select FORM **S**ettings to display the database settings sheet (see fig. 18.3). Look at the basic and the form ranges in the top left portion of the screen. Notice the range names (such as SALES_DB) that appear next to each range in the settings sheet. Symphony created these range names when generating the database.

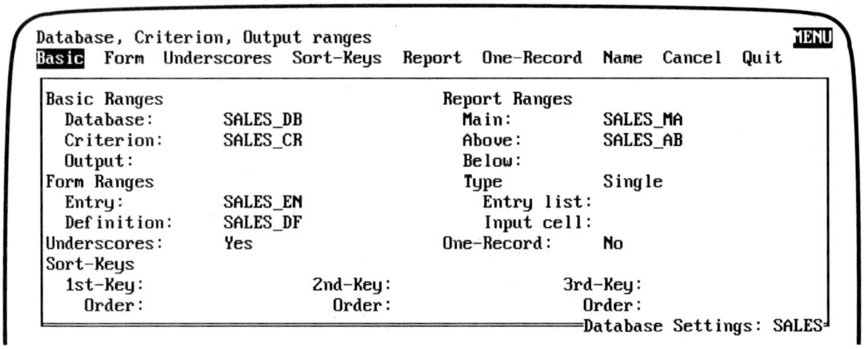

Fig. 18.3.

The database settings sheet.

```
Database, Criterion, Output ranges                                    MENU
Basic  Form  Underscores  Sort-Keys  Report  One-Record  Name  Cancel  Quit

Basic Ranges                         Report Ranges
   Database:      SALES_DB              Main:         SALES_MA
   Criterion:     SALES_CR              Above:        SALES_AB
   Output:                              Below:
Form Ranges                             Type          Single
   Entry:         SALES_EN                Entry list:
   Definition:    SALES_DF                Input cell:
Underscores:      Yes                  One-Record:    No
Sort-Keys
   1st-Key:                2nd-Key:                3rd-Key:
     Order:                  Order:                  Order:
                                                =Database Settings: SALES
```

4. Select **B**asic **D**atabase. The database range (SALES_DB or A28..E29) holds all the database records. Right now, the database has only one record, but as you input more records, Symphony expands this range to include the new records.

5. Press Enter to accept this range.

6. Select **C**riterion. The criterion range (SALES_CR or A23..E24) is where you enter selection criteria when you search for a record or want a list of only certain records in the database.

7. Press Enter to accept this range.

8. Select **Q**uit **F**orm **E**ntry. The entry range (SALES_EN or A1..A7) should look familiar to you. This range holds the input form you use for data entry.

9. Press Enter to accept this range.

10. Select **D**efinition. The definition range (SALES_DF or A14..H18) is where you enter the formula for any computed fields (such as QUOTA in the example). You also use this range to enter formats for date and numeric fields and to indicate other special settings for the input form.

11. Press Enter to accept the definition range.

12. Select **Q**uit **Q**uit.

Entering Formulas

As mentioned in the preceding section, QUOTA is a computed field. Although you specified that it was a computed field when you generated the database, you haven't yet entered the formula. In this example, the quota should be 110 percent of the current year's sales. Enter in the definition range the formula that makes this calculation by following these steps:

1. Switch to SHEET mode.

2. Go to the definition range by pressing GoTo (F5) and entering **SALES_DF**.

3. Move the cell pointer to the Formula column in the QUOTA row (cell E18).

4. Enter the formula **+B17*110%** (see fig. 18.4).

   Note: Formulas for computed fields always refer to cells in the Value column (column B). If you want to transform input with a formula (for example, to ensure that what is typed for the last name is in initial capital letters), the formula you use must refer to the Input column (column G).

5. Switch back to FORM mode.

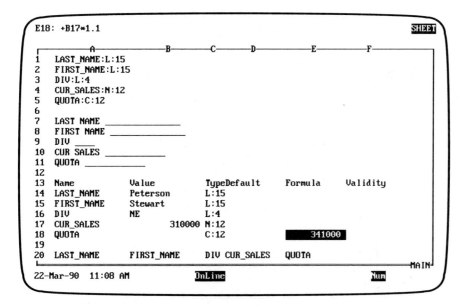

Fig. 18.4.

Entering a formula in the definition range.

Because you entered the first record before writing the formula, you must recalculate the record. Record 1 should be displayed, so simply press the Calc (F8) key. The figure **341000** appears in the QUOTA field for that record.

Entering Records

Follow these steps to enter a record and see how the quota is automatically calculated once you enter the current year's sales:

1. Press PgDn to display a blank form.
2. Type **Jones** in the LAST_NAME field and press Enter.
3. Enter **Robert** in the FIRST_NAME field.
4. Enter **NW** (for Northwest) in the DIV field.
5. Enter **300000** in the CUR_SALES field. Symphony automatically calculates QUOTA and displays **330000** in that field.
6. Press Ins to insert the record.

Refer to figure 18.5 to enter the remaining records in the database.

Fig. 18.5.
The database records.

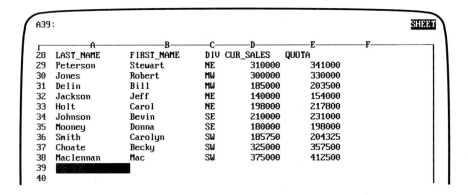

	LAST_NAME	FIRST_NAME	DIV	CUR_SALES	QUOTA
28	LAST_NAME	FIRST_NAME	DIV	CUR_SALES	QUOTA
29	Peterson	Stewart	NE	310000	341000
30	Jones	Robert	MW	300000	330000
31	Delin	Bill	MW	185000	203500
32	Jackson	Jeff	NE	140000	154000
33	Holt	Carol	NE	198000	217800
34	Johnson	Bevin	SE	210000	231000
35	Mooney	Donna	SE	180000	198000
36	Smith	Carolyn	SW	185750	204325
37	Choate	Becky	SW	325000	357500
38	Maclennan	Mac	SW	375000	412500
39					
40					

As you enter the additional records, remember that you type each row in figure 18.5 on a separate form. Use the Ins key to insert the record. When you finish entering the records, save the file with the same name, responding that you want to replace the file.

Maintaining the In-RAM Database

Once you generate a database and enter data into it, you need to keep the database accurate and up-to-date. At times, you may want to locate specific records so that you can edit the data or look up information. Having the data sorted in a meaningful order helps you organize and find information.

Sorting the Data

If you have ever had to sort anything manually, you know how tedious the process is. Fortunately, the computer is a star when it comes to sorting.

Sorting in Symphony is a two-step process. First, you must specify the sort *key* (the field by which you want to sort) in the settings sheet. Second, you tell Symphony to perform the record sort.

To sort the SALES database by the LAST_NAME field, follow these steps:

1. Select FORM **S**ettings **S**ort-Keys **1**st-Key. The screen temporarily switches to SHEET mode, and the cell pointer is located within the database range.

2. Point to cell A29 in the LAST_NAME column and press Enter. Although you can point to any cell in the LAST_NAME column, pointing to the cell that contains the first record makes Symphony display **LAST_NAME** instead of just the cell address as the 1st-Key (see fig. 18.6).

3. Type **A** to select **A**scending order.

4. Select FORM **R**ecord-Sort **A**ll to sort all the records.

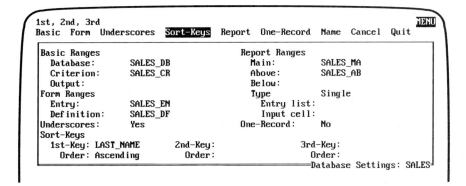

Fig. 18.6.
The settings sheet with 1st-Key specified.

Follow these steps to browse through the records. Notice that the records are now arranged alphabetically by last name.

1. Press Home to go to the first record.

2. Press PgDn and PgUp to look at the records.

3. Press End to go to the last record.

Finding a Record

If you have dozens, hundreds, or thousands of records in a database, you need a faster way of going to a specific record than the PgDn and PgUp keys, even if the database is sorted. The **C**riteria command gives you that speed. You enter in a criterion record what you are seeking, and Symphony displays the matching record for you. You can then look up or update information in the record.

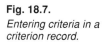

Because the SALES database is small, you really don't need to use the **Criteria** command to locate a record. But you can use the database to get an idea of how this command works on a larger database.

Follow these steps to use the **Criteria** command to look up Smith's quota:

1. Select FORM **Criteria Edit**. A blank criterion record appears.
2. Next to the LAST NAME field, enter **Smith** (see fig. 18.7).
3. Press PgUp to go back to the database.
4. Select FORM **Criteria Use** to invoke the criteria. The record for Smith appears. What is her quota?

Fig. 18.7.

Entering criteria in a criterion record.

```
┌──────────────────────────────────────────────────────────────────────────┐
│ Editing Criterion Record 1 of 1                                     EDIT   │
│ Enter LAST_NAME                                                            │
│  ┌──────────────────────────────────────────────────────────────────────┐ │
│  │ LAST NAME Smith_____                                             │ │
│  │ FIRST NAME _____                                            │ │
│  │ DIV ____                                                              │ │
│  │ CUR SALES _____                                                │ │
│  │ QUOTA _____                                                    │ │
│  │                                                                      │ │
│  │                                                                      │ │
│  │                                                                      │ │
│  │                                                                      │ │
│  │                                                                      │ │
│  │                                                                      │ │
│  │                                                                      │ │
│  │                                                                      │ │
│  └──────────────────────────────────────────────────────────────────────┘ │
│ └SALES════════════════════════════════════════════════════════════MAIN┘ │
│  Criteria Edit                                           Calc      Num     │
└──────────────────────────────────────────────────────────────────────────┘
```

The message **(1 Match)** displays in the control panel. This message tells you that only one record matches the search criteria. In other words, only one Smith is located in the database.

When a criterion record is in use, as it is now, you can look only at the selected record or records. If you try to look at other records by pressing PgUp or PgDn, Symphony beeps. If you want to view the entire database again, you must tell Symphony to ignore the criteria. Follow these steps to view the entire database again:

1. Select FORM **Criteria Ignore**. Notice that the **(1 Match)** message in the control panel disappears.
2. Press PgUp and PgDn to confirm that the entire database is now accessible.

In the previous example, you knew exactly how *Smith* was spelled, so you had no trouble locating the record. Sometimes, though, you may not be sure of the spelling. In that case, you use a wild card to help locate the record. Suppose that you want to look up information for a sales person whose name begins with *J*. Follow these steps to perform the search:

1. Select FORM **C**riteria **E**dit. Notice that the last search criteria (**Smith**) is still in the form. You can type right over this criteria.

2. Next to the LAST_NAME field, enter **J***. The asterisk is a wild card that tells Symphony to accept all characters in place of the *

3. Press PgUp.

4. Select FORM **C**riteria **U**se. The first record that matches the criteria appears on-screen, and the control panel displays the message (**Match 1 of 3**), as shown in figure 18.8.

5. Press PgDn to look at the three records.

```
Editing Record 6 of 10 (Match 3 of 3)                          FORM
Enter LAST_NAME

 LAST NAME Jones_____
 FIRST NAME Robert_____
 DIV MW__
 CUR SALES 300000_____
 QUOTA 330000_____
```

Fig. 18.8.
The first record that meets the criteria.

Deleting a Record

You are searching for Jackson's record. His sales are so bad, you want to fire him. Delete him from the database by following these steps:

1. Press PgUp or PgDn to display Jackson's record. Look at how poor his sales record is.

2. Press the Del key to delete the record.

3. Select **Y**es to confirm your intention.

Once you delete a record, it is gone forever. This is a major difference between the in-RAM database manager and the @BASE database manager. With the @BASE database manager, you mark and unmark records for deletion. You actually delete @BASE database records in a separate step.

Editing a Record

Editing a record in FORM mode is similar to editing a cell in SHEET mode. You can replace what is in the field by typing over the data, or you can use the Edit (F2) key to modify the contents.

Follow these steps to correct Johnson's last name to *Johanson.*

1. If necessary, press PgUp or PgDn to display Johnson's record.
2. With the cursor in the LAST_NAME field, press Edit (F2).
3. Press the right-arrow key until the cursor is on the first *n* in *Johnson.*
4. Type **a**. The record should look like figure 18.9.
5. Press Enter.

Fig. 18.9.

After editing a criterion record.

```
Editing Record 5 of 10  (Match 2 of 3)                    FORM
Enter LAST_NAME

LAST NAME Johanson_____
FIRST NAME Bevin_____
DIV SE___
CUR SALES 210000_____
QUOTA 2310000_____
```

Creating Reports with the In-RAM Database

To print a database report in Symphony, you specify the database (not a range) as the source for the report. The report prints in the order in which the database is currently sorted, using the criteria currently specified—even if you select **C**riteria **I**gnore.

Printing the Default Report

Print the report that Symphony automatically set up for you when you generated the database. The default report prints all fields with the field names above each column.

Reports use the last criteria entered. Because you want the entire database to print, delete the criterion record before printing. Follow these steps to delete the criterion record:

1. Select FORM **C**riteria **E**dit to display the criterion record.
2. Press the Del key to delete the record.
3. Select **Y**es to confirm.
4. Press PgUp.

Follow these steps to print the report:

1. Select SERVICES **P**rint **S**ettings **S**ource **D**atabase **SALES**. (You can either type **SALES** or select it from a list by moving the cursor.)

2. Select **Q**uit to exit from the **S**ettings menu.

3. Select **A**lign **G**o to print. The report should look similar to figure 18.10.

```
LAST NAME       FIRST NAME    DIV   CUR SALES    QUOTA
Choate          Becky         SW       325000    357500
Delin           Bill          MW       185000    203500
Holt            Carol         ME       190000    217000
Jackson         Jeff          ME       140000    154000
Johanson        Bevin         SE       210000    231000
Jones           Robert        MW       300000    330000
Maclennan       Mac           SW       375000    412500
Mooney          Donna         SE       100000    198000
Peterson        Stewart       NE       310000    341000
Smith           Carolyn       SW       185750    204325
```

Fig. 18.10.
The printed report.

4. Select **P**age to feed the paper out of the printer. (Some printers may require that you issue an additional **P**age command before you can tear off the sheet.)

5. Select **Q**uit.

Modifying the Report

To modify the report, you must be familiar with the report ranges Symphony automatically sets up when it generates the database. The *above range* (SALES_AB) consists of the report column headings, which by default are simply the field names. You edit this range if you want to change the content or alignment of the column headings. The *main range* (SALES_MA) prints once for each record in the database. Each cell in this range references the appropriate field in the database. If you want to format the data in the report, this range is the one to change.

The report would look better if the numbers had commas and if the column headings above the numbers were aligned on the right. Follow these steps to format the numbers in the main range to the **P**unctuated format:

1. Press Switch (Alt-F9) to switch to SHEET mode.

2. Press GoTo (F5) and enter **SALES_MA**.

3. Move the cell pointer to cell D21.

4. Select SHEET **F**ormat **P**unctuated.

5. Type **0** for the number of decimal places and press Enter.

6. Highlight the range D21..E21. The screen should look like figure 18.11. Press Enter.

Fig. 18.11.

Aligning labels in the above range.

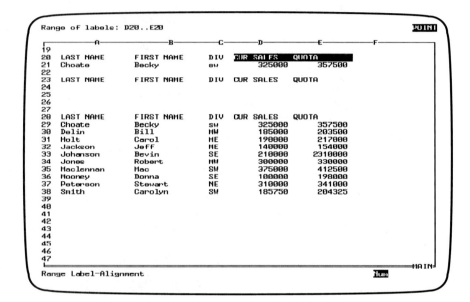

```
Range of labels: D20..E20                                                    POINT
        A          B          C       D          E            F
19
20  LAST NAME   FIRST NAME   DIV   CUR SALES   QUOTA
21  Choate      Becky        sw       325000      357500
22
23  LAST NAME   FIRST NAME   DIV   CUR SALES   QUOTA
24
25
26
27
28  LAST NAME   FIRST NAME   DIV   CUR SALES   QUOTA
29  Choate      Becky        SW       325000      357500
30  Delin       Bill         MW       185000      203500
31  Holt        Carol        ME       198000      217000
32  Jackson     Jeff         ME       140000      154000
33  Johnson     Bevin        SE       210000      231000
34  Jones       Robert       MW       300000      330000
35  Maclennan   Mac          SW       375000      412500
36  Mooney      Donna        SE       100000      198000
37  Peterson    Stewart      NE       310000      341000
38  Smith       Carolyn      SW       185750      204325
39
40
41
42
43
44
45
46
47
                                                            MAIN
Range Label-Alignment                                       Num
```

The above range is directly above the main range. Follow these steps to right-align the column headings over the numbers:

1. Move the cell pointer to the cell containing CUR_SALES, cell D20.

2. Select SHEET **R**ange **L**abel-Alignment **R**ight.

3. Highlight the range D20..E20. The screen should resemble figure 18.11. Press Enter.

Follow these instructions to reprint the report. Symphony remembers that you already specified the database as the source.

1. Press Switch (Alt-F9) to switch to FORM mode.

2. Select SERVICES **P**rint **G**o. The report should look similar to figure 18.12.

3. Select **P**age to feed the paper out of the printer. (With some printers, you may have to issue an additional **P**age command before you can tear off the sheet.)

LAST NAME	FIRST NAME	DIV	CUR SALES	QUOTA
Choate	Becky	SW	325000	357500
Delin	Bill	MW	185000	203500
Holt	Carol	ME	190000	217000
Jackson	Jeff	ME	140000	154000
Johanson	Bevin	SE	210000	2310000
Jones	Robert	MW	300000	330000
Maclennan	Mac	SW	375000	412500
Mooney	Donna	SE	100000	198000
Peterson	Stewart	NE	310000	341000
Smith	Carolyn	SW	185750	204325

Fig. 18.12.
The printed results.

Creating the @BASE Database

To begin creating the @BASE on-disk database you use in this part of the chapter, follow these steps:

1. Load the Symphony program. A blank worksheet appears, and you are in SHEET mode.

2. Attach @BASE by selecting SERVICES **A**pplication **A**ttach and choosing BASEFUNC.APP. Select **A**ttach again and choose BASE.APP. Select **A**ttach a third time and choose BASEUTL.APP. Select **Q**uit to return to the SHEET window.

3. Change to the BASE window environment by pressing Type (Alt-F10) and selecting BASE.

4. Press Menu (F10) to display the menu shown in figure 18.13.

```
Open   Close  Use  Define  Modify  Extract  Field-Rename  Post        MENU
File   Data  Criteria  Settings  Utility
Alias          File name
```

Fig. 18.13.
The @BASE menu.

5. Select **F**ile **D**efine.

6. Enter **SALES** as the name of the database you are defining.

   Note: You can use the same name for in-RAM databases and @BASE on-disk databases. The in-RAM database is saved in a worksheet file with the extension WR1; the on-disk database is saved in a database file with the extension DBF.

7. Enter the field names, types, lengths, and, for the two numeric fields, the number of decimal places. Figure 18.14 shows the screen after you enter this information.

Notice that because the @BASE add-in lacks computed fields, the QUOTA field is defined as numeric. Later in this chapter, you see how to use macros to compute the value for the QUOTA field. You also see that the Option Pac add-in provides an easy way to produce computed fields.

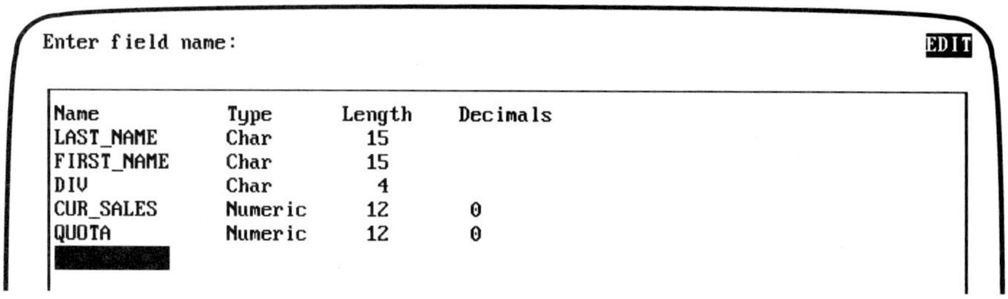

Fig. 18.14.

Defining the @BASE database.

```
Enter field name:                                              EDIT

| Name       | Type    | Length | Decimals |
| LAST_NAME  | Char    | 15     |          |
| FIRST_NAME | Char    | 15     |          |
| DIV        | Char    | 4      |          |
| CUR_SALES  | Numeric | 12     | 0        |
| QUOTA      | Numeric | 12     | 0        |
```

8. Press Enter after entering the data in figure 18.14. Press Esc.
9. Select **S**ave and accept **SALES** as the database alias.

@BASE automatically generates an entry form using the database definition you provided. Enter a record with this entry form by following these steps:

1. Select **D**ata **F**orm and accept **SALES** as the database.
2. Type **Peterson** in the LAST_NAME field and press Enter.
3. Enter **Stewart** in the FIRST_NAME field.
4. Enter **NE** in the DIV field.
5. Enter **310000** in the CUR_SALES field. The screen looks like figure 18.15.
6. Press Ins to insert the record into the database.

Enter the remaining records. Be sure that you press Ins after each record. Once you enter all 10 records, an empty entry form displays.

Last Name	First Name	Division	Current Sales
Delin	Bill	NW	185000
Jones	Robert	NW	300000
Jackson	Jeff	NE	310000
Holt	Carol	NE	198000
Johanson	Bevin	SE	210000
Mooney	Donna	SE	180000
Smith	Carolyn	SW	185750
Choate	Becky	SW	325000
MacLennen	Mac	SW	375000

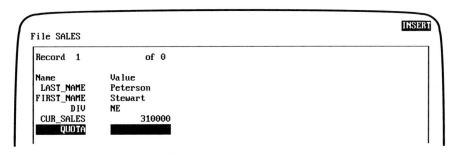

Fig. 18.15.
Entering a record using the @BASE entry form.

Maintaining the @BASE Database

Just as when you create an in-RAM database, once you create an @BASE database, you must keep the database accurate and up to date. At times, you may want to locate specific records so that you can edit the data or look up information. Having the data sorted in a meaningful order helps you organize and find information.

Sorting the Database

Symphony's in-RAM database manager provides up to three sort keys, although you can add additional sort levels. With the @BASE database manager, you can specify up to 256 sort keys: one for every possible database field. In these steps, however, you just sort by one field, LAST_NAME:

1. Press Esc to leave the entry form and return to the @BASE menu.

2. Select **D**ata **S**ort and accept **SALES** as the database file.

3. Because the cursor is already on the LAST_NAME field, press Enter and select **A**scending for the sort order.

4. Press Esc to indicate that you have selected all the sort keys for this operation.

5. Select **O**verwrite and **E**xecute to complete the sort.

Viewing the Sorted Database

Follow these steps to use the browse screen to view all the sorted records at the same time:

1. Select **D**ata **B**rowse.

2. Accept **SALES** as the database file.

3. Select **A**ll to see all the database fields. The screen looks like figure 18.16. Notice that the QUOTA field is still empty.

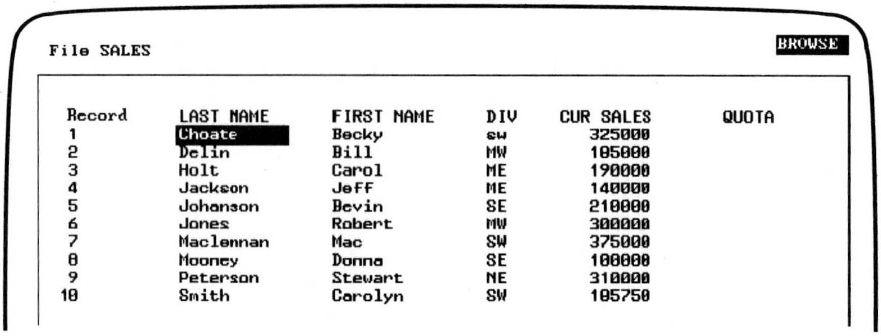

Fig. 18.16.

The browse screen after sorting the database.

```
File SALES                                                          BROWSE

   Record    LAST NAME    FIRST NAME    DIV    CUR SALES    QUOTA
   1         Choate       Becky         SW        325000
   2         Delin        Bill          MW        105000
   3         Holt         Carol         ME        190000
   4         Jackson      Jeff          ME        140000
   5         Johanson     Bevin         SE        210000
   6         Jones        Robert        MW        300000
   7         Maclennan    Mac           SW        375000
   8         Mooney       Donna         SE        100000
   9         Peterson     Stewart       NE        310000
   10        Smith        Carolyn       SW        105750
```

Creating a Macro To Compute a Field

Because you don't want to manually calculate the sales quota for each person in the database, and because the basic @BASE add-in doesn't offer computed fields, you have to use macros and some @DB functions to compute the value for the QUOTA field. Don't worry if the macros confuse you a little; Chapter 21 covers macros in greater detail.

Follow these steps to create a macro that computes the value of the QUOTA field:

1. Press Switch (Alt-F9) to switch to SHEET mode.

2. Enter **RESULT** in cell A1.

3. Enter **COUNTER** in cell A2.

4. Enter **VALUE** in cell A3.

5. Press Menu (F10) and select **R**ange **N**ame **L**abels **R**ight. Highlight cells A1 through A3 and press Enter to assign the range names in column A to the adjacent cells in column B.

6. Enter '**\M** in cell A5.

7. Press Menu (F10) and select **R**ange **N**ame **L**abels **D**own. Indicate A5 to assign the range name \M to cell A6. By assigning \M to the first cell of the macro, you can invoke the macro by pressing Alt-M.

8. Refer to figure 18.17 and type the rest of the macro as shown.

9. Give cell A11 the range name SET_QUOTA by placing the cursor on cell A10 and issuing **R**ange **N**ame **L**abels **D**own.

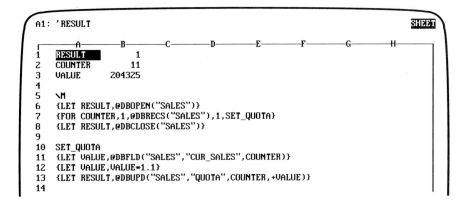

A1: 'RESULT   **SHEET**

```
       A         B        C        D        E        F        G        H
1    RESULT            1
2    COUNTER          11
3    VALUE        204325
4
5    \M
6    {LET RESULT,@DBOPEN("SALES")}
7    {FOR COUNTER,1,@DBRECS("SALES"),1,SET_QUOTA}
8    {LET RESULT,@DBCLOSE("SALES")}
9
10   SET_QUOTA
11   {LET VALUE,@DBFLD("SALES","CUR_SALES",COUNTER)}
12   {LET VALUE,VALUE*1.1}
13   {LET RESULT,@DBUPD("SALES","QUOTA",COUNTER,+VALUE)}
14
```

Fig. 18.17.
A macro to fill in the QUOTA field.

Understanding the Use of @DB Functions in the Macro

Several of the @DB functions in these macros return a value to indicate whether they are successful. The @DBOPEN, @DBUPD, and @DBCLOSE functions used in these macros all return 1 if they are successful and 0 if they are not. For this simple set of macros, the values returned by these functions are ignored to prevent the macros from becoming too complex. In Chapter 21 you learn the technique of "conditional branching" and use these values to detect and correct possible errors (like files that cannot be opened or updated).

Running the Macro

After you carefully check your screen entries to make sure that they match figure 18.17, you're ready to run the macro and have it calculate the sales quotas. Then you can switch back to the BASE window and check your results.

Follow these steps to run the macro:

1. Press Alt-M. The **Macro** indicator at the bottom of the screen appears to show that the macro has started. Because the database has only 10 records, the macro finishes quite quickly and the **Macro** indicator disappears.

2. When the **Macro** indicator disappears, press Switch (Alt-F9) to switch back to the BASE window.

   Note: If pressing Switch (Alt-F9) doesn't take you to the BASE window, press Type (Alt-F10), select BASE, and press Enter. You may encounter this problem if you changed the window type to DOC, GRAPH, FORM, or COMM after you switched from the BASE window to the SHEET window.

3. Select BASE **F**ile **O**pen. Select SALES and accept **SALES** as the alias.

4. Select BASE **D**ata **B**rowse.

5. Accept **SALES** as the database file.

6. Select **A**ll to see all the database fields. The screen looks like figure 18.18. Notice that the QUOTA field contains the computed value of 110% of CUR_SALES.

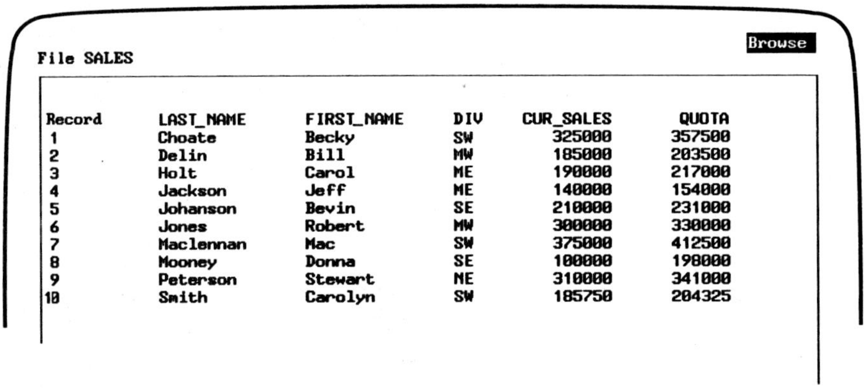

Fig. 18.18.

The browse screen after running the macro.

```
File SALES                                                          Browse

Record    LAST_NAME     FIRST_NAME    DIV    CUR_SALES    QUOTA
1         Choate        Becky         SW       325000     357500
2         Delin         Bill          MW       185000     203500
3         Holt          Carol         ME       198000     217000
4         Jackson       Jeff          ME       140000     154000
5         Johanson      Bevin         SE       210000     231000
6         Jones         Robert        MW       300000     330000
7         Maclennan     Mac           SW       375000     412500
8         Mooney        Donna         SE       100000     198000
9         Peterson      Stewart       ME       310000     341000
10        Smith         Carolyn       SW       185750     204325
```

Finding a Record

If you have a large number of records in a database, you need a faster way of going to a specific record than the down and up arrows in the browse screen or the PgDn and PgUp keys in the entry-form screen, even if the database is sorted. The **C**riteria command gives you that speed. You enter in a criterion record what you are seeking, and @BASE displays the matching record for you. You can then look up or update information in the record.

Because the SALES database is small, you really don't need the **C**riteria command to locate a record. But you still can use the command to get an idea of how it works on a larger database.

Enter the criteria to select Smith's record by following these steps:

1. Select BASE **C**riteria **P**rompt and accept **SALES** as the database file. @BASE presents the fields in the SALES database for your selection as shown in figure 18.19.

2. Because the LAST_NAME field is already highlighted, press Enter to select it as the field to which selection conditions will be applied. (If you want to apply criteria to another field, move the cursor to highlight the correct field before pressing Enter). The screen now looks like figure 18.20.

Name	Type	Length	Decimals
LAST_NAME	Char	15	
FIRST_NAME	Char	15	
DIV	Char	4	
CUR_SALES	Numeric	12	0
QUOTA	Numeric	12	0

Fig. 18.19.

The criteria-prompt screen displaying the fields for selection.

LAST_NAME

=	(Equal)
<>	(Not equal)
>	(Greater than)
>=	(Greater than or equal)
<	(Less than)
<=	(Less than or equal)

Fig. 18.20.

The criteria-build screen.

3. Select = to indicate that you will enter a value in the criterion string that LAST_NAME must equal. The prompt `Enter value:` appears.

4. Enter **Smith** as the value that LAST_NAME must equal. The screen now looks like figure 18.21.

5. Select **Q**uit from the list of options displayed on-screen to indicate that you are done entering criteria. The @BASE menu reappears. The AND and OR choices cause @BASE to redisplay the fields as in figure 18.19. You can then enter additional criteria to either narrow or broaden the record-selection criteria.

LAST_NAME="Smith"

Quit
And
Or

Fig. 18.21.

The list of criteria options.

Viewing the Database with Criteria Selected

When a criteria is in use, as it is now, you can only view records that match the criteria. If you want to view all the records again, you must use the BASE **C**riteria **C**ancel command.

To view Smith's record in the browse screen, follow these steps:

1. Select **D**ata **B**rowse and accept **S A L E S** as the database file.

2. Select **A**ll to accept all fields for viewing. The screen looks like figure 18.22. Because only one database record matches the LAST_NAME="smith" criteria, only one line is displayed in the browse screen.

Fig. 18.22.

The browse screen showing the located record.

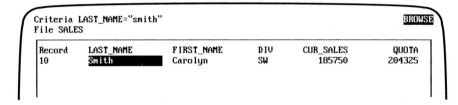

You may find the entry form easier to understand than the browse screen. Instead of displaying all the fields in one row, the entry form displays each field in a separate row. To switch from the browse screen to the entry form, follow these steps:

1. Press Esc to return to the @BASE menu.

2. Select **D**ata **F**orm and accept **S A L E S** as the database. Smith's form is displayed. Because the criteria LAST_NAME="smith" is active, you cannot use PgDn or PgUp to display other records in the database.

In the previous example, you knew exactly how *Smith* was spelled, so you had no trouble locating the record. Sometimes, though, you may not be sure of the spelling. In that case, you can use a wild card to help locate the record. Suppose that you want to look up information for a sales person whose name begins with *J*. Follow these steps to perform the search:

1. Select **C**riteria **E**dit. Notice that the search criteria LAST_NAME="smith" is still in effect. You can edit this criteria.

2. Move the cursor to the left and use the Backspace key to remove *smith*. Enter **J*** between the quotation marks. The asterisk is a wild card that tells Symphony to accept all characters in place of the *.

3. Select **D**ata **B**rowse and accept **S A L E S** as the database file.

4. Select **A**ll to accept all fields for viewing. The screen now shows the three records of the sales people whose last names start with the letter *J* (see fig. 18.23).

```
Criteria LAST_NAME="J*"                                          BROWSE
File SALES

     Record      LAST NAME      FIRST NAME    DIV    CUR SALES    QUOTA
     4           Jackson        Jeff          ME        140000    154000
     5           Johanson       Bevin         SE        210000    231000
     6           Jones          Robert        MW        300000    330000
```

Fig. 18.23.
The browse screen with criteria set to LAST_NAME="J".*

Deleting a Record

When you used the wild card to search for all records that start with *J*, you were looking for Jeff Jackson's record. He received a job offer from another company and is leaving the group. Follow these steps to delete his record from the database:

1. Press the ↑ or ↓ to highlight Jackson's record.

2. Press the Del key to mark this record for deletion. An asterisk appears to the left of the record, indicating that this record is marked for deletion.

3. Press Del again to unmark Jackson's record. Instead of deleting the record in the browse screen, you decide to use the entry-form screen. (The method for deleting a marked record is the same whether you mark the record in the browse screen or the entry-form screen.)

Follow these steps to switch back to the entry-form screen and delete Jackson's record there:

1. Press Esc to return to the @BASE menu.

2. Select **D**ata **F**orm and accept **SALES** as the database. Press PgUp or PgDn to display Jackson's record.

3. Press Del to mark this record for deletion. The entry form displays the message ***** DELETED ***** to show you that a record is marked for deletion (see fig. 18.24).

Once you delete a record, it is gone forever. With the @BASE database manager, however, you can mark and unmark records for deletion. You actually delete the records in a separate step, so the process is safer than with Symphony's in-RAM database.

Marking Jackson's record for deletion is just the first step; next you actually delete the record. Follow these steps to "pack" the database file:

1. Press Esc to return to the @BASE menu. Select **D**ata **D**elete **P**ack and accept **SALES** as the database file.

2. @BASE gives you one more chance to back out. Because you're certain you want to delete Jackson's record, select **E**xecute and press Enter.

Fig. 18.24.

The entry-form screen with Jackson's record marked for deletion.

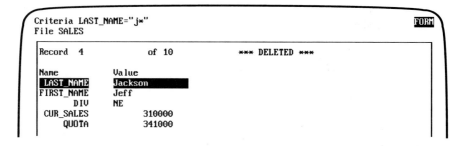

```
Criteria LAST_NAME="j*"                                    FORM
File SALES

Record   4              of 10           *** DELETED ***

Name            Value
 LAST_NAME      Jackson
FIRST_NAME      Jeff
      DIV       NE
 CUR_SALES          310000
     QUOTA          341000
```

3. Return to the browse screen and verify that Jackson's record is gone.

Editing a Record

Editing a record in the browse screen is similar to editing a cell in the SHEET window. You can replace what is in the field by typing over the data, or you can use the Edit (F2) key to modify the contents.

Follow these steps to correct Johnson's last name to *Johanson*.

1. If necessary, press the up or down arrow to display Johnson's record.
2. With the cursor in the LAST_NAME field, press Edit (F2).
3. Press the left-arrow key until the cursor is on the first *n* in *Johnson*.
4. Type **a**. The record should look like figure 18.25.
5. Press Enter.

Fig. 18.25.

Editing Johnson's name to change it to Johanson.

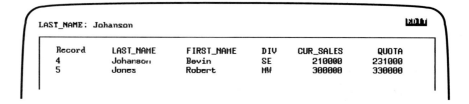

```
LAST_NAME: Johanson                                        EDIT

 Record    LAST_NAME    FIRST_NAME    DIV    CUR_SALES    QUOTA
 4         Johanson     Bevin         SE        210000    231000
 5         Jones        Robert        MW        300000    330000
```

Creating Reports with @BASE

The @BASE add-in database manager does not include a direct means of producing printed reports. Instead, you must use either the SHEET or DOC window, depending on the application. Most typical database reports, for example, use the SHEET window. A form letter, on the other hand, is easier to produce in the DOC window.

Transferring the @BASE File to the SHEET Window

A report similar to the default database report produced using Symphony's FORM window is easy with @BASE and a SHEET window. Of course, you do have to be aware that an @BASE database can be too large to fit in a Symphony worksheet. If the database is too large, use record-selection criteria to narrow the report.

@BASE uses any active criteria when it transfers data to a SHEET window. Because you want to transfer the entire database into the SHEET window for printing, follow these steps to cancel all criteria before doing the transfer:

1. Return to the @BASE menu. If you're still in the browse screen press Esc. If you're at the BASE main window with no menu displayed, press Menu (F10).
2. Select **C**riteria **C**ancel and accept **SALES** as the database file.

Follow these steps to transfer the data to the SHEET window:

1. Select **D**ata **T**ransfer **I**mport and accept **SALES** as the database file.
2. Select **A**ll because you want to transfer all database fields to the SHEET window. The screen shifts temporarily to the SHEET window and displays the prompt **Enter start of output range:**. Symphony suggests cell A1 as the start of the output range (or the current cursor position if the worksheet isn't blank).
3. Press Enter to accept A1 as the start of the output range. The screen shifts back to the BASE window with the menu showing. @BASE places copies of the database field names in the top row of the output range and the places records directly below.

Viewing and Printing the Transferred Data

Follow these steps to switch to the SHEET window before you can specify the print range and print the report:

1. Press Esc to return to the BASE main window (with no menu showing). Remember that you must return to the BASE main window before you can switch to another window or use Symphony's Services (F9) key.

2. Press Switch (Alt-F9) to switch to the SHEET window. The screen should look similar to figure 18.26.

Fig. 18.26.

The result of Data Transfer Import.

```
A1: "Recno                                                          SHEET
┌──────A───────────B────────────────C──────────D─────────E─────────F──
1    Recno LAST_NAME      FIRST_NAME      DIV       CUR_SALES      QUOTA
2        1 Choate         Becky           SW          325000     357500
3        2 Delin          Bill            MW          185000     203500
4        3 Holt           Carol           NE          198000     217800
5        4 Johanson       Bevin           SE          210000     231000
6        5 Jones          Robert          MW          300000     330000
7        6 MacLennen      Mac             SW          375000     412500
8        7 Mooney         Donna           SE          180000     198000
9        8 Peterson       Stewart         NE          310000     341000
10       9 Smith          Carolyn         SW          185750     204325
11
```

Unlike the in-RAM database manager's default report, the @BASE **D**ata **T**ransfer **I**mport command produces a report that takes into account the contents of each field. Notice that for the three numeric fields, Recno, CUR_SALES, and QUOTA, the field labels in row 1 are right-aligned. The field labels above the character fields are left-aligned.

This report would look better if the numbers had commas. Follow these steps to format the numbers in the CUR_SALES and QUOTA columns to the **P**unctuated format:

1. Move the cursor to cell E2.

2. Select SHEET **F**ormat **P**unctuated.

3. Type **0** for the number of decimal places and press Enter.

4. Highlight the range E2..F10 and press Enter. The screen should look like figure 18.27.

The report is now ready to print. If you don't want to include the Recno column in the print range, exclude column A when you specify the print range. Follow these steps to print the report:

1. Select SERVICES **P**rint **S**ettings **S**ource **R**ange and highlight B1..F10 (this range excludes the Recno column from the report). Press Enter.

2. Select **Q**uit; then select **G**o to begin printing. The report should look like figure 18.28.

3. Select **P**age to feed the paper out of the printer. (For some printers, you may have to issue **P**age several times before you can tear off the sheet.)

```
A1: "Recno                                                            SHEET
┌───────A────────B───────────────C──────────D─────────E──────────F──────
1      Recno LAST_NAME     FIRST_NAME      DIV      CUR_SALES       QUOTA
2       1 Choate          Becky           SW         325,000     357,500
3       2 Delin           Bill            MW         185,000     203,500
4       3 Holt            Carol           NE         198,000     217,800
5       4 Johanson        Bevin           SE         210,000     231,000
6       5 Jones           Robert          MW         300,000     330,000
7       6 MacLennen       Mac             SW         375,000     412,500
8       7 Mooney          Donna           SE         180,000     198,000
9       8 Peterson        Stewart         NE         310,000     341,000
10      9 Smith           Carolyn         SW         185,750     204,325
11
```

Fig. 18.27.
Formatting the range E2..F10 as **P***unctuated with zero decimal places.*

```
LAST_NAME       FIRST_NAME      DIV      CUR_SALES       QUOTA
Choate          Becky           SW         325,000     357,500
Delin           Bill            MW         185,000     203,500
Holt            Carol           NE         198,000     217,800
Johanson        Bevin           SE         210,000     231,000
Jones           Robert          MW         300,000     330,000
MacLennen       Mac             SW         375,000     412,500
Mooney          Donna           SE         180,000     198,000
Peterson        Stewart         NE         310,000     341,000
Smith           Carolyn         SW         185,750     204,325
```

Fig. 18.28.
The printed report.

Producing @BASE Statistical Reports

The @BASE database manager has the capacity to generate a crosstabular report showing either the count of database entries that have the same value for a field (such as the number of sales people in each division) or the sum of entries that contain the same entry in another field (such as the sum of CUR_SALES by division). These reports are difficult to produce using the in-RAM database manager; using @BASE they're quite straightforward.

As a business owner, you're concerned about the results your business is producing. You want to be sure that the number of sales people in each division is matched to the sales figures. You decide to use @BASE crosstab reports to compare each division to see where you need to concentrate your pep talks.

Although the crosstab report is generated in the SHEET window, you must switch back to the BASE window to issue the commands to produce the report. Begin by erasing the existing report which you no longer need:

1. Press the Home key to move the cursor to cell A1.
2. Select SHEET **E**rase.
3. Press End Home to highlight the entire report.
4. Press Enter to erase the report.

Generating the Crosstabular Report

Follow these steps to generate the crosstab statistical report:

1. Press Switch (Alt-F9) to switch back to the BASE window.

2. Select **F**ile **U**se **S**et and accept **SALES** as the database file. Once you set a database file, you don't have to specify that file for future **D**ata commands during the current session.

3. Select **D**ata **C**rosstab. The database field names display for your selection.

4. Move the cursor to DIV and press Enter. @BASE displays the message **1 selected** to the right of the DIV field (see fig. 18.29).

NAMES

Name	Type	Length	Decimals	
LAST_NAME	Char	15		
FIRST_NAME	Char	15		
DIV	Char	4		1 Selected
CUR_SALES	Numeric	12	0	
QUOTA	Numeric	12	0	

Fig. 18.29.

Selecting the DIV field for the crosstab report.

5. Press Esc to indicate that you are done selecting fields.

6. Select **G**enerate; the screen shifts to SHEET mode and shows the prompt **Enter key values label row: A1**. Press Enter to accept cell A1 as the start of the first crosstab table.

7. Select **C**ount because you want a report showing the count of the number of records in each division. @BASE briefly displays the message **Pass 1 of 1** and returns to the menu.

Generating the Second Crosstabular Report

You have generated the first report showing the count of sales people in each division. Now you want to expand the report to include the sum of the CUR_SALES field for each division so that you can determine how well each division stacks up on a per-person basis. Follow these steps to generate such a report:

1. Select **D**ata **C**rosstab. The field names appear for your selection.

2. You want the second table to be broken down by the same classifications, so move the cursor to DIV and press Enter.

3. Press Esc to indicate that the fields have been selected.

4. Select **G**enerate; the screen shifts to SHEET mode and displays the prompt `Enter key values label row: A1`.

5. You don't want the second crosstab table to overwrite the first one, so move the cursor to cell C1 and press Enter to start the table at cell C1.

6. Select **S**um because you want the table to show the sum of the CUR_SALES field values for each division. Because you have to instruct @BASE which field or fields you want to sum, the screen displays the field names.

7. Move the cursor to CUR_SALES and press Enter.

8. Press Esc to generate the second crosstab table.

Viewing and Modifying the Crosstabular Tables

To view the crosstab tables, you must first switch back to the SHEET window. Then you can add formulas to show how the sales people in each division are doing.

1. Press Esc to return to the BASE main window.

2. Press Switch (Alt-F9) to return to the SHEET window. The screen should look like figure 18.30.

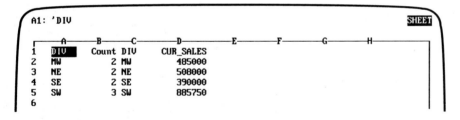

Fig. 18.30.
The crosstab reports.

You want to see the current sales per sales person in each division. Follow these steps to add the appropriate formulas:

1. Move the cursor to cell E2 and enter the formula **+D2/B2**.

2. Select SHEET **F**ormat **P**unctuated.

3. Enter **0** for zero decimal places.

4. Press Enter to accept **E2** as the range to format.

5. Select SHEET **C**opy and press Enter to accept **E2** as the FROM range.

6. Highlight E3..E5 as the TO range and press Enter. The screen should look like figure 18.31.

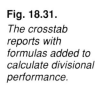

Fig. 18.31.

The crosstab reports with formulas added to calculate divisional performance.

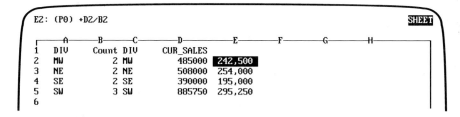

Clearly, the SE division sales people are having problems. The final results show that the three sales people in the SW division are doing about 50% more business each than those in the SE division. The @BASE data crosstab feature made it easy to compare the results for each division.

Using the @BASE Option Pac

The Option Pac is an optional extension for @BASE that provides several useful features. If you haven't purchased the Option Pac, you cannot do the following exercises, but follow along anyway. This section gives you an idea of what the Option Pac offers; you then can decide if it includes features you need.

Attaching the Option Pac

The @BASE Option Pac consists of two new Symphony add-ins. One, BASEOPTF.APP, replaces BASEFUNC.APP and provides the additional @functions. The other, BASEOPT.APP, adds the balance of the Option Pac features to the BASE menu. You must attach the add-ins in the proper order.

To attach @BASE and the Option Pac, follow these steps:

1. Select SERVICES **A**pplication **A**ttach.
2. Highlight BASEOPTF.APP and press Enter.
3. Select **A**ttach, highlight BASE.APP, and press Enter.
4. Select **A**ttach, highlight BASEOPT.APP, and press Enter.
5. Select **A**ttach, highlight BASEUTL.APP, and press Enter.
6. Select **Q**uit to return to the worksheet.

You also can attach @BASE and the Option Pac automatically every time you load Symphony using the SERVICES **C**onfiguration **O**ther **A**pplication **S**et command. This method is not recommended, however, because of the large amount of memory used by these add-ins. The exact amount of memory used is difficult to determine because system configurations (such as the quantity of expanded memory) vary greatly. An additional point to consider is that you cannot detach Symphony add-ins like BASEFUNC.APP and BASEOPTF.APP that add new @functions, so they continue to use memory even when you no longer use them. You have to exit from Symphony and restart the program to regain the memory used by these add-ins.

Indexing the Database

Suppose that you want to access the SALES database sorted either by last name or current sales. One way to do this is to specify LAST_NAME as one index and CUR_SALES as the other. Depending on your needs, you can use the index that shows the database in the necessary order.

To index the database, follow these steps:

1. Press Switch (Alt-F9) to switch back to the BASE window.

2. Press Menu (F10) to access the @BASE menu (fig. 18.32 shows the new menu with the **O**ptions selection added).

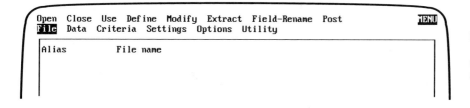

Fig. 18.32.
The @BASE menu with the Option Pac added.

3. Select **F**ile **O**pen and highlight SALES.DBF.

4. Press Enter and accept **SALES** as the database alias.

5. Select **E**xclusive as the method of access.

6. Select **F**ile **U**se **S**et and accept **SALES** to set SALES as the database file to use.

7. Select **O**ptions **I**ndex **F**ile **P**rompt.

8. Enter **LASTNAME** as the index file name and accept **LASTNAME** as the alias. The screen displays the field names from the SALES database.

   Note: When @BASE asks for the index file name, you should specify a name that reminds you of the field name being indexed. The index file name does not have to be the same as the database file name.

9. Because the cursor is already on LAST_NAME, press Enter to select LAST_NAME as the indexed field.

10. Press Esc and select **E**xecute to generate the index file.

11. Select **D**ata **B**rowse **A**ll to view the database. The screen should look like figure 18.33.

Fig. 18.33.

The browse screen using the index LASTNAME.

```
┌─────────────────────────────────────────────────────────────────BROWSE┐
│ File SALES                      Index LASTNAME                          │
│ ┌─────────────────────────────────────────────────────────────────────┐│
│ │Record    LAST_NAME      FIRST_NAME      DIV      CUR_SALES      QUOTA ││
│ │1         Choate         Becky           SW          325000     357500 ││
│ │2         Delin          Bill            MW          185000     203500 ││
│ │3         Holt           Carol           NE          198000     217800 ││
│ │4         Johanson       Bevin           SE          210000     231000 ││
```

When you use an indexed database, the browse screen shows the currently active index at the top of the screen. In figure 18.33, you can see that LASTNAME is the current index.

Adding a Second Index to the Database

To access the database in order of current sales results, add a second index as described in the following steps:

1. Press Esc to return to the menu.

2. Select **O**ptions **I**ndex **F**ile **P**rompt and enter **CURSALES** for the index file name.

3. Accept **CURSALES** as the index alias. The field-selection screen appears.

4. Move the cursor to CUR_SALES and press Enter.

5. Press Esc and select **E**xecute to generate the CURSALES index file.

Selecting an Index

If you have more than one index file, you must select which index file to use to display the records. Once you establish the index files, selecting an index file is much faster than sorting a large database. You don't see much difference with the small number of records in the SALES database, but you certainly do on a large database.

To select the CURSALES index file, follow these steps:

1. Select **O**ptions **I**ndex **F**ile **S**elect. The screen displays two choices: LASTNAME and CURSALES.

2. Select CURSALES.

3. View the database records using **D**ata **B**rowse **A**ll. The screen should look like figure 18.34.

Using index files to display the database records affects only the order in which the records are accessed. The Recno field in figure 18.34 shows that the record numbers haven't changed, only their displayed order.

```
                                                           BROWSE
  File SALES                 Index CURSALES

  Record    LAST_NAME      FIRST_NAME    DIV      CUR_SALES        QUOTA
  7         Mooney         Donna         SE          180000       198000
  2         Delin          Bill          MW          185000       203500
  9         Smith          Carolyn       SW          185750       204325
  3         Holt           Carol         NE          198000       217800
  4         Johanson       Bevin         SE          210000       231000
  5         Jones          Robert        MW          300000       330000
  8         Peterson       Stewart       NE          310000       341000
  1         Choate         Becky         SW          325000       357500
  6         MacLennen      Mac           SW          375000       412500
```

Fig. 18.34.

The browse screen using the index CURSALES.

Joining Files To Create Relational Databases

As your business grows, you will want more complete information from the database. You may, for example, want to display the address of each sales person's divisional office. One way to do this is to add extra fields to the SALES database and type the address information for each record. With a small database, the task may not be too time consuming; when you grow to several hundred sales persons, however, you will want a better way.

Instead of adding fields to the SALES database, create a new database called DIVN and join the two in a relational manner.

Creating the Second Database

Follow these steps to define the new database:

    1. Press Esc to return to the @BASE menu.

    2. Select **F**ile **D**efine.

    3. Enter **DIVN** as the database name.

    4. Enter the field names, types, and lengths as shown in figure 18.35.

    5. Press Esc.

    6. Select **S**ave and accept **DIVN** as the database alias.

Entering Records in the Second Database

Because the SALES database is currently set as the database to use, you must first cancel that setting before you can enter data into the DIVN database. Select **F**ile **U**se **C**ancel to cancel SALES as the current database.

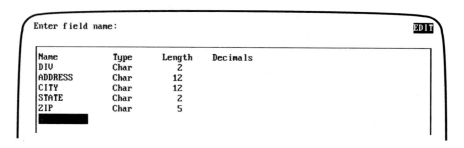

Fig. 18.35.
The DIVN database field definitions.

Enter records into the DIVN database using the entry form @BASE generated with the database definition you provided. Follow these steps to enter records into the DIVN database:

1. Select **Data Form** and accept **DIVN** as the database.
2. Enter **NE** in the DIV field.
3. Enter **123 Main** in the ADDRESS field.
4. Enter **Boston** in the CITY field.
5. Enter **MA** in the STATE field.
6. Type **01234** in the ZIP field.
7. Press Ins to insert the record.

Refer to figure 18.36 and enter the remaining records. Be sure to press Ins after each record.

Fig. 18.36.
The DIVN database.

Joining the Databases

Before you can join the databases, you must create an index of the divisions in the DIVN file. Follow these steps to create an index:

1. Select **Options Index File Prompt** and enter **DIVN** for the index file name.
2. Accept **DIVN** as the index alias. The field-selection screen appears.
3. Select DIV and press Enter.
4. Press Esc and select **Execute** to generate the index file.

Once the DIVN database file has been indexed, you can join (or *link*) the two files.

1. Select **O**ptions **L**ink.

2. Specify **SALES** as the primary file (the *primary file* is the file containing information unique to each record).

3. Specify **DIVN** as the lookup file (the *lookup file* contains the data shared by several records). The screen shows the field names in the lookup file.

4. Select ADDRESS, CITY, STATE, and ZIP as joined fields: point to each field in turn and press Enter. The screen should look like figure 18.37.

   Note: DIV is not selected as a joined field because it is the indexed field common to both database files. The value of DIV in SALES.DBF is used to look up the values of the joined fields in DIVN.DBF.

5. Press Esc and select **E**xecute to complete the joining.

NAMES

Name	Type	Length	Decimals	
DIV	Char	2		
ADDRESS	Char	12		1 Selected
CITY	Char	12		2 Selected
STATE	Char	2		3 Selected
ZIP	Char	5		4 Selected

Fig. 18.37.
Selecting the joined fields.

Viewing the Joined Databases

Once you join the two database files, you can view the results. Follow these instructions to view the joined databases:

1. Select **D**ata **B**rowse.

2. Select the SALES database.

3. Choose **S**elected to look at only certain fields. The fields in the SALES database and the joined fields are displayed.

4. Select LAST_NAME, DIV, ADDRESS, CITY, STATE, and ZIP as the fields to view: point to each field in turn and press Enter.

5. Press Esc to complete the selections. The screen should look like figure 18.38. Notice that the names of the joined fields (ADDRESS, CITY, STATE, and ZIP) appear in lowercase letters. The Option Pac displays joined and computed fields (which it calls *virtual* fields) in lowercase letters. You cannot edit, index, or sort based on these fields.

Fig. 18.38.

The browse screen showing the joined fields.

```
                                                                    BROWSE
  File SALES                        Index CURSALES

  Record     LAST_NAME      DIV     address      city       state  zip
  7          Mooney         SE      45 Swamp Rd  Tampa      FL     12345
  2          Delin          MW      17935 Texas  Plymouth   MN     55440
  9          Smith          SW      3500 Bacon   Sparks     NV     89502
  3          Holt           NE      123 Main     Boston     MA     01234
  4          Johanson       SE      45 Swamp Rd  Tampa      FL     12345
  5          Jones          MW      17935 Texas  Plymouth   MN     55440
  8          Peterson       NE      123 Main     Boston     MA     01234
  1          Choate         SW      3500 Bacon   Sparks     NV     89502
  6          MacLennen      SW      3500 Bacon   Sparks     NV     89502
```

Using Computed Fields

The Option Pac provides a much easier method for computing a field value than the basic @BASE database manager does. In an example earlier in this chapter, you used a macro to calculate the value for the QUOTA field. In this section, you create a computed field that calculates the increase between current sales and the quota.

Follow these steps to create a computed field:

1. Press Esc to return to the @BASE menu.

2. Select **O**ptions **C**omputed_field **C**reate.

3. Select SALES as the database file. @BASE displays the prompt `Enter field name:`.

4. Enter **INCREASE** as the name of the computed field.

5. Select **N**umeric for the field type, **8** for the field length, and **0** decimal places. @BASE displays the prompt `Enter field definition:`.

6. Type the formula **+QUOTA−CUR_SALES** and press Enter.

You now can view the records with the new computed field using either the browse screen or the entry form. To use the entry form, follow these instructions:

1. Select **D**ata **F**orm.

2. Select SALES as the database. The screen should look like figure 18.39. Remember that computed, or virtual, field names appear in lowercase letters, regardless of how you type them.

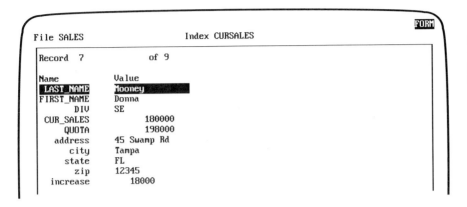

Fig. 18.39.
The entry-form screen showing computed fields.

Using View Files

You have done considerable work creating joined and computed fields. If you close the database files or leave @BASE, these "virtual" fields disappear. "Virtual" fields don't really exist in the database; they exist only as long as the database is open.

To prevent the loss of the joined and computed fields, use the **View S**ave command. When you use **View S**ave, you can open the view file later, and the virtual fields are redefined automatically. Follow these steps to save a view file:

1. Press Esc to return to the @BASE menu.
2. Select **O**ptions **V**iew **S**ave.
3. Choose the SALES database file.
4. Type **SALES** as the view file name and press Enter.

Using the Option Pac @Functions in an Example

You created two index files for the SALES database: LASTNAME and CURSALES. This section uses a simple example that combines @DB and @NDX functions to open a database and an index file.

Follow these instructions to enter formulas in the SHEET window:

1. Press Esc to return the BASE main window.
2. Press Switch (Alt-F9) to switch to the SHEET window.
3. Move the cursor to cell A1; type **@DBOPEN("SALES")** and press Enter.
4. Move to cell A2; type **@NDXOPEN("SALES","LASTNAME")** and press Enter.

5. Move to cell A3; type **@DBFLD("SALES","LAST_NAME",**
   @NDXFIRST("SALES","J",@TRUE)) and press Enter.

6. Move to cell A4; type **@DBCLOSE("SALES")** and press Enter.

Once you enter the formulas, the screen should look like figure 18.40. If you made any errors entering the formulas and had to edit any of them, you may have to press Calc (F8) a few times.

Fig. 18.40.

An example of the use of Option Pac @functions.

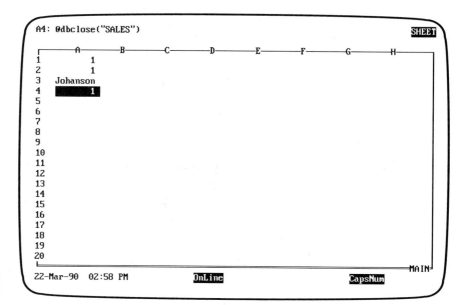

Chapter Summary

In this hands-on practice session, you reviewed data-management basics in Symphony's FORM window and the BASE window. You generated a database, entered data, sorted the data, located records according to different search criteria, and printed and modified simple reports in both environments. You also sampled the @BASE Option Pac and saw the added functions it provides.

Chapter 19 introduces you to Symphony's COMM environment for data communications.

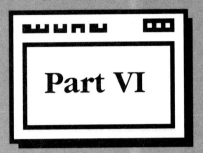

Part VI

Symphony Communications Module

*Using the Symphony
Communications Module*

*Learning Communications:
Hands-On Practice*

19

Using the Symphony Communications Module

With Symphony's COMM window, you can use your personal computer for two-way data communications. For example, you can receive database information from a corporate mainframe or a minicomputer; hook up to a time-sharing service to get the latest information on news, stocks, weather, and other current topics; dial into a computer bulletin board; or link up with a friend's microcomputer to exchange Symphony models, information, or gossip.

Like the other Symphony functions, the communications environment is surprisingly strong and rivals the power of many stand-alone packages. In addition to standard file-transfer capability, Symphony offers custom terminal emulation, data capture and translation, and a powerful script language. The program has some minor weaknesses, however, such as a limited set of file-transfer protocols (the rules by which computers exchange information). Symphony also does not support synchronous communications; see "Understanding Asynchronous and Synchronous Transmissions" later in this chapter. In general, though, you should be pleasantly surprised at the COMM window's power.

Symphony enables you to connect with many different kinds of computers; just follow the simple rules outlined in the next section: "Communicating Successfully—Some Guidelines." The chapter then explains how to connect with an electronic bulletin board system so that you can copy public-domain software programs. That section is followed by an explanation of how to communicate with another person's microcomputer if that person also has Symphony. You may even be able to communicate with someone else's PC if that person uses another communications program. In short, this chapter provides enough background to enable you to make good use of Symphony's communications environment.

Communicating Successfully— Some Guidelines

Symphony's COMM window is a powerful feature, but you can become discouraged with it easily if you run into early problems. The following guidelines provide some background about Symphony's COMM window and let you know what you can expect from the program.

Using Modems and Acoustic Couplers

Reminder:

Modems enable you to communicate with other computers across telephone lines.

To communicate successfully with Symphony, you must have a modem or an acoustic coupler. (You also can connect two microcomputers with a serial cable and a "null modem," or you can hard-wire your computer to a mainframe or minicomputer, but these tasks are beyond the scope of this book.) A *modem* (*mo*dulator-*dem*odulator) is a device that converts digital signals in your computer into analog tones that can travel over telephone lines. Modems can be external devices connecting the serial (RS-232) interface on your computer to a telephone cable, or they can be internal devices on a board directly connected to your computer and to a telephone line.

An *acoustic coupler* is another type of modem, and requires that you place a standard telephone receiver in the rubber cradles of the coupler. Otherwise, acoustic couplers are hooked up like any other external modem. Because the most frequent problems with any kind of modem are poor cable connections, make sure that the connections between the computer and the telephone line are sound. You seldom see acoustic couplers these days; most modems today are the direct-connect type. Direct-connect modems offer many advantages such as auto-dialing, higher speed, and better transmission quality. Figure 19.1 shows the three kinds of modems discussed.

Fig. 19.1.
Types of modems.

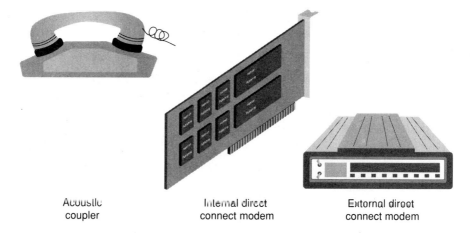

Acoustic coupler

Internal direct connect modem

External direct connect modem

Understanding Asynchronous and Synchronous Transmissions

Symphony supports *asynchronous communications transmission.* This term means that a clock in the computer times the sampling of incoming data and the recording of the number of bits in each sample. The clock "ticks" according to the transmission speed you specify (the *baud rate* or *bits per second*). Because the asynchronous-transmission technique leaves most of the timing work up to the computer, you can use relatively inexpensive modems easily.

Most mainframe computers, however, use *synchronous communications transmission.* With this kind of transmission, the modem provides a clock signal to detect the bits being received. The host computer also provides a master-clock signal to its attached modem. For purposes of timing, and for a variety of other reasons too complex to go into here, this type of transmission requires more complex and expensive modems.

The major advantage of synchronous communications transmission is that you can transmit data faster. In the past, low to medium speeds (0 to about 1200 baud, or bits per second) were associated with asynchronous transmission; higher speeds (anything above 1200 baud) were achieved with synchronous transmission. Symphony can support asynchronous transmissions up to 9600 baud, although 2400 baud is about the fastest you normally use on dial-up services. CompuServe is an example of a *dial-up* or *time-sharing service.* Because modems for speeds greater than 2400 baud are often expensive and frequently require special telephone lines, the higher baud rates are usually used only for direct connection to another computer.

> **Reminder:**
> *Symphony supports asynchronous communications transmissions up to 9600 baud.*

Perhaps in the future, Symphony will support synchronous communications transmission. For now, however, any computer with which you use Symphony to communicate must follow the asynchronous-transmission method. Most systems designed to communicate with personal computers follow the asynchronous convention, so you should not have much trouble. However, you probably will not be able to communicate with a sophisticated mainframe not normally used to communicate with microcomputers.

Understanding Protocol Methods

Symphony supports three different protocols for file transfer: XMODEM, CompuServe B, and BLAST. *Protocol* is another name for the rules established to exchange information between computers. A communications protocol is required to ensure that computers send and receive data accurately. You indicate the protocol method that Symphony will use when you install Symphony, selecting from XMODEM/B and BLAST. The INSTALL program offers XMODEM and CompuServe B as one choice, even though they are two different protocols.

> **Reminder:**
> *Protocols are standard procedures in which computers exchange information.*

XMODEM protocol, developed by Ward Christensen, has become a standard in the microcomputer industry. When you use Symphony's file-transfer capability, both computers must use XMODEM protocol. Nearly all PC-communications programs offer XMODEM as one of their file-transfer options. As a result, you will find that XMODEM is almost always one of the available choices offered in a menu for any dial-up service.

B protocol is a special protocol you can use with the CompuServe Information Service. Although CompuServe also supports XMODEM, the advantage to using B protocol is that file transfers are done completely through CompuServe. With XMODEM, you must tell both CompuServe and Symphony that you want to transfer a file. When you use B protocol, the name of the file to be sent and received is sent automatically; when you use XMODEM, you must manually provide to both systems the name of the file. Another advantage to B protocol is slightly faster file transmission due to larger blocks of data being transmitted by the programs.

Symphony also supports BLAST protocol. If you want to communicate with a mainframe that uses this protocol, select BLAST. You cannot use BLAST to send files between two microcomputers.

Setting Protocol Parameters

Once the specifics about types of modems, transmissions, and protocols are clear to you, the next step for successful communications with Symphony is to make sure that you correctly set all the parameters for protocol. These parameters include baud rate, byte length, number of stop bits to be transmitted, and parity. Table 19.1 describes each parameter.

Table 19.1
Protocol Parameters

Parameter	Description
Baud rate	Speed (bits per second) at which data is transmitted. Can vary between 0 and 9600, but most frequent settings are 300, 1200, and 2400.
Word length	The number of bits (binary digits) to be transmitted in a byte. Can be set to either 7 or 8 bits.
Stop bits	The number of bits following each data word. Asynchronous transmission usually requires the addition of stop bits. Choices are 1 or 2.
Parity	During parity checking, the individual *on* bits are added, the total is an odd or even number. Choices are odd, even, or none.

Normally, you don't have to worry about choosing the protocol parameters. Parameters are usually specified by the computer with which you are trying to communicate. Always match the two computers' settings for baud rate, byte length, stop bits, and parity.

Reminder:
Make sure that your computer and the computer with which you want to communicate are using the same parameters.

> ### Tip
> Although Symphony, like most good communications programs, gives you a wide variety of communications settings, only two groups of parameters are commonly in use today. After selecting the proper baud rate (which is almost always 1200 or 2400), you can set word length to 7, parity to even, and stop bits to 1; or word length to 8, parity to none, and stop bits to 1. These two groups of parameters settings are often expressed as *7E1* and *8N1*. If you have a problem connecting to another computer, first try 2400 baud and parameters 8N1; then try 2400, 7E1; then try 1200, 8N1; finally try 1200, 7E1. In nearly every case, one of these settings works properly.

Selecting the Proper Driver

The final step for successful communications is making sure that you select the proper driver set. The options presented during installation are Hayes (and compatibles) and Popcom (and compatibles). If you don't have a Hayes or Popcom modem, check your modem's documentation to see whether it is compatible with either of these brands. If so, you can make the appropriate selection. If you aren't sure with which type of driver set your modem is compatible, select Hayes because most modems sold are "Hayes compatible." (This term just means that the modem can understand the same commands as a Hayes modem. "Hayes compatible" and other modems can usually "talk" to each other.)

Connecting to a Bulletin Board System

One common use for a computer with a modem is to connect with an electronic bulletin board system (BBS). Electronic bulletin boards generally offer public-domain software you can download (copy) to your computer. *Public-domain software* are programs (word processors, games, utilities, and so on) available to whoever wants them, free of charge. Sometimes you are requested to send the author a donation if you like the program, but payment is purely voluntary.

Most BBSs offer an electronic mail system through which you can send and receive messages from other BBS users, such as *The World of Lotus* or *PCMagnet* on CompuServe. If you have a computer-related problem, you can leave a "help!" message in the mail system; if you're lucky, a fellow computer guru will respond with a solution. This resource can be invaluable when you are stumped with a computer dilemma. Many BBS users are quite experienced with computers and can be knowledgeable resources for you.

So how do you discover BBSs in your area? Your best bet is to contact a local computer users' group. Most of these groups have a bulletin board for their members or can steer you towards other BBSs. So your next question is, "How do I find out about local computer users' groups?" Magazines such as *Lotus* and *PC World* list users' groups on a regular basis. Your local newspaper may list users' group meetings in the community news section. Many computer dealers have information on local groups as well.

Before you connect with a BBS, you must first find out what protocol parameters it uses. The protocol your computer uses must match the BBS's protocol. Most BBS listings show the necessary parameters in a form like 2400-8N1 (meaning 2400 baud, 8-bit word length, no parity, and 1 stop bit). If you can't find a listing of the parameters, try the procedure given in the tip following table 19.1.

Most BBSs use the following parameters:

300, 1200, or 2400 baud

8-bit byte length

1 stop bit

No parity

Changing the Default Settings

Now that you are familiar with the standards required for a BBS, you are ready to select the first set of COMM window settings. Figure 19.2 shows the settings that appear when you select a COMM window and choose **S**ettings from the main COMM menu. Lotus provides these default settings with the program.

Note: Unless you specified to the INSTALL program that you're going to use communications and have a modem, you cannot make any selections from the COMM settings sheet.

Once you modify the settings sheet, you can store the settings in a communications configuration file (CCF) that you can retrieve whenever you want to use those settings. If you are using one of the popular information services (such as CompuServe), you can retrieve the appropriate communications configuration file included with Symphony. The CCF files packaged with Symphony are ADP, COMPUSRV, DOWJONES, MCI, and SOURCE. These files are located on the Help and Tutorial disk (5.25-inch floppy disks) or the Program, Help and Tutorial disk (3.5-inch floppy disks). You can use the files as they are given to you, or you can modify them as needed.

```
Speed and type of transmission                                        MENU
Interface  Phone  Terminal  Send  Break  Handshaking  Capture  Login  Name  Quit
┌───────────────────────────────────────────────────────────────────┐
│  Interface              Terminal              Send                  │
│    Baud:      110         Screen:   Window      EOL:       \m       │
│    Parity:    None        Echo:     No          Delay:     0        │
│    Length:    7           Linefeed: No          Response:  \j       │
│    Stop bits: 1           Backspace: Backspace  Format:    No       │
│    Comm Port: COM1        Wrap:     Yes         Break:     60       │
│  Phone                    Delay:    0         Handshaking           │
│    Type:      Pulse       Translation:          Inbound:   Yes      │
│    Dial:      60            (none)              Outbound:  Yes      │
│    Answer:    15                              Capture:              │
│    Number:                                      Range:     No       │
│                                                 Printer:   No       │
│                                   ════Communications Settings: ═    │
└───────────────────────────────────────────────────────────────────┘
```

Fig. 19.2.
The COMM settings sheet.

Note: None of the CCF files supplied with Symphony contain a telephone number to call to access the service. You must obtain the correct local access number as well as an account number and password before you can use these services. Chapter 20 provides helpful information about signing up with a service.

To create new settings, the first step is to create a new settings sheet name. Select **S**ettings **N**ame, choose **S**ave, and type a new settings name, such as BBS, for Bulletin Board System.

Reminder:
Select Settings Name to assign a name to a settings sheet that contains information you plan to use again.

Changing the Interface Settings

Once you name the new settings sheet, you are ready to change the interface settings. When you select **S**ettings **I**nterface, the following choices appear:

Baud   **P**arity   **L**ength   **S**top-Bits   **C**omm-Port

Most of these terms should already be familiar to you. When you select the **B**aud option, Symphony gives you these choices:

Menu Choice	Baud Rate
1	110
2	150
3	300
4	600
5	1200
6	2400
7	4800
8	9600

For this example, assume that you are using a 1200-baud modem, so select option **5**. When you select **I**nterface **P**arity, Symphony gives you the choices of **1** (None), **2** (Odd), and **3** (Even). As mentioned earlier, most bulletin board systems require that you choose option **1**, no parity.

Select the **L**ength option to see the choices **1** (7 bits) and **2** (8 bits). To select a character length of 8 bits, choose option **2**. Select the **S**top-Bits option and choose **1** stop bit from the menu. Using the **C**omm-Port option, you indicate which communications port (either **1** or **2**) on the computer you are using. The default setting is COM1, but this choice depends on your hardware configuration. Figure 19.3 shows the COMM settings sheet after you have selected all the new interface settings.

Fig. 19.3.

After selecting new interface settings.

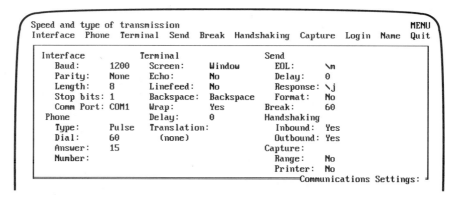

Changing the Phone Settings

After selecting the interface settings, the next logical step in specifying communications settings is to choose the phone settings. When you select **S**ettings **P**hone, the following choices appear:

Type **D**ial-Time **A**nswer-Time **N**umber

Reminder:

If your modem has an auto-dial feature, specify the number to be dialed with the Settings Phone Number command.

The phone settings you want depend on the kind of modem you are using. If your modem has an auto-dial feature, you can select **N**umber and enter the number for the bulletin board system. Symphony then dials the number for you when you tell the program to do so. If your modem is incapable of auto-dialing, however, you must dial the number yourself.

Cue:

Use commas in a telephone number to make Symphony pause before continuing with the number.

Assume for now that you have a modem with auto-dial capabilities and that you are calling from a business phone where you have to dial 9 to get an outside line before you dial the number. After Symphony dials the 9, you want the program to pause momentarily (to wait for the connection to the outside line) before entering the telephone, or access, number. By entering a series of commas between the 9 and the phone number, you can have Symphony pause for as long as you need. The length of the pause that a comma produces is difficult to gauge. But Lotus recommends five commas as a good starting point. For this example, select **S**ettings **P**hone and then select **N**umber. Enter the following string:

9,,,,,6382762

You must also indicate the type of phone you are using with the **T**ype option. (You can skip this option if your modem is incapable of auto-dialing.) If you have standard rotary-dial service, select **P**ulse. Select **T**one if you have push-button service.

Select the **D**ial-Time option to specify the maximum time in seconds that Symphony spends dialing and trying to make a connection after you issue **P**hone **C**all, the command that initiates calling. The default setting is 60 seconds, which normally works fine.

Select the **A**nswer-Time option to specify the maximum number of seconds that Symphony spends answering a call when you issue **P**hone **A**nswer. The default is 15 seconds, which is sufficient under normal circumstances. **D**ial-Time and **A**nswer-Time work through a modem's auto-dial and auto-answer features, so don't worry about these commands if your modem does not have these features. Figure 19.4 shows the COMM settings after you have made all the phone settings.

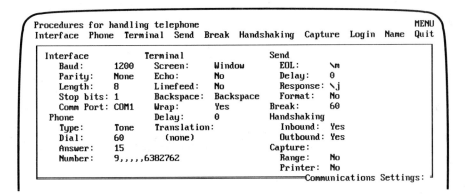

Fig. 19.4.
After selecting new phone settings.

Changing the Terminal Settings

The next step in specifying communications settings is to designate the terminal settings. These settings are used to match the characteristics of the COMM window in which you are working to the characteristics of the service (or computer) you are calling. In practice, you can set several of the terminal settings after you establish a connection with the service. In some cases, you must see how the remote computer reacts to your input before you change the settings. In other cases, you can adjust the settings before you establish the

Cue:
You can set some of the terminal settings after you establish a connection with the remote computer.

connection. When you select **S**ettings **T**erminal, you can choose from these options:

Screen   **E**cho   **L**inefeed   **B**ackspace   **W**rap   **D**elay   **T**ranslation

The **S**creen option lets you eliminate the box that encloses the COMM window. Some remote computers require that you have a full 25-line display (specifically, when you are trying to emulate the VT100 display terminal). Because you are trying to run a standard IBM PC, XT, AT, or PS/2 connection in this example, however, leave the **S**creen option set to **W**indow, the default, rather than changing it to **F**ull-Screen.

The **E**cho option controls whether the characters you type are displayed on-screen. Normally, you want to have your input displayed so that you can see whether it is correct. If you are connecting with a full-duplex system, you can leave the setting at **N**o. Full-duplex systems "echo" the characters you type automatically; half-duplex systems (which allow only one-way communication) do not. Therefore, the **E**cho option is normally set to **Y**es for half-duplex systems.

If you are not sure whether the system you are working on is full-duplex or half-duplex, you can set this option after you establish the connection. If you see two characters for every one you type, set the option to **N**o. If you see no characters when you type, set **E**cho to **Y**es. If you see three characters for every character you type, your modem is probably also echoing characters. Turn off this feature on your modem and then set the **E**cho option to **N**o.

Linefeed, the third **T**erminal option, is another option that you can set once you are connected to the remote computer. A few computers do not supply a linefeed. If your messages write over one another on the same line, set **L**inefeed to **Y**es. In this example, assume that the remote system supplies a linefeed, so leave this option set to **N**o.

The **B**ackspace option determines the character deleted by the Backspace key. By default, whenever you press the Backspace key, the cursor moves one character to the left and erases the character in that space. By setting this option to **D**elete, you can have the Backspace key delete the character on which the cursor rests, and have all the characters to the right of the cursor shift one place to the left. Normally, you leave this setting on the default, which is **B**ackspace.

If long lines that you type or that are returned to you from the other computer do not wrap around to the next line, you must set the **W**rap option to **Y**es. The default is **Y**es; keep this setting for the current example.

Reminder:

Use the Settings Terminal Delay command to specify a delay period between transmission of characters.

Use the **D**elay option to set the delay between transmissions of characters. The unit of measure is 1/128 of a second; Lotus says that typical settings range from 30 to 60. You may find, however, that a smaller setting is sufficient. You must set this option by trial and error. (For the current example, chose a setting of 10.) The **D**elay option is particularly important for slowing down the transmission of

characters as you are logging onto another computer. A good indicator of the
need to increase the delay is when the other computer appears to be losing
the characters you send it. Of all the **T**erminal options, the **D**elay option
requires the most experimenting. This option is one of the most important ones
you have for controlling the interaction between your microcomputer and a
remote computer system.

Use the **T**ranslation option to choose the current character-code translation
table. Specify this option when you are using an international character set to
communicate with a remote computer, or if you are an expert user and have
devised a special translation table. You have the following choices after
selecting **T**ranslation:

Default **N**ational **C**ustom **G**enerate

In most cases, including the current example, leave the option set to **D**efault.
For more information about character-code translation tables, see the discussion
in Chapter 7 on the use of translation tables.

If you have attached the application add-in for DEC VT100 terminal emulation,
an additional **T**erminal option appears: **V**T100. This option gives you access to
another settings sheet so that you can modify special screen characteristics
(such as color, scrolling speed, and cursor appearance) of a VT100 terminal.
Figure 19.5 shows the COMM settings sheet that appears if you've attached the
VT100 add-in and have selected **S**ettings **V**T100.

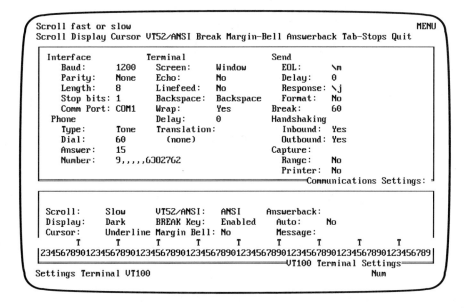

Fig. 19.5.

*The settings sheet
with the VT100
add-in attached.*

Figure 19.6 shows the COMM settings sheet after you have set the terminal settings. Only the **D**elay option has been changed from the default.

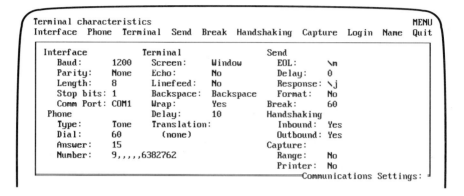

Fig. 19.6.

After selecting new terminal settings.

```
Terminal characteristics                                              MENU
Interface  Phone  Terminal  Send  Break  Handshaking  Capture  Login  Name  Quit

  Interface              Terminal              Send
    Baud:       1200        Screen:    Window      EOL:       \m
    Parity:     None        Echo:      No          Delay:     0
    Length:     8           Linefeed:  No          Response:  \j
    Stop bits:  1           Backspace: Backspace   Format:    No
    Comm Port:  COM1        Wrap:      Yes        Break:      60
  Phone                     Delay:     10        Handshaking
    Type:       Tone        Translation:           Inbound:   Yes
    Dial:       60            (none)               Outbound:  Yes
    Answer:     15                               Capture:
    Number:     9,,,,,6382762                      Range:     No
                                                   Printer:   No
                                            Communications Settings:
```

Setting Up a Log-in Sequence

Setting up a log-in sequence with a remote computer is one of the most interesting aspects of Symphony's COMM window. You have several options with which you can work. One has already been mentioned: the **S**ettings **T**erminal **D**elay command. The other options are part of the **S**ettings **L**ogin command. Figure 19.7 shows the command menu and settings sheet that appear when you select **S**ettings **L**ogin.

Fig. 19.7.

*The **S**ettings **L**ogin command menu and settings sheet.*

```
Number of seconds to wait for log-in to succeed                      MENU
Maximum-Time  Repeat-Time  A  B  C  D  E  F  G  H  I  J  New  Quit

    Count  Send (maximum time 0)           Receive (repeat time 0)
  A  1
  B  1
  C  1
  D  1
  E  1
  F  1
  G  1
  H  1
  I  1
  J  1
                                                    Login Settings:
```

The **L**ogin menu is the place where you store strings to be sent to the remote computer (called the *send strings*) and the responses you are expecting in return (the *receive strings*). Suppose that during the log-in sequence to a local bulletin board system, you expect the following sequence of events:

Reminder:
*Use the **Settings** Login command to specify the information you want to send and the data you expect to receive.*

1. Once you get the **CONNECT** message, the BBS displays a series of messages and then asks **What is your FIRST name?**.

2. You respond with your first name and press Enter.

3. The BBS returns the message **What is your LAST name?**.

4. You respond with your last name and press Enter.

5. The BBS asks you to **Enter your password:**.

6. You type your password and press Enter.

Once this information has been provided, you are logged onto the system and can send messages to other users, download files, and use any other services the BBS offers. (These services are usually displayed on a menu.)

Entering Send and Receive Strings

To automate the log-in sequence, you can enter send and receive strings in the **L**ogin menu. Figure 19.8 displays the finished log-in sheet. First, select the **A** option from the **L**ogin menu. When you do, Symphony shows you the following options:

Count **S**end **R**eceive **Q**uit

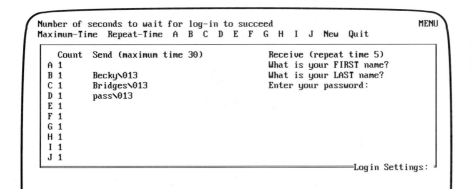

Fig. 19.8.
After setting up the log-in sequence.

In this remote system, you must receive something (the question `What is your FIRST name?`) before you can send anything. Therefore, **A** has no send string. To enter the first receive string, select **R**eceive and type **What is your FIRST name?** after the prompt. This string is the one that you want to appear on-screen before Symphony transmits a send string. In other words, when Symphony receives this string from the remote computer, the program sends the next string (the B string) automatically. You are finished with the **A** option, so select **Q**uit from the **A** menu.

Tip

A good method of determining the exact wording of the receive strings is to log in manually and capture the entire log-in sequence to a range in a worksheet. Refer to "Capturing Data to a Range" later in this chapter for details.

Tip

Because Symphony examines the text it receives from the remote computer and waits until it gets the receive string, you don't have to include the entire string in the log-in sheet. In this case, for example, you can enter just **FIRST name?**, **name?**, or **?** as the receive string. Keeping the receive string short is wise because you have less chance of making a typing error. Typing errors such as an extra space or an incorrectly capitalized letter can cause problems.

The receive string should always include the last characters you expect the other computer to transmit, because Symphony begins to transmit the send string as soon as it receives the specified receive string. If you specify an incorrect receive string, Symphony never transmits the send string, and the log-in process fails. If that happens, you must complete the log-in sequence manually or hang up, edit the log-in sequence, and try again.

Select **B** to enter the next set of send and receive strings. To enter the first send string, select **S**end and enter **Becky\013** (or use *your* first name followed by \013). The \013 signals the Enter key. If you forget to include the \013, the remote computer will never see the response and won't send the next prompt. Then select **R**eceive and enter **What is your LAST name?**. Finally, select **Q**uit from the **B** menu.

Select **C** and enter **Bridges\013** (or use *your* last name) as the send string. Enter the string **Enter your password:** as the receive string. Then select **Q**uit from the **C** menu.

For the **D** option, enter a send string (enter **pass\013** or whatever your password is). You do not need a receive string for this option because the prompt for the password is the last string in the log-in sequence you receive from the remote computer.

Tip

Instead of entering your password as a send string, you may want to enter it yourself when you log in to a remote computer system. If your password is contained in a log-in string, anyone who uses your computer can log in and use your account at will.

You may have noticed that you didn't change the **C**ount option. The **C**ount option designates the number of times you want to transmit the send string. Because you need to send each string only once, you left **C**ount set to the default of 1 for this example.

Note: Some remote computers require that you send a series of Enters at the beginning of the log-in sequence. If so, enter **\013\013\013** as the send string for option **A** to send three Enters (or however many Enters the remote computer expects).

Specifying the Maximum-Time Option

After specifying the send and receive strings, you must enter a value, in whole seconds, for the **M**aximum-Time option of the **L**ogin menu. Use the **M**aximum-Time option to specify the maximum number of seconds that Symphony waits for the log-in sequence to succeed. This amount includes all the time needed for sending and receiving during the log-in sequence. The **M**aximum-Time setting varies depending on how much sending and receiving you want to accomplish in the log-in sequence. For the current example, a good setting is 30 seconds. You can use a value as small as 10 seconds, but 10 seconds may not be enough time if the remote computer is slow in responding. If the **M**aximum-Time setting is reached before the log-in sequence is completed, Symphony interrupts the log-in sequence and issues an error message.

Note: If you set the **M**aximum-Time option too high, a failed log-in sequence can tie up the phone line until Symphony times out. Setting a high time-out value can be expensive in this situation, especially if you are dialing long distance.

Reminder:
Set the Maximum-Time option to the number of seconds you want Symphony to wait for the entire log-in sequence to be completed.

Specifying the Repeat-Time Option

The **R**epeat-Time option is used to set the number of seconds you want Symphony to delay before retransmitting a send string. The **R**epeat-Time option only applies if you set the **C**ount option to a number higher than the default of 1. If, for example, Symphony transmits a send string and the bulletin board system responds immediately, Symphony transmits the next send string immediately. The other system may be slow, however, in responding to the send string. You don't want Symphony to get ahead by sending another string before receiving a response to the first one. Therefore, if you set the **C**ount option to a value higher than 1, you must set the **R**epeat-Time option to allow the other computer enough time to respond. Because the **C**ount option remains at the default of 1 for the current example, the repeat time is not important.

Striking the right balance between too much and not enough time for the **R**epeat-Time option requires some experimenting. Allowing extra time is not a problem if you set the **M**aximum-Time option high enough to allow the entire log-in sequence to be completed.

Refer again to figure 19.8 to see how the **L**ogin settings sheet appears after you enter all the settings. Notice that the **M**aximum-Time and **R**epeat-Time settings appear above the Send and Receive columns, respectively.

Changing Handshaking Settings

Cue:

Most computers use the same kind of handshaking: XON/XOFF. You probably won't have to change the Handshaking option.

Handshaking refers to whether Symphony uses XON/XOFF (Ctrl-Q/Ctrl-S) protocol when communicating with a remote computer. If you have ever used the DOS TYPE command and pressed Ctrl-S to stop a file from displaying and Ctrl-Q to start displaying again, you have used XON/XOFF protocol. (Don't confuse XON/XOFF with the Christensen XMODEM protocol; the two are entirely different.) Most manufacturers adhere to the XON/XOFF standard, so most remote computers recognize the Ctrl-Q and Ctrl-S characters. Some computers have their own variations of handshaking protocol, however, and require different control characters. On rare occasion you may have to disable Symphony's handshaking in order to communicate with one of these computers. Even if handshaking is disabled, however, you can still manually issue Ctrl-S to stop the display (not the transmission) of a communications session, and then use Ctrl-Q to start the display again.

Symphony has two controls for handshaking: **I**nbound and **O**utbound. (You access the **H**andshaking options from the **S**ettings menu.) If you set **H**andshaking **O**utbound to **Y**es, you are indicating that Symphony can start and stop a remote computer's transmission by issuing XON/XOFF signals. If you set **H**andshaking **I**nbound to **Y**es, you are indicating that the remote computer can stop Symphony's transmission by XON/XOFF signals. The default setting for both **I**nbound and **O**utbound is **Y**es; you probably do not need to change these settings.

Starting Communications

Now that you have an understanding of most of the COMM settings, you are ready to start communications. You can change any of the COMM settings while you are in the middle of a communications session, so don't worry if you are not sure about a particular setting. Try the settings you think are most appropriate, and change them one by one if they don't work properly.

Phoning

Suppose that you have a modem with auto-dial capability and that you have specified a bulletin board system's access number with the **S**ettings **P**hone **N**umber command. You now want Symphony to dial the number for you. To do so, select **P**hone from the main COMM menu. The following menu choices appear:

Call **W**ait-Mode **A**nswer **H**angup **D**ata-Mode **V**oice-Mode

Note: The **P**hone **C**all command is described in this section; the other commands are described in "Using the Other COMM Phone Options" later in this chapter.

When you select **C**all and press Enter, you should hear some strange beeping noises from the modem as it dials the number. A **Dialing...** message appears at the top of the screen. When Symphony makes a connection with the remote system, you should hear a high-pitched tone over the speaker. (If Symphony does not make the connection, an error message appears on-screen.) After a short while, the high-pitched tone stops, and you are ready to begin the log-in sequence. Be sure to wait until the modem stops making the high-pitched tone before proceeding. Usually the modem displays a message on-screen to tell you it is connected. Hayes-compatible modems display the message **CONNECT** or **CONNECT 2400**. If you set the modem for short (or terse) responses, the message is either 1 or 10.

> **Reminder:**
> *After dialing the remote computer, wait until the modem stops making the high-pitched tone before beginning the log-in sequence.*

Note: If your modem does not have an auto-dial feature, you must dial the phone number yourself. When you hear the high-pitched tone over the receiver, flip the switch on your modem from Voice to Data, and you are ready to start the log-in sequence.

Starting the Log-in Sequence

After connecting to the remote system, select **L**og-in from the main COMM menu (don't confuse the COMM **L**og-in command with the COMM **S**ettings **L**ogin command). Symphony displays the letters A through J. You have already entered the log-in sequence for the current example in the **S**ettings **L**ogin settings sheet, so select **A**. Symphony starts the log-in sequence by looking for receive string A and displaying the message **Logging in...** at the top of the screen. If the log-in settings you specified are working properly, you should not have to touch the computer again until you are completely logged into the remote computer.

Note: If you select any letter option other than **A**, Symphony starts the log-in sequence with the send string you select. Send and receive strings associated with letters before the one you selected are ignored. For example, if you select option **C**, Symphony ignores the send and receive strings for options **A** and **B** and starts with the send string for option **C**.

Symphony continues sending strings until the program reaches an empty line in the **L**ogin settings sheet. If the log-in settings are not correct, however, you may have to halt the log in sequence in midstream (by pressing Ctrl-Break and Esc) and enter the log-in sequence manually. If this situation occurs, enter a different value for the **S**ettings **T**erminal **D**elay command and try logging in again.

Using Phone-and-Login

Cue:

Use the Settings Name Phone-and-Login command to dial and log-in with one command.

As an alternative to using the **P**hone command to dial the number and the **L**og-in command to begin your log-in sequence, you can use the COMM **S**ettings **N**ame **P**hone-and-Login command. Before invoking this command, you must create a named settings sheet containing all the correct interface parameters, the phone number, and the log-in sequence. Use the COMM **S**ettings **N**ame **C**reate command to save and name the settings.

When you invoke the **P**hone-and-Login command, you are prompted for a settings-sheet name. Once you type the name or select the name of an existing settings sheet from the list, Symphony retrieves the settings sheet, dials the number, and begins the log-in sequence. As you can see, **P**hone-and-Login is a powerful, time-saving command.

Using the Other COMM Phone Options

In addition to the **P**hone **C**all command, explained in "Phoning," earlier in this chapter, the COMM **P**hone menu offers several other useful options. Following is a brief description of each:

Wait-Mode	Used to place the modem in auto-answer mode. Selecting **P**hone **W**ait-Mode **Y**es sends a command string to your modem instructing it to automatically answer the next incoming call. This command is useful if you are expecting a call from another computer. Issue this command before your phone rings.
Answer	Instructs the modem to take the telephone line off-hook and answer a call. Issue this command after the phone begins to ring. Use **P**hone **W**ait-Mode **Y**es to make the answering process a bit more automatic.

Hangup	Instructs the modem to break the current connection and place the phone line "on-hook" (telephone terminology for "hang up the phone"). Issue this command to make sure that your modem has disconnected the phone call.
Data-Mode	Instructs the modem to switch to data mode from voice mode. In data mode, the modem generates a high-pitched carrier tone and attempts to connect with a modem on the other end of the line. Use this command after you place a call manually.
Voice-Mode	Instructs the modem to stop generating the high-pitched tone so that you can pick up the phone and speak with another person. This command does not break the phone connection or terminate the call.

Copying to the Printer

While you are in a COMM window, you can have Symphony send to the printer a copy of all data that appears on-screen, including all the data sent by the remote computer and all the data you type. The command to initiate printing is **S**ettings **C**apture **P**rinter. When you have begun printing, the `Capture` message appears at the bottom of the screen.

Once you start copying to the printer, you can stop the procedure at any time by using the Capture key (F4 on IBM PC, XT, AT, and PS/2 computers and compatibles). To start copying again, press Capture (F4) a second time. You also use the Capture key when capturing data in a range in the worksheet, as explained in the following section. (The Capture key is the only special-function key used in a COMM window.)

Capturing Data in a Range

After you have logged onto the bulletin board system and found some interesting data, you may want to capture that data in a range in Symphony. Captured data is stored in a worksheet as labels; you can use the captured data immediately in a DOC window if you set the capture range to a single column. If you want to use the data as numbers, however, you must convert it to a usable form before you can perform calculations, make a graph, play "what if," and so on.

Before you can capture data, however, you must designate in the worksheet a capture range where you want the data placed as it comes in. The capture range can be located anywhere in the worksheet. Just make sure that the range you designate is large enough (both in width and length) to contain all the data you want to capture.

Reminder:
Specify a capture range in the worksheet before you capture data from the remote computer.

Suppose, for example, that a friend left you an electronic message on the bulletin board. To capture the message in a range in a Symphony worksheet, use the **S**ettings **C**apture **R**ange command and the Capture (F4) key. When you issue **C**apture **R**ange, Symphony temporarily shifts to the SHEET environment so that you can enter a capture range. A good technique is to make the capture range a little larger than you think you need. If the capture range fills up, you must erase the capture range (by using the **S**ettings **C**apture **E**rase command), reset the capture range to a larger size, reissue the bulletin board's command to read a message, and start capturing again.

Tip

If you want to use the captured data in a DOC window, specify the capture range as A1..A8192 and allow the data to "spill over" as long labels in column A. If you specify a multicolumn capture range, you find that although the data is still captured as labels, you cannot use the data in a DOC window because each cell only contains a label as long as the current column width.

If the capture range is A1..H200, for example, the columns have the default width of 9, and the first line of text you capture is *The quick brown fox catches the hens sleeping*, cell A1 contains *The quick*, cell B1 contains *brown fox*, C1 has *catches*, D1 has *the hens*, and E1 contains *sleeping*. If you try to edit these entries in a DOC window, you can edit only what is in A1. By capturing the data in one column, however, you can change to a DOC window and edit properly.

You use the Capture (F4) key to capture data in a COMM window. After you set the capture range and want to begin capturing data, press the Capture key and choose **R**ange **Y**es to initiate the process. When you have captured all the data you want, press the Capture key again, followed this time by **R**ange **N**o.

Converting Numbers to a Usable Form

When you have captured numerical data from a remote computer, you need a way to convert the data to numbers for use in calculations, graphs, and the like. You have two ways to accomplish this conversion: by using @functions, such as @DATEVALUE, @TIMEVALUE, and @VALUE; or by using the **Q**uery **P**arse command.

Note: You can remain connected to the other computer while you convert data. If you pay for connect time with the other computer, however, you may want to log off before you convert the data.

Setting the Capture-Range Column Widths

Before you can convert numerical data to a usable form, you must make sure that you capture the data properly. Suppose that you have captured the data that appears in figure 19.9 and you want to convert it for use in a graph.

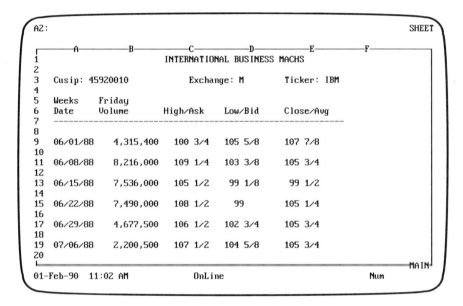

Fig. 19.9.
Sample spreadsheet data.

If you plan to use @functions to convert the data to a useful form, you should set the capture range for the data in figure 19.9 as A1..E8192. Because the capture range is several columns wide, Symphony enters the data for Weeks Date, Friday Volume, High/Ask, Low/Bid, and Close/Avg in separate columns. Remember to indicate a capture range that is wide enough if you want Symphony to maintain columnar separation.

Reminder:
Specify a multiple-column capture range if you plan to use @functions to convert the data.

In addition, if you plan to use @functions to convert the data, you must set the column widths to conform to the data you are capturing. If you leave the columns set to the default width of 9, Symphony may not split the data where you prefer. The best way to determine the column widths for your data is to experiment. The column widths for figure 19.9 were set to the following:

Column	Width
A	9
B	13
C	12
D	12
E	12

If you plan to use the **Q**uery **P**arse command to convert the data, set a capture range that is one column wide: A1..A8192. Then, all the data for each row will be written in one long label.

Using @Functions To Convert Data

To use @functions to convert the data in figure 19.9 from labels to numbers, switch to a SHEET window and go to an out-of-the-way area of the worksheet. You then can use the following formulas to convert the data in row 9:

Variable	Function
Weeks Date	@DATEVALUE(A9)
Friday Volume	@VALUE(B9)
High/Ask	@VALUE(C9)
Low/Bid	@VALUE(D9)
Close/Avg	@VALUE(E9)

Once you have the formulas for the first row, copy them to succeeding rows. Then use the SHEET **R**ange **V**alues command to change to numbers the formulas in the out-of-the-way range and to copy them over the original label data. If the formulas return ERR, you may have to adjust the column widths and recapture the data. You also may want to use @CLEAN and @TRIM to remove control characters and extra spaces from the strings of data. If the remote computer adds "strange" characters like these, you may find it difficult to convert the strings without cleaning them up first. @CLEAN and @TRIM are discussed in Chapter 6.

Using Query Parse

The second technique for converting string data to numbers, the **Q**uery **P**arse command, is much easier than using @functions. To use **Q**uery **P**arse, you must be familiar with the FORM window (see Chapter 17).

Suppose that you have captured the data in figure 19.9. Because you plan to use **Q**uery **P**arse to convert the data, capture the data in a one-column capture range (A1..A20). One advantage to using **Q**uery **P**arse is that you don't have to determine beforehand how to split the data into separate columns. Another advantage is that the single-column capture range prevents you from having to recapture the data if you select incorrect widths for the data fields.

The first step to using **Q**uery **P**arse on captured data is to create a simple input form using a DOC (or SHEET) window. Be careful if you use a DOC window; you don't want to disturb the data you have just captured. The best location for

Caution:
If you use a DOC window to create the input form, be careful not to disturb the captured data in the DOC window.

entering the fields for the input form is below or to the right of the captured data.

To create the input form, type the name of the first field and a colon. For example, type **Weeks Date:** (see fig. 19.10). Then type the letter of the field type (**D** for date, **L** for label, **N** for numeric, or **T** for time) and another colon. Finally type the length of the field (the column width needed to parse the input string properly) and press Enter. To calculate the correct field lengths, you will probably have to count the character positions in the input string. For example, suppose that you captured the following string:

01-Jun-90   43154000   100.75   105.625   107.875

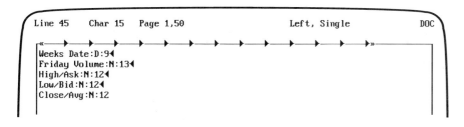

Fig. 19.10.
Input-form fields for the Query Parse command.

You count the positions like this:

```
                    1111111111222222222233333333334444444444455555555555
          12345678901234567890123456789012345678901234567890123456789

          01-Jun-90      43154000      100.75     105.625     107.875
```

In this example, the Weeks Date field occupies positions 1 through 9 and requires a field length of 9. The second field occupies positions 10 through 22, so you must specify a field length of 13 to include the entire range. The third field occupies positions 23 through 34, so you must specify a field length of 12. The fourth field occupies positions 35 through 46; specify a field length of 12. The last field occupies positions 47 through 58 and requires a field length of 12.

After you create the input form, switch to a FORM window and issue the **G**enerate command, which causes Symphony to generate the input form and the important ranges for the database. You are now ready to issue the **Q**uery **P**arse command.

To enter the command, switch from a FORM to a SHEET window and issue **Q**uery **P**arse. Symphony asks you for the range to be parsed. Be sure to indicate all columns in which the data is displayed (in this example, A1..E20) even though the data is contained in only one column. Although the capture range may contain all kinds of unrelated data (such as titles and log-in sequences), Symphony conveniently discards all the lines that do not conform to the field definitions you supply. After you enter the range to be parsed, Symphony asks for a review range. This range is where Symphony puts all the nonconforming lines. Choose an out-of-the-way place for the review range. After you enter the review range, Symphony executes the **Q**uery **P**arse. Figure 19.11 shows the results after column widths were adjusted and the field labels were set to right-alignment. Notice that the Weeks Date field automatically was given D1 format because it was defined as a date field.

Fig. 19.11.

The results of converting data with **Q**uery **P**arse.

```
A68: 'Weeks Date                                                    SHEET
      ┌────A────────B────────C────────D────────E────────F──────────┐
   66 │                                                             │
   67 │                                                             │
   68 │ Weeks Date Friday Volume   High/Ask   Low/Bid   Close/Avg   │
   69 │ 01-Jun-88     4315400       100.75    105.625    107.875    │
   70 │ 08-Jun-88     8216000       109.25    103.375    105.75     │
   71 │ 15-Jun-88     7536000       105.5      99.125     99.5      │
   72 │ 22-Jun-88     7490000       108.5         99     105.25     │
   73 │ 29-Jun-88     4677500       106.5     102.75     105.75     │
   74 │ 06-Jul-88     2200500       107.5     104.625    105.75     │
   75 │                                                             │
```

Saving Settings

Reminder:

Save the communications settings before you exit Symphony.

Before you exit Symphony, make sure that you save your settings in a communications configuration file. To save the settings, issue the **S**ettings **N**ame **S**ave command. Symphony saves the settings to a file with the extension CCF on the Symphony Program disk (or to the Symphony program directory if you loaded Symphony from the hard disk). After you save the settings, you can retrieve them by selecting the **S**ettings **N**ame **R**etrieve command. If you want Symphony to retrieve the settings for you automatically every time you boot the program, you can enter the name of the CCF file in the SERVICES **C**onfiguration **C**ommunications command and select **U**pdate to save the new configuration. For more on modifying and updating the SERVICES **C**onfiguration menu, see Chapter 2.

Ending a Session

Each bulletin board system has its own command for logging off. For example, you may have to enter **x** to exit. On systems like CompuServe, you enter **bye** or **off** to exit. Be sure to log off properly; some systems continue accumulating connect time and continue billing your account for a period of time if you hang up without logging off. If your modem has an auto-hangup feature, select **P**hone **H**angup from the main COMM menu. This command causes Symphony to signal your modem to hang up the phone. If you do not have the auto-hangup feature, flip the switch on your modem from Data to Voice.

Communicating with Another Microcomputer

At some point, you will probably want to use the COMM environment to communicate with another Symphony user. In fact, you should make a special point of trying this type of communication. Call up a friend who also has Symphony and try passing messages and data back and forth. You will learn a great deal about Symphony's COMM environment by experimenting.

Matching the Interface Settings

When you are communicating with another microcomputer, your first concern should be that you both have the same interface settings. For example, if one modem can be set at either 300 or 1200 baud, and the other modem can be set only at 300, both must be set at the lower rate. The settings for parity, length, and stop bits also must be the same.

When you send files back and forth using the **F**ile-Transfer **S**end and **F**ile-Transfer **R**eceive commands, Symphony temporarily modifies the interface settings to accommodate the protocol. (For example, XMODEM protocol is 8-bit word length, no parity, and 1 stop bit.) When the file transfer is complete, Symphony adjusts the settings back to what they were originally. No specific action is required on your part. One reason that many BBSs use 8-bit word length is that some PC communications programs don't make the changes so gracefully. In fact, 8N1 has become the most common setting for communications between PCs. The **F**ile-Transfer **S**end and **F**ile-Transfer **R**eceive commands are described in "Transferring Files," later in this chapter.

Reminder:
When you communicate with another microcomputer, make sure that the parameters are set the same.

Making the Connection

Once you coordinate the interface settings for both computers, you are ready to make the connection. Suppose that your friend is the caller and you are the receiver of the call. After your friend uses the **P**hone **C**all command to dial your number, you use the **P**hone **A**nswer command to have Symphony automatically answer the call. As Symphony is working, it displays the message **Answering...** at the top of the screen. Alternatively, you can issue the **P**hone **W**ait-Mode **Y**es command before your friend calls to make sure that your PC and modem are ready to answer the call. This method has the advantage of not requiring you to manually tell the modem to answer after the phone rings.

Cue:
*Use the **P**hone Wait-Mode **Y**es command to make the modem ready to answer a call without your help.*

Just how long Symphony attempts to answer the call depends on the **S**ettings **P**hone **A**nswer-Time setting you specified. The default setting of 15 seconds is usually more than enough time when you know you are being called.

Because Symphony does not have a special indicator to let you know when you are being called, you have to rely on signals from your modem. If the modem is equipped with a speaker, you can hear noises when someone is calling. If you are not in a COMM window, you must switch to one to issue the **P**hone **A**nswer command. (For modems not equipped with an auto-answer feature, the **P**hone **A**nswer command has no effect.) If you set the **P**hone **W**ait-Mode command to **Y**es, your modem automatically answers a call after a preset number of rings, determined by a setting on the modem.

Tip

Hayes-compatible modems display messages on-screen to advise you of the progress of an incoming or outgoing call. These messages can be either short (terse) or long (verbose), depending on the settings of the modem's switches and internal memory configuration. You can issue a command in the COMM window to set the modem messages to terse or verbose by typing **ATV0** for terse or **ATV1** for verbose (all modem commands must be typed in uppercase letters).

You type the AT commands at any point in a COMM window. Anything you type in a COMM window is automatically sent to the modem.

The following list shows typical modem messages:

Terse	Verbose	Terse	Verbose
0	OK	5	CONNECT 1200
1	CONNECT	6	NO DIAL TONE
2	RING	7	BUSY
3	NO CARRIER	8	NO ANSWER
4	ERROR	10	CONNECT 2400

On 1200-baud modems, only the first four verbose messages are usually available.

If your modem is not equipped with an auto-answer feature, keep the modem set to Voice mode. When someone calls you, flip the switch from Voice to Data and you are ready to send messages.

Sending Messages

Reminder:

Make sure that Settings Terminal Echo is set to Yes on both systems, or you cannot "chat" with the other person.

After you have made the connection, you are automatically in "chat" mode where everything you type is also seen on the other person's screen, and everything the other person types displays on your screen. Be sure that you set **S**ettings **T**erminal **E**cho to **Y**es on both systems or you won't be able to see what you're typing. If you want to send a long message that you have previously typed in a SHEET or DOC environment, you can use the COMM **T**ransmit-Range command.

When you issue the **T**ransmit-Range command, Symphony temporarily shifts to the SHEET environment so that you can designate the range to be sent. After you designate the range and press Enter, Symphony immediately shifts back to the COMM environment and transmits the specified message.

Note: If your message stretches across several columns, make sure that you designate all the columns involved. If you point to only the first column (as you may do if the message is a long label), Symphony transmits only the first portion of the message (just as it prints only the highlighted area if you designated a print range in a SHEET window).

In general, transmitting messages is awkward in Symphony, but you can automate the process. Chapter 22 shows how to use the Symphony Command Language to make sending messages a simple task. Transferring messages that you've saved previously in files is easier and more reliable, as you see in "Transferring Files" later in this chapter.

Sending Ranges

You can use the **T**ransmit-Range command to send other data. For example, you may want to send a portion of an inventory spreadsheet or the latest figures you received on T-bill auction rates.

When you use **T**ransmit-Range to send ranges, you must make sure that you have selected the proper options for the **S**ettings **S**end command. When you select **S**ettings **S**end, Symphony returns the following choices:

    End-of-Line **D**elay **R**esponse **F**ormat

The **E**nd-of-Line option is used to enter an end-of-line terminator. Symphony uses the specified terminator between lines of data when you issue the **T**ransmit-Range command. The end-of-line terminator is a three-digit ASCII control code (or letter equivalent) preceded by a backslash. For example, the most common end-of-line indicator is \013 (or its equivalent \M or Control-M), the carriage-return character. This indicator is the default setting for Symphony and is the end-of-line terminator to use when communicating with another Symphony user.

Note: An appendix in the Symphony reference manual has a complete listing of all the ASCII and Lotus International Character Set (LICS) codes. The appendix also explains the use of these codes in the Symphony COMM window.

The **D**elay option sets the number of seconds you want Symphony to wait before sending consecutive lines of a range. The default setting is 0, the setting to use when communicating with another Symphony user. Some time-sharing services are slow to accept new data, however, and you may have to enter a delay time when sending a range to these services.

Sometimes you will want to have Symphony read a string from a remote computer before sending a data range. To have Symphony read the string, you must choose the **R**esponse option and enter the string. Suppose that the remote computer is running a line editor that is currently in EDIT mode. After you send a command to switch the editor from EDIT to INSERT mode, you want to have Symphony read the editor's response before sending a range. If the editor's prompt is **INSERT**, enter this string in the **R**esponse setting. Some electronic mail services use the colon as a prompt, which you should enter as the **R**esponse setting. For the current example, leave the response string blank. When you get into more sophisticated applications later, such as using the Lotus Command Language to send data ranges, you may want to include a response string.

Cue:

Use Settings Send Format No when sending a Symphony document to a person who uses another word processor.

If you are transmitting a Symphony document, you can use the **F**ormat option to include (or not include) DOC mode's special symbols (hard tabs, hard returns, indents, page breaks, and format lines). If you specify **F**ormat **Y**es, these special symbols are included with the document when you transmit it. If you specify **F**ormat **N**o, the symbols are not transmitted. When sending a document to another Symphony user, you probably want to include the word processing symbols. When sending a document to someone who uses another word processor, specify **F**ormat **N**o so that that person doesn't receive special symbols the system cannot understand.

Transferring Files

Symphony gives you two options for sending data back and forth between your computer and another Symphony user's machine. As described previously, you can use the **T**ransmit-Range command to transmit a portion of a file. Unfortunately, the receiving Symphony user must capture the data as lines of text when you transmit data this way. Alternatively, you can use the **F**ile-Transfer **S**end and **R**eceive commands. These commands are used to transfer entire files by means of Symphony's XMODEM file-transferring capabilities. One of the main advantages of XMODEM file transfer is that you keep the separation between cell entries. Another advantage is that error checking takes place as the file is being transferred. When you use **T**ransmit-Range, no error checking takes place, and any noise on the phone lines can cause errors in what the receiving computer receives.

When you issue the **F**ile-Transfer **S**end command to transfer a file to another Symphony user, Symphony first requests the name of the file you are transferring. (Remember that you are not limited to sending only Symphony files.) Suppose that the name of the file you select is SALES.WR1. After you enter this name, Symphony displays the following message on your screen:

```
Sending file: SALES.WR1
Waiting for connection...
```

The user of the receiving computer must issue the **F**ile-Transfer **R**eceive command and specify the name of the file to be received. One problem often encountered in the file-transfer process is that the receiving user may forget to type the complete file name with its extension. In this example, the complete file name SALES.WR1 is necessary. If the receiving user typed only **SALES** and left off the **.WR1**, the file would be transferred but couldn't be retrieved as a Symphony worksheet until it was renamed SALES.WR1. If the receiving user has already issued the **F**ile-Transfer **R**eceive command, you probably will not see the second line of the message. Instead, Symphony shows some variation of the following message:

```
Sending file: SALES.WR1
1024 out of 2048 sent, 0 errors corrected
```

As Symphony transmits the file, the numbers in the second line of the message are constantly updated to reflect the status of the transfer. Incidentally, the receiving user's screen shows the same messages with the word `Sending` replaced by `Receiving`. The receiving user's screen, however, doesn't include the file's size, only the number of bytes already sent.

With all the error-checking that occurs, transferring a file can take a substantial amount of time. For example, transferring approximately 5,000 bytes takes three to four minutes at 300 baud. At 1200 baud, the file transfers in about one minute; at 2400 baud, the file transfers in about 30 seconds.

If the remote computer you are working with does not support XMODEM, CompuServe B, or BLAST protocol, you must use Symphony's **S**ettings **C**apture **R**ange command to transfer a file from the remote computer to Symphony. Sometimes this technique is the only way to get data from a remote computer into Symphony. Because no error-checking occurs when you capture data in a range, you may get some strange characters mixed with the data. If you do, use the @CLEAN function to remove the control characters, and then carefully edit the result to correct any other errors.

Chapter Summary

In this chapter, you have learned about Symphony's COMM window through two examples: accessing a bulletin board system and communicating with another Symphony user. In many ways Symphony's COMM window is quite sophisticated. Chapter 20 provides a hands-on practice session for working with Symphony's communications. In Chapter 22, you find examples of how to use the Symphony Command Language to help streamline some of the COMM window operations. With the Command-Language additions, Symphony provides a powerful communications capability.

20

Learning Communications: Hands-On Practice

In Chapter 19 you read how you can use Symphony's COMM mode to connect with an electronic bulletin board system and with another microcomputer running Symphony. In this hands-on practice chapter, you connect with the popular CompuServe Information Service. This time-sharing service offers current and historical information on a wide variety of subjects: financial news, stocks, weather, travel, and, of course, computers. You can even play games and go shopping while you are on-line!

In this session, you access *The World of Lotus*, a special information service that Lotus Development Corporation has set up on CompuServe. With this service, you can leave messages about a problem you are having with Symphony; a Lotus employee, or perhaps another Symphony user, may offer help. The service also provides lists of other resources (magazines, books, and users' groups). In addition, you can download a variety of files to use with Symphony: new drivers, add-in applications, worksheet templates, macros, utilities, and so on. These files are free; you pay only for your CompuServe connect time.

In this practice session, you first modify the CompuServe communications configuration file included with Symphony and create a log-in sequence to automate the process of logging onto CompuServe. Once you connect with CompuServe, you enter *The World of Lotus*, capture data in a worksheet so that you can read the data later, and download a small worksheet file.

This chapter makes the following assumptions:

❏ You have installed Symphony for communications and have indicated XMODEM/B protocol during installation.

❏ Your modem is installed.

❏ You know the local access number for CompuServe. (A phone list comes with your CompuServe information packet.)

❏ You have already set up a CompuServe account and have a user ID and a password.

Note: If you are not yet a CompuServe subscriber, call the CompuServe Customer Service Department at 1-800-848-8990 for information on becoming one. You can receive current details about such things as local access numbers, sign-up charges, connect-time charges, and other information. Most other services provide similar information.

Changing Settings

Lotus includes in the Symphony package communications configuration files for several popular information services, one of which is CompuServe. Because creating a communications settings sheet from scratch can be confusing to the novice "telecommunicator," you will appreciate that Lotus has specified the settings for you. All you have to do is add the local CompuServe access number to the settings sheet. Depending on your modem, you may have to change the baud rate.

Modifying a Communications Configuration File

If you copied all the Symphony disks to your hard disk, the CompuServe communications configuration file (COMPUSRV.CCF) should be in the Symphony directory. If you are working from 5.25-inch floppy disks, COMPUSRV.CCF is on the Help and Tutorial disk. If you have 3.5-inch disks, the communications configuration files are on the Program, Help and Tutorial disk.

Follow these steps to load Symphony and retrieve the COMPUSRV.CCF file:

1. Load the Symphony program. A blank worksheet appears, and you are in SHEET mode.

2. Press the Type key (Alt-F10) and select **COMM** to display a COMM window.

3. Select COMM **S**ettings **N**ame **R**etrieve.

4. Select **COMPUSRV.CCF** and press Enter. The settings sheet should look like figure 20.1.

Note: If COMPUSRV.CCF is not listed, you may have to switch disks or directories. If you are using a hard disk, make sure that the Symphony directory (the one with the program files) is displayed. If it's not, change the path. If you are using 5.25-inch disks, make sure that the Help and Tutorial disk is in drive A. If you are using 3.5-inch disks, make sure that the Program, Help and Tutorial disk is in drive A. If you cannot locate COMPUSRV.CCF, enter the settings as shown in figure 20.1.

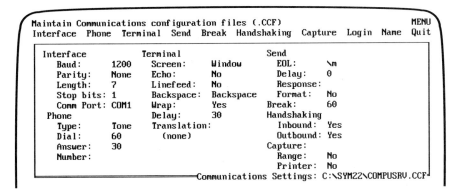

Fig. 20.1.
The settings sheet for the CompuServe communications configuration file.

Enter your local CompuServe access number into the settings sheet by following these steps:

1. Select COMM **S**ettings **P**hone **N**umber.

2. Enter the number.

   Note: If you are calling from a business phone that requires you to dial 9 to get an outside line, type **9,,,,,** and then type the CompuServe phone number.

Designating a capture range before you log onto CompuServe is a good idea; when you specify a capture range, you can save information as it displays on the screen. Follow these steps to designate a capture range:

1. Select **C**apture **R**ange from the **S**ettings menu.

2. Specify the range **A1..A8192**. The settings sheet should look similar to figure 20.2.

Specifying a capture range in the settings sheet automatically turns on the Capture feature; thus, as soon as you log onto the other computer, everything on your screen is saved into the worksheet. Because you don't want to turn on the Capture feature until the middle of the session, turn Capture off by following these steps:

1. Press Esc until you are out of the COMM menu. Notice the **Capture** message at the bottom of the screen.

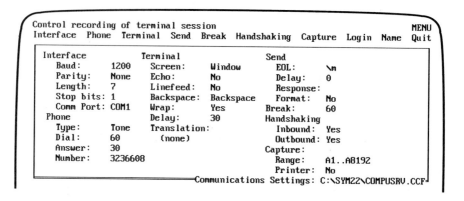

Fig. 20.2.

The settings sheet after entering the local CompuServe access number and designating a capture range.

2. Press the Capture (F4) key.

3. Select **R**ange **N**o. The `Capture` message disappears.

Make any other necessary changes to the sheet (baud rate, phone type, and so on).

Automating the Log-in Sequence

CompuServe, like most electronic bulletin board systems, requires you to answer a few questions to identify yourself after you connect. This process is called *logging on* or *logging in.* To save yourself the trouble of entering your user ID and password each time you access CompuServe, you can create a log-in sequence that automatically logs on for you.

To log onto CompuServe, you follow this sequence:

1. You dial the local access number and wait for your modem to connect. Most modems first make a high-pitched noise, silence the speaker, and then provide an on-screen message telling you a connection has been made.

2. You issue a Control-C to tell the network that you want to connect to CompuServe.

3. You type your user ID number and press Enter. CompuServe responds with `Password:`.

4. You type your password and press Enter.

Begin entering the send and receive strings into the log-in sheet. The first keystroke that CompuServe looks for after you connect is a Control-C. A Control-C, represented by \003, is the first send string. (Recall that Appendix A of the Symphony reference manual shows you how to send control characters. Just as the carriage-return character can be sent as Control-M or \013, Control-C is sent as \003. In your worksheet, a Control character appears with a ^ preceding it. Control-C looks like ^C.)

Follow these steps to enter the send and receive strings you use to log onto CompuServe:

1. Select COMM **S**ettings **L**ogin. You see the menu in figure 20.3.

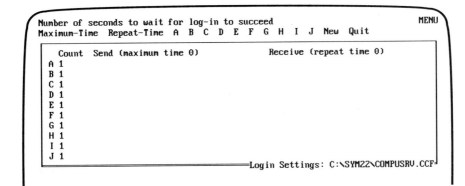

```
Number of seconds to wait for log-in to succeed                    MENU
Maximum-Time  Repeat-Time  A  B  C  D  E  F  G  H  I  J  New  Quit

    Count  Send (maximum time 0)              Receive (repeat time 0)
  A 1
  B 1
  C 1
  D 1
  E 1
  F 1
  G 1
  H 1
  I 1
  J 1
                                    Login Settings: C:\SYM22\COMPUSRV.CCF
```

Fig. 20.3.
The Login menu.

2. Select **A S**end.
3. Enter **\003**.
4. Select **R**eceive.
5. Enter **User ID:**.
6. Select **Q**uit.

Follow these steps to enter the next set of send and receive strings in the **B** option:

1. Select **B S**end.
2. Enter your user ID number (for example, **72106,2551**) followed by **\013**.
3. Select **R**eceive.
4. Enter **Password:**.
5. Select **Q**uit.

Enter the last send string in the **C** option. (CompuServe sends no more strings for the log-in sequence after it receives your password.) If you prefer to enter your password manually instead of saving it in the log-in sequence you can skip the following steps.

1. Select **C S**end.
2. Enter your password (for example, **ralph*morter**) followed by **\013**.
3. Select **Q**uit.

Whether or not your modem has auto-answer and auto-dial capabilities, you should now enter values for the **M**aximum-Time and **R**epeat-Time options on the **S**ettings **L**ogin menu. **M**aximum-Time is the total amount of time (in seconds) that Symphony waits for the entire log-in sequence to succeed. **R**epeat-Time is the amount of time (in seconds) that Symphony waits between issuing a send string and resending it if you've set the **C**ount option to a number larger than 1.

Follow these steps to set the **M**aximum-Time and **R**epeat-Time options:

1. Select **M**aximum-Time from the **S**ettings **L**ogin menu.

2. Enter **30**.

3. Select **R**epeat-Time.

4. Enter **5**. The log-in sequence should look similar to figure 20.4.

Fig. 20.4.

The log-in sequence.

```
Number of seconds to wait for log-in to succeed                    MENU
Maximum-Time  Repeat-Time  A  B  C  D  E  F  G  H  I  J  New  Quit

     Count  Send (maximum time 30)          Receive (repeat time 5)
   A  1     \003                            User ID:
   B  1     72106,2551\013                  Password:
   C  1     ralph*morter\013
   D  1
   E  1
   F  1
   G  1
   H  1
   I  1
   J  1
                                    Login Settings: C:\SYM22\COMPUSRV.CCF
```

5. Select **Q**uit to go back to the **S**ettings menu.

6. Select **N**ame **S**ave to save your modifications.

7. Press Enter to keep the same name (COMPUSRV.CCF) and select **Y**es to replace.

Connecting with CompuServe

If your modem does not have auto-dialing capability, you must dial the CompuServe access number yourself. Turn on your modem, dial the number, and, after you connect, switch your modem from Voice to Data mode.

If your modem does have an auto-dial feature, you can use a Symphony command to dial the telephone number that you previously entered in the settings sheet. Make sure that your modem is turned on and follow these steps:

1. Select COMM **P**hone **C**all. The phone number you entered in the settings sheet appears.

2. Press Enter to dial CompuServe. If your modem has a speaker, you may hear your modem dialing the number; Symphony also displays the message **Dialing...** in the upper left corner of the screen. When your computer successfully connects with CompuServe, you briefly hear a high-pitched tone and see on-screen the message **CONNECT**.

Congratulations! You have successfully accessed a remote computer. You are now ready to begin the log-in sequence you created and enter *The World of Lotus*. Follow these steps:

1. Select COMM **S**ettings **L**ogin **A**. You see CompuServe ask several questions (the receive strings you specified), and the responses automatically fill in (the send strings you entered). Eventually, you see the CompuServe menu and a prompt to **Enter choice number !** as shown in figure 20.5.

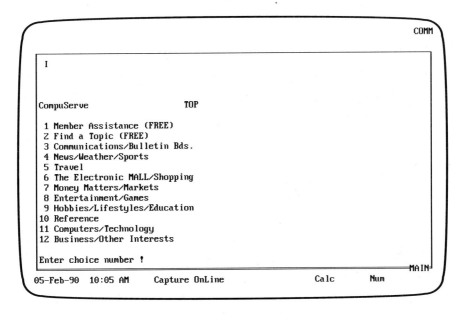

Fig. 20.5.
The CompuServe Top menu.

2. Enter **go lotus**. The World of Lotus menu appears, as shown in figure 20.6.

Capturing Data in a Range

Because you are charged by the minute while you are logged onto an information service, you may want to save information to a worksheet range so that you can read the data after you log off. You have already indicated the

Fig. 20.6.
The World of Lotus menu.

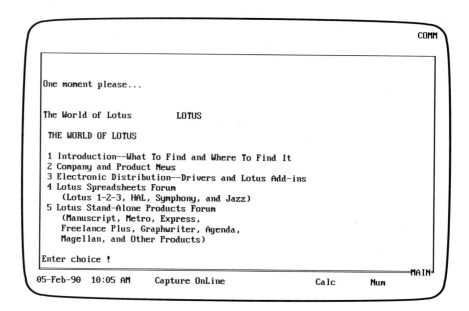

```
                                                                    COMM

One moment please...


The World of Lotus            LOTUS

  THE WORLD OF LOTUS

  1 Introduction--What To Find and Where To Find It
  2 Company and Product News
  3 Electronic Distribution--Drivers and Lotus Add-ins
  4 Lotus Spreadsheets Forum
      (Lotus 1-2-3, HAL, Symphony, and Jazz)
  5 Lotus Stand-Alone Products Forum
      (Manuscript, Metro, Express,
      Freelance Plus, Graphwriter, Agenda,
      Magellan, and Other Products)

  Enter choice !
                                                                   MAIN
  05-Feb-90  10:05 AM       Capture OnLine              Calc      Num
```

capture range where data can be stored in the worksheet. Use the Capture (F4) key to indicate when you want to capture the data.

When you see something on-screen that you want to capture for perusal later, follow these steps:

1. Press the Capture (F4) key.

2. Select **R**ange **Y**es. The `Capture` message appears at the bottom of the screen. Everything that appears on-screen until you turn off CAPTURE mode is stored in the worksheet range you previously specified.

3. When you want to stop capturing data to the capture range, press Capture (F4) again and select **R**ange **N**o. You can start and stop the data capture as often as you like; Symphony adds to the bottom of the existing material.

Downloading a File

The World of Lotus contains a data library of files you can download: worksheet templates, utilities, macros, and so on. Before you can download any of the files in the data library, you must first join the Lotus Spreadsheets group (you incur no extra charge to join any of CompuServe's forum groups). Joining a forum just means that you supply your name as a member of the group.

Follow these steps to access the data library:

1. If you have not already done so, connect to CompuServe and enter **go lotus** to go to The World of Lotus main menu.

2. Enter **4** to select Lotus Spreadsheets Forum. The menu should look similar to the one shown in figure 20.7.

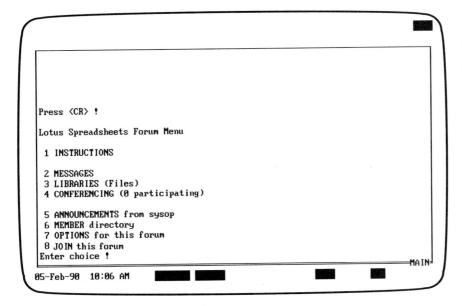

Fig. 20.7.
The Lotus Spreadsheets Forum menu.

```
Press <CR> !

Lotus Spreadsheets Forum Menu

 1 INSTRUCTIONS

 2 MESSAGES
 3 LIBRARIES (Files)
 4 CONFERENCING (0 participating)

 5 ANNOUNCEMENTS from sysop
 6 MEMBER directory
 7 OPTIONS for this forum
 8 JOIN this forum
Enter choice !
                                              MAIN

05-Feb-90  10:06 AM
```

3. Enter **8** to select JOIN this forum. You are prompted to enter your name.

4. Enter your name and confirm it.

5. Enter **3** to see the data libraries menu. The menu should look similar to the one shown in figure 20.8.

6. Enter **10** to select LOTUS Magazine.

Follow these steps to use CompuServe's browse command to locate files about Symphony and to download a file:

1. Enter **1** to select BROWSE thru files. CompuServe displays the prompt `Enter keywords (e.g. modem) or <CR> for all`. This prompt asks you to enter *keywords* (words you want to search for) or to press Enter (represented by `<CR>`) to browse through all the files in the data library.

2. Enter **symphony** as the keyword for which you want to search the library. CompuServe displays the prompt `Oldest files in days or <CR> for all`.

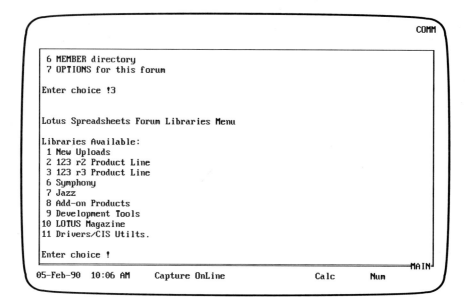

Fig. 20.8.

The Lotus Spreadsheets Forum Libraries menu.

```
                                                                    COMM
  6 MEMBER directory
  7 OPTIONS for this forum

  Enter choice !3


  Lotus Spreadsheets Forum Libraries Menu

  Libraries Available:
   1 New Uploads
   2 123 r2 Product Line
   3 123 r3 Product Line
   6 Symphony
   7 Jazz
   8 Add-on Products
   9 Development Tools
  10 LOTUS Magazine
  11 Drivers/CIS Utilts.

  Enter choice !
                                                               ⊣MAIN⊢
  05-Feb-90  10:06 AM     Capture OnLine         Calc      Num
```

3. Press Enter for all. Your screen will look similar to the one shown in figure 20.9.

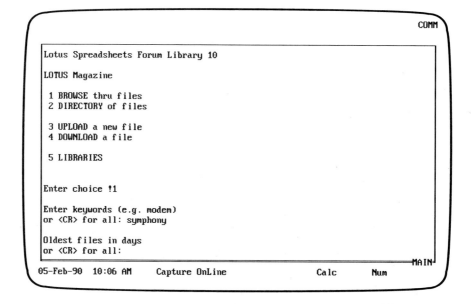

Fig. 20.9.

The LOTUS Magazine menu and the BROWSE thru files prompts.

```
                                                                    COMM
  Lotus Spreadsheets Forum Library 10

  LOTUS Magazine

   1 BROWSE thru files
   2 DIRECTORY of files

   3 UPLOAD a new file
   4 DOWNLOAD a file

   5 LIBRARIES


  Enter choice !1

  Enter keywords (e.g. modem)
  or <CR> for all: symphony

  Oldest files in days
  or <CR> for all:
                                                               ⊣MAIN⊢
  05-Feb-90  10:06 AM     Capture OnLine         Calc      Num
```

In these steps, you specified that you want to look for files that relate to Symphony. After each file is displayed, the prompt **Press <CR> for next or type CHOICES** appears. When you find a file that looks interesting, type **CHOICES** at the prompt and press Enter. In the example screen shown in figure 20.10, you've found a file named MS8809.ARC, which you're going to download. Looking at the description, you see that the file is small—3138 bytes; it won't take too long to transfer.

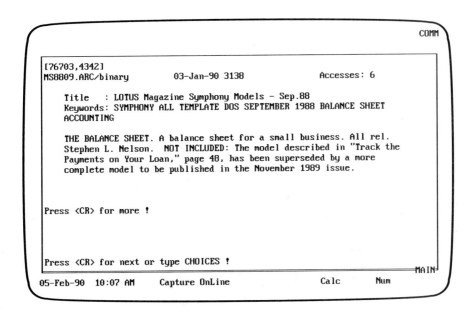

```
                                                                    COMM

  [76703,4342]
  MS8809.ARC/binary          03-Jan-90 3138              Accesses: 6

      Title    : LOTUS Magazine Symphony Models - Sep.88
      Keywords: SYMPHONY ALL TEMPLATE DOS SEPTEMBER 1988 BALANCE SHEET
      ACCOUNTING

      THE BALANCE SHEET. A balance sheet for a small business. All rel.
      Stephen L. Nelson.  NOT INCLUDED: The model described in "Track the
      Payments on Your Loan," page 48, has been superseded by a more
      complete model to be published in the November 1989 issue.



  Press <CR> for more !



  Press <CR> for next or type CHOICES !
                                                                    MAIN
  05-Feb-90  10:07 AM    Capture OnLine            Calc      Num
```

Fig. 20.10.
A description of a file named MS8809.ARC.

Follow these instructions to download the file:

1. If the message **Press <CR> for more** is displayed, press Enter.

2. When you see the message **Press <CR> for next or type CHOICES**, type **CHOICES** and press Enter.

3. Enter **2** to download the file you've looked at with the browse option. The Library Protocol menu (similar to the one shown in fig. 20.11) appears.

4. Enter **2** to select CompuServe B+ and original B.

5. When the prompt **File name for your computer:** appears, enter the name of the file that you want to download. In this case, enter **MS8809.ARC**.

   Note: To download the file to your default Symphony file directory, just enter the file name. You also can specify a path name in front of the file name if you want to download the file to another directory.

Fig. 20.11.

*The Library
Protocol menu.*

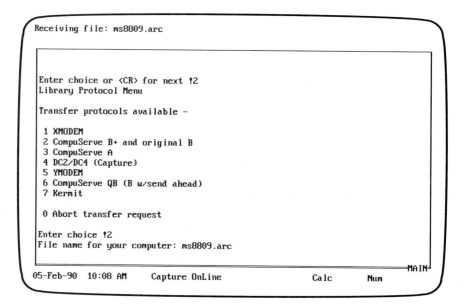

```
Receiving file: ms8809.arc

Enter choice or <CR> for next !2
Library Protocol Menu

Transfer protocols available -

 1 XMODEM
 2 CompuServe B+ and original B
 3 CompuServe A
 4 DC2/DC4 (Capture)
 5 YMODEM
 6 CompuServe QB (B w/send ahead)
 7 Kermit

 0 Abort transfer request

Enter choice !2
File name for your computer: ms8809.arc
                                                    MAIN
05-Feb-90  10:08 AM     Capture OnLine              Calc      Num
```

As the file downloads, you see a status message in the control panel that reads `Receiving file: MS8809.ARC, xx bytes received, 0 errors corrected`, where *xx* is a number that increases to the file size (in this case, 3138).

Because most files on Compuserve are stored in a compressed format to save connect time when you're downloading them, you also must download a small program that can uncompress the files after they're on your system. You only need to download this program once; when you download files in the future, you can use this copy of the program.

Follow these steps to download the program that uncompresses files:

1. Once you have downloaded MS8809.ARC, enter **4** to return to the Lotus Spreadsheets Forum Library 10 menu in figure 20.9.

2. Enter **5** to return to the Lotus Spreadsheets Forum Libraries menu shown in figure 20.12.

3. Select **11**, Drivers/CIS Utilts (see fig. 20.12).

4. Select **1** to browse through the utilities files.

5. Enter **arc** as the keyword for which you want to search. Press Enter to select all files, regardless of age.

6. When you find a file with a description similar to the one for ARCE4C.EXE (shown in fig. 20.13), download it by typing **choices** at the prompt and selecting **2** to download

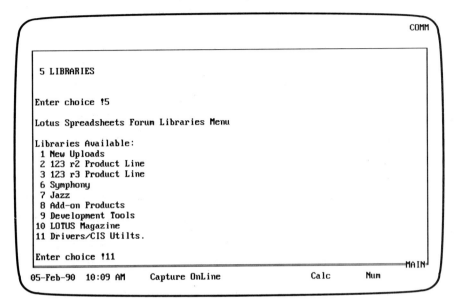

```
                                                              COMM

   5 LIBRARIES


   Enter choice !5

   Lotus Spreadsheets Forum Libraries Menu

   Libraries Available:
    1 New Uploads
    2 123 r2 Product Line
    3 123 r3 Product Line
    6 Symphony
    7 Jazz
    8 Add-on Products
    9 Development Tools
   10 LOTUS Magazine
   11 Drivers/CIS Utilts.

   Enter choice !11
                                                           MAIN
   05-Feb-90  10:09 AM    Capture OnLine        Calc    Num
```

Fig. 20.12.
Choosing the Drivers/CIS Utilts library.

```
                                                              COMM

   or <CR> for all:



   [76067,1203]
   ARCE4C.EXE/binary       19-Jun-89 10219          Accesses: 862

      Title   : Latest version of ARCE, free unarchiving program
      Keywords: ARCHIVE UNARCHIVE UNCOMPRESS ARC ARCE ARC-E BUERG

      Latest version of Vern Buerg's unarchiving utility. This version
      is compatible with all forms of .ARC archive files. Note that it
      will not work with the new PKware .ZIP files or any of the other
      new compression programs. Free program. DOWnload with a protocol
      and just type ARCE at the DOS prompt; this is a self-extracting
      file which will unarchive itself into a documentation file and the
      actual executable file.


   Press <CR> for more !
                                                           MAIN
   05-Feb-90  10:10 AM    Capture OnLine        Calc    Num
```

Fig. 20.13.
A description of ARCE4C.EXE.

When the file transfer of the program to uncompress files is complete, log off of CompuServe. Follow these steps:

   1. Press Enter when the `Receiving file: ARCE4C.EXE`
      message in the control panel disappears.

2. Enter **bye**. CompuServe displays a message telling you how long you were connected and then hangs up. Your modem displays the message **NO CARRIER**, telling you that the connection has ended.

3. Turn off your modem.

Don't forget that while you were logged onto CompuServe, you captured the session to the worksheet. You should save the worksheet to a file by following these instructions:

1. Press Alt-F9 to switch to SHEET mode.

2. Select SERVICES **F**ile **S**ave.

3. Enter the file name. You can read or print this file later.

Before you can retrieve the MS8809.ARC file, you must uncompress it. Exit Symphony and change to the directory where you saved the downloaded files. If you downloaded the ARCE4C.EXE program, enter **ARCE4C** at the DOS prompt. The ARCE program is extracted from ARCE4C. Once the ARCE program is extracted, use it to uncompress MS8809.ARC by typing the following:

ARCE MS8809

Two files, 88_09_84.WR1 and MS8809.DOC, are extracted from MS8809.ARC. Now return to Symphony, retrieve the 88_09_84.WR1 worksheet, and see what it contains. Follow these steps:

1. Select SERVICES **F**ile **R**etrieve.

2. Enter **88_09_84**.

This file contains a small-business balance sheet. You can find many other models available on CompuServe's forums as well. In addition to *The World of Lotus*, you can find spreadsheet models in the PC Magazine libraries (type **go pcmagnet** instead of **go lotus** after you log onto CompuServe).

Chapter Summary

In this practice chapter, you modified the CompuServe communications configuration file (COMPUSRV.CCF) included with the Symphony program. You then used your modem to connect with CompuServe's computer and accessed a special information service called *The World of Lotus*. You used Symphony communications commands to capture data in a worksheet range and to download a small spreadsheet file.

Part VII

Symphony Macros and the Command Language

Creating and Using Macros

Introducing the Command Language

Creating and Using Macros

Imagine a hand emerging from your computer and typing Symphony commands for you as you sit back and relax. This idea is what macros are all about. You can reduce multiple keystrokes to a two-keystroke operation with Symphony macros: Press two keys, and Symphony does the rest, whether you are formatting a range, creating a graph, or printing a spreadsheet.

In this chapter, you learn how to do the following:

❏ Create, edit, and debug macros

❏ Create macros for use in SHEET, DOC, GRAPH, COMM and FORM environments

❏ Document and name macros

❏ Create and use a Macro Library Manager

Examining the Macro

In its most basic form, a macro is like a storehouse of keystrokes. These keystrokes can be commands or simple text and numeric entries. You can use a macro rather than the keyboard to issue a command or to enter data in the Symphony worksheet.

If you are a Symphony novice, you may think macros are something to leave to Symphony gurus and computer programmers. However, this chapter shows you how easy macros are to build, and gives you a number of macros that you can create and use immediately. Even if you are new to Symphony, you can begin experimenting with macros.

Building the Macro

Once you have decided what you want a macro to do (for example, format a cell in currency format with 0 decimal places), perform the following basic steps:

1. Enter the macro keystrokes in a worksheet cell.
2. Name the macro.
3. Invoke the macro, using the name you gave it.
4. Correct any errors in the macro.

The following section, "Creating Macros," discusses steps 1 and 2. The sections titled "Naming Macros" and "Debugging Macros," discuss steps 3 and 4.

Creating Macros

Suppose that you want to create a simple macro that formats the current cell in the **C**urrency format with **0** decimal places. To execute this command manually, perform the following steps:

1. Press MENU (F10).
2. Select **F**ormat.
3. Select **C**urrency.
4. Type **0**.
5. Press Enter.
6. Press Enter again to format only the current cell.

You can create this macro in two different ways: enter the macro into the worksheet exactly as you enter any other label (by typing all the characters); or use the Learn mode to have Symphony type in the macros for you. (Learn mode is discussed in the next section.) Here is how the macro looks in a worksheet cell:

```
{MENU}fc0~~
```

{MENU} is the special macro keyword used to bring up the menu. The **fc** stands for **F**ormat **C**urrency, and the **0** tells Symphony that you want no digits displayed to the right of the decimal.

At the end of the macro are two characters called tildes. When used in a macro, the tilde (~) represents the Enter key. In this case, the two tildes signal two presses of the Enter key. If you are entering this command from the keyboard, you press Enter twice: once after supplying the 0 for the number of decimals, and again to signal that the format applies to the current cell.

Symphony also uses symbols other than the ~ to represent keystrokes. For example, look at the following macro:

{MENU}fc0~{END}{RIGHT}~

This macro is similar to the one just discussed, except that this version also causes the cell pointer to move. You can use this macro to format an entire row rather than just one cell. Notice the phrase {END}{RIGHT} in the macro. The {END} stands for the End key on the keyboard. The {RIGHT} represents the → key. {END}{RIGHT} has the same effect in the macro as these two keys would have if you typed them in sequence from the keyboard. The pointer moves to the next boundary in the row between blank cells and cells that contain data.

Symphony uses symbols like these to represent all the special keys on the IBM PC, AT, and PS/2 keyboards. In every case, the name of the function key (such as RIGHT for the →, or CALC for function key F8) is enclosed in braces. For example, {UP} represents the ↑ key, {TAB} stands for the Tab key, and {EDIT} represents the Edit (F2) key.

Table 21.1 shows the complete list of special key representations. If you are manually entering the keystrokes for the macro, you must use these representations to enter the keys or commands. If you are using Learn mode, Symphony enters these representations for you as you press the corresponding keys or commands.

Table 21.1
Macro Key Representations

Function Keys	
Representation	*Corresponding Key*
{ABS}	F3 in SHEET window
{CALC}	F8 in SHEET window
{CAPTURE}	F4 in COMM window
{CAPTURE}	Alt-F4 in DOC window
{DRAW}	Alt-F8
{EDIT}	F2 in SHEET and FORM window
{ERASE}	F4 in DOC window
{GOTO}	F5
{HELP}	F1
{INDENT}	F3 in DOC window
{JUSTIFY}	F2 in DOC window
{LEARN}	Alt-F5
{MENU} or {M}	F10

Table 21.1—(continued)

Function Keys

Representation	Corresponding Key
{SERVICES} or {S}	F9
{SPLIT}	Alt-F3
{SWITCH}	Alt-F9
{TYPE}	Alt-F10
{USER}	F7
{WHERE}	Alt-F2 in DOC window
{WINDOW}	F6
{ZOOM}	Alt-F6

Cursor-Movement Keys

Representation	Corresponding Key
{BIGLEFT}	Ctrl-←
{BIGRIGHT}	Ctrl-→
{DOWN}	↓
{END}	End
{HOME}	Home
{LEFT}	←
{PGDN} or {BIGDOWN}	PgDn
{PGUP} or {BIGUP}	PgUp
{RIGHT}	→
{UP}	↑

Other Special Keys

Representation	Corresponding Key
{BACKSPACE} or {BS}	Backspace
{BREAK}	Ctrl-Break
{DELETE}	Del
{ESCAPE} or {ESC}	Esc
{INSERT}	Ins
{TAB}	Tab
{?}	Causes macro to pause and wait for input from keyboard, macro resumes execution after you press Enter
	Enter

Word-Processing Accelerator Keys	
Representation	*Corresponding Key*
{AUTO}	Ctrl-J
{CASE}	Ctrl-X
{COPY}	Ctrl-C
{DLEFT}	Ctrl-T
{DLINE}	Ctrl-D
{DRIGHT}	Ctrl-Y
{DWORD}	Ctrl-Backspace
{FORMAT}	Ctrl-F
{MERGE}	Ctrl-O
{MOVE}	Ctrl-M
{NEXTPAGE}	Ctrl-PgDn
{PAGE}	Ctrl-N
{PASTE}	Ctrl-P
{REPLACE}	Ctrl-R
{SEARCH}	Ctrl-S
{TOPAGE}	Ctrl-PgUp

Note that you must type a label prefix (such as an apostrophe) before any macro that begins with a non-text character (/, \, +, −, or any number). Otherwise, Symphony interprets the macro characters as numbers or commands, which it immediately executes.

Because 240 characters is the maximum number of characters that can fit in a cell, you can type up to 240 characters for each macro in a single cell. If your macro has more than 240 characters, you can continue typing in the cell directly underneath. (Do not leave a blank line, because the macro stops when it reaches a blank cell.) You may want to divide the macro into consecutive cells before the 240-character limit is reached. By placing different functions of a long macro on separate lines, your macro is easier to read. Compare the two macros in figure 21.1.

Reminder:
When you exceed the 240-character maximum, use the cell directly underneath. If you leave a blank line, the macro stops operating when it reaches a blank cell.

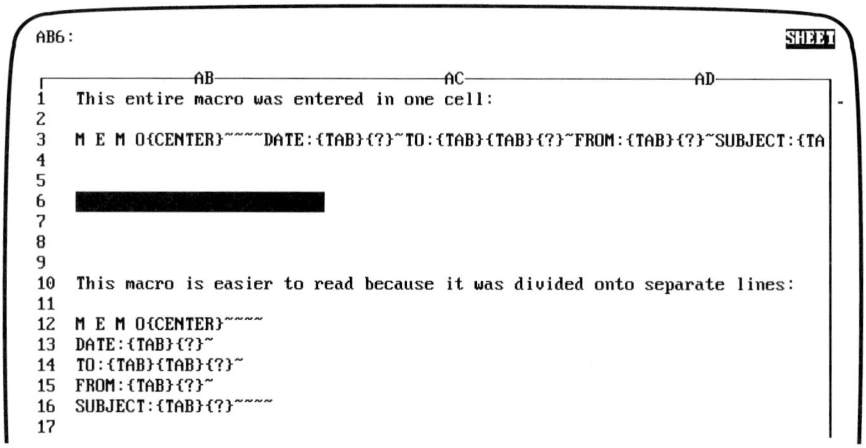
AB6:
SHEET
AB
AC
AD
1 This entire macro was entered in one cell:
2
3 M E M O{CENTER}~~~~DATE:{TAB}{?}~TO:{TAB}{TAB}{?}~FROM:{TAB}{?}~SUBJECT:{TA
4
5
6
7
8
9
10 This macro is easier to read because it was divided onto separate lines:
11
12 M E M O{CENTER}~~~~
13 DATE:{TAB}{?}~
14 TO:{TAB}{TAB}{?}~
15 FROM:{TAB}{?}~
16 SUBJECT:{TAB}{?}~~~~
17

Fig. 21.1.
Two macros compared

Using the Learn Mode

The Learn mode is a powerful Symphony feature that writes macros for you. As you type the keystrokes, Learn records them and places them in a designated area that you select. You can use the keystrokes as they are, or edit them to arrive at your final macro, or incorporate the saved keystrokes into a full-scale macro application. Also, using Learn reduces the opportunity for macro errors.

To use the Learn mode, perform the following steps:

1. Designate a range of cells to record the keystrokes by invoking the **G**lobal **S**ettings sheet (use the SERVICES **S**ettings **L**earn **R**ange command).
2. Turn the Learn mode on by pressing Alt-F5. The `Learn` mode indicator appears at the bottom of the screen.
3. Press the keystrokes you want Symphony to record for you.
4. Turn the Learn mode off by pressing Alt-F5. The `Learn` mode indicator disappears from the screen.

Reminder:
Remember to turn off Learn mode after entering the keystrokes to be recorded.

A common mistake when using the Learn mode is failing to turn it off after entering the keystrokes to be recorded. At a minimum, this causes excess keystrokes at the end of the learn range that must be removed.

If you type too long without turning the Learn mode off, Symphony stops, and an error message telling you that the learn range is full appears at the bottom of the screen. To regain control of the keyboard, press Esc and remove the extra keystrokes from the learn range.

Figure 21.2 shows keystrokes recorded in the Learn mode (B6). These keystrokes assign the **C**urrency **F**ormat with **0** places after the decimal to a specific range of cells (for example, the cell on which the cursor rests and three cells to the right). The keystrokes do not become a macro until you assign a range name to them.

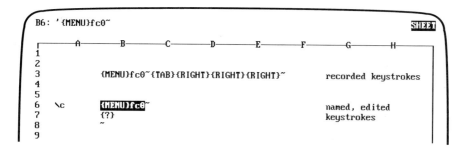

Fig. 21.2.
Keystrokes recorded in the Learn mode.

In figure 21.2, A6 shows keystrokes that also were captured in the Learn mode; however, they create a macro because they are named and edited. The {?} macro command replaces the {TAB}{RIGHT}{RIGHT}{RIGHT}. The {?} enables the macro to pause so that the user can format any range of cells.

Tip

The Learn mode records every keystroke. If you make a mistake, Learn records it and you must go back later and edit out the problem. For example, you press F10 **R**ange ESC **E**rase Return. You wanted to erase a cell, but accidentally pressed *R* for **R**ange. {MENU}r{ESC}~ is recorded.

Using Function Key Grammar

To specify more than one use of a special key, you can include repetition factors inside the braces of a special-key phrase. For example, you can use the following statements:

{PGUP 3}

{RIGHT JUMP}

These statements tell you to press PgUp three times in a row, and then press → the number of times indicated by the value in the cell with a range name JUMP.

Placing Macros

The safest place to put macros is in their own window, with a restrict range specified. This method keeps you from accidentally overwriting or erasing part of a macro as you create your model. Also, when you put macros in a window, you can move to them quickly by pressing Window (F6).

You can create a macro window anywhere outside the active area of your model. Because most models rarely require more than 26 columns, column AA is a practical location for your macros. To create the window, use the SERVICES **W**indow **C**reate command. Enter **MACRO** as the window name, select **SHEET** as the window type, and press Enter to accept the entire screen as the area.

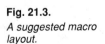

Reminder:

It is important that you restrict the range of the window.

The next step is to restrict the range of the window. You must include this step or you defeat the main purpose of creating a window. With a restrict range specified, you do not run the risk of accidentally destroying macros when you make changes to your model. Select **R**estrict **R**ange and designate a range for storing macros (for example, AA..IV8192).

You must also set the restrict range of other windows so that they do not overlap with MACRO's restrict range. For example, if the window settings sheet for MAIN shows a restrict range of AA..IV8192, then row deletions in MAIN can inadvertently alter lines of code in the MACRO window.

Documenting Your Macros

The macros that you create in this chapter are simple and require little explanation. But the more commands a macro executes, the more difficult the macro is to understand. Suppose that you created a complex macro that you have not looked at for a month, but now need to modify. Without built-in explanations that tell you what each step of the macro does, you may have a difficult time making modifications. That's where documentation comes in. Whenever you create a macro, place comments (documentation) next to each step so that you can determine exactly what the macro does. The best method is to place the comments in the column to the right of the macro next to the macro steps. For example, in the macro in figure 21.3, the macro name is in column AA, the macro itself is in column AB, and the comments are in column AC.

Fig. 21.3.

A suggested macro layout.

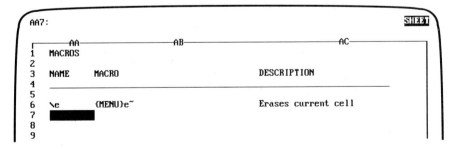

Naming Macros

A macro that you have entered in the worksheet as a label (or a series of labels) must be given a name before you can invoke the macro. Ranges containing macros are assigned names just like any other range. The following types of macro names are available:

- ❏ A single alphabetic character, preceded by a backslash (\). For example, you may want to name the format macro \f.

- ❏ A name of up to 15 characters long (the standard limit for range names). Although the first method is easier and faster, use the second method if you like longer, more descriptive macro names.

- ❏ A number (1 through 10) preceded by a backslash (\). For example, you can name a macro \10.

Using Range Name Create

Suppose that you just built the macro shown in figure 21.4. Now you need to name this macro so that you can invoke it from the keyboard. You have decided to name the macro \d (for dollar). You should choose a name that in some way describes the macro. In this case, for example, you could choose the name \d (for dollar) or \f (for format). You may want to name this macro \$, but because the dollar sign is not a letter, \$ is not a legal macro name.

Reminder:
It is always a good idea to choose a name that in some way describes the macro.

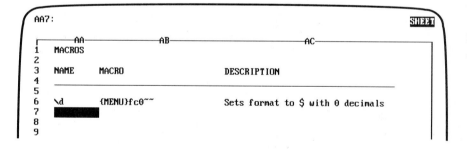

Fig. 21.4.
A sample macro.

To assign the name from the SHEET environment, invoke the command **R**ange **N**ame **C**reate. Next, type the name you selected—\d—and press Enter. Finally, Symphony prompts you for the range to name. If the cell pointer is currently on cell AB6, which is where the macro itself is located, press Enter to sign the name to the cell. Otherwise, you must move the cell pointer to the appropriate cell, or type the cell coordinates from the keyboard.

Most macros require more than one row in the spreadsheet. For example, look at the simple two-row macro in figure 21.5.

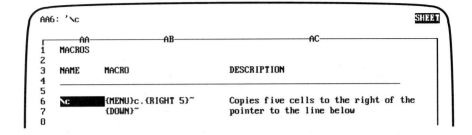

Fig. 21.5.
A simple two-row macro.

To name this macro, you need to assign a name to only the first cell in the range that contains the macro. In this case, assign the name \c to cell AB6. You can indicate the entire range, AB6..AB7, but it is not necessary.

Using Range Name Labels Right

Another way to name cells is with the SHEET **R**ange **N**ame **L**abels **R**ight command. This method works only if you have typed the macro names next to the keystrokes. The **L**abels **R**ight command enables you to name a range by using the contents of the cell immediately to the left as the range name. For example, suppose that you had created the macros in figure 21.6.

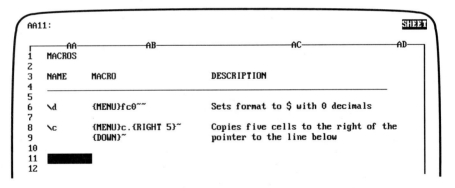

Fig. 21.6.
Two sample macros.

Reminder:

One of the best ways to name macros and associated ranges is by using the Labels Right option.

With your cell pointer on cell AA6, you can name both macros at once with the SHEET **R**ange **N**ame **L**abels **R**ight command. When asked for the label range, highlight the range AA6..AA8. Symphony assigns the name \d to cell AB6, and the name \c to cell AB8.

If you are documenting your macros properly, you already have the names in the sheet; therefore, using the **L**abels **R**ight option is a simple and convenient way to name all your macros simultaneously.

Executing Macros

You execute, or invoke, macros whose names consist of a backslash and a letter (for example, \d) by pressing Macro (Alt) and at the same time pressing the letter name of the macro. For example, if the macro you want to use is named \d, you invoke the macro by pressing Alt-D. The \ symbol in the name is a representation of the Alt key.

Macros you named with regular range names are invoked with the User key (F7). When you press the User key, a **User** indicator appears at the lower right corner of the screen. You can then enter the name of the macro you want to execute. As you type the characters in the name, they appear in place of the User indicator. If you enter a macro name longer than four characters, the name scrolls across the indicator.

If you assigned a number as the macro name (for example, \2), you invoke the macro by pressing the User key followed by the function key of the name (F2, in this case).

As soon as you issue the command, the macro starts to run. If the macro is free of bugs and pause instructions, it continues to run until finished. You may be amazed at its speed. The commands are issued faster than you can see them.

You can store many macro keystrokes or commands in a single cell. Some macros that are especially long or include special commands are easier to understand when written in two or more cells (see examples in Chapter 21, "Creating and Using Macros"). When Symphony starts executing a macro, the program continues in the first cell until all the keystrokes stored there have been used. Symphony then moves down one cell to continue execution. If that cell is blank, or contains a number or a numeric formula, the program stops. If that cell contains more macro commands, however, Symphony continues reading down the column until it reaches the first blank cell.

Automating Macros

Symphony offers an exciting macro feature called automatic macro execution. This technique enables you to create a special macro that executes automatically when you retrieve the file that contains the macro. To use the automatic macro you must first create the macro just like you create any other macro. Then you specify the macro's name in the SERVICES Settings Auto-Execute Set command.

An even more powerful feature is Symphony's capability to load a file automatically into the worksheet. Use the SERVICES Configuration Auto command and specify the name of the file you want Symphony to retrieve each time you load the program. Select Update to save the new configuration. If that file contains an autoexecute macro, the macro automatically executes when you load Symphony.

Use these automatic features to create self-contained programs in the Symphony worksheet. Pressing the Alt or User key is not required to start the macro in these cases. When combined with menus and the other useful macro commands, the automatic execution feature makes macros a remarkably user-friendly tool.

Later in this chapter, the section titled "Making Simple Macros," shows an autoexecute macro in an autoload file.

Debugging Macros

Sometimes a macro does not work perfectly the first time. Errors that cause the program to malfunction are called "bugs" and the process of eliminating them is called "debugging." Your macros most often have fewer bugs when you use the learn mode to write them instead of manually entering keystrokes for the functions to be performed.

Recognizing Common Errors

Like all computer programs, the Symphony command processor is a literal creature with no capability to discern an error in the code. For example, you may recognize immediately that {GATO} is a misspelling of {GOTO}. But the command processor tries to execute the macro as is. The misspelled word generates an error.

If you enclose in braces a phrase that is not a key name or a command keyword, Symphony returns the following error message:

```
Unrecognized key Range name{...}(A1)
```

{...} represents the invalid key name and (A1) tells you that the error occurred in cell A1.

Consequently, you must be extremely careful when you build your macros so that they have no errors. Even misplaced spaces and tildes can cause difficulty for Symphony.

The biggest problem most beginners experience when creating macros is forgetting to represent all of the required Enter keystrokes. This omission can lead to some dismaying results. For example, the missing ~ after the {RIGHT 5} in the macro in figure 21.7 causes the {DOWN} command to be included in the definition of the FROM range of the SHEET Copy command, instead of defining the TO range. The result of running this macro is that the Copy command is stopped in the middle of its execution because of the missing tilde, as shown in figure. 21.8.

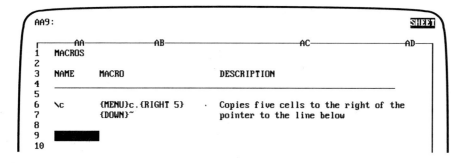

Fig. 21.7.
A macro with a missing ~.

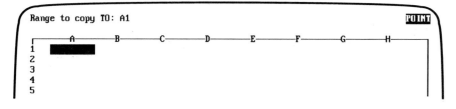

Fig. 21.8.
The result of running the macro with the missing ~.

Another big problem with Symphony macros is that the cell references included in macros are always absolute: The references do not change when cells are moved about or deleted from the sheet. For example, the following macro erases the contents of cell A6:

> {MENU}eA6~

But suppose that you use the SHEET **M**ove command to move the contents of cell A6 to B6. Because cell references in formulas automatically adjust when cells are moved, you may expect the macro to read as follows:

> {MENU}eB6~

If you try this example, however, you see that the macro has not changed.

If you think about it for a second, this rigidity makes perfect sense. A macro is nothing but a label, and you would not expect other labels to change when the sheet is changed. For example, if you created the label A15A15A15A15, you would not expect it to change to C15C15C15C15 if you inserted two columns in the sheet to the left of column A. Macros are no different.

The absolute nature of cell references within macros is a strong argument in favor of using range names. A range name remains associated with the same range even if you move that range. Range names within macros (and other formulas) follow the cells to which the names apply, thus eliminating the absolute reference problem.

Reminder:
By using range names in your macros you eliminate the absolute reference problem.

However, avoid using range names that are also macro keywords or key representations. For example, do not create a range name called EDIT. Your macro will not run correctly if you use macro keywords as range names. Also, never name a range with a cell address (for example, ID1). In the latter case, Symphony responds to the cell address rather than the address of the range.

Stepping through a Buggy Macro

Like programs written in other programming languages, Symphony macros often need to be debugged before you can use them. Symphony has a tool that helps make debugging much simpler: the Step function. With this release of Symphony, macro commands are now shown at the bottom of the screen; before, they were executed without you seeing them. This feature makes it significantly easier to follow a macro step by step. When Symphony is in Step mode, all macros are executed one step at a time. Symphony literally pauses between each keystroke stored in the macro. Thus you can follow the macro's execution.

Step through the buggy macro in figure 21.7. This macro was supposed to copy the contents of the current cell and five cells to its right to the next line. If you look at figure 21.8 to see the results of executing the macro, you see no indication that the second line has been included in the FROM range. All you know is that the macro ends with the program waiting for you to specify the TO range.

When you discover an error, you must first exit the macro and change to READY mode by pressing Ctrl-Break and Esc.

But if you do not know what the macro's problem is, your next step is to enter Step mode and rerun the macro. To invoke the single-step mode, press Alt-F7. The message **Step** appears at the bottom of the screen.

The **Step** message disappears as soon as you press Alt-C to execute the \c macro. Also, the date and time just below the lower left edge of the border is replaced by the macro's first line **{MENU}c.{RIGHT 5}**. You can move the macro forward one step at a time by pressing any key, although you may find the space bar the most convenient.

As you repeatedly press the space bar, the macro advances one keystroke or step at a time. For example, the cursor in the border below the screen initially rests on **{MENU}**, but it moves to **c** after the space bar is tapped once, as shown in figure 21.9. When one line is completed, the next line of macro code appears below the screen border.

As you step through the macro, you see each command appear in the control panel. In this example, the \ macro was executed with the cell pointer in cell A1. Just before the error occurs, the control panel looks like the one shown in figure 21.10. Because the macro does not have a tilde after the **FROM** range is specified, the **TO** range is included as part of the **FROM** range.

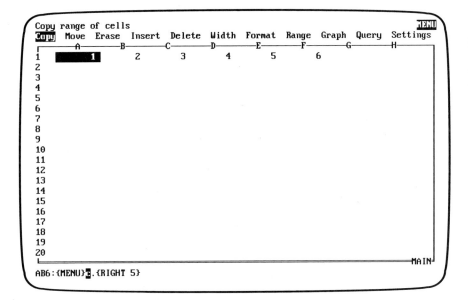

Fig. 21.9.
The macro code below the screen border.

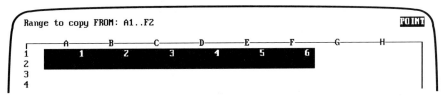

Fig. 21.10.
The control panel before the error.

Thanks to single-step mode, you can easily pinpoint the error's location in the macro. Once you identify the error, you can exit Step mode by pressing Alt-F7 again. Abort the macro by pressing Ctrl-Break and Esc; then you are ready to repair the macro's error.

Editing the Macro

Fixing an error in a macro is as simple as editing the cell that contains the erroneous code. You need not rewrite or rename the cell. You need only to change the element in error.

In this example, first move the pointer to cell AB6, then press F2 to enter EDIT mode. Because the error is a missing ~, fixing the macro is easy. Just type ~ and press Enter.

Editing complex macros is no different from editing this simple macro. Just use Symphony's cell editor (F2) to correct the cell that contains the error.

Making Simple Macros

Now that you know the different macro commands available in Symphony, and have a general understanding of Symphony's work environments, you may be seeking ways you can use macros to speed up tasks you do frequently. To get you started, this section provides practical examples of macros for Symphony's work environments.

Look through the following macros, select the ones you find most useful, and enter them in your macro library. To enter any of the macros in this section, you should follow the steps outlined in the previous sections. As a reminder, you need to take the following steps:

1. Enter the keystrokes, either manually or automatically (with Learn mode), in a worksheet cell.

   Note: Some of the macros contain special macro commands (for example, {?}) that you cannot enter with Learn mode. In these cases, you can either edit the special macro commands into the recorded keystrokes as displayed in figure 21.2, or you can enter these commands manually.

2. Name the macro with the SHEET **R**ange **N**ame **C**reate or **R**ange **N**ame **L**abels **R**ight command.

3. Invoke the macro with either the Alt or User key, depending on the type of name you give the macro.

4. Debug the macro and correct any errors.

Creating Utility Macros for Any Environment

You can use the following macros in any of Symphony's five environments because these macros all use commands invoked by the SERVICES key. As you know, the SERVICES menu contains commands applicable to all work environments. The utility macros are listed in figure 21.11. Included are macros to save, retrieve, and print files.

Saving the Macro

Normally, resaving a file with the same name takes five keystrokes. Also, the keystrokes are slightly different if you replace the file than if you save the file under a new file name. Because saving is so important, you should make the process as quick and painless as possible by creating save macros.

The save and replace macro (\r) is as follows:

{SERVICES}f3 y

```
 AA2:                                                      SHEET
┌──────────────────────────────────────────────────────────────┐
│    ┌AA────────────AB──────────────────AC──────────AD───────┐  │
│  1 │ UTILITY MACROS (ANY ENVIRONMENT)                       │  │
│  2 │ ████████████                                           │  │
│  3 │ NAME      MACRO                 DESCRIPTION             │  │
│  4 │ ───────────────────────────────────────────────────── │  │
│  5 │                                                        │  │
│  6 │ \r        {SERVICES}fs~y        Saves and replaces a file│ │
│  7 │                                                        │  │
│  8 │ \b        {SERVICES}fs{?}~      To save a backup version of a│
│  9 │           y{ESC}               file                    │  │
│ 10 │                                                        │  │
│ 11 │ \p        {SERVICES}pagpq       Prints with specified source range│
│ 12 │                                                        │  │
│ 13 │ \q        {SERVICES}pssc        Cancels prior print range, then│
│ 14 │           sr{?}~qagpq             pauses for new print range before│
│ 15 │                                   printing page        │  │
│ 16 │                                                        │  │
│ 17 │ AUTO      {SERVICES}fr{MENU}    Autoexec macro in an autoload worksheet│
│ 18 │                                   that displays a list of files to retrieve│
│ 19 │                                                        │  │
│ 20 │                                                        │  │
│    └────────────────────────────────────────────────MAIN┘  │
│ 10-Feb-90  04:06 PM                                          │
└──────────────────────────────────────────────────────────────┘
```

Fig. 21.11.
Utility macros for any environment.

This macro displays the SERVICES menu, selects **F**ile **S**ave, presses Enter to keep the same name, and selects **Y**es to replace.

You must be careful never to use this macro on a file you have not named yet. If you do, you replace the first file in your directory with this new worksheet.

Consequently, you may want your save macro to pause before replacing the file or even give you an option of selecting a new name so that the old file remains intact. The pause macro is as follows:

> {SERVICES}fs{?}~
>
> y{ESC}

Caution:

Never use the {SERVICES}fs~y macro on a file you have not named yet. If you do, you replace the first file in your directory with this new worksheet.

This macro displays the SERVICES menu, selects **F**ile **S**ave, and then pauses so that you can enter whatever you want. If you press return, the macro copies over the file you retrieved. The {ESC} on the second line has no effect.

If you enter a new file name when the macro pauses, the worksheet is stored under the new name, and the original file remains undisturbed. Although the y on the second line appears in the control panel, the {ESC} following it removes it from the control panel so it has no effect.

Printing the Macro

One of the first macros you may want to create is a printing macro. You will love the convenience of simply pressing two keys (such as Alt-P) to print. The following \p macro prints in DOC mode, or in any other mode as long as you have specified the **S**ource **R**ange:

{SERVICES}pagpq

This macro displays the SERVICES menu, selects the **P**rint command, **A**ligns the paper, prints with **G**o, gives a **P**age-Advance, and selects **Q**uit to leave the **P**rint menu.

The \p macro prints the document with the current settings for margins, source range, headers, footers, and so on. If you want the macro to ask you for a **S**ource **R**ange, create the following macro:

{SERVICES}psscsr{?}~

qagpq

This macro displays the SERVICES menu, selects the **P**rint command, and then selects **S**ettings **S**ource **C**ancel. The **S**ource **C**ancel removes any previous source range settings just before the **S**ource **R**ange command requests a range to print.

Reminder:

By using the Source Cancel sequence, the macro always enters the worksheet at the point the macro was invoked.

When the {?} macro command pauses the macro so that you can enter the **S**ource **R**ange, enter the range by pointing and highlighting or by typing a range of cells marked by a cell address. As soon as you press Enter, the macro continues executing. Without the **S**ource **C**ancel sequence, the macro would enter the worksheet at the {?} pause in either of two points: where the macro was invoked; or, at the top left corner of the prior-source range. With the **S**ource **C**ancel sequence, the macro always enters the worksheet at the point the macro was invoked.

See Chapter 22 for a print macro that uses the Symphony Command Language to print multiple copies of a worksheet or document.

Making the Autoexecuting Macro

The first thing many users do once they load Symphony is retrieve a file. By creating a file-retrieving macro and specifying it as an autoexecuting macro in an autoloading worksheet, you can have Symphony automatically display a list of file names from which you can choose.

Here is how you make a file-retrieving macro: First, in a blank work sheet, create the following macro:

{SERVICES}fr{MENU}

After displaying the SERVICES menu, this macro invokes the **F**ile **R**etrieve command and uses MENU (F10) to display the files in an alphabetical, multi-column list. Give the macro a name such as AUTO. Specify the macro as autoexecuting by selecting the SERVICES Settings Auto-Execute command. Enter **AUTO** for the range.

Also save the file with a name like AUTO. Specify this file as autoloading by selecting the SERVICES **C**onfiguration **A**uto command. Enter the name **AUTO**. Select **U**pdate to save the settings.

Now, whenever you load Symphony, you can simply point to the file you want to retrieve and press Enter.

Caution:
Make sure you specify the path for the auto-load worksheet or that the auto-load worksheet is in the initial default directory specified by the SERVICES Configuration File command.

Creating Macros in the SHEET Environment

This section describes how to create macros that draw horizontal and vertical lines, sum a column of numbers, set column widths, and move the cell pointer during data entry. The macros are listed in figure 21.12.

```
AA2:                                                              SHEET
    ┌────AA────────────AB────────────────────────AC──────────────AD────
    1   MACROS IN THE SHEET ENVIRONMENT
    2   ██████████
    3   NAME      MACRO                     DESCRIPTION
    4   ──────────────────────────────────────────────────────────────
    5   \h        {MENU}ir~                 Inserts horizontal line
    6             \_~{menu}c~.
    7
    8   \v        {MENU}ic~                 Inserts vertical line
    9             {MENU}ws1~
   10             '¦~{MENU}c~.
   11
   12   \a        @SUM(                     Adds a column of numbers
   13             {UP}.{END}{UP}
   14             )~
   15
   16   \w        {MENU}ws{?}~{RIGHT}       Sets column widths
   17             {BRANCH \w}
   18
   19   \e        {?}{DOWN}{BRANCH \e}      Data-entry macro
   20
    └──────────────────────────────────────────────────────────MAIN┘
    12-Apr-90  12:28 AM            InLine                     Caps
```

Fig. 21.12.

Sample macros for the SHEET environment.

A Macro To Draw Horizontal Lines

You can improve the legibility and appearance of worksheets by adding dashed lines under column headings and above total rows. The \h macro assumes that you have not left a blank line for the dashed line, so the macro inserts a row before creating the dashed line. The macro is as follows:

{MENU}ir~

'\-~{MENU}c~.

This macro selects **I**nsert **R**ow from the SHEET menu, enters the repeating label (\-), selects SHEET **C**opy, presses Enter for the FROM range, and presses a period to anchor the TO range. Because your lines vary in length, the macro stops so that you can highlight the number of cells into which you want to copy.

A Macro To Draw Vertical Lines

Vertical lines help users read a large worksheet. The \v macro assumes that you are inserting the lines after the worksheet is completed; consequently, the macro begins by inserting a column.

Create the macro as follows:

```
{MENU}ic~
{MENU}ws1~
'|~{MENU}c~.
```

In the first line, the \v macro selects **Insert Column** from the SHEET menu. Then in the succeeding lines, the macro selects SHEET **W**idth **S**et, enters **1** for the column width, enters a vertical bar with the label prefix ('|), selects SHEET **C**opy, presses Enter for the FROM range, and presses a period to anchor the TO range. Again, the macro stops to let you define the length of the line.

A Macro To Sum a Column

Because adding up a column of numbers is a common spreadsheet task, the \a macro would be a perfect "addition" to your macro library. The macro is as follows:

```
'@SUM(
{UP}.{END}{UP}
)~
```

This summing macro begins the @SUM function, moves the pointer up one cell to the bottom of the column, anchors with a period, moves the pointer to the top of the column with *{END}{UP}*, ends the formula with a), and presses Enter.

The macro uses two shortcuts with which you may not be familiar:

Reminder:
The summing macro uses two shortcuts designed to save you time.

❏ Begin the range definition at the bottom rather than the top. This method is faster because the pointer need not move all the way to the top and then back to the bottom. Thus, *{UP}* moves the cell pointer to the bottom of the column.

❏ *{END}{UP}* highlights until reaching a blank cell, so that the macro finds the top of the column of numbers (if no blank cells exist in the range you are summing).

The \a macro works only if the cell above the pointer contains a value or label. If the cell is blank, the macro sums the wrong range.

A Macro To Set Column Widths

Use the \w macro when you need to set the column widths of several consecutive columns. That macro is as follows:

{MENU}ws{?}~{RIGHT}

{BRANCH \w}

This macro invokes the SHEET **W**idth **S**et command, then pauses for you to enter a column width. The macro next presses Enter, moves the pointer to the next column to the right, and then automatically re-executes. This automatic looping is accomplished by using the {BRANCH} command in Symphony Command Language. This command transfers control to the {MENU} command that starts the macro.

This program, however, is what is called an infinite loop: it continues endlessly. So how do you stop it? Like you stop any macro, by pressing Ctrl-Break and Esc.

You can build similar macros for any command (such as formatting) that you want to repeat several times for consecutive columns or rows.

A Macro for Data-Entry

Data entry often involves entering a series of numbers down a column. With the \e macro, your PC keyboard has some of the same convenience as an enhanced keyboard; you no longer need to toggle between numbers and arrows on the 10-key numeric keypad; you can turn Num Lock on to enter numbers; and the macro takes care of moving the cell pointer. The data-entry macro is as follows:

{?}{DOWN}{BRANCH \e}

This macro pauses to let you enter data; moves the pointer down one cell; and loops back to the beginning, pausing for you to enter the next number.

Before invoking the macro, press the Num Lock key so that you can use the 10-key pad to enter numbers. To move to the next column for entering more numbers, turn Num Lock off (or hold down the Shift key) and press the arrow and other placement keys on the 10-key pad. Then, reactivate Num Lock and resume using the macro. When there are no more numbers to enter, press Ctrl-Break and Esc to stop the macro and return to normal keyboard control.

If you enter data across rows, you can change the {DOWN} statement to {RIGHT}.

Making Macros in the DOC Environment

Because word processing often involves repetitive tasks, you probably have created a set of macros you use regularly and keep them in your macro library. Figures 21.13 and 21.14 display some word processing macros. You may see the need for other macros as you edit, and you can create them "on the fly" to speed up a repetitive editing process.

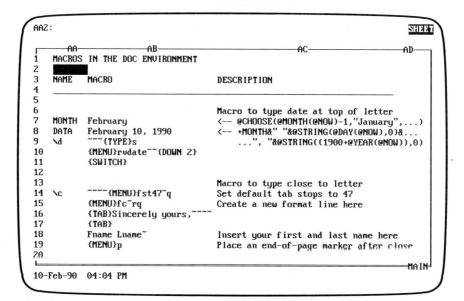

Fig. 21.13.

Sample macros for the DOC environment.

Fig. 21.14.

Sample macros for the DOC environment.

This section includes macros for correcting typing mistakes (transposing letters and words), moving a paragraph, and erasing a paragraph. Also, several macros help to prepare memos and letters. A pair of Spelling Checker macros, shown in figure 21.15, conclude the presentation of DOC-mode macros.

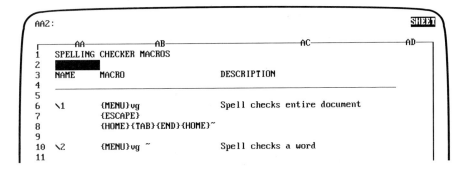

Fig. 21.15.

Sample Spelling Checker macros.

The Letter-Transposition Macro

One common typographical error is transposed letters. For example, you may type *recieve* rather than *receive*. The \l macro uses the DOC **M**ove command to correct the error. That macro is as follows:

    {MENU}m~{LEFT}~

The \l macro displays the DOC menu, selects **M**ove, presses Enter, moves the cell pointer to the left, and again presses Enter.

To invoke the macro, place the cell pointer on the second transposed letter and press Alt-L.

The Word-Transposition Macro

Another useful macro for editing in a DOC window is the word-transposition macro, which enables you to transpose two words located next to each other. Like the letter-transposition macro just described, the word-transposition macro (\w) uses the DOC **M**ove command to correct the error. The macro is as follows:

    {MENU}m ~{BIGRIGHT 2}~

This macro selects DOC **M**ove, presses the space bar to highlight the word, presses Enter, presses Ctrl-→ twice to move to the target location, and finally presses Enter.

The cell pointer should be on the first letter of the first transposed word when you invoke this macro with Alt-W.

The Paragraph-Moving Macro

A paragraph is one of the most common blocks of text you move in a document. The \m macro highlights a paragraph and stops so that you can enter the target location. Make the macro as follows:

{END}{UP}{MENU}m

{END}{DOWN}{DOWN}~

This handy macro moves the cell pointer to the beginning of the paragraph, selects DOC **M**ove, moves the cell pointer to the end of the paragraph, and presses Enter. Remember that the {END}{UP} combination moves the cell pointer to the beginning of the paragraph, as {END}{DOWN} moves the cell pointer to the end of the paragraph. Note the extra {DOWN} in the macro. This instruction highlights the line after the paragraph, so that you do not have spacing problems after the move.

To invoke the paragraph-moving macro, press Alt-M with the cell pointer placed anywhere in the paragraph except on the first character. The macro executes until it reaches the **Move TO where?** prompt. At this point, you should move the cell pointer to the location in your document to which you want the paragraph moved. Finally, press Enter to complete the move operation.

The Paragraph-Erasing Macro

Although Symphony Release 2.2 has accelerator keys for erasing words, lines, and parts of lines, you may want to create macros for deleting other blocks of text. The \e macro erases a paragraph. The macro is as follows:

{END}{UP}{ERASE}

{END}{DOWN 2}~

Reminder:

Before invoking the macro, make sure that the cell pointer is anywhere in the paragraph except the first character.

The macro moves the cell pointer to the beginning of the paragraph, presses Erase, highlights to the end of the paragraph, and presses Enter. Before invoking the macro, make sure that the cell pointer is anywhere in the paragraph except the first character. When executing this macro, you may get a syntax error message. The message is faulty, as the macro clearly works when executed manually.

This macro is very similar to the one that moves a paragraph macro. The erasing macro simply substitutes {ERASE} for {MENU}m; the erasing macro is also concluded under macro control by the final tilde. However, the down-arrow keystroke that moves to the end of the paragraph and the second down-arrow keystroke that moves to the line after the paragraph, are merged into one pair of braces (for example, {DOWN 2}).

The Memo Macro

The memo macro (MEMO) enters the constant headings (TO:, FROM:, and so on) of a memo and then pauses for you to enter the variable information. That macro is as follows:

MEMO{CENTER}~~~~

DATE:{TAB}{?}~

TO:{TAB}{TAB}{?}~

FROM:{TAB}{?}~

SUBJECT:{TAB}{?}~~~

The MEMO macro types and centers the word **MEMO**, presses Enter four times to get blank lines, enters **DATE:**, presses Tab, pauses for you to type, and presses Enter. These steps are repeated for each memo heading line. You may need to change this macro to conform to your company's memo format. If the memos are always from the same person, you can fill in the name next to FROM: instead of pausing the macro at that point.

Execute this macro by pressing User (F7) and entering **MEMO**.

The Date-Typing Macro

The \d in figure 21.14 automatically types the current date wherever the cursor is positioned. First, it computes the date as a string function based on the function @NOW. Next, it presses the return key three times and enters the sheet environment. In that environment, it uses the **R**ange **V**alues command to enter the value of DATE into the current cursor location; then, it moves the cursor down two rows. Finally, it switches back to the DOC mode from the SHEET environment. The macro is as follows:

MONTH	@CHOOSE(@MONTH(@NOW)-1,"January",...,"December")
DATE	+MONTH&" "&@STRING(@DAY(@NOW),0)&", "&... ...@STRING((1900+@YEAR(@NOW)),0)
\d	~~~{TYPE}s {MENU}rvdate~~{DOWN 2} {SWITCH}

Two formulas are used to compute the date. The first one with a range name of MONTH uses an @CHOOSE function to translate a number from 1 through 12 based on @NOW to a month name (for example, February). The second formula concatenates the month name with day and the year. These values are first derived from @NOW and then converted to labels with the @STRING function.

The Letter-Closing Macro

The second macro in figure 21.14 types the close of a letter for its user. The next to the last line of this macro needs to be updated with the name of the person signing the letter. The macro is as follows:

```
\c      ~~~~{MENU}fst47~q
        {MENU}fc~rq
        {TAB}Sincerely yours,~~~~
        {TAB}
        Fname Lname~
        {MENU}p
```

The macro starts by setting a default tab of 47. This has the effect of placing the first letter after a tab in the 48th position on a line. The next macro line creates a format line based on this new default format line; the new format line is positioned where the cursor currently rests. The macro code in rows 16 through 18 types the close. The last line places an end-of-page marker just after the close.

Spelling Checker Macros

Once you have attached the Spelling Checker add-in, you can use either of the Spelling Checker macros shown in figure 21.15. The first one (\1) specifies the entire document for the spell-check range, and the second one (\2) checks only the current word.

The \1 macro is as follows:

```
\1      {MENU}vg
        {ESCAPE}
        {HOME}{TAB}{END}{HOME}~
```

The \1 macro selects **V**erify **G**o from the DOC menu, presses Esc to unanchor, moves the cell pointer to the beginning of the document, re-anchors with Tab, highlights to the end of the document, and presses Enter. The \2 macro is as follows:

```
\2      {MENU}vg ~
```

Reminder:

You will not see the correction menu if Spelling Checker finds no misspelled words.

The second Spelling Checker macro selects DOC **V**erify **G**o, presses the space bar to highlight the word, and presses Enter. This macro assumes that the cell pointer is at the beginning of the word you want to check and that a space follows the word. You execute these two macros with the User key. For example, to invoke the first macro, press User (F7) and then press F1. After the macro has executed, the correction menu displays, and you can correct the spelling errors in the document. (***Note:*** You will not see the correction menu if Spelling Checker finds no misspelled words.)

Creating Macros in the GRAPH Environment

Some useful macros for the GRAPH environment are listed in figure 21.16. These examples include macros to view a graph, select and view one of many graphs, and print a graph.

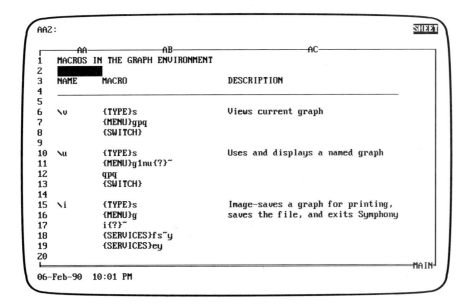

Fig. 21.16.
Sample macros in the GRAPH environment.

The Graph-Preview Macro

Unlike 1-2-3, Symphony does not have a Graph function key that displays the current graph. In Symphony, you have to go to the menu—unless you create the \v macro as follows:

```
{TYPE}s
{MENU}gpq
{SWITCH}
```

This preview macro changes the window type to SHEET, selects the **G**raph **P**review command, exits the Graph menu with **Q**uit, and switches window type.

You can execute the macro in any window type, because the first line begins by changing to a SHEET window. The last instruction in the macro switches you back to the window type you were in before executing the macro.

The macro pauses when the graph is displayed because this pause is an inherent part of the **P**review command. Press any key to continue macro execution.

The Choose-a-Graph Macro

When you have multiple graphs in a file, each graph has a name, and many keystrokes are required to load the graph settings and then look at the graph. The \u macro displays the list of graph names so that you can select the one you want, and then displays that graph. The macro is as follows:

{TYPE}s

{MENU}g1nu{?}~

qpq

{SWITCH}

This macro changes the window type to SHEET, selects **G**raph **1**st-**S**ettings **N**ame **U**se, pauses to let you highlight the graph name, and presses Enter. Then the macro selects **Q**uit to exit the **S**ettings menu, **P**reviews the graph, **Q**uits the Graph menu, and switches window type.

The choose-a-graph macro is similar to the graph preview macro, except that the choosing macro enables you to select the graph before previewing. Like the preview macro, this macro pauses when the graph is displayed. Press any key, and the macro continues to execute.

The Graph-Printing Macro

To print a graph, you need to save both the graph and the file and then exit Symphony. Use the \i macro when you have only one graph to print. The macro is as follows:

{TYPE}s

{MENU}gp

i{?}~

{SERVICES}fs~y

{SERVICES}ey

The \i macro changes the window type to SHEET, selects **G**raph **P**review, selects **I**mage-Save, pauses to let you enter a file name, and presses Enter. Then the macro selects SERVICES **F**ile **S**ave, presses Enter to keep the same name, selects **Y**es to replace, and selects SERVICES **E**xit **Y**es to leave Symphony.

The macro previews the graph so that you can make sure it is the one you want to print (press Ctrl-Break and Esc if you see the wrong graph). The macro assumes that you have previously saved the worksheet file. Also, this macro requires that you give the graph file a new name when you **I**mage-Save. If you do not, the macro will not work.

Reminder:
When you Image-Save, give the graph file a new name or the macro will not work.

Making Macros in the COMM Environment

Several simple COMM macros are listed in figure 21.17. These macros automatically dial a number in the worksheet, disconnect a call, log into a remote computer, and capture data to a printer during a communications session.

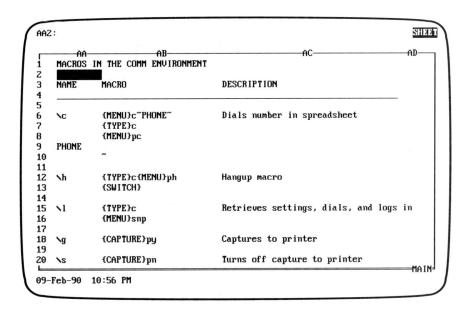

Fig. 21.17.

Sample macros for the COMM environment.

The Auto-Dialing Macro

The COMM environment does not limit you to dialing other computers. If you have a modem that can auto-dial, you can build a simple macro that dials a phone number in a worksheet cell. The \c macro is useful if you have a phone list in a spreadsheet or database. You must be in a SHEET window with the cell pointer on the number you want to dial before invoking this macro. The macro is as follows:

Reminder:
You must be in a SHEET window with the cell pointer on a number you want to dial before invoking the Auto-Dialing macro.

```
\c        {MENU}c~PHONE~
          {TYPE}c
          {MENU}pc
PHONE
          ~
```

This macro selects **C**opy from the SHEET menu, presses Enter to copy from the current cell, enters **PHONE** as the range name to copy to, changes the window type to COMM, selects **P**hone **C**all, and presses Enter to dial the number. Notice the empty cell in the macro next to the word PHONE. This cell is the cell to which the phone number is copied. You should use the **R**ange **N**ame command to name this cell PHONE.

The auto-dialing macro is different from the other macros you have learned so far, because it is dynamic; a different phone number is copied into PHONE each time you invoke the macro.

If you use this macro to dial a person, you can pick up the phone as soon as the party answers. You can use the following hangup macro when you want to disconnect the call.

The Hangup Macro

You can think of the hangup macro as a companion to the auto-dialing macro. You can use the \h macro to disconnect any call, whether the call was placed to another person or to a remote computer. That macro is as follows:

    {TYPE}c{MENU}ph
    {SWITCH}

The macro changes to a COMM window type, selects **P**hone **H**angup from the COMM menu, and then switches back to the last environment you were in.

The Log-in Macro

Symphony's **P**hone-and-Log-in command retrieves a COMM **S**ettings sheet, dials the number, and logs into a remote computer. Even though this single command combines three separate commands, it still takes six keystrokes to execute. The \l macro executes in two. The macro is as follows:

    {TYPE}c
    {MENU}snp

This compact macro first changes the window type to COMM, then selects **S**ettings **N**ame **P**hone-and-Login. The macro stops at the point where you are asked to enter a communications configuration file name. You can select the name, and then the macro will dial the number and log in for you.

The Capture Macro

When logged onto a remote computer, you may want to print what appears on your screen so that you have a hard-copy record of your communications session. Most times, though, you do not want to print everything; you want to turn the printing on when important information displays and turn it off when menus and other unimportant messages appear. You can control printing with the \g and \s macros. Those macros are as follows:

> \g{CAPTURE}py

This simple macro presses the **C**apture key and selects **P**rinter **Y**es.

> \s{CAPTURE}pn

Conversely, the \s macro presses the **C**apture key and selects **P**rinter **N**o.

If you want to capture the data to a spreadsheet **R**ange rather than to the **P**rinter, substitute *r* for *p* in the two previous macros.

Creating Macros for the FORM Environment

Simple macros to use in the FORM environment are listed in figure 21.18. These macros speed up searching and sorting in a FORM window.

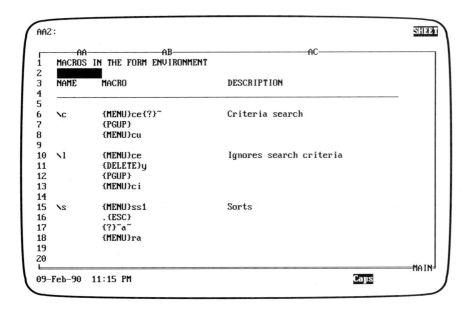

Fig. 21.18.
Sample macros for the FORM environment.

The Search Macro

To find records in a FORM window, you must complete a criterion record and instruct Symphony to use this criteria. The \c macro performs these commands automatically. That macro is as follows:

{MENU}ce{?}~

{PGUP}

{MENU}cu

First, the macro selects **Criteria Edit** from the FORM menu and pauses for you to enter criteria. Then the macro returns to the database and selects **Criteria Use.**

When the criterion record displays and the macro pauses, use only the arrow keys to move between fields. If you press Enter, the macro continues executing before you have a chance to fill in the criteria.

After invoking this macro, you can look at only the records that satisfy the specified criteria. To see all the database records again, use the \i macro to **I**gnore the criteria. Create the macro as follows:

{MENU}ce

{DELETE}y

{PGUP}

{MENU}ci

This macro selects **Criteria Edit** from the FORM menu, presses Del, confirms the deletion with **Y**es, returns to the database, and selects **Criteria Ignore.**

Note that the \i macro deletes the criterion record. Although this step is not mandatory, it is a good idea, because the criteria are *not* ignored during printing.

The Sort Macro

Sorting requires two steps in Symphony. First, you specify the field by which you want to sort. Second, you perform the sort. The \s macro performs both steps. The macro is as follows:

{MENU}ss1

'.{ESC}

{?}~a~

{MENU}ra

The sort macro selects **Settings Sort-Keys 1**st-Key from the FORM menu, presses period then Esc, and pauses to let you point to the sort field. Then the macro specifies **A**scending order and selects **R**ecord-Sort **A**ll.

Reminder:

To determine whether a range is anchored, place a period before {ESC} in the macro.

The second line of this macro contains a trick that is useful when you do not know whether a range is anchored. You cannot just use the Esc key, because if the range is not anchored, Esc cancels the command. But if you place a period before {ESC} in the macro, you can ensure that the range is indeed anchored before you press Esc to unanchor.

Making The Macro Library Manager

With Symphony Release 1.1 and later releases, you get an add-in application called the Macro Library Manager. With this add-in, if you have macros that you use in more than one worksheet, you do not need to create them in every worksheet. The Macro Library Manager enables you to create macros that are stored in a separate part of working memory (RAM) and can be invoked from any worksheet. Symphony saves the macros both to memory and to a disk file with an MLB file extension. This way the macros are ready for you to invoke and also are saved permanently.

Symphony provides a different set of commands to manage these libraries of macros. After you create and debug the macros, you save the range containing the macros in a macro library, where they sit ready to be invoked from any worksheet. You can load a macro into memory and can retrieve a worksheet and invoke the macro. When you retrieve another worksheet, it does not wipe out the macro in that separate area of memory (nicknamed hyperspace). When you save a worksheet range, however, Symphony erases the macro from the worksheet so that you can clear out any commonly used macros from any worksheet.

Accessing the Macro Library Manager

Because the Macro Library Manager is an add-in application, you must attach it before you can use it. Once the Macro Library Manager is attached, the SERVICES menu provides a new choice: **M**acros. Selecting that option brings up the Macro Library Manager commands. To attach the Manager, take the following steps:

1. Press SERVICES and select **A**pplication from the menu.

2. Select **A**ttach and then move the cell pointer to MACROMGR.APP to select it. (If you have a two floppy drive system, be sure that the Help and Tutorial disk [5.25-inch], or the Program, Help, and Tutorial disk [3.5-inch], which contains the APP files, is in drive A.)

From then on, you just press SERVICES **M**acros whenever you need to access the Macro Library Manager menu.

Creating a Macro Library in Hyperspace

When you create a macro library, Symphony moves a range out of your worksheet and stores it in two places: RAM memory and a permanent disk file. The macro range can consist of any number of macros, and each library can contain up to 16,376 cells.

- To save a range to a macro library, you call up the SERVICES menu and select **M**acros and then **S**ave. Symphony prompts you for a file name under which to store the library, and a worksheet range to be stored. At this point you also can add a password to the library file. In its usual "last chance to back out" style, Symphony informs you whether the library already exists on disk or in memory and asks whether you want to go ahead with the operation. If you respond **Y**es, Symphony erases from the worksheet the range and any range names contained in it and saves the new range to RAM (hyperspace) and to a disk file (for permanent storage). Symphony automatically adds the file extension MLB to the file name you specify.

Ordinarily, however, when you are not creating or modifying the macro, you do not need or want to have it in the worksheet before putting it into hyperspace. You use the **M**acros **L**oad command, which copies the macro library directly from disk to memory.

Invoking Macros from the Library

The macros contained in a library are callable from any worksheet even though you cannot "see" them. The big advantage, of course, is that you do not have to store multipurpose macros separately in every worksheet in which you need them.

Once a library is stored in memory (hyperspace), you call up a macro in the usual way. A macro stored in a pass-protected library does not require that you use the password to invoke the macro. The password protection is used only to prevent any unauthorized user from editing the macro.

Reminder:

Avoid using the same range name for macros in different libraries.

If you try executing a macro whose range name is in your active worksheet and in one or more libraries, Symphony looks to the current worksheet first, and then to the libraries in the order in which they were loaded into memory. That order is the same order that appears in the control panel when you select **M**acros **E**dit, **R**emove, or **N**ame-List. The program runs the first macro found with the selected name. For that reason, you should avoid using the same range name for macros in different libraries. Figure 21.19 shows the flow of macro libraries to and from hyperspace, disk, and worksheet.

If you have forgotten what range names are contained in a library in memory, you can display a list of the names with the **M**acros **N**ame-List command. This command is similar to the SHEET window's **R**ange **N**ame **T**able command except that only the range names are listed with **N**ame-List. No cell range definitions are listed, because the library has no cell coordinates. After you indicate which library in memory you want, Symphony prompts you for a location in the worksheet to place the table. The table is simply a one-column listing of all the range names associated with that library.

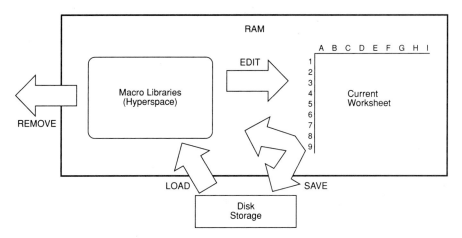

Fig. 21.19.
The flow of macro libraries.

Modifying a Library

When you need to modify or just look at a macro in a library, you must bring the library into your active worksheet. You do that with the **M**acros **E**dit command, which prompts you for the name of a library to copy from memory into the worksheet. You cannot bring a library directly from disk into the worksheet; the library must be loaded into memory first. If the library file is password-protected, Symphony prompts you for the password.

You may have ranges with the same names in the worksheet and in the library you are bringing in. Symphony has a way of resolving that conflict. The program prompts you to **I**gnore (and drop) any library range names that conflict with worksheet range names or to **O**verwrite the worksheet range name definitions with those from the incoming library. Again, the safe practice is to avoid the problem by naming your range names uniquely.

Symphony prompts you for a location in the worksheet to place the entire library. You will need an empty range of cells because Symphony overwrites whatever is there. Remember that Symphony copies the entire library. You cannot select only certain macros or ranges to load.

Reminder:
Symphony copies the entire library. You cannot select only certain macros or ranges to load.

Removing a Macro

After you edit and test a macro library again, you may want to save the range back into a library, either the one from which it came or a new one. Use the **M**acros **S**ave command to remove the range from the worksheet again.

At times, you may want to remove a library from memory entirely, perhaps to free up some memory for a larger worksheet or for other libraries. Symphony provides a **M**acros **R**emove command for that purpose. Note that this command does not erase the library file from the disk. To erase an MLB disk file containing a macro library, use the normal SERVICES **F**ile **E**rase command, which now includes an additional option of **M**acro-Library files.

Using Range Names and Cell Coordinates

You must observe three important rules when creating and working with macro libraries:

1. Macro statements that use any worksheet menu commands (such as **C**opy, **M**ove, and so on) cannot contain library range names. The statements must always refer to cells in the worksheet only. Look at the following statements contained in a library:

COPY_OUT	{GOTO}D1~{MENU}cOUT~~
COPY_IN	{GOTO}E1~{MENU}cIN~~
STATE_OUT	{GOTO}D3~+OUT~
STATE_IN	{GOTO}E3~+IN~
IN	999

   If the cell named OUT is in the current worksheet, and the cell named IN is only in the library but not in the worksheet, the COPY_OUT and STATE_OUT macros would work correctly, but COPY_IN and STATE_IN would not. They would stumble over the range name IN.

2. Formulas should not cut across libraries or between a library and the worksheet. Range names or cell references in a formula in a library must refer to that library. Otherwise, the formulas evaluate as meaningless. Similarly, any cell references in a worksheet formula must not refer to cells or ranges in a library. Look at the following macros that are contained in a macro library; both FORMULA_IN and FORMULA_OUT contain formulas (+IN and +OUT, respectively), and the cell named IN contains the label '{SERVICES}FB:

FORMULA_IN	{SERVICES}FB
FORMULA_OUT	{SERVICES}FB
IN	{SERVICES}FB

   Again, the cell named OUT is in the worksheet and contains the label '{SERVICES}FB. FORMULA_IN works fine because the cell it refers to (IN) is contained in the same library. FORMULA_OUT does nothing; it is a formula referring to a cell in the worksheet, so the formula is blank in the macro library.

3. Command language statements can refer to cells in another library or in the worksheet. For example, {LET E2,IN} or {MENUBRANCH MENU1} work whether IN and MENU1 are range names in a library or in a worksheet.

Using Macro Libraries for @Base and Allways

The @Base and Allways applications, which are standard with Symphony 2.2, add powerful new features. However, this additional capability is gained at the expense of greater memory demands. The file memory requirements of @Base and Allways are so great that you cannot run both applications at once.

Furthermore, Allways can require even greater memory as it develops images to send to the printer. Therefore, another application, such as MACROMGR.APP, need not cause problems at the time Allways is attached, but it may represent a drain on memory resources before a Symphony session with the Allways add-in concludes. For these reasons, you may want to remove some other applications from memory when running Allways.

Attaching the @Base application is especially involved because three or four add-in files need to be attached to run it. The number of add-ins needed for @Base depends on how much capability you want to access. Also, when detaching the @Base environment only two to three add-in files can be detached. Because the process is relatively involved to perform manually and not straightforward to program, it is displayed in figure 21.20.

The macro library application presented in this section automatically loads the Macro Library Manager if it is not already in memory. Upon your command, it will attach or detach either the @Base or Allways add-ins.

The master control for the whole application is in an auto-loading worksheet named B&AINOUT.WR1. This worksheet is shown in figure 21.21. Five macros are included in this worksheet—one of which is an auto-executing macro (AUTO).

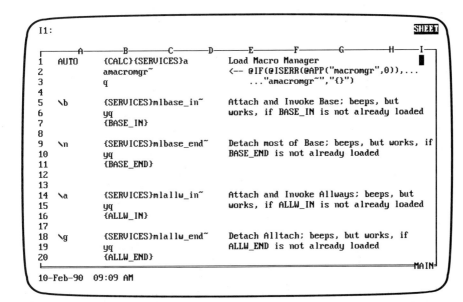

Fig. 21.20.
Macros to attach and detach @Base and Allways applications.

Fig. 21.21.

Master control macros for @Base and Allways.

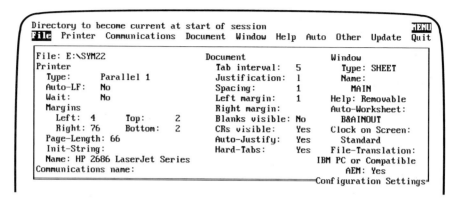

```
Directory to become current at start of session                        MENU
File  Printer  Communications  Document  Window  Help  Auto  Other  Update  Quit

File: E:\SYM22                    Document              Window
Printer                            Tab interval:    5     Type: SHEET
  Type:       Parallel 1           Justification:   1     Name:
  Auto-LF:    No                   Spacing:         1       MAIN
  Wait:       No                   Left margin:     1     Help: Removable
  Margins                          Right margin:          Auto-Worksheet:
    Left:   4       Top:     2     Blanks visible: No       B&AINOUT
    Right: 76       Bottom:  2     CRs visible:    Yes    Clock on Screen:
  Page-Length: 66                  Auto-Justify:   Yes      Standard
  Init-String:                     Hard-Tabs:      Yes    File-Translation:
  Name: HP 2686 LaserJet Series                           IBM PC or Compatible
Communications name:                                        AEM: Yes
                                                        Configuration Settings
```

Figure 21.21 shows the Symphony **C**onfigurations **S**ettings sheet, which causes the master control worksheet to be loaded automatically. Notice in the third column of **S**ettings that B&AINOUT is entered under **A**uto-Worksheet; this causes the worksheet to load automatically at the start of a Symphony session. As shown by the first entry in the left column of the **C**onfiguration **S**ettings, the default directory is E:\SYM22. Because no path is set under the **A**uto-Worksheet setting, the auto-loading worksheet must be in E:\SYM22.

Although B&AINOUT.WR1 loads automatically at the start of a Symphony session, the application also is meant to be retrieved at any time during a session. By retrieving the application, you can attach or detach the @Base and Allways add-ins during a session.

In figure 21.20, the @IF in the second line of the AUTO macro is either a null macro command ({}) or a sequence of keystrokes to attach MACROMGR.APP. The {CALC} command in the first line of AUTO evaluates the @IF. This technique ensures that the Macro Library Manager is available, but avoids an error that would occur if you tried to attach it when it is already in memory.

The @IF function's representation depends on two other nested functions. The inner function of the pair is *@APP("macromgr",0)*. Th *@APP* function evaluates to **0** if the Macro Library Manager is attached, else it is ERR. The outer function of the nested pair (*@ISERR* checks if @APP evaluates to ERR. When the inner function is ERR, the outer function is **1**, otherwise it is **0**.

While each of the four other macros in B&AINOUT have a distinct function, they all have the same structure. The macros load BASE_IN.MLB, BASE_END.MLB, ALLW_IN.MLB, and ALLW_END.MLB. These macro library files contain a single macro with the same name as the file. Because the macros in B&AINOUT parallel each other, you can understand all of them by discussing any one of them.

The \b macro loads BASE_IN.MLB into hyperspace in its first and second lines. The third line of \b executes a subroutine call to a macro in hyperspace named BASE_IN.

Figure 21.22 shows, for economy of space, the four macro libraries in a single worksheet (in the application, each macro is in a separate worksheet file).

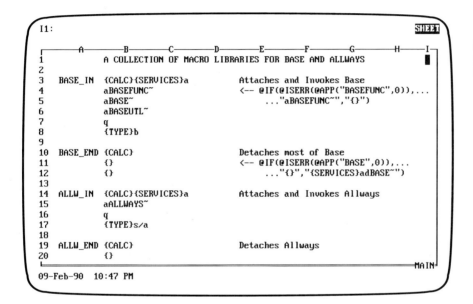

Fig. 21.22.
Four macro libraries.

All these macro libraries use the same @IF technique described for the AUTO macro of B&AINOUT. In the case of the BASE_IN macro, we attach three add-in files: BASEFUNC, BASE, and BASEUTL. After the files are attached, the macro starts the BASE add-in environment by entering **b** in response to the TYPE key name list.

Because function macro libraries cannot be detached in a Symphony session, only two of the @Base add-in files can be detached (BASE.APP and BASEUTL.APP). The macro BASE_END detaches the two files. Figure 21.22 shows two null commands for this macro, but the comment with the @IF formula to the side shows that the line can change if BASE and BASEUTL are already loaded.

The ALLW_IN and ALLW_END have a parallel structure to BASE_IN and BASE_END. However, Allways macros manipulate a single add-in file (ALLWAYS.APP).

This Macro Library application can be expanded easily to permit the detaching of the Macro Library Manager. Such an addition offers the Allways add-in more space in which to develop files for the printer. You will not be able to run macros from memory after detaching MACROMGR.APP, but Allways will continue to function.

Chapter Summary

By making it a practice to create macros for your most frequent Symphony tasks, you save time and increase efficiency. Think of the operations you perform most often, jot down the keystrokes needed to complete each operation, and begin your own macro library. As you become experienced in creating and using keyboard macros, begin experimenting with the Command Language. Turn to Chapter 22 and learn about Symphony's Command Language.

22

Introducing the Command Language

In addition to keyboard macro capabilities, Symphony contains a powerful set of commands offering many of the ingredients of a full-featured programming language. This set of commands is called the *Symphony Command Language*. With the Command Language, you can customize and automate Symphony for your worksheet applications.

In the preceding chapter, you learned how to automate keystrokes to save precious time by streamlining work functions. This chapter explains the various Command Language commands you can use to perform a variety of programming tasks. This chapter is not designed to teach programming theory and concepts, but rather to introduce you to the capabilities of programming with the Command Language.

If you have a burning desire to try your hand at programming, or you want to become your company's Symphony expert (creating models to amaze every department), or you are interested in developing template models to distribute on the open market, you should begin by reading this chapter.

Why Use the Command Language?

Programs created with the Command Language give you added control and flexibility in the use of your Symphony files. With the Command Language, you control such tasks as accepting input from the keyboard during a program, performing conditional tests, repeatedly performing a sequence of commands, and creating user-defined command menus.

715

Reminder:

Use the Command Language as a full-featured programming language to develop custom worksheets.

You can use the Command Language as a full-featured programming language to develop custom worksheets for specific business applications. For example, by developing Command Language programs that teach users exactly how to enter and change data on a worksheet, you can ensure that data is entered correctly. With this type of program, novice users of an application do not have to be familiar with all the Symphony commands and operations.

Using the Command Language is nothing mysterious. After learning the concepts and the parts of the Command Language discussed in this chapter, you'll be ready to develop programs that do the following:

❏ Create menu-driven spreadsheet and database models

❏ Accept and control input from a user

❏ Manipulate data within and between files

❏ Execute tasks a predetermined number of times

❏ Control program flow

❏ Set up and print multiple reports

❏ Make intelligent decisions based on user input

❏ Execute multiple programs based on decisions made within programs

As you become more experienced with the Command Language, you can take advantage of its full power to do these tasks:

❏ Disengage or redefine the function keys

❏ Develop a complete business system—from order entry to inventory control to accounting

❏ Operate Symphony as a disk-based database system—limiting the size and speed of the file operation only to the size and speed of the hard disk

If you want to take Symphony to its practical limits, the Command Language is the proper vehicle, and your creativity can be the necessary fuel.

What Is the Command Language?

Reminder:

Command Language commands can be used within Command Language programs and keyboard macros.

The Symphony Command Language is a set of more than 40 invisible commands. These commands are called *invisible* because, unlike the command instructions you invoke through the Symphony menu and function keys, the Command Language commands cannot be invoked from the keyboard. You can use these commands only within Command Language programs or keyboard macros. The terms *program* and *macro* are used interchangeably throughout this chapter

The Command Language program in figure 22.1 is an example of the use of the Command Language.

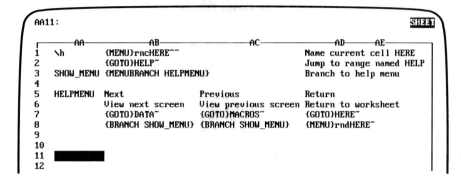

Fig. 22.1.
*Command
Language program
using
MENUBRANCH
and BRANCH.*

With commands such as MENUBRANCH and BRANCH, you can create custom menus to assist and prompt a user. The program in figure 22.1 begins by creating a range name wherever the user has positioned the cell pointer before invoking the program. The second line displays a custom help screen. The third line uses the MENUBRANCH command to display a menu with three options: Next (select the next help screen), Previous (select the previous help screen), or Return (return to the original cell-pointer position in the worksheet). The BRANCH command in the last line of the first two menu options causes the program to redisplay the menu after the user has selected either the next or the previous help screen.

As you read this chapter, you learn about the commands for accepting input, for program control, for decision-making operations, for data manipulation, for program enhancement, and for file manipulation.

The Elements of Command Language Programs

The commands discussed in this chapter are used most often with the keyboard macros discussed in Chapter 21. In the examples that follow, you see how to use macros with the Command Language to produce complete, efficient programs that take Symphony's macro capability far beyond simply automating keystrokes.

Command Language programs can contain the Command Language commands and all the elements that can be included in macros. Programs can include the following:

❏ Keystrokes used for selecting Symphony commands (for example, {MENU}fc0)

❏ Range names and cell addresses

Reminder:
*Command
Language pro-
grams can contain
Command
Language com-
mands and all the
macro elements.*

❏ Keywords for moving the cell pointer (see Chapter 21 for a list of keywords)

❏ Keywords for function keys (see Chapter 21)

❏ Keywords for editing (see Chapter 21)

❏ Keywords for accelerator keys (see Chapter 21)

❏ Key representation for Enter: ~

❏ Command Language commands

The Syntax of the Command Language

Reminder:

Command Language commands are represented in curly braces.

Like the keywords used in macros, all commands in the Command Language are enclosed in braces. Just as you represent the right-arrow key in a macro as {RIGHT}, you enclose a command such as QUIT in braces: {QUIT}.

Many commands, however, require additional arguments within the braces. The arguments that follow commands have a syntax similar to the grammar used in Symphony @functions. The general format of commands that require arguments is as follows:

{COMMAND *argument1,argument2,...,argumentN*}

An argument can consist of numbers, strings, cell addresses, range names, formulas, and @functions.

The command and its arguments are separated by a space; for most commands, arguments are separated by commas (with no spaces). As you study the syntax for the specific commands described in this chapter, keep in mind the importance of following the conventions for spacing and punctuation. For example, when you use the BRANCH command to transfer program control to a specific location in the program, you must follow the word BRANCH with the cell address or range name indicating where the program should branch.

The Methods of Working with Command Language Programs

With Command Language programs, as with macros, you must keep several considerations in mind to ensure that your programs are efficient and error free. You begin by defining which actions you want the program to perform and determining the sequence of actions. Then you develop the program, test it, and practically always debug it.

If you have created keyboard macros, you have a head start toward creating Command Language programs, which share many of the conventions used in keyboard macros. If you haven't experimented with Symphony macros, you should do so before trying to develop Command Language programs. You also may want to review Chapter 21's detailed discussions of creating, using, and debugging macros, because many of the concepts are the same in Command Language programs.

Like keyboard macros, Command Language programs should be carefully planned and positioned on the worksheet. Create a window for your Command Language programs, specifying a restrict range so that changes to the worksheet do not affect the programs.

You enter Command Language programs just as you enter macros—as text cells. You must precede with a label prefix any line that begins with a nontext character such as /, \, (, +, and – so that Symphony does not interpret the characters that follow as numbers or commands.

Reminder:
Precede with a label prefix any line in a Command Language program that begins with a nontext character.

After you decide where to locate the program and have begun to enter program lines, keep several considerations in mind.

First, remember to document Command Language programs as you document macros—to the right of each program line. Because Command Language programs are usually more complex than macros, documenting each line is essential. A documented program is easier to debug and change than an undocumented one.

Note: Most of the programs shown in this chapter are fully explained in the text and therefore do not include documentation within the figures. This practice conserves space in the figures and also allows the presentation of advanced programs.

Second, remember to name Command Language programs in the same way you name macros. Refer to Chapter 21's section on "Naming Macros" for a review of the three types of macro names. Enter the program name in the cell directly to the left of the program's first line. Use Symphony's SHEET **R**ange **N**ame **L**abels **R**ight command to name the Command Language program. If you want the program to be invoked automatically as soon as you open the worksheet file, specify the macro as an autoexecuting macro with the SERVICES **S**ettings **A**uto-Execute command.

After you develop and start to run your program, you almost certainly will have to debug it. Like macros, Command Language programs are subject to such problems as missing tildes (~), misspelled keywords, or the use of cell addresses that remain absolute in the program but have changed in a worksheet application. You can solve the cell-address problem by using range names in place of cell addresses wherever possible.

To debug Command Language programs, use Symphony's STEP mode as you do for simple keyboard macros. Before you execute the program, press Step (Alt-F7) to invoke STEP mode. Then execute your Command Language program. Press any key or the space bar to activate each operation in the program. When you discover an error, press Step (Alt-F7) again to turn off STEP mode, press Esc, and edit the program.

The Command Language Commands

Using the power of the program's Command Language, you can make Symphony applications easier to use; you can enhance the features of Symphony's regular commands; and you can customize Symphony for special worksheet applications. The following sections group the Command Language commands into six categories: accepting input, program control, decision-making operations, data manipulation, program enhancement, and file manipulation.

Commands for Accepting Input

The {?}, GET, GETLABEL, GETNUMBER, and LOOK commands provide for all possible types of input into a Symphony worksheet (see table 22.1). You also can use these commands to provide the user with a friendlier interface than that of Symphony's standard commands and operations. For example, you can use these commands to create prompts that help the user enter data more easily and quickly. These commands also make it easy to perform simple validity checks on the input before storing it in the worksheet.

Table 22.1
Commands for Accepting Input

Command	Description
{?}	Accepts any type of input
{GET}	Places the first character from the DOS type-ahead buffer into *location*; removes the character from the buffer
{GETLABEL}	Accepts a label into *location*
{GETNUMBER}	Accepts a number into *location*
{LOOK}	Places the first character from the DOS type-ahead buffer into *location*; leaves the character in the buffer

The {?} Command

The {?} command causes the program to pause while you enter any type of information. During the pause, no prompt is displayed in the control panel. You can move the cell pointer to direct the location of the input. The program continues executing after you press Enter. The format for the {?} command is as follows:

{?}

For example, the following one-line program combines macro commands and a Command Language command to create a file-retrieve program:

{SERVICES}fr{MENU}{?}

This program displays all files in the current drive and then pauses to accept input from you. In this instance, you can either type the name of a viewed file or move the cell pointer to a file name and press Enter.

The GET Command

The GET command places a single keystroke from the DOS type-ahead buffer into a target cell. Because the keystroke is intercepted before it reaches the Symphony processor, it can be assigned nonstandard functions. A keystroke retrieved with the GET command removes the keystroke from the type-ahead buffer.

The GET command does not necessarily pause a macro like the {?} command. If one or more keystrokes are already in the type-ahead buffer, the command retrieves the first keystroke. If no keystrokes are in the buffer, the GET command pauses macro operation. However, any single keystroke is enough to continue the macro. The format for the GET command is as follows:

Reminder:
GET intercepts keystrokes from the DOS type-ahead buffer before they reach the Symphony processor.

{GET *location*}

This command accepts a single keystroke into the range defined by *location*. In the example shown in figure 22.2, the GET statement traps two individual keystrokes; all other keystrokes are ignored (or rather, the program beeps at them and briefly displays a message stating what the two appropriate keystrokes are).

When the macro starts at \k in cell B9, it expects the cursor to be resting in one of the following four cells: A1, A3, A5, or A7. Presuming that no keystrokes are in the DOS type-ahead buffer, the GET command pauses until a key is pressed; that keystroke is stored in the range KEY, which is tested in cell B10. If the keystroke is an up or down arrow, the worksheet is recalculated and control is transferred to OKINPUT.

Any other keystroke causes the program to beep. This sound is followed by a message which appears briefly in the control panel. The message is displayed only briefly because it is followed immediately by an Esc keystroke representation that removes it from the control panel.

A vertical-lookup formula in OKINPUT translates the up-arrow or down-arrow keystroke so that the cursor remains in one of the four legitimate cells. The initial @CELLPOINTER argument of the @VLOOKUP function always matches one of the values in ROW (the range E3..E6). If the keystroke is an up arrow, the lookup is in column D; otherwise it is in column F.

Fig. 22.2.

Using the GET command with a vertical rolling-bar menu.

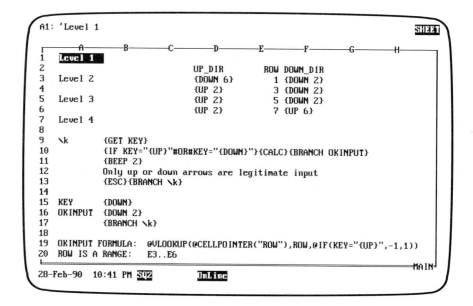

```
A1: 'Level 1                                                            SHEET
  A          B          C          D          E          F          G      H
1  Level 1
2                                          UP_DIR          ROW DOWN_DIR
3  Level 2                                 {DOWN 6}          1 {DOWN 2}
4                                          {UP 2}            3 {DOWN 2}
5  Level 3                                 {UP 2}            5 {DOWN 2}
6                                          {UP 2}            7 {UP 6}
7  Level 4
8
9  \k         {GET KEY}
10            {IF KEY="{UP}"#OR#KEY="{DOWN}"}{CALC}{BRANCH OKINPUT}
11            {BEEP 2}
12            Only up or down arrows are legitimate input
13            {ESC}{BRANCH \k}
14
15 KEY        {DOWN}
16 OKINPUT    {DOWN 2}
17            {BRANCH \k}
18
19 OKINPUT FORMULA:   @VLOOKUP(@CELLPOINTER("ROW"),ROW,@IF(KEY="{UP}",-1,1))
20 ROW IS A RANGE:    E3..E6
                                                                        MAIN
28-Feb-90  10:41 PM  SCZ          InLine
```

The OKINPUT formula shows how you can use GET to assign nonstandard actions to a keystroke. For example, the up-arrow key causes the cursor to move up two cells—not just one. If the cursor is in row 1, an up-arrow keystroke causes the cursor to move *down* 6 cells.

Cue:

Use GET to pause a macro so that the user can read a message.

Figure 22.3 shows a simple use of the GET command that improves on the basic macro shown in figure 22.2. In this version of the macro, the GET command in B14 pauses the macro after the error message displays in the control panel. Any keystroke causes the message to disappear. Now, the user can view the message in the control panel and press a key when finished reading it. This macro assumes that the DOS type-ahead buffer is empty or contains at most a single keystroke when the macro starts. If two or more keystrokes are in the buffer, the error message does not remain on-screen until the user presses a key to clear it.

Another use of GET is shown in figure 22.4. Suppose that you are writing an inventory program and want to prompt the user to make a one-keystroke choice to enter data on premium-quality or regular-quality widgets. Figure 22.4 shows a program you can use in such an application.

In this example, the GET command pauses the program while the user enters a single letter from the keyboard; the program then stores that entry in a cell named CODE. Notice that the program displays the user prompt in the cell named MAIN. If you want a prompt to appear in the control panel rather than in the worksheet, use the GETLABEL or GETNUMBER command.

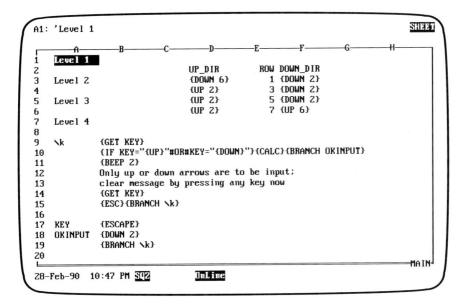

Fig. 22.3.
Using the GET command to pause for an error message.

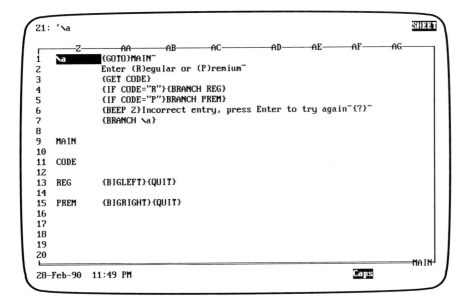

Fig. 22.4.
Using the GET command to allow one-character input.

Note: When the control panel is empty, any keystrokes you type appear in the control panel. This is how you can display a message without the GETLABEL or GETNUMBER command (see figs. 22.2 and 22.3).

The LOOK Command

The LOOK command, like the GET command, checks the DOS type-ahead buffer. However, LOOK does not pause a macro if the buffer is empty, nor does it remove a keystroke from the buffer when it copies the first keystroke in the buffer.

The general form of the command is as follows:

{LOOK *location*}

Reminder:

Use LOOK to copy the first keystroke in the DOS type-ahead buffer.

If any keys have been pressed since the type-ahead buffer was last accessed, LOOK places a representation of the first keystroke in the specified cell *location*. LOOK can be used with GET to examine a keystroke before removing it from the type-ahead buffer. The LOOK command, in conjunction with other commands, also can be used to interrupt processing until you press a key.

When LOOK is executed, it checks the type-ahead buffer and copies the first character into the indicated *location*. Thus, you can type a character at any time, and the program finds it when the LOOK command is executed. You then can test the contents of *location* with an IF statement. Because the character is not removed from the type-ahead buffer, you must make provisions to use the character or dispose of it before the program ends or needs keyboard input (use the GET or GETLABEL command to dispose of the character in the buffer).

In the program shown in figure 22.5, the LOOK statement examines the type-ahead buffer and places the first keystroke in the cell named STROKE. If no keys have been pressed, the LOOK statement blanks the cell, leaving only a label prefix. Although program execution is not halted by the LOOK command, the effect of this three-line program is that the program stops. Line 3 makes the program loop until a key is pressed, satisfying the IF condition in line 2. (For more information, see the discussions of the IF and BRANCH commands.)

Fig. 22.5.

Using the LOOK command.

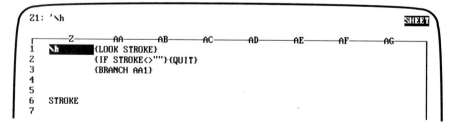

As a simple test of the LOOK command, try the example in figure 22.6. This program causes the computer to beep until you press a key. Each time LOOK is encountered, Symphony checks the keyboard buffer and copies into INTERRUPT the first character in the buffer. An IF statement checks the contents of INTERRUPT and branches accordingly. The GETLABEL command at the end of the program disposes of the keystroke that interrupted the loop.

Cue:

Use LOOK to create a loop that effectively halts a program.

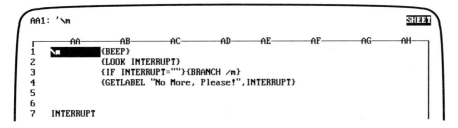

Fig. 22.6.
Using LOOK to stop a beeping program.

The LOOK command is especially helpful if you build a lengthy program to process, such as a stock-portfolio database, and you want to be able to stop processing at certain points in the program. You can use LOOK and an IF statement similar to that in figure 22.6 at several places in the program. When you press a key, the program stops the next time a LOOK is executed. If you do not touch the keyboard, the program continues processing.

Figure 22.7 shows how LOOK can be used with the GET command. Whether a keystroke generates cursor movement or not, the program branches to EMPTY?.

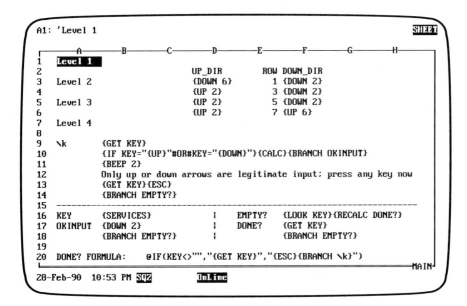

Fig. 22.7.
Using LOOK with the GET command.

The EMPTY? routine examines the type-ahead buffer just after it is accessed by a GET command. The EMPTY? routine removes remaining keystrokes in the buffer before returning control to \k for more processing. Emptying the keyboard buffer after a keystroke is processed stops a user from looping the program continuously merely by holding down a single key.

The GETLABEL Command

The GETLABEL command accepts any type of entry from the keyboard and enters it as a label. For example, you can type a telephone number without first typing a label prefix. The format for the GETLABEL command is as follows:

{GETLABEL *prompt,location*}

The specified *prompt* (which must be a string enclosed in quotation marks) is displayed in the control panel. The characters entered in response to the prompt are placed as a label in the cell specified by *location* when you press the Enter key.

In the example in figure 22.8, the GETLABEL statement displays a prompt and accepts a label date into cell AA19. The second line of the program places in cell AA20 a formula that converts the label date to a numerical date and then formats the cell to appear as a date.

Fig. 22.8.

Using GETLABEL to allow input of a label date.

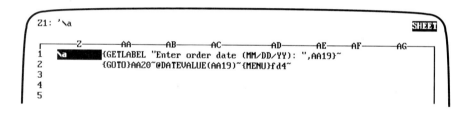

```
Z1: '\a                                                      SHEET
       -Z-------AA------AB------AC-------AD------AE----AF----AG-
  1   \a        {GETLABEL "Enter order date (MM/DD/YY): ",AA19}~
  2             {GOTO}AA20~@DATEVALUE(AA19)~{MENU}fd4~
  3
  4
  5
```

Figure 22.9 shows how to use GETLABEL with the IF, BRANCH, and BEEP commands (discussed later in this chapter) to prompt for a part description.

Fig. 22.9.

Using GETLABEL with other commands for more complex string input.

```
Z1: '\w                                                      SHEET
       -Z-------AA------AB------AC-------AD------AE----AF----AG-
  1   \w        {GETLABEL "Enter the description: ",DESC}
  2             {IF DESC="ROUND"}{BRANCH WRONG}
  3             ~
  4
  5   WRONG     {BEEP 0}
  6             {GETLABEL "NO ROUND WIDGETS! PRESS ENTER",DESC}
  7             {BRANCH \w}
  8
  9   DESC
 10
```

You can add a second GETLABEL command to this program so that if you make an incorrect entry, an error message displays, and the program pauses until you press any key. Remember, however, that whatever you enter in response to the **NO ROUND WIDGETS!** prompt is stored in DESC.

The GETNUMBER Command

The GETNUMBER command accepts only numerical entries. The format for GETNUMBER is as follows:

{GETNUMBER *prompt,location*}

The specified *prompt* (which must be a string enclosed in quotation marks) is displayed in the control panel; the numerical input entered in response to the prompt is placed in *location* when you press Enter.

In the example in figure 22.10, the GETNUMBER statement displays a prompt and accepts a numerical entry into cell AB10. The second line copies that numerical entry into the next available row in column A (the @COUNT function finds the next open row in column A).

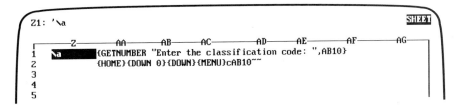

Fig. 22.10.
Using GETNUMBER for numerical input.

Figure 22.11 shows how you can use GETNUMBER in an inventory program. Here GETNUMBER prompts for a part number. If the user does not enter a number between 0 and 9999, the program displays the message **INVALID PART NUMBER! PRESS ENTER** and prompts the user to enter another number.

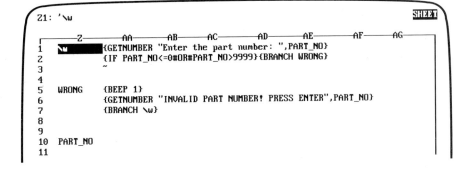

Fig. 22.11.
Using GETNUMBER in an inventory application.

Commands for Program Control

The commands shown in table 22.2 enable varying degrees of control in Symphony programs. These commands, used alone or in combination with decision-making commands, afford you extremely specific control of program flow.

Table 22.2
Commands for Program Control

Command	Description
{BRANCH}	Continues program execution at *location*
{MENUBRANCH}	Prompts the user with the menu found at *location*
{MENUCALL}	Works like MENUBRANCH, except that control returns to the statement after the MENUCALL
{RETURN}	Returns from a program subroutine
{QUIT}	Ends program execution
{ONERROR}	Traps errors, passing control to *branch*
{BREAKOFF}	Disables the Ctrl-Break key
{BREAKON}	Enables the Ctrl-Break key
{WAIT}	Waits a specified amount of time
{DISPATCH}	Branches indirectly by way of *location*
{DEFINE}	Specifies cells for subroutine arguments
{RESTART}	Cancels a subroutine

The BRANCH Command

The BRANCH command causes program control to pass unconditionally to the cell address indicated by *location*. The general format of the BRANCH command is as follows:

{BRANCH *location*}

Reminder:

BRANCH transfers macro control from the current location to the location specified in the command.

The program begins reading commands and statements at the cell indicated by *location*. Program control does not return to the line from which it was passed unless directed to do so by another BRANCH statement.

In the example in figure 22.12, the first line places the cell pointer in cell R34 and then executes an @COUNT function. The second line passes program control to cell F13, regardless of any commands that follow the BRANCH command. The program then executes commands beginning in cell F13.

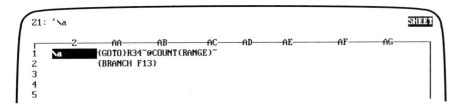

Fig. 22.12.
*Using BRANCH to
pass program
control to cell F13.*

BRANCH is an unconditional command unless it is preceded by an IF statement, as in the following example:

Reminder:
*BRANCH
statements are
made conditional
when used with IF
statements.*

> {IF C22="alpha"}{BRANCH G24}
>
> {GOTO}S101~

The IF statement must be in the same cell to act as a conditional-testing statement. For more information, see "The IF Command" later in this chapter.

Suppose that three separate companies are under your corporate umbrella, and that you have written a program to add and modify records in a corporate personnel database. Figure 22.13 shows a portion of such a program. Depending on how the user of the program responds to the **Enter Company (R, A, or C):** prompt, you want the program to branch to a different place in the program and prompt the user further for data specific to that company.

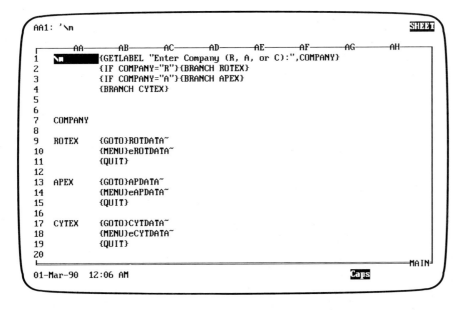

Fig. 22.13.
*Using BRANCH in
a database
application.*

The BRANCH statements in the \m program cause the flow of program execution to shift to the different company routines. In this example, the

BRANCH statements are coupled with IF statements to shift execution conditionally, depending on the user's response. After the program executes a company routine, the QUIT statement at the end of the routine causes program execution to stop.

You may prefer that execution return to the \m program or to another program after completing the company routine. You can arrange this setup in one of two ways:

❏ Replace the QUIT statements at the end of the company routines with {BRANCH \m} statements to return to \m

❏ Replace the BRANCH statements in \m with subroutine calls (discussed later in this chapter) and then include in the subroutine a BRANCH to the point where execution should continue

Remember two important points about BRANCH statements. First, they cause a permanent shift in the flow of statement execution (unless you use another BRANCH statement). Second, BRANCH statements are most often used in combination with IF statements.

The MENUBRANCH Command

Reminder:

MENUBRANCH defines and displays a menu consisting of from one to eight selections.

The MENUBRANCH command defines and displays in the control panel a menu-selection structure from which you can initiate as many as eight individual programs. You select menu items as you make selections from a Symphony command menu: either by highlighting the selection and pressing Enter or by typing the first letter of the selection name. The form of the MENUBRANCH command is as follows:

{MENUBRANCH *location*}

location is the range where the menu is located. The menu invoked by the MENUBRANCH command can consist of one to eight consecutive columns in the worksheet. Each column corresponds to one item in the menu. The upper left corner of *location* must refer to the first menu item; otherwise, you receive the error message `Invalid use of Menu macro command`.

Each menu item consists of three or more rows in the same column. The first row is the menu-option name. Choose option names that begin with different letters. If two or more options begin with the same letter, and you try to type the first letter to access an option, Symphony selects the first option with the letter you specified. That option may not be the one you want.

The second row in the menu range contains descriptions of the menu items. The description is displayed in the top row of the control panel when the cell pointer highlights the name of the corresponding menu option. The first 73 characters of a description are shown in the control panel. The description row must be present, even if it is blank.

The third row begins the actual program command sequence. Once the individual programs have been executed, program control must be directed by statements at the end of each individual program.

No empty columns can exist between menu items; the column immediately to the right of the last menu item must be empty. You can supplement the Symphony menu structure by creating a full-screen menu. For example, figure 22.7 uses a rolling-bar menu; this type of menu, with its on-screen instructions, can use all or most of a screen to supplement the Symphony menu structure.

Reminder:
Menu options must be in contiguous cells; the column to the right of the last menu item must be empty.

In figure 22.14, the MENUBRANCH statement produces a menu structure that begins in cell AB4. The individual programs begin in row 6 in each cell. Each of these programs must contain a statement to continue once the main task has been completed. For example, row 6 in figure 22.14 continues the main task for each option.

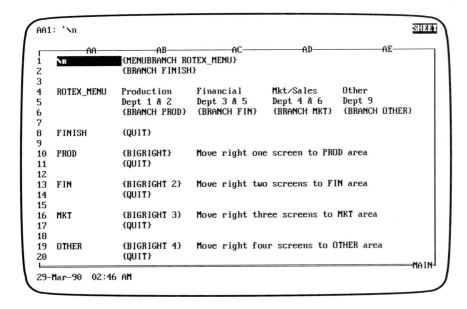

Fig. 22.14.

A program using the MENUBRANCH command.

When the MENUBRANCH statement is executed, Symphony displays in the control panel the menu beginning at cell ROTEX_MENU. (**Note:** You must use SHEET **R**ange **N**ame **L**abels **R**ight to assign the name ROTEX_MENU to the cell in which the label **Production** resides. **P**roduction is the first menu item.)

The top line of the control panel contains a description of whatever menu item is currently highlighted. For instance, when you move the cell pointer to **Financial**, the description **Dept 3 & 5** appears on the top line of the control panel.

Suppose that you want to select the second menu item (**Financial**). As mentioned previously, you select it the same way you do any Symphony menu item: by pressing Enter after you position the cursor on that option, or by typing the first letter of the menu item. After you select **F**inancial from the menu, the next statement to be executed is {BRANCH FIN}.

If, instead of selecting a menu item, you press the Esc key, Symphony stops displaying the menu items and executes the next command after the MENUBRANCH command: {BRANCH FINISH}.

Tip

If you have a multilevel menu structure, you can make the Esc key function as it does in the Symphony command menus (backing up to the previous menu). After the current MENUBRANCH command, place a BRANCH to the previous level's MENUBRANCH. When you press Esc, this BRANCH backs you up to the previous menu.

The MENUCALL Command

The MENUCALL command is identical to the MENUBRANCH command except that Symphony executes the menu program as a subroutine (see the tip about subroutines later in this section). Once the individual menu programs have been executed, program control returns to the cell immediately below the cell containing the MENUCALL statement. The format of the MENUCALL command is as follows:

    {MENUCALL *location*}

Figure 22.15A shows most of a macro that controls init strings for a LaserJet printer. Figure 22.15B shows the complete macro printed on a LaserJet printer. An advantage of the macros (\s, \p, LASINIT, ORIENT, LINES, and PITCH) is that they relieve the user of recalling the init strings that control orientation, lines per inch, and pitch. Furthermore, the macro has the built-in "intelligence" to adjust the page-length setting so that it is consistent with the lines-per-inch init string.

This macro system will rarely be needed because the ALLWAYS add-in, which does an outstanding job of controlling the LaserJet printer, is standard with Symphony 2.2. However, ALLWAYS can set very demanding memory requirements. If your worksheet requires large amounts of memory, it may be incompatible with ALLWAYS. If this is the case, the macro system in figure 22.15B—or a slight variation of this system—may be just what you need to simplify the management of LaserJet printing.

This macro system generally starts with the invocation of the \s macro. The best way to start is to clear the previous init strings by selecting the **C**lear option after starting \s. Typing **c** for **C**lear removes any previous init strings, reinvokes the default printer settings, sets the page-orientation variable, O_CODE, to "p", and

```
A5:                                                              SHEET
      A          B              C              D
1   \s MACRO IS FOR SETTING
2      ORIENTATION (portrait or landscape)
3      LINES PER INCH (6 or 8 lines per inch)
4      PITCH (pica or compressed)
5   ████████
6   \p MACRO IS FOR
7      SENDING PAGE IMAGE TO PRINTER
8      EJECTING LAST PAGE FROM PRINTER
9
10  O_CODE    1
11
12  \s        {SERVICES}psmni
13            {MENUCALL LASINIT}
14            qq
15
16  \p        {SERVICES}pagpq
17
18
19
20
21  LASINIT  Orientation       Lines/in.         Pitch
22           Portrait or landscape 6 or 8 lines/in. pica or compressed
23           {MENUCALL ORIENT}  {MENUCALL LINES} {MENUCALL PITCH}
24
25
26  ORIENT   Portrait          Landscape
27           Print upright     Print sideways
28           \027\&l00~        \027\&l1O~
29           {let O_CODE,"p"}  {let O_CODE,"l"}
30
31  LINES          6               8
32               6 lines/in.      8 lines/in.
33           \027\&l6D~p145~q  \027\&l8D~p160~q
34
35  PITCH    PICA              COMPRESSED
36           10 chars/in.      16.6 chars/in.
37           \027(s10H~        \027(s16.6H~
38
39  FORMULA...
40  ...IN C33 +"\027\&l8D~p1"&@IF(O_CODE="p","80","60")&"~q"
                                                            MAIN
28-Feb-90  10:59 PM SQ2       OnLine
```

Fig. 22.15A.
Using MENUCALL to control a LaserJet printer.

makes the page-length setting equal 60 before quitting the print settings sheet and the macro.

You control the orientation, lines per inch, and pitch by selecting the appropriate option from the LASINIT subroutine menu. When you select an option, another MENUCALL command is executed. Therefore, LASINIT is a subroutine which can, in turn, call one of three other subroutines (ORIENT, LINES, or PITCH).

When you use MENUCALL, Symphony returns to the statement immediately following the MENUCALL whenever it encounters a blank cell or a RETURN command. Suppose that you select the **P**ortrait option in the ORIENT subroutine. After setting the appropriate init string and setting O_CODE equal to "p", the **P**ortrait routine encounters a blank cell. This cell causes control to pass back to the row after {MENUCALL ORIENT} in LASINIT. Because this cell

Reminder:
MENUCALL returns to the statement immediately following the MENUCALL whenever it encounters a blank cell or a RETURN.

Fig. 22.15B.

A printout from the MENUCALL LaserJet macro with landscape orientation, 6 lines per inch, and compressed print.

```
\s MACRO IS FOR SETTING
    ORIENTATION (portrait or landscape)
    LINES PER INCH (6 or 8 lines per inch)
    PITCH (pica or compressed)

\p MACRO IS FOR
    SENDING PAGE IMAGE TO PRINTER
    EJECTING LAST PAGE FROM PRINTER

O_CODE    l

\s        {SERVICES}psmni
          {MENUCALL LASINIT}
          qq

\p        {SERVICES}pagpq


LASINIT  Orientation          Lines/in.      Pitch            Clear
         Portrait or landscape 6 or 8 lines/in. pica or compressed Clear init string
         {MENUCALL ORIENT}    {MENUCALL LINES} {MENUCALL PITCH}  {ESC}\027E~i{ESC}~
                                                                 {let O_CODE,"p"}
                                                                 pl60~qqq
ORIENT   Portrait             Landscape                         {QUIT}
         Print upright        Print sideways
         \027\&l00~           \027\&l10~
         {let O_CODE,"p"}     {let O_CODE,"l"}

LINES         6                    8
              6 lines/in.          8 lines/in.
         \027\&l60~pl45~q      \027\&l80~pl60~q

PITCH    PICA                 COMPRESSED
         10 chars/in.         16.6 chars/in.
         \027(s10H~           \027(s16.6H~
```

is also blank, macro control passes to the last line of the \s macro. The qq statement in that cell causes the macro to quit the print settings sheet.

So that a print-settings selection reliably ejects a full page and concurrently starts the next page at the top of a sheet, you must make sure that the page-length setting is appropriate. For example, in landscape mode there are 7.5 inches of printing space from the top to the bottom default margins; at 8 lines per inch, this results in 60-line pages. The portrait mode contrasts with this by making available 10 inches of print space from the top to the bottom default margins, resulting in 80-line pages at 8 lines per inch.

The formula in cell C33 dynamically adjusts the page-length setting based on the page orientation and the lines-per-page selection; this formula is shown at the bottom of figure 22.15A. A similarly structured formula sets the page length to either 45 or 60 for the 6 lines-per-inch selection.

Keep in mind that pressing Esc has the same effect with MENUCALL as it does with MENUBRANCH. Execution shifts to the statement following the MENUCALL statement. You can use the Esc-key technique to back up to preceding menus only if you want this technique to also apply when the MENUCALL command finishes executing.

The advantage of MENUCALL is that you can call the same menu from several different places in a program and continue execution from the calling point after MENUCALL is finished. You enjoy this advantage whenever you use subroutines.

Tip

The MENUCALL statement should give you some feel for calling subroutines. Quite a bit more, however, can be involved in calling standard (nonmenu) subroutines.

A *subroutine* is an independent program that can be run from within the main program. Calling a subroutine is as easy as enclosing the name of a routine in braces; for example {SUB} calls the subroutine named SUB. When Symphony encounters a name in braces, the program passes control to the named routine. When the subroutine is finished (when Symphony encounters a blank cell or a RETURN command), program control passes back to the command in the cell below the cell that called the subroutine.

Why use subroutines? You can duplicate a simple subroutine by using two BRANCH commands. But by using a subroutine, you can execute the subroutine from any number of locations within the main program.

The RETURN Command

The RETURN command indicates the end of subroutine execution and returns program control to the cell immediately below the cell that called the subroutine. When Symphony encounters a RETURN command, program control passes to the main program (or another subroutine) at the location after the subroutine call. Do not confuse RETURN with QUIT, which ends the program completely. You can use RETURN with the IF statement to return conditionally from a subroutine. The form of this command is as follows:

Reminder:
RETURN signifies the end of a subroutine and returns program control to the cell immediately below the cell that called the subroutine.

{RETURN}

The first line of the macro in figure 22.16 places the cell pointer in AA101 and calls the subroutine SUB. After SUB is executed, the RETURN command passes control to the next command after the subroutine call (in this case, the second line of the \a macro). This statement places the cell pointer in the Home position and copies the range of cells entered by the subroutine into the range whose upper left corner is identified by the Home position.

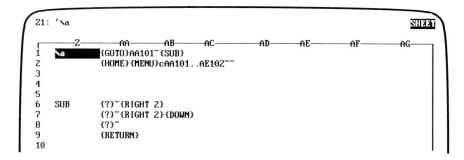

Fig. 22.16.
Using the RETURN command.

Symphony also ends a subroutine and returns to the calling routine when it encounters, while executing the subroutine, a cell that either is blank or contains a numeric value. Although this method of returning from a subroutine works, use the RETURN command because it documents the fact that a particular set of macro keywords and Command Language instructions is intended to be a subroutine.

Figure 22.17 shows a timing test of the RETURN versus blank-line method of terminating a subroutine. The blank-line method is 53 percent faster in this case than using the RETURN method of returning from a subroutine. The times for the 53-percent savings were achieved on a 386-based PC compatible, running under Windows/386 with Symphony 2.2 in two separate windows. The blank-line times are achieved with the code as shown. The RETURN times are achieved by moving the two orphan RETURN statements in cells E14 and E17 to cells E13 and E16 (to make them part of the SUB1 and SUB2 subroutines). Subroutines that use more menu commands instead of Symphony macro commands will sometimes show little or no difference between the two ways of ending a subroutine.

The preferred method for ending a macro depends on the circumstances. If speed is critical, you may want to use macro commands instead of Symphony menu commands whenever possible. If you need speed, you may prefer to use the blank-line method of ending a routine. When you use Symphony menu commands for quick-and-dirty macro implementation, you may prefer the RETURN command; the statement's self-documenting characteristic may be more important than the slightly longer return time.

The QUIT Command

Reminder:

Place QUIT at the end of a program; do not place QUIT at the end of a subroutine

The QUIT command forces the program to terminate unconditionally. Even without a QUIT command, the program terminates if it encounters (within the program sequence) a cell that is empty or contains an entry other than a string. It is good practice, however, to put a QUIT statement at the end of your programs to indicate that you intend execution to stop. (Conversely, do not put a QUIT command at the end of a program that you intend to call as a subroutine.) The form of the QUIT command is as follows:

{QUIT}

In the following example, the QUIT command forces the program sequence to terminate unconditionally:

{HOME}{SERVICES}fs~y{QUIT}

When QUIT is preceded by an IF conditional-testing statement, as in figure 22.18, termination of the program depends on the IF statement.

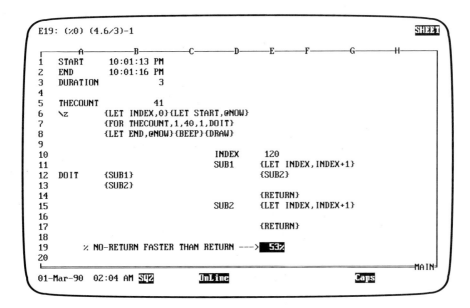

Fig. 22.17.

A timing test for the RETURN versus blank-line method of terminating a subroutine.

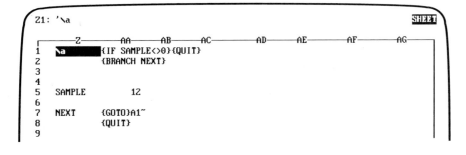

Fig. 22.18.

Using QUIT with an IF statement.

The ONERROR Command

The processing of Command Language programs is normally interrupted if a system error (such as **Disk drive not ready**) occurs during execution. By sidestepping system errors that normally cause program termination, the ONERROR command allows programs to proceed. The general format of the command is as follows:

{ONERROR *branch,message*}

The ONERROR command passes program control to the cell indicated by *branch*; any errors can be recorded in the cell specified by *message*; *message* is an optional argument.

Cue:

Place the ONERROR statement early in the program, before any errors are encountered.

As a general rule, always make sure that the program executes the ONERROR statement before an error occurs. Therefore, you may want to include an ONERROR statement near the start of your programs. Because you can have only one ONERROR statement in effect at a time, you should take special precautions to write your programs so that the right message appears for each error condition.

In figure 22.19, the ONERROR statement acts as a safeguard against leaving drive A empty or not closing the drive door. If an error occurs, program control passes to the cell named ERROR. This cell contains a GETLABEL statement that prompts you to correct the error.

Fig. 22.19.

Using ONERROR to prompt users to close the drive door.

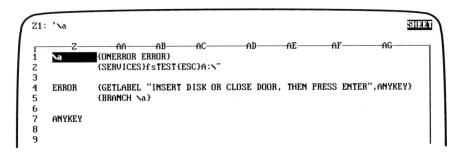

The best place to put an ONERROR statement is directly above the program line that you think may cause an error. For example, suppose that your program is about to copy a portion of the current worksheet to a disk file, using the SERVICES **F**ile **X**tract command. A system error occurs if the drive is not ready or the disk is full. Therefore, you should include a strategically placed ONERROR command (see fig. 22.20).

In figure 22.20, the ONERROR statement causes the program to branch to a cell called BAD_DRV if an error occurs. A copy of the error message that Symphony issues is entered in a cell called BAD_DRV_MSG. The first statement in the BAD_DRV routine moves the cell pointer to an out-of-the-way cell (cleverly called OUT_OF_WAY_CELL). Next, the message **Disk drive is not**

ready is entered in the worksheet, followed by **Prepare drive and press Enter**. The program pauses for you to press Enter. Finally, the program branches back to \p to try again.

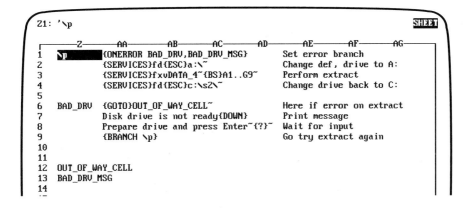

Fig. 22.20.

Using an ONERROR statement to retry disk access.

Ctrl-Break presents a special problem for the ONERROR statement. Because Ctrl-Break causes an error condition, the ONERROR statement is invoked when you press Ctrl-Break to halt the macro. Therefore, a good technique when you plan to use the ONERROR statement is to disable Ctrl-Break after you debug the program. (See the following discussion of the BREAKOFF command.) By disabling Ctrl-Break, you can prevent the confusion that can arise with an untimely error message.

The BREAKOFF Command

The easiest way to stop a program is to issue a Ctrl-Break command. But Symphony can eliminate the effect of a Ctrl-Break while a program is executing. By including a BREAKOFF command in a program, you can prevent a user from stopping the program before its completion. Before you use a BREAKOFF statement, however, you must be certain that the program has been fully debugged.

The BREAKOFF command disables the Ctrl-Break command during program execution. The form of the BREAKOFF command is as follows:

{BREAKOFF}

BREAKOFF is used primarily to prevent a user from interrupting a process and destroying the integrity of data in the worksheet. You do not need to use BREAKOFF unless you are developing sophisticated programs; but, in such applications, BREAKOFF can be an important safeguard against user-caused problems.

The BREAKON Command

To restore the effect of Ctrl-Break, use the BREAKON command. The form of this command is as follows:

{BREAKON}

You probably will want a simple one-line program that issues BREAKON, just in case something happens to the original program during execution. You also may want to make sure that the last statement in your program before QUIT is BREAKON.

Cue:

Place BREAKON at a point in the program where execution can safely stop.

Because any Ctrl-Break keystrokes in the keyboard buffer are executed as soon as the BREAKON command is executed, be sure that the BREAKON is at a place where the program can safely stop. Figure 22.21 demonstrates how you can use the BREAKOFF and BREAKON commands.

Fig. 22.21.

Using the BREAKOFF and BREAKON commands.

```
Z1: '\a                                                          SHEET
┌───────Z────────AA───────AB───────AC───────AD──────AE──────AF────
│   1  \a              {LET PREVIOUS_NUMBER,1}
│   2                  {GETNUMBER "Enter number: ",FACTORIAL}
│   3                  {BREAKOFF}
│   4                  {FOR COUNTER,1,FACTORIAL,1,FACT_RTN}
│   5                  1.6E+25
│   6                  {BREAKON}
│   7                  {QUIT}
│   8
│   9  FACT_RTN        {LET PREVIOUS_NUMBER,+PREVIOUS_NUMBER*COUNTER}
│  10                  {RETURN}
│  11
│  12  COUNTER               26
│  13  FACTORIAL             25
│  14  PREVIOUS_NUMBER  1.6E+25
│  15
```

The WAIT Command

The WAIT command causes the program to pause until, or for, an appointed time. The general form of the WAIT command is as follows:

{WAIT *argument*}

In this syntax, *argument* specifies the appointed time or the time to elapse. The WAIT statement in figure 22.22 allows the error message to be displayed for three seconds before erasing it and looping back to extract another keystroke from the type-ahead buffer.

The \k macro in figure 22.22 can be compared with figures 22.2 and 22.3. In figure 22.2, the error message can flash across the control panel before the user has the chance to read it. Figure 22.3 provides a pause, but requires the user to press a key to clear the message from the control panel. The WAIT command provides a three-second pause so that the user can view the message.

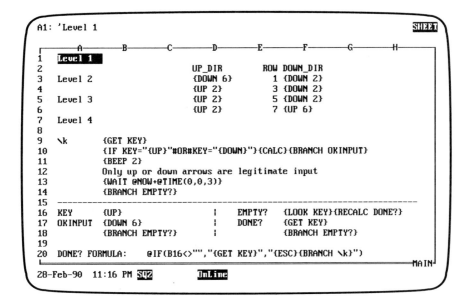

Fig. 22.22.
Using WAIT to control the duration an error message is displayed.

The serial-time-number *argument* must contain a date plus a time. If you want the program to wait until 6:00 P.M. today to continue, you can use the expression {WAIT @INT(@NOW)+@TIME(18,00,00)}. To make the program pause for 50 seconds, use the expression {WAIT @NOW+@TIME(0,0,50)}.

Reminder:
The serial-time-number argument must contain a date and a time.

The DISPATCH Command

The DISPATCH command is similar to the BRANCH command. The DISPATCH command, however, branches indirectly to a location specified by the value contained in *location*. The form of the command is as follows:

{DISPATCH *location*}

location should contain a cell address or range name as the destination of the DISPATCH. If the cell referred to by *location* does not contain a valid cell reference or range name, an error occurs, and program execution either stops with an error message or transfers to the location specified by the current ONERROR command.

The DISPATCH *location* must be a cell reference or range name that points to a single-cell reference. If *location* is either a multicell range or a range that contains a single cell, the DISPATCH acts like a BRANCH statement and transfers execution directly to *location*.

Reminder:
The location to which DISPATCH transfers control must be a single cell.

In figure 22.23, the DISPATCH statement selects the subroutine to be executed based on the input in the cell NUMBER generated by the GETLABEL statement. The string formula in the DISPATCH command concatenates the word *SUB* and the menu-selection number entered by the user. Because the name of every subroutine begins with the word SUB, the DISPATCH command passes program control to the subroutine specified by the user.

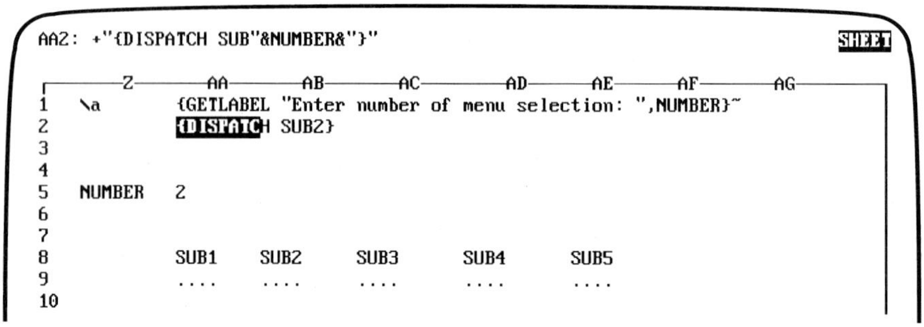
AA2: +"{DISPATCH SUB"&NUMBER&"}"
SHEET
Z AA AB AC AD AE AF AG
1 \a {GETLABEL "Enter number of menu selection: ",NUMBER}~
2 {DISPATCH SUB2}
3
4
5 NUMBER 2
6
7
8 SUB1 SUB2 SUB3 SUB4 SUB5
9 ....
10

Fig. 22.23.
An example of the DISPATCH command.

The DEFINE Command

An important subroutine feature of Symphony is the capability of passing arguments, using the keyword version of the subroutine call only. A subroutine called with arguments must begin with a DEFINE statement that associates each argument with a specific cell location. The form of the subroutine call with arguments is as follows:

{DEFINE *loc1:type1,loc2:type2,...*}

In this syntax, *loc1*, *loc2*, and so on are names or cell references for the cells in which to place the arguments passed from the main program. You can use one or more arguments, separated by commas. *type* can be either STRING or VALUE and is optional; if not specified, the default is STRING.

If an argument is of *type* STRING, the text of the corresponding argument in the subroutine call is placed in the indicated cell as a string value (label).

If an argument is of *type* VALUE, the corresponding argument in the subroutine call is treated as a formula, and its numeric or string value is placed in the argument cell. An error occurs if the corresponding argument in the subroutine call is not a valid number, string, or formula. You do not, however, have to put a string in quotation marks or have a leading + sign in a formula that uses cell references.

Suppose that you have an application where you must repeatedly convert strings to numbers and display the numbers in **C**urrency format. Rather than enter the same code at several different places in the program, you decide to write a subroutine. Figure 22.24 shows how the subroutine might appear. (The SHEET **R**ange **N**ame **L**abels **R**ight command was used to define all the range names in this example.)

The first statement in the program is a GETLABEL statement that reads a string value into the cell named INPUT_STRING. Line 2 calls a subroutine named STR_2_NO and passes the arguments INPUT_STRING (the name of the cell containing the input string) and RETURN_NUMBER (the name of the cell where the formatted number is to be stored).

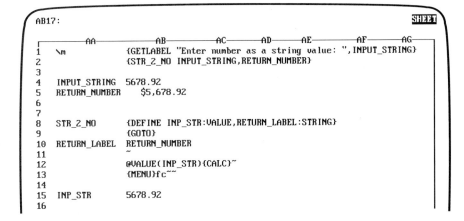

AB17:   SHEET

	AA	AB	AC	AD	AE	AF	AG
1	\m	{GETLABEL "Enter number as a string value: ",INPUT_STRING}						
2		{STR_2_NO INPUT_STRING,RETURN_NUMBER}					
3							
4	INPUT_STRING	5678.92					
5	RETURN_NUMBER	$5,678.92					
6							
7							
8	STR_2_NO	{DEFINE INP_STR:VALUE,RETURN_LABEL:STRING}					
9		{GOTO}					
10	RETURN_LABEL	RETURN_NUMBER					
11		~					
12		@VALUE(INP_STR){CALC}~					
13		{MENU}fc~~					
14							
15	INP_STR	5678.92					
16							

Fig. 22.24.

An example of a subroutine call with parameters.

The STR_2_NO subroutine begins with a DEFINE statement, which defines where and how the arguments passed to the subroutine from \m are to be stored. Any subroutine that receives arguments passed from its calling macro must begin with a DEFINE statement.

The DEFINE statement in STR_2_NO specifies two cells, INP_STR and RETURN_LABEL, that will hold the two arguments passed from \m. If the number of arguments in the subroutine call does not agree with the number of arguments in the DEFINE statement, an error occurs.

The DEFINE statement specifies that the first argument in the subroutine call is to be evaluated and its value placed in INP_STR. The first argument is the cell reference INPUT_STRING; the DEFINE statement places the value in cell INPUT_STRING—the string "5,678.92"—in INP_STR.

The DEFINE statement also specifies that the text of the second argument in the subroutine call is to be placed into cell RETURN_LABEL as a string. Because the text of the second argument is *RETURN_NUMBER*, the string "RETURN_NUMBER" is placed in cell RETURN_LABEL.

The cell containing the second argument is located in the body of the subroutine. This technique is used to enable the subroutine to return a value to a location designated by the caller. In this example, the location RETURN_NUMBER is passed to the subroutine as a string value. The subroutine uses the passed value as the argument of a GOTO statement that places the cell pointer on the output cell. This technique is one of two primary ways to return information to the calling routine. The other way to return information is to place it in a specified cell used every time the subroutine is called.

After the subroutine places the cell pointer on the output cell, the subroutine continues by converting the string in INP_STR to a number and placing the resulting numeric value in the output cell.

Reminder:

Any subroutine that receives arguments passed from its calling macro must begin with a DEFINE statement.

Passing arguments to and from subroutines is important if you want to get the most from Symphony's subroutine capabilities. Subroutines with arguments simplify program coding and make macros easier to trace. Subroutine arguments are almost essential when you are developing a subroutine to perform a common function that you use again and again. They are also one of the trickiest parts of the Symphony Command Language.

The RESTART Command

Although you normally return from a subroutine by coming back to the command immediately after the subroutine call, you can abort that process. You may want to prevent a subroutine from returning in special circumstances (for example, when the user inputs a code to stop the macro).

The way Symphony knows where a subroutine should return after completion is through a subroutine stack. A *stack* is simply a list of cell addresses. When one subroutine terminates routinely, Symphony passes control to the address at the top of the stack; this address is the cell after the one that made the subroutine call. If one subroutine calls another, the second routine returns control to the point after its call from the first subroutine. The first subroutine, in turn, returns control to the main program.

Reminder:

RESTART clears the subroutine stack and continues execution.

The RESTART command clears the subroutine stack, but continues execution. The result is the same as a quit after the last command in the subroutine. The syntax of the command is as follows:

{RESTART}

Figure 22.25 shows how the RESTART command functions. In normal operation, SUB prompts the user sequentially for a product description, item #, and price. If the user presses Enter without providing any data for either the item # or price prompts, the entry is cleared, E_LINE is set to "yes" (to terminate looping within SUB) and the RESTART command is executed.

When the RESTART command is executed, the subroutine stack is cleared. Therefore, after the final LET command in SUB, control fails to pass back to the main calling program (\a) and E_LINE is assigned the value `With Restart, it stops here!`. If control were to return to \a, E_LINE would have the value `It never gets to this point`.

Commands for Making Decisions

The Command Language's decision-making commands, shown in table 22.3, give you the capability of a true programming language such as BASIC. With these commands, you can test for numeric and string values. The IF command provides the kind of conditional logic available in many high-level languages. FOR and FORBREAK offer conditional looping capabilities, enabling you to control how many times a set of statements is activated.

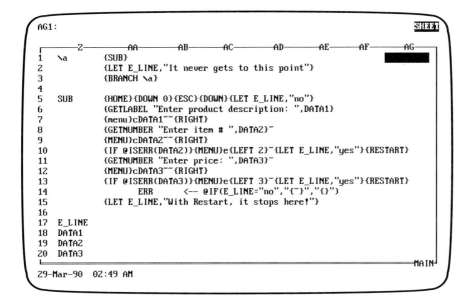

```
AG1:                                                                  SHEET
    ┌──Z─────────AA──────AB──────AC──────AD─────AE──────AF──────AG──┐
  1  \a          {SUB}                                           ███████
  2               {LET E_LINE,"It never gets to this point"}
  3               {BRANCH \a}
  4
  5  SUB          {HOME}{DOWN 0}{ESC}{DOWN}{LET E_LINE,"no"}
  6               {GETLABEL "Enter product description: ",DATA1}
  7               {menu}cDATA1~~{RIGHT}
  8               {GETNUMBER "Enter item # ",DATA2}~
  9               {MENU}cDATA2~~{RIGHT}
 10               {IF @ISERR(DATA2)}{MENU}e{LEFT 2}~{LET E_LINE,"yes"}{RESTART}
 11               {GETNUMBER "Enter price: ",DATA3}~
 12               {MENU}cDATA3~~{RIGHT}
 13               {IF @ISERR(DATA3)}{MENU}e{LEFT 3}~{LET E_LINE,"yes"}{RESTART}
 14               ERR      <-- @IF(E_LINE="no","{~}","{}")
 15               {LET E_LINE,"With Restart, it stops here!"}
 16
 17  E_LINE
 18  DATA1
 19  DATA2
 20  DATA3
    └──────────────────────────────────────────────────────────MAIN┘
  29-Mar-90  02:49 AM
```

Fig. 22.25.
A demonstration of RESTART in a database application.

Table 22.3
Commands for Making Decisions

Command	Description
{IF}	Conditionally executes statements after IF
{FOR}	Activates a loop (loop count is placed in *counter*)
{FORBREAK}	Terminates a FOR loop

The IF Command

The IF statement uses if-then-else logic to evaluate the existence of certain numeric and string values. Commonly used to control program flow and enable the program to perform based on criteria provided by the user, the Command Language's IF command is the functional equivalent of the IF command in BASIC. The form of the IF command is as follows:

{IF *condition*}{*true*}

{*false*}

If the logical expression (*condition*) is true, the remaining commands on the same line are executed. (These commands ordinarily include a BRANCH command to skip the {*false*} statements.) If the expression is false, execution skips the commands after the IF command on the current line and continues on the next line.

Reminder:
If the condition is true, the commands on the same line as the IF are executed; otherwise execution continues with the following line.

As the following examples show, IF statements can check for a variety of conditions, including the position of the cell pointer, a specific numeric value, or a specific string value. In figure 22.26, for example, the IF statement checks to see whether the current location of the cell pointer is row 200. If it is, program control passes to AA4, where a QUIT command is executed. If the cell pointer is not on row 200, the cell pointer moves down a row, accepts input, and branches back to cell AA1, where the IF statement again checks to see whether the cell pointer is located on row 200.

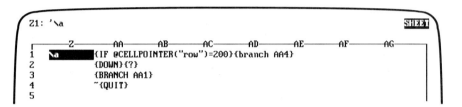

Fig. 22.26.

Using IF to check the cell pointer.

Figure 22.27 shows how you can use IF to evaluate a cell's value. The IF statement evaluates the value in cell R18. If cell R18 contains a negative value, the program converts that value to 0 and halts program execution. If the value in cell R18 is 0 or greater, the second line replaces the value in cell R18 with the value represented by the equation R18*.55.

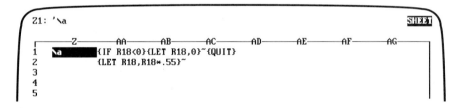

Fig. 22.27.

Using IF to evaluate a cell value.

The IF command also can evaluate a value entered by a user. You can, for example, develop IF statements that complete different operations depending on user input.

The macro in figure 22.28 facilitates the entry of numbers or labels down the columns of worksheet; the macro performs one of three functions depending on user input. In one case, it accepts user input in a cell. In another case, it moves to the top of a new column for more input, and, in the third case, it simply quits.

Like the macro in figure 22.26, the one in figure 22.28 first checks to see if the row is equal to 200. If the cell pointer is in row 200, the macro branches to DONE, which contains the QUIT command. If the cell pointer is not in row 200, the program moves the cursor down one row and waits for the user to enter something from the keyboard. After the user presses Enter, the program takes over again and places the keyboard entry into the current cell with a tilde.

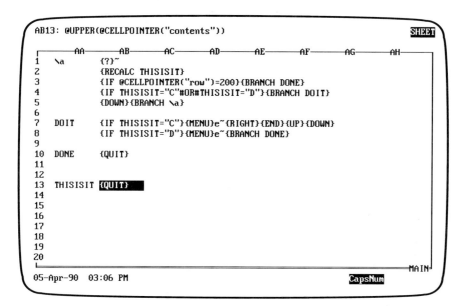

```
AB13:  @UPPER(@CELLPOINTER("contents"))                                    SHEET
        AA        AB        AC        AD        AE        AF        AG        AH
1     \a        {?}~
2               {RECALC THISISIT}
3               {IF @CELLPOINTER("row")=200}{BRANCH DONE}
4               {IF THISISIT="C"#OR#THISISIT="D"}{BRANCH DOIT}
5               {DOWN}{BRANCH \a}
6
7     DOIT      {IF THISISIT="C"}{MENU}e~{RIGHT}{END}{UP}{DOWN}
8               {IF THISISIT="D"}{MENU}e~{BRANCH DONE}
9
10    DONE      {QUIT}
11
12
13    THISISIT  {QUIT}
14
15
16
17
18
19
20
                                                                        MAIN
05-Apr-90   03:06 PM                                           CapsNum
```

Fig. 22.28.
Using IF in an if-then-else formulation.

After the entry is placed in a cell, the formula in the range THISISIT transforms the entry to an uppercase label. If THISISIT is an uppercase *C* or *D*, the program branches to the range DOIT; otherwise the program branches to back to \a.

The IF statement in row 4 shows an if-then-else style of macro programming. When the IF statement is true, it executes the *then* clause (that is, BRANCH DOIT). When the IF statement is false, it executes the *else* clause (that is, {DOWN}{BRANCH\a}).

DOIT erases the cell's contents and branches to DONE if THISISIT equals *D*. When THISISIT equals *C*, the cell's contents are erased, the cursor is positioned for the next column of entries, and a branch to \a is executed to accept more input in the new column.

The FOR Command

The FOR command is used to control the looping process in a program by calling a subroutine to be executed a certain number of times. FOR enables you to define the exact number of times the subroutine is executed. The form of the FOR command is as follows:

{FOR *counter,start,stop,step,routine*}

Reminder:
FOR controls the number of times a subroutine is executed.

The FOR statement contains five arguments. The *counter* argument is a cell that acts as the counter mechanism for the loop structure. The *start* argument is the starting number for the counter mechanism; *stop* is the completion number for the counter mechanism. The *step* argument is the incremental value for the counter mechanism; *routine* is the name of the subroutine to be executed. Arguments *start*, *stop*, and *step* can be values, cell addresses, or formulas. Arguments *counter* and *routine* must be range names or cell addresses. Because multiple loops are permitted, be careful of the logical flow of multiple-looping structures.

Notice how FOR is used in the simple example in figure 22.29. The FOR in the first line of the program controls how many times the program loops to format a column of values. The FOR statement begins by using the range named COUNT as a counter to keep track of how many times the program loops. The second argument, 1, is the start number for the counter; the next argument, 5, is the stop number; the fourth argument is the value by which the counter is to be incremented after each loop. The last argument, FORMAT, is the name of the routine to be executed.

Fig. 22.29.
Using FOR to control the number of loops in a formatting program.

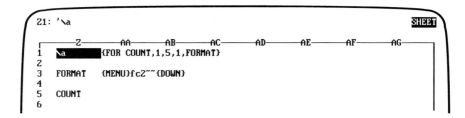

The FORBREAK Command

Reminder:
FORBREAK ends processing of a FOR loop.

If you want to end the processing of a FOR command based on something other than the number of iterations, such as a conditional test, you can use the FORBREAK command. When you use this command, Symphony interrupts the processing of the FOR command and continues execution with the command following the FOR.

Figure 22.30 shows the FORBREAK command in action. The \a macro was stopped in its third iteration of the FOR loop by a Ctrl-Break key combination.

The FORMAT routine assigns the **C**urrency format to a cell and moves down to the next cell in the column. If it encounters a blank cell before the 500th iteration, the FOR loop is terminated by the FORBREAK command. When FORBREAK is executed, control passes back to the second row of the main routine, and the cursor moves to the top of the column of formatted entries. In this example, the FOR statement encounters a blank cell (cell AF7) in its sixth repetition; the FORBREAK command is then executed.

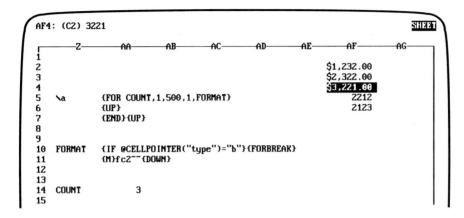

Fig. 22.30.
A macro that uses the FORBREAK command.

Commands for Manipulating Data

The LET, PUT, CONTENTS, and BLANK commands allow precise placement of data within worksheet files. These commands, which are listed in table 22.4, function similarly to such menu commands as **C**opy, **M**ove, and **E**rase but provide capabilities that go beyond simple copy, move, and erase operations.

Table 22.4
Commands for Manipulating Data

Command	Description
{LET}	Places the value of *expression* in *location*
{PUT}	Puts the specified *value* into the cell specified by *col* and *row* within *range*
{CONTENTS}	Stores the contents of *source* to *destination*
{BLANK}	Erases the cell or range

The LET Command

The LET command places a value or string in a target cell location without the cell pointer having to be at the location. LET is extremely useful, for example, for placing criteria in a database criterion range. The form of the LET command is as follows:

{LET *location,expression*}

This command places the value of *expression* in *location*.

Reminder:
LET places a value or string in a specified location.

In the \b macro in figure 22.31, the LET statement in row 8 is executed only if the condition in the IF statement is true; the LET statement in row 9 is executed only if the condition is false. The LET statement in row 8 places a label in a cell; row 9 places a value represented by the formula in a cell.

Fig. 22.31.

Using LET with an IF statement.

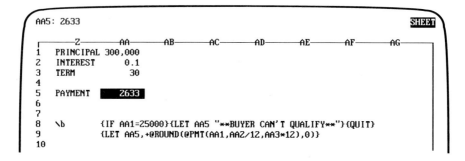

Figure 22.32 shows how to use LET in an application that takes a master file and saves it under a new name: that of a client code number. The program begins with a GETLABEL statement that prompts the user for a client code number; the number is placed in cell B3. The LET statement duplicates in the cell named CODE the client code number. The macro then invokes the SERVICES File Save command and uses the name in CODE to name the file.

Fig. 22.32.

Using LET in a program that saves files.

```
AA3:                                                              SHEET
        ──Z──────AA───────AB───────AC──────AD──────AE──────AF──────AG──
1       \a      {GETLABEL "Enter Client Code #: ",B3}~{LET CODE,B3}
2               {SERVICES}fs{ESC}c:\CLIENTS\
3       CODE    ▔▔▔▔▔▔▔▔▔▔▔▔~
4
5
```

You can use a string value with the LET command. In fact, you can even use a string formula. For example, if the cell named FIRST contains the string "Robert", and LAST holds the string "Hamer", the following statement stores "Robert Hamer" in NAME:

{LET NAME,FIRST&" "&LAST}

Like the DEFINE command, the LET command enables you to specify :STRING and :VALUE suffixes after the *expression* argument. The STRING suffix stores the text of the argument in the specified location, whereas the VALUE suffix evaluates the argument as a string or numeric formula and places the result in the specified location. When a suffix is not specified, LET stores the argument's numeric or string value if the argument is a valid formula; otherwise, the text of the argument is stored.

The LET command in the following example stores "Robert Hamer" in NAME:

{LET NAME,FIRST&" "&LAST:VALUE}

The LET command in this example, on the other hand, stores the string *FIRST&"
"&LAST* in NAME:

{LET NAME,FIRST&""&LAST:STRING}

You can duplicate the LET command by moving the cell pointer to the
appropriate location with GOTO and entering the appropriate value into
the cell. The LET command, however, has the major advantage that it does not
disturb the current location of the cell pointer. Overall, the LET command is a
convenient and useful means of specifying the value of a cell from within a
program.

Reminder:
*LET does not
disturb the position
of the cell pointer
when it places a
value in a cell
location.*

The PUT Command

The PUT command places a value in a target cell location determined by the
intersection of a row and a column in a defined range. The form of the PUT
command is as follows:

{PUT *range,col,row,value*}

The PUT statement contains four arguments. The *range* argument defines the
range into which the value is to be placed. The *col* argument defines the column
offset within *range*; *row* defines the row offset within *range*. The *value*
argument indicates the value to be placed in the cell location. The *range*
argument can be a range name or cell address. The *col, row,* and *value*
arguments can be values, cell references, or formulas.

For example, the following PUT statement places the contents of the cell named
ARG4 in the range named TABLE at the intersection defined by the values in
cells S1 and S2:

{PUT TABLE,S1,S2,ARG4}

Reminder:
*The row and
column offset
numbers follow the
same conventions
used by functions
(the first column is
column 0, the
second is column 1,
and so on).*

Figure 22.33 shows the results of different variations of this command. Keep in
mind that the row and column offset numbers follow the same conventions
used by functions (the first column is number 0, the second is number 1, and
so on).

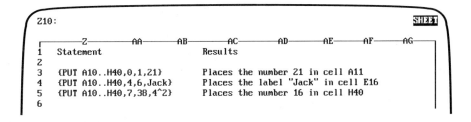

Fig. 22.33.
*Using PUT to enter
numbers and
labels.*

The CONTENTS Command

The CONTENTS command stores the contents of a *source* cell in a *destination* cell. The command also can optionally assign cell *width* and cell *format* to the destination cell. If *width* or *format* are not specified, the CONTENTS command uses the column width and format of the source to format the string. The form of the CONTENTS command is as follows:

{*CONTENTS destination,source,width,format*}

For example, the following CONTENTS statement places the contents of the cell named HERE in the cell named THERE, gives the individual cell a width of 11, and formats the entry as a full international date (121):

{CONTENTS THERE,HERE,11,121}

Cue:

Use the format codes to format the destination cell.

The number **121** used to format the destination cell was taken from the list of CONTENTS command format numbers that appears in table 22.5. This table also supplies the format numbers for the other examples in this section.

Table 22.5
Numeric Format Codes for CONTENTS Command

Code	Destination String's Numeric Display Command
0	Fixed, 0 decimal places
1-15	Fixed, 1 to 15 decimal places
15-31	Scientific, 0 to 15 decimal places
32-47	Currency, 0 to 15 decimal places
48-63	Percent, 0 to 15 decimal places
64-79	Comma, 0 to 15 decimal places
112	+/- Bar Graph
113	General
114	D1 (DD-MMM-YY)
115	D2 (DD-MM)
116	D3 (MMM-YY)
121	D4 (Full International date format: MM/DD/YY)
122	D5 (Partial International date format: MM/DD)
119	D6 (HH:MM:SS AM/PM time format)
120	D7 (HH:MM AM/PM time format)
123	D8 (Full International time format)
117	Text
118	Hidden
127	Current window's default display format

Suppose that you want to copy the number 123.456 from cell A21 to cell B25 and change the number to a string while you copy. The statement for this step is as follows:

　　{CONTENTS B25,A21}

The contents of cell B25 are displayed as the string **'123.456** with a left-aligned label-prefix character (').

Suppose that you want to change the width of the string when you copy it. Rather than have the string display as **123.456**, you want it to display as **123.4**. To get this result, change the statement to this:

　　{CONTENTS B25,A21,6}

This second statement uses a width of 6 to display the string. Symphony truncates the least significant digits of the number to create the string. If the number cannot be displayed in the specified width using the specified format, Symphony places a string of asterisks (*****) in the cell instead. (This method works just like Symphony's normal worksheet-formatting commands.)

Reminder:
Formatting with CONTENTS is similar to formatting with the SHEET Format and SHEET Settings Format commands.

Finally, suppose that you want to change the display format of the string while you copy it and change its width. The following command changes the display format to **Currency 0**:

　　{CONTENTS B25,A21,5,32}

The result of the statement is the number **$123**.

In the following examples of the CONTENTS command, 123.456 is the number in cell A21, the width of column A is 9, and the display format for cell A21 is **Fixed 2**.

Command	Result
{CONTENTS B25,A21}	Displays the number **123.46** in cell B25, using the **Fixed 2** format.
{CONTENTS B25,A21,4}	Uses a width of 4 and the **Fixed 2** format. The result is **★★★★**.
{CONTENTS B25,A21,5,0}	Displays the number **123** in cell B25, using the **Fixed 0** format.

The CONTENTS command is rather specialized but very useful in situations that require converting numeric values to formatted strings. CONTENTS can convert long numeric formulas to strings, using the **Text** format. This application is particularly useful for debugging purposes.

The BLANK Command

The BLANK command erases a range of cells in the worksheet. Although this command works similarly to the SHEET **E**rase command, using BLANK in Command Language programs has an advantage: BLANK is faster than SHEET **E**rase because BLANK works outside the menu structure. The form of the BLANK command is as follows:

{BLANK *location*}

In this syntax, *location* is the range to be erased.

In the example in figure 22.34, the BLANK statement erases RANGE1. The second line executes the {BLANK RANGE2} statement only if the IF statement tests true.

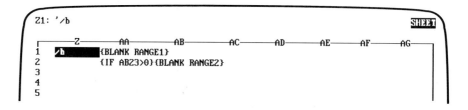

Commands for Enhancing Programs

The commands shown in table 22.6 can "dress up" a program or recalculate a portion of a worksheet. With skillful placement, these commands can add the polish that a solid program structure needs to become a smooth, easy-to-use application. This catchall group of maintenance-oriented commands includes commands to sound the computer's speaker, control the screen display, selectively recalculate portions of the worksheet, and invoke communications commands. Two commands in this group (WINDOWSOFF and PANELOFF) can increase significantly the execution speed of large Command Language programs.

The BEEP Command

The BEEP command activates the computer's speaker system to produce one of four tones. The form of the BEEP command is as follows:

{BEEP *number*}

or

{BEEP}

Table 22.6
Commands for Enhancing Programs

Command	Description
{BEEP}	Sounds one of the computer's four beeps
{PANELOFF}	Suppresses display of the control panel
{PANELON}	Displays the control panel
{WINDOWSOFF}	Suppresses the redrawing of the current window
{WINDOWSON}	Enables the redrawing of the current window
{INDICATE}	Resets the control panel indicator to *string*
{RECALC}	Recalculates a specified portion of the worksheet in row-by-row fashion
{RECALCCOL}	Recalculates a specified portion of the worksheet in column-by-column fashion
{PHONE}	Phones a remote computer
{HANDSHAKE}	Sends a single-line message to a remote computer

The optional *number* argument can be a number from 0 through 3. Each number produces a different tone. (Numbers greater than 3 produce a tone like their modulo 4 equivalent in the range 0 through 3). The BEEP command is commonly used to alert a user to a specific condition in the program or to draw the user's attention to an item.

The following BEEP statement produces a sound if the condition presented in the IF statement is true. If the statement is false, program control passes to the cell below the IF statement.

    {IF A35>50}{BEEP 2}

The PANELOFF Command

The PANELOFF command freezes the control panel, prohibiting the display of additional program commands in the control panel during program execution. You can use this command effectively to keep a specific message in the control panel, regardless of the cell pointer's current location. Be aware, however, that the PANELOFF command prevents the display of prompts from GETLABEL and GETNUMBER statements. The form of the PANELOFF command is as follows:

Reminder:
PANELOFF prevents the further display of commands and messages in the control panel.

    {PANELOFF}

In figure 22.35, the PANELOFF command in line 1 suppresses the control panel's display of the **C**opy command in line 2.

Fig. 22.35.
*Using PANELOFF
and PANELON.*

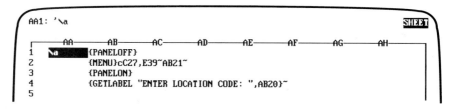

The PANELON Command

The PANELON command unfreezes the control panel. This command is commonly used immediately before a GETLABEL or GETNUMBER command. The form of the PANELON command is as follows:

{PANELON}

In figure 22.35, the PANELON command reactivates the control panel so that the prompt for the GETLABEL statement is displayed.

The WINDOWSOFF Command

Reminder:
*WINDOWSOFF
prevents the screen
from changing,
regardless of what
commands the
macro issues.*

By using the WINDOWSOFF command, you can freeze the lower part of the screen and have just the control panel show the changes that occur as a result of the commands activated in the program. The WINDOWSOFF command freezes the current screen display, regardless of whether the program is executing. WINDOWSOFF is particularly useful when you are creating applications to be used by novice Symphony users. WINDOWSOFF enables you to display only those screen changes that the user must see, freezing other changes that can confuse a beginner. The form of the WINDOWSOFF command is as follows:

{WINDOWSOFF}

In the following example, the WINDOWSOFF command prevents the automatic screen-rebuilding associated with the SHEET **C**opy command and the Calc key:

{WINDOWSOFF}
{MENU}cS24~Z12~{CALC}

Cue:
*Use
WINDOWSOFF
and PANELOFF to
improve execution
time.*

Using the WINDOWSOFF and PANELOFF commands can have a significant effect on program execution time. In a sample complex application, use of WINDOWSOFF and PANELOFF to freeze the screen reduced execution time by 50 percent: from 5 to 2 1/2 minutes. Speed improvement depends, of course, on the particular application.

You can use WINDOWSOFF with PANELOFF to create a graph "slide show" for business meetings. These commands enable you to display a sequence of graphs uninterrupted by intervening worksheet screens.

The program in figure 22.36 demonstrates how to use WINDOWSOFF and PANELOFF to eliminate screen shifting and to reduce execution time for such a presentation. The PANELOFF and WINDOWSOFF commands in AB1 suppress redrawing of the window and panel. Lines AB2 through AB8 display four different graphs, turning the window display on and off as needed. (Windows must be turned back on before each preview so that the graph can be seen.) In line AB9, the PANELON command restores function of the control panel. The program ends by returning the worksheet display with the cell pointer located at the Home position.

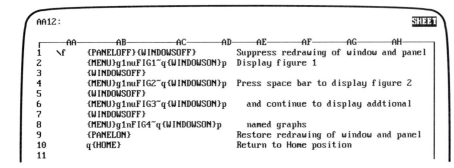

Fig. 22.36.
Using WINDOWSOFF and PANELOFF for a graphics slide show.

Be aware that if something goes wrong with a program while the WINDOWSOFF command is in effect, you can get into trouble. Unless you have a simple one-line program already preset for issuing the WINDOWSON command, you may have to reboot Symphony and start the application over again to recover the use of the screen. Therefore, you should develop and test your programs without the WINDOWSOFF and WINDOWSON commands; add these commands to the debugged and tested program.

Cue:
Add WINDOWSOFF and PANELOFF after you debug and test the program.

The WINDOWSON Command

The WINDOWSON command unfreezes the screen, allowing display of executing program operations. The command enables display of the on-screen consequences of Symphony menu selections. The form of the WINDOWSON command is as follows:

    {WINDOWSON}

In figure 22.36, the WINDOWSON command is used throughout the program so that the graphs can be seen when you preview.

Figure 22.37 shows how to use WINDOWSON along with the other three screen-control commands (WINDOWSOFF, PANELON, and PANELOFF) in subroutines that can substantially remove screen jitter. These commands can give your macros a more professional appearance. In addition, the ON and OFF subroutines shown in figure 22.37 significantly reduce the time for a macro to complete.

Fig. 22.37.

Using screen-updating commands in subroutines.

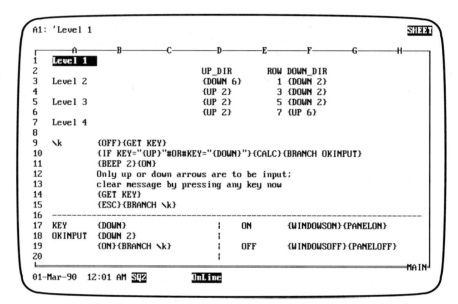

```
A1: 'Level 1                                                          SHEET

     ┌───A────────B────────C────────D────────E────────F────────G────────H────┐
   1 │Level 1                                                                  │
   2 │                                 UP_DIR       ROW DOWN_DIR                │
   3 │ Level 2                         {DOWN 6}       1 {DOWN 2}                │
   4 │                                 {UP 2}         3 {DOWN 2}                │
   5 │ Level 3                         {UP 2}         5 {DOWN 2}                │
   6 │                                 {UP 2}         7 {UP 6}                  │
   7 │ Level 4                                                                  │
   8 │                                                                         │
   9 │ \k        {OFF}{GET KEY}                                                 │
  10 │           {IF KEY="{UP}"#OR#KEY="{DOWN}"}{CALC}{BRANCH OKINPUT}         │
  11 │           {BEEP 2}{ON}                                                   │
  12 │           Only up or down arrows are to be input;                       │
  13 │           clear message by pressing any key now                         │
  14 │           {GET KEY}                                                     │
  15 │           {ESC}{BRANCH \k}                                              │
  16 │        ───────────────────────────────────────────────────────        │
  17 │ KEY       {DOWN}                   ┆   ON       {WINDOWSON}{PANELON}     │
  18 │ OKINPUT   {DOWN 2}                 ┆                                     │
  19 │           {ON}{BRANCH \k}          ┆   OFF      {WINDOWSOFF}{PANELOFF}   │
  20 │                                   ┆                                     │
     └────────────────────────────────────────────────────────────────MAIN──┘
     01-Mar-90  12:01 AM SQ2              OnLine
```

Figure 22.37 is a variant of the rolling-bar program shown in figure 22.3. By using the OFF and ON subroutines, the movement of the cursor from Level 1 to Level 4 when you press ↑ now appears continuous. These two subroutines let the cursor show at only two positions—before and after the move. The intermediate cursor movements that occur as the cursor moves down six rows are not displayed.

The call to the OFF subroutine halts screen updating before a keystroke is retrieved from the type-ahead buffer by the {GET KEY} statement. If an up or down arrow is pressed, screen updating is turned on again just after the cursor is relocated; the ON subroutine call in the last line of OKINPUT accomplishes this. The branch back to \k turns off screen updating again.

The ON subroutine call after the BEEP in row 11 allows the error message to be displayed. After the user clears the message by pressing any key, the branch to \k turns off screen updating again.

Note: When you quit a macro, the window and the panel are turned back on automatically, even if the macro didn't do so before finishing. However, you still have to refresh the screen (by pressing Enter, for example) if WINDOWSOFF was in effect when the macro finished.

The INDICATE Command

The INDICATE command alters the mode indicator in the upper right corner of the screen. This command is commonly used to provide custom indicators. The INDICATE command accepts a string argument of up to seven characters. If the string is longer, Symphony uses only the first seven characters. When you use INDICATE, you must enter a string; you cannot use a cell address or range name. The form of the INDICATE command is as follows:

{INDICATE *string*}

Suppose that you want to display the message **START** in the upper right corner of the screen. You can use the following INDICATE command:

{INDICATE START}

The **START** message remains on display until you exit Symphony, unless you clear the indicator using this command:

{INDICATE}

To blank out the indicator completely, you can use this command:

{INDICATE ""}

To summarize, {INDICATE} lets Symphony regain control of the indicator; {INDICATE ""} keeps the indicator blank regardless of what Symphony does.

The RECALC and RECALCCOL Commands

Two commands, RECALC and RECALCCOL, enable you to recalculate a portion of the worksheet. Recalculating parts of the worksheet can be useful in large worksheets where recalculation time is long and where you need to recalculate certain values in the worksheet before you proceed to the next step in the macro. The commands for partial recalculation have the following form:

{RECALC *location,condition,iteration_number*}

and

{RECALCCOL *location,condition,iteration_number*}

In these syntaxes, *location* is a range or range name that specifies the cells whose formulas are to be recalculated. The *condition* and *iteration_number* arguments are optional.

If you include the *condition* argument, the range is recalculated repeatedly until *condition* has logical value of TRUE (1). The *condition* argument must be either a logical expression or a reference to a cell within the recalculation range that contains a logical expression. If *condition* is a reference to a cell outside the recalculation range, the value of *condition*, either TRUE (1) or FALSE (0), does not change, and *condition* does not control the partial recalculation.

If you include the *iteration_number* argument, you also must specify the *condition* argument (use the value 1 to make *condition* always TRUE). *iteration_number* specifies the number of times that formulas in the location range are to be recalculated.

The macro in figure 22.38 is similar to the one shown in figure 22.28. The macro in figure 22.38 is designed to run properly when the recalculation method is set to manual; the macro in 22.28 does not run properly unless the recalculation method is set to automatic.

Fig. 22.38.

Using the RECALC command.

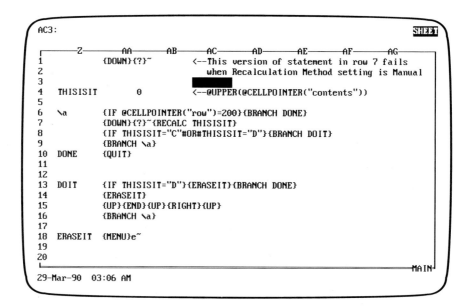

```
AC3:                                                                SHEET
        ┌───Z────────AA──────AB──────AC──────AD──────AE──────AF──────AG──
        1              {DOWN}{?}~         <--This version of statement in row 7 fails
        2                                    when Recalculation Method setting is Manual
        3
        4    THISISIT        0              <--@UPPER(@CELLPOINTER("contents"))
        5
        6    \a         {IF @CELLPOINTER("row")=200}{BRANCH DONE}
        7               {DOWN}{?}~{RECALC THISISIT}
        8               {IF THISISIT="C"#OR#THISISIT="D"}{BRANCH DOIT}
        9               {BRANCH \a}
        10   DONE       {QUIT}
        11
        12
        13   DOIT       {IF THISISIT="D"}{ERASEIT}{BRANCH DONE}
        14               {ERASEIT}
        15               {UP}{END}{UP}{RIGHT}{UP}
        16               {BRANCH \a}
        17
        18   ERASEIT    {MENU}e~
        19
        20                                                                       MAIN
        29-Mar-90  03:06 AM
```

Recalculating manually is a good idea when you have a large worksheet with many formulas that depend on values being repetitively updated. However, you probably won't have to recalculate every formula for each new entry. Using RECALC is a fast way to update a selected set of formulas.

The RECALC in line 7 ensures that THISISIT is based on the most recent user input. Formulas that depend on THISISIT may not work properly, but IF statements which reference its value will access a value for THISISIT based on the most recent input—provided that a RECALC command for the range is issued first. Therefore, the IF statements on lines 8 and 13 work properly.

Reminder:

RECALC calculates row by row; RECALCCOL calculates column by column.

The RECALC and RECALCCOL commands differ in the order in which cells in the specified range are recalculated. The RECALC command performs the calculations by row: all the cells in the first row of the range are recalculated, then all the cells in the second row, and so on. The RECALCCOL command performs the calculations by column: all the cells in the first column of the range are recalculated, then all the cells in the second column, and so on. In both commands, only cells within the specified range are recalculated.

Use RECALC to recalculate the range when the formulas in the range refer only to cells in rows above or to the left in that range. Use RECALCCOL to recalculate the range when formulas in the range refer only to cells above or in columns to the left in the range.

Note: You may have to use CALC instead of RECALC or RECALCCOL if formulas in the range refer to cells below or to the right.

Include in the recalculation range only those cells you want to recalculate. The formulas in the recalculation range can refer to values in cells outside the range; however, those values are not updated by RECALC or RECALCCOL.

When either the RECALC or RECALCCOL command is executed, the partial recalculation occurs immediately. The results do not appear on-screen, however, until the screen is redrawn. Program execution may continue for some time before a command that updates the screen is executed. In the interim, the recalculated numbers, although not visible on-screen, are available for use in calculations and conditional tests.

If the program ends and you want to be sure that the recalculated numbers are on-screen, use the PgUp and PgDn keys to move the window away from and back to the recalculated range. The act of looking away and back again updates the screen and displays the current values in the recalculated range.

You may have to use CALC, RECALC, or RECALCCOL after commands such as LET, GETNUMBER, and {?}. You do not have to recalculate after invoking Symphony commands such as SHEET **C**opy and **M**ove; Symphony automatically recalculates the affected ranges after such commands, even during program execution.

Caution: Recalculating a portion of the worksheet can cause some formulas (those outside a recalculated range that reference formulas within the range) to fail to reflect current data. If this situation occurs in your application, be sure to perform a general recalculation (using {CALC}) at some point before the end of the program.

The PHONE Command

The PHONE command enables you to phone a remote computer without having to switch to a COMM window. The general form of this command is as follows:

{PHONE *phone_number_string*}

Figure 22.39 shows an example of how to use the PHONE command. Notice that *phone_number_string* is the range name PHONE_NO. You also can use a string formula for the argument.

Reminder:
Use PHONE to phone a remote computer without switching to a COMM window.

Fig. 22.39.

A program that uses the PHONE and HANDSHAKE commands.

```
AA20:                                                            SHEET
      ┌──AA────────AB────────AC────────AD────────AE────────AF────────AG────────AH──┐
  1   │  \c        {WAIT @TIME(22,00,00)}
  2   │            {PHONE PHONE_NO}{BRANCH NO_GO}
  3   │            {HANDSHAKE "CPS\013","USER ID:",10}
  4   │            {HANDSHAKE "76030.10\013","Password:",10}
  5   │            .
  6   │            .
  7   │            {HANDSHAKE "\013","!",240,CAPTURE_RANGE}
  8   │            {HANDSHAKE "bye\013","Off",20}
  9   │
 10   │  NO_GO     {GETLABEL "COULD NOT CONNECT!",MSG}
 11   │
```

Notice the BRANCH statement that follows the PHONE statement in cell AB2. If Symphony is unable to make a connection, the program executes the statement following the PHONE command in the same line (in this case, {BRANCH NO_GO}). If a connection is made, however, the next statement that Symphony executes is on the line below the PHONE statement.

The HANDSHAKE Command

Reminder:

Send a single-line message to a remote computer with HANDSHAKE.

You can send single-line messages to a remote computer without having to switch to a COMM window. The command to send messages is HANDSHAKE, and its general form is as follows:

{HANDSHAKE *send_string,receive_string,seconds,capture_ location*}

The *send_string* argument is the string you want to send; *receive_string* is the string you expect from the remote computer in response to *send_string*. The *seconds* argument is the number of seconds you want to allocate for sending *send_string* and receiving *receive_string*. This number is the maximum amount of time you want Symphony to take to complete the transaction. Symphony moves immediately to the next statement when *receive_string* is read. The final argument, *capture_location*, is optional. It indicates where you want Symphony to save any text that the remote computer sends before sending the expected *receive_string* (but not including *receive_string*).

Suppose that after establishing a connection to a computer service that provides stock information, you want to send all the log-in messages and menu responses for calling up stock information on the remote system. The HANDSHAKE statements in figure 22.39 show how you can do this.

In the first HANDSHAKE statement, notice that the *send_string* argument includes the string **CPS** followed by the decimal ASCII code for the Enter key (**\013**). You must use the decimal ASCII code, or the HANDSHAKE statement does not work properly. Send the \013 code whenever the remote computer expects the Enter key; otherwise the remote computer cannot process your input correctly.

The second HANDSHAKE statement is similar to the first: it sends the user-ID number and receives the **Password:** prompt from the remote computer.

The next HANDSHAKE statement is only slightly different from the first two. Because this statement includes a *capture_location* argument, issuing this statement causes Symphony to save the text that precedes the receive string (in this case, the text that precedes "!") on the same line in the capture location. In practice, you rarely need to include a *capture_location* argument. Do not confuse this argument with the capture range required for capturing large amounts of data.

Note: An advantage to being in a COMM window when you run this macro is that you can see how the other computer responds to the macro's input.

The combination of the WAIT, PHONE, and HANDSHAKE statements makes the delayed accessing of remote systems quite easy.

Commands for Manipulating Files

Eight commands give Symphony the capability of opening, reading, writing, and closing a sequential data file containing ASCII text data. This capability allows Symphony applications to read and write files used by other business applications. Although the SERVICES **F**ile **I**mport command provides a limited capability to manipulate foreign files, the file-manipulation commands listed in table 22.7 provide a capability equal to the sequential-file commands in BASIC or other programming languages.

Table 22.7
Commands for Manipulating Files

Command	Description
{OPEN}	Opens a file for reading, writing, or both
{CLOSE}	Closes a file opened with OPEN
{READ}	Copies the specified characters from the open file to *location*
{READLN}	Copies the next line from the open file to *location*
{WRITE}	Copies a string to the open file
{WRITELN}	Copies a string plus a carriage-return, line-feed sequence to the open file
{SETPOS}	Sets a new position for the file pointer
{GETPOS}	Records the position of the file pointer in *location*
{FILESIZE}	Records the size of the open file in *location*

> **Warning**
>
> The file-manipulation commands are programming commands. To read from and write to foreign files successfully, you must understand exactly how these commands work and how the sequential files you are manipulating are organized. If you write to a file containing another application, be sure to back up the file before trying to write to it from Symphony.
>
> If you keep this warning in mind, this group of commands can open up the world of outside files to your Symphony applications. If you need to process external data files, these commands make it possible to do the job with Symphony.

In this section, the term *file pointer* refers to a byte position in a file. *Bytes* are basic units of data in a file (for example, characters in a text file). Bytes are numbered starting at 0 and incrementing through the file. The file pointer is a place marker in an open file.

The OPEN Command

Reminder:

Use OPEN to access a file from or to which you want to read or write data.

The OPEN command opens a disk file, providing access so that you can write to or read from that file. The form of the OPEN command is as follows:

{OPEN *filename,access_mode*}

The *filename* argument is a string, an expression with a string value, or a single-cell reference to a cell that contains a string or a string expression. The string must be a valid DOS file name or path name. A file in the current directory can be specified by its name and extension. A file in another directory may require a drive identification, a subdirectory path, or a complete DOS path in addition to the file name and extension.

The *access_mode* argument is a single-character string that specifies whether you want to read only ("R"), write only ("W"), both read from and write to the file ("M"), or restrict access to the end of the file ("A"). The following chart explains the values that the *access_mode* argument can assume:

"R" (Read)   Opens an existing file and allows access with the READ and READLN commands. You cannot write to a file opened with Read access.

"W" (Write)   Opens a new file with the specified name and allows access with the WRITE and WRITELN commands. Any existing file with the specified name is erased and replaced by the new file.

"M" (Modify)   Opens an existing file with the specified name and allows access with both read (READ AND READLN) and write (WRITE and WRITELN) commands.

"A" (Append)   Opens an existing file and positions the file pointer at the end of the file. Append access allows access with WRITE and WRITELN commands.

Symphony allows only one file to be open at a time. If you want to work with more than one file in an application, you must close one file before opening and using the next file.

The OPEN command succeeds if it can open the file with the access you requested. If the OPEN command succeeds, program execution continues with the cell below the OPEN command. Any commands after the OPEN statement in the current cell are ignored.

The OPEN command can fail with an ERROR if the disk drive is not ready. If the access mode is Read or Modify, but the file does not exist in the indicated directory, the OPEN command fails and program execution continues with the commands after the OPEN command in the current cell. You can place one or more commands after the OPEN command in the same cell to deal with the failure. The most common practice is to place a BRANCH or a subroutine call after the OPEN command to transfer control to a subroutine that handles the failure.

Reminder:
If OPEN fails, program execution continues with the commands after the OPEN command in the current cell.

Following are some examples and explanations of the OPEN command:

{OPEN "PASTDUE",R}{BRANCH FIXIT}

Opens the existing file named PASTDUE in the current directory for reading. If the file cannot be opened, branches to the routine FIXIT.

{OPEN "C:\DATA\CLIENTS.DAT",W}

Opens the new file named CLIENTS.DAT in drive C, subdirectory DATA, for writing.

{OPEN FILE,M}{BRANCH RETRY}

Opens the file whose name is in cell FILE for Modify access. If the file cannot be opened, branches to the routine RETRY.

Figure 22.40 shows an example that uses all the file commands except the READ and WRITE commands (which are similar to READLN and WRITELN). The program named \o uses the OPEN command to open a user-specified file. This program shows how to deal with **Disk drive not ready** and **File not found** errors. Next, the OPEN command is used with the BRANCH command. This BRANCH handles such problems as a **File not found** error.

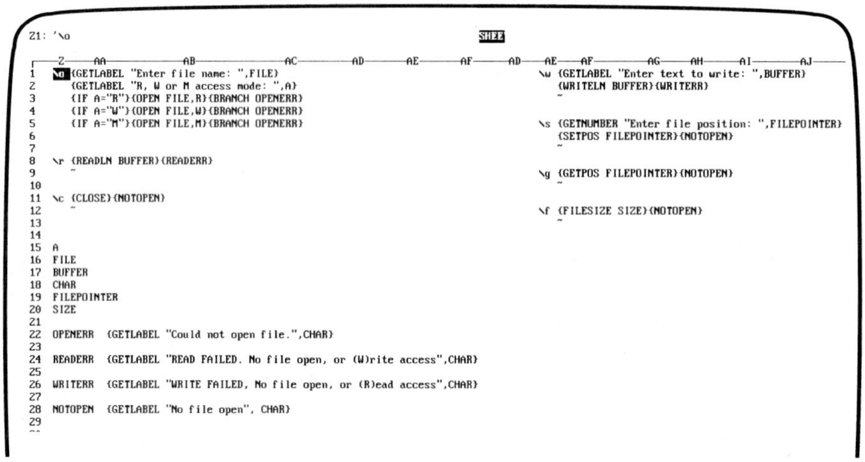

Fig. 22.40.

A program that uses the file-manipulation commands.

```
Z1: '\o                                              SHEET
    -Z-----AA--------AB---------AC-----AD----AE----AF----AD---AE----AF------AG-----AH------AI-----AJ----
1   \o {GETLABEL "Enter file name: ",FILE}                    \w {GETLABEL "Enter text to write: ",BUFFER}
2      {GETLABEL "R, W or M access mode: ",A}                     {WRITELN BUFFER}{WRITERR}
3      {IF A="R"}{OPEN FILE,R}{BRANCH OPENERR}
4      {IF A="W"}{OPEN FILE,W}{BRANCH OPENERR}
5      {IF A="M"}{OPEN FILE,M}{BRANCH OPENERR}             \s {GETNUMBER "Enter file position: ",FILEPOINTER}
6                                                             {SETPOS FILEPOINTER}{NOTOPEN}
7      ~
8   \r {READLN BUFFER}{READERR}
9      ~                                                    \g {GETPOS FILEPOINTER}{NOTOPEN}
10
11  \c {CLOSE}{NOTOPEN}                                     \f {FILESIZE SIZE}{NOTOPEN}
12
13
14
15     A
16     FILE
17     BUFFER
18     CHAR
19     FILEPOINTER
20     SIZE
21
22     OPENERR  {GETLABEL "Could not open file.",CHAR}
23
24     READERR  {GETLABEL "READ FAILED. No file open, or (W)rite access",CHAR}
25
26     WRITERR  {GETLABEL "WRITE FAILED, No file open, or (R)ead access",CHAR}
27
28     NOTOPEN  {GETLABEL "No file open", CHAR}
29
```

The CLOSE Command

The CLOSE command closes the currently open file. If no file is open, the CLOSE command has no effect. CLOSE does not take an argument. The CLOSE command is particularly important for files that you are writing or modifying. You can lose the last data written to a file that you don't close. The form of the CLOSE command is as follows:

{CLOSE}

Under most circumstances, Symphony automatically takes care of a file that you do not close, but you should make it a practice to use CLOSE when you finish using any file opened with OPEN. Better safe than sorry. Use of the CLOSE command is shown in the macro labeled \c in figure 22.40.

The READ Command

The READ command reads a specified number of characters from the currently open file, beginning at the current file-pointer location. The form of the READ command is as follows:

{READ *bytecount,location*}

Reminder:

READ places as a label the specified number of characters from an open file into the indicated cell location.

In this syntax, *bytecount* is the number of bytes to read, and *location* is the cell to read into. READ places the specified number of characters from the file into the *location* cell as a label. *bytecount* can be any number between 1 and 240, the maximum number of characters in a Symphony label. If *bytecount* is greater than the number of characters remaining in the file, Symphony reads the remaining characters into *location*. After the READ command finishes, the file pointer is positioned at the character following the last character read.

For example, the following statement transfers information from the open file into the cell location named INFO:

{READ NUM,INFO}

The amount of information transferred is determined by the contents of the cell named NUM, which can contain either a value or a formula.

The READ command is useful when you want to read a specific number of characters into the worksheet. A data file that contains fixed-length records, for example, can be read conveniently with the READ command when *bytecount* is set to equal the record length.

You should not use READ with ASCII text files from a word processor or text editor. Such files generally have variable-length lines terminated with a carriage-return, line-feed sequence. Such lines can be read better with the READLN command. Although figure 22.40 does not contain an example of the READ command, READ is used much like READLN in the figure's \r macro.

The READLN Command

The READLN command reads one line of information from the currently open file, beginning at the file pointer's current position. The READLN command form is as follows:

{READLN *location*}

The characters read are placed in the specified *location* in the current worksheet. For example, the following statement copies a line from an open file into the cell named HERE:

{READLN HERE}

The line on which the file pointer is located can be determined by the SETPOS command. (SETPOS is discussed later in this chapter.)

Use READLN to read a line of text from a file whose lines are delimited by carriage-return, line-feed combinations. For example, use READLN to read the next line from an ASCII text file. ASCII text files can be created with Symphony's SERVICES **P**rint **S**ettings **D**estination **F**ile command. Also referred to as *print files*, these files are assigned the PRN file extension by Symphony. READLN is best suited to reading files that are print images. The macro labeled \r in figure 22.40 shows the use of READLN.

Reminder:
Use READLN instead of READ to read a line from a file that has carriage-return, line-feed combinations at the ends of the lines.

> **Tip**
>
> If no file is open, or if the file was opened with Write access, the READ or READLN command is ignored and program execution continues in the same cell. Otherwise, after the READ or READLN command is completed, program execution continues on the next line. You should place a BRANCH or subroutine call after the READ or READLN statement to handle the problem of an unexecuted READ or READLN statement.

The WRITE Command

The WRITE command writes a string of text to the currently open file. The WRITE command has the following form:

> {WRITE *string*}

Cue:

Use WRITE to write to a file that contains fixed-length database records.

The *string* argument can be a literal string, a range name, or a cell reference to a single cell that contains a string or a string expression. Because WRITE does not place a carriage-return, line-feed sequence at the end of the string, you can use multiple WRITE commands to concatenate text on a single line. WRITE is well-suited to creating or updating a file that contains fixed-length database records. Although figure 22.40 does not contain an example of the WRITE command, this command is used in much the same way as is the WRITELN command in the \w macro in that figure.

If the file pointer is not at the end of the file, Symphony overwrites existing characters in the file. If the file pointer is at the end of the file, Symphony extends the file by the number of characters written. And if the file pointer is past the end of the file (see the discussion of the SETPOS command), before writing the characters, Symphony extends the file to the position of the file pointer and then adds the string.

The WRITELN Command

Reminder:

WRITELN places a carriage-return, line-feed sequence after the last character written.

The WRITELN command is identical to the WRITE command except that WRITELN places a carriage-return, line-feed sequence after the last character written from the string. The WRITELN command form is as follows:

> {WRITELN *string*}

WRITELN is useful when the file being written or updated uses a carriage-return, line-feed sequence to mark the end of the lines or records. In many applications, you can use several WRITEs to write a line to the file, then issue a WRITELN to mark the end of the line. The WRITELN command is shown in the \w macro in figure 22.40.

The SETPOS Command

The SETPOS command sets the position of the file pointer to a specified value. The form of the command is as follows:

{SETPOS *file_ position*}

The *file_ position* argument is a number, or an expression resulting in a number, that specifies the character at which you want to position the pointer. The first character in the file is position 0, the second is position 1, and so on.

Reminder:

The first character in a file is at file-pointer position 0; the second character is at position 1; and so on.

Suppose that you have a database file with 100 records, each 20 bytes long. To access the first record, you can use these commands:

{SETPOS 0}

{READ 20,BUFFER}

To read the 20th record, you can use these commands:

{SETPOS (20–1)*20}

{READ 20,BUFFER}

Nothing prevents you from setting the file pointer past the end of the file. If you set the file pointer at or past the end and execute a READ or READLN command, the READ or READLN does nothing, and program execution continues with the next command on the same line. If you set the file pointer at or past the end and execute a WRITE or WRITELN command, Symphony extends the file to the length specified by the file pointer, and then, starting at the file pointer, writes the characters.

Warning: If you inadvertently set the file pointer to a large number with SETPOS and write to the file, Symphony attempts to expand the file and write the text at the end of the file. If the file does not fit on the disk, the WRITE command does nothing, and program execution continues with the next command on the same line. If the file does fit on the disk, Symphony extends the file and writes the text at the end of the file.

If a file is not currently open, SETPOS does nothing, and execution continues with the next command on the same line as the SETPOS command. If no error results from the SETPOS command, execution continues on the next line of the program. You should place a BRANCH command or a subroutine call after the SETPOS command to handle the problem of an unexecuted statement. The use of SETPOS is shown in the \s program in figure 22.40.

The GETPOS Command

The GETPOS command enables you to record the file pointer's current position. The form of this command is as follows:

{GETPOS *location*}

The current position of the file pointer is placed in the cell indicated by *location*, where *location* is either a cell reference or a range name. If *location* points to a multicell range, the value of the file pointer is placed in the upper left corner of the range.

The GETPOS command is useful to record the location of something you want to find again. You can use GETPOS to mark the current place in the file before you use SETPOS to move the file pointer to another position. You can use GETPOS, for example, to record the locations of important items in a quick-reference index. The use of GETPOS is shown in the \g macro in figure 22.40.

The FILESIZE Command

The FILESIZE command returns the length of the opened file in bytes. The form of the command is as follows:

{FILESIZE *location*}

FILESIZE determines the current length of the file and places this value in the cell referred to by *location*, where *location* can be a cell reference or range name. If *location* refers to a multicell range, the file size is placed in the cell in the upper left corner of the range. The use of FILESIZE is shown in the \f macro in figure 22.40.

A Command Language Application

Although Symphony's **P**rint menu provides most of the capabilities needed for a variety of worksheet-printing tasks, you cannot use the **P**rint menu to print multiple copies of a single report automatically. To print multiple copies of the same report, you must repeatedly select the commands for aligning paper and beginning the print operation. With Symphony's Command Language, you can create a program to accomplish these tasks. You can enhance the program by adding help screens and prompts that will help users solve problems that may occur during the print operation.

Figure 22.41 shows a Command Language program for printing multiple copies of a report. Notice that this program includes 10 of the commands discussed in the previous sections of this chapter. These commands include the following:

❑ Commands for accepting input: GET, GETNUMBER, and LOOK

❑ Commands for program control: BRANCH, MENUCALL, and BREAKOFF

```
 21: '\p                                                            SHEET
   ┌───Z──────AA─────AB─────AC─────AD─────AE─────AF─────AG─────
   1   \p      {GETNUMBER "Enter number of copies: ",STOP}~
   2           {IF @ISERR(STOP)}{BEEP}{BRANCH \p}
   3           {PANELOFF}{BREAKOFF}{GOTO}MSG_SCRN~
   4           {WINDOWSOFF}{FOR COUNT,1,STOP,1,PRINT}~{BEEP 3}{WINDOWSON}
   5
   6   COUNT           1
   7   STOP            4
   8   INTERRUPT
   9   MESSAGE
  10
  11   PRINT   {LOOK INTERRUPT}
  12           {IF INTERRUPT="{MENU}"}{BRANCH ABORT}
  13           {SERVICES}pagpq
  14
  15   ABORT   {BEEP 2}{GET MESSAGE}~
  16           {MENUCALL MSG}
  17           {QUIT}
  18
  19   MSG                         - PRINT JOB ABORTED AT YOUR REQUEST -
  20           {Press Enter to end macro execution (printer may not stop immediate
  21           {CALC}{RETURN}
  22
```

Fig. 22.41.
A Command Language program that prints multiple copies of a report.

❏ Decision-making commands: IF and FOR

❏ Program-enhancement commands: BEEP and PANELOFF

In the program's first line, the GETNUMBER command prompts you for the number of copies to be printed. For example, if you want four copies, enter **4** in response to the prompt **Enter number of copies:**. The GETNUMBER command stores the number in the range STOP (cell AA7). Notice the companion error-checking routine for GETNUMBER in the program's second line.

In line 3, PANELOFF prevents movement on the control panel (so that you aren't distracted); BREAKOFF disables Ctrl-Break; and a message screen (with the range name MSG_SCRN) is incorporated into the worksheet. This message screen informs you that the print job is in progress and explains what to do if something goes wrong (see fig. 22.42). Notice that cell AJ9 in figure 22.42 uses a string formula to tell you how many copies are to be printed.

Cue:
Use a full-screen help screen to display a message during macro execution.

In figure 22.41, two additional range names (INTERRUPT and MESSAGE) appear in lines 8 and 9, respectively. The PRINT subroutine contains a LOOK statement followed by an IF statement, both of which use the range INTERRUPT. Two other subroutines, ABORT and MSG, are used also. (The range to be printed must be predefined.)

Fig. 22.42.

The message displayed by the print program.

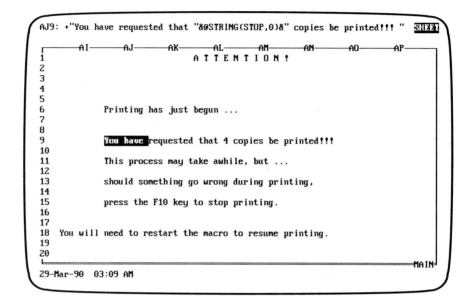

```
AJ9: +"You have requested that "&@STRING(STOP,0)&" copies be printed!!! "   SHEET
      r----AI-------AJ-------AK-------AL------AM------AN------AO-------AP----
      1                        A T T E N T I O N !
      2
      3
      4
      5
      6              Printing  has  just  begun ...
      7
      8
      9              You have requested that 4 copies be printed!!!
     10
     11              This process may take awhile, but ...
     12
     13              should something go wrong during printing,
     14
     15              press the F10 key to stop printing.
     16
     17
     18   You will need to restart the macro to resume printing.
     19
     20
      L                                                             MAIN
      29-Mar-90   03:09 AM
```

When you run the program, the following actions take place. First, the prompt **Enter number of copies:** is displayed in the control panel. After you enter a number, a message screen similar to the one shown in figure 22.42 appears. The string formula in cell AJ9 is updated with the value entered in STOP, confirming the number of copies to be printed. You are told to press F10 if you want to interrupt the print operation. At this point, printing begins.

Suppose that you requested the wrong number of copies to be printed. As soon as you press F10, the computer beeps, the menu message **– PRINT JOB ABORTED AT YOUR REQUEST –** appears in the control panel, and you are instructed to **Press Enter to end macro execution** (see fig. 22.43).

Fig. 22.43.

Message showing that the print job has been aborted.

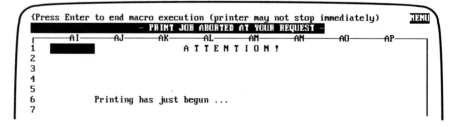

```
{Press Enter to end macro execution (printer may not stop immediately)   MENU
              – PRINT JOB ABORTED AT YOUR REQUEST –
      r----AI-------AJ-------AK-------AL------AM------AN------AO-------AP----
      1
      2                        A T T E N T I O N !
      3
      4
      5
      6              Printing  has  just  begun ...
      7
```

How did all these steps occur? The essential elements in this method of stopping the program are the LOOK and IF statements in the PRINT subroutine.

LOOK checks the type-ahead buffer to see whether anything was typed during program execution. If something was typed, the first character is copied into the range named INTERRUPT. If a function key was pressed, the name representation for that function key is stored in INTERRUPT. In this program, each time LOOK is executed, Symphony checks INTERRUPT to see whether anything is stored there. For instance, if you press F10, {MENU} is stored in INTERRUPT.

INTERRUPT is then evaluated by the IF statement, which indicates that if INTERRUPT contains the string "{MENU}", the program should branch to the subroutine ABORT; otherwise, the program should print the worksheet. Note that you must press F10 to stop printing. Pressing any other key causes a false condition in the IF statement, and the print routine executes. Because both LOOK and IF are part of PRINT, these two commands are executed whenever the FOR statement executes the loop; INTERRUPT is checked on every pass.

When program control moves to ABORT, no additional reports are printed. ABORT causes the computer to beep and issues the GET command to clear the keyboard buffer (LOOK doesn't do this). ABORT then displays the menu message stored in MSG. Because {MENUCALL MSG} is used, the {RETURN} in the MSG subroutine sends the program back to ABORT when you press Enter. Because the cell after {MENUCALL MSG} contains QUIT, the program ends.

Figure 22.44 shows what happens if you press F10 during program execution. Because you pressed F10, the range name INTERRUPT contains the string "{MENU}". Notice that the range name MESSAGE also contains "{MENU}" (GET put the string there). Because {MENU} has already done its job with LOOK and is now useless, MESSAGE is nothing more than the "wastebasket" where GET sends all unwanted characters.

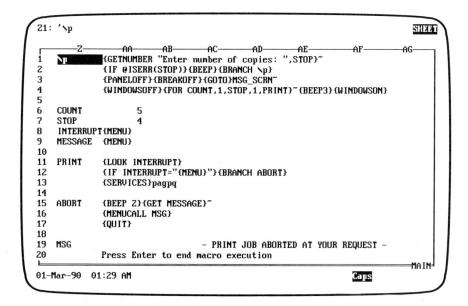

Fig. 22.44.

The print program after the F10 key has been pressed.

This example is a sophisticated program for a special application that uses many Symphony capabilities, including string formulas and keyword commands. You may want to use this program if you occasionally print multiple copies of long reports (or even if you print multiple copies of short reports).

Other Command Language Programs

The following examples include some Command Language programs that you can use in Symphony's SHEET, GRAPH, COMM, and FORM environments.

A Program to Avoid Fatal Macro Errors

Cue:

*Use OPEN instead of **F**ile **R**etrieve to avoid a fatal macro error.*

When you try to retrieve a file that does not exist with Symphony's **F**ile **R**etrieve command, a fatal error results. This kind of error terminates macro control. The Symphony OPEN macro command enables you to check for the existence of a file before you actually retrieve it. You should use OPEN to avoid one kind of fatal error for a macro.

Figure 22.45 shows the problem and a solution. The problem is in macro \a. This macro fails and halts execution when FILENAME does not exist in DIRECTORY. You have to press Esc after the error to regain control of the keyboard.

Fig. 22.45.

Avoiding a fatal error with the OPEN command.

```
H1:                                                              SHEET
 ┌──────A───────B───────C───────D───────E───────F───────G───────H──┐
 1   DIRECTORY    a:
 2   FILENAME     temp
 3   FILESTRING   "a:temp.wr1"      <---- +QUOTE&DIRECTORY&FILENAME&".wr1"&QUOTE
 4   OUTCOME
 5   QUOTE               "
 6
 7   NOTE: \a will fail if FILENAME does not exist
 8   \a          {SERVICES}fd{ESC}
 9               a:~               <---- +DIRECTORY&"~"
10               {SERVICES}fr
11               temp~             <---- +FILENAME&"~"
12
13   note: \b checks to see if FILENAME exists before attempting a retrieve
14   \b          {OPEN "a:temp.wr1",R}{LET OUTCOME,FAILED}~{QUIT}      <---¦
15               {LET OUTCOME,SUCCEEDED}                                   ¦
16               {CLOSE}~                                                  ¦
17               {WAIT @NOW+@TIME(0,0,3)}{BRANCH \a}                       ¦
18                                                                        ¦
19                                                                        ¦
20   \b FORMULA: +"{OPEN "&FILESTRING&",R}{LET OUTCOME,FAILED}~{QUIT}" ----¦
 └────────────────────────────────────────────────────────────────MAIN┘
   29-Mar-90  02:52 AM
```

Macro \b serves as a front-end to \a to prevent the fatal error. If FILENAME does not exist in DIRECTORY, the user is informed by the **FAILED** entry in OUTCOME. Next, the \b macro quits, but it could just as easily branch to a new location and continue. In any event, the macro avoids the possibility of a fatal error that can halt macro \a when \a is run by itself.

The trick to \b is the operation of OPEN in Read mode. When the file to be opened does not exist, the command performs any remaining commands on the same line before executing commands on the next line. Therefore, if FILENAME is not in DIRECTORY, OUTCOME is set to **FAILED**, the screen is updated by the tilde representing an Enter keystroke, and the macro quits.

If FILENAME does exist in DIRECTORY, OUTCOME is set to **SUCCEEDED**. The file is closed, and the WAIT command pauses the computer so that you can see the message **SUCCEEDED** in the OUTCOME cell before the program branches back to \a to retrieve another file. The SUCCEEDED outcome is coded to occur in an if-then-else style: the SUCCEEDED outcome is the else clause, and the trapped error is the then clause.

A Program To Image-Save a Series of Graphs

The graph-printing macro in Chapter 21 was designed to print a single graph. If you want to print more than one graph in a file, use the program in figure 22.46. This program displays the graph menu (line 1), has you select which graph you want to print, and previews the graph so that you can make sure you chose the correct one (line 2). Line 3 of the macro invokes the **I**mage-Save command and pauses for you to enter a file name for the graph. In line 4, the program asks if you want to print another graph and stores your response in a cell named ANSWER. If you pressed Y for Yes, the program branches back to the cell named ANOTHER and prompts for the next graph. If you pressed anything but Y, the file is saved with the same name, and the macro exits from Symphony.

Cue:
*Use a macro to invoke the **G**raph Image-Save command multiple times.*

After you run this macro, all the graphs are saved in PIC files, and you can load the PrintGraph program to print the graphs.

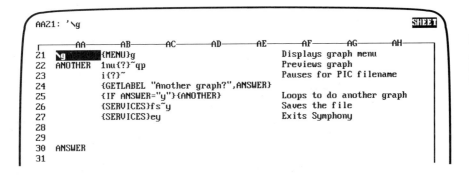

Fig. 22.46.
A program to image-save a series of graphs.

A Program To Auto-Dial

Cue:

Use a series of macros to automate a phone-dialing task using a database of telephone numbers.

If you have a worksheet or database file of phone numbers, you can create several programs that automatically dial each number in the list. Figure 22.47 shows an auto-dialing program. The \d dialing program dials the telephone number on which the cell pointer is located, and the \h hang-up program disconnects the call when you are finished, moves the pointer to the next number, and reactivates the \d program.

Fig. 22.47.

A program that includes auto-dialing and auto-hang-up macros.

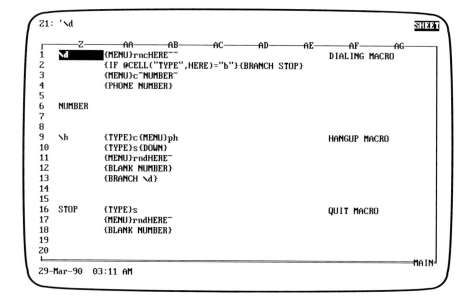

The first line of \d assigns the range name HERE to the current cell. Line 2 uses the IF command to test whether the cell is blank. If so, the program branches to the STOP subroutine. STOP deletes the range name HERE, erases the number in NUMBER, and quits the program's execution.

If the current cell is not blank, however, the third line in the \d program is executed. This line copies the telephone number (the current cell) into the cell named NUMBER. Line 4 dials the number with the PHONE command.

The first line in the \h program hangs up the phone. The second line switches to SHEET mode and moves the pointer down one cell to the next phone number. The next two lines are housekeeping commands that delete the range name HERE and erase the last phone number from the cell named NUMBER. Notice that the program uses the Command Language BLANK command, which is faster than the SHEET **E**rase command. The last line of the hang up program branches back to the dialing program.

A Program To Redial

If you frequently get a busy signal when dialing an electronic bulletin board or information service, you can use the redialing program in figure 22.48 to redial continuously until you connect.

Cue:
Use a macro to automatically redial a phone until you get a connection.

All you have to do is press Esc if you get a busy signal (or no answer), and the macro dials the number again. This program assumes that you have entered the phone number into the communications settings sheet.

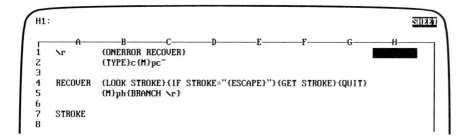

Fig. 22.48.
A program to redial a telephone number.

The first line of the macro sets a trap for an error condition (such as a no-carrier error caused by a busy signal). The next line of the macro changes to the COMM environment and dials the number. The {GET STROKE} line puts the next keystroke you type into a cell named STROKE. The IF statement tests the contents of the STROKE cell. If you pressed Esc, the program hangs up the phone, branches back to the beginning of the program, and dials again. If you pressed any other key, the macro ends.

A Program To Create Entry Forms

A program that can help you make more efficient use of the FORM environment is one for building entry forms. Figure 22.49 shows a looping macro that takes field name, type, and length information and builds a range that is ready for the FORM **G**enerate command.

Cue:
Use a macro to prompt for field name, type, and length information necessary for a database entry form.

The first line of the macro uses the WINDOWSOFF command to eliminate the shifting of the screen when data is entered.

The range name LOOP marks the place in the code to which the macro branches after entering in the worksheet all the information associated with a field name. The cell named LOOP contains the first of three GETLABEL commands. The first GETLABEL retrieves the field name and places it in a cell called NAME. (NAME and all the other cells used as the target-location cells for the GETLABEL commands are listed below the macro.) The second GETLABEL retrieves the field-type designation; the third GETLABEL retrieves the field length. The RECALC statement recalculates the cell called COMBO, which concatenates NAME, DATATYPE, and LENGTH (including the appropriate colons) when those fields contain entries. The RECALC statement is essential here, or else the formula will reflect the entry from the previous loop.

Fig. 22.49.

A program to generate a database.

```
AB6: '{MENU}rvCOMBO~~                                           SHEET

        AA      AB        AC      AD      AE      AF      AG      AH
1    MAIN     {WINDOWSOFF}
2    LOOP     {GETLABEL "Enter field name: ",NAME}
3             {GETLABEL "Enter (N)umber,(L)abel,or (D)ate: ",DATATYPE}
4             {GETLABEL "Enter length: ",LENGTH}
5             {RECALC COMBO}
6             {MENU}rvCOMBO~~
7             {GETLABEL "More fields? (Y/N): ",ANSWER}
8             {IF ANSWER="Y"}{DOWN}{BRANCH LOOP}
9             {WINDOWSON}
10            {TYPE}F{MENU}G~~~
11            ,{END}{UP}~
12
13
14
15   NAME
16   DATATYPE
17   LENGTH
18   COMBO            ERR
19   ANSWER
20                                                             MAIN

29-Mar-90  03:14 AM
```

The formula stored in the cell named COMBO is as follows:

+NAME&@IF(DATATYPE<>"",":"&DATATYPE&@IF(LENGTH<>"",":"&LENGTH,""),"")

This formula concatenates the DATATYPE and LENGTH strings to the NAME string only if DATATYPE and LENGTH contain entries. Otherwise, just the NAME string appears in COMBO.

Note: Do not leave spaces in the formula for documentation purposes, or the formula generates a syntax-error message.

After the RECALC statement, the next statement uses the SHEET **R**ange **V**alues command to copy COMBO to the cell where the cursor is currently positioned. As you recall, **R**ange **V**alues converts the formula to an actual value as the command copies from one location to another.

Next, another GETLABEL command asks whether more fields exist for this input form. The IF statement that follows determines whether the answer is Y; if it is, the statements to the right of the IF are executed (the cell pointer moves down to the next row and the macro loops back to LOOP). If you respond with anything other than Y, the next line is executed. Window display is turned back on, and the **G**enerate command creates the database.

Programs To Change Default Values

Symphony lets you specify one default value for each field in a database so that if most of your records contain a certain value, you don't have to enter this value into each record. Sometimes, though, you have several values that appear frequently in a field. With some simple macros, you can quickly change the default values on-the-fly as you enter data.

Defaults are specified by entering values in the Default column of the database's definition range. For this example, assume that the two values commonly used in the CITY field of a database are San Francisco and San Jose. Also assume that the default cell for the CITY field in this sample database is cell D12.

Consider these two macro programs:

        \1   {LET D12,San Francisco}
              {CALC}{ESC}
        \2   {LET D12,San Jose}
              {CALC}{ESC}

The first program, \1, puts **San Francisco** into D12 and recalculates so that the new default is reflected. The second program, \2, puts San Jose into D12. Because the LET statement is used to place the values, you can execute these programs at any time in any window environment. When you want to activate a new default, press the User (F7) key followed by the appropriately numbered function key (F1 or F2 in this example).

An Address-Entry and Mailing-Label System

The final application presented in this chapter is actually a system comprised of two macro programs, a data-entry area, and a data-storage area. The first macro accepts address lines by referencing data-entry and data-storage areas. The second macro prints two-across labels by referencing these same two areas in reverse order; in this application, the data-entry area helps you input addresses for the first macro and lay out labels for the second.

Cue:

Use a series of macros to simplify data entry and automate the printing of two-across mailing labels.

Figure 22.50 shows the data-entry area. It starts with a header title line; you may want to replace the title of this sample firm—CAB—with the name of your company. Following the title are five address lines. The data-storage area can be anywhere in the worksheet that has blank rows. In this example, however, the first vacant cell of the storage area is named LINE 1.

The macro code to facilitate the entry of address lines into the data-entry area is shown in figure 22.51. This macro assumes that the INPUT.APP add-in that comes with Symphony is already attached.

Fig. 22.50.

The data-entry area for the mailing-label application.

```
B3: A                                                              SHEET
   ┌──────A──────────────B──────────────C──────────────D─────────
 1 │ CAB Address Input/Output Form
 2 │
 3 │ Line 1    ████████████████████████████████
 4 │ Line 2
 5 │ Line 3
 6 │ Line 4
 7 │ Line 5
 8 │
 9 │
10 │
11 │ 1) Enter address one line at a time.
12 │ 2) Use Up/Down or Left/Right arrow keys to move from one line to the next.
13 │ 3) End input by presssing Escape or Enter without typing anything new
14 │    on a line.
15 │
```

Fig. 22.51.

The macro for the address entry in the mailing-label application.

```
IA11: '\a                                                         SHEET
   ┌──IA──────IB──────IC──────ID──────IE──────IF──────IG──────IH──
 3 │ \p       {SERVICES}sgyq{RETURN}
 4 │ \u       {SERVICES}sgnq{RETURN}
 5 │ OFF      {WINDOWSOFF}{PANELOFF}{RETURN}
 6 │ ON       {WINDOWSON}{PANELON}{RETURN}
 7 │ DONE     yes
 8 │
 9 │ CLEAR    {MENU}e.{DOWN 4}~
10 │
11 │ \a       {GOTO}B3~{OFF}{GOTO}A1~
12 │          {MENU}rpp{TAB}{DOWN 6}{RIGHT}~
13 │          {MENU}rpa{ESCAPE}{DOWN 2}{RIGHT}{TAB}{DOWN 4}~
14 │          {\p}
15 │          {MENU}ri{TAB}{DOWN 6}{RIGHT}{ON}~
16 │          {OFF}{\u}{GOTO}B3~{MENU}rt{END}{DOWN}~LINE 1~{CLEAR}
17 │          {GOTO}LINE 1~{DOWN}
18 │          /rncLINE 1~~/rndLINE 1~/rncLINE 1~~
19 │          {LET DONE,""}{GETLABEL "Done (YES/NO)?",DONE}
20 │          {HOME}{GOTO}B3~{ON}
21 │          {IF DONE="YES"}{QUIT}
22 │          {BRANCH \a}
   └──────────────────────────────────────────────────────────MAIN┘
02-Apr-90  10:06 PM
```

The INPUT-APP add-in restricts cursor movement to an unprotected range within a protected range. In this application, the unprotected range is B3..B7 in figure 22.50; the protected range is A1..B7. On-screen instructions in rows 11 through 14 of figure 22.50 explain how to enter an address record after it is completed (you press Enter without typing any new input on a line—it does not matter if there is already something on the line).

Rows 11 through 14 of figure 22.51 set up the protected and unprotected ranges. The **R**ange **I**nput command is invoked in row 15. After **R**ange **I**nput is invoked, the cursor-movement commands set up the **R**ange **I**nput range so that the user can enter address lines. When the user signals the end of the input, the macro turns off screen updating by calling the OFF routine (see line 16 in fig. 22.51).

Once the macro resumes control, the **R**ange **T**ranspose command is used to copy the address lines to LINE 1, the next vacant row in the data-storage area. The address lines are erased from the data-entry area with the subroutine call to CLEAR. Next, the LINE 1 range in the storage area is moved down one row.

In the last part of the macro, a GETLABEL command prompts the user to enter YES or NO to signal whether all address entry is completed. Unless the user replies **YES**, the program branches back to \a for more address input. When the user replies with **YES** to the prompt, the macro quits.

The mailing-label macro in figure 22.52 shows how to print two-across labels. The print parameters are set for an Epson LQ-800 printing on Avery brand two-across labels. Two-across labels are attractive for mass-mailing label production because printing goes faster than with one-across labels. Three-across and four-across labels are available, but require a printer with an extra-wide carriage.

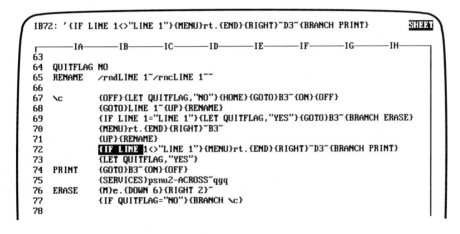

```
IB72: '{IF LINE 1<>"LINE 1"}{MENU}rt.{END}{RIGHT}~D3~{BRANCH PRINT}        SHEET

     -IA-------IB-------IC-------ID------IE------IF------IG------IH-
63
64   QUITFLAG  NO
65   RENAME    /rndLINE 1~/rncLINE 1~~
66
67   \c        {OFF}{LET QUITFLAG,"NO"}{HOME}{GOTO}B3~{ON}{OFF}
68             {GOTO}LINE 1~{UP}{RENAME}
69             {IF LINE 1="LINE 1"}{LET QUITFLAG,"YES"}{GOTO}B3~{BRANCH ERASE}
70             {MENU}rt.{END}{RIGHT}~B3~
71             {UP}{RENAME}
72             {IF LINE 1<>"LINE 1"}{MENU}rt.{END}{RIGHT}~D3~{BRANCH PRINT}
73             {LET QUITFLAG,"YES"}
74   PRINT     {GOTO}B3~{ON}{OFF}
75             {SERVICES}psnu2-ACROSS~qgq
76   ERASE     {M}e.{DOWN 6}{RIGHT 2}~
77             {IF QUITFLAG="NO"}{BRANCH \c}
78
```

Fig. 22.52.
The macro for printing two-across labels in the mailing-label application.

The macro in figure 22.52 accesses a range of address records in the format created by the macro in figure 22.51. The \c macro assumes that the range name LINE 1 points to a blank cell just below the first line of the last label in the range. Successive labels are on each row going up the range until a cell with the contents **LINE 1** is encountered; this is the marker for the end of the labels.

The pairs of labels for the two-across forms are constructed in the display area shown in figure 22.50. Three adjacent columns (B, C, and D) are used to simulate the two-across form. Column C simulates the gap between the labels in columns B and D; the width of column C is set to 6. The widths of columns B and D are set to 30. These widths are less than the theoretical maximum to accommodate some lack of precision in form alignment.

The macro in figure 22.52 starts at \c by setting the range QUITFLAG to NO and moving the cursor to cell B3. The screen is updated to show the cursor's location by turning the screen ON and then OFF (the ON and OFF routines use

WINDOWSON, PANELON, WINDOWSOFF, and PANELOFF). Next, the cursor moves to LINE 1, so that the contents of the next cell can be checked. If that cell contains **LINE 1**, QUITFLAG is set to YES. If the cell contains anything other than **LINE 1**, the label in that row is transposed to the cell in B3. The second label is constructed in a similar fashion; rows 71 and 72 show the code.

As long as at least one label is left, it is printed. Printing is accomplished with the aid of the print settings sheet named 2-ACROSS. This sheet sets the print range. It also sets page breaks to NO so that printing starts at the very top of a form without leaving space for headers.

After printing, the print range (B3..D8) is erased. If QUITFLAG equals NO, the macro branches to \c to print at least one new mailing label. Otherwise, the macro comes to a halt at the blank in cell IB78.

Chapter Summary

As you work with the Symphony Command Language, you soon discover that this powerful spreadsheet program has an extremely potent programming language.

Although Symphony's Command Language makes many things possible, be aware of some practical limitations. For example, because Symphony is RAM-based, you must limit the size of the worksheet files. Database files, with the new @BASE add-in, can be as large as DOS allows (32 MB). Memory-management improvements new with Symphony 2.2 dramatically improve the amount of RAM you can use with expanded memory.

Symphony may not always execute programming commands with lightning speed because it is based on an interpreter that decodes each command before executing it. Several tips for making macros go faster are discussed in this chapter (turning screen updating off, using macro commands instead of menu commands where possible, and avoiding the use of RETURN). A trade-off exists between development time and execution time. Techniques for speeding macro execution are sometimes difficult to program.

If you are an adventurer who wants to develop efficient, automated, customized models, the Command Language is for you. This chapter has provided the groundwork for developing such models. As you become more experienced with the Command Language, turn to other Que publications for help in becoming an expert Command Language programmer.

Part VIII

Quick Reference Guide to Using Symphony

Troubleshooting Section

Using the Symphony Command Reference

Appendix A: Installing Symphony

Appendix B: Allways Menu Map and PrintGraph Menu Map

Index

Troubleshooting

Troubleshooting Installation

INSTALLATION PROBLEM #1:

You can't print, and you can't display graphs on a color monitor.

Explanation: The program requires a file, called a *driver set*, that describes the equipment used in your system. This file must have the extension SET. When you execute Symphony, the program looks for the file LOTUS.SET, which contains the driver set. The Setup disk contains an initial driver set called LOTUS.SET. (You can find the driver set after the Setup program decompresses it.) This driver set uses a Universal Text Display driver that works with almost any display but has no support for printers and cannot display graphs.

Solution: Run the Install program and follow the prompts to describe your computer system. If you don't give the driver set a special name, Install names it LOTUS.SET.

If you use different displays on your computer system, you may need several driver sets. Use Install to set up different driver sets and give them individual names. To tell the program to use a driver set other than LOTUS.SET, specify the name of the SET file when you execute the program.

For example, if you have a VGA card and monitor, you may want to use the 80-column-by-34-row display in some cases and the 80-column-by-60-row display in others. Set up two separate SET files by running Install and select the appropriate settings. Name one driver set 80X34.SET and the other 80X60.SET.

When you want to use the 80-column-by-34-row display, invoke Symphony by typing **SYMPHONY 80X34** at the DOS prompt; to use the 80-column-by-60-row display, type **SYMPHONY 80X60**.

If you always use the same display with your system, let Install name the driver set LOTUS.SET. When you start Symphony, you don't have to type the name of the driver set file because Symphony looks automatically for LOTUS.SET.

INSTALLATION PROBLEM #2:

When loading Symphony, the system hangs with a blank screen, forcing you to reboot.

Explanation: The default Universal Text Display driver works with almost any display. If you have a color monitor, however, and try to start the program with a driver installed for a monochrome monitor, or vice versa, you hang the system.

Solution: First, if your driver set is not named LOTUS.SET, make sure that you specified the proper driver set when you executed Symphony. For example, suppose that LOTUS.SET is set for a monochrome display and COLOR.SET is set for a color monitor. Be sure to specify COLOR.SET when you use a color monitor. If you have only the LOTUS.SET file, rerun Install and check the driver set to make sure that it is set for the type of monitor you are using.

Alternative Explanation: Two sets of switches located within an IBM Personal Computer tell the computer what kind of monitor, how much memory, how many floppy disk drives you have, and so on. The XT contains one set of switches. Although the AT has no switch settings, its SETUP program serves the same purpose.

One of the switch settings on the PC or XT tells the computer whether you have a math coprocessor chip installed. This special chip can perform math functions many times faster than the regular microprocessor in your computer.

If you do not have a math coprocessor, but the switch settings indicate that you do, the system hangs as soon as you try to run the program.

You may have owned your computer for years and not been aware that this switch setting is incorrect; the computer operates properly as long as you do not run programs that try to use the math coprocessor. Some editions of the *IBM Guide to Operations*, which is part of the standard documentation package shipped with most computers, show the switch settings reversed.

Alternative Solution: If you do not have a math coprocessor, set the switch indicated in your guide to the ON position, even if the guide states otherwise.

If you have an AT, run the SETUP program and make sure that you do not indicate that you have a math coprocessor if none is installed. If you have a Personal System/2, this type of error cannot occur because no switch settings or SETUP programs exist.

INSTALLATION PROBLEM #3:

You have access to several printers and plotters that you use occasionally to print worksheets and graphs, but keeping track of all the driver sets for these different configurations is difficult.

Explanation: Symphony lets you use only the printers and plotters in your driver set. If you put all the output devices in different driver sets, you must remember which driver set to use whenever you execute the program.

Solution: Do not set up different driver sets for each printer or plotter. Put all the printers and plotters in one set.

You must use more than one driver set only when you change either the physical display or the way Symphony displays information, which is an option with some display systems. (With a VGA card, for example, you can display text in 25-row-by-80-column, 34-row-by-80-column, or 60-row-by-80-column mode.)

If you switch equipment and use different printers and plotters, you can install them all in one driver set. Whenever you specify a text printer, Install asks whether you have another printer. If you sometimes attach another printer to your system, answer **Y**es and then select the other printer. You can specify as many as four text printers and four different graphics printers. Repeat the step for any printers or plotters that you might attach to your computer for printing graphs. For example, if you use a printer to print both spreadsheets and graphs, specify it twice (once as a text printer for Symphony and once as a graphics printer for PrintGraph).

Because the program does not expect more than one printer or plotter to be used at a time, you can install more than one, even when only one is attached. Then, while you're working in Symphony, use SERVICES **C**onfiguration **P**rinter **N**ame to select the printer currently attached to your computer. If you want the printer you choose to remain the default, select SERVICES **C**onfiguration **U**pdate (this command saves the defaults to disk; whenever you start Symphony, the same defaults are in effect).

If you attach printers to different ports on your computer, you must use SERVICES **C**onfiguration **P**rinter **T**ype to tell Symphony which printer interface to use. Parallel printers usually are `Parallel 1`. If you have more than one parallel-printer port, specify the one to which the printer is connected. If you use a serial printer, specify which serial port you're using (usually `Serial 1`). If you use a local-area network, and printed output is redirected to another computer, you may have to specify DOS device LPT1:, LPT2:, LPT3:, or LPT4:. (Use SERVICES **C**onfiguration **P**rinter **T**ype to specify the DOS device.)

With the PrintGraph program, use **S**ettings **H**ardware **P**rinter to specify the printer or plotter. Symphony then lists all the graph printers and plotters included in your driver set (see fig. T.1). Use **S**ettings **H**ardware **I**nterface to specify the correct LPT (parallel) or COM (serial) port. After you make the changes, use **S**ettings **S**ave to make the new settings the default.

Fig. T.1.

A list of all graph output devices in the driver set.

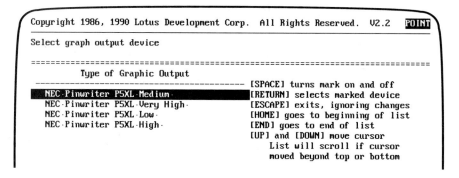

```
Copyright 1986, 1990 Lotus Development Corp.  All Rights Reserved.  V2.2  POINT

Select graph output device

=================================================================================
      Type of Graphic Output
----------------------------------------------- [SPACE] turns mark on and off
  NEC-Pinwriter P5XL-Medium·              [RETURN] selects marked device
  NEC-Pinwriter P5XL-Very High·           [ESCAPE] exits, ignoring changes
  NEC-Pinwriter P5XL-Low·                 [HOME] goes to beginning of list
  NEC-Pinwriter P5XL-High·                [END] goes to end of list
                                          [UP] and [DOWN] move cursor
                                              List will scroll if cursor
                                              moved beyond top or bottom
```

INSTALLATION PROBLEM #4:

You can't find your printer listed in the list of printers.

Explanation: Lotus Development supplies a large number of printer drivers but doesn't directly support every printer.

Solution: Most PC printers have switches you can set to control the command set they use. If your printer can be set to emulate the IBM Graphics printer or an Epson printer, set the switches and then select the type of printer being emulated.

Alternative Solution: Many printer manufacturers supply printer driver files for use with Lotus 1-2-3 and Symphony. Contact your printer manufacturer to see if these drivers are available. If they are, use the **A**dvanced **O**ptions selection in the Install program to add the drivers to the library.

INSTALLATION PROBLEM #5:

You can't find your modem listed in the list of modems.

Explanation: Most PC direct-connect modems are Hayes compatible.

Solution: Select Hayes as the modem type.

INSTALLATION PROBLEM #6:

You bought extra memory for your computer but Symphony doesn't show it when you select SERVICES **S**ettings.

Explanation: Symphony can use only *conventional* and *expanded* memory. Memory added on to an 80286, 80386, or 80486 system is usually *extended* memory, which Symphony cannot use.

Solution: Use an expanded-memory driver to convert some or all the extended memory to expanded memory. DOS V4.01 includes such a driver (the driver is called EMM386.SYS, and it works with DOS V3.1 or higher on 80386 and 80486 systems). Many extended-memory boards also include expanded-memory drivers.

Troubleshooting the Symphony Spreadsheet

Problems with Data Entry

DATA ENTRY PROBLEM #1:

After you type a label that starts with a number, Symphony beeps and puts you in EDIT mode.

Explanation: When you begin typing information in a cell, Symphony changes the SHEET mode indicator in the screen's upper right corner to either LABEL or VALUE. If the first character you type is a number or a symbol used in a formula, Symphony assumes that you are typing a value. If you then type any character that is invalid for a value entry and press Enter, Symphony beeps, moves the cursor to the first character it rejects, and switches to EDIT mode.

Solution: To type a label such as **353 Sacramento Street**, you must first type a label prefix, such as an apostrophe ('), so that Symphony knows you are working with a label. If you forget to enter the prefix and Symphony beeps, press Home and insert the prefix.

If the label is a valid numeric entry, instead of an error you get a numeric calculation you don't want. For example, if you type **842-7162** as a telephone number, Symphony evaluates the entry as a formula and displays **–6320**. Edit the field to change it from a number to a label.

DATA ENTRY PROBLEM #2:

When you finish writing a complex formula, Symphony beeps and switches to EDIT mode. If you can't find the error immediately, you have to press Esc. You lose the entire formula and have to start again.

Explanation: When you type an invalid formula, Symphony does not accept the entry and switches to EDIT mode. You must provide a valid entry before you can continue.

Solution: Make the formula a valid entry by converting it to a label: press Home, type an apostrophe, and press Enter. Then you can work on the problem until you find and correct the error. Or you can work on another part of the worksheet and return to the formula later.

One common reason that Symphony rejects a formula is the use of an unnamed range name. If you forgot to create a range name, convert the formula to a label, create the range name, and then edit the formula to remove the label prefix.

Tip

Here is a method for debugging complex formulas. For example, suppose that you enter this formula in a cell:

@IF(@ISERR(A1/A2),@IF(A2=0),0,@ERR),A1/A2)

When you press Enter, Symphony beeps and switches to EDIT mode. If the error isn't obvious, you are stuck. You cannot exit EDIT mode unless you either fix the error or press Esc, erasing the contents of the cell. But because Symphony accepts anything as a label, you can insert a label prefix at the beginning of the entry and then press Enter. Copy the formula to another cell and work on the formula until you find the error.

In this case, begin by eliminating the compound @IF from the formula. To do so, copy the formula to a blank cell (a work area) and erase the middle @IF statement, replacing it with a 0 (zero):

@IF(@ISERR(A1/A2),0,A1/A2)

Because this formula works, the problem must be in the @IF statement you erased. Again, copy the original formula to the work area. Now delete everything except the middle @IF:

@IF(A2=0),0,@ERR)

You can see that you should erase the right parenthesis that follows A2=0. Make the change and test it:

@IF(A2=0,0,@ERR)

When this segment works, erase the work cell and correct the original formula:

@IF(@ISERR(A1/A2),@IF(A2=0,0,@ERR),A1/A2)

You may write formulas that are longer and more complex than this example. To debug them, simply convert them to labels and test them, one part at a time.

Problems with Circular References

CIRCULAR REFERENCE PROBLEM #1:

The `Circ` indicator suddenly appears after you enter a formula.

Explanation: Whenever the worksheet is recalculated and a `Circ` indicator appears at the bottom of the screen, Symphony is warning you about a circular reference. Circular references are formulas that refer to themselves, either directly or indirectly. Because they are usually errors, you should correct circular references as soon as they occur.

An example of the most common *direct* circular reference is shown in figure T.2. In this example, the @SUM function includes itself in the range to be summed. Whenever the worksheet recalculates, this sum increases.

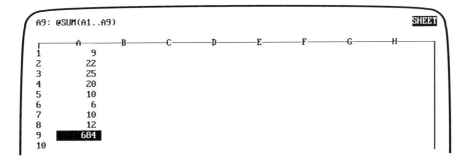

Fig. T.2.
A direct circular reference.

Solution: Change the @SUM formula to include the cells through A8, but excluding A9; the `Circ` indicator disappears.

CIRCULAR REFERENCE PROBLEM #2:

The `Circ` indicator appears after you enter a formula, but the formula does not refer to itself.

Explanation: Symphony is warning you about an *indirect* circular reference, which is tricky to find and to fix. No formula refers to itself, but two or more formulas refer to each other. For example, each formula in figure T.3 seems reasonable, but A1 refers to A3, A2 refers to A1, and A3 refers to A2. You have no way of evaluating these formulas. The numbers increase whenever the worksheet recalculates.

Fig. T.3.

An indirect circular reference.

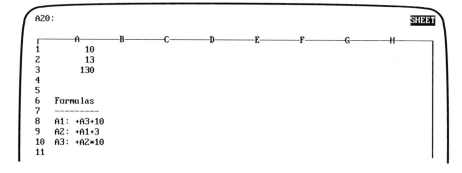

Solution: If you can't find an obvious reason for the **C i r c** indicator, use SHEET **S**ettings to find the cell location of the circular reference (see fig. T.4). If, after looking at the formula in the specified cell, you still cannot find the problem, write down the formula and check the contents of every cell referenced. You will eventually track down the problem.

Fig. T.4.

SHEET Settings showing a circular reference.

```
Set default label alignment (left, right, center)               MENU
Label-Prefix  Recalculation  Titles  Format  Width  Zero  Auto-Link  Quit

   Circular          A1
   Label-Prefix:     '
                                              Titles
   Recalculation                                 Columns: 0
      Method:         Automatic                  Rows:    0
      Order:          Optimal                    Format:  (G)
      Iterations:     1                          Width:   9
                                              For window: MAIN
   Zero Suppression: No
   Auto-Link:  Yes
                                                     Sheet Settings
```

Alternative Explanation: @CELL("width") can cause an annoying circular reference if you use the cell address that contains this function to determine the width of the column that contains the formula. For example, if cell C9 contains the following formula, a circular reference results:

@CELL("width",C9..C9)

Alternative Solution: Because all the cells in a column are the same width, change the formula to refer to another cell in the same column:

@CELL("width",C8..C8)

CIRCULAR REFERENCE PROBLEM #3:

You have a formula that is *supposed* to be a circular reference, and you don't know how many times to recalculate to get the correct answer.

Explanation: Even deliberate circular references can be a problem. Figure T.5 shows a profit calculation in which total profit depends on the amount of the executive bonus, but the bonus is based on profits—a legitimate circular reference. Every time Symphony recalculates, the profit figure comes closer to the right answer. The problem lies in knowing how many recalculations you need. The general answer is that you must recalculate until the change in the results is insignificant.

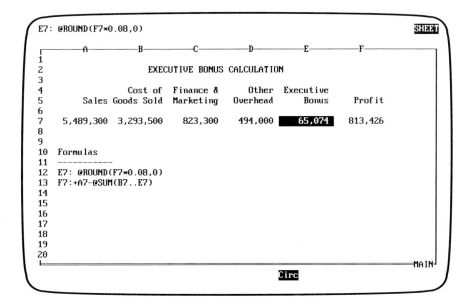

Fig. T.5.
A deliberate circular reference.

Solution: You can recalculate manually if you have a one-time calculation and a small worksheet. Use @ROUND to set the required precision. In figure T.5, the bonus is rounded to whole dollars. Then press Calc (F8) to calculate the worksheet until the profit number does not change. In the example shown in figure T.5, you must calculate the worksheet five times before the profit figure stops changing.

If the numbers change often, and you want to recalculate automatically, use the macro in figure T.6 to recalculate the profit information until PROFIT is equal to OLD PROFIT in cell F3. Figure T.6 shows the result of executing the macro. In most cases, cell F3 would be hidden. This macro works because RECALC proceeds row-by-row, and F3 is above PROFIT. If OLD PROFIT were below PROFIT, this macro would not work because the two numbers would always be the same and the macro would stop at the first RECALC.

Fig. T.6.

A macro that automatically solves a circular reference.

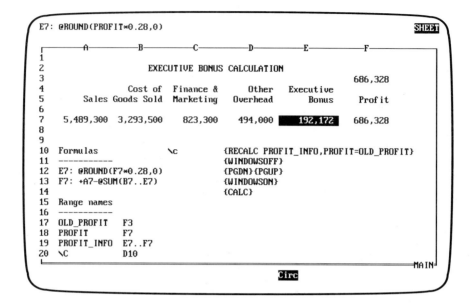

```
E7:  @ROUND(PROFIT*0.28,0)                                              SHEET
         A          B         C          D          E          F
  1
  2                      EXECUTIVE BONUS CALCULATION
  3                                                            686,328
  4                 Cost of   Finance &     Other    Executive
  5          Sales Goods Sold  Marketing   Overhead     Bonus      Profit
  6
  7      5,489,300 3,293,500    823,300    494,000  ▌192,172      686,328
  8
  9
 10    Formulas               \c          {RECALC PROFIT_INFO,PROFIT=OLD_PROFIT}
 11    ----------                         {WINDOWSOFF}
 12    E7: @ROUND(F7*0.28,0)              {PGDN}{PGUP}
 13    F7: +A7-@SUM(B7..E7)               {WINDOWSON}
 14                                       {CALC}
 15    Range names
 16    ----------
 17    OLD_PROFIT    F3
 18    PROFIT        F7
 19    PROFIT_INFO   E7..F7
 20    \c            D10
                                                                    MAIN
                                Circ
```

CIRCULAR REFERENCE PROBLEM #4:

An ERR is created in one of the cells in an intentional circular reference, which causes all the cells in the circular reference also to return ERR. You remove the source of the ERR, but the remaining cells continue to show an ERR.

Explanation: Cells that depend on a cell that returns an ERR also return an ERR. If two or more cells with ERR refer to each other, the result is always ERR. Once the cells in the circular reference have been "contaminated," you may not be able to eliminate all the ERRs after you correct the original error no matter how many times you recalculate.

Solution: First break the circular reference; then correct the error and recalculate. The fastest way to break the circular reference is to copy the cells that evaluate to ERR to a work area and then erase the original cells. Next calculate the worksheet, which should cause the ERR indicators to disappear. Finally, copy the formulas back to the original cells and erase the work area.

Problems with ERR

ERR PROBLEM #1:

A formula that had been working correctly suddenly changes to ERR.

Explanation: A valid formula can be destroyed by certain subsequent entries. When Symphony cannot evaluate part of a formula, it changes that part of the formula to ERR, and the result is ERR.

Moves, deletions, and certain entries can destroy or invalidate a formula. If you move a cell or a range to a cell referenced in a formula, Symphony replaces the reference with ERR (see fig. T.7).

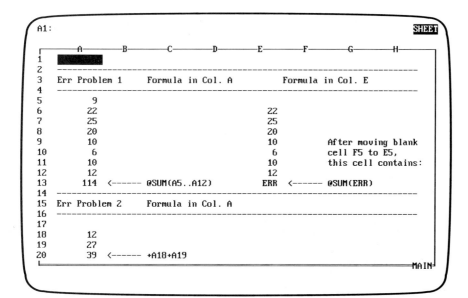

Fig. T.7.
Moving cells to turn a formula to ERR.

Solution: If you want to move a value into a cell after you refer to that cell in a formula, you cannot use the SHEET **M**ove command. Instead, you must use SHEET **C**opy to copy the cell and then erase the original cell.

If you want to move a formula to a cell after you have referred to the cell in a formula, again you cannot use the SHEET **M**ove command. Instead, you must use SHEET **C**opy, following these steps:

1. Edit the formula to convert it to a label.
2. Copy the label to the cell.
3. Edit the label to convert it back to a formula.
4. Erase the original cell.

You convert the formula to a label to prevent relative-cell references from changing when you copy the formula.

If you want the cell references to change when you copy the formula to its new location, just copy the cell as a formula.

ERR PROBLEM #2:

Formulas change to ERR after you delete a row or a column somewhere else in the worksheet.

Explanation: Although you seldom deliberately delete a row or column containing information used in formulas, deleting such information accidentally is not unusual. The SHEET **D**elete **R**ows or **C**olumns command deletes the entire row or column in the window without giving you a chance to inspect the entire row or column; you see only the usual screenful of cell entries. Information contained in the row or column may be somewhere off-screen. Figure T.7 shows a formula (in cell B20) before row 18 was deleted. Figure T.8 shows the effect of deleting the row; the referenced cell changes to ERR.

Fig. T.8.

Deleting cells to turn a formula to ERR.

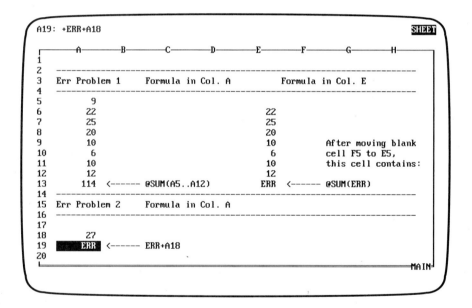

```
A19: +ERR+A18                                                    SHEET

       ┌───A────────B────────C────────D─────E─────F─────G─────H───
     1 │
     2 │ ----------------------------------------------------------------
     3 │ Err Problem 1      Formula in Col. A        Formula in Col. E
     4 │ ----------------------------------------------------------------
     5 │        9
     6 │       22                                 22
     7 │       25                                 25
     8 │       20                                 20
     9 │       10                                 10        After moving blank
    10 │        6                                  6        cell F5 to E5,
    11 │       10                                 10        this cell contains:
    12 │       12                                 12
    13 │      114   <------ @SUM(A5..A12)        ERR  <------ @SUM(ERR)
    14 │ ----------------------------------------------------------------
    15 │ Err Problem 2      Formula in Col. A
    16 │ ----------------------------------------------------------------
    17 │
    18 │       27
    19 │      ERR   <------ ERR+A18
    20 │                                          .
       └────────────────────────────────────────────────────────MAIN
```

Solution: Avoid this problem by checking the worksheet carefully before you delete rows or columns. To check a row, move the cell pointer to the row and then press End ← and End → to move to the beginning and end of the row in the active window. Use End ↓ and End ↑ to move to the end and beginning of the column in the window.

Even this method is not foolproof. A formula can legitimately refer to a blank cell in a row or column that is completely blank. Perhaps the cell is to contain data that has not yet been entered. If you delete this blank row or column, the formula that refers to the cell in that row or column changes to ERR.

The most foolproof way to avoid this error is to do the following:

1. Save the worksheet.
2. In a blank cell, put an @SUM formula that sums the entire active area (from A1 to End Home).
3. Delete the row or column and, if recalculation is set to **M**anual, press Calc (F8).

If the @SUM formula changes to ERR, you know that somewhere a cell changed to ERR when you deleted the row or column. Search the worksheet until you find the ERR. If a formula is in error, correct it. If the deleted row or column is needed, retrieve the worksheet you saved before the deletion.

ERR PROBLEM #3:

String formulas change to ERR after you erase a cell or a range.

Explanation: With numeric formulas, it usually does not matter whether a cell contains a number or a string or whether it is blank. Blank cells and cells containing strings are treated as zeros in numeric calculations.

String formulas, however, are not as forgiving as numeric formulas. A string formula results in ERR if any referenced cell is blank or contains numeric values. If you erase a cell used in a string formula, the string formula changes to ERR. This change may be acceptable if you plan to enter new data in the cell. Figure T.9 shows some examples of numeric and string formulas.

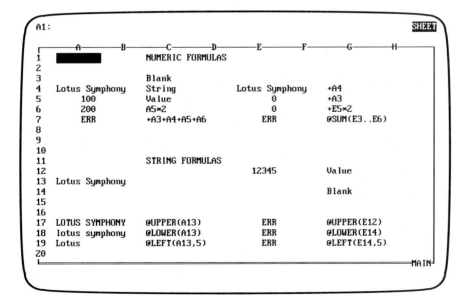

Fig. T.9.

Blank cells and numbers causing ERR in string formulas.

Solution: If you are sure that you will complete the blank cells before you print the worksheet, nothing needs to be done. In fact, the ERR can remind you that data is missing.

If the data is optional, you must trap the possible error in the formula. You can test for a null string in the cell before referencing the cell in the formula. A blank cell is treated as though it contains a null string (""). For example, the following formula concatenates the strings in A1 and B1 if both contain strings:

+A1&B1

If A1 always contains a string and B1 can be blank, change the formula to the following:

+A1&@IF(@CELL("type",B1..B1)="b","",B1)

If A1 is either blank or a number, the result is ERR, and Symphony warns you that something is wrong. If B1 is blank, no error occurs, and the formula equates to the contents of A1.

Here's another formula that behaves in a similar manner:

+A1&@S(B1..B1)

The @S function avoids errors, filtering out anything that is not a string. This formula works if B1 contains a label or number, or is blank.

Problems with Memory Management

MEMORY PROBLEM #1:

While working on a large worksheet, you run out of memory.

Explanation: Symphony 1.1 solved part of the problem by providing an improved method of memory management for blank cells. But running out of memory is still one of the most common problems in Symphony. People tend to keep building bigger and more complex worksheets. These users eventually run out of memory and then have to redesign the entire worksheet.

Solution: You have several options to avoid running out of memory. But because none of these methods is foolproof, use SERVICES **S**ettings to check available memory as you build large worksheets.

Proper worksheet design is the best way to avoid memory problems. Don't try to put an entire accounting system into one worksheet. And don't try to use one worksheet for all your product-line forecasts, even if the worksheets for all the product lines are identical. Instead, build separate worksheets based on a single template. Not only do properly designed worksheets save memory, they also speed recalculation. (The larger the worksheet, the longer you wait whenever you recalculate.)

Sophisticated analysis models can require a dozen or more separate worksheets. Each of these worksheets can print a detailed report or (for a smaller, consolidated report) extract data to be combined into a summary report. Use the SERVICES **F**ile **C**ombine **A**dd command to consolidate similar worksheets into a summary worksheet. If you use Symphony 2.2, you also can link supporting files into a summary worksheet.

Alternative Solution: Another way to avoid memory problems is to make sure that your computer has the maximum amount of memory. If you want to build large worksheets, you need at least 640K, the maximum amount of memory that normal programs can use. Memory has become so inexpensive that most of the new computers on the market, including the IBM Personal System/2, include at least 640K of standard memory. If your computer comes with 256K, you can add 384K for as little as $100 to $150.

Because Symphony users wanted to build increasingly larger worksheets, Lotus (working with Intel and Microsoft) developed the LIM expanded memory specification (EMS). This hardware and software specification lets a program use memory that exceeds the 640K limit. To use expanded memory, a program must know about EMS. Although you cannot use EMS with older programs, you can use as many as four megabytes of expanded memory with Symphony 1.1 and later releases. Because a normal memory board doesn't work with more than 640K, however, you must buy a special memory expansion board designed to be an EMS board.

Expanded memory works in both the PC (and compatibles) and the AT (and compatibles). AST Research, Inc., has devised an extended EMS called EEMS. Both EMS and EEMS boards provide the same expansion capabilities for Symphony worksheets.

Using expanded memory does not solve all memory problems. Although certain parts of worksheets—labels, formulas, decimal numbers, and integers larger than 32,767—use expanded memory, everything else must be in conventional memory (up to 640K). In addition, every cell stored in expanded memory uses four bytes in regular memory. You can have a maximum of about 100,000 individual cell entries before you run out of conventional memory, which means that you can run out of memory and still have megabytes of expanded memory that you have not used (and cannot use).

Alternative Solution: In some situations, you may want to disable Symphony 2.2's Advanced Expanded Memory (AEM) feature with the SERVICES **C**onfiguration **O**ther **M**emory **N**o command. With some large applications, you may run out of conventional memory with AEM enabled even though you have expanded memory available.

Alternative Solution: If you find you don't use all five Symphony environments, you may want to consider using ExtraK with Symphony. ExtraK is a Symphony add-in that works with Symphony releases 1.1 and later; the add-in enables you to unload environments you don't use (with the exception of the SHEET environment), freeing memory for your applications. Depending on the environments you unload, you can reclaim between 35K and 94K of conventional memory.

Alternative Solution: Because formulas take up more space than numbers, you can use formulas to build a worksheet and then, by using SHEET **R**ange **V**alues, convert the formulas to numbers. Use this method with any numbers that do not change when you update the worksheet. (Be sure to save the original template with the unconverted formulas, in case you later discover that you need the formulas.)

Because the results of the SHEET **R**ange **W**hat-If command are numbers, not formulas, you can save memory by converting large tables of formulas to data tables. Then repeat the SHEET **R**ange **W**hat-If command to recalculate the tables if the values in the input cells change. Do not use this technique in a large worksheet if you frequently need to recalculate the data table—recalculating can take several minutes or even hours.

Alternative Solution: The shape of the active area can affect the total amount of memory used by the worksheet. The *active area* is defined as a rectangle starting in cell A1 and ending in the last row and last column that contains data or a range format, or is unprotected. For example, a worksheet with a value in G3 and a format in A12 has an active area from A1 to G12. A worksheet with cell AF4 unprotected and a label in B300 has an active area from A1 to AF300.

Although Lotus says that the memory-management scheme for Symphony 1.1 and later releases uses no memory for empty cells, this statement does not appear to be true. For example, putting the number 1 in cells A1, A2, B1, and B2 uses 32 bytes of memory. Putting the number 1 in cells A1, A8192, IV1, and IV8192 uses 65,536 bytes of memory. (In fact, simply formatting or unprotecting those four cells uses 65,536 bytes—even though you enter no data at all in the worksheet!)

If memory is a problem, keep proper worksheet design in mind as you create the application. Also, keep the shape of the occupied cells in the worksheet as small as possible. To move the cursor to the lower right corner of the active area of any worksheet, press End Home. You may be surprised to discover that a stray entry is costing you quite a bit of memory.

Alternative Solution: If you frequently move, insert, and delete rows and columns when you build large worksheets, you may run out of memory. When you move data or delete rows and columns, not all the memory is recovered. You usually can recover the memory by saving the worksheet and retrieving it again.

Troubleshooting Symphony Commands

Problems with Range Names

RANGE NAME PROBLEM #1:

A range name that was valid suddenly results in an ERR.

Explanation: You can cause once-valid formulas to result in ERR when you move or delete cells and ranges in the worksheet (see the section on avoiding ERR problems). These operations also can cause range names to be lost. A range and its range name both are identified by the upper left cell and the lower right cell in the range. If you assign the range name SALES, for example, you must specify the range's upper left and lower right cells, such as D5..H16. If you move the contents of another cell or range to one of these corner cells, the range name is lost. Suppose, for example, that you are working with the range name table shown in figure T.10. If you use the SHEET **D**elete **R**ows command to delete row 9, you affect the lower corner cells for the ranges EXPENSES, PERCENT, PROFITS, and SALES, as shown in figure T.11. The formulas summing those ranges now produce ERR. As you can see, you lose only those range names whose upper left or lower right corners are affected.

```
A1: 'DEPARTMENT                                                    SHEET
       A          B          C          D          E          F
  1  DEPARTMENT       SALES    EXPENSES    PROFITS    % PROFIT
  2
  3  DEPT 1      171,734.00  134,464.00   37,270.00     21.70%
  4  DEPT 2      188,721.00  166,332.00   22,389.00     11.86%
  5  DEPT 3      130,504.00   85,280.00   45,224.00     34.65%
  6  DEPT 4      155,347.00  127,667.00   27,680.00     17.82%
  7  DEPT 5      149,857.00  106,888.00   42,969.00     28.67%
  8  DEPT 6      129,909.00  114,287.00   15,622.00     12.03%
  9  DEPT 7      134,361.00  123,487.00   10,874.00      8.09%
 10
 11    TOTALS  1,060,433.00  858,405.00  202,028.00     19.05%
 12
 13
 14                          EXPENSES    C3..C9
 15                          PERCENT     E3..E9
 16                          PROFITS     D3..D9
 17                          SALES       B3..B9
 18                          TOTALS      B11..E11
 19
 20
                                                              MAIN
 15-May-90   04:13 PM                                   Num
```

Fig. T.10.
A range name table.

Fig. T.11.

The range name table after moving and deleting.

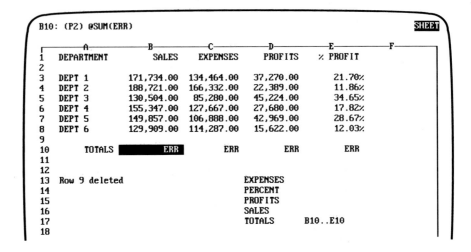

```
 B10: (P2) @SUM(ERR)                                              SHEET

      ┌────A────────────B───────────C──────────D─────────E─────────F──────
    1 │ DEPARTMENT         SALES     EXPENSES     PROFITS    % PROFIT
    2 │
    3 │ DEPT 1         171,734.00  134,464.00   37,270.00     21.70%
    4 │ DEPT 2         188,721.00  166,332.00   22,389.00     11.86%
    5 │ DEPT 3         130,504.00   85,280.00   45,224.00     34.65%
    6 │ DEPT 4         155,347.00  127,667.00   27,680.00     17.82%
    7 │ DEPT 5         149,857.00  106,888.00   42,969.00     28.67%
    8 │ DEPT 6         129,909.00  114,287.00   15,622.00     12.03%
    9 │
   10 │      TOTALS         ERR         ERR         ERR          ERR
   11 │
   12 │
   13 │ Row 9 deleted                   EXPENSES
   14 │                                 PERCENT
   15 │                                 PROFITS
   16 │                                 SALES
   17 │                                 TOTALS      B10..E10
   18 │
```

Solution: Although both ranges and range names are lost in the same manner, you can more easily audit such errors by using range names. Keep a current table of range names in all your worksheets. After you make any changes to the worksheet, re-create the range name table and look for blank cells next to range names.

Caution: If you use a release of Symphony prior to Release 2.2, you may have noticed that something strange happens when you lose a range name, and then save and later retrieve the file: the lost range names no longer are lost. Any cell that was erased or had data moved into it, however, is changed to cell IV8192. This idiosyncrasy can have a disastrous effect on macros that use range names. To avoid these problems, create a range name table. You should check the table and the worksheet frequently for blank cells, ERR, or IV8192.

Release 2.2, however, does not have this problem. When a range is lost, Symphony retains the range name. The range name is, in essence, unassigned, and may be reassigned.

RANGE NAME PROBLEM #2:

A valid formula seems to change automatically to an incorrect cell reference.

Explanation: Incorrectly assigned range names also can cause formulas to change. Macro users, for example, commonly use macros that name the current cell HERE, move the cell pointer wherever it's needed to complete the macro, and then return the cell pointer to HERE. This process can cause problems if you reassign the range name HERE without first deleting the range name. When you simply reassign a range name to a different cell or range, any formulas that refer to the old cell or range change to refer to the new cell or range. If you delete the range name first, however, the formula that referred to the range name will be changed to refer to the cell or cells that made up that range.

In figure T.12, cell A3 is named HERE; the formula in A6 refers to A3. Figure T.13 shows the same worksheet after the name HERE has been reassigned to refer to D3 rather than A3. Notice that the formula in A6 now refers to D3.

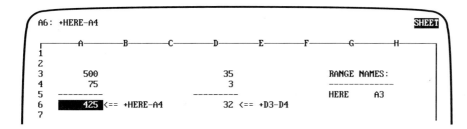

Fig. T.12.
A formula using the range name HERE.

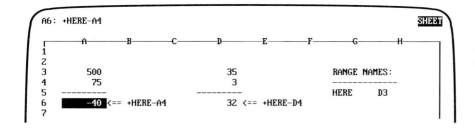

Fig. T.13.
The formula after HERE is reassigned.

Solution: To avoid this problem, always use SHEET **R**ange **N**ame **D**elete before you use SHEET **R**ange **N**ame **C**reate to reassign a range name. If HERE had been deleted before being reassigned, the formula in A6 would have changed to +A3–A4, and the formula in D6 would have correctly taken on the name HERE, changing to +HERE–D4.

RANGE NAME PROBLEM #3:

A range name looks correct in the range name table, but the macros and formulas that refer to the named range do not work properly.

Explanation: This problem occurs when you use a range name that is also a cell address. If you set up a complex report and give the individual pages the range names P1, P2, and P3, the printed report will contain only the contents of cells P1, P2, and P3. Further, suppose that you give a macro the range name GO2, and then enter the statement {BRANCH GO2} within the macro code, so that the routine will start over when it reaches the BRANCH statement. Rather than branching back and starting over, however, the macro will branch to cell GO2, and probably will stop at a blank cell.

Solution: Never name a range with a combination of one or two letters and a number. Don't even use a range name such as TO4; a range name that is not a valid cell address in the current version of Symphony may be a valid cell address in a future release.

Problems with Relative and Absolute Addressing

ADDRESSING PROBLEM #1:

After you copy a formula to other cells, the copied formulas are wrong, because they now contain incorrect addresses.

Explanation: Whenever you copy a formula from one cell to another, Symphony automatically adjusts the formula's relative cell addressing. Relative addressing is so natural and automatic, you probably stop thinking about it after a while.

Suppose, for example, that cell A4 contains the following formula:

    +A1+A2−A3

When the cell pointer is positioned in A4, the program displays this formula in the control panel. You think of the formula as meaning the following:

Add the contents of A1 and A2 and subtract the contents of A3.

If you copy the formula from A4 to B4, Symphony adjusts the formula so that it reads as follows:

    +B1+B2−B3

This result, which is exactly what an experienced Symphony user might expect, is based on the concept of relative addressing. Symphony recognizes the formula's addresses in terms of their relationship to the cell that contains the formula. That is, Symphony interprets the formula in A4 as follows:

Add the contents of the cell three rows up to the cell two rows up, and subtract the contents of the cell one row up.

When you copy the formula into cell B4, therefore, the formula itself does not change. Only the relative cell addresses change.

Sometimes, however, you might not want the cell references to change when you copy a formula. If you copy the cell references as relative addresses, the wrong formula results. In figure T.14, for example, the formula for % OF TOTAL SALES was written in C2, and then copied to each cell in the range C3 C13. The relative addressing adjustment changes the formula in C3 from +B2/B14 to +B3/B15, and so on down the range.

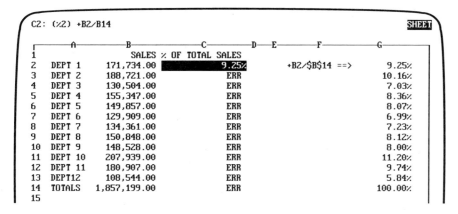

Fig. T.14.
*ERRs after copying
a formula with
relative cell
addressing.*

Solution: Specify an address as absolute when you write the formula, not when you copy it. To make an address absolute, prefix the column letter and the row number with a dollar sign ($). If you use the pointing method to specify a range or a cell address, make the address absolute by pressing Abs (F3) when you point to the cell. If you type a cell address manually, make the address absolute by pressing F3 after you type the address.

The formula in C2 should be +B2/$B$14. When you copy this formula, the relative address (B2) changes, but the absolute address ($B$14) does not change. The results of the correct formulas are shown in column G.

Problems with Recalculation

RECALCULATION PROBLEM #1:

As your worksheets become larger, recalculation becomes annoyingly slow.

Explanation: Whenever you add or change a cell, Symphony recalculates the entire worksheet. At first, this recalculation is almost instantaneous, and you can ignore the delay. As you add more complex formulas and string functions, however, the delay noticeably increases and becomes annoying. Your work can slow down dramatically if you add data to many cells in a large worksheet.

Solution: The first solution is to check the recalculation order, by selecting the SHEET **S**ettings command. If the settings sheet shows that the recalculation order is **N**atural, select the commands **R**ecalculation **O**rder **O**ptimal to change the recalculation setting to **O**ptimal. When you make this change, Symphony recalculates formulas only when you modify their data.

If recalculation still takes a long time, the second solution is to change recalculation to **M**anual by using the SHEET **S**ettings **R**ecalculation **M**ethod **M**anual command. You experience no delay the next time you make an entry, because no recalculation occurs. If Symphony later detects that the information in some cells may be incorrect, the **CALC** indicator appears at the bottom of the screen.

Press Calc (F8) when you want the program to recalculate the worksheet. The **CALC** indicator disappears until you make another entry.

RECALCULATION PROBLEM #2:

When you print reports after updating the worksheet, some of the printed data is incorrect. You may have a similar problem when you use the SERVICES **F**ile **X**tract **V**alues and SHEET **R**ange **V**alues commands. In all cases, the resulting values are not current.

Explanation: When recalculation is set to **M**anual, a formula's current value may be incorrect if you change the information in cells that are referenced by the formula. If recalculation is not set to **A**utomatic, you cannot expect Symphony commands to recalculate the worksheet (even when a correct answer depends on recalculation).

Solution: If you use a macro to print reports, to extract data as values, or to convert formulas to values with the SHEET **R**ange **V**alues command, add {CALC} to the macro before it executes the commands. If you don't use a macro, press Calc (F8) to recalculate manually.

RECALCULATION PROBLEM #3:

When you use the SERVICES **F**ile **C**ombine **A**dd (or **S**ubtract) command to transfer information from another worksheet, the transferred data is not current.

Explanation: This problem is related to the preceding one. If you save a file that recalculates manually, and then combine all or part of that file into another worksheet, the current values of the formulas may be incorrect (even if the current worksheet is set to recalculate automatically).

The SERVICES **F**ile **C**ombine **A**dd and **S**ubtract commands use the current values of the formulas in the source file. Unless these formulas are recalculated before their values are combined into another worksheet, the combined values may be incorrect. On the other hand, the **F**ile **C**ombine **C**opy command can bring formulas, rather than just their values, into the worksheet. When you use the **F**ile **C**ombine **C**opy command, you do not have to be concerned about whether the source file has been recalculated.

Solution: In this case (unlike the preceding problem, in which you can calculate the worksheet immediately before executing the command), you must calculate the source worksheet before saving it. If you use a macro to save your worksheet, add {CALC} to the macro before it saves the file. If you don't use a macro, recalculate manually by pressing Calc (F8) before you save the file.

RECALCULATION PROBLEM #4:

You want to see only a few values on a large worksheet that takes a long time to recalculate, but you are spending an inordinate amount of time recalculating.

Explanation: On large, complex models that can take several minutes to recalculate, you almost always should use manual recalculation. But when you are building or changing the model, or entering data in one section, you want to keep the values current in the area in which you are working. If you must repeatedly press Calc (F8), however, you lose time waiting for the program to recalculate the entire worksheet.

Solution: If you want to recalculate only part of a worksheet, you can do so in one of several ways.

To recalculate a single cell, simply edit the cell. Press Edit (F2) and then press Enter.

To recalculate a range of cells, copy the range to itself. Figure T.15 shows a range that is part of a large worksheet. To recalculate the cells in only the range BC65..BH75, copy the range BC65..BH75 to BC65. All the cells in the range recalculate when Symphony copies them to themselves.

```
BC65: (P0) @SUM(D3..D48)                                          SHEET
┌─────BB────────BC────────BD────────BE────────BF────────BG────────BH────
│59           Summary Totals from the Budget Detail
│60           ----------- This Year -----------      ------ Next Year ------
│61
│62             Actual    Budget    Forecast  Variance   Budget    Budget
│63             YTD       YTD       Full Year  YTD       YTD       Full Year
│64
│65  Region 1  125,876   100,900    167,415   (24,976)  163,800   218,400
│66  Region 2  114,056    98,600    151,694   (15,456)  155,600   207,467
│67  Region 3  122,868   133,600    163,414    10,732   195,000   260,000
│68  Region 4  112,611   124,600    149,773    11,989   180,900   241,200
│69  Region 5  106,903   115,400    142,181     8,497   168,900   225,200
│70  Region 6  104,307    85,800    138,728   (18,507)  138,000   184,000
│71  Region 7  118,989   140,700    158,255    21,711   200,200   266,933
│72  Region 8  125,247   101,300    166,579   (23,947)  163,900   218,533
│73  Region 9  148,397   131,500    197,368   (16,897)  205,700   274,267
│74
│75  Totals  1,079,254 1,032,400  1,435,407   (46,854) 1,572,000 2,096,000
│76
```

Fig. T.15.
A range that is part of a large worksheet.

If you want to use a macro to recalculate part of a worksheet, use the macro commands RECALC and RECALCCOL.

RECALCULATION PROBLEM #5:

Because your worksheet is large, you keep recalculation on **M**anual and use the partial-recalculation methods described in the preceding solution. But partial recalculation sometimes yields incorrect results.

Explanation: When you recalculate the entire worksheet, Symphony uses optimal calculation as the default. In other words, Symphony only recalculates those formulas that are affected by changes. Unless you change the recalculation order to **R**owwise or **C**olumnwise, Symphony always calculates a cell after calculating the results of all the cells to which that cell refers (this is called the "natural order" of recalculation). This type of recalculation avoids problems that occurred in older spreadsheet programs, which could calculate only across rows or down columns. With natural-order calculation, you can place formulas anywhere in the worksheet; with other calculation methods, formulas are correct after one recalculation only when they refer to cells above or to the left of the cell being recalculated. Formulas that refer to a cell address below and to the right of the cell being recalculated are known as *forward references*.

The worksheet shown in figure T.16 contains forward references and shows the formulas before any recalculation. Notice that C1 contains a zero. The zero is replaced with 100 before each calculation. Figures T.17 and T.18 show the results of different methods of recalculation. Certain combinations produce correct results, but others are incorrect.

Fig. T.16.

Formulas with forward references.

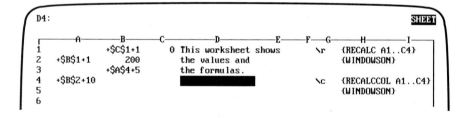

Fig. T.17.

The worksheet after being recalculated by column.

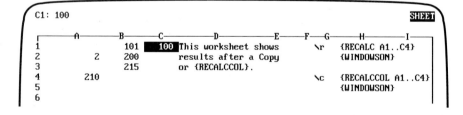

Fig. T.18.

The worksheet after being recalculated by row.

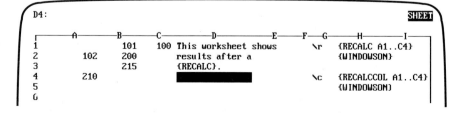

Figure T.17 shows the results after a **C**opy or RECALCCOL command recalculates the formulas by column. The formula in A2 is incorrect because it was calculated while cell B1 still contained a value of 1. Later, column B was calculated, and cell B1 became 101, but it was too late to change the value in A2. The other formulas are correct.

Figure T.18 shows the results after a RECALC recalculates the formulas by row. The formula in B3 is incorrect because it was calculated while cell A4 still contained a value of 10. Later, row 4 was calculated, and cell A4 became 210, but it was too late to change the value in B3. The other formulas are correct.

Solution: No complete solution to the problem exists. You can get complete natural-order recalculation only by recalculating the entire worksheet. If you know the structure of the data and the formulas, however, you can make sure that you get the correct answers from partial recalculation.

First, be sure to recalculate all the cells that are referenced by the formulas in the area you want to recalculate. Suppose, for example, that you want to recalculate part of a large worksheet (see fig. T.19). If you change the discount rate in BA60 and then recalculate the range BD65..BD75, you'll get an incorrect answer because the average discounts are not recalculated. To get the correct answer, recalculate the range BC65..BD75. (Note that you do not have to include cell BA60 in the recalculation because that cell contains a number and is not affected during worksheet recalculation.)

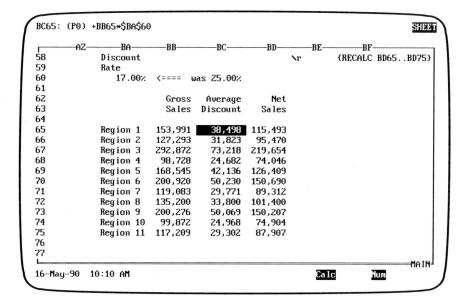

Fig. T.19.
A range that is part of a large worksheet.

Try to avoid forward references in an area in which you want partial recalculation. If forward references are not present, the partial recalculations can work.

If you cannot avoid forward references, you can still get the correct answer if you pay attention to how partial recalculation proceeds. When you copy a range or use RECALCCOL, the program recalculates each cell, starting at the upper left corner of the range and continuing down each column. When it reaches the bottom of each column, Symphony starts recalculating at the top of the next column in the range.

If you use RECALC, the program recalculates each cell, starting at the upper left corner of the range and continuing across each row. When it reaches the last cell of a row, Symphony continues recalculating at the first cell in the next row.

The following rules apply to partial recalculation:

1. If you use Copy or RECALCCOL for a partial recalculation, the results may be incorrect for a formula that refers to another formula that is either in a column to its right or below it in the same column.

2. If you use RECALC for a partial recalculation, the results may be incorrect for a formula that refers to another formula that is either in a row below it or to its right in the same row.

3. Regardless of the recalculation method you use, the results will . always be correct for formulas that refer to cells containing values.

If you must use partial recalculation on a range that contains forward references, the only solution involves more than one recalculation. You must use RECALC or RECALCCOL once for every nested forward reference in the range. A nested forward reference is a formula that refers forward to a formula that refers forward (and so on) to a cell. Figure T.20 shows a series of forward references. Each RECALC resolves one additional forward reference.

After you determine how many nested forward references must be recalculated, add that number of RECALC or RECALCCOL statements to your macro.

Miscellaneous Problems

DATA DESTRUCTION PROBLEM #1:

You use the SHEET **M**ove command to move a range of cells, and you end up losing data.

Explanation. The SHEET **M**ove command does not insert the cells you are moving; it copies the source cells' contents over the target cells.

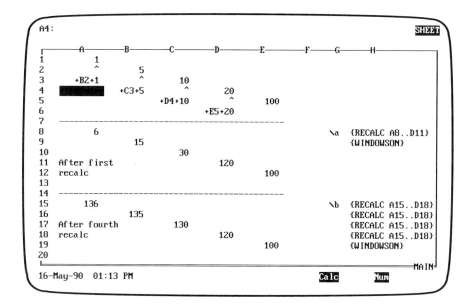

Fig. T.20.
A series of forward references.

Solution: Before you issue the **M**ove command, insert rows or columns (or both, if necessary) to hold the moved cells.

DATA DESTRUCTION PROBLEM #2:

When you use the SERVICES **F**ile **C**ombine **C**opy command to combine data from two files, you lose data.

Explanation: The **F**ile **C**ombine **C**opy command brings in the specified range or file beginning at the cell pointer's location in the target worksheet. If any data is in the area, it is overwritten with the data from the source file.

Solution: First, save the target file so that you can recover the original file if anything unexpected happens. Next, position the cell pointer where you want the data to begin in the target worksheet, and make sure that you have sufficient room for the data. Then you can issue the SERVICES **F**ile **C**ombine **C**opy command.

DATA DESTRUCTION PROBLEM #3:

Occasionally, by making a mistake with the SHEET **C**opy, **M**ove, or **D**elete commands, you destroy part of the worksheet and then must painstakingly reconstruct it.

Explanation: Unlike modeling languages and statistical analysis packages, spreadsheets such as Symphony do not separate the model from the data. (The model is composed of formulas and macros that do not change. The data is the information that you continually enter and change.) When you use Symphony to modify data, you risk accidentally changing the model, as well.

Solution: Always keep a backup copy of all worksheets. (Keep two or three backup copies of critical worksheets.) Then, if you destroy a worksheet, you can recover it from the backup file. You also can keep a backup copy of your worksheet model, without any data. This type of backup is discussed later in this section.

You can use the **P**rotection option to prevent the worksheet from being destroyed. Protected cells cannot be changed. If you try to change a protected cell, the program beeps and displays a warning message, but does not accept any changes to the cell's contents.

Use the SHEET **R**ange **P**rotect **A**llow-Changes command to unprotect the cells you want to be able to modify. However, you should not allow changes to be made to cells that contain important text or formulas. After you have built the worksheet and are ready to use it, turn on the global protection feature by issuing SERVICES **S**ettings **G**lobal-Protection **Y**es before you enter data. Only the cells that were unprotected now can be changed.

TEMPLATE PROBLEM #1:

At the beginning of each month, you must carefully erase all the data from the preceding month to prepare for the new month. If any of the preceding month's data is accidentally left in the worksheet, the information for the new month will be incorrect.

Explanation: This problem is related to the preceding one. Because Symphony does not distinguish between the model and the data, the program cannot present a blank model for the next month's data.

Solution: Although Symphony cannot distinguish between the model and the data, you can. Build a model, or template; that is, a worksheet that contains all the necessary formulas, formats, and macros, but no data. Save this worksheet and make a backup copy. Then use this model every month to start the new month. After you add data to the file, always be sure to save it under a different name from that of the template. For example, you might name a budget template BUDGET. Retrieve BUDGET every month, saving it as BUD0890 in August 1990, BUD0990 in September 1990, and so on.

Alternative Solution: Rather than using the SHEET **E**rase command to erase each range of data, use the SERVICES **F**ile **C**ombine **S**ubtract command. Start by saving the file. Then, with the file still on the screen, place the cell pointer in cell A1. Issue the SERVICES **F**ile **C**ombine **S**ubtract command and combine the same file. All values are subtracted from themselves, leaving zeros in the data-entry cells. Formulas and labels remain unchanged.

Troubleshooting Functions

FUNCTIONS PROBLEM #1:

You get apparent rounding errors, even when you have not rounded off.

Explanation: When you use formats such as **F**ixed, **P**unctuated, and **C**urrency with a fixed number of decimal places, Symphony keeps the number to 15 decimal places but rounds off the display. Figure T.21A shows the formula results without any formatting; figure T.21B shows the apparent rounding errors resulting after the cells are formatted with 0 decimal places.

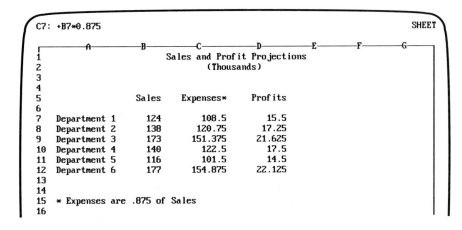

Fig. T.21A.
Formula results without formatting.

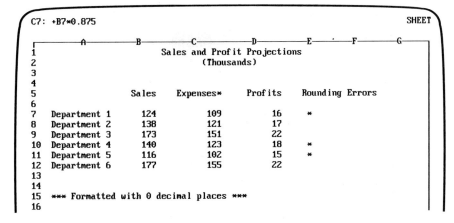

Fig. T.21B.
Apparent rounding errors after cells are formatted.

Solution: To avoid such rounding errors, use the @ROUND function to round off numbers to the same precision shown in the display (see fig. T.21C).

Fig. T.21C.

Rounding errors eliminated by @ROUND.

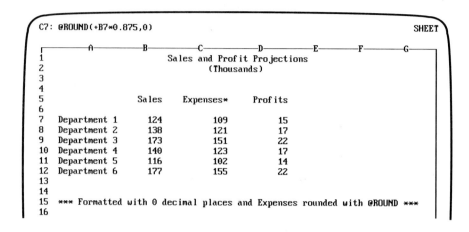

```
C7:  @ROUND(+B7*0.875,0)                                          SHEET
      ───A───────B───────C───────D───────E───────F───────G──
   1                   Sales and Profit Projections
   2                        (Thousands)
   3
   4
   5                  Sales     Expenses*      Profits
   6
   7   Department 1    124         109            15
   8   Department 2    138         121            17
   9   Department 3    173         151            22
  10   Department 4    140         123            17
  11   Department 5    116         102            14
  12   Department 6    177         155            22
  13
  14
  15   *** Formatted with 0 decimal places and Expenses rounded with @ROUND ***
  16
```

FUNCTIONS PROBLEM #2:

You get ERR when you try to combine numbers and strings.

Explanation: Although Symphony has a full complement of string functions, you cannot mix strings and numbers in the same function. Figure T.22A shows the effect of trying to build an address by using words from strings and a number for the ZIP code.

Fig. T.22A.

An error when numbers mix with strings.

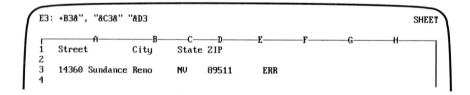

```
E3:  +B3&", "&C3&" "&D3                                          SHEET
      ───A───────B─────C───D───────E───────F───────G───────H──
   1   Street      City     State ZIP
   2
   3   14360 Sundance Reno    NV      89511        ERR
   4
```

Solution: Use the @STRING function to convert a number to its equivalent string (see fig. T.22B). Then you can use the converted number in a string function.

Fig. T.22B.

A function that converts a number to a string.

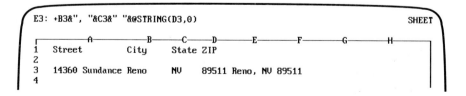

```
E3:  +B3&", "&C3&" "&@STRING(D3,0)                               SHEET
      ───A───────B─────C───D───────E───────F───────G───────H──
   1   Street      City     State ZIP
   2
   3   14360 Sundance Reno    NV      89511 Reno, NV 89511
   4
```

FUNCTIONS PROBLEM #3:

You want to use string functions on a field, but you are not sure whether a number or a string will be entered in the field.

Explanation: All functions work on either strings or numbers, but not on both. If you don't know what a cell contains, and you guess incorrectly, you risk getting ERR or an incorrect result.

Solution: You can test a cell to see whether it contains a number or a string and then, depending on the contents of the cell, use the appropriate functions. Suppose, for example, that you want to concatenate the contents of A1 and B1. You can use the following formula:

   +A1&B1

The ampersand (&), which is a string concatenation operator, causes an error if either A1 or B1 is blank or contains a number. Assume that you know A1 contains a string but that you don't know whether B1 contains a string, a number, or is blank. To concatenate B1 to A1 only if B1 contains a string, use the following formula:

   A1&@S(B1)

The @S function (a filter) does nothing if the cell contains a string, but returns a null string if the cell does not contain a string. The formula therefore results in either A1 (if B1 does not contain a string) or in A1&B1 (if B1 contains a string).

To concatenate the contents of B1 regardless of whether it contains a number or a string, you need a more complex formula (see fig. T.23).

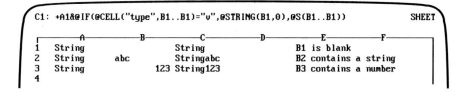

Fig. T.23.
A formula that handles numbers, strings, or blank cells.

In the formula in the control panel of figure T.23, if the type is "v" (for value), the contents of the cell are converted to a string. If the cell is blank, the @S function filters it out, and the cell is ignored. If the cell contains a string, the @S function does nothing, and the two strings are concatenated.

FUNCTIONS PROBLEM #4:

Your averages are returning incorrect results.

Explanation: The @AVG function adds the values in the specified range and divides by the number of nonblank cells in that range. If the range contains any labels, they are counted in the total number of nonblank cells, and the average is incorrect.

Solution: Never include labels (such as the dashed line at the bottom of the column) in the average range. The first example in figure T.24A includes the dashed line in the average range and results in an incorrect average. The second example specifies the correct range (no labels included).

Also, make sure that cells that appear blank don't have a space entered in them, because a space in a cell is considered a label. You can tell if a cell contains a space by placing the cell pointer in the cell and looking in the control panel. If you see an apostrophe, a space is there. Use SHEET **E**rase to erase the space. The first example in figure T.24B has a space in one of the cells in the average range, so the total is incorrectly divided by 3. The average range in the second example contains a cell erased with the SHEET **E**rase command, so the total is correctly divided by 2.

Fig. T.24A.

Including labels in a range to average.

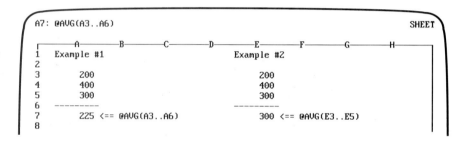

Fig. T.24B.

Including cells with spaces in a range to average.

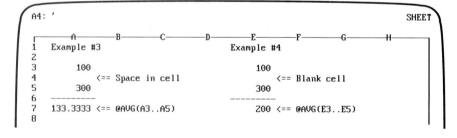

FUNCTIONS PROBLEM #5:

A spreadsheet you've been using seems to show incorrect results after you upgrade to Symphony 2.2.

Explanation: The functions that require range arguments were changed slightly in Symphony 2.2. Functions such as @CELL and @COUNT, which previously required a single cell to be expressed as a range—(A1..A1) instead of (A1) for example—no longer have this requirement. However, @COUNT returns a value of 1 when given a single-cell argument regardless of the contents of the cell; the formula @COUNT(A1..A1) returns 0 if A1 is blank.

Solution: Instead of using @COUNT to examine the contents of a single-cell range, use @CELL. @CELL("type",A1) returns **b** if A1 is blank, **v** if it contains a numeric value, and **l** if it contains a label.

FUNCTIONS PROBLEM #6:

A database report that used @S to include the string value of a field worked fine during testing. Once you deleted the test records, however, the reports showed the field labels instead of the data.

Explanation: The @S formula refers to the first record in the database. This record is contained in the row directly below the field labels. When you deleted the test records, Symphony reset the range names for each database field to the row containing the field labels.

Solution: Whenever you delete all the records from a Symphony database, change the window type to SHEET, move the cursor to the top left cell of the database, and issue a **R**ange **N**ame **L**abels **D**own command. Highlight all the field labels and press Enter.

Alternative Solution: Symphony 2.0 and later releases have included an option on the SHEET **S**ettings menu for **Z**ero **S**uppression. Setting this option to **Y**es means that any formulas that evaluate to 0 are displayed as blank. This setting is not saved with the worksheet and must be reselected every time you use the worksheet. One problem with zero suppression, however, is that all zeros—not just those resulting from a string formula—are suppressed.

FUNCTIONS PROBLEM #7:

The @CHOOSE formula seems to return the wrong value.

Explanation: @CHOOSE selects the first argument in the list if the key value evaluates to 0, the second if it evaluates to 1, and so on.

Solution: Be sure that you structure the @CHOOSE argument list to account for the offset numbering system. Consider this formula:

    @CHOOSE(@MOD(@NOW,7),"Sun","Mon","Tue","Wed","Thu","Fri","Sat")

This formula is incorrect because the 0 argument should be "Sat". You can correct the formula by moving "Sat" to the beginning of the list.

FUNCTIONS PROBLEM #8:

Boxes you drew on-screen using the @CHAR function don't appear on the printout when you print the worksheet.

Explanation: The line-drawing characters you can produce with @CHAR are not printable. In some cases, they represent printer-control characters and can cause your printer to "lock up" or produce unexpected results.

Solution: Use the ALLWAYS add-in to draw lines and boxes that will print.

FUNCTIONS PROBLEM #9:

The @APP function returns ERR even if an add-in application is attached.

Explanation: The first argument in the @APP function must be the application name contained within quotation marks (" ") without the APP extension.

Solution: Make sure that you spell the application's name correctly and do not include the APP extension. The following formula displays `ERR` if DOS.APP is not attached and `DOS application is attached` if it is:

    @APP("DOS","DOS application is attached")

Troubleshooting File Operations

FILE PROBLEM #1:

Your hard disk contains so many files that you have trouble finding the files you want. File operations are slow in executing.

Explanation: A single hard disk can hold thousands of files. If that many files were placed in one subdirectory, however, you would not be able to keep track of them. Further, DOS slows down significantly if a single subdirectory contains more than approximately 112 or 224 files (depending on which version of DOS you use). If you try to put all your files in the root directory, DOS reaches an absolute limit and won't let you save additional files.

Solution: Set up separate subdirectories for different applications and users.

The default directory should contain the subdirectory of files that you use most often. To specify this subdirectory, use the SERVICES **C**onfiguration **F**ile command.

To reach files in other subdirectories, use the SERVICES **F**ile **D**irectory command. This command changes the directory until you either use SERVICES **F**ile **D**irectory again or return to the default directory by quitting and re-entering Symphony.

FILE PROBLEM #2:

You want to retrieve a file that is not in the default directory, but you cannot remember which directory contains the file.

Explanation: You can see only the files in the current directory. The file you want is in another directory, but Symphony does not list all the disk's directories.

Solution: Select SERVICES **F**ile **L**ist and, depending on the type of file you're looking for, choose **W**orksheet, **P**rint, **G**raph, or **A**ll. Symphony displays a list of all files of that type and all subdirectories within the current directory. To search forward through a chain of directories, move the cursor to the directory you want and press Enter. To search backwards through the chain of directories, use the Backspace key. When you locate your file, use the SERVICES **F**ile **D**irectory or **F**ile **R**etrieve commands to retrieve the file. For ASCII files, use SERVICES **F**ile **I**mport.

Alternative Solution: Attach the DOS add-in application (DOS.APP), and use the SERVICES **D**OS command to suspend Symphony temporarily and return to DOS. This method makes the DOS TREE command available to you; you can use the TREE, CD, and DIR commands to find the subdirectory and file that you want.

After you locate the file, return to Symphony by typing **EXIT** at the DOS prompt. Then you can use the SERVICES **F**ile **D**irectory or SERVICES **F**ile **R**etrieve commands to read the file.

FILE PROBLEM #3:

While building a large file, you fear making a mistake that will destroy part of the file and cost you hours of work.

Explanation: Sooner or later, every computer user destroys part or all of an important file. The greater your proficiency in Symphony, the larger and more complex the files you can build—and the more disastrous the errors you can make.

Solution: Once you destroy a file, you may not be able to restore it. The only solution may be to avoid the problem by preparing for it.

You can best prepare for this problem by frequently saving your file as you make changes or write macros. Be sure, however, to save the file under a different name each time. If you use the same file name, you might save the file two or three times after making a disastrous error before discovering the error. By saving the worksheet under different file names, however, you can revert back several generations, if necessary.

If you are developing a worksheet, for example, save it under a name that includes a sequence number (such as BUDGET1, BUDGET2, BUDGET3, and so on). When you reach BUDGET10 and have done some testing, you can consider erasing BUDGET1; after saving BUDGET11, consider erasing BUDGET2, and so on. At least once during each development session, save the file to a floppy disk. This backup copy is an additional safeguard.

Remember that time spent storing data is minimal, compared with the time you might have to spend re-entering lost data and rebuilding lost macro-driven files.

FILE PROBLEM #4:

Some of the formulas brought in by SERVICES **F**ile **C**ombine **C**opy are meaningless.

Explanation: Using SERVICES **F**ile **C**ombine **C**opy is similar to using SHEET **C**opy within a worksheet. The same rules about relative addressing apply in both instances. Suppose that you combine a range from a worksheet on disk into the current worksheet. If this combined range contains formulas that refer to other cells in the same range, the formulas maintain their relationship with the cells they reference, and continue to yield correct results after being combined into the current worksheet. If the combined range contains formulas that refer to cells outside the range, however, these formulas become references to cells in the current worksheet. These formulas may become meaningless, and yield incorrect results.

For example, figure T.25 shows the result of combining the data in J10..K15. Because the formula in K10 refers to cell G10, which is a blank cell in this worksheet, the result in K10 is 0. In the original worksheet, the corresponding cell contained a price, and the formula gave a correct result.

Fig. T.25.

*Meaningless formulas after a **File** **Combine** operation.*

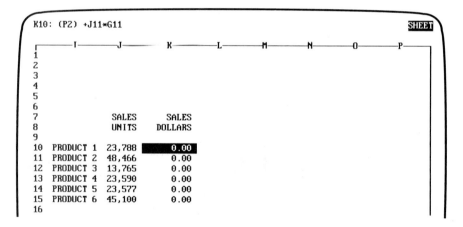

Solution: You can use SERVICES **F**ile **C**ombine **A**dd to combine values from another worksheet into the current worksheet. The command converts the source worksheet's formulas into values. If you don't want any of the formulas from the source worksheet, simply use SERVICES **F**ile **C**ombine **A**dd for the entire range. If you want to pull in some of the formulas from the source worksheet, first use **F**ile **C**ombine **C**opy to get the formulas. Then, to get the numbers, use **F**ile **C**ombine **A**dd on a different range.

The SERVICES **F**ile **C**ombine **A**dd command, however, has drawbacks of its own. As Symphony executes the command, the program checks each cell in the current worksheet. If a cell is blank or contains a number, the corresponding value from the file being combined is added to that cell. If the cell in the current worksheet contains a formula, Symphony skips that cell, regardless of what the corresponding cell's contents in the file being combined may contain. Further, remember that **File Combine Add** brings in only numeric values, not strings.

FILE PROBLEM #5:

You use the SERVICES **File Combine Add** command and get old values.

Explanation: Before combining, **File Combine Add** automatically converts to values any formulas in the range to be combined (even if you select the **Formulas** option). If the source worksheet is set for manual recalculation and was saved without first being recalculated, some of the formulas may not reflect current values.

Solution: If you intend to use a worksheet later in a **File Combine** operation (adding or subtracting), always calculate the worksheet before saving it.

FILE PROBLEM #6:

After you use SERVICES **File Import Numbers** to read in an ASCII file, some of the information is lost, and some of the surviving data is scrambled.

Explanation: The **File Import Numbers** command works only when the data in the ASCII file is in a precise format. Each field must be separated by commas or spaces, and each string must be enclosed in double quotation marks. Symphony ignores data that is not in this format, but imports whatever data the program recognizes as numbers. Ordinarily, the result is a useless mess.

Solution: Using SERVICES **File Import Text**, read in the ASCII data as a series of long labels. Then use SHEET **Query Parse** to separate the data into individual cells that Symphony can use.

FILE PROBLEM #7:

When attempting to save a backup copy, you use SERVICES **File Directory** to change to drive A, and then use SERVICES **File Save** to save the file. Later, you notice that the file was not saved on drive A.

Explanation: When you save a file, Symphony remembers the entire path that was last used to save the file or, if you haven't saved the file, to retrieve it. The program does not consider the current directory. Even if you change the directory before executing SERVICES **File Save**, Symphony still saves the file in the original directory.

Suppose, for example, that your file BUD0810 was read from the default directory (in this case, C:\SYMPHONY).

You change the directory to A:\ and then use SERVICES File Save. Symphony ignores the fact that the current directory is A:\ and displays the default path:

```
Enter save file name: C:\SYMPHONY\BUD0810
```

The file is saved again in C:\SYMPHONY.

Solution: Clear the entire old path by pressing Esc and retyping the file name. Because you gain nothing by changing the current directory, leave it alone and include drive A in the file name. In this example, after you select the SERVICES File Save command, the following prompt appears:

```
Enter save file name: C:\SYMPHONY\BUD0810
```

Press Esc, and the path and file name disappear from the prompt:

```
Enter save file name:
```

At this prompt, type **A:\BUD0810** and then press Enter. The file is saved on drive A.

Caution: The next time you save this file, Symphony will save it on drive A unless you reverse the process and enter the old path, including drive C.

FILE PROBLEM #8:

When you try to retrieve a password-protected file, Symphony displays the error message `Incorrect password`. You cannot retrieve the file.

Explanation: You must enter the password exactly as you assigned it, including the same capitalization. In other words, passwords are case-sensitive.

Solution: Try entering the password in all uppercase letters. If the error message reappears, enter the password again in all lowercase letters.

Troubleshooting Allways

ALLWAYS PROBLEM #1:

After setting up Symphony to have Allways attach automatically, you tried to invoke Allways from the control panel and could not find Allways in the menu options.

Explanation: Allways becomes part of the control-panel menu options only when you are in the SHEET environment.

Solution: From the DOC environment, use SERVICES Application Invoke and select Allways from the control-panel menu.

Alternative Solution: Make certain that you are in the SHEET environment either by using the TYPE (Shift-F10) key or by configuring Symphony with SHEET as the default mode.

ALLWAYS PROBLEM #2:

When you retrieve a worksheet, you find that the Allways formats moved to different cells.

Explanation: When you modify a worksheet in Symphony and Allways is detached (not in memory), the modifications are not incorporated in the Allways file.

Solution: Whenever you use Symphony to modify a worksheet formatted with Allways, make sure that Allways is attached so that the Allways formats are synchronized with the worksheet changes.

ALLWAYS PROBLEM #3:

Your printout of a worksheet is missing the top parts of some characters.

Explanation: The tops of characters do not print when the row height is not tall enough for the fonts the row contains. This condition commonly results when you manually adjust the height of a row (most likely to occur with soft fonts).

Solution: Set the **W**orksheet **R**ow **A**uto command so that Allways automatically adjusts the row height.

ALLWAYS PROBLEM #4:

You get an `Out of memory` error when you try to invoke Allways, even though you successfully invoked it before.

Explanation: Not enough memory is available to load Allways; too many other add-in programs may be attached. The most common cause of this error is that the Spelling Checker add-in has been attached.

Solution: Detach the add-in that is using the most memory. If you want to detach the Spelling Checker add-in, select SERVICES **A**pplication **D**etach and highlight the Spelling Checker add-in.

ALLWAYS PROBLEM #5:

The soft fonts and graphs you print are low quality.

Explanation: The graphic resolution of your printer controls the quality of the soft fonts and graphs. Check the number of dots-per-inch (resolution) supported by your printer.

Solution: Select the fonts in the Allways listing that have `printer` next to them. Fonts with this designation are either built into the printer or are available on a cartridge. If you have a problem with low-quality graphs, do not insert graphs into your worksheet.

Alternative Solution: If your printer supports a higher resolution, select **P**rint **C**onfiguration **R**esolution and specify the highest resolution that your printer supports.

ALLWAYS PROBLEM #6:

You get duplicate borders on your worksheet printouts.

Explanation: Allways prints everything defined in the worksheet's print range.

Solution: Do not include the defined borders in the print range. Check to see what is defined as the borders in the Allways Layout command menu option; omit the cells included in the border range from the print range.

ALLWAYS PROBLEM #7:

You selected a few cells to be used as top and bottom borders, but Allways printed the entire row.

Explanation: Allways is designed to use an entire row for top and bottom borders and an entire column for left borders, no matter how many cells in the row or column you specify.

Solution: Use **F**ormat **S**hade **W**hite to "eliminate" cell contents from a printout. By using this menu option, you can print only a portion of a row or column for the border.

ALLWAYS PROBLEM #8:

Your Allways worksheets print in a different font than you see when you print with Symphony.

Explanation: When you first use Allways, the add-in uses a default set of fonts. These fonts are not the same fonts Symphony uses for printing.

Solution: Use **F**ormat **F**ont **R**eplace to change Allways' default font to the font you are accustomed to using with Symphony.

ALLWAYS PROBLEM #9:

You have a printer with a manual feed slot and a standard 8 1/2-by-11-inch paper tray. When you attempt to feed legal-size paper manually, you get paper jams.

Explanation: Even though the printer is set to manual feed, Allways overrides the printer settings. In effect, Allways assumes that 8 1/2-by-11-inch paper is being used, even though the printer is set up to accept legal size paper.

Solution: Set the **P**rint **C**onfiguration **B**in option to **2** (Manual Feed) to avoid paper jams with legal-size paper.

ALLWAYS PROBLEM #10:

After changing the appearance of the Symphony worksheet with Allways, you retrieve the Symphony file and invoke Allways, but the worksheet shows none of the enhancements.

Explanation: Enhancements made to a Symphony worksheet with Allways are stored in a file with the ALL extension. These changes to the worksheet are not saved until the worksheet is saved in Symphony.

Solution: After making changes to a worksheet with Allways, quit the Allways program and return to Symphony. Select SERVICES **F**ile **S**ave to save the worksheet to a Symphony file to keep the changes.

Troubleshooting Windows

WINDOW PROBLEM #1:

You have used the SERVICES **W**indow **P**ane command to divide the screen into two windows. You no longer want the second window, but when you delete it, the first window is still only half the screen's width (see fig. T.26).

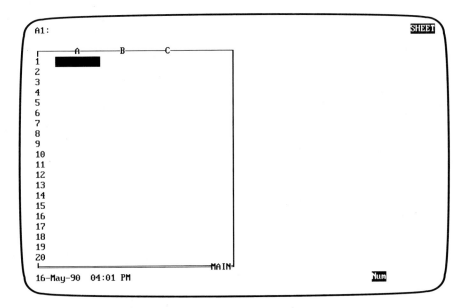

Fig. T.26.
A window with half the screen width.

Explanation: Deleting a window does not change the size of any existing windows.

Solution: Select the SERVICES **W**indow **L**ayout command and highlight the entire screen to make the window full-screen again.

Alternative Solution: You can press Zoom (Alt-F6) to enlarge a window to full size, but this solution is only temporary. The window returns to its previous size when you turn off the Zoom (Alt-F6) or when you display another window by pressing Window (F6) or the SERVICES **W**indow **U**se command.

WINDOW PROBLEM #2:

When typing in a DOC window you have created, you get the `Not enough room in Restrict range` message, and you can't type any more. When inserting rows in a SHEET window, you get a similar message, saying `Selected range not within Restrict range`.

Explanation: If you have specified a restrict range for a window, Symphony displays these error messages when you try to go beyond that range.

Solution: Expand the window's restrict range by using the SERVICES **W**indow **S**ettings **R**estrict **R**ange command.

WINDOW PROBLEM #3:

When you press Window (F6) to move between windows, you are unable to go to one of the windows.

Explanation: Window (F6) does not move to hidden windows. At some point you must have used the SERVICES **W**indow **H**ide command to conceal the elusive window.

Solution: Issue the SERVICES **W**indow **U**se or **W**indow **E**xpose command to retrieve the hidden window.

WINDOW PROBLEM #4:

You don't like the order in which the windows are displayed when you press Window (F6).

Explanation: The window order corresponds to the order in which the windows were created, unless you have used the **W**indow **U**se command. **W**indow **U**se changes the order of the window stack by placing the specified window after the current window.

Solution: Decide on the order in which the windows should appear. Determine which window is current (as indicated by a double line at the bottom of the window). Issue the SERVICES **W**indow **U**se command and select the window that should succeed the current window. Repeat the command for each window that you want to reorder. Figure T.27 shows, for example, that as you press Window (F6), Symphony activates the windows in clockwise order, from MAIN to 1, to 2, to 3. If you want to reverse the order, place the pointer in the MAIN window and select SERVICES **W**indow **U**se **3**. Then put the pointer in window 2 and select SERVICES **W**indow **U**se **1**.

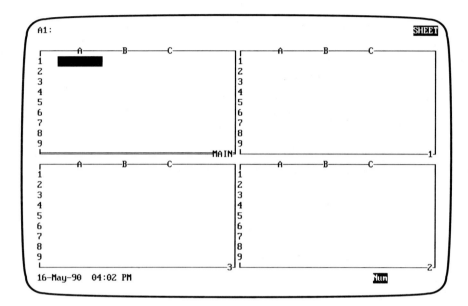

Fig. T.27.
A sample window layout.

WINDOW PROBLEM #5:

You have a window that does not take up the entire screen, and you don't like window's on-screen position.

Explanation: By default, windows are anchored where you create them. But you can move them.

Solution: Select SERVICES **W**indow **L**ayout to highlight the current window, and press Scroll Lock. When you press any of the cursor-movement keys (arrows, PgUp, PgDn, Ctrl-→, and Ctrl-←) the highlighted window moves. Press Enter when you are satisfied with the location.

WINDOW PROBLEM #6:

You have created many windows in a file, each with specific restrict ranges. Although the windows enable you to organize your data effectively, they are sometimes too restrictive, because you continually hit the end of each window's restrict range as you try to examine the entire worksheet.

Explanation: If you restrict the range of every window, including the default window MAIN, you can never move freely through the entire worksheet.

Solution: Leave the MAIN window with the default restrict range of the entire worksheet (A1..IV8192). You can use the SERVICES **W**indow **H**ide command to hide the window until you need to look at it again. You can display the window again by issuing either **W**indow **U**se or **W**indow **E**xpose.

Troubleshooting Word Processing

WORD PROCESSING PROBLEM #1:

When you change the tab settings in a format line, the text does not move to the new tab stops.

Explanation: You can configure Symphony release 2.0 and later for two types of tabs: hard and soft. If you choose hard tabs, as in figure T.28A, a tab character is inserted when you press the Tab key. When you retrieve the file later, the text moves to new tab stops when you change the settings. If you choose soft tabs, as in figure T.28B, the tab character is not saved in the file. Instead, spaces are inserted where the tab character was, and additional spaces are not inserted when you change tab settings. Releases of Symphony before 2.0 do not support hard tabs at all.

Fig. T.28A.
Symphony configured for hard tabs.

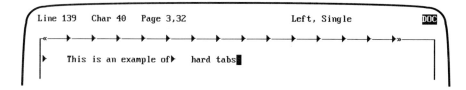

Fig. T.28B.
Symphony configured for soft tabs.

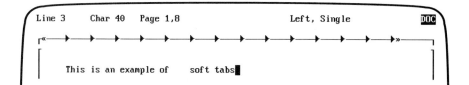

Solution: Use the SERVICES **C**onfiguration **D**ocument **H**ard-Tabs command and specify **Y**es to configure Symphony to use hard tabs.

Tip

Symphony displays any tab characters you insert in the current document, regardless of whether Symphony is configured for hard tabs or soft tabs. The SERVICES **C**onfiguration **D**ocument **H**ard Tabs setting is effective only when you save and then retrieve the document file.

WORD PROCESSING PROBLEM #2:

You get the message `Cannot alter this area of document` when you try to edit in a DOC window.

Explanation: The text you are trying to edit was entered in a SHEET or OUTLN window. You can use DOC mode to edit text created in SHEET mode only if the text was entered as a left-aligned label in the leftmost column of the window. If the text is in the leftmost column but is centered, right-aligned, a repeating label, or a value, you cannot edit it. Additionally, you cannot use DOC mode to edit section markers created in the OUTLN window. An asterisk displays in the control panel when you place the cursor on a noneditable line.

Solution: Switch to SHEET or OUTLN mode and use the Edit (F2) key to edit these cells.

WORD PROCESSING PROBLEM #3:

As you are entering new text, the words do not wrap to the next line.

Explanation: Automatic wordwrap only works in Insert mode. If you forget to turn Overtype mode off when editing, new text does not wrap. Also, wordwrap is turned off if you set **J**ustification to **N**one.

Solution: Turn Overtype mode off by pressing the Ins key. The `Ovr` indicator at the bottom of the screen disappears. Alternatively, change the justification with the DOC **F**ormat **S**ettings **J**ustification command. If justification was turned off in a format line you created, edit it with the DOC **F**ormat **E**dit **C**urrent **J**ustification command. You may need to press the Justify (F2) key to realign the paragraph.

WORD PROCESSING PROBLEM #4:

The Backspace key deletes but leaves a blank space where the character was; the text to the right of the cursor does not shift to the left as text usually does.

Explanation: In Insert mode, the Backspace key deletes to the left of the cursor and slides text to the right of the cursor to the left to close up the space. In Overtype mode, the Backspace key deletes to the left of the cursor and leaves the space open. Figure T.29 shows how blank space is left after backspacing the words `to come` in Overtype mode.

Solution: Turn Overtype mode off by pressing the Ins key. The `Ovr` indicator at the bottom of the screen disappears. Press Justify (F2) to justify the paragraph and remove the spaces.

Fig. T.29.

The space left after backspacing in Overtype mode.

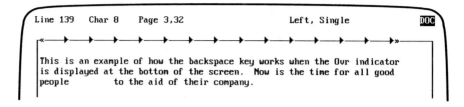

```
Line 139   Char 8   Page 3,32              Left, Single        DOC
«———→——→——→——→——→——→——→——→——→——→——→——→»
This is an example of how the backspace key works when the Ovr indicator
is displayed at the bottom of the screen.  Now is the time for all good
people           to the aid of their company.
```

WORD PROCESSING PROBLEM #5:

Symphony doesn't seem to be paying attention to the number of spaces you insert. Sometimes, when you put in one space, Symphony adds another when it justifies the paragraph. Other times, when you press two spaces, Symphony subtracts one. If you want more than two spaces, Symphony does not let you have more than one or two.

Explanation: Symphony follows spacing rules when justifying paragraphs. If a word contains no vowels and ends with a period (*Mr.*, for example), Symphony allows only one space after the period. If a word has at least one vowel and ends with a period, question mark, or exclamation point, *and* the next word begins with a capital letter, Symphony puts two spaces after the period. If the next word is not capitalized, only one space is inserted.

Solution: If you need more or fewer spaces than Symphony's justification rules permit, use hard spaces to override the rules. Unlike soft spaces, hard spaces are not altered as Symphony justifies paragraphs. Instead of entering spaces as you normally do, press Compose (Alt-F1) and press the space bar twice. A raised dot appears on-screen. Repeat this process for each space.

Tip

Use hard spaces when you need to keep two words together on one line. If you want to keep the words *Mr. Johnson* together instead of letting *Mr.* print on one line and *Johnson* wrap to the next, place a hard space between *Mr.* and *Johnson*. Symphony treats the phrase as a single word.

WORD PROCESSING PROBLEM #6:

When you type a capital letter or a number followed by a period at the left margin, these characters slide to the left of the margin (see fig. T.30).

Explanation: Symphony assumes that you want a hanging indent if you type letters or numbers followed by a period or colon. A *hanging indent* is a line with characters that stick out to the left of a line. Hanging indents are often used to create outlines.

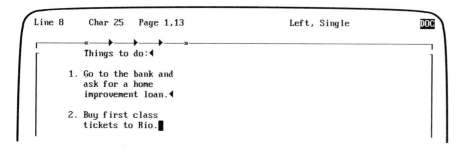

Fig. T.30.
Hanging indents automatically formatted when you type a number and a period.

Solution: Control the left margin with the SERVICES **P**rint settings rather than the DOC **F**ormat settings. First, set the left margin so that no room exists for hanging characters. In other words, use DOC **F**ormat **S**ettings **L**eft to set the left margin to 1. Second, control the left margin in the print settings sheet with the SERVICES **P**rint **S**ettings **M**argins **L**eft command.

WORD PROCESSING PROBLEM #7:

You can't get the Indent (F3) key to work properly. The text doesn't wordwrap to where you want it.

Explanation: The Indent key wraps text to wherever you pressed Indent (that is, where the indent symbol appears).

Solution: Use the space bar or Tab key to position the cursor where you want the text to wrap; then press Indent (F3). Consider figure T.31. To indent the first paragraph, position the cursor at the beginning of the paragraph, press the Tab key, and then press Indent. To indent the second paragraph, position the cursor in front of the character **1.** and press Tab twice. Move the cursor after the period, press the space bar five times, and then press Indent (F3).

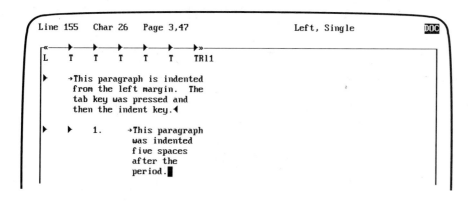

Fig. T.31.
Examples of indented paragraphs.

WORD PROCESSING PROBLEM #8:

You want to use DOC mode to edit a DOS batch file, but every time you make a change, all the lines jumble together and make the file unusable.

Explanation: Whenever you set DOC **F**ormat **S**ettings **A**uto-Justify to the default **Y**es, Symphony tries to rejustify the current paragraph whenever you make a change (such as adding or deleting characters to make a line wrap).

Solution: Before editing the DOS batch file, set DOC **F**ormat **S**ettings **A**uto-Justify to **N**o. As you edit the file, make sure that you don't press Justify (F2); that action causes Symphony to rejustify the current paragraph regardless of the **A**uto-Justify setting.

WORD PROCESSING PROBLEM #9:

The Spelling Checker takes too long to correct a spelling error, even though you specified a single word as the spell-check range.

Explanation: If you set DOC **F**ormat **S**ettings **A**uto-Justify to the default **Y**es, Symphony rejustifies the rest of the document after spell checking even a single word.

Solution: Set DOC **F**ormat **S**ettings **A**uto-Justify to **N**o before running the Spelling Checker. To quickly justify the document before printing, select DOC **J**ustify **A**ll-Remaining.

Alternative Solution: If you know that a word is misspelled, have the Spelling Checker show you the correct spelling (issue DOC **V**erify **G**o to invoke the Spelling Checker). Write down the correct spelling displayed on-screen; instead of pressing Enter to select the correct spelling, press Esc and select **Q**uit. Edit the word manually in the DOC window.

Troubleshooting Printing

PRINTING PROBLEM #1:

Sometimes when you print, you get about 10 blank lines in the middle of the page.

Explanation: Symphony keeps track of the number of lines on the page whenever it prints. If the final page of the report ends on line 35, for example, Symphony knows there are 31 lines left on the page. But if you use the form-feed button on your printer or use the printer knob to roll the paper out manually, Symphony doesn't know it. The program thinks you are still on line 35 even though you are back on line 1. The next time you print, Symphony inserts a page break where the program thinks the end of the page is, but this spot is the middle of the page.

Solution: After you manually adjust the paper to the top of the page, use the SERVICES **P**rint **A**lign command to tell Symphony the printer is now at the top of the page.

Alternative Solution: Don't use the printer controls to feed out the paper. Use the SERVICES **P**rint **P**age-Advance or **L**ine-Advance commands to eject the paper. With this method, Symphony always knows the line on which the page the print head is located

PRINTING PROBLEM #2:

When you print a document, the right ends of some lines are truncated.

Explanation: Symphony looks at two sets of margins when printing a document: the margins in the document format settings and the margins in the print settings. The print margin settings are added to the format margin settings when the document is printed. The print settings right margin must be greater than the sum of the left margin in the document format settings, the left margin in the print settings sheet, and the right margin in the document format settings. If the right margin in the print settings is less than this sum, some (or all) of the lines are cut off when you print.

Solution: Making the print settings right margin a very large number doesn't hurt; just make sure that this number is greater than the sum of all the other margins. Therefore, when printing a document, use the SERVICES **P**rint **S**ettings **M**argins **R**ight command and type a large number, such as the maximum of 240.

PRINTING PROBLEM #3:

You have specified double-spacing in the print settings sheet, but the document is still single-spaced when it prints.

Explanation: When you print from a DOC window, the document format settings have priority over the print settings. Therefore, whatever spacing is specified in the document format is used when the document is printed.

Solution: Use the DOC **F**ormat **S**ettings **S**pacing **2** command to double-space the document before printing.

PRINTING PROBLEM #4:

Even though you specified top and bottom margins of 0, several blank lines still appear at the top of the page.

Explanation: Symphony considers the top margin to be the number of lines from the top of the page to the header line. Whether or not you enter a header, Symphony reserves one line for the header and two lines for the space between the header and body text. Likewise, three lines are reserved at the bottom for the footer.

Solution: If you need every line on the page for your report, select SERVICES **P**rint **S**ettings **P**age **B**reaks **N**o so that the headers, footers, and page-break margins are suppressed.

Alternative Solution: If you want to fit more lines on the page but also want top and bottom margins, you can enter an initialization string for your printer to condense the print vertically by printing more than 6 lines per inch. If you do this, you also must change the page length (use SERVICES **P**rint **S**ettings **P**age **L**ength). For example, the initialization string for 8 lines per inch on an Epson RX-80 is \027\065\009. The corresponding page length is 88 (8 lines per inch times an 11-inch page).

PRINTING PROBLEM #5:

The footer is not printed on the last page of a multipage report.

Explanation: Symphony does not automatically advance to the top of the next page when it finishes printing. Therefore, Symphony does not print the footer on the last page until you tell the program to advance to the next page or until you exit the program.

Solution: Do not use the form-feed button on the printer to eject the last page. Instead, use the SERVICES **P**rint **P**age-Advance command; the paper will advance, and the footer will print.

Alternative Solution: Put a hard-page break on the last line of the source range. Use the DOC **P**age command to insert the page-break symbol in the first column, last row, of the source range. Alternatively, you can enter | :: (a vertical line and two colons) in the leftmost column you are printing from the SHEET window.

PRINTING PROBLEM #6:

You have a multiple-page report that spans different sections of the worksheet. Specifying all the different print ranges is a laborious task.

Explanation: The program remembers only the last print range specified. If a report has multiple print ranges, you must specify each one whenever you print the report.

Solution: Give each page or print range a descriptive name (RANGE1, RANGE2, and so on). Then create a macro that prints each range (see fig. T.32).

PRINTING PROBLEM #7:

Your print macro usually works as you want it to, but after you change the print options (to print a different report), the standard reports print incorrectly.

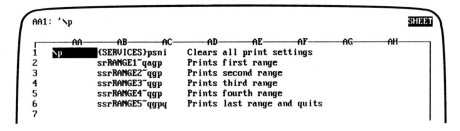

Fig. T.32.
A simple print macro.

Explanation: Symphony remembers the print settings from the last report you printed. If you print a special report on wider paper—or with different margins, headers, footers, and print-initialization strings, for example—these settings affect the next report you print with the macro.

Solution: Use SERVICES **P**rint **S**ettings **N**ame **C**reate to create a print settings sheet containing the particular settings you need to print the report. At the beginning of your print macro, use the SERVICES **P**rint **S**ettings **N**ame **U**se command to retrieve this settings sheet before printing.

Alternative Solution: At the beginning of your print macro, use the SERVICES **P**rint **S**ettings **N**ame **I**nitial-Settings command to reset all printer options to their defaults and to clear everything else (see the first line of fig. T.32). Then have the macro specify the printer options you want. In this way, you can include in one worksheet several print macros that don't interfere with one another.

PRINTING PROBLEM #8:

After you make changes to the worksheet, your reports sometimes print data that is not current.

Explanation: In manual recalculation mode, Symphony prints the worksheet as of the last recalculation.

Solution: If you specify the printing options manually, press the Calc (F8) key before you issue the **P**rint command. If you use a macro to print, begin the macro with {CALC}.

PRINTING PROBLEM #9:

When you set up print ranges, you considered margins and the six lines reserved for headers and footers. But the program occasionally skips a page between pages.

Explanation: You can use one of two methods to skip to the next page when you print reports: you can specify a long report and let Symphony skip automatically to a new page whenever it prints a full page or encounters a page-break code, or you can specify individual print ranges for each page and use the

Page-Advance command to tell the program to skip to the next page. Under certain conditions, the two methods conflict, and both send a page break to the printer, which results in a blank page.

With top and bottom margins of 0, you can have a one-page print range of as many as 60 lines. If Symphony encounters a print range of exactly 60 lines, the program automatically tells the printer to skip to the next page. If your macro also sends a page break, you get a blank page.

Solution: Either restrict your print ranges to 59 lines (minus the number of lines for top and bottom borders) or do not issue a **P**age-Advance command after a 60-line page.

PRINTING PROBLEM #10:

You do not want to print certain information in the middle of a print range.

Explanation: Suppose that you have documented assumptions, shown intermediate results that clarify a calculation, and added comments to make your worksheets easier to understand. You may not want to include this information in the final printed reports.

Solution: This problem has several solutions. Select those that best meet your needs.

Two solutions skip only rows:

❏ Specify multiple print ranges that skip any rows you do not want printed. (This method is practical only if you use a macro to print and if you do not add comments after completing the worksheet.)

❏ Use a special label prefix, the vertical bar (I), to tell Symphony not to print a row. Whenever Symphony sees this label prefix in the leftmost cell of a row in a print range, the program skips that row. Except for printing, this label prefix and the left-aligned label prefix (') act the same way. The contents of the cell are displayed normally.

This solution skips one or more columns in the middle of a print range:

❏ Use the SHEET **W**idth **H**ide command to hide the column before you print it. Then, after you have printed the range, "unhide" the column by selecting SHEET **W**idth **D**isplay.

PRINTING PROBLEM #11:

You want to print a report twice. But instead of starting at page 1, the second copy begins with the next page number of the first copy.

Explanation: With Symphony, you can build a report from many separate sections of a worksheet. If you use page numbers in headers or footers, every page starts with the next page number because the program assumes that you are producing one report.

Solution: Issue the **A**lign command after a **P**age-Advance command to instruct Symphony to start again at page 1. Because **A**lign also tells the program that you have adjusted the paper to the top of the page, always issue the **P**age-Advance command before the **A**lign command to prevent pages from being misaligned. Another way to change the page number is with the **P**rint **S**ettings **P**age **N**umber **P**rint-Number command. Enter the first page number you want printed in the header or footer.

PRINTING PROBLEM #12:

You don't want to bother specifying individual print ranges for a long report over and over again.

Explanation: If your report is more than five pages long, setting up the range names, settings sheets, and writing the macro to print the report can be a tedious process. If the report is likely to grow longer as time passes (if it contains year-to-date details, for example), you want to avoid having to continue adding range names and settings and changing the macro.

Solution: Let Symphony automatically break up the report. Symphony forces a page break after every full page and automatically inserts any headers or footers you specify. If you specify borders, Symphony prints them on every page; you simply specify one print range.

Symphony also splits vertically a report that is too wide to print on a single page. The program prints as much material as possible on one page and then prints the "right side" of the report on separate pages. You can leave these pages separate or tape them together to make a wide report.

PRINTING PROBLEM #13:

You let Symphony handle page breaks automatically, but the program separates information you want to keep on one page.

Explanation: When you specify a long report and let the program separate it automatically into pages, every page has the same number of print lines. But the report may contain information you do not want separated: paragraphs of explanation, or multiple-line descriptions of accounts, for example.

Solution: Leave the report as one print range, and insert page-break characters manually wherever you want a page to end. To insert a page-break character, move the cell pointer to the cell in the leftmost column of the row at which you want to start a new page. Then use the DOC **P**age command to instruct

Symphony to insert a row above the cell pointer and put a page-break character (|::) in the cell. Alternatively, you can insert a row in the spreadsheet and type the page-break character (|::) into a cell.

PRINTING PROBLEM #14:

When you used the DOC **P**age command to specify a page break, the command inserted a row through a macro, spreadsheet, or database in the same row as the print range.

Explanation: Symphony inserts a page break by inserting a row across the entire window. The blank row is inserted through anything that spans that row.

Solution: Rather than use DOC **P**age to insert a page break, indicate where you want the new page by typing the page-break character as a label.

In the leftmost column of the row where you want the new page, type the page-break character—a vertical-bar label prefix followed by two colons (|::). Symphony treats this label as a page-break character, except that no blank row is inserted in the worksheet. Remember that you must type the page-break character in a blank line in your print range because the row with the page-break character does not print.

Alternative Solution: Restrict the range for the window containing the print range so that inserted rows don't affect other areas of the file. Use the SERVICES **W**indow **S**ettings **R**estrict **R**ange command.

PRINTING PROBLEM #15:

You used the **P**rint **S**ettings **I**nit-String command to tell the printer to print compressed print. But the report wraps to a new line after 72 characters, even though additional space remains on the line.

Explanation: The **I**nit-String command indicates how many characters are printed per inch. The number of characters printed on each line is specified in the margin settings.

Solution: Whenever you change the print pitch, change the right margin. With a default left margin of 4 and a default right margin of 76, the 72-character print line matches the standard 72 data characters that Symphony displays on-screen.

If you change the line spacing to something other than six lines per inch, you also must change the page length to match the new setting.

PRINTING PROBLEM #16:

When you try to print a worksheet, the error message `No printer driver loaded` appears.

Explanation: This error message displays when you have not run the Symphony Install program or if you did not select a text printer driver when you ran the Install program.

Solution: Start the Install program and select a text printer driver by using the Change Selected Equipment option from the Install main menu. Then select the Text Printer(s) option and follow the instructions on-screen to select the text printer driver. When you are done, make sure that you select Save Changes from the Install menu options.

PRINTING PROBLEM #17:

The top of printed pages displays strange characters.

Explanation: You selected a printer driver during installation that does not match the type of printer you have. Although you may have selected the correct printer manufacturer, you may not have selected the model compatible with the selected printer driver.

Solution: Start the Install program and use the Change Selected Equipment menu option. Then choose Text Printer(s) and reselect the appropriate printer driver. You may have to confer with a technical-resource person or a computer dealer to determine which driver works best with your printer.

Alternative Solution: You may want to run the Install program and select Unlisted from the manufacturer list and Complete Compatibility from the printer-model list. Doing so selects a generic printer driver that works with most printers and gives you adequate printer output. Although this driver may limit the use of some of the features of your printer, it does produce a printout.

PRINTING PROBLEM #18:

You cannot print a full-page graph with your HP LaserJet printer.

Explanation: You may have exceeded the internal printer memory with resident soft fonts loaded from another application. This is especially true if you have more than 512K of internal printer memory. If you have only 512K of internal printer memory, you cannot print a full-page high-density graph on a LaserJet printer.

Solution: If you have more than 512K of internal printer memory, clear out the soft fonts by resetting the printer. If you have less than 512K of internal memory, you may want to purchase additional printer memory; alternatively, decrease the size or resolution of the graph.

PRINTING PROBLEM #19:

You cannot print two half-sized graphs on the same page with your HP LaserJet or HP DeskJet printer.

Explanation: LaserJet or DeskJet printers cannot print in the bottom half-inch of the page.

Solution: In the PrintGraph program, select **S**ettings **I**mage **S**ize **M**anual and enter the following settings:

Top	0.395
Left	1.102
Height	4.191
Width	5.805

Troubleshooting Graphing

GRAPHING PROBLEM #1:

You created several different graphs and used the **I**mage-Save command to save each one. After you printed the graphs in PrintGraph, you discovered a minor mistake in the first graph. When you went back into Symphony, you discovered that you no longer had the settings for the first graph—the **P**review command displays the last graph you created. You have to redefine all the graph's settings from scratch to correct the minor error.

Explanation: Each time you create a new graph, the previous graph's settings are lost because Symphony can have only one current graph in each window. The fact that you saved the graph with **I**mage-Save is irrelevant; **I**mage-Save creates a graph file with a PIC extension that is used for printing purposes only—you cannot view or change the PIC file in Symphony.

Solution: Although Symphony can have only one active graph in a window, you can save a library of graphs within the worksheet. Before creating a new graph, use the SHEET **G**raph (or GRAPH) **1**st-Settings **N**ame **C**reate command to save the settings under a name you choose. Then enter the specifications for that graph.

Repeat this process for each graph, giving each group of settings a different name. To recall any graph, issue the SHEET **G**raph (or GRAPH) **1**st-Settings **N**ame **U**se command and either type the name of the graph or point to its name in the list of graph names. If you are working in a GRAPH window, you can use GRAPH **A**ttach to view a named graph.

When you save the worksheet, the graph names and settings are saved also. Be sure to save the worksheet; if you forget to save, the names and settings are lost.

GRAPHING PROBLEM #2:

You are creating and naming graphs, but the settings for the different graphs get all mixed up.

Explanation: The SHEET **G**raph (or GRAPH) **1**st-Settings **N**ame **C**reate command assigns the name you specify to whatever settings are currently displayed in the settings sheets. If you create one graph and change the settings before you name the next graph, the changes you make are recorded in the first graph.

Solution: First name the graph, then change the settings, rather than the other way around.

GRAPHING PROBLEM #3:

You don't like the patterns used by some of the graph ranges.

Explanation: Symphony has a fixed set of patterns for each graph range (X, and A through F). By default, the A-range is assigned pattern 2; the B-range, pattern 3; and so on. You may find that looking at two particular patterns next to each other, however, strains your eyes (see fig. T.33).

Solution: Use SHEET **G**raph (or GRAPH) **1**st-Settings **H**ue to assign different patterns to the data ranges. Figure T.34 shows the same graph as figure T.33 with the A-range set to hue 1 and the B-range set to hue 7.

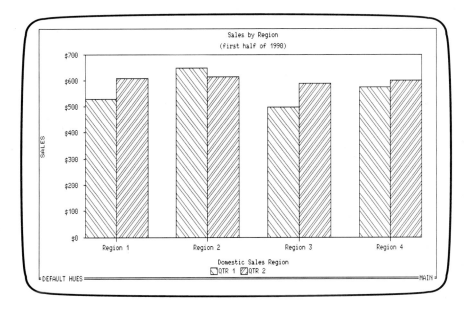

Fig. T.33.

Default patterns for the A-range and B-range.

Fig. T.34.
A graph with modified hues.

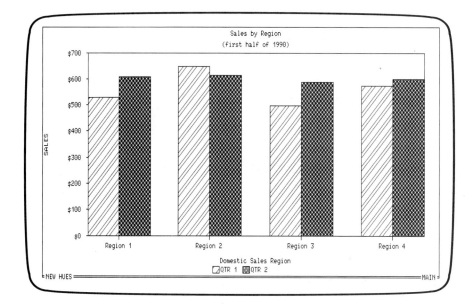

GRAPHING PROBLEM #4:

You want extra space between the bars in your graphs, but the program automatically puts them right next to each other.

Explanation: In a bar graph with multiple ranges, each bar touches the one next to it even if ample room exists to separate them.

Solution: You can specify a range of blank cells (or zeros) as a "dummy" graph range. Symphony displays the dummy range as a bar with zero height, which is the same as a space between the bars. The bar graph in figure T.35 shows the A and C ranges, which contain data, separated by B and D ranges of blank cells.

The blank B range produces the extra space between the A and C ranges, that is, between first and second quarter data. The blank D range provides additional space between the sets of bars, that is, between each region. If you don't specify a D range, equal amounts of space appear between each bar, making it difficult to tell which bar goes with which region.

GRAPHING PROBLEM #5:

You are graphing data in thousands; numbers higher than 1,000 represent millions. Symphony automatically scales the data and adds the deceiving notation **(Thousands)** to the y-axis.

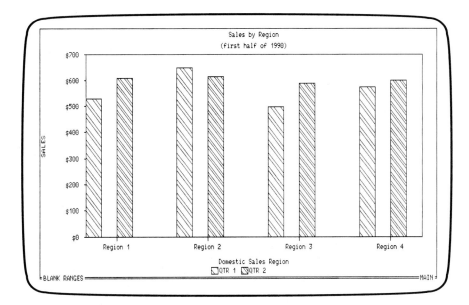

Explanation: This problem can be extremely confusing. Symphony assumes that all the numbers you graph represent individual units. If the largest numbers are greater than 1,000, Symphony automatically scales the numbers into thousands and adds the notation **(Thousands)** to the y-axis. You cannot stop this automatic scale indicator.

If you graph information that you have already "converted" to thousands (or millions, or more) in the worksheet (as is frequently done on a financial statement), the **(Thousands)** indicator that Symphony puts on the graph is incorrect.

Figure T.36 shows a table of sales data for the first three quarters. The numbers are in thousands of dollars. Note that one of the numbers in the table (in cell D5) is larger than 1,000. Figure T.37 shows the graph of this data with the incorrect y-axis scale indicator.

Solution: Although you cannot stop the automatic scale indicator, you can change the data. If you add three zeros to each cell in figure T.36, the graph is labeled **(Millions)** rather than **(Thousands)**, as shown in figure T.38.

GRAPHING PROBLEM #6:

Your graph's x-axis labels overlap.

Explanation: You can fit only a limited number of x-axis labels on a graph before the labels start to overlap (see fig. T.39).

Fig. T.36.

A spreadsheet with numbers in the thousands.

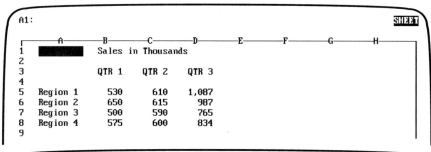

Fig. T.37.

Incorrect use of the scaling notation (Thousands).

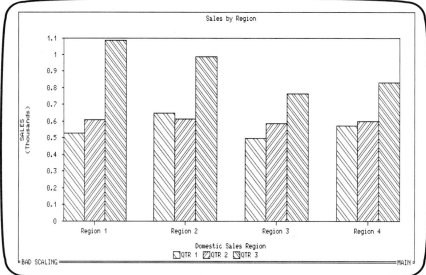

Fig. T.38.

Correct use of the scaling notation (Millions).

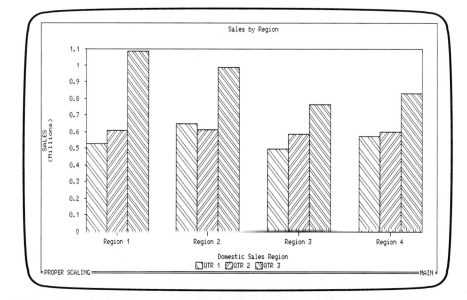

Solution: Use the SHEET **G**raph (or GRAPH) **2**nd-Settings **O**ther **S**kip command to skip a specific number of x-axis labels between the entries displayed on the graph. Figure T.40 shows the same graph as figure T.39 after **S**kip **2** is specified.

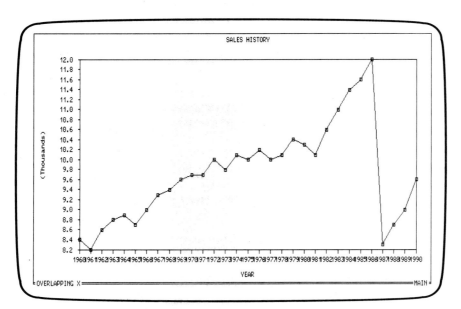

Fig. T.39.
Overlapping x-axis labels.

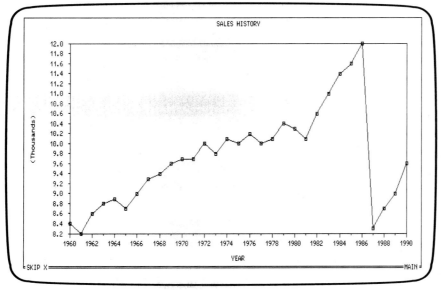

Fig. T.40.
Skipping every second x-axis label.

GRAPHING PROBLEM #7:

After waiting 30 minutes for a graph to print, you discover an error and must print the graph again.

Explanation: This problem is a common one. The graph display does not show exactly what the printed graph looks like. For example, the display doesn't show the different fonts you can specify for the text portion of a graph, and you can easily overlook missing legends or incorrect data on the display version of a graph.

Solution: Speed up the process of printing a graph by specifying the lowest possible resolution for your printer. Select **S**ettings **H**ardware **P**rinter from the PrintGraph menu to look at a list of all the printers and densities included in the printer's driver set (see fig. T.41). For example, the Epson printer in figure T.41 offers low and high density; the HP LaserJet printer offers medium and high density. Depending on the density at which you print, the difference in print time for a full-page graph can be a few minutes or a half-hour or more. Although the lowest density may not be acceptable for presentations, you can use low density to print a review copy of the graph.

Fig. T.41.

Choosing a low-density printer to speed printing.

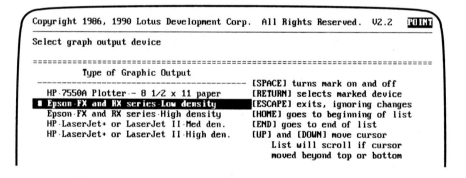

Alternatively, you can print a review copy quickly by specifying an unusually small size. To do so, choose **S**ettings **I**mage **S**ize **M**anual from the PrintGraph menu and then specify a small **W**idth and **H**eight for the test print. To produce a graph that covers one-eighth of a page, for example, specify a **W**idth of **3.25** inches and a **H**eight of **2.345** inches. (These numbers are half the sizes you use to print a half-page graph.)

When you are confident that the graph is correct, print it full-size in the highest print density available for your printer.

GRAPHING PROBLEM #8:

Your pie graph looks like someone blew it up with a stick of dynamite: every piece is exploded (see fig. T.42).

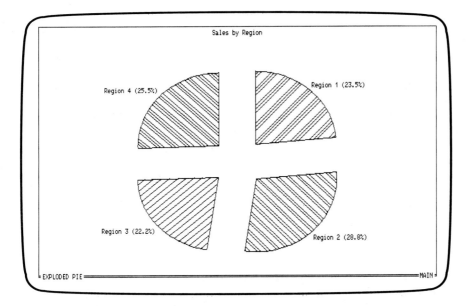

Fig. T.42.
*A pie graph with all
the slices exploded.*

Explanation: Pie graphs use the A-range for the graphing values and the B-range for the shading/exploding codes. If a value in the B-range is over 100, the pie slice is separated from the rest of the pie—that is, it is exploded. If all values in the B-range are over 100, all the pieces of the pie are exploded. If you didn't mean to explode sections of the pie graph, you probably have a B-range left over from another graph.

Solution: Cancel the B-range with the SHEET **G**raph (or GRAPH) **1**st-Settings **C**ancel **E**ntire-Row **B** command. If you want shading in the pie slices, set up a B-range with values between 1 and 7. Figure T.43 shows the pie graph after the B-range has been corrected.

GRAPHING PROBLEM #9:

The top part of some or all of the bars in a bar graph are truncated (see fig. T.44).

Explanation: Symphony always tries to fit the graph into the scales you specify. If you set the upper limit of a scale too low, the resulting graph simply shows as much of the data as can be squeezed into the allotted space. For example, if you set the upper limit at 10 and the lower limit at 0—but your data values are all greater than 10—the result is the graph shown in figure T.44.

Solution: Look at the values in your spreadsheet and locate the highest value; the upper limit of your scale should be equal to or greater than this value. Use the SHEET **G**raph (or GRAPH) **2**nd-Settings **Y**-Scale **T**ype **M**anual-Linear command to reset the lower and upper limits.

Fig. T.43.

The pie graph after canceling the B-range and resetting the pattern values.

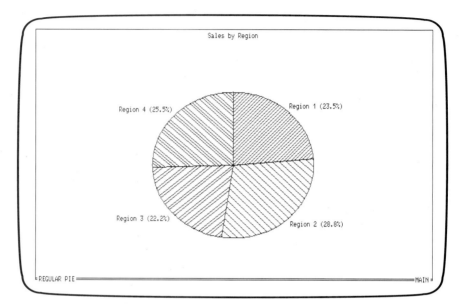

Fig. T.44.

A bar graph showing inadequate scale upper limits.

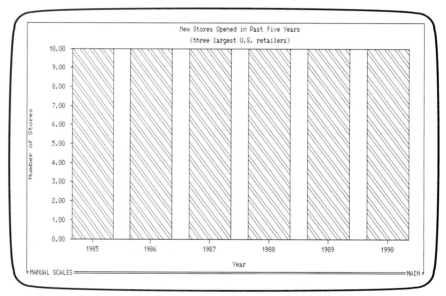

Troubleshooting Data Management

DATA MANAGEMENT PROBLEM #1:

You enter a criterion, but all the records are selected.

Explanation: When you choose SHEET **Q**uery **F**ind, **E**xtract, **U**nique, or **D**elete, or FORM **C**riteria **U**se, Symphony uses the criterion as a filter to select records from the database. If the criterion is not exact, these **Q**uery commands do not work correctly.

Solution: Issue the FORM **S**ettings **B**asic **C**riterion command (or SHEET **Q**uery **S**ettings **B**asic **C**riterion). When Symphony highlights the old range, check it carefully, looking for the following errors:

  1. Does the criterion range contain any blank rows? (See fig. T.45.) This error is the most common one in criterion ranges that select all records. Each row is a separate selection test; if a record in the database passes any one test, that record is selected. Because a blank row has no tests, all records are selected. Make sure that only the field names and the rows containing criteria are highlighted.

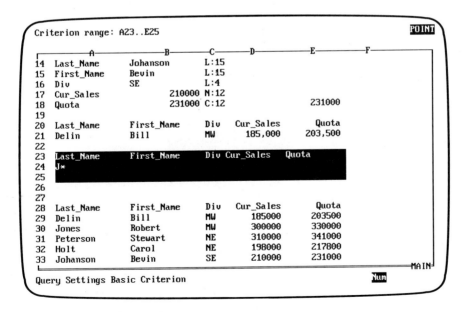

Fig. T.45.

A criterion range with a blank row.

2. Do any compound tests use #NOT# or <> (not equal)? Such compound tests can be extremely tricky and can produce results just the opposite of the results you are trying to produce. Here is an example of an erroneous compound test:

    +B5<>100#OR#B5<>200

The purpose of this test is to select all records except those in which the value in column B is *either* 100 or 200. This written statement makes sense, but the effect of the test (the formula) is to select all records in which the value in column B is anything *but* 100 or 200. If the value is 100, it passes the test because it is not 200; if the value is 200, it passes the test because it is not 100. The correct way to write the test is as follows:

    +B5<>100#AND#B5<>200

DATA MANAGEMENT PROBLEM #2:

You enter a criterion, but none of the records is selected.

Explanation: Each field in a criterion record (or a row in a criterion range) can be a separate test. To be selected, a record must pass all the tests in the same criterion record or row. If you write the selection tests incorrectly, it may be impossible for a record to pass all of them. This problem is most common when you use the #AND#, #OR#, and #NOT# operators in selection tests.

Solution: Carefully check the selection tests in the criterion records or range for tests such as the following:

    +NUMBER>100#AND#NUMBER<0

This test tells Symphony to select records only when the value is both greater than 100 and less than 0. Because this result is impossible, no records are selected.

Also, make sure that the test's format matches the data in the field you are testing. If you use label matches or string functions on numeric data, or if you use number matches on strings, nothing is selected.

DATA MANAGEMENT PROBLEM #3:

You printed a database report, and not all records printed, even though you selected FORM **C**riteria **I**gnore.

Explanation: Symphony uses the worksheet criterion range as a filter to select records from the database. **C**riteria **I**gnore only affects the *display* of records in FORM mode. Even though you specified that you want to ignore the criterion, the criterion is still in effect for SHEET **Q**uery commands and the printing of reports.

Solution: Use SHEET **E**rase to erase the criterion from the criterion range. You can also delete the criterion record by displaying the criterion record with FORM **C**riteria **E**dit and then pressing the Del key.

DATA MANAGEMENT PROBLEM #4:

A SHEET **Q**uery **F**ind command works correctly, but SHEET **Q**uery **E**xtract (or **U**nique) does not.

Explanation: Because **F**ind does not use the output range, unlike **E**xtract and **U**nique, something must be wrong with that range.

Solution: The field names in the output range must match the field names in the database. If the names do not match, Symphony selects the correct records but does not copy any fields to the output range. To ensure that the field names match, copy them from the database. You can use selected fields instead of all database fields if you like, but the labels at the top of the output range must still match the field names exactly.

DATA MANAGEMENT PROBLEM #5:

When you extract records, you get the message `Too many records for output range`, and only some of the records that should have been extracted are displayed in the output range.

Explanation: As your database grows, the output from **E**xtract commands grows also. When you define an output range, you can define the number of rows you want Symphony to use. If the output of the **E**xtract (or **U**nique) command contains more records than you have specified, the **Q**uery stops, and you get an error message.

Solution: Specify as the output range only the row containing the field names. Symphony treats this specification as allowing the use of as many rows as necessary for **E**xtract or **U**nique. If you use this solution, however, be sure that nothing is below the output range. If there is, you lose valuable data; the next time you issue an **E**xtract or **U**nique command, Symphony erases everything below the field names before copying the selected records. (The program even erases data that is far below the area needed for copying the selected records.)

Alternative Solution: Enlarge the size of the output range and then rerun the **E**xtract.

DATA MANAGEMENT PROBLEM #6:

You inserted more records into your database, but these new records are not sorted according to the sort key you specified.

Explanation: Sorting records involves two steps. First, you use FORM **S**ettings **S**ort-Keys (or SHEET **Q**uery **S**ettings **S**ort-Keys) to specify the sort key, then you perform the **R**ecord-Sort. The sort key is stored in the settings sheet, so you only need to make this specification once. You must still use **R**ecord-Sort, however, after new records are added to the file.

Solution: After adding new records to a database, issue the FORM **R**ecord-Sort command.

Alternative Explanation: If you're using the @BASE database manager add-in, new records are added to the end of the database.

Alternative Solution: After adding new records to an @BASE database, issue the BASE **D**ata **S**ort command.

Alternative Solution: Consider buying the @BASE Option Pac and indexing the database. Indexed databases are automatically displayed in sorted order.

DATA MANAGEMENT PROBLEM #7:

You print a database report, but the column widths are not correct, and some of the columns display asterisks.

Explanation: When you generate a database, Symphony sets column widths for each field according to the field length you specified. Symphony uses the column widths of the current window when printing reports. If you are not in the FORM window when you issue the SERVICES **P**rint command, Symphony uses the column widths of whatever window you are in.

Solution: Make sure that before you issue the SERVICES **P**rint command when you are in the FORM window in which you created the database.

Alternative Solution: Set up a report-layout window using the correct column widths and make that window current before printing. This approach is especially useful if you want to modify the database reports so that records print on multiple lines.

DATA MANAGEMENT PROBLEM #8:

You specified two sort keys, and you no longer want the second key. The Backspace and the Esc keys, however, don't clear the key.

Explanation: Once you specify a sort key, the only way to clear it is with the **C**ancel command.

Solution: In a SHEET window, issue the SHEET **Q**uery **S**ettings **C**ancel **S**ort-Keys command. In a FORM window, use the FORM **S**ettings **C**ancel **S**ort-Keys command. All sort keys are cleared, and you must then reenter the **1**st-Key.

DATA MANAGEMENT PROBLEM #9:

You're in the BASE window but you cannot switch to any other window mode or use the SERVICES menu.

Explanation: You can't switch to another mode or use the SERVICES menu in the BASE window unless you're at the BASE main screen.

Solution: Press the Esc key until you return to the BASE main screen (see figure T.46).

Fig. T.46.
The BASE main screen.

DATA MANAGEMENT PROBLEM #10:

You attached the @BASE add-in and later detached it but ran out of memory when you tried to load another add-in or a large file.

Explanation: Any Symphony add-in that adds @functions, such as BASEFUNC.APP and BASEOPTF.APP, contains what is known as an *Undetachable_Flag* that prevents it from being detached. Once you loaded one of these add-ins, it remains attached until you exit from Symphony.

Solution: If you're attaching add-ins, be sure to attach first those like BASEFUNC.APP or BASEOPTF.APP that add @functions. Then, if you detach add-ins, Symphony can detach the other add-ins and recover the memory they were using even though it cannot detach the @function add-in.

Alternative Solution: If you set SERVICES **C**onfiguration **O**ther **A**dd-in to automatically attach add-ins, don't include BASEFUNC.APP or BASEOPTF.APP.

Alternative Solution: If you have attached @function add-ins, be certain that they aren't set to be automatically attached (modify SERVICES **C**onfiguration **O**ther **A**dd-in if necessary) and exit from Symphony. Restart Symphony without attaching the add-ins.

DATA MANAGEMENT PROBLEM #11:

After you copied some formulas that use @DB functions, the copies don't work properly.

Explanation: The criteria in @DB functions do not adjust when you copy the formulas using SHEET **C**opy.

Solution: Use BASE **U**tility **C**riteria-Copy to copy formulas that contain @DB functions.

DATA MANAGEMENT PROBLEM #12:

Your worksheet contains several @DB functions that seem to produce incorrect results.

Explanation: The @DB functions don't use natural order recalculation. Forcing @DB formulas to calculate in the order you think they should is very difficult. Also, because @DB formulas move to the end of the formula-recalculation stack when you edit them, worksheets that calculated properly before you edited some formulas may not calculate properly afterwards.

Solution: Use SHEET **S**ettings **R**ecalculation **I**terations to set the recalculation iterations to a number higher than the default of 1. The exact number necessary may be difficult to determine, but should be high enough so that pressing the Calc (F8) key a second time doesn't change any results.

Alternative Solution: Set the recalculation method to **C**olumn-by-Column or **R**ow-by-Row to force the formulas to recalculate in a particular order.

Alternative Solution: Use the @DB functions in macros to ensure that they are processed in the desired order.

Troubleshooting Communications

COMMUNICATIONS PROBLEM #1:

You are unable to connect with a remote computer. When you dial the number, you get garbage on the screen, never connect, or immediately disconnect.

Explanation: The interface settings (baud, parity, length, stop bits) for the remote computer must exactly match yours. If they are not identical, you cannot communicate successfully.

Solution: Double-check the interface settings. When in doubt, use 1200 baud, no parity, 8-bit word length, and 1 stop bit. Most information services and electronic bulletin boards use these settings.

Alternative Explanation: Too much static on the phone lines may be preventing a good connection.

Alternative Solution: If the problem lies in the phone lines, take these steps:

1. Try dialing again later.
2. Try connecting at a lower baud rate (300 or 1200). Higher baud rates are more sensitive to static.
3. If you are dialing another computer user, have the other user call you.

4. Use another long-distance carrier. Some carriers have more static than others. By dialing **10288** before the phone number, you can access AT&T's lines. By dialing **10333** before the phone number, you can access US Sprint's fiber-optic network, which usually has the least line noise of any carrier. If you normally use another carrier, AT&T and US Sprint generally bill through your local phone company.

COMMUNICATIONS PROBLEM #2:

You try to use the COMM **S**ettings **I**nterface command, but Symphony won't let you change any of the options.

Explanation: When you installed Symphony, you indicated that you did not plan to use communications. You cannot change the interface settings if you have not installed Symphony for communications use.

Solution: Run the Install program and answer **Y**es when asked Do you plan to use communications?.

COMMUNICATIONS PROBLEM #3:

You are on-line with another PC user, and you connected with the following settings: 1200 baud, even parity, 7-bit word length, and 1 stop bit (see fig. T.47). Although you were successful in connecting and typing messages back and forth, you cannot transfer a file successfully.

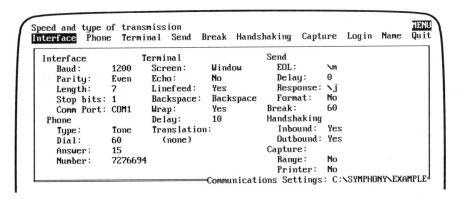

Fig. T.47.
Sample communications settings.

Explanation: Successful telecommunications require that both computers use the same protocol settings. You were able to connect because both you and the other user specified 7 bits, even parity, and 1 stop bit. During file-transfer operation, however, Symphony automatically changes these settings to 8 bits, no parity, and 1 stop bit. If the other PC's communications program doesn't also use these settings during file transfer, you cannot transfer files.

Solution: If you plan to transfer files, you and the other user should specify 8 bits, no parity, and 1 stop bit as the interface settings.

COMMUNICATIONS PROBLEM #4:

When you are use the **P**hone-and-Login command, the log-in starts before the connection is made, and the system hangs with a **WAIT** message. But if you phone and log in separately, everything works fine.

Explanation: With the **P**hone-and-Login command, Symphony dials the number and then waits for the **Online** indicator to display at the bottom of the screen before starting the log-in sequence. If the **Online** message is displayed before dialing, Symphony prematurely starts the log-in sequence.

Solution: The premature display of the **Online** message is usually caused by an incorrect switch setting in the modem. If you have a Hayes 1200 modem, switch 6 must be in the off (open) position. If you have a Hayes 1200B modem, switch 3 must be off (open).

Tip

Many modems follow a standard switch layout. The following table shows a typical switch pattern used with external modems.

Switch	On Position	Off Position
1	Verbose mode	Terse mode
2	Send result code	Do not send result code
3	Echo commands	Do not echo commands
4	Enable auto answer	Disable auto answer
5	DTR followed	DTR forced ON
6	DCD reflects on-line	DCD forced ON
7	Modem recognizes AT commands	Modem does not recognize AT commands
8	Position not used	

If your modem uses this same switch pattern, a good starting point is to set all the switches to the On position.

COMMUNICATIONS PROBLEM #5:

When you are connected to a remote computer, everything you type appears twice (for example, **HHEELLLLOO**).

Explanation: You are communicating with a full-duplex computer that automatically sends back to you the characters you type. In addition, Symphony is also displaying the characters you type. The result is that every character you type appears twice (an *echo*).

Solution: Change the **E**cho setting on the settings sheet to **N**o (select COMM **S**ettings **T**erminal **E**cho **N**o). See figure T.47.

COMMUNICATIONS PROBLEM #6:

When you are connected to a remote computer, you can't see anything you type.

Explanation: You are communicating with a half-duplex computer that does not send back to you the characters you type. In addition, Symphony is not displaying the characters you type.

Solution: Change the **E**cho setting on the settings sheet to **Y**es (select COMM **S**ettings **T**erminal **E**cho **Y**es).

COMMUNICATIONS PROBLEM #7:

When you are connected to a remote computer, the Enter key moves the cursor back to the beginning of the same line; the cursor doesn't move down to the next line.

Explanation: The Enter key is producing a carriage return but not a line feed. The **L**inefeed setting in the settings sheet controls whether a linefeed is given.

Solution: Change the **L**inefeed setting on the settings sheet to **Y**es (select COMM **S**ettings **T**erminal **L**inefeed **Y**es). See figure T.47.

COMMUNICATIONS PROBLEM #8:

You can't get any response from your modem; it does not dial a phone number.

Explanation: The modem isn't connected properly.

Solution: Check to make certain that the modem has power, is turned on, is connected to an operating phone line, and is plugged into the correct serial port on your computer. Many PCs have two serial ports; the COMM **S**ettings **I**nterface **C**omm **P**ort setting must match the port to which the cable is connected. Try changing the setting from COM1 to COM2.

Alternative Solution: Serial and parallel ports on PCs use different connectors. Be sure to buy the proper cable made for PC use. Mainframe computers often use nonstandard cables that allow you to connect a modem to the parallel port.

Alternative Explanation: The modem is being interfered with by another device like a mouse.

Solution: If you have a mouse connected and are unable to use your modem, try unplugging the mouse and rebooting the computer. If the modem works, try switching the ports to which the mouse and modem are connected.

Alternative Explanation: No communications configuration file is being loaded so Symphony is trying to communicate with your modem at the default 110 baud. Most modems cannot communicate below 300 baud.

Alternative Solution: Use SERVICES **C**onfiguration **C**ommunications **S**et to set a communications configuration file to be automatically loaded when you start Symphony. Be sure to select **U**pdate after selecting the CCF file.

Troubleshooting Macros

MACRO PROBLEM #1:

You write a macro. When you try to execute it with the Alt key, the macro fails to start and the beeper sounds.

Explanation: You must use a precise name format for macros invoked with the Alt key. The range name must be exactly two characters: the first is a backslash; the second is a letter (from A to Z). If you name your macro anything else, Symphony cannot execute it with the Alt key. You must use the User (F7) key for other types of macro names.

Solution: Use SHEET **R**ange **N**ame **C**reate to check the macro's range name. Symphony lists, in alphabetical order, all the range names in the worksheet. Range names that start with a backslash are at the end of the list. If you don't see the macro's name listed, you haven't named the macro. Even experienced programmers make this seemingly trivial mistake, which is the most common reason a macro won't work.

If the range name is in the list, make sure that you have included the backslash. For example, although the letter A is a valid range name, it is not a valid name for a macro to be started with the Alt key.

Another common error is to use a slash (/) rather than a backslash (\) when you name a macro. If the range name is in the list, check carefully to make sure that the name starts with a backslash.

If the macro name is listed and looks valid, highlight it and press Enter. Symphony highlights the range with that name. The range should contain only one cell—the first cell of the macro. The contents of the first cell of the macro must be a label or a string-valued function. If the cell is blank or contains a numeric value, the macro does not work.

MACRO PROBLEM #2:

You have a macro named \7, but it does not work when you press Alt-7. You know that the name 7 is assigned to the first cell of the macro and that the first cell is a label. The macro does not beep when you attempt to start it, but a backslash appears in the control panel.

Explanation: You do not start macros named \1 through \10 like those named \a through \z. Numbered macros can be started in one of two ways: press User (F7) followed by the function key that corresponds to the number 1 through 10, or press User (F7) followed by the backslash (\) and the name of the macro.

Solution: Start the first and second macros in figure T.48 by pressing the F7 function key. After releasing F7, press F7 to start \7 or F10 to start \10.

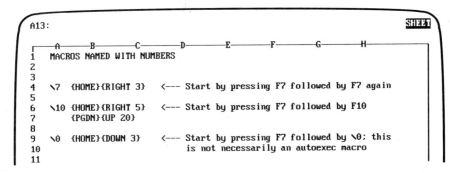

Fig. T.48.
Starting numbered macros.

Unlike 1-2-3, Symphony does not automatically start a macro with the name \0. Because no function key is designated F0, you cannot use the same method to start a \0 macro you use to start macros named \1 through \10.

Start a macro named \0 by pressing User (F7) and typing **\0**. Press Enter to end the name and start the macro. You can use the technique of typing the macro name for macros named \1 through \10 as well.

MACRO PROBLEM #3:

After you write a few macros, you move some data. The macros now refer to the wrong addresses.

Explanation: Macros are not like formulas; the addresses in macros do not change automatically when you move data used by the macro. In fact, a macro is nothing more than a label. Symphony does not adjust the contents of labels when you move data, because the program does not know that labels contain addresses.

Solution: **Never** use cell addresses in macros. Always give range names to all the cells and ranges you use in macros, and use these range names in the macros. If you move these ranges or insert and delete rows and columns, the range names adjust automatically, and the macro continues to refer to the correct cells and ranges.

MACRO PROBLEM #4:

Your macro seems to work correctly, but after you execute the macro, the display is wrong.

Explanation: Symphony does not update the display or recalculate the worksheet during certain macro commands. Figure T.49A shows a macro (\a) that has just been executed. Although the contents of cell A1 should be 100, the cell is blank. Although the worksheet is set for automatic recalculation, the `Calc` indicator is on.

Fig. T.49A.

A macro that does not update the display.

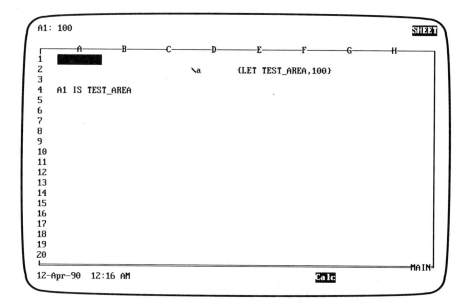

Solution: To display the update, add a tilde (~), a DRAW command, or a CALC command to the end of the macro. If you add any of these to the end of the macro shown in figure T.49A, Symphony displays **100** as the contents of A1, and the `Calc` indicator vanishes (see fig. T.49B). With the new recalculation function that updates only formulas dependent on cells changed since the last recalculation, the CALC command does not necessarily pause a program excessively. If you use a macro command such as RECALC or RECALCCOL, you have to move the screen to update the display. For example, after you issue RECALC, you (or the macro) must press Esc or an arrow key to update the screen.

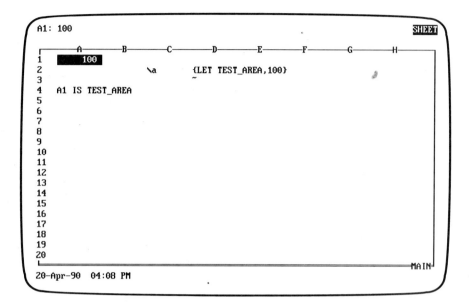

Fig. T.49B.
The macro after adding ~ to update the display.

MACRO PROBLEM #5:

A relatively short macro never seems to stop running. The macro repeatedly branches back on itself and never moves on to the next step or stops running (the macro has an infinite loop).

Explanation: Figure T.50A shows a simple macro with an infinite loop. The first line in \a sets cell A1 to 100. The second line branches back to the first line as long as the value in cell A1 is 100. Because the value in A1 is always 100 and the macro test no other values, the program repeatedly loops back on itself.

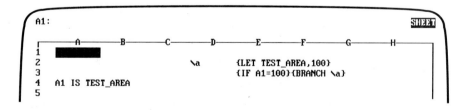

Fig. T.50A.
A macro with an infinite loop.

Solution: If a macro with an infinite loop is running, you must halt the macro. You then have to gain control of the keyboard and fix the code. Halt a macro with an infinite loop by pressing Ctrl-Break. Then press Esc to gain control of the keyboard.

After you terminate the infinite loop, you must fix the code. You can often find the point at which a program loops back on itself by using Symphony's Step (Alt-F7) function.

Figure T.50B shows one correction for the infinite loop shown in figure T.50A. A special flag named REPEAT? is set so that the program monitors whether a loop back causes it to repeat itself.

Fig. T.50B.

The macro with a flag to test for an infinite loop.

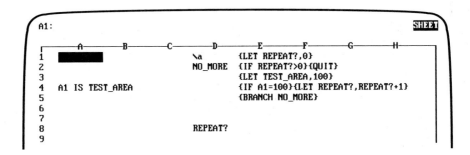

MACRO PROBLEM #6:

Although the logic of the macro appears correct, the macro never works properly. Critical values do not seem to be current, even when recalculation is on **A**utomatic.

Explanation: On a large worksheet, macros would execute slowly if Symphony recalculated the entire worksheet after every macro command. Symphony seldom recalculates the worksheet while a macro executes. If critical values change during execution, the macro uses the old values—not the current ones.

Solution: Determine which cells and ranges must be recalculated to make the macro work correctly and then add RECALC or RECALCCOL statements to the macro where necessary. A complete worksheet recalculation with CALC works also but usually is extremely slow.

The macro shown in figure T.51A tests incorrectly for a valid entry. In this macro, GETNUMBER finds the old value because the test in IP_TEST (cell C12) is not updated after GETNUMBER. To correct the problem, add a RECALC command to the macro (see fig. T.51B). If the worksheet is set for automatic recalculation, you can use a tilde instead of RECALC; if the worksheet is set for manual recalculation, you must use RECALC or RECALCCOL.

In figure T.51B, the macro branches to PROCESS if the test in C12 is TRUE and branches to ERROR_ROUTINE if the test is FALSE. You can make the PROCESS and ERROR_ROUTINE routines perform whatever processing you need in the worksheet.

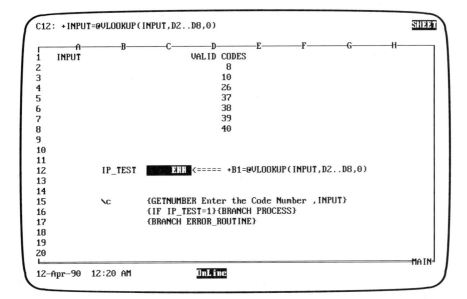

Fig. T.51A.

A macro that requires recalculation to work correctly.

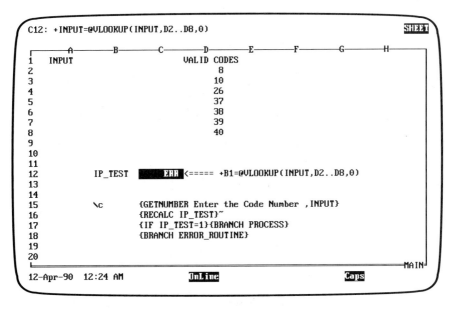

Fig. T.51B.

Adding a RECALC to the macro.

MACRO PROBLEM #7:

When using a simple GOTO command in an application with more than one window, the macro comes to an abrupt halt with an error message about restrict ranges.

Explanation: Figure T.52 shows the problem. The \a macro attempts to move the cursor with a GOTO command to the range named RIGHTHERE. The problem is that \a is in AREA_1, and RIGHTHERE is in AREA_2, a different window with a nonoverlapping restrict range. The message at the bottom of the screen alerts the user that the range is outside the current window's restrict range.

Fig. T.52.

Two macros to move outside a restrict range.

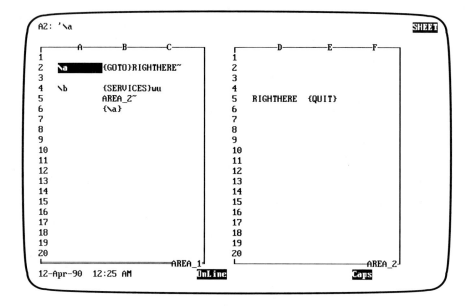

Solution: Regain control from the fatal error condition by pressing Ctrl-Break and then pressing Esc to regain access to the keyboard.

The \b macro shows one solution to the fatal error in \a. The macro changes the current window to the one containing the range to which you want to move the cursor. After changing the window to AREA_2, the \a macro works properly. Notice that \b, which does not generate an error, executes a subroutine call to \a.

MACRO PROBLEM #8:

You need to change a macro that you wrote earlier, but you can't remember how it works.

Explanation: This common problem surprises users when they first start to work with macros. After having painstakingly written, tested, and debugged a macro, you use it successfully in your worksheet. Because you wrote the macro, you know exactly what it does and how it operates. When you have to change it, you are amazed that you can't remember how it works.

Even people who write Symphony macros for a living have this problem. They write the macro quickly but have difficulty figuring it out a few months later.

Solution: Structure and document your macros carefully and consistently. Keep each macro short, and design it to perform only one operation. Instead of trying to cram the entire macro onto one line, keep each line of macro code short. Put all the range names to the left of the cell with that name, and put comments to the right of each macro statement. Write your comments in plain language, and explain why the macro does what it does.

To make your macros easy to read, use uppercase and lowercase letters consistently. Always use lowercase letters for menu commands, and uppercase letters for range names and functions. Macro keywords can be either uppercase or lowercase, but be consistent in all your macros. (For example, all keywords in this book are uppercase.)

Consider the following example:

```
\h {MENU}rncHERE~~{GOTO}HELP~{?}{ESC}
   {GOTO}HERE~{MENU}rndHERE~
```

Notice that a poorly constructed, undocumented macro is confusing. This macro is a subroutine that provides the operator with a page of help text (at the range name HELP). When the operator reads the information and presses Enter, the macro returns the cursor to range name HERE (its position before the macro executed).

Figure T.53 shows the same macro code after its structure has been improved and documented.

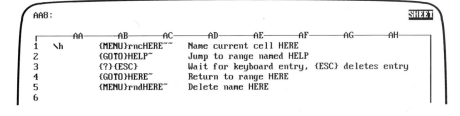

Fig. T.53.
A well-constructed macro.

MACRO PROBLEM #9:

Although your macro seems correct, it starts to beep in the middle of some commands and puts some commands as a label in a cell.

Explanation: The macro may look correct, but Symphony is not interpreting the macro in the way you anticipated. Either something is missing, or the macro contains extraneous keystrokes.

Solution: This problem commonly occurs if you forget to include tildes (to indicate Enter) in a macro. You can use one of two methods to find errors:

1. Press Step (Alt-F7) to put macro execution in single-step mode. When you execute the macro, Symphony executes only one keystroke and then waits for you to press any key. When you press a key, you signal the program to execute the next macro keystroke. As you watch the macro execute in slow motion, you usually can see exactly where the error lies. (With some macros, this single-step approach can be painfully slow.)

2. Play "computer" and execute the macro manually. First, print the macro; then replay it from the keyboard, doing exactly as the macro indicates, keystroke-by-keystroke. Unless the problem is a recalculation problem that happens only during macro execution, you will find the error if you follow the script faithfully. If the macro works when you execute it manually, change recalculation to manual and try again.

Alternative Solution: You may have created a range name with the same name as a macro key names (such as {MENU} or {TYPE}). If you make this mistake, Symphony uses the range name rather than the function of the key. Consequently, if you name a cell MENU, Symphony never displays the menu invoked with the Menu (F10) key. If you are having trouble with your macro, look at your range names and check them against a list of macro key names (see fig. T.54).

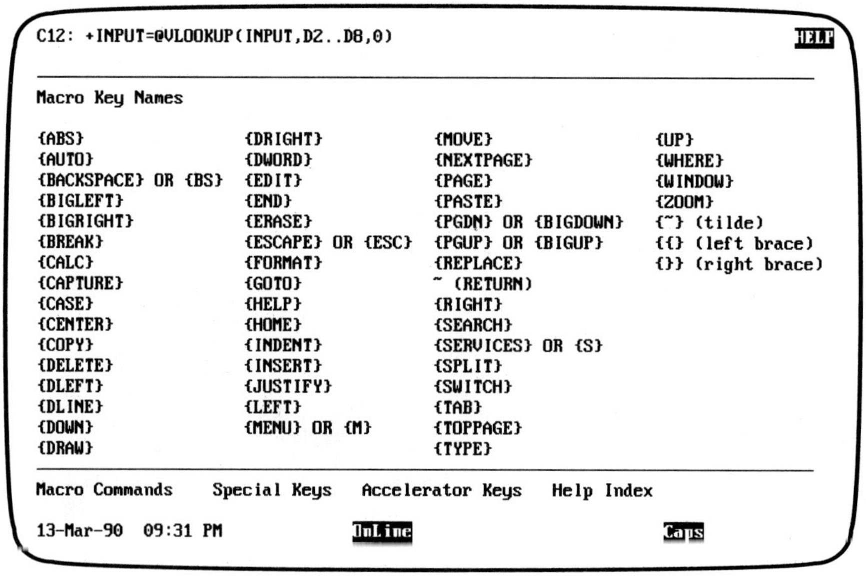

Fig. T.54.
A list of macro key names.

```
C12: +INPUT=@VLOOKUP(INPUT,D2..D8,0)                         HELP

Macro Key Names

{ABS}                   {DRIGHT}        {MOVE}              {UP}
{AUTO}                  {DWORD}         {NEXTPAGE}          {WHERE}
{BACKSPACE} OR {BS}     {EDIT}          {PAGE}              {WINDOW}
{BIGLEFT}               {END}           {PASTE}             {ZOOM}
{BIGRIGHT}              {ERASE}         {PGDN} OR {BIGDOWN} {~} (tilde)
{BREAK}                 {ESCAPE} OR {ESC} {PGUP} OR {BIGUP} {{} (left brace)
{CALC}                  {FORMAT}        {REPLACE}           {}} (right brace)
{CAPTURE}               {GOTO}          ~  (RETURN)
{CASE}                  {HELP}          {RIGHT}
{CENTER}                {HOME}          {SEARCH}
{COPY}                  {INDENT}        {SERVICES} OR {S}
{DELETE}                {INSERT}        {SPLIT}
{DLEFT}                 {JUSTIFY}       {SWITCH}
{DLINE}                 {LEFT}          {TAB}
{DOWN}                  {MENU} OR {M}   {TOPPAGE}
{DRAW}                                  {TYPE}

Macro Commands    Special Keys    Accelerator Keys    Help Index

13-Mar-90  09:31 PM            InLine                      Caps
```

MACRO PROBLEM #10:

You have written a series of handy macros for your worksheet, but you can't remember all their names.

Explanation: You can name 26 macros (A to Z) for execution with the Alt key, 10 macros for execution with the function keys, and an unlimited number of macros with regular range names. Remembering the names of 20 or more macros in several worksheets boggles the mind.

Solution: Use menus to execute macros. Menus are easier to learn than many of the macro keywords. You can have a large macro-driven worksheet with hundreds of macros, only one of which (\m, for example) is executed from the keyboard. You use this one macro to bring up a main menu. A series of hierarchical menus can contain any number of macros, each of which can have any valid range name. (Only macros executed from the keyboard require special names that start with a backslash.)

If you use more than five macros, even if they are for your own use only, put them in a menu so that you won't have to remember their names.

MACRO PROBLEM #11:

You wrote a macro containing an error. The macro destroyed your worksheet.

Explanation: A macro can do anything you can do from the keyboard. A macro can erase all or part of the worksheet, quit Symphony, and erase a file on the disk. If you don't prepare for possible catastrophic errors, you can lose hours—even days—of work.

Solution: Always save your worksheet before you test a macro. Then, if the macro destroys something, you still have the data on disk. If part of the macro saves the file, make sure that you first save it with a different name. Saving the file is futile if the macro erases most of the worksheet and then saves the destroyed file with the name of the original file.

In fact, using a macro to save a file automatically is so dangerous that you should save your files manually until you are completely familiar with macro programming and the Command Language. Some people believe it is too dangerous to ever save file from a macro.

MACRO PROBLEM #12:

While debugging a macro, the macro changed some critical values from the initial condition. After you find and attempt to fix the bug, you need to reset these critical values so that you can retest the revised macro code.

Explanation: Figure T.55 shows a worksheet with two macros. The \a macro terminated in a fatal error. As you can see, the program attempts to move the cursor to an illegitimate cell. Even after you change the cell reference from IZ1 to a legitimate cell address, the program can still fail to run properly because of logical errors (for example, suppose the IF condition in row 10 is VAL1>12 instead of VAL1>9).

Fig. T.55.

An erroneous macro and a macro to reset some range names to be initially blank.

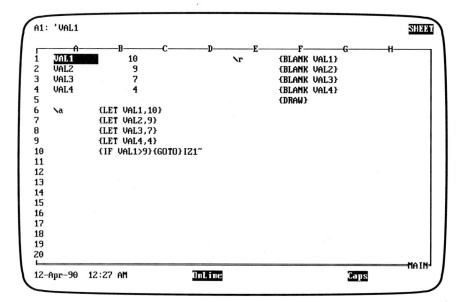

To test the program properly, you need to reset the worksheet to its initial condition, but you still want to retain the program fix. The \r macro accomplishes this. \r blanks the ranges VAL1, VAL2, VAL3, and VAL4, and then redraws the screen so that you can visually verify its action.

Solution: The \r macro shows an approach to debugging macros. Namely, you reset constants and other worksheet settings to their initial condition before retesting some code. This approach makes it easy to eliminate bugs at a variety of points in a macro program.

Using Symphony
Command Reference

Topic	Command Sequence	Command Description
SHEET Environment:		
Appearance	{MENU} **F**ormat	Change the appearance of a cell containing a number or date
	{MENU} **S**ettings **F**ormat	Specify default format for values that are entered.
	{MENU} **S**ettings **Z**ero	Select to or not to suppress the display of zeros in the worksheet
Calculation	{MENU} **S**ettings **R**ecalculation	Change how Symphony recalculates in SHEET mode
	{MENU} **S**ettings **R**ecalculation **M**ethod	Switch between Automatic and Manual recalculation
	{MENU} **S**ettings **R**ecalculation **O**rder	Select among Natural, Column-by-Column, Row-by-Row, or Optimal recalculation
	{MENU} **S**ettings **R**ecalculation **I**terations	Set the number of times the worksheet calculates (used with circular references)
	{MENU} **S**ettings **A**uto-Link	Select to or not to automatically link to other worksheets
Copy	{MENU} **C**opy	Copy a range
	{MENU} **R**ange **T**ranspose	Copy data from a column to a row or from a row to a column

Topic	Command Sequence	Command Description
	{MENU} **R**ange **V**alues	Copy the values only from a formula
Default	{MENU} **S**ettings	Display current SHEET mode settings
Deletion	{MENU} **E**rase	Erase a range
	{MENU} **D**elete **C**olumns	Delete a column in a window observing windows restrict ranges
	{MENU} **D**elete **R**ows	Delete a row in a window observing windows restrict range
	{MENU} **D**elete **G**lobal **C**olumn	Delete a column ignoring windows restrict ranges
	{MENU} **D**elete **G**lobal **R**ow	Delete a row in a worksheet ignoring windows restrict ranges
	{MENU} **R**ange **N**ame **D**elete	Delete a range name
	{MENU} **Q**uery **D**elete	Delete records from a database according to specific criteria
Distribution	{MENU} **R**ange **D**istribution	Calculate the frequency distribution of a range of cells
Fill	{MENU} **R**ange **F**ill	Fill a range of cells with values or formulas
Graph save	{MENU} **G**raph **I**mage-Save	Save the current graph settings to a disk file
Graph settings	{MENU} **G**raph **1**st-Settings	Change the basic graph settings
	{MENU} **G**raph **2**nd-Settings	Change the advanced graph settings
Graph view	{MENU} **G**raph **P**review	Display the current graph
Hide/Display	{MENU} **W**idth **H**ide	Hide column(s) in a worksheet
	{MENU} **W**idth **D**isplay	Redisplay hidden column(s)
Insertion	{MENU} **I**nsert **C**olumns	Insert a column in a window observing windows restrict ranges
	{MENU} **I**nsert **R**ows	Insert a row in a window observing windows restrict ranges

Topic	Command Sequence	Command Description
	{MENU} **I**nsert **G**lobal **C**olumn	Insert a column ignoring windows restrict ranges
	{MENU} **I**nsert **G**lobal **R**ow	Insert a row in a worksheet ignoring windows restrict ranges
Labels	{MENU} **R**ange **L**abel-Alignment	Center, Left- or Right-justify a label in a cell
	{MENU} **S**ettings **L**abel-Prefix	Change default label prefix
Move	{MENU} **M**ove	Move a range
Name creation	{MENU} **R**ange **N**ame **C**reate	Create a range name
	{MENU} **R**ange **N**ame **L**abels	Assign range names by using labels in the worksheet
Name deletion	{MENU} **R**ange **N**ame **R**eset	Clear all range names in the worksheet
Name list	{MENU} **R**ange **N**ame **T**able	Create a list of all range names and associated ranges in the worksheet
Parse	{MENU} **Q**uery **P**arse	Copy long labels into a database
Protection	{MENU} **R**ange **P**rotect	Allow or disallow changes to be made to the contents of a cell
Query	{MENU} **Q**uery **S**ettings	Change the database and associated ranges
	{MENU} **Q**uery **F**ind	Search for records in a database according to specific criteria
	{MENU} **Q**uery **E**xtract	Copy records from a database according to specific criteria
	{MENU} **Q**uery **U**nique	Copy unique records from a database according to specific criteria
Sort	{MENU} **Q**uery **R**ecord-Sort	Sort records in a database with the option of eliminating duplicate records
Titles	{MENU} **S**ettings **T**itles	Keeps rows or column from leaving the screen when you scroll the worksheet

Topic	Command Sequence	Command Description
What-If	{MENU} **R**ange **W**hat-If **1**-Way	Calculate formula using a table with single variables
	{MENU} **R**ange **W**hat-If **2**-Way	Calculate formula using a table with two variables
Width	{MENU} **W**idth **S**et	Change the column width
	{MENU} **W**idth **R**estore	Restore the column width to the default width
	{MENU} **S**ettings **W**idth	Set default column width for all columns

DOC Environment:

Topic	Command Sequence	Command Description
Appearance	{MENU} **F**ormat **S**ettings **B**lanks	Display a character for each space (each space displayed as a dot)
	{MENU} **F**ormat **S**ettings **CR**s	Display a character for each carriage return (each carriage return displayed as a triangle)
Copy	{MENU} **C**opy	Copy a block in a document
Deletion	{MENU} **E**rase	Erase a block in a document
Justify	{MENU} **J**ustify **P**aragraph	Rejustify a single paragraph in a document
	{MENU} **J**ustify **A**ll-Remaining	Rejustify all paragraphs in a document from the cursor position to the end of the document
	{MENU} **F**ormat **S**ettings **J**ustification	Set the default justification for the document (None, Left, Even, Center)
	{MENU} **F**ormat **S**ettings **A**uto-Justify	Select to or not to automatically rejustify a paragraph when each key is typed
Line spacing	{MENU} **F**ormat **S**ettings **S**pacing	Set the default spacing for the document (Single, Double, Triple)
Margins/ Tabs	{MENU} **F**ormat **C**reate	Create a new format line in a document (left and right margins and tabs, justification, spacing, name a format line)

Topic	Command Sequence	Command Description
	{MENU} **F**ormat **E**dit	Edit an existing format line in a document (left and right margins and tabs, justification, spacing, name a format line)
	{MENU} **F**ormat **S**ettings **T**abs	Set the default interval of tabs for the document
	{MENU} **F**ormat **S**ettings **L**eft	Set the default left margin for the document
	{MENU} **F**ormat **S**ettings **R**ight	Set the default right margin for the document
Move	{MENU} **M**ove	Move a block in a document
Name creation	{MENU} **L**ine-Marker	Assign a name to or remove a name from a line marker
Name use	{MENU} **F**ormat **U**se-Named	Use a named format line in a document (left and right margins and tabs, justification, spacing)
Page break	{MENU} **P**age	Insert a page break
Search	{MENU} **S**earch	Search through a document for a character string
	{MENU} **R**eplace	Search through a document for a character string and replace with another character string

GRAPH Environment:

Topic	Command Sequence	Command Description
Color	{MENU} **1**st-Settings **H**ue	Set color or hatching patterns for each range
	{MENU} **2**nd-Settings **O**ther **C**olor	Display a graph in color or in black and white using hatch patterns
Graph settings	{MENU} **1**st-Settings **S**witch	Display the 2nd-Settings menu
	{MENU} **1**st-Settings **C**ancel	Cancel a range, format, data-label, legend, hue or all settings for one range.
	{MENU} **2**nd-Settings **S**witch	Display the 1st-Settings menu
Grid	{MENU} **2**nd-Settings **O**ther **G**rid	Place either a vertical or horizontal grid on the graph, both grids, or no grid

Topic	Command Sequence	Command Description
Labels	{MENU} **1**st-Settings **D**ata-Labels	Assign a label to each range that will appear on the graph
	{MENU} **2**nd-Settings **T**itles **F**irst	Enter the first title at the top of the graph
	{MENU} **2**nd-Settings **T**itles **S**econd	Enter the second title at the top of the graph
	{MENU} **2**nd-Settings **T**itles	Enter the title displayed along the X-axis bottom of the graph
	{MENU} **2**nd-Settings **T**itles **Y**-axis	Enter the title displayed along the left-side of the graph
	{MENU} **2**nd-Settings **O**ther **H**ide	Hide a graphs titles and scales
Legend	{MENU} **1**st-Settings **L**egend	Assign a legend to each range that will appear on the graph
Line type	{MENU} **1**st-Settings **F**ormat [**X,A-F**] **L**ines	Select to display a range in a line or XY graph with lines only
	{MENU} **1**st-Settings **F**ormat [**X,A-F**] **S**ymbols	Select to display a range in a line or XY graph with symbols only
	{MENU} **1**st-Settings **F**ormat [**X,A-F**] **B**oth	Select to display a range in a line or XY graph with both lines and symbols
	{MENU} **1**st-Settings **F**ormat [**X,A-F**] **N**either	Select to display a range in a line or XY graph with neither lines nor symbols
Name	{MENU} **1**st-Settings **N**ame **I**nitial-Settings	Restore the initial graph settings
	{MENU} **2**nd-Settings **N**ame **I**nitial-Settings	Restore the initial graph settings
Name creation	{MENU} **1**st-Settings **N**ame **C**reate	Create a name for a graph's settings
	{MENU} **2**nd-Settings **N**ame **C**reate	Create a name for a graph's settings
Name deletion	{MENU} **1**st-Settings **N**ame **D**elete	Delete a named graph settings
	{MENU} **2**nd-Settings **N**ame **D**elete	Delete a named graph settings

Topic	Command Sequence	Command Description
	{MENU} **2**nd-Settings **N**ame **R**eset	Clear all named settings
Name use	{MENU} **1**st-Settings **N**ame **U**se	Use a named graph's settings
	{MENU} **1**st-Settings **N**ame **P**revious	Use a previous graph settings
	{MENU} **1**st-Settings **N**ame **N**ext	Use the next graph settings
	{MENU} **2**nd-Settings **N**ame **U**se	Use a named graph's settings
	{MENU} **2**nd-Settings **N**ame **P**revious	Use a previous graph settings
	{MENU} **2**nd-Settings **N**ame **N**ext	Use the next graph settings
Names deletion	{MENU} **1**st-Settings **N**ame **R**eset	Clear all named settings
Pie	{MENU} **2**nd-Settings **O**ther **A**spect	Change the roundness of a pie chart
Range creation	{MENU} **1**st-Settings **R**ange	Select a range on the worksheet to plot (A-F or X)
Save	{MENU} **I**mage-Save	Save a graph to a file for printing or importing into another program
Select	{MENU} **A**ttach	Select a graph to display
Type	{MENU} **1**st-Settings **T**ype	Select a graph type (line, bar, stacked-bar, xy, pie, High-Low-Close-Open)
X-Axis	{MENU} **2**nd-Settings **X**-Scale **T**ype	Select how values are to be displayed on the X-Axis
	{MENU} **2**nd-Settings **X**-Scale **F**ormat	Format the values on the X-Axis
	{MENU} **2**nd-Settings **X**-Scale **E**xponent	Set the scaling factor for the X-Axis (exponential)
	{MENU} **2**nd-Settings **X**-Scale **W**idth	Set the width for the X-Axis
	{MENU} **2**nd-Settings **O**ther **S**kip	Display every nth X range entry
	{MENU} **2**nd-Settings **O**ther **O**rigin	Specify at what value the x-axis is drawn (bar graph only)

Topic	Command Sequence	Command Description
Y-Axis	{MENU} **2**nd-Settings **Y**-Scale **T**ype	Select how values are to be displayed on the Y-Axis
	{MENU} **2**nd-Settings **Y**-Scale **F**ormat	Format the values on the Y-Axis
	{MENU} **2**nd-Settings **Y**-Scale **E**xponent	Set the scaling factor for the Y-Axis (exponential)
	{MENU} **2**nd-Settings **Y**-Scale **W**idth	Set the width for the Y-Axis
FORM Environment:		
Criteria	{MENU} **C**riteria **U**se	Select records for use based on criteria
	{MENU} **C**riteria **I**gnore	Ignore entered criteria so that all records are selected
	{MENU} **C**riteria **E**dit	Change criteria for selecting records
Database creation	{MENU} **G**enerate	Create a new database and all necessary ranges
Entry form	{MENU} **S**ettings **F**orm	Set the ranges for the entry and definition ranges
	{MENU} **S**ettings **U**nderscores	Display, don't display the underscores marking each field in an entry form
Field insertion	{MENU} **F**ield	Insert, delete and move fields in a database
Name	{MENU} **S**ettings **N**ame **I**nitial-Settings	Restore the database settings sheet to its initial settings
Name creation	{MENU} **S**ettings **N**ame **C**reate	Save the database settings sheet with a name
Name deletion	{MENU} **S**ettings **N**ame **D**elete	Delete a named database settings sheet
	{MENU} **S**ettings **N**ame **R**eset	Reset all named database settings sheets
Name use	{MENU} **S**ettings **N**ame **U**se	Use a named database settings sheet
	{MENU} **S**ettings **N**ame **P**revious	Use the previous named database settings sheet
	{MENU} **S**ettings **N**ame **N**ext	Use the next named database settings sheet

Topic	Command Sequence	Command Description
Range creation	{MENU} **S**ettings **B**asic	Set the ranges for the database, criterion and output ranges
Range deletion	{MENU} **S**ettings **C**ancel	Cancel the Basic, Form, or Report ranges, and Sort-Keys
Record	{MENU} **I**nitialize	Replaces information in a record with initial values, and blanks fields that have no initial values
	{MENU} **S**ettings **O**ne-Record	Treat a database as one record
Report	{MENU} **S**ettings **R**eport	Specify the ranges for the Report range (Main, Above, Below, Type)
Sort	{MENU} **R**ecord-Sort **U**nique	Sort all records based on sort-keys, eliminating duplicate records
	{MENU} **R**ecord-Sort **A**ll	Sort all records based on sort-keys
	{MENU} **S**ettings **S**ort-Keys	Specify the 1st, 2nd and 3rd sort keys for sorting the database
Use database	{MENU} **A**ttach	Make available a database and entry form

COMM Environment:

Topic	Command Sequence	Command Description
Answer	{MENU} **P**hone **W**ait-Mode	Set your modem to answer calls automatically
	{MENU} **P**hone **A**nswer	Manually answer an incoming call
Backspace	{MENU} **S**ettings **T**erminal **B**ackspace	Destructive or nondestructive Backspace key
Break	{MENU} **B**reak	Send a break character to a remote computer
Capture	{MENU} **S**ettings **C**apture	Capture incoming data to a printer, range or file
Dial	{MENU} **P**hone **C**all	Dial another computer
Echo	{MENU} **S**ettings **T**erminal **E**cho	Specify whether characters sent to a remote computer should also be echoed to the screen

Topic	Command Sequence	Command Description
Handshake	{MENU} **S**ettings **H**andshaking	Specify whether Inbound or Outbound handshaking should take place
Hangup	{MENU} **P**hone **H**angup	Disconnect from a call
Interface	{MENU} **S**ettings **I**nterface **B**aud	Specify the speed that your modem transmits data
	{MENU} **S**ettings **I**nterface **P**arity	Specify the parity (none, odd, even)
	{MENU} **S**ettings **I**nterface **L**ength	Specify the number of databits for each character (7 or 8)
	{MENU} **S**ettings **I**nterface **S**top-Bits	Specify the number of stop bits for each character (1, 2)
	{MENU} **S**ettings **I**nterface **C**omm-Port	Specify the communications port number (COM1 or COM2)
Line	{MENU} **S**ettings **T**erminal **W**rap	Wrap characters to the next line when end of line is reached
	{MENU} **S**ettings **S**end **E**nd-of-Line	Characters that should be sent at the end of a line
Linefeed	{MENU} **S**ettings **T**erminal **L**inefeed	Specify if a line feed should be issued after each carriage return
Login	{MENU} **L**ogin	Send a predefined login sequence to the remote computer
	{MENU} **S**ettings **L**ogin	Specify different login character strings that can be transmitted
Name	{MENU} **S**ettings **N**ame **R**etrieve	Load a named communication settings file
	{MENU} **S**ettings **N**ame **P**hone-and-Login	Load a communications settings file, call the number, and issue a login string
Name creation	{MENU} **S**ettings **N**ame **S**ave	Save the current settings to a disk file
Name deletion	{MENU} **S**ettings **N**ame **E**rase	Delete a communications settings file
Phone	{MENU} **P**hone **D**ata-Mode	Switch to data transmission, cannot use phone for voice
	{MENU} **P**hone **V**oice-Mode	Switch from data transmission to voice
	{MENU} **S**ettings **P**hone **T**ype	Pulse or touch-tone phone line

Topic	Command Sequence	Command Description
Phone number	{MENU} **S**ettings **P**hone **N**umber	The phone number that Symphony should dial
Screen	{MENU} **S**ettings **T**erminal **S**creen	Use the full screen or only a window for the terminal
Time	{MENU} **S**ettings **P**hone **D**ial-Time	The amount of time Symphony should wait for a remote computer to answer
	{MENU} **S**ettings **P**hone **A**nswer-Time	The amount of time Symphony should wait when answering a call from a remote computer
	{MENU} **S**ettings **T**erminal **D**elay	Amount of time to wait before each character is sent
	{MENU} **S**ettings **S**end **D**elay	Amount of time to wait after a line is transmitted
	{MENU} **S**ettings **B**reak	Length of time that a break transmission should be
Translation	{MENU} **S**ettings **T**erminal **T**ranslate	Translate characters to another character set
Transmit	{MENU} **T**ransmit-Range	Send a range to a remote computer
	{MENU} **F**ile-Transfer	Send or Receive a file
	{MENU} **S**ettings **S**end **R**esponse	Characters that remote computer sends after receiving a line of text
	{MENU} **S**ettings **S**end **F**ormat	Specify whether Symphony DOC mode formatting characters should be sent

A

Installing Symphony

Before you can use Symphony, you need to complete the following maintenance operations:

1. Run the SETUP program on the Setup Disk to do the following:
   a. Initialize the disk by adding your name and company.
   b. Create a Symphony directory on your hard disk.
   c. Transfer the compressed program files to your hard disk.
   d. Decompress the files.
2. Run the INSTALL program to tell Symphony about your hardware configuration.

The Symphony package contains ten 5.25-inch disks or five 3.5-inch disks. The 3.5-inch disks have about twice the capacity of the 5.25-inch disks, so some of the 3.5-inch disks have the same files as two of the 5.25-inch disks. The disks and their programs are as follows:

5.25-inch disks	*3.5-inch disks*
Symphony Setup Disk	Symphony Setup Disk
Symphony Disks 2-6	Symphony Disks 2-3
Allways Setup Disk	Allways Setup Disk
Allways Disks 2-4	Allways Disk 2

Making the Initial Setup

The procedures for preparing and using the disks that come with Symphony are as follows:

1. Place the original Symphony Setup Disk in the diskette drive. You may use either drive A: or B: but you cannot use a copy of the Symphony Setup Disk.

2. Make the diskette drive the current drive by typing A: (or B: if using the B: drive) at the DOS prompt.

3. Type **SETUP C:\SYMPHONY A:** and press Enter to start the Setup program.

   Note: you can substitute another directory for **\SYMPHONY** if you prefer. Also, if you are running the Setup program from drive B:, substitute B: for A: in the command.

4. Follow the instructions shown on the screen for recording your name and your company name.

   Note: The names you enter become a permanent part of your copy of Symphony and cannot be changed; be sure to enter them carefully.

5. When prompted, change the diskettes so the Setup program can copy the files to the hard disk. Once all of the files have been copied, Setup will decompress them. This process can take between three and 15 minutes depending on your system.

Installing Symphony's Drivers

You next need to install driver programs to tailor Symphony for your particular computer system. Drivers are programs that reside in a file called MASTER.LBR, or as separate files provided by your computer, printer, or video card manufacturer. These files store information about your specific system—the display, printer, plotter, modem, and so on. You can create one or many driver files, depending on your needs. For example, if you want to run Symphony on a desktop PC that is capable of displaying graphics in multicolor, and also run the program on a laptop PC that displays graphics and text in one color, then two separate driver files will enable you to run Symphony on both computers whenever you like.

When you make your driver selection, review the options carefully. Whether or not your system can display graphs and text at the same time, and in color, depends on several factors, including color cards and the type of monitor(s) you are using.

Some equipment selections enable you to view text and graphics only at different times on the screen (Separate mode). An IBM color monitor with a color card, for example, will display graphs and text in color, but not at the same time. Some dual monitor combinations, on the other hand, enable you to view color graphs on one screen and text on the other at the same time (Dual mode). Finally, other equipment options permit you to simultaneously view graphs and text on the screen (Combined mode).

Before you begin to run the Install program, prepare a list of equipment you plan to use. First, Symphony has to know what kind of display hardware you have. For example, a color monitor uses graphics control characters that are different from those for a monochrome monitor equipped with a graphics card displaying regular black-and-white graphs. Second, Symphony needs to know what kind of text printer(s) you have. Third, Symphony asks you to indicate the graphics printer(s) or plotter(s), if any, you plan to use. And finally, Symphony needs information about your modem so that you can use the Symphony communications feature. A list of driver options is shown in figure A.1.

```
CHANGE   SELECTED   EQUIPMENT

                                    Select Return to Main Menu if
                                    you have finished using this
  Return to Main Menu               menu.  If you want help making
  Screen Display                    decisions about how to set up
  Text Printer(s)                   Symphony for your equipment,
  Graphics Printer(s)               select First-Time Installation
  Communications Options            from the Install main menu.
  Save Changes
  Exit Install Program
```

Figure A.1.
A list of driver options.

To select drivers, you need to consider not only the kinds of equipment required to run Symphony, but also the optional equipment that you can use. As mentioned in Chapter 1, the following hardware is required to install Symphony:

- ❏ The IBM Personal Computer, XT or AT, PS/2, or compatibles, with at least 512K of RAM (640K with add-ins)
- ❏ One floppy drive and one hard drive with at least 5M of storage (4M for Symphony and 1M for Allways)
- ❏ A monochrome monitor or a graphics monitor (single color or multicolor)
- ❏ A keyboard

The following optional equipment enables you to use all of Symphony's features:

❏ Printer (parallel or serial port)

❏ Modem or acoustic coupler

❏ Additional monitor

Also, if you have an add-on memory board (which can bring your system up to 640K of RAM) or an expanded memory board (enabling use of up to 4M of RAM), you can use more of Symphony's worksheet area.

Note: Symphony does not use extended memory. If you have a system with an 80286, 80386, or 80486 microprocessor and extended memory, you must use an expanded memory driver that meets the Lotus/Intel/Microsoft Expanded Memory Specification (LIM specification, versions 3.2 and 4.0) to convert extended memory to expanded memory. One such driver, EMM386.SYS, is included with MS-DOS 4.01 for use on 80386 and 80486 systems.

When installing drivers, you must provide information for all required equipment, but you can select only the sections for the optional equipment you will be using. For example, if you are not going to use a plotter or modem, the Symphony Install program enables you to skip the steps for adding these pieces of equipment to the driver set. Following is the procedure for selecting drivers to run Symphony with your equipment (for these examples we'll assume that you have the Symphony files located on drive C: in a directory called **C:\SYMPHONY**):

1. Be sure your DOS prompt indicates that **C:** is the current drive. If it is not, enter **C:** at the DOS prompt.

2. Change to the Symphony directory by entering
   CD \SYMPHONY at the DOS prompt.

3. Load the Install program by typing **INSTALL** and pressing Enter. You also may select Install from the Symphony ACCESS menu if you prefer. In that case, type **ACCESS,** press Enter, and then select Install by pressing the letter **I** after the menu screen appears.

4. Choose **F**irst-Time Installation the first time around. Follow the step-by-step directions that appear on the screen for creating and naming the driver. If you are creating only one driver, you should use the default driver name "LOTUS." If you are creating two or more drivers, you must name each driver differently.

Once you have completed installing your copy of Symphony, the program should be ready to run with your equipment. You also can use the Install program to modify a driver set that you have previously created and to create additional driver sets if needed. One use for additional driver sets is for running Symphony with different systems containing different monitors—one with a color monitor and one with a monochrome monitor, for example.

Adding Advanced Options

The Symphony Install program also offers a selection called **A**dvanced **O**ptions. This selection allows you to fine-tune your Symphony driver set by adding new drivers or modifying the choices in the current set. If your computer, printer, or video card manufacturer has provided separate files designed to take advantage of special features of your equipment, you'll use **A**dvanced **O**ptions to add those drivers to a file called SINGLE.LBR. Once you have done this, you can modify your current driver set to include them.

Adding New Drivers

Suppose, for example, that your printer manufacturer has provided a diskette with special printer drivers for using your printer with 1-2-3 and Symphony. These drivers might allow your 24-pin printer to print color graphics or special fonts. To add these drivers to Symphony's selections, follow these steps:

1. Copy the special drivers to the **C : \ SYMPHONY** directory.

   Note: Driver files for 1-2-3 and Symphony always have the extension .DRV.

2. Run the Install program.

3. Select **A**dvanced **O**ptions from the main menu.

4. Select **A**dd **N**ew **D**rivers to **Li**brary from the **A**dvanced **O**ptions menu (see fig. A.2).

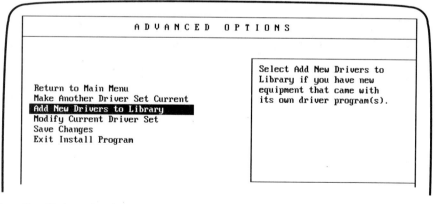

Fig. A.2.
*The **A**dvanced **O**ptions menu.*

Install will then display a message telling you that any new drivers must be in the Symphony directory. Press Enter to confirm this and the drivers will automatically be added to SINGLE.LBR. Once this step is complete the screen will display the message:

    READY You can select any of the new drivers
    from the Install menus

Modifying the Driver Set

Once you have added new drivers to SINGLE.LBR, you are ready to modify your existing LOTUS.SET (or other .SET file if you have used another name) to include the new drivers. To do so follow these steps:

1. Select **M**odify **C**urrent **D**river **S**et on the **A**dvanced **O**ptions menu.

2. Select the particular driver you wish to modify from the list (as shown in figure A.3).

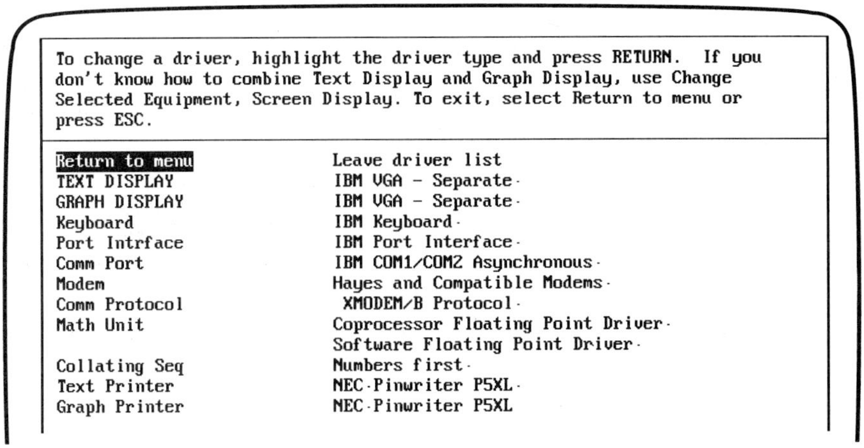

Fig. A.3.

Symphony driver options.

```
To change a driver, highlight the driver type and press RETURN.  If you
don't know how to combine Text Display and Graph Display, use Change
Selected Equipment, Screen Display. To exit, select Return to menu or
press ESC.

Return to menu        Leave driver list
TEXT DISPLAY          IBM VGA - Separate·
GRAPH DISPLAY         IBM VGA - Separate·
Keyboard              IBM Keyboard·
Port Intrface         IBM Port Interface·
Comm Port             IBM COM1/COM2 Asynchronous·
Modem                 Hayes and Compatible Modems·
Comm Protocol          XMODEM/B Protocol·
Math Unit             Coprocessor Floating Point Driver·
                      Software Floating Point Driver·
Collating Seq         Numbers first·
Text Printer          NEC-Pinwriter P5XL·
Graph Printer         NEC-Pinwriter P5XL
```

As an example, suppose that you received special printer drivers for your NEC P5XL printer. You would move the cursor down to highlight **T**ext **P**rinter and press Enter. A list of text printer drivers is then displayed. Move the cursor to NEC and press Enter. Choose the new driver selection for the P5XL by highlighting it and pressing Enter. You will then be returned to the driver options screen (fig. A.3) where you also should make a selection for **G**raph **P**rinter in the same manner. Once your selections are complete, return to the main menu, save your changes, and exit the install program.

Installing Allways

Before you can use the Allways add-in, you must also run the Allways Setup program. Allways uses the graphics features of your monitor and printer to enhance report printing. If your system does not support graphics you will not be able to use Allways. To install Allways follow these steps:

1. Make sure the current directory is the Symphony program directory. Enter the command **CD \SYMPHONY** and press Enter if necessary.
2. Type the command **AWSETUP** and press Enter.
3. Select **F**irst-Time Installation from the menu and press Enter.
4. Accept `C:\SYMPHONY` as the directory for the files.

    Note: you must install Allways in the Symphony program directory.

Allways then examines your system to determine which display card and monitor are installed. In most cases the selection is correct and you can accept the display type shown. Next, you must indicate the type of printer you have. After you have done this, you are prompted to insert the Allways diskette that contains the driver for the printer you selected. You may now leave the Allways Setup program and return to DOS.

Configuring the Printer and the Files Directory

After drivers are installed, you must set the configuration for the printer and the default directory for worksheet file storage. Symphony helps in this process by saving certain default settings from session to session. Lotus provides a default configuration for all settings, but you may want to change some of those choices.

You access the settings for the printer by invoking SERVICES **C**onfiguration **P**rinter after you have loaded Symphony. You then access the setting for the default directory for file storage by choosing SERVICES **C**onfiguration **F**ile. The default directory for transferring data to and from disk storage is the Symphony program directory. You may want to change this by specifying a data directory.

Running Symphony on Diskettes

Symphony Release 2.2 must be installed on a hard disk. It is possible, however, to run Symphony from diskette drives after it has been installed on a hard disk. For example, suppose that you use a desktop PC that has a hard disk, and you use a laptop PC when traveling on business. Once you have installed Symphony on your desktop PC, you can copy files to diskettes and run Symphony on your laptop. Note, however, that you will have to give up many of Symphony's extras in order to fit the necessary files on diskettes.

The minimum necessary files you will need are:

File	Size (K)
LOTUS.SET	53132 ← will vary depending on equipment
SYMPHONY.CMP	222359
SYMPHONY.CNF	1143
SYMPHONY.DYN	25675
SYMPHONY.EXE	49920

These five files will just fit on a 360K diskette. Because most laptop PCs use 720K diskettes, however, you may want to include SYMPHONY.HLP (162361K), which is the Symphony Help file.

If your laptop happens to use 1.44M diskettes, you can include most of the Symphony and add-in files on one diskette. However, you must choose which add-ins are important. Because each case will be different, it is not possible to suggest the exact list of files to include. The following files suggest several ideas:

File	Purpose
*.AFL	Allways fonts
*.APD	Allways drivers
*.APP	Symphony add-in applications
*.CCF	Communications configuration settings
*.CFG & *.CNF	Configuration settings
ACCESS.COM	Symphony Access Menu
TRANS.COM	The file translate utility
AWEMM.COM, AWSETUP.DAT & AWSETUP.EXE	(Used to setup Allways)
CHGDIR.EXE, DSKROOM.EXE, INFLATE.EXE, INSTALL.EXE, MASTER.LBR, SINGLE.LBR, and FLATE.RI	(Used to install Symphony)
SYMPHONY.*	Necessary to run Symphony
PGRAPH.EXE	Printgraph program
*.FNT	Printgraph font files
*.IILP	Help files
*.VWA	VIEWER files

Allways Menu Map

Worksheet | Format | Graph | Layout | Print | Display | Special | Quit

Format

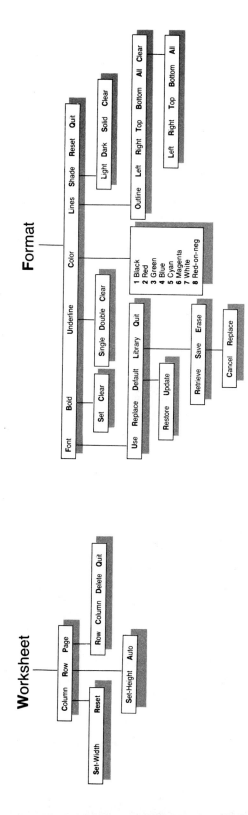

Font | Bold | Underline | Color | Lines | Shade | Reset | Quit

Set | Clear

Single | Double | Clear

1 Black
2 Red
3 Green
4 Blue
5 Cyan
6 Magenta
7 White
8 Red-on-neg

Light | Dark | Solid | Clear

Outline | Left | Right | Top | Bottom | All | Clear

Left | Right | Top | Bottom | All

Use | Replace | Default | Library | Quit

Restore | Update

Retrieve | Save | Erase

Cancel | Replace

Worksheet

Column | Row | Page

Set-Width

Reset

Set-Height | Auto

Row | Column | Delete | Quit

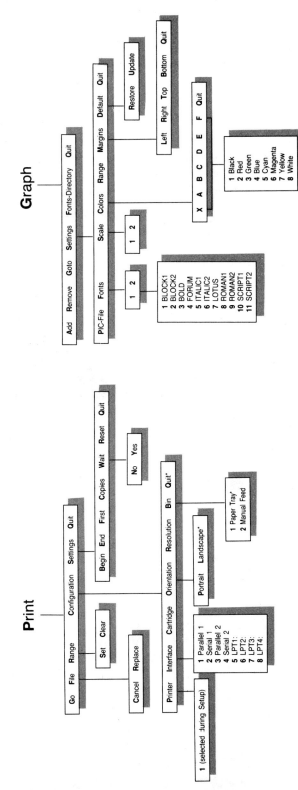

Print

Go File Range Configuration Settings Quit

Set Clear

Cancel Replace

Begin End First Copies Wait Reset Quit

No Yes

Printer Interface Cartridge Orientation Resolution Bin Quit*

Portrait Landscape*

1 Paper Tray*
2 Manual Feed

1 (selected during Setup)

1 Parallel 1
2 Serial 1
3 Parallel 2
4 Serial 2
5 LPT1:
6 LPT2:
7 LPT3:
8 LPT4:

Graph

Add Remove Goto Settings Fonts-Directory Quit

PIC-File Fonts Scale Colors Range Margins Default Quit

1 2

1 2

Restore Update

Left Right Top Bottom Quit

X A B C D E F Quit

1 Black
2 Red
3 Green
4 Blue
5 Cyan
6 Magenta
7 Yellow
8 White

1 BLOCK1
2 BLOCK2
3 BOLD
4 FORUM
5 ITALIC1
6 ITALIC2
7 LOTUS
8 ROMAN1
9 ROMAN2
10 SCRIPT1
11 SCRIPT2

*Depending on your printer,
these selections may be different.

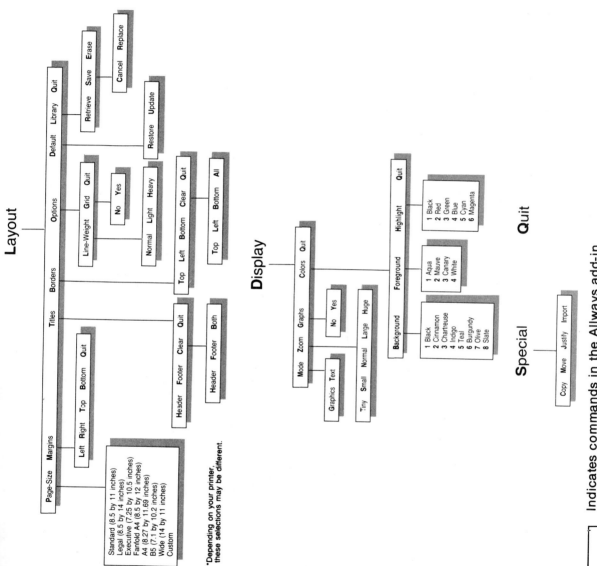

Layout

Page-Size   Margins   Titles   Borders   Options   Default   Library   Quit

Standard (8.5 by 11 inches)
Legal (8.5 by 14 inches)
Executive (7.25 by 10.5 inches)
Fanfold A4 (8.5 by 12 inches)
A4 (8.27 by 11.69 inches)
B5 (7.1 by 10.2 inches)
Wide (14 by 11 inches)
Custom

*Depending on your printer,
these selections may be different.

Left   Right   Top   Bottom   Quit

Header   Footer   Clear   Quit

Header   Footer   Both

Line-Weight   Grid   Quit

No   Yes

Normal   Light   Heavy

Top   Left   Bottom   Clear   Quit

Top   Left   Bottom   All

Retrieve   Save   Erase

Cancel   Replace

Restore   Update

Display

Mode   Zoom   Graphs   Colors   Quit

Graphics   Text

No   Yes

Tiny   Small   Normal   Large   Huge

Background   Foreground   Highlight   Quit

1 Black
2 Cinnamon
3 Chartreuse
4 Indigo
5 Teal
6 Burgundy
7 Olive
8 Slate

1 Aqua
2 Mauve
3 Canary
4 White

1 Black
2 Red
3 Green
4 Blue
5 Cyan
6 Magenta

Special

Copy   Move   Justify   Import

Quit

Indicates commands in the Allways add-in
program that comes with Symphony Release 2.2

PrintGraph Menu Map

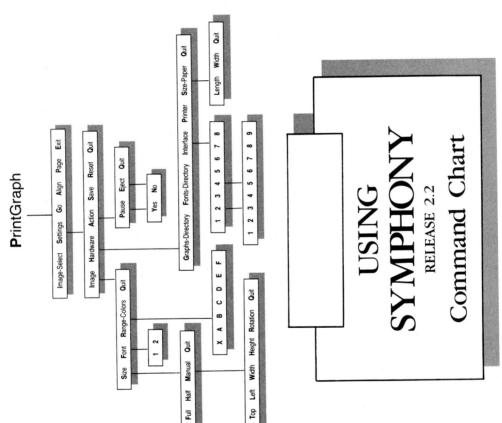

PrintGraph

Image-Select Settings Go Align Page Exit

Image Hardware Action Save Reset Quit

Pause Eject Quit

Yes No

Graphs-Directory Fonts-Directory Interface Printer Size-Paper Quit

1 2 3 4 5 6 7 8

1 2 3 4 5 6 7 8 9

Length Width Quit

Size Font Range-Colors Quit

1 2

Full Half Manual Quit

X A B C D E F

Top Left Width Height Rotation Quit

USING
SYMPHONY
RELEASE 2.2
Command Chart

Que Corporation
11711 N. College Avenue
Carmel, IN 46032

INDEX

— A —

above range, 601-602
Abs (F3) key, 65, 138-139, 805
@ABS function, 167
absolute cell addressing, 131,
133-136, 138, 804-805
absolute value, 167
accelerator keys, 66, 287
Allways, 398
Ctrl-B (Begin Print Attribute),
269-271
Ctrl-Backspace (Delete Word
Left), 270, 287
Ctrl-C (Copy Text), 269
Ctrl-D (Delete Line), 270, 287,
320
Ctrl-E (End Print Attribute),
270-271
Ctrl-F (Format), 270, 311
Ctrl-J (Auto-Justification), 269,
274, 304
Ctrl-M (Move), 270, 288, 330
Ctrl-N (Page), 270, 308
Ctrl-O (Merge), 270
Ctrl-P (Paste Text), 270, 287,
289-290, 320-321
Ctrl-PgDn (Next Page), 270
Ctrl-PgUp (Top Page), 270
Ctrl-R (Replace), 270, 296,
298, 331
Ctrl-S (Search), 270, 296, 298
Ctrl-T (Delete Text to Start of
Line), 269, 287, 321
Ctrl-X (Capitalize Characters),
269
Ctrl-Y (Delete Text to Right
End of Line), 270, 287, 321
DOC window, 269-270
ACCESS File-Translate command,
239
ACCESS SYSTEM menu, 28, 40-
41, 239, 476, 884

@ACOS function, 171
Add Record to Database (Ins)
key, 515
add-in applications, 11, 43
@BASE, 23, 35, 53, 505, 510,
563-590, 592, 599, 603-
604, 711-714, 852-853
activating, 53
Allways, 35, 393-430, 445,
460, 711-714, 732-734,
817, 822-825
SETUP, 886-887
attaching, 53, 204-205
DEC VT100 terminal
emulation, 639
ExtraK, 799-800
Freelance Plus, 460
Graphwriter II, 460
INPUT.APP, 779-780
Lotus Magellan VIEWER, 34-
35, 230
Macro Library Manager, 707-
714
Option Pac, 587-590, 604,
618-626, 852
PrintGraph, 40-41, 445, 475-
500, 775, 787-788, 840,
846
Spelling Checker, 26, 333-344,
823-832
Text Outliner, 26, 28, 333,
344-367
Translate, 40
addition (+) operator,
ADP.CCF file, 634
Advanced Expanded Memory
(AEM), 37-38
Advanced Options, 788, 885-886
AFS file extension, 406
Align PrintGraph command, 484-
485
ALL file extension, 400, 422, 825

Allways add-in application, 35,
393-430, 445, 460, 732-734,
817
adding lines, 407-408
and Macro Library Manager,
711-714
attaching, 394
boldfacing data in cells, 404
color on-screen, 405, 427-428
commands, selecting from
menus, 399
control panel, 395-396
copying cell formats, 429
default fonts, 406
displaying text and graphics,
424-426
editing worksheets, 400
enlarging or reducing
worksheet display, 424-
425
fonts, 405-407, 419
formatting commands, 403-
410, 428-429
graphics display mode, 397
graphs, 410-412
headers and footers, 417
help system, 400
importing worksheet formats,
429
installing, 394, 886-887
justifying text, 429
landscape and portrait
orientation, 420
library of page layouts, 415
lines, changing weight, 416
main menu, 396, 399
memory requirements, 393
menu map, 889-892
moving cell formats, 429-430
physical dimensions of pages,
417
print settings, 422

893

MS-DOS User's Guide, Special Edition
Developed by Que Corporation

A special edition of Que's best-selling book on MS-DOS, updated to provide the most comprehensive DOS coverage available. Includes expanded EDLIN coverage, plus **Quick Start** tutorials and a complete **Command Reference** for DOS Versions 3 and 4. A **must** for MS-DOS users at all levels!

Order #1048
$29.95 USA
0-88022-505-X, 900 pp.

Using Computers in Business
by Joel Shore

This text covers all aspects of business computerization, including a thorough analysis of benefits, costs, alternatives, and common problems. Also discusses how to budget for computerization, how to shop for the right hardware and software, and how to allow for expansions and upgrades.

Order #1020
$22.95 USA
0-88022-470-3, 450 pp.

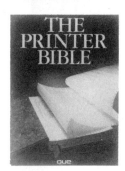

The Printer Bible
by Scott Foerster

From basic printer concepts and purchasing analysis to networking, maintenance, and troubleshooting, *The Printer Bible* is the ultimate printer information resource! Covers all kinds of printers —including laser-jet and dot matrix—and provides troubleshooting tips and a glossary of printer terms. A definite best-seller!

Order #1056
$24.95 USA
0-88022-512-2, 550 pp.

Using DOS
Developed by Que Corporation

The most helpful DOS book available! Que's *Using DOS* teaches the essential commands and functions of DOS Versions 3 and 4 —in an easy-to-understand format that helps users manage and organize their files effectively. Includes a handy **Command Reference**.

Order #1035
$22.95 USA
0-88022-497-5, 550 pp.